41

Real Life Real History

Beaten Unconscious on the Senate Floor
297

22   **Skull Jewelry** becomes fashionable

41   **Pocahontas**—Then and Now

81   **Ink!** The Man With the Tattooed Face

144   **Jefferson's Photocopier**

163   **Backslapping George Washington**

198   **Taking the Leap:** The Worker Who Leaped Off Niagara Falls

238   **The Unthinkable:** Women Speaking to Mixed Audiences

291   **"From the Wrong Side of the Tracks"**—What It Meant to Be

297   **Beaten Unconscious** on the Senate Floor

22

144

163

U.S

A NARRATIVE History

Volume 1

McGraw Hill

Boston   Burr Ridge, IL   Dubuque, IA   Madison, WI   New York   San Francisco   St. Louis
Bangkok   Bogotá   Caracas   Kuala Lumpur   Lisbon   London   Madrid   Mexico City
Milan   Montreal   New Delhi   Santiago   Seoul   Singapore   Sydney   Taipei   Toronto

U.S. A NARRATIVE HISTORY

AUTHORS
James West Davidson   **Brian DeLay**
Christine Leigh Heyrman   **Mark H. Lytle**   **Michael B. Stoff**

Vice President and Editor-in-Chief   **Michael J. Ryan**
Publisher   **Frank Mortimer**
Sponsoring Editor   **Jon-David Hague**
Director of Development   **Rhona Robbin**
Development Editor   **Sora Kim**
Marketing Manager   **Pamela Cooper**
Marketing Specialist   **Clare Cashen**
Senior Production Editor   **Mel Valentín**
Production Assistant   **Rachel J. Castillo**
Manuscript Editor   **Stacey Sawyer**
Art Editor   **Sonia Brown**
Art Manager   **Robin Mouat**
Cover Designer   **Preston Thomas**
Text Designer   **Jeanne Calabrese**
Photo Research Coordinator   **Nora Agbayani**
Photo Research   **Photo Search, Inc.**
Media Project Manager   **Ronald Nelms, Jr.**
Senior Production Supervisor   **Richard DeVitto**

Higher Education

U*S/A NARRATIVE HISTORY, Volume 1

Published by McGraw-Hill, a business unit of The McGraw-Hill Companies, Inc., 1221 Avenue of the Americas, New York, NY 10020. Copyright © 2009 by The McGraw-Hill Companies, Inc. All rights reserved. No part of this publication may be reproduced or distributed in any form or by any means, or stored in a database or retrieval system, without the prior written consent of The McGraw-Hill Companies, Inc., including, but not limited to, any network or other electronic storage or transmission, or broadcast for distance learning.

Some ancillaries, including electronic and print components, may not be available to customers outside the United States.

1 2 3 4 5 6 7 8 9 0 WCK/WCK 0 9 8

Stand-alone text: ISBN: 978-0-07-338546-4; MHID: 0-07-338546-8

Vol. 1 of a Two-Vol. Set: ISBN: 978-0-07-731338-8; MHID: 0-07-731338-0

Vol. 1-2 Set: ISBN: 978-0-07-731539-9; MHID: 0-07-731539-1

The text was set in 10.5/12 Times Roman by Argosy Publishing, and printed on acid-free 45# Influence Gloss by Quebecor World.

Cover images: Front cover: top: Image Source/Jupiterimages; bottom: Library of Congress, Prints & Photographs Division, [LC-BH82- 4140]; **Inside front cover:** Royalty-Free/Corbis; **Back cover:** Polka Dot Images/Jupiterimages.

Because this page cannot legibly accommodate all acknowledgements for copyrighted material, credits appear at the end of the book, and constitute an extension of this copyright page.

Library of Congress Cataloging-in-Publication Data

US : a narrative history / James West Davidson . . . [et al.]. – 1st ed. v. cm.

Includes bibliographical references and index.
ISBN-13: 978-0-07-338546-4 (v. 1 : alk. paper)
ISBN-10: 0-07-338546-8 (v. 1 : alk. paper)
ISBN-13: 978-0-07-723621-2 (v. 2 : alk. paper)
ISBN-10: 0-07-723621-1 (v. 2 : alk. paper)

1. United States–History–Textbooks. I. Davidson, James West. II. Title: U.S. III. Title: United States.
E178.1.U83 2009
973–dc22

2008043055

p. 18

Brief Contents

1 The First Civilizations of North America **2**

2 Old Worlds, New Worlds [1400–1600] **18**

3 Colonization and Conflict in the South [1600–1750] **38**

4 Colonization and Conflict in the North [1600–1700] **60**

5 The Mosaic of Eighteenth-Century America [1689–1771] **80**

p. 158

6 Toward the War for American Independence [1754–1776] **100**

7 The American People and the American Revolution [1775–1783] **120**

8 Crisis and Constitution [1776–1789] **138**

9 The Early Republic [1789–1824] **158**

10 The Opening of America [1815–1850] **186**

11 The Rise of Democracy [1824–1840] **204**

12 The Fires of Perfection [1820–1850] **224**

13 The Old South [1820–1860] **242**

14 Western Expansion and the Rise of the Slavery Issue [1820–1850] **262**

15 The Union Broken [1850–1861] **286**

16 Total War and the Republic [1861–1865] **308**

17 Reconstructing the Union [1865–1877] **334**

p. 334

The River JAMES

Contents

1 **The First Civilizations of North America** 2

Preview 3

A Continent of Culture 4

Cultures of Ancient Mexico 5

Cultures of the Southwest 6

Cultures of the Eastern Woodlands 7

Cultures of the Great Plains 8

Cultures of the Great Basin 8

Cultures of the Pacific Northwest 8

Cultures of the Subarctic and the Arctic 9

Innovations and Limitations 9

America's Agricultural Gifts 9

Landscapers 10

The Shape of a Problem 11

Animals and Illness 12

Crisis and Transformation 14

Enduring Cultures 14

North America on the Eve of Contact 15

Significant Events 16

Chapter Summary 16

Additional Reading 17

2 **Old Worlds, New Worlds [1400–1600]** 18

Preview 19

Eurasia and Africa in the Fifteenth Century 21

Europe's Place in the World 21

Africa and the Portuguese Wave 22

Sugar and the Origins of the Atlantic Slave Trade 23

Spain in the Americas 24

The Spanish Beachhead in the Caribbean 24

Conquest of the Aztecs 26

The Columbian Exchange 26

The Crown Steps In 27

The Search for North America's Indian Empires 29

Religious Reform Divides Europe 30

The Teachings of Martin Luther 30

The Contribution of John Calvin 31

French Huguenots and the Birth of Spanish Florida 31

The English Reformation 32

England's Entry into America 32

The Ambitions of Gilbert, Raleigh, and Wingina 33

A Second Roanoke – and Croatoan 35

AFTER THE FACT:
Early Modern Goth 22

Significant Events 36

Chapter Summary 36

Additional Reading 37

3 Colonization & Conflict in the South [1600–1750] 38

Preview 39

Spain's North American Colonies 41

The Founding of a "New" Mexico 41

The Growth of Spanish Florida 43

Pope and the Pueblo Revolt 43

English Society on the Chesapeake 44

The Virginia Company 45

Reform and a Boom in Tobacco 46

War with the Confederacy 46

The Founding of Maryland and the Renewal of
  Indian Wars 47

Changes in English Policy in the Chesapeake 48

Chesapeake Society in Crisis 48

Bacon's Rebellion and Coode's Rebellion 48

From Servitude to Slavery 49

Africa and the Atlantic Slave Trade 49

A Changing Chesapeake Society 52

From the Caribbean to the Carolinas 53

Paradise Lost 53

The Founding of the Carolinas 54

Carolina, Florida, and the Southeastern Slave Wars 54

White, Red, and Black: The Search for Order 56

The Founding of Georgia 57

AFTER THE FACT:
The Mystery of the Sawed-Off Foot 42

Significant Events 58

Chapter Summary 59

Additional Reading 59

4 Colonization & Conflict in the North [1600–1700] 60

Preview 61

France in North America 62

The Origins of New France 62

New Netherlands, the Iroquois, and the Beaver
  Wars 63

The Lure of Mississippi 64

The Founding of New England 65

The Puritan Movement 65

The Pilgrim Settlement at Plymouth Colony 66

The Puritan Settlement at
Massachusetts Bay 67

**Stability and Order in Early
New England 68**

A Puritan New Englander Wrestles
with Her Faith 70

Communities in Conflict 70

Goodwives and Witches 71

The People in the Way 71

Metacom's War 72

The Mid-Atlantic Colonies 73

English Rule in New York 73

The Founding of New Jersey 73

Quaker Odysseys 74

Patterns of Growth 74

Quakers and Politics 75

Adjustments to Empire 76

The Dominion of New England 76

Royal Authority in America in 1700 76

Significant Events 78

Chapter Summary 78

Additional Reading 79

**5   The Mosaic of Eighteenth-Century
America [1689–1771] 80**

Preview 81

Forces of Division 83

Immigration and Natural Increase 84

The Settlement of the Backcountry 84

Social Conflict on the Frontier 85

Boundary Disputes and Tenant Wars 86

Eighteenth-Century Seaports 86

Social Conflict in Seaports 89

**Slave Societies in the Eighteenth-Century
South 89**

The Slave Family and Community 90

Slavery and Colonial Society in French Louisiana 91

Slave Resistance in Eighteenth-Century British
North America 91

Enlightenment and Awakening in America 91

The Enlightenment in America 92

The First Great Awakening 93

The Aftermath of the Great Awakening 93

**Anglo-American Worlds of the
Eighteenth Century 94**

English Economic and Social
Development 94

Inequality in England and America 95

Politics in England and America 95

The Imperial System before 1760 96

Toward the Seven Years' War 97

AFTER THE FACT:
Enlightened Witchcraft? 92

Significant Events 98

Chapter Summary 99

Additional Reading 99

**6   Toward the War for American
Independence [1754–1776] 100**

Preview 101

The Seven Years' War 102

The Years of Defeat 102

The Years of Victory 103

Postwar Expectations 104

The Imperial Crisis 104

New Troubles on the Frontier 104

George Grenville's New Measures 106

The Beginning of Colonial Resistance 108

Riots and Resolves 109

Repeal of the Stamp Act 110

The Townshend Acts 111

The Resistance Organizes 111

The International Sons of Liberty 112

The Boston Massacre 112

Resistance Revived 113

The Empire Strikes Back 113

Toward the Revolution 114

The First Continental Congress 114

The Last Days of the British Empire in
America 115

The Fighting Begins 116

Paine's Common Sense 117

Significant Events 118

Chapter Summary 118

Additional Reading 119

7 The American People and the American Revolution [1775–1783] 120

Preview 121

The Decision for Independence 122

The Second Continental Congress 123

The Declaration 123

American Loyalists 123

The Fighting in the North 124

The Two Armies at Bay 124

Laying Strategies 126

The Campaigns in New York and New Jersey 126

Capturing Philadelphia 127

Disaster for the British at Saratoga 128

The Turning Point 128

The American Revolution as a Global War 128

Winding Down the War in the North 129

War in the West 130

The Home Front in the North 131

The Struggle in the South 131

The Siege of Charleston 131

The Partisan Struggle in the South 131

Greene Takes Command 132

African Americans in the Age of Revolution 133

The World Turned Upside Down 134

Surrender at Yorktown 134

Significant Events 136

Chapter Summary 136

Additional Reading 137

8 Crisis and Constitution [1776–1789] 138

Preview 139

Republican Experiments 140

The State Constitutions 140

From Congress to Confederation 141

The Temptation of Peace 142

The Temptations of the West 142

Foreign Intrigues 142

Disputes among the States 143

The More Democratic West 144

The Northwest Territory 144

Slavery and Sectionalism 145

Wartime Economic Disruption 147

Republican Society 148

The New Men of the Revolution 148

The New Women of the Revolution 148

Mary Wollstonecraft's Vindication 149

Seduction Literature and the Virtues of Women 149

Republican Motherhood and Education for Women 149

The Attack on Aristocracy 150

From Confederation to Constitution 151

The Jay-Gardoqui Treaty 151

Shay's Rebellion 151

Framing a Federal Constitution 152

The Virginia and New Jersey Plans 152

The Deadlock Broken 153

Ratification 153

AFTER THE FACT:
Skirting the Issue 150

Significant Events 156

Chapter Summary 156

Additional Reading 157

9 The Early Republic [1789–1824] 158

Preview 158

1789: A Social Portrait 161

Semisubsistence and Commercial Economies 162

The Constitution and Commerce 163

The New Government 164

Washington Organizes the Government 164

Hamilton's Financial Program 164

The Emergence of Political Parties 166

Americans and the French Revolution 166

Washington's Neutral Course 167

The Federalists and the Republicans Organize 167

The 1796 Election 167

Federalist and Republican Ideologies 168

The Presidency of John Adams 168

The Naval War with France 168

Suppression at Home 169

The Election of 1800 170

John Marshall and Judicial Review 170

The Political Culture of the Early Republic 171

Popular Participation in Political Festivals 171

African-American Celebrations 171

Jefferson in Power 172

The New Capital City 172

Jefferson's Philosophy 173

Jefferson's Economic Policies 173

Whites and Indians in the West 173

The Miami Confederacy Resists 173

Doubling the Size of the Nation 174

Pressure on Indian Lands and Culture 175

White Frontier Society 176

The Beginnings of the Second Great Awakening 176

The Prophet, Tecumseh, and the Pan-Indian Movement 177

The Second War for American Independence 179

The Embargo 179

Madison and the Young Republicans 180

The Decision for War 181

The British Invasion 181

America Turns Inward 182

Monroe's Presidency 183

AFTER THE FACT: Man or God and How to Tell the Difference 167

Significant Events 184

Chapter Summary 184

Additional Reading 185

10 The Opening of America [1815–1850] 186

Preview 187

The Market Revolution 189
The New Nationalism 189
The Cotton Trade 189
The Transportation Revolution 189
Revolution in Communications 190
The Postal System 191
Agriculture in the Market Economy 191
John Marshall and the Promotion of Enterprise 192

The Restless Temper 193
Population Growth 193
The Restless Movement West 193
Urbanization 193

The Rise of Factories 194
Technological Advances 194
Textile Factories 195
Lowell and the Environment 196
Industrial Work 197
The Labor Movement 197
Sam Patch and a Worker's "Art" 198

Social Structures of the Market Society 199
Economic Specialization 199
Materialism 199
Wealth and the Emerging Middle Class 199
Social Mobility 200
A New Sensitivity to Time 200

Prosperity and Anxiety 201
The Panic of 1819 201

Significant Events 202
Chapter Summary 202
Additional Reading 203

11 The Rise of Democracy [1824–1840] 204

Preview 205

Equality and Opportunity 207

The New Political Culture of Democracy 207
The Election of 1824 208
Social Sources of the New Politics 208

Jackson's Rise to Power 210

President to the People 210
The Political Agenda in the Market Economy 211

Democracy and Race 211
Accommodate or Resist? 211
Trail of Tears 211
Free Blacks in the North 212
The African American Community 213
Racism Strikes a Deeper Root 214

The Nullification Crisis 215
The Growing Crisis in South Carolina 215
The Nullifiers Nullified 216

The Bank War 216
The National Bank and the Panic of 1819 216
The Bank Destroyed 217
Jackson's Impact on the Presidency 218

Van Buren and Depression 219
"Van Ruin's" Depression 219
The Whigs Triumph 220

The Jacksonian Party System 220
Democrats, Whigs, and the Market 220
The Social Bases of the Two Parties 221

AFTER THE FACT:
The Bank and Bare-Knuckled Boxers 217

Significant Events 222
Chapter Summary 222
Additional Reading 223

12 The Fires of Perfection [1820–1850] 224

Preview 225

Revivalism and the Social Order 227

Finney's New Measure and New Theology 227

Religion and the Market Economy 228

The Rise of African American Churches 229

Women's Sphere 229

The Ideal of Domesticity 229

The Middle-Class Family in Transition 230

American Romanticism 231

The Transcendentalists 231

The Age of Reform 232

Utopian Communities 232

The Mormon Experience 233

Socialist Communities 233

The Temperance Movement 234

Educational Reform 234

The Asylum Movement 235

Abolitionism 235

The Beginnings of the Abolitionist Movement 235

The Spread of Abolitionism 237

Opponents and Divisions 237

The Women's Rights Movement 238

The Schism of 1840 238

Reform Shakes the Party System 239

The Maine Law 239

Abolitionism and the Party System 239

Significant Events 240

Chapter Summary 240

Additional Reading 241

13 The Old South [1820–1860] 242

Preview 242

The Social Structure of the Cotton Kingdom 245

Deep South, Upper South 245

The Rural South 247

Distribution of Slavery 247

Slavery as a Labor System 247

Class Structure of the White South 249

The Slaveowners 249

Tidewater and Frontier 249

The Master at Home 250

The Plantation Mistress 251

Yeoman Farmers 251

Poor Whites 252

The Peculiar Institution 252

Work and Discipline 253

Slave Maintenance 253

Resistance 254

Slave Culture 255

The Slave Family 255

Songs and Stories of Protest and Celebration 256

The Lord Calls Us Home 256

The Slave Community 257

Free Black Southerners 257

Southern Society and the Defense of Slavery 259

The Virginia Debate of 1832 259

The Proslavery Argument 259

Closing Ranks 259

AFTER THE FACT:
Steamboat Manifests and Starvation 255

Significant Events 260

Chapter Summary 260

Additional Reading 261

14 Western Expansion and the Rise of the Slavery Issue [1820–1850] 262

Preview 263

Manifest (and Not So Manifest) Destiny 266

The Roots of the Doctrine 266

The Mexican Borderlands 266

The Texas Revolution 267

The Texas Republic 268

The Trek West 270

The Overland Trail 270

Women on the Overland Trail 271

Indians and the Trail Experience 271

The Political Origins of Expansion 271

Tyler's Texas Ploy 271

To the Pacific 272

Provoking a War 272

Indians and Mexicans 273

Opposition to the War 274

The Price of Victory 274

The Rise of the Slavery Issue 275

New Societies in the West 276

Farming in the West 276

The Gold Rush 278

Instant City: San Francisco 279

The Migration from China 279

The Mormons in Utah 280

Shadows on the Moving Frontier 280

Escape from Crisis 281

A Two-Faced Campaign 282

The Compromise of 1850 282

Away from the Brink 283

AFTER THE FACT:
Hide and Go Seek 273

Significant Events 284

Chapter Summary 284

Additional Reading 285

15 The Union Broken [1850–1861] 286

Preview 287

Sectional Changes in American Society 290

The Growth of a Railroad Economy 290

Railroads and the Prairie Environment 291

Railroads and the Urban Environment 291

Rising Industrialization 291

Immigration 293

Southern Complaints 294

The Political Realignment of the 1850s 295

The Kansas-Nebraska Act 295

The Collapse of the Second American Party System 295

The Know-Nothings 296

The Republicans and Bleeding Kansas 297

The Caning of Charles Sumner 297

The Election of 1856 298

The Worsening Crisis 298

The Dred Scott Decision 298

The Lecompton Constitution 299

The Lincoln-Douglas Debates 299

The Beleaguered South 301

The Road to War 301

A Sectional Election 301

Secession 302

The Outbreak of War 303

The Roots of a Divided Nation 304

Significant Events 306

Chapter Summary 306

Additional Reading 307

16 Total War and the Republic [1861–1865] 308

Preview 309

The Demands of Total War 311

Political Leadership 312

The Border States 312

Opening Moves 313

Blockade and Isolate 313

Grant in the West 314

Eastern Stalemate 315

Emancipation 317

The Logic of Events 317

The Emancipation Proclamation 317

African Americans' Civil War 318

Black Soldiers 318

The Confederate Home Front 319

The New Economy 319

New Opportunities for Southern Women 319

Confederate Finance and Government 320

Hardship and Suffering 320

The Union Home Front 321

Government Finances and the Economy 321

A Rich Man's War 321

Women and the Workforce 321

Civil Liberties and Dissent 322

Gone to Be a Soldier 323

Discipline 323

Camp Life 324

The Changing Face of Battle 324

Hardening Attitudes 324

The Union's Triumph 325

Lincoln Finds His General 326

War in the Balance 328

The Twilight of the Confederacy 329

Significant Events 332

Chapter Summary 332

Additional Reading 333

17 Reconstructing the Union [1865–1877] 334

Preview 335

Presidential Reconstruction 337

Lincoln's 10 Percent Plan 337

Reconstruction under Andrew Johnson 337

The Failure of Johnson's Program 338

Johnson's Break with Congress 339

The Fourteenth Amendment 340

THE FIFTEENTH AMENDMENT.
CELEBRATED MAY 19TH 1870.

The Election of 1866 **340**

Congressional Reconstruction 341

Post-Emancipation Societies in the Americas **341**

The Land Issue **342**

Impeachment **342**

Reconstruction in the South 342

Black and White Republicans **342**

Reforms under the New State Governments **344**

Economic Issues and Corruption **344**

Black Aspirations 344

Experiencing Freedom **345**

The Black Family **345**

The Schoolhouse and the Church **345**

New Working Conditions **346**

Planters and a New Way of Life **346**

The Abandonment of Reconstruction 347

The Grant Administration **348**

Growing Northern Disillusionment **349**

The Triumph of White Supremacy **349**

The Disputed Election of 1876 **350**

Racism and the Failure of Reconstruction **351**

AFTER THE FACT:
Minstrels, Carnivals, and Ghosts **349**

Significant Events 352

Chapter Summary 351

Additional Reading 353

Features

What do you think happened to the Roanoke colonists?

129 Would the American colonies have won their independence without the military assistance of France?

141 Should the electoral college be abolished?

176 Was there any strategy that Indian nations between the Appalachians and the Mississippi could have adopted to halt white expansion?

189 Did the Market Revolution benefit most Americans?

208 Did the period between the American Revolution and the 1830s bring about a significant democratization in American politics?

230 Did the status of women improve in the United States between the American Revolution and the Civil War?

253 What role did race play in maintaining the institution of slavery? Could a system of white or Indian slavery have existed as easily?

274 Was the U.S.-Mexican War justified?

301 Was the Civil War an "irresistible conflict," as Senator William Seward of New York insisted, or could it have been avoided?

312 Was Lincoln justified in suspending habeas corpus? Was the Bush administration justified in doing so in the war in terror?

340 Did the South or the North win the Civil War?

OPINION

6 If your outstretched arm represented North America's human history, contact with Europe would happen around the second knuckle of your index finger, with the fingertips being the present. Why do you think students learn so little about the Americas prior to 1492?

33 What do you think happened to Roanoke colonists?

40 Would you have opposed slavery if you had lived in the seventeenth century?

66 Do you think that the Puritans committed to religious freedom?

86 Was the most critical sectional division in eighteenth-century America between North and South or between East and West?

113 Were the whigs right to worry about the dangers of a standing army? If so, does our standing army pose a danger today?

POINT OF VIEW

15 Wilderness America?

72 Squanto's Advice

104 The Seven Years' War

148 The Impact of the American Revolution

190 The Market Revolution

227 The Second Great Awakening

304 Democracy's Limitations

317 The Presence of Death

POINT OF VIEW

The Second Great Awakening

"The wave of popular religious movements that broke upon the United States in the half century after independence did more to Christianize American society than any thing before or since. Nothing makes that point more clearly than the growth of Methodist and Baptist movements among white and black Americans."

—Nathan Hatch, *The Democratization of American Christianity*

Features

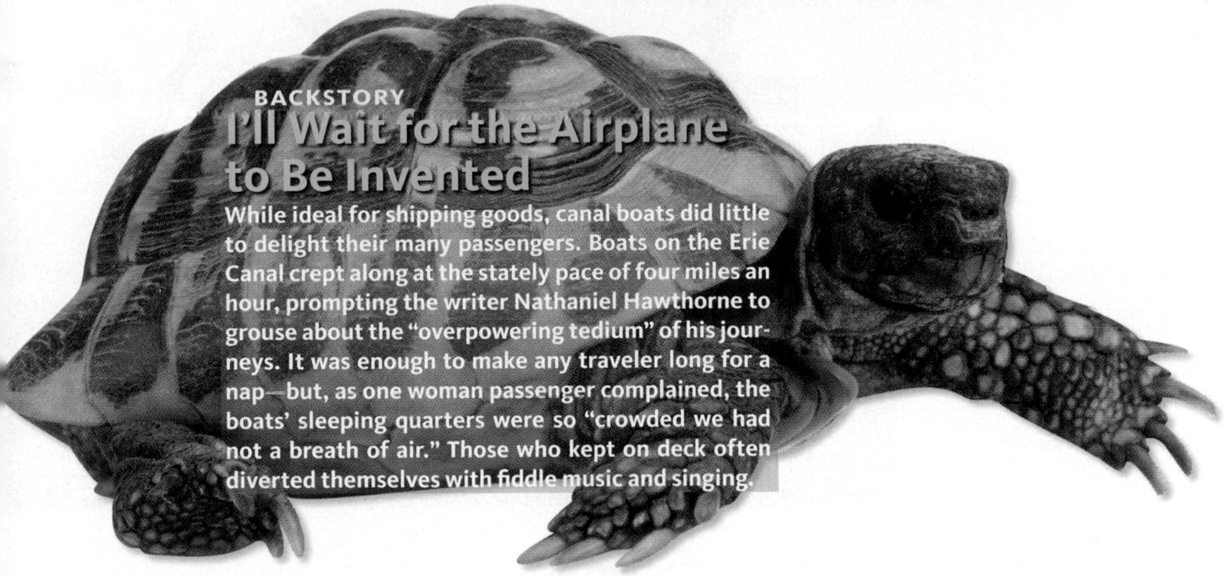

BACKSTORY

BACKSTORY

I'll Wait for the Airplane to Be Invented

While ideal for shipping goods, canal boats did little to delight their many passengers. Boats on the Erie Canal crept along at the stately pace of four miles an hour, prompting the writer Nathaniel Hawthorne to grouse about the "overpowering tedium" of his journeys. It was enough to make any traveler long for a nap—but, as one woman passenger complained, the boats' sleeping quarters were so "crowded we had not a breath of air." Those who kept on deck often diverted themselves with fiddle music and singing.

BACKSTORY

14 Aztec Rest Stops and Recycling

29 Perceptions of Savagery

52 Manly Men

63 The Power of Dreams

97 Not-So-Poor Richard

111 Spirits of Independence

131 A Killer on All Continents

147 The Contagion of Liberty

163 Forbidding George

192 I'll Wait for the Airplane to Be Invented

212 Great White Father?

231 An Ecumenical Spirit

254 Dizzy from Thirst

267 The First Illegal Immigration Crisis

296 Anti-Catholic Violence

324 Hospitals

339 Manning the Barricades

THEN & NOW

41 Seeing What We Want to See

144 But How Many Dots per Inch?

235 "Friends" and Neighbors

299 Political Debate Tactics

Then & Now

SEEING WHAT WE WANT TO SEE

Pocahontas, daughter of the mighty weroance Powhatan and wife of English colonist John Rolfe, has long fascinated non-natives. In the first image from 1616 she is represented as a high-status English lady. The second image, from the 1995 Disney film, portrays her as a gorgeous and innocent child of nature. Now as then, we see in her what we want to.

Features

AFTER THE FACT

22 Early Modern Goth
42 The Mystery of the Sawed-Off Foot
92 Enlightened Witchcraft?
150 Skirting the Issue
167 Man or God and How to Tell the Difference
217 The Bank and the Bare-Knuckled Boxers
255 Steamboat Manifests and Starvation
273 Hide and Go Seek
349 Minstrels, Carnivals, and Ghosts

WITNESS
Fleeing the Stamp Act Mob

"I had been [gone] but a few minutes before the hellish crew fell upon my house with the rage of devils and in a moment with axes split down the doors and entered my son being in the great entry heard them cry damn him he is upstairs we'll have him . . . they began to take the slate and boards from the roof and were prevented only by the approaching daylight from a total demolition of the building."

AFTER THE FACT
Minstrels, Carnivals, and Ghosts

The costumes of Ku Klux Klan night riders—pointed hoods and white sheets—have become a staple of history books. In fact, not all the KKK wore costumes, and those who did sported a variety of outfits. But why use such outlandish, often elaborate disguises? To hide the identity of members, according to some accounts, or to terrorize freedpeople into thinking they were being menaced by Confederate ghosts. But clearly African Americans knew these were living, mortal enemies. Though simpler masks would have hidden identities, the guns that they brandished were far more frightening than any "ghostly" robes.

One historian has suggested that the KKK performances took their cues from traditions already a part of American popular culture: the costumes of Mardi Gras and similar carnivals, as well as the humorous sketches of minstrel shows. In behaving like minstrel performers or carnival revelers, KKK members may have had other audiences in mind. Northerners who read accounts of their doings could be lulled into thinking that the repressive night rides were just humorous pranks, not a threat to Radical rule. For southern Democrats, KKK rituals provided a way to reassert a sense of white supremacy. Klansmen might have been defeated in war, but their theatrical night rides helped overturn the social order of Reconstruction, just as carousers at carnivals disrupted the night. The ritual garb provided more innocent cover for a campaign of intimidation that often turned deadly.

WITNESS

12 What are these ancient ruins?
26 A Conquistador in the Aztec Markets
46 The Indian War of 1622
70 Is There a God?
93 Benjamin Franklin at a Whitefield Revival
109 Fleeing the Stamp Act Mob
132 Partisan War in the Backcountry
146 North Carolina Federalists Post an Insulting Cartoon
181 Impressed by the British Navy
194 The Mere Love of Moving
211 Jackson's Tumultuous Inauguration
229 A Slave's Conversion Experience
253 Resistance and Discipline on a Cotton Plantation
278 In the Gold Diggings
301 John Brown's Impact
329 A Georgia Plantation Mistress in Sherman's Path
350 Mississippi Redeemers

1 The First Civilizations of North

From the air, this serpentine mound fashioned thousands of years ago still stands out in bold relief. Located in southern Ohio, it extends from the snake's coiled tail at the left of the photo to the open mouth at the top right, which is pointed in the direction of the summer solstice sunset. The snake's tail points toward the winter solstice sunrise.

America

THE POWER OF A HIDDEN PAST

Stories told about the past have power over both the present and the future. Until recently, most students were taught that American history began several centuries ago—with the "discovery" of America by Columbus, or with the English colonization of Jamestown and Plymouth. History books ignored or trivialized the continent's precontact history. But the reminders of that hidden past are everywhere. Scattered across the United States are thousands of ancient archaeological sites and hundreds of examples of monumental architecture, still imposing even after centuries of erosion, looting, and destruction.

Man-made earthen mounds, some nearly 5,000 years old, exist throughout eastern North America in a bewildering variety of shapes and sizes. Many are easily mistaken for modest hills, but others evoke wonder. In present-day Louisiana an ancient town with earthworks took laborers an estimated 5 million work hours to construct. In Ohio a massive serpent effigy snakes for a quarter-mile across the countryside, its head aligned to the summer solstice. In Illinois a vast, earthen construct covers 16 acres at its base and once reached as high as a 10-story building. »

WHAT'S TO COME

4 A CONTINENT OF CULTURES

9 INNOVATIONS AND LIMITATIONS

14 CRISIS AND TRANSFORMATION

Observers in the colonial and revolutionary eras looked on such sites as curiosities and marvels. George Washington, Thomas Jefferson, and other prominent Americans collected ancient artifacts, took a keen interest in the excavation of mounds, and speculated about the Indian civilizations that created them. Travelers explored these strange mounds, trying to imagine in their mind's eye the peoples who had built them. In 1795 the Reverend James Smith traced the boundaries of a mound wall that was strategically placed to protect a neck of land along a looping river bend in the Ohio valley. "The wall at present is so mouldered down that a man could easily ride over it. It is however about 10 feet, as near as I can judge, in perpendicular height. . . . In one place I observe a breach in the wall about 60 feet wide, where I suppose the gate formerly stood through which the people passed in and out of this stronghold." Smith was astonished by the size of the project. "Compared with this," he exclaimed, "what feeble and insignificant works are those of Fort Hamilton or Fort Washington! They are no more in comparison to it than a rail fence is to a brick wall."

But in the 1830s and 1840s, as Americans sought to drive Indians west of the Mississippi and then confine them on smaller and smaller reservations, many began thinking differently about the continent's ancient sites. Surely the simple and "savage" people just then being expelled from American life could not have constructed such inspiring monuments. Politicians, writers, and even some influential scientists dismissed the claim that North America's ancient architecture had been built by the ancestors of contemporary Indians and instead attributed the mounds to peoples of Europe, Africa, or Asia—Hindus, perhaps, or Israelites, Egyptians, or Japanese. Many nineteenth-century Americans found special comfort in a tale about King Madoc from Wales, who supposedly shipwrecked in the Americas in the twelfth century and had left behind a small but ingenious population of Welsh pioneers who built the mysterious mounds before being overrun by Indians. The Welsh hypothesis seemed to offer poetic justice, because it implied that nineteenth-century Indians were only receiving a fitting punishment for what their ancestors had done to the remarkable mound builders from Wales.

These fanciful tales were discredited in the late nineteenth and early twentieth centuries. In recent decades archaeologists working across the Americas have discovered in more detail how native peoples built the hemisphere's ancient architecture. They have also helped to make clear the degree to which prejudice and politics have blinded European-Americans to the complexity, wonder, and significance of America's history before 1492. Fifteen thousand years of human habitation in North America allowed a broad range of cultures to develop, based on agriculture as well as hunting and gathering. In North America a population in the millions spoke hundreds of languages. Cities evolved as well as towns and farms, exhibiting great diversity in their cultural, political, economic, and religious organization. «

A CONTINENT OF CULTURES

Most archaeologists agree that the Western Hemisphere's first human inhabitants came from northeastern Asia. At least 15,000 years ago B.P.[1] during the most recent Ice Age, small groups of people began crossing the Bering Strait, then a narrow bridge of land connecting Siberia to Alaska. Gradually these **nomads** filtered southward, some following the Pacific coastline in small boats, but most making their way down a narrow, glacier-free corridor along the eastern base of the Rocky Mountains and onto the northern Great Plains. There they found and hunted a stunning array of huge mammals, so-called megafauna. These animals included mammoths that were twice as heavy as elephants, giant bison, sloths that were taller than giraffes, several kinds of camels, and terrifying, 8-foot long lions. Within a few thousand years the descendants of these Siberians, people whom

nomad a member of a group of people who have no fixed home and who move about, usually seasonally, in pursuit of food, water, and other resources.

---

[1] Before the Present, used most commonly by archaeologists when the time spans are in multiple thousands of years. This text will also use C.E. for Common Era, equivalent to the Christian Era or A.D.; B.C.E. is Before the Common Era, equivalent to B.C.

↑ Aztec merchants, or pochtecas, spoke many languages and traveled on foot great distances throughout Mesoamerica and parts of North America. This one carries a cane and bears a sack of trade goods, topped off by a parrot.

seeds, and edible plants; those in the Pacific Northwest relied mainly on fishing; and those east of the Mississippi, besides fishing and gathering, tracked deer and bear and trapped smaller game animals and birds. Over these same centuries, distinct groups developed their own languages, social organizations, governments, and religious beliefs and practices. Technological and cultural unity gave way to regional diversity as the first Americans learned how to best exploit their particular environments.

Cultures of Ancient Mexico >> To the south, pioneers in **Mesoamerica** began domesticating plants 10,000 years ago. Over the next several thousand years farmers added other crops, including beans, tomatoes, and especially corn, to an agricultural revolution that would transform life through much of the Americas. Because many crops could be dried and stored, agriculture allowed these first farmers to settle in one place.

> **Mesoamerica** the area stretching from present-day central Mexico southward through Honduras and Nicaragua, in which pre-Columbian civilizations developed.

By about 1500 B.C.E., farming villages began giving way to larger societies, to richer and more advanced cultures. As the abundant food supply steadily expanded their populations, people began specializing in certain kinds of work. While most continued to labor on the land, others became craftworkers and merchants, architects and artists, warriors and priests. Their built environment reflected this social change as humble villages expanded into skillfully planned urban sites that were centers of trade, government, artistic display, and religious ceremony.

The Olmecs, the first city builders in the Americas, constructed large plazas, pyramidal structures, and sculpted enormous heads chiseled from basalt. The Olmec cultural influence gradually spread throughout Mesoamerica, perhaps as a result of their trade with neighboring peoples. By about 100 B.C.E., the Olmecs' example had inspired the flowering of Teotihuacán from a small town in central Mexico into a metropolis of towering pyramids. The city had bustling marketplaces, palaces decorated with mural paintings that housed elite warriors and priests, schools for their children, and sprawling suburbs for commoners. At its height, around 650 C.E., Teotihuacán spanned more than ten square miles and had a population of perhaps a quarter million—larger even than that of Rome at the time.

Columbus would wishfully dub "Indians," had spread throughout the length and breadth of the Americas.

As the new world of the Americas was settled, it was changing dramatically. The last Ice Age literally melted away as warmer global temperatures freed the great reservoirs of water once locked in glaciers. A rise in sea levels inundated the Bering Strait, submerging the land bridge, and creating new lakes and river systems. The emergence of new **ecosystems**— climates, waterways, and land environments in which humans interacted with other animals and plants—made

> **ecosystem** a community and/or region studied as a system of functioning relationships between organisms and their environments.

for ever greater diversity. The first human inhabitants of the Americas had fed, clothed, warmed, and armed themselves by hunting megafauna, and few of these giants survived the end of the Ice Age. As the glaciers receded, later generations had to adapt to changing conditions. They adjusted by hunting smaller animals with new, more specialized kinds of stone tools and by learning to exploit particular places more efficiently.

So it was that between 10,000 and 2,500 years ago, distinctive regional cultures developed among the peoples of North America. Those who remained in the Great Plains turned to hunting the much smaller descendants of the now-extinct giant bison; those in the deserts of the Great Basin survived on small game,

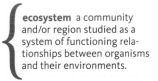

Technological and cultural **unity** gave way to regional **diversity** as the first Americans learned how to best **exploit** their particular environments.

and tribute from the several million other peoples in the region subjugated by the Aztecs.

Unsurpassed in power and wealth, in technological and artistic attainments, theirs was also a highly stratified society. The Aztec ruler, or Chief Speaker, shared governing power with the aristocrats who monopolized all positions of religious, military, and political leadership, while the commoners—merchants, farmers, and craftworkers—performed all manual labor. There were slaves as well, some captives taken in war, others from the ranks of commoners forced by poverty to sell themselves or their children.

More impressive still were the achievements of the Mayas, who benefited from their contacts with both the Olmecs and Teotihuacán. In the lowland jungles of Mesoamerica they built cities filled with palaces, bridges, aqueducts, baths, astronomical observatories, and pyramids topped with temples. Their priests developed a written language, their mathematicians discovered the zero, and their astronomers devised a calendar more accurate than any then existing. In its glory, between the third and ninth century C.E., the Mayan empire boasted some 50 urban centers scattered throughout the Yucatán Peninsula, Belize, Guatemala, and Honduras.

But neither the earliest urban centers of the Olmecs nor the glittering city-state of Teotihuacán survived. Even the enduring kingdom of the Mayas had collapsed by 900 C.E. Like the ancient civilizations of Greece and Rome, they thrived for centuries and then declined. Scholars still debate the reasons for their collapse. Military attack may have brought about their ruin, or perhaps their large populations exhausted local resources.

Mayan grandeur was eventually outdone in the Valley of Mexico. In the middle of the thirteenth century, the Aztecs, a people who had originally lived on Mesoamerica's northern frontiers, swept south and settled in central Mexico. By the end of the fifteenth century, they ruled over a vast empire from their capital at Tenochtitlán, an island metropolis of perhaps a quarter of a million people. At its center lay a large plaza bordered by sumptuous palaces and the Great Temple of the Sun. Beyond stood three broad causeways connecting the island to the mainland, many other tall temples adorned with brightly painted carved images of the gods, zoological and botanical gardens, and well-stocked marketplaces. Through Tenochtitlán's canals flowed gold, silver, exotic feathers and jewels, cocoa, and millions of pounds of maize—all trade goods

Cultures of the Southwest >> Mesoamerican crops and farming techniques began making their way north to the American Southwest by 1000 B.C.E. At first the most successful farmers in the region were the Mogollon and Hohokam peoples, two cultures that flourished in New Mexico and southern Arizona during the first millennium C.E. Both tended to cluster their dwellings near streams, which allowed them to adopt the systems of irrigation as well as the maize cultivation of central Mexico. The Mogollon came to be the master potters of the Southwest. The Hohokam pioneered vast and complex irrigation systems in arid southern Arizona that allowed them to support one of the largest populations in precontact North America.

Their neighbors to the north, in what is now known as the Four Corners of Arizona, Colorado, New Mexico, and Utah, are known as the Anasazi. The Anasazi adapted corn, beans, and squash to the relatively high altitude of the Colorado Plateau

If your outstretched arm represented North America's human history, contact with Europe would happen around the second knuckle of your index finger, with the fingertips being the present. Why do you think students learn so little about the Americas prior to 1492?

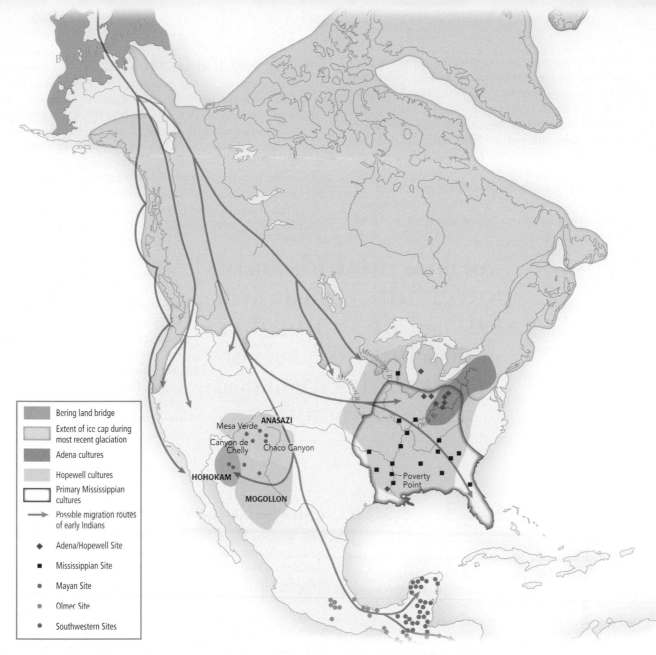

Legend:

- Bering land bridge
- Extent of ice cap during most recent glaciation
- Adena cultures
- Hopewell cultures
- Primary Mississippian cultures
- → Possible migration routes of early Indians
- ◆ Adena/Hopewell Site
- ■ Mississippian Site
- ● Mayan Site
- ● Olmec Site
- ● Southwestern Sites

Map labels: Mesa Verde, ANASAZI, Canyon de Chelly, Chaco Canyon, HOHOKAM, MOGOLLON, Poverty Point, Mississippi R., Missouri R., Ohio R., Bering Strait

EARLY PEOPLES OF NORTH AMERICA

Migration routes across the Bering Strait from Asia were taken by peoples whose descendants created the major civilizations of ancient Americans. The influence of Mesoamerica is most striking among the cultures of the Southwest and the Mississippians.

and soon parlayed their growing surplus and prosperity into societies of considerable complexity. Their most stunning achievements were villages of exquisitely executed masonry buildings—apartment-like structures up to four stories high and containing hundreds of rooms at places such as Mesa Verde (Colorado) and Canyon de Chelly (Arizona). Scores of sites in Chaco Canyon (New Mexico), the largest center of Anasazi settlement, were linked to the wider region by hundreds of miles of wide, straight roads.

Besides their impressive dwellings, the Anasazi filled their towns with religious shrines, astronomical observatories, and stations for sending signals to other villages. Their craftworkers fashioned delicate woven baskets,

beautiful feather and hide sashes, decorated pottery, and turquoise jewelry that they traded throughout the region and beyond. For nearly a thousand years, Anasazi civilization prospered, reaching its zenith between about 900 and 1100 C.E. During those three centuries, the population grew to approximately 30,000 spread over 50,000 square miles, a total area larger than present-day California.

Cultures of the Eastern Woodlands

>> East of the Mississippi, Indian societies prospered in valleys near great rivers (Mississippi, Ohio, Tennessee, and Cumberland), the shores of the Great Lakes, and

the coast of the Atlantic. Everywhere the earliest inhabitants depended on a combination of fishing, gathering, and hunting—mainly deer but also bear, raccoon, and a variety of birds. Around 2000 B.C.E., some groups in the temperate, fertile Southeast began growing the gourds and pumpkins first cultivated by Mesoamerican farmers, and later they also adopted the cultivation of maize. But unlike the ancient peoples of the Southwest, most Eastern Woodland peoples continued to subsist largely on animals, fish, and nuts, all of which were abundant enough to meet their needs and even to expand their numbers.

Indeed, many of the mysterious earthen mounds that would so fascinate Europeans were built by peoples who did not farm. About 1000 B.C.E. residents of a place now known as Poverty Point in northeastern Louisiana fashioned spectacular earthworks—six semicircular rings that rose nine feet in height and covered more than half a mile in diameter.

> **All these mounds attest powerfully not only to the skill and sheer numbers of their builders but also to the complexity of these ancient societies.**

Although these structures might have been sites for studying the planets and stars, hundreds of other mounds—built about 2,000 years ago by the Adena and the Hopewell cultures of the Ohio and Mississippi valleys—served as the burial places of their leading men and women. Alongside the corpses mourners heaped their richest goods—headdresses of antlers, necklaces of copper, troves of shells and pearls—rare and precious items imported from as far north as Canada, as far west as Wyoming, and as far east as Florida. All these mounds attest powerfully not only to the skill and sheer numbers of their builders but also to the complexity of these ancient societies, their elaborate religious practices, and the wide scope of their trading networks.

Even so, the most magnificent culture of the ancient Eastern Woodlands, the Mississippian, owed much of its prominence to farming. By the twelfth century C.E. these peoples had emerged as the premier city-builders north of the Rio Grande, and their towns radiated for hundreds of miles in every direction from the hub of their trading network at Cahokia, a port city of several thousand located directly across from present day St. Louis at the confluence of the Missouri and the Mississippi rivers. Cahokia's many broad plazas teemed with farmers hauling their corn, squash, and beans and with craftworkers and merchants plying their wares. But what commanded every eye were the structures surrounding the plazas—more than 100 flat-topped pyramidal mounds crowned by religious temples and elite dwellings.

Cultures of the Great Plains >>

Cahokia's size and power depended on consistent agricultural surpluses. Outside the Southwest and the river valleys of the East, agriculture played a smaller role in shaping North American societies. On the Great Plains, for example, some people did cultivate corn, beans, squash, and sunflowers, near reliable rivers and streams. But more typically Plains communities depended on hunting and foraging, migrating to exploit seasonally variable resources. Plains hunters pursued game on foot; the horses that had once roamed the Americas became extinct after the last Ice Age. Sometimes large groups of people worked together to drive bison over cliffs or to trap them in corrals. The aridity of the Plains made it a dynamic and unpredictable place to live. During times of reliable rainfall, bison populations boomed, and hunters flocked to the region. But sometimes centuries passed with lower-than-average precipitation, and families abandoned the plains for eastern river valleys or the foothills of the Rocky Mountains.

Cultures of the Great Basin >>

Some peoples west of the Great Plains also kept to older ways of subsistence. Among them were the Numic-speaking peoples of the Great Basin, which includes present-day Nevada and Utah, eastern California, and western Wyoming and Colorado. Small family groups scoured their stark, arid landscape for the limited supplies of food it yielded, moving with each passing season to make the most of their environment. Men tracked elk and antelope and trapped smaller animals, birds, even toads, rattlesnakes, and insects. But the staples of their diet were edible seeds, nuts, and plants, which women gathered and stored in woven baskets to consume in times of scarcity. Several families occasionally hunted together or wintered in common quarters, but because the desert heat and soil defied farming, these bands usually numbered no more than about 50 people.

Cultures of the Pacific Northwest >>

The rugged stretch of coast from the southern banks of present-day British Columbia to northern California has always been an extraordinarily rich natural environment. Its mild climate and abundant rainfall yield forests lush with plants and game; its bays and rivers teem with salmon and halibut, its oceans with whales and porpoises, and its rocky beaches with seals, otters, abalone, mussels, and clams. Agriculture was unnecessary in such a bountiful place. From their villages on the banks of rivers, the shores of bays, and the beaches of low-lying offshore islands, the ancestors of the Nootkans, Makahs, Tlingits, Tshimshians, and Kwakiutls speared or netted salmon, trapped sea mammals, gathered shellfish, and launched canoes. The largest of these craft, from which they harpooned whales, measured 45 feet bow to stern and nearly 6 feet wide.

By the fifteenth century these fecund lands supported a population of perhaps 130,000. They also permitted a culture with the leisure time needed to create works of art as well as an elaborate social and ceremonial life. The peoples of the Northwest built houses and canoes from red cedar; carved bowls and dishes from red alder; crafted paddles and harpoon shafts, bows, and clubs from Pacific yew; and wove baskets from bark and blankets from mountain goat wool. They evolved a society with sharp distinctions among nobles, commoners, and slaves, the last group being mainly women and children captured in raids on other villages. Those who were free devoted their lives to accumulating and then redistributing their wealth among other villagers in elaborate potlatch ceremonies in order to confirm or enhance their social prestige.

Cultures of the Subarctic and the Arctic >> Most of present-day Canada and Alaska were inhospitable to agriculture. In the farthest northern reaches—a treeless belt of Arctic tundra—temperatures fell below freezing for most of the year. The Subarctic, although densely forested, had only about 100 frost-free days each year. As a result, the peoples of both regions survived by fishing and hunting. The Inuit, or Eskimos, of northern Alaska harvested whales from their umiaks, boats made by stretching walrus skin over a driftwood frame and that could bear more than a ton of weight. In the central Arctic, they tracked seals. The inhabitants of the Subarctic, both Algonquian-speaking peoples in the East and Athapaskan speakers of the West, moved from their summer fishing camps to berry patches in the fall to moose and caribou hunting grounds in the winter.

INNOVATIONS AND LIMITATIONS

The first Americans therefore expressed, governed, and supported themselves in a broad variety of ways. And yet they shared certain core characteristics, including the desire and ability to reshape their world. Whether they lived in forests, coastal regions, jungles, or prairies, whether they inhabited high mountains or low deserts, native communities experimented constantly with the resources around them. Over the course of millennia, nearly all the hemisphere's peoples found ways to change the natural world in order to improve and enrich their lives.

America's Agricultural Gifts >> No innovation proved more crucial to human history than native manipulation of plants. Like all first farmers, agricultural pioneers in the Americas began experimenting accidentally. Modern-day species of corn, for example, probably derive from a Mesoamerican grass known as teosinte. It seems that ancient peoples gathered teosinte to collect its small grains. By selecting the grains that best suited them and bringing them back to their settlements, and by returning the grains to the soil through spillage or waste disposal, they unintentionally began the process of

⌃ Theodore de Bry, *Florida Indians Planting Maize*. Both men and women were portrayed as involved in agriculture. Except for the digging stick at the center rear, however, the farming implements drawn by the artist are European in origin.

domestic cultivation. Soon these first farmers began deliberately saving seeds from the best plants and sowing them in gardens. In this way, over hundreds of generations, American farmers transformed the modest teosinte grass into a staple crop that would give rise to the hemisphere's mightiest civilizations.

Indeed, ever since contact with Europe, the great breakthroughs in Native American farming have sustained peoples around the world. In addition to corn, the first Americans gave humanity scores of varieties of squash, potatoes, beans, and other basic foods. Today, plants domesticated by indigenous Americans account for three-fifths of the world's crops, including many that have revolutionized the global diet. For good or ill, a handful of corn species occupies the center of the contemporary American diet. In addition to its traditional forms, corn is consumed in chips, breads, and breakfast cereals; corn syrup sweeteners are added to many of our processed foods and nearly all soft drinks; and corn is fed to almost all animals grown to be consumed, even farmed fish.

Other Native American crops have become integral to diets all over the world. Potatoes revolutionized northern European life in the centuries after contact, helping to avert famine and boost populations in several countries. Ireland's population tripled in the century after the introduction of potatoes. Beans and peanuts became prized for their protein content in Asia. And in Africa, corn, manioc, and other new-world crops so improved diets and overall health that the resulting rise in population may have offset the population lost to the Atlantic slave trade.

> Of the 14 large mammal species that humans successfully domesticated before 1900, how many were indigenous to the Americas?
>
> a. 10
> b. 7
> c. 4
> d. 1
>
> Key: d—the llama

today, after several centuries of disuse, overgrowth, and even deliberate destruction, human-shaped landscapes dating from the precontact period still cover thousands of square miles of the Americas.

Recently, scholars have begun to find evidence of incredible manipulation of landscapes and environments in the least likely of places. The vast Amazon rainforest has long been seen by westerners as an imposing symbol of untouched nature. But it now seems that much of the Amazon was in fact made by people. Whereas farmers elsewhere in the world domesticated plants for their gardens and fields, farmers in the Amazon cultivated food-bearing trees for thousands of years, cutting down less useful species and replacing them with ones that better suited human needs. All told there are more than 70 different species of domesticated trees throughout the Amazon. At least one-eighth of the nonflooded rainforest was directly or indirectly created by humans. Likewise, native peoples laboriously improved the soil across as much as a tenth of the Amazon, mixing it with charcoal and a variety of organic materials. These managed soils are more than 10 times as productive as untreated soils in the Amazon. Today, farmers in the region still eagerly search for the places where precontact peoples enriched the earth.

Native North Americans likewise transformed their local environments. Sometimes they moved forests. Anasazis cut down and transported more than 200,000 trees to construct the floors and the roofs of the monumental buildings in Chaco Canyon. Sometimes they moved rivers. By taming the waters of the Salt and Gila Rivers in present-day Arizona with the most extensive system of irrigation canals anywhere in precontact North America, the Hohokam were able to support large populations in a desert environment. And sometimes they moved the land itself. Twenty-two million cubic feet of earth were moved to construct just one building in the Mississippian city of Cahokia.

Indians also employed fire to systematically reshape landscapes across the continent. Throughout North America's great eastern and western forests, native peoples periodically set low fires to consume undergrowth and fallen trees. In this way the continent's first inhabitants managed

[I]t now seems that much of the Amazon was in fact made by people.

Landscapers >> Plant domestication requires the smallest of changes, changes farmers slowly encourage at the genetic level. But native peoples in the precontact Americas transformed their world on grand scales as well. In the Andes, Peruvian engineers put people to work by the tens of thousands, creating an astonishing patchwork of terraces, dykes, and canals designed to maximize agricultural productivity. Similar public-works projects transformed large parts of central Mexico and the Yucatan. Even

forests and also animals. Burning enriched the soil and encouraged the growth of grasses and bushes prized by game animals such as deer, elk, beaver, rabbit, grouse, and turkey. The systematic use of fire to reshape forests helped hunters in multiple ways: it increased the overall food supply for grazing animals, it attracted those animal species hunters valued most, and, by clearing forests of ground debris, fire made it easier to track, kill, and transport game. Deliberate burns transformed forests in eastern North America to such an extent that bison migrated from their original ranges on the plains and thrived far to the east. Thus, when native hunters from New York to Georgia brought down a buffalo, they were harvesting a resource that they themselves had helped to create.

The Shape of a Problem >> No matter how great their ingenuity, the first Americans were constrained by certain natural realities. One of the most important is so basic that it is easy to overlook. Unlike Eurasia, which stretches across the northern hemisphere along an east-west axis, the Americas fall along a north-south axis, stretching nearly pole to pole. Consequently, the Americas are broken up by tremendous geographic and climactic diversity, making communication and technology transfer far more difficult than it was in the Old World.

Consider the agricultural revolution in Eurasia. Once plants and animals were first domesticated in the Fertile Crescent around 10,000 years ago, they quickly began spreading east and west. Within 1,500 years these innovations had been adopted in Greece and India. A thousand years later the domesticated plants and animals of the Fertile Crescent had reached central Europe, and, from there, it took perhaps 200 years for them to be embraced in present-day Spain. Eurasia's east-west axis facilitated these transfers. Locations at roughly the same latitude share the same seasonal variation, have days of the same length, and often have similar habitats and rates of precipitation, making it relatively easy for plants and animals to move from one place to the next.

In contrast, the north-south orientation of the Americas erected natural

[T]he north-south orientation of the Americas erected natural barriers to plant and animal transfer.

barriers to plant and animal transfer. Mesoamerica and South America, for example, are about as far apart as the Balkans and Mesopotamia. It took roughly 2,000 years for plants and animals domesticated in Mesopotamia to reach the Balkans. But because Mesoamerica and South America are separated by tropical, equatorial lowlands, it took domesticated plants such as corn several thousand years to jump between the two regions. Sometimes the transfer never happened at all before European contact. South American potatoes would have thrived in central Mexico, but the tropics stopped their northward migration. Equatorial jungles also denied Mesoamerican societies the llama and the alpaca, domesticated more than 5,000 years ago in the Andes. One wonders what even greater heights the Olmec, Toltec, Mayan, and Aztec civilizations would have achieved if they had had access to these large creatures as draft animals and reliable sources of protein.

⌃ Fewer large mammal species were available for domestication in the Americas, perhaps because the first wave of humans on the continent contributed to mass extinctions. Native Americans did domesticate dogs, shown here in a watercolor-and-ink sketch of a Mandan dog sled painted by Karl Bodmer in 1834.

Dramatic variations in climate likewise delayed the transfer of agriculture from Mexico to regions north of the Rio Grande. Archaeologists have recently discovered evidence of 10,000-year-old domesticated squash in a cave in southern Mexico, an indication that agriculture began in the Americas nearly as early as anywhere else in the world. Yet squash and corn were not cultivated in the present-day American Southwest for another 7,000 years, and the region's peoples did not embrace a fully sedentary, agricultural lifestyle until the start of the Common Era. Major differences in the length of days, the growing season, average temperatures, and rainfall between the Southwest and central Mexico meant that farmers north of the Rio Grande had to experiment for scores of generations before they had perfected crops suited to their particular environments. Corn took even longer to become a staple crop in eastern North America, which is why we do not see major urban centers arise there until approximately 1000 C.E.

By erecting barriers to communication and the spread of technology, then, the predominantly north-south orien-

WITNESS
What are these ancient ruins?

"I have often observed while travelling thro' this country, a number of round hillocks, raised from 15 feet high and under and from 50 to 100 yards around them. It seems evident that those places are not natural, but the work of man. The only question seems to be, 'What were they made for?' Some have supposed that they were once places of defence. But the most probable opinion is, that they are burying places of the former inhabitants of this country."

tation of Americas made it more difficult for the hemisphere's inhabitants to build on one another's successes. Had American innovations spread as quickly as innovations in Eurasia, the peoples of the Western Hemisphere would likely have been healthier, more numerous, and more powerful than they were when Europeans first encountered them in 1492.

Animals and Illness >> One other profound
difference between the Eurasian world and the Americas concerned animals and disease. Most diseases affecting humans originated from domesticated animals, which came inevitably into frequent and close contact with the humans who raised them. As people across Eurasia embraced agriculture and started living with one

> After [1492], European colonizers discovered the grim advantage of their millennia-long dance with disease.

another and with domesticated animals in crowded villages, towns, and cities, they created ideal environments for the evolution and transmission of infectious disease. For example, measles, tuberculosis, and smallpox all seem to have derived from diseases afflicting cattle.

Eurasians therefore paid a heavy price for living closely with animals. Yet in the long run, the continent's terrible illnesses hardened its population. Victims who survived into adulthood enjoyed acquired immunity to the most common diseases: that is, if they had already encountered a particular illness as children, their immune systems would recognize and combat the disease more effectively in the event of reinfection. By the fifteenth century, then, Eurasian bodies had learned to live with a host of deadly communicable diseases.

But Native American bodies had not. With a few important exceptions, including tuberculosis, pneumonia, and possibly herpes and syphilis, human populations in the western hemisphere seem to have been relatively free from major communicable pathogens. Insofar as most major diseases emerge from domesticated animals, it is easy enough to see why. Indigenous Americans domesticated turkeys, dogs, Muscovy ducks, and Guinea pigs but raised only one large mammal—the llama or alpaca (breeds of the same species).

This scarcity of domestic animals had more to do with available supply than with the interest or ability of their would-be breeders. The extinction of most species of megafauna soon after humans arrived in the Americas deprived the hemisphere of 80 percent of its large mammals. Those that remained, including modern-day bison, elk, deer, and moose, were more or less immune to domestication because of peculiarities in their dispositions, diets, rates of growth, mating habits, and social characteristics. In fact, of the world's 148 species of large mammals, only 14 were successfully domesticated before the twentieth century. Of those 14, only one—the ancestor to the llama/alpaca—remained in the Americas following the mass extinctions. Eurasia, in contrast, was home to 13—including the five most common and adaptable domestic mammals: sheep, goats, horses, cows, and pigs.

With virtually no large mammals to domesticate, Native Americans were spared the nightmarish effects of most of the world's major communicable diseases—until 1492. After that date, European colonizers discovered

INDIANS OF NORTH AMERICA, CIRCA 1500

Establishing the location of native groups in maps of precontact America is always problematic, since many peoples undertook major migrations in the contact period, boundaries between groups were fluid, and many of the names applied to native communities differ from what those communities called themselves before colonization. Nonetheless, this map depicts the rough location of important native peoples and their main modes of subsistence on the eve of contact.

the grim advantage of their millennia-long dance with disease. Old-world infections that most colonizers had experienced as children raged through indigenous communities, usually doing greatest damages to adults whose robust immune systems reacted violently to the novel pathogens. Often native communities came under attack from multiple diseases at the same time. Combined with the wars that attended colonization and the malnutrition, dislocation, and despair that attend wars, disease would kill native peoples by the millions while European colonizers increased and spread over the land. Despite their ingenuity and genius at reshaping plants and environments to their advantage, native peoples in the Americas labored under crucial disadvantages compared to Europe—disadvantages that would contribute to disaster after contact.

CRISIS AND TRANSFORMATION

With its coastal plains, arid deserts, broad forests, and vast grassy plains, North America has always been a place of tremendous diversity and constant change. Indeed, many of the continent's most dramatic changes took place in the few centuries before European contact. Because of a complex and still poorly understood combination of ecological and social factors, the continent's most impressive civilizations collapsed as suddenly and mysteriously as had those of the Olmecs and the Mayas of Mesoamerica. In the Southwest, the Mogollon culture went into eclipse around the twelfth century, the Hohokam and the Anasazi by about the fourteenth. In the Eastern Woodlands, the story was strikingly similar. Most of the great Mississippian population centers, including the magnificent city of Cahokia, had faded by the fourteenth century.

Enduring Cultures >> The survivors of these crises struggled to construct new communities, societies, and political systems. In the Southwest, descendents of the Hohokam withdrew to small farming villages that relied on simpler modes of irrigation. Anasazi refugees embarked on a massive, coordinated exodus from the Four Corners region and established new, permanent villages in Arizona and New Mexico that the Spaniards would collectively call the Pueblos. The Mogollons have a more mysterious legacy, but some of their number may have

Average life expectancy was only 16.5 years.

helped establish the remarkable trading city of Paquime in present-day Chihuahua. Built around 1300, Paquime contained more than 2,000 rooms and had a sophisticated water and sewage system unlike any other in the Americas. The city included 18 large mounds, all shaped differently from one another, and three ballcourts reminiscent of those found elsewhere in Mexico. Until its demise sometime in the fifteenth century Paquime was the center of a massive trading network, breeding macaws and turkeys for export and channeling prized feathers, turquoise, sea shells, and worked copper throughout a huge region.

The dramatic transformations remaking the Southwest involved tremendous suffering. Southwesterners had to rebuild in unfamiliar and oftentimes less productive places. Although some of their new settlements endure even to this day, many failed. Skeletal analysis from an abandoned pueblo on the Rio Grande, for example,

indicates that the average life expectancy was only 16.5 years. Moreover, drought and migrations increased conflict over scarce resources. The most successful new settlements were large, containing several hundred people, and constructed in doorless, defensible blocks, or else set on high mesas to ward off enemy attacks. These changes were only compounded by the arrival of Athapaskan-speaking peoples (known to the Spanish as Apaches and Navajos) in the century or two before contact with Europeans. These hunters and foragers from western Canada and Alaska moved in small bands, were sometimes friendly, sometimes hostile toward different Pueblos, and eventually became key figures in the postcontact Southwest.

In the Eastern Woodlands, the great Mississippian chieftainships never again attained the glory of Cahokia, but key traditions endured in the Southeast. In the lower Mississippi valley, the Natchez maintained both the temple mound-building tradition and the rigid social distinctions of Mississippian civilization. Below the chief, or "Great Sun," of the Natchez stood a hereditary nobility of lesser "Suns" who demanded respect from the lowly "Stinkards," the common people. Other Muskogean-speakers rejected this rigid and hierarchical social model and gradually embraced a new, more flexible system of independent and relatively **egalitarian** villages that forged confederacies to better cope with outsiders. These groupings would eventually mature into three of the great southeastern Indian confederacies: Creek, Choctaw, and Chickasaw.

egalitarian exhibiting or asserting a belief in the equality of humans in a social, political, or economic context.

To the North lived speakers of Iroquoian languages, roughly divided into a southern faction including Cherokees and Tuscaroras, and a northern faction including the powerful Iroquois and Hurons. Like Muskogeans to the South, these Iroquoian communities mixed farming with a hunting/gathering economy and lived in semi-permanent towns. The distinctive feature of Iroquois and Huron architecture was not the temple mound but rather the longhouse (some stretching up to 100 feet in length). Each sheltered as many as 10 families.

The Algonquians were the third major group of Eastern Woodlands people. They lived along the Atlantic seaboard and the Great Lakes in communities smaller than

BACKSTORY
Aztec Rest Stops and Recycling

As one Spanish conqueror wrote home, "on all the roads they have shelters made of reeds or straw or grass so that they can retire when they wish to do so, and purge their bowels unseen by passers-by, and also in order that their excrement shall not be lost," because it was used to cure skins and produce salt.

those of either the Muskogeans or the Iroquois. By the fifteenth century the coastal communities from southern New England to Virginia had adopted agriculture to supplement their diets, but those in the colder northern climates with shorter growing seasons depended entirely on hunting, fishing, and gathering plants such as wild rice.

Cultures of equal and even greater resources persisted and flourished during the fifteenth century in the Caribbean, particularly on the Greater Antilles—the islands of present-day Cuba, Haiti and the Dominican Republic, Jamaica, and Puerto Rico. Although the earliest inhabitants of the ancient Caribbean, the Ciboneys, probably came from the Florida peninsula, it was the Tainos, later emigrants from northern South America, who expanded throughout the Greater Antilles and the Bahamas. Taino chiefs known as *caciques*, along with a small number of noble families, ruled island tribes, controlling the production and distribution of food and tools and exacting tribute from the great mass of commoners, farmers, and fisherfolk. Attending to these elites were the poorest Taino peoples—servants who bedecked their masters and mistresses in brilliant diadems of feathers, fine woven textiles, and gold nose and ear pieces and then shouldered the litters on which the rulers sat and paraded their finery.

North America on the Eve of Contact >>

By the end of the fifteenth century, 5 to 10 million people lived north of the Rio Grande—with perhaps another million living on the islands of the Caribbean—and they were spread among more than 350 societies speaking nearly as many distinct languages. (The total precontact population for all of the Americas is estimated at between 57 and 112 million.)

These millions lived in remarkably diverse ways. Some peoples relied entirely on farming; others on hunting, fishing, and gathering; still others on a combination of the two. Some, such as the Natchez and the Iroquois, practiced matrilineal forms of kinship, in which women owned land, tools, and even children. Among others, such as the

Algonquians, patrilineal kinship prevailed, and all property and prestige descended in the male line. Some societies, like those of the Great Plains and the Great Basin in the West, the Inuit in the Arctic, and the Iroquois and Algonquians in the East, were roughly egalitarian, whereas others, like many in the Caribbean and the Pacific Northwest, were rigidly divided into nobles and commoners and servants or slaves. Some, such as the Natchez and the Taino, were ruled by powerful chiefs; others, such as the Algonquians and the Pueblos, by councils of village elders or heads of family clans; still others in the Great Basin, the Great Plains, and the far North looked to the most skillful hunter or the most powerful shaman for direction. Those people who relied on hunting practiced religions that celebrated their kinship with animals and solicited their aid as guardian spirits, while predominantly agricultural peoples sought the assistance of their gods to make the rain fall and the crops ripen.

The total precontact population for all of the Americas is estimated at between 57 and 112 million.

When Europeans first arrived in North America, the continent north of present-day Mexico boasted an ancient and rich history marked by cities, towns, and prosperous farms. At contact it was a land occupied by several million men, women, and children speaking hundreds of languages and characterized by tremendous political, cultural, economic, and religious diversity. This diversity was heightened by the north/south orientation of the Americas rather than the east/west orientation of Eurasia, since the spread of crops and animals in temperate regions was impeded by the tropical zones of the equator. The isolation from European diseases would make their arrival after 1492 even more devastating. Before 1492, though, the civilizations of North and South America remained populous, dynamic, and diverse.

For most of our nation's short history, we have not wanted to remember things this way. European Americans have had a variety of reasons to minimize and belittle the past, the works, even the size of the native populations that ruled North America for 99 percent of its human history. In 1830, for example, President Andrew Jackson delivered an address before Congress in which he tried to answer the many critics of his Indian removal policies. Although "humanity has often wept over the fate of the aborigines of this country," Jackson said, the Indians' fate was as natural and inevitable "as the extinction of one generation to make room for another." He reminded his listeners of the mysterious mounds that had so captivated the founding fathers. "In the monuments and fortresses of an unknown people, spread over the extensive regions of the West, we behold the memorials of a once powerful race, which was exterminated, or has disappeared, to make room for the existing savage tribes." Just as the architects of the mounds supposedly met their end at the hands of these "savage tribes," the president concluded, so, too, must Indians pass away before the descendents of Europe. "What good man would prefer a country covered with forests and ranged by a few thousand savages, to our extensive republic, studded with cities, towns, and prosperous farms; embellished with all the improvements which art can devise, or industry execute; occupied by more than twelve millions of happy people, and filled with all the blessings of liberty, civilization, and religion!"

Indeed, stories told about the past have power over both the present and the future. Jackson and many others of his era preferred a national history that contained only a few thousand ranging "savages" to one shaped by millions of indigenous hunters, farmers, builders, and inventors. Yet every generation rewrites its history, and what seems clear from this latest draft is the rich diversity of American cultures on the eve of contact between the peoples of Eurasia, Africa, and the Americas. We are still struggling to find stories big enough to encompass not only Indians from across the continent but also those who have come from all over the world to forge this complex, tragic, and marvelous nation of nations.

CHAPTER SUMMARY

During the thousands of years after bands of Siberian nomads migrated across the Bering Strait to Alaska, their descendants spread throughout the Americas, creating civilizations that rivaled those of ancient Europe, Asia, and Africa.

- Around 1500 B.C.E. Mesoamerica emerged as the hearth of civilization in the Western Hemisphere, a process started by the Olmecs and brought to its height by the Mayans and Aztecs.
  - These Mesoamerican peoples devised complex ways of organizing society, government, and religious worship and built cities remarkable for their art, architecture, and trade.
  - Both commerce and migration spread cultural influences throughout the hemisphere, notably to the islands of the Caribbean basin and to North America, an influence that endured long after these empires declined.
- The adoption of agriculture gave peoples in the Southwest and the Eastern Woodlands the resource security necessary to develop sedentary cultures of increasing complexity. These cultures eventually enjoyed great achievements in culture, architecture, and agriculture.
- Inhabitants of the Great Plains, the Great Basin, the Arctic, and the Subarctic evolved their own diverse cultures, relying for subsistence on fishing, hunting, and gathering.
- Peoples of the Pacific Northwest boasted large populations and prosperous economies as well as an elaborate social, ceremonial, and artistic life.

Significant Events

First humans arrive in the Americas	Agriculture begins in the Western Hemisphere	Agriculture spreads from Mesoamerica to the present-day Southeast		The Olmecs begin to build the first Mesoamerican cities		Adena culture reaches its height in North America
AT LEAST 15,000 B.C.E.	CA. 10,000–7000	CA. 2000	CA. 1700–700	CA. 1500	CA. 1000	CA. 500–100
			Poverty Point flourishes in present-day Louisiana		ca. 1000 Agriculture spreads from Mesoamerica to the present-day Southwest	

- The native inhabitants of the Americas transformed their environments in a variety of ways, from pioneering crops that would eventually feed the world to terraforming mountains and jungles.
- Nonetheless, natural constraints would leave Native Americans at a disadvantage compared to Europe. The continent's north-south orientation inhibited the spread of agriculture and technology, and a lack of domesticatable animals compared to Europe left Native Americans with little protection against disease.
- For reasons that remain unclear, many of North America's most impressive early civilizations had collapsed by the end of the fifteenth century. In their wake a diverse array of cultures evolved across the continent.
  - In the Southwest, Pueblo Indians were joined by Athapaskan speaking hunters and foragers in an arid landscape.
  - In much of eastern North America, stratified chiefdoms of the Mississippian era gave way to more egalitarian confederacies of independent villages subsisting on farming and hunting.
- Although Americans in the nineteenth, twentieth, and even twenty-first centuries have been slow to recognize the fact, the societies of precontact America were remarkably populous, complex, and diverse. Their influence would continue to be felt in the centuries after contact.

Additional Reading

The best descriptions of ancient American civilizations are offered by Brian M. Fagan, *Kingdoms of Gold, Kingdoms of Jade: The Americas before Columbus* (1991); and, especially, Charles C. Mann, *1491: New Revelations of the Americas before Columbus* (2005). For North America specifically, see Alice Beck Kehoe, *America before the European Invasions* (2002). For the Southwest, see Stephen Plog, *Ancient Peoples of the Southwest* (1997). For the Eastern Woodlands, see George R. Milner, *The Moundbuilders: Ancient Peoples of Eastern North America* (2005). Roger G. Kennedy, *Hidden Cities: The Discovery and Loss of Ancient North American Civilization* (1994), gives a fascinating account of how white Americans responded to the ruins of ancient American cultures. For the consequences of axis alignment and of domesticated animals, see the captivating work by Jared Diamond, *Guns, Germs, and Steel: The Fates of Human Societies* (1998).

For the cultures of precontact Mexico, see Michael D. Coe and Rex Koontz, *Mexico: From the Olmecs to the Aztecs* (5th ed., 2002). For exhaustive surveys of all regional cultures in North America, see William C. Sturtevant, general editor, *Handbook of North American Indians*, 20 volumes projected (1978–). Carl Waldman, *Atlas of the North American Indian* (1985), is also an excellent source of information, offering much more than good maps.

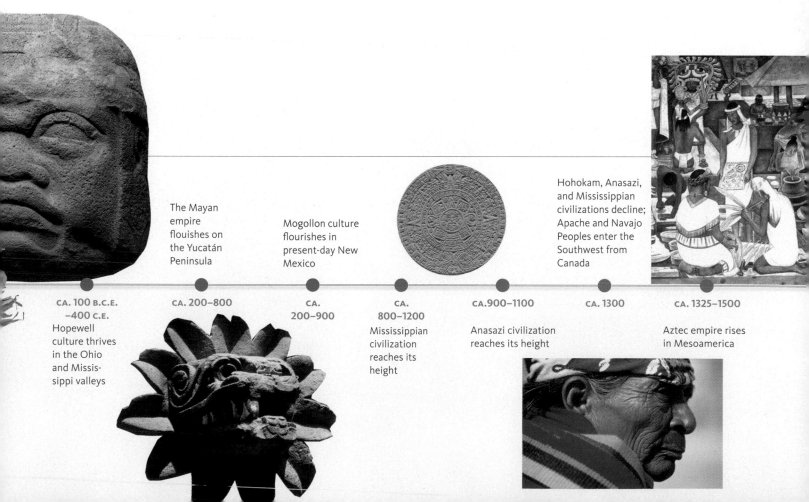

CA. 100 B.C.E. –400 C.E.
Hopewell culture thrives in the Ohio and Mississippi valleys

CA. 200–800
The Mayan empire flouishes on the Yucatán Peninsula

CA. 200–900
Mogollon culture flourishes in present-day New Mexico

CA. 800–1200
Mississippian civilization reaches its height

CA. 900–1100
Anasazi civilization reaches its height

CA. 1300
Hohokam, Anasazi, and Mississippian civilizations decline; Apache and Navajo Peoples enter the Southwest from Canada

CA. 1325–1500
Aztec empire rises in Mesoamerica

2 Old New

WHAT'S TO COME

21 **EURASIA AND AFRICA IN THE FIFTEENTH CENTURY**

24 **SPAIN IN THE AMERICAS**

29 **THE SEARCH FOR NORTH AMERICA'S INDIAN EMPIRES**

30 **RELIGIOUS REFORM DIVIDES EUROPE**

32 **ENGLAND'S ENTRY INTO AMERICA**

With sails bellying in a gale, the Dutch ship in this painting has furled the rest of its canvas to prevent the masts from being blown off. Sailors from western Europe risked much as they crossed the Atlantic in search of fish, silver, gold, and other commodities to trade.

Worlds

Worlds

1400–1600

FISHING NETS AND FAR HORIZONS

All the world lay before them. Or so it seemed to mariners from England's seafaring "West Country" coasts, pushing toward unknown lands in the far Atlantic.

The scent of the new land came first—not the sight of it, but the smells, perhaps the scent of fir trees wafted from beyond the horizon, delicious to sailors who had felt nothing but the rolling sea for weeks on end. Straightaway the captain would call for a lead to be thrown overboard to sound the depths. At its end was a hollowed-out socket with a bit of tallow in it, so that some of the sea bottom would stick when the lead was hauled up. A good sailing master could tell where he was by what came up— "oozy sand" or perhaps "soft worms" or "popplestones" as big as beans. »

Through much of the fifteenth century the search for cod had drawn West Country sailors north and west, toward Iceland. In the 1480s and 1490s a few English tried their luck farther west. They returned with little to show for their daring until the coming of an Italian named Giovanni Caboto, called John Cabot by the English. Cabot, who hailed from Venice, obtained the blessing of King Henry VII to hunt for unknown lands. From the port of Bristol his lone ship set out to the west in the spring of 1497.

This time the return voyage brought news of a "new-found" island where the trees were tall enough to make fine masts and the codfish were plentiful. After returning to Bristol, Cabot marched off to London to inform His Majesty, received 10 pounds as his reward, and with the proceeds dressed himself in dashing silks. The multitudes of London flocked after him, wondering over "the Admiral"; then Cabot returned triumphantly to Bristol to undertake a more ambitious search for a northwest passage to Asia. He set sail with five ships in 1498 and was never heard from again.

By the 1550s Cabot's island, now known as Newfoundland, attracted 400 vessels annually, fishermen not only from England but also from France, Portugal, and Spain. The harbor of present-day St. John's, Newfoundland, served as the informal hub of the North Atlantic fishery. Sailors from three kingdoms dropped anchor there, to take on supplies in the spring, trade with native peoples, or to prepare for the homeward voyage in autumn. There was eager conversation at this meeting place, for these seafarers knew as much as anyone—if not more—about the new world of wonders that was opening to Europeans. They were acquainted with names such as Cristoforo Colombo, the Italian from Genoa whom Cabot might have known as a boy. They listened to Portuguese tales of sailing around the Horn of Africa in pursuit of spices and to stories of Indian empires to the south, rich in gold and silver that Spanish treasure ships were bringing home.

Indeed, Newfoundland was one of the few places in the world where so many ordinary folk of different nations could gather and talk, crammed aboard dank ships moored in St. John's harbor, huddled before blazing fires on its beaches, or crowded into smoky makeshift taverns. When the ships sailed home in autumn, the tales went with them, repeated in the tiniest coastal villages by those pleased to have cheated the sea and death one more time. Eager to fish, talk, trade, and take profits, West Country mariners were almost giddy at the prospect of Europe's expanding horizons.

Most seafarers who fished the waters of Newfoundland's Grand Banks remain unknown today. Yet it is well to begin with these ordinary fisherfolk, for the European discovery of the Americas cannot be looked on simply as the voyages of a few bold explorers. Adventurers such as Christopher Columbus and John Cabot were only the most visible representatives of a much larger expansion of European peoples and culture that began in the 1450s. That expansion arose out of a series of gradual but telling changes in the fabric of European society—changes reflected in the lives of ordinary seafarers as much as in the careers of explorers decked out in silks.

Some of these changes were technological, arising out of advances in the arts of navigating and shipbuilding and the use of gunpowder. Some were economic, involving the development of trade networks such as those linking Bristol with ports in Iceland and Spain. Some were **demographic,**

demographic factors relating to the characteristics of populations. Demography is the study of populations, looking at such aspects as size, growth, density, and age distribution.

bringing about a rise in Europe's population after a devastating century of plague. Other changes were religious, adding a dimension of devout belief to the political rivalries that fueled discoveries in the Americas. Yet others were political, making it possible for kingdoms to centralize and extend their influence across the ocean. Portugal, Spain, France, and England—all possessing coasts along the Atlantic—led the way in exploration, spurred on by Italian "admirals" such as Caboto and Colombo, Spanish *conquistadores* —"conquerors"—such as Hernán Cortés and Francisco Pizarro, and English sea dogs such as Humphrey Gilbert and Walter Raleigh. Ordinary folk rode these currents, too. The great and the small alike were propelled by forces that were remolding the face of Europe—and were beginning to remold the face of the world. «

EURASIA AND AFRICA IN THE FIFTEENTH CENTURY

In 1450, however, the Western European kingdoms that would one day dominate much of the world still sat at the fringe of an international economy that revolved around China. By a variety of measures Ming China was the richest, most powerful, and most advanced society in the world. All Eurasia sought Chinese goods, especially spices, ceramics, and silks, and Chinese ships sped these goods to faraway ports. Seven times between 1405 and 1433, China's "treasure fleet"—300 ships manned by 28,000 sailors and commanded by Zheng He (pronounced "Jung Huh")—unfurled its red silk sails off the south China coast and traveled as far as the kingdoms of eastern Africa. The treasure fleet's largest craft were nine-masted junks measuring 400 feet long, sporting multiple decks and luxury cabins. By comparison, Columbus's largest ship in 1492 was a mere 85 feet long, and the crew aboard all three of his ships totaled just 90 men. Political turbulence led Chinese leaders to ground their trading fleet and end the long-distance voyages. But Chinese luxuries, most transported overland, continued to be Eurasia's most sought-after commodities.

The next mightiest powers in the Old World were not European kingdoms but rather huge Islamic empires, especially the Ottomans in the eastern Mediterranean. The Ottomans rose to prominence during the fourteenth and fifteenth centuries, gaining control of critical trade routes and centers of commerce between Asia and Europe. Their greatest triumph came in 1453, when the sultan Mehmed II conquered Constantinople (now Istanbul), the ancient and supposedly impregnable Christian city that straddled Europe and Asia. Mehmet's stunning victory sounded alarms throughout Europe.

Europe's Place in the World >> Europe's
rulers had good reason for alarm. Distant from Asia's profitable trade and threatened by the Ottomans' military might, most of the continent remained fractious and vulnerable. During the fourteenth and the fifteenth centuries, 90 percent of Europe's people, widely dispersed in small villages, made their living from the land. But warfare, poor transportation, and low grain yields all created food shortages, and undernourishment produced a population prone to disease. Under these circumstances life was, to paraphrase the English philosopher Thomas Hobbes, nasty, brutish, and usually short. One-quarter of all children died in the first year of life. People who reached the age of 40 counted themselves fortunate.

It was also a world of sharp inequalities, where nobles and aristocrats enjoyed several hundred times the income of peasants or craftworkers. It was a world with no strong, centralized political authority, where kings were weak and warrior lords held sway over small towns and tiny fiefdoms. It was a world of violence and sudden death, where homicide, robbery, and rape occurred with brutal frequency. It was a world where security and order of any kind seemed so fragile that most people clung to tradition and feared change.

But Europe was changing, in part because of a great calamity. Between the late 1340s and the early 1350s, bubonic plague—known as the Black Death—swept away one quarter of Europe's population. Some urban areas lost 70 percent of their people to the disease. The Black Death disrupted both agriculture and commerce, and provoked a spiritual crisis that resulted in violent, unsanctioned religious movements, scapegoating of marginal groups, even massacres of Jews. Although Europeans seem to have met recurrent outbreaks of the disease with less panic, the sickness continued to disrupt social and economic life.

⌃ During the sixteenth century, West Country fisherfolk from England sailed from harbors such as Plymouth, shown here. Such seaports were small; the fortifications dotting the coastline and a wall around the town itself were used to defend against invaders.

Yet the sudden drop in population relieved pressure on scarce resources. Survivors of the Black Death found that the relative scarcity of workers and consumers made for higher wages, lower prices, and more land. These changes promoted an overall expansion of trade. In earlier centuries Italian merchants had begun encouraging commerce across Europe and tapping into trade from Africa, the Middle East, and, when able, from Asia. By the late fifteenth century Europe's merchants and bankers had devised more efficient ways of transferring the money generated from manufacturing and trade, and established credit in order to support commerce across longer distances. Wealth flowed into the coffers of traders, financiers, and landlords, creating a pool of capital that investors could plow into new technologies, trading ventures, and, eventually, colonial enterprises.

The direction of Europe's political development also laid the groundwork for overseas colonization. After 1450 strong monarchs in Europe steadily enlarged their power at the expense of warrior lords. Henry VII, the founder of England's Tudor dynasty, Francis I of France, and Ferdinand and Isabella of Spain began the trend, forging modern nation-states by extending their political control over more territory, people, and resources. Such larger, more centrally organized states were able to marshal the resources necessary to support colonial outposts and to sustain the professional armies and navies capable of creating and protecting overseas empires.

Africa and the Portuguese Wave »

European expansion began with Africa. For centuries, African spices, ivory, and gold had entered the Eurasian market either through ports on the Indian Ocean or through the Sahara Desert and into the Mediterranean Sea. Powerful African kingdoms controlled the routes through which these prized commodities moved, while Islamic expansion in the fifteenth century made competition all the more intense. European merchants yearned to access West African markets directly, by ship. But navigational and shipbuilding technology was not yet up to the challenge of the Atlantic's prevailing currents, which sped ships south along Africa's coast but made the return voyage virtually impossible.

Portugal was the first to solve this problem and tap directly into West African markets, thanks in large part to Prince Henry "the Navigator," as he became known. An ardent Catholic and a man who dreamed of turning back Islam's rising tide, Henry understood that direct commerce with West Africa would allow his kingdom to circumvent the costly trans-Sahara trade. To forward his vision, Henry funded exploratory voyages, established a maritime school, and challenged sailors and engineers to conquer the problem of the current. The Portuguese responded by developing the caravel, a lighter, more maneuverable ship that could sail better against contrary winds and in rough seas. More seaworthy than the lumbering galleys of the Middle Ages, caravels combined longer, narrower hulls—a shape built for speed—with triangular lateen sails, which allowed for more flexible steering. The caravel allowed the Portuguese to regularly do what few Europeans had ever done, sail down Africa's west coast and return home. Other advances, including a sturdier version of the Islamic world's astrolabe, enabled Portugal's vessels to calculate their position at sea with unprecedented accuracy.

As the Portuguese pressed southward along the Atlantic rim of sub-Saharan Africa, they began to meet peoples who had never encountered Europeans or even possessed any knowledge of other continents. On catching their first sight of a Portuguese expedition in 1455, villagers on the Senegal River marveled at the strangers' clothing and their white skin. As an Italian member of that expedition recounted, some Africans "rubbed me

Early Modern Goth

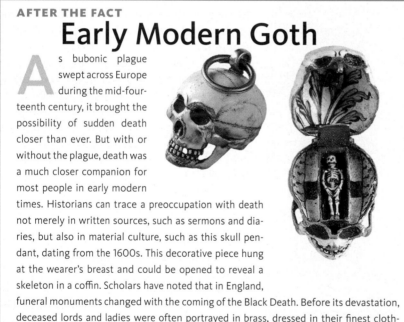

As bubonic plague swept across Europe during the mid-fourteenth century, it brought the possibility of sudden death closer than ever. But with or without the plague, death was a much closer companion for most people in early modern times. Historians can trace a preoccupation with death not merely in written sources, such as sermons and diaries, but also in material culture, such as this skull pendant, dating from the 1600s. This decorative piece hung at the wearer's breast and could be opened to reveal a skeleton in a coffin. Scholars have noted that in England, funeral monuments changed with the coming of the Black Death. Before its devastation, deceased lords and ladies were often portrayed in brass, dressed in their finest clothing. Afterward, the monuments increasingly featured death masks, contorted corpses or skeletons with serpents slinking among their bones. To make yet another contrast, if one does a Google or Yahoo! image search today of the phrase "skull pendant," a host of modern jewelry comes up. In what ways do such fashions reflect their modern culture in the same sort of ways that the skull pendants of the sixteenth and seventeenth century reflected theirs?

<< This stately ivory mask made by an African artist in the early sixteenth century for the Court of Benin (present-day Nigeria) is adorned with 10 bearded heads of white men, representing Portuguese explorers and traders who had first arrived in Benin in 1472.

with their spittle to discover whether my whiteness was dye or flesh."

But the Portuguese were wrong to mistake such acts of innocence for economic or political naïveté. Formidable African chiefdoms and states were eager to trade with Europeans but intent on protecting already established commercial networks. Portugal could not simply take what it wanted from West Africa. With few exceptions, it proved impossible for European powers to colonize territory in West Africa before the nineteenth century, because the region's people were too many and too organized. Furthermore, malaria would kill between one-fourth and one-half of all Portuguese unwise enough to try and stay. To succeed, the newcomers had to seek partners. As the Portuguese built forts and trading houses on the coast, they gave tribute or taxes to local powers in return for trading privileges. The Portuguese offered textiles, especially, but also raw and worked metal goods, currency (in the form of cowry shells), and beads. In return Africans gave up prized commodities such as gold, ivory, and malaguetta pepper. Portuguese traders also expressed interest in another commodity, one that would reshape the wider Atlantic world: slaves.

Sugar and the Origins of the Atlantic Slave Trade >> Unfree labor has existed in nearly all human societies. Although the norms, characteristics, and economic importance of slavery have varied widely over time and place, men, women, and children have been held as slaves from before recorded history to the present. (U.S. and international organizations estimate that today there are as many as 27 million people held in some form of labor bondage and that nearly 1 million unfree people are sold across international borders every year.)

By the Middle Ages, elites in Europe had largely abandoned the slave culture of the Roman Empire and relied instead on serfs or peasants for labor. Slaves became more important as status symbols than as workers, and most were young white women. Indeed, the word "slave" comes originally from "Slav"; Slavic girls and women from the Balkans and the coasts of the Black Sea were frequent targets of slave raids.

But European slavery began to change again following the Crusades. In 1099 Christian forces captured Jerusalem from the Seljuk Turks and discovered sugar plantations that the Turks had cultivated in the Holy Land. Crusaders recognized sugar's economic potential. But because sugar required intense work during planting and close tending during the growing season, they found it a difficult commodity to produce. On maturity the crop had to be harvested and processed 24 hours a day to avoid being spoiled. In short, sugar demanded cheap, pliable labor, and the newly arrived crusaders relied in part on slaves.

When Islamic forces under the famed leader Saladin reconquered Jerusalem in the twelfth century, European investors established new plantations on eastern Mediterranean islands. In addition to being labor intensive, though, sugar was a crop that quickly exhausted soils and forced planters to move operations regularly. Plantations spread to new islands, and by the early 1400s sugar was even being grown in Portugal. As production expanded, planters had to work harder than ever to obtain the necessary labor because of the Black Death and because Turkish conquests restricted European access to the traditional slaving grounds of the eastern Mediterranean and the Balkans.

Thus by the fifteenth century the Portuguese were already producing sugar on slave-run plantations, but they were seeking new crop land and new sources of slaves. Once again Prince Henry's vision enhanced his kingdom's economic interests. While Portugal's merchants were establishing trading posts along the west coast of Africa,

⌃ The rich, volcanic soils of the Azores, the Canaries, and Madeira proved ideal for growing sugar. These islands in the eastern Atlantic were a stepping-stone to later plantations in the Americas, such as the one pictured in this engraving by Theodore de Bry from 1596.

Iberian mariners were discovering or rediscovering islands in the eastern Atlantic: the Canaries, Madeira, and the Azores, islands with rich, volcanic soils ideally suited to sugarcane. By the late 1400s sugar plantations were booming on the Atlantic islands, staffed by West African slaves. By 1550, people of African descent accounted for 10 percent of the population of Lisbon, Portugal's capital city.

Now convinced that they could reach coveted Asian markets by sea, ambitious Portuguese mariners sailed their caravels farther and farther south. In 1488 Bartolomeu Dias rounded the Cape of Good Hope on the southern tip of Africa, sailing far enough up that continent's eastern coast to claim discovery of a sea route to India. Ten years later Vasco da Gama reached India itself, and Portugal's interests ultimately extended to Indochina and China.

Portuguese geographers had long felt certain that travel around Africa was the shortest route to the Orient, but an Italian sailor disagreed. Cristoforo Colombo had spent a decade gaining experience from Portugal's master mariners. He also threw himself into research, devouring Lisbon's books on geography and cartography. Columbus (the Latinized version of his name) became convinced that the fastest route to China lay west, across the uncharted Atlantic Ocean. He appealed to Portugal's king to support an exploratory voyage, but royal geographers scoffed at the idea. They agreed that the world was round but insisted (correctly, as it turns out) that the globe was far larger than Columbus had calculated, making any westward route impractical. Almost a decade of rejection had grayed Columbus's red hair, but—undaunted—he packed up in 1485 and took his audacious idea to Spain.

SPAIN IN THE AMERICAS

He arrived a few years too early. Spain's monarchs, Ferdinand and Isabella, rejected Columbus's offer because they were engaged in a campaign to drive the Muslims out of their last stronghold on the Iberian Peninsula, the Moorish kingdom of Granada. But in 1492 Ferdinand and Isabella took Granada and completed their reconquest of Spain, or *reconquista*. Flush with victory, the pair listened to Columbus argue

reconquista military reconquest of the Iberian peninsula from Islamic Moors of Africa by European Christian rulers.

> He coasted along Cuba and Hispaniola, expecting at any moment to catch sight of gold-roofed Japanese temples or fleets of Chinese junks.

that a westward route to Asia would allow Spain to compete with Portugal and generate enough revenue to continue the reconquest, even into the Holy Land itself. Ignoring the advice of their geographers, the monarchs agreed to his proposal.

Columbus's first voyage across the Atlantic could only have confirmed his conviction that he was destiny's darling. His three ships, no bigger than fishing vessels that sailed to Newfoundland, plied their course over placid seas, south from Seville to the Canary Islands and then due west. On October 11, a little more than two months after leaving Spain, branches, leaves, and flowers floated by their hulls, signals that land lay near. Just after midnight, a sailor spied cliffs shining white in the moonlight. On the morning of October 12, the *Niña*, the *Pinta,* and the *Santa Maria* set anchor in a shallow sapphire bay, and their crews knelt on the white coral beach. Columbus christened the place San Salvador (Holy Savior).

The Spanish Beachhead in the Caribbean >> Like many men of destiny, Columbus mistook his true destination. At first he confused his actual location, the Bahamas, with an island near Japan. He coasted along Cuba and Hispaniola (today's Haiti and Dominican Republic), expecting at any moment to catch sight of gold-roofed Japanese temples or fleets of Chinese junks. He encountered instead a gentle, generous people who knew nothing of the Great Khan but who welcomed the newcomers profusely. Columbus's journals note that they wore little clothing, but they did wear jewelry—tiny pendants of gold suspended from the nose. He dubbed the Taino people "Indians"—inhabitants of the Indies.

It would take some years before other mariners and geographers understood clearly that these newfound islands and the landmasses beyond them lay between Europe and Asia. One of the earliest geographers to do so was the Florentine Amerigo Vespucci, who first described Columbus's Indies as *Mundus Novus,* a "New World." Rather than dub the new lands "Columbia," a German mapmaker called them "America" in Vespucci's honor. The German's maps proved wildly successful, and the name stuck.

Unlike the kingdoms of West Africa, the Taino chiefdoms lacked the military power to resist European aggression. And Europeans decided that the societies they encountered were better suited to be ruled than partnered with. Moreover, while the newfound islands eventually presented their own threats to European health, they seemed a good deal more inviting than the deadly coast

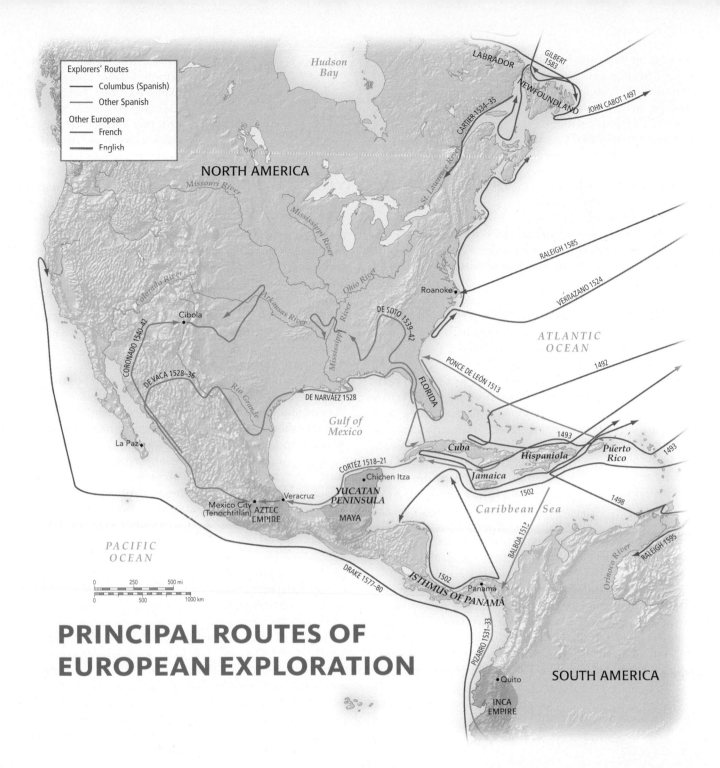

PRINCIPAL ROUTES OF EUROPEAN EXPLORATION

Explorers' Routes
— Columbus (Spanish)
— Other Spanish
Other European
— French
— English

NORTH AMERICA

Hudson Bay

Missouri River

Mississippi River

Colorado River

Arkansas River

Ohio River

St. Lawrence River

LABRADOR

GILBERT 1583

NEWFOUNDLAND

CARTIER 1534–35

JOHN CABOT 1497

RALEIGH 1585

VERRAZANO 1524

Roanoke

DE SOTO 1539–42

CORONADO 1540–42

Cibola

DE VACA 1528–36

Rio Grande

Mississippi River

DE NARVÁEZ 1528

PONCE DE LEÓN 1513

ATLANTIC OCEAN

1492

La Paz

Gulf of Mexico

FLORIDA

1493

Cuba

Hispaniola

Puerto Rico

1493

Jamaica

1502

1498

CORTÉZ 1518–21

Chichen Itza

Veracruz

Mexico City (Tenochtitlán)

AZTEC EMPIRE

YUCATAN PENINSULA

MAYA

Caribbean Sea

BALBOA 1513

PACIFIC OCEAN

DRAKE 1577–80

ISTHMUS OF PANAMÁ

1502

Panamá

Orinoco River

RALEIGH 1595

PIZARRO 1531–33

SOUTH AMERICA

Quito

INCA EMPIRE

0   250   500 mi
0   500   1000 km

---

of West Africa. Hints of gold, a seemingly weak and docile population, and a relatively healthy climate all insured that Columbus's second voyage would be one of colonization rather than commerce. During the 1490s and early 1500s, Spanish colonizers imposed a brutal regime upon the Tainos, slaughtering native leaders and forcing survivors to toil in mines and fields.

Only a few Spaniards spoke out against the exploitation. Among them was Bartolomé de las Casas, a man who spent several years in the Caribbean, participating in conquests and profiting from native labor. Eventually Las

Casas renounced his conduct and, as a Dominican friar, became a tireless foe of Spanish cruelties toward Indians. He railed against the "unjust, cruel, and tyrannical" war waged to force the native peoples into "the hardest, harshest, and most heinous bondage to which men or beasts might ever be bound into." Las Casas's writings, translated throughout Europe and illustrated with gruesome drawings, helped give rise to the "Black Legend" of Spanish atrocities in the Americas.

The warnings had some effect, but not for decades. Within a generation of Columbus's landfall, the Taino population had nearly collapsed from war, overwork, malnutition, despair, and strange new Eurasian diseases. Ambitious Spaniards began scouring the Caribbean basin, discovering new lands and searching for new populations of Indians to subjugate or enslave in place of the vanishing Tainos. Soon the Bahamas were depopulated by Spanish slavers, and conquests had done to present-day Cuba, Jamaica, and Puerto Rico what they first had done to Hispaniola.

[A]n Indian **witness** noted that "the Spaniards . . . picked up the **gold** and fingered it **like monkeys.** . . . Their bodies swelled with **greed.**"

Conquest of the Aztecs >> Would-be con-

quistadors turned their eyes to the mainland. In 1519 an expedition led by the impetuous Hernán Cortés made contact with native peoples on Mexico's gulf coast. They spoke of an oppressive imperial people who occupied a fantastic city to the West. These were the Aztecs.

Aztecs had much in common with Spaniards. Both societies were predominantly rural, with most inhabitants living in small villages and engaging in agriculture. In both places, merchants and specialized craftworkers clustered in cities, organized themselves into guilds, and clamored for protection from the government. Aztec noble and priestly classes, like those in Europe, took the lead in politics and religion, demanding tribute from the common people. Finally, both societies were robustly expansionist, bent on bringing new lands and peoples under their control.

Yet critical differences between these two peoples shaped the outcome of their meeting. The Aztecs lacked the knowledge of ocean navigation, metal tools and weaponry, and firearms. Equally important, the relatively young Aztec empire had not yet established total control over central Mexico. Formidable peoples remained outside Aztec domination, and conquered city-states

within the empire bitterly resented Aztec rule. Cortés exploited that weakness. Massing an army of disgruntled native warriors, he and his men marched inland to the mighty Aztec capital Tenochtitlán, home to more people (roughly a quarter million) than any city then existing in Europe. When the emperor Moctezuma's ambassadors met Cortés on the road and attempted to appease him with gold ornaments and other gifts, an Indian witness noted that "the Spaniards . . . picked up the gold and fingered it like monkeys. . . . Their bodies swelled with greed." The newcomers were welcomed into the city as honored guests but soon seized Moctezuma and took him captive. For months Cortés ruled the empire indirectly, but the Aztecs drove the Spanish out after Moctezuma's death.

In the midst of this victory the city encountered another foe—smallpox. Geographically isolated from Eurasia and its complex disease environment, the Aztecs and all other native peoples in the Americas lacked the acquired immunity that gave Europeans a degree of protection against Old-World pathogens. The resulting **virgin soil epidemics**—so called because the victims had no prior exposure—took a nightmarish toll. Smallpox claimed millions in central Mexico between 1520 and 1521. This, too, presented Cortés with opportunities. Supported by a massive Indian force, he put Tenochtitlán to siege, killing tens of thousands before the ragged, starving survivors surrendered in August of 1521. The feared Aztec empire lay in ruins. Conquistadors fanned out from central Mexico, overwhelming new populations and eventually learning of another mighty kingdom to the South. Again relying on political faction, disease, technological advantages, and luck, by 1532 Spaniards under Francisco Pizarro and his brothers had conquered the Incan empire in South America, which in certain regards outshone even the Aztecs.

virgin soil epidemic epidemic in which the populations at risk have had no previous contact with the diseases that strike them and are therefore immunologically almost defenseless.

The Columbian Exchange >> Virgin

soil epidemics, which contributed to the collapse of many Indian populations, were only one aspect of a complex web of interactions between the flora and fauna of the Americas on the one hand and those of Eurasia and Africa on the other. Just as germs migrated along with

Columbian Exchange transition of people, plants, insects, and microbes between the two hemispheres, initiated when—Columbus reached the Americas in 1492.

humans, so did plants and animals. These transfers, begun in the decades after Columbus first landed in the Caribbean, are known by historians as the **Columbian Exchange**, and they had far-reaching effects on both sides of the Atlantic. Europeans brought a host of American crops home with them, as seen in Chapter 1 (pages 2–17). They also most likely brought syphillis, an American disease that broke out across Europe in more virulent form than ever before. Europeans brought to the Americas the horses and large dogs that intimidated the Aztecs; they brought oranges, lemons, figs, and bananas from Africa and the Canary Islands. Escaped hogs multiplied so rapidly that they overran some Caribbean islands, as did European rats.

The Columbian exchange was not a short-lived event. In a host of different ways it reshaped the globe over the next 500 years as travel, exploration, and colonization brought cultures ever closer. Instead of smallpox, today bird flu from Asia or the West Nile virus threatens populations worldwide. But the exchanges of the sixteenth century were often more extreme, unpredictable, and far-reaching, because of the previous isolation of the two hemispheres.

Key: b

Spanish conquistadores compared the Aztec capital to what European city?

a. London

b. Venice

c. Paris

d. Madrid

The Crown Steps In >>

Proud conquistadors did not long enjoy their mastery in the Americas. Spain's monarchs, who had just tamed an aristocracy at home, were not about to allow a colonial nobility to arise across the Atlantic. The Crown bribed the conquistadors into retirement—or was saved the expense when men such as Francisco Pizarro were assassinated by their own followers. The task of governing Spain's new colonies passed from the conquerors to a small army of officials, soldiers, lawyers, and Catholic bishops, all appointed by the Crown, reporting to the Crown, and loyal to the Crown. Headquartered in urban centers such as Mexico City (formerly Tenochtitlán), an elaborate, centralized bureaucracy administered the Spanish empire, regulating nearly every aspect of economic and social life.

⌃ Both the Aztecs and the Spanish tried to understand the new in terms of the familiar. Hence an Aztec artist portrayed Cortés as an Indian with strange clothes and a stranger beard (*left*), whereas a European artist depicted Moctezuma in the style of a Greco-Roman warrior (*right*).

SPANISH AMERICA, CA. 1600

By 1600, Spain was extracting large amounts of gold and silver from Mexico and South America, as well as profits from sugar plantations in the Caribbean. Each year Spanish treasure ships ferried bullion from mines such as the one at Potosí to the Isthmus of Panama, where it was transported by land to the Caribbean coast, and from there to Spain. An expedition from Acapulco sailed annually to the Philippines as well, returning with Asian spices and other trade goods.

Few Spaniards besides imperial officials settled in the Americas. By 1600, only about 5 percent of the colonial population was of Spanish descent, the other 95 percent being Indian, African, or of mixed heritage. Even by 1800 only 300,000 Spanish immigrants had come to live in the Americas. Indians often remained on the lands that they had farmed under the Aztecs and the Incas, now paying Spanish overlords their taxes and producing livestock for export. More importantly, Indians paid for the new order through their labor, sometimes as slaves but more often through an evolving administrative system channeling native workers to public and private enterprises throughout the Americas. The Spanish also established sugar plantations in the West Indies; these were worked by black slaves who by 1520 were being imported from Africa in large numbers.

Spain's colonies returned even more spectacular profits by the 1540s—the result of huge discoveries of silver in both Mexico and Peru. Silver mining developed into a large-scale capitalist enterprise requiring substantial investment. European investors and Spanish immigrants who had profited from cattle raising and sugar planting poured their capital into equipment and supplies used to mine the silver deposits more efficiently: stamp mills, water-powered crushing equipment, pumps, and mercury. Whole villages of Indians were pressed into service in the mines, joining black slaves and free European workers employed there.

By 1570 the town of Potosí, the site of a veritable mountain of silver, had become larger than any city in either Spain or its American empire, with a population of 120,000. Local farmers who supplied mining centers with food and Spanish merchants in Seville who exported European goods to Potosí profited handsomely. So, too, did the Spanish Crown, which claimed one-fifth of all extracted silver. During the sixteenth century, some 16,000 tons of the precious metal were exported from Spanish America to Europe.

THE SEARCH FOR NORTH AMERICA'S INDIAN EMPIRES

Riches and glory radicalized Spanish expectations. Would-be conquistadors embarked on an urgent race to discover and topple the next Aztec or Incan Empire, a race to become the next Cortés or Pizarro. The prevailing mood was captured by the portrait of a Spanish soldier that adorns the frontispiece of his book about the West Indies. He stands with one hand on his sword and the other holding a pair of compasses on top of a globe. Beneath is inscribed the motto "By compasses and the sword/More and more and more and more."

Some of the most ambitious adventurers felt certain that more lands and riches would be found in the North. The Spanish had probed the North American coast up to present-day South Carolina, looking for slaves. But Juan Ponce de León, the conquerer of Puerto Rico, launched the first official expedition to the mainland, which he named Florida in 1513. Everywhere he met armed resistance and was repulsed, for the inhabitants had come to despise Spaniards as slave raiders. Eight years later, he returned, only to be mortally wounded in a battle with Calusa Indians.

Still, the dreams of northern Indian empires persisted. In 1528 Pánfilo de Narváez, a red-bearded veteran from the conquest of Cuba, led a major expedition back to Florida. Ignoring advice from his second-in-command, Alvar Núñez Cabeza de Vaca, Narváez separated from his main force near Tampa Bay and led 300 men on a harrowing march in search of riches. For months Narváez plundered

> **Disillusioned and desperate, 242 survivors lashed together makeshift rafts and tried to sail along the Gulf Coast to Mexico. Weeks later proud Narváez and most of his men had disappeared at sea.**

his way through Florida, while the men fell ill or fell victim to Indian archers, whose longbows could bury an arrow six inches into a tree. Disillusioned and desperate, 242 survivors lashed together makeshift rafts and tried to sail along the Gulf Coast to Mexico. Weeks later proud Narváez and most of his men had disappeared at sea, whereas Cabeza de Vaca and a handful of survivors washed up on islands off the Texas coast.

Local Indian groups then turned the tables and made slaves of the Spaniards. After years as prisoners, Cabeza de Vaca and three others, including an African slave named Esteban, escaped to make an extraordinary trek across Texas and northern Mexico. Somewhere in present-day Chihuahua they passed through what had been the trading hinterland of Paquime, and Cabeza de Vaca noted an enduring regional commerce in feathers and "green stones"—turquoise. Finally, in July 1536 a shocked party of Spanish slavers stumbled across the four rag-tag castaways and brought them to Mexico City.

The stories the four men told of their ordeal inspired two more massive expeditions to the north. The first, led by Hernán de Soto, scoured the southeast's agricultural villages searching for gold and taking whatever he wanted: food, clothing, luxury goods, even young women whom he and his men "desired both as servants and for their foul uses. . . ." De Soto's men became the first and last Europeans to glimpse several declining Mississippian chiefdoms, echoes of Cahokia's ancient majesty. Some native communities resisted, inflicting substantial losses on the expedition. Others feigned friendship and sent de Soto to hunt gold in neighboring villages, thus ridding themselves of a great danger and directing it at enemies instead. De Soto's men never found the treasures they sought as they traveled through much of the present-day South (see the map, page 25). But the expedition's cruel and destructive foray did hasten the transformation of the southeastern chiefdoms into decentralized confederacies.

Spanish ambition met a similar fate in the West. In 1539, 29-year-old Francisco Vázquez de Coronado led 300 Spaniards and 1,000 Mexican Indian warriors north into the present-day American Southwest. Coronado was emboldened by tales of cities more wondrous than

Tenochtitlán, but his brash confidence began to fail him when instead he found only mud and straw pueblos inhabited by modest farmers. Desperate to turn his hugely expensive expedition to advantage, Coronado sent men in all directions. To the west, his scouts were blocked by the vastness of the Grand Canyon. Others traveled east, forcing themselves on the Pueblo peoples of the Upper Rio Grande, descendants of the Anasazi. Finally Coronado followed an Indian he dubbed the Turk out onto the Great Plains in search of a rumored kingdom called Quivira. Perhaps the Turk had in mind one of the easternmost Mississippian chiefdoms, but the frustrated conquistador became convinced he had been deceived. He had the Turk strangled somewhere in present-day Kansas and in 1542 returned to Mexico, where crown authorities tried him for inflicting "great cruelties" on Indians.

Such North American expeditions ruined conquistadors such as Coronado and de Soto, but Spain could afford these blunders. It had taken vast wealth from the Americas, conquered the hemisphere's mightiest peoples, and laid claim to the bulk of the new world. Yet for most of the sixteenth century rival European powers took little interest in the Americas. England's fishermen continued to explore the North Sea, Labrador, and Newfoundland. Portugal discovered and laid claim to Brazil. France launched expeditions along North America's eastern shoreline (Giovanni da Verrazano, 1524) and the St. Lawrence River Valley (Jacques Cartier, 1534, 1535, and 1541). These efforts proved important in the long run, but for most of the century Spain could treat the Americas as their own.

They owed that luxury, in part, to religious upheaval in Europe. During the second decade of the sixteenth century—the same decade in which Cortés laid siege to Tenochtitlán—religious changes of enormous significance began spreading through Europe. That revolution in Christianity, known as the Protestant Reformation, occupied European attentions and eventually figured as a crucial force in shaping the history of the Americas.

RELIGIOUS REFORM DIVIDES EUROPE

During the Middle Ages, the Roman Catholic Church defined what it meant to be a Christian in western Europe. Like other institutions of medieval society the Catholic

> By the fifteenth century the Catholic Church and the papacy had become enormously powerful but increasingly indifferent to popular religious concerns.

Church was a hierarchy. At the top was the pope in Rome, and under him were the descending ranks of other church officials—cardinals, archbishops, bishops. At the bottom of the Catholic hierarchy were parish priests, each serving his own village, as well as monks and nuns living in monasteries and convents. But medieval popes were weak, and their power was felt little in the lives of most Europeans. Like political units of the era, religious institutions of the Middle Ages were local and decentralized.

Between about 1100 and 1500, however, as the monarchs of Europe grew more powerful so, too, did the popes. The Catholic Church acquired land throughout Europe, and its swelling bureaucracy added to church income from tithing (taxes contributed by church members) and from fees paid by those appointed to church offices. In the thirteenth century, church officials also began to sell "indulgences." For ordinary believers who expected to spend time after death purging their sins in purgatory, the purchase of an indulgence promised to shorten that punishment by drawing on a "treasury of merit" amassed by the good works of Christ and the saints.

By the fifteenth century the Catholic Church and the papacy had become enormously powerful but increasingly indifferent to popular religious concerns. Church officials meddled in secular politics. Popes and bishops flaunted their wealth, while poorly educated parish priests neglected their pastoral duties. At the same time, popular demands for religious assurance grew increasingly intense.

The Teachings of Martin Luther ››

Into this climate of heightened spirituality stepped Martin Luther, who abandoned studying the law to enter a monastery. Like many of his contemporaries, Luther was consumed by fears over his eternal fate. He was convinced that he was damned, and he could not find any consolation in the Catholic Church. Catholic doctrine taught that a person could be saved by faith in God and by his or her own good works—by leading a virtuous life, observing the sacraments (such as baptism, the Mass, and penance), making pilgrimages to holy places, and praying to Christ and the saints. Because Luther believed that human nature was innately evil, he despaired of being able to lead a life that "merited" salvation. If men and women are so bad, he reasoned, how could they ever win their way to heaven with good works?

Luther finally drew on the Bible to break through his despair. It convinced him that God did not require fallen humankind to earn salvation. Salvation, he concluded, came by faith alone, the "free gift" of God to undeserving sinners. The ability to live a good life could not be the *cause* of salvation but its *consequence:* once men and women believed that they had saving faith, moral behavior was possible. Luther elaborated that idea, known as "justification by faith alone," between 1513 and 1517.

Luther was ordained a priest and then assigned to teach at a university in Wittenberg, Germany. He became increasingly critical, however, of the Catholic Church as an institution. In 1517 he posted on the door of a local church 95 theses attacking the Catholic hierarchy for selling salvation in the form of indulgences.

The novelty of this attack was not Luther's open break with Catholic teaching. Challenges to the church had cropped up throughout the Middle Ages. What was new was the passion and force behind Luther's protest. Using the blunt, earthy Germanic tongue, he expressed the anxieties of many devout laypeople and their outrage at the church hierarchy's neglect. The "gross, ignorant asses and knaves at Rome," he warned, should keep their distance from Germany, or else "jump into the Rhine or the nearest river, and take . . . a cold bath."

The pope and his representatives in Germany at first tried to silence Martin Luther, then excommunicated him. But opposition only pushed Luther toward more radical positions. He asserted that the church and its officials were not infallible; only the Scriptures were without error. Every person, he said, should read and interpret the Bible for himself or herself. In an even more direct assault on church authority, he advanced an idea known as "the priesthood of all believers." Catholic doctrine held that salvation came only through the church and its clergy, a privileged group that possessed special access to God. Luther asserted that every person had the power claimed by priests.

Although Luther had not intended to start a schism within Catholicism, independent Lutheran churches were forming in Germany by the 1520s. During the 1530s Luther's ideas spread throughout Europe, where they were eagerly taken up by other reformers.

The Contribution of John Calvin >>

Luther's most influential successor was John Calvin, a French lawyer turned theologian. Calvin agreed with Luther that men and women could not merit their salvation. But, whereas Luther's God was a loving deity who extended his mercy to sinful humankind, Calvin conceived of God as awesome, all-knowing and all-powerful—the controlling force in human history that would ultimately triumph over Satan. To bring about that final victory, to usher in his heavenly kingdom, God had selected certain people as his agents, Calvin believed. These people—"the saints," or "the elect"—had been "predestined"

> **elect** in theology, those of the faithful chosen, or "elected" by God for eternal salvation.

by God for eternal salvation in heaven.

Calvin's emphasis on predestination led him to another distinctively Protestant notion—the doctrine of calling. How could a person learn whether he or she belonged to the elect who were saved? Calvin answered: strive to behave like a saint. God expected his elect to serve the good of society by unrelenting work in a "calling," or occupation, in the world. In place of the Catholic belief in the importance of good works, Calvin emphasized the goodness of work itself. Success in attaining discipline and self-control, in bringing order into one's own life and the entire society, revealed that a person might be among the elect.

⌃ Protestants such as Luther and Calvin placed greater emphasis on the Word of Scripture rather than church rituals controlled by priests and bishops. In this seventeenth-century portrait of John Calvin, sacred words from scripture literally help define him.

Calvin fashioned a religion to change the world. Whereas Luther believed that Christians should accept the existing social order, Calvin called on Christians to become activists, reshaping society and government to conform with God's laws laid down in the Bible. He wanted all Europe to become like Geneva, the Swiss city that he had converted into a holy commonwealth in which the elect regulated the behavior and morals of everyone else. And unlike Luther, who wrote primarily for a German audience, Calvin addressed his most important book, *The Institutes of the Christian Religion* (1536), to Christians throughout Europe. Reformers from every country flocked to Geneva to learn more about Calvin's ideas.

French Huguenots and the Birth of Spanish Florida >>

The Protestant Reformation shattered the unity of Christendom in Western Europe. Spain, Ireland, and Italy remained firmly Catholic. England, Scotland, the Netherlands, Switzerland, and France developed either dominant or substantial Calvinist constituencies. Much of Germany and Scandinavia opted for Lutheranism. As religious groups competed for political power and the loyalties of believers, brutal wars swept sixteenth-century Europe. France experienced some of the worst violence. An influential group of Huguenots (Calvin's

French followers) saw in North America a potential refuge from religious persecution. Under Jean Ribault, 150 Huguenots in 1562 established a simple village on Parris Island off present-day South Carolina. That experiment ended in desperation and cannibalism, but two years later Ribault led another, larger group to a site south of present-day Jacksonville, Florida. Here, at Fort Caroline, the Huguenots nurtured a cordial relationship with the local Timucua Indians. It seemed a promising start.

But Spanish authorities in the Caribbean took the Huguenots for a triple threat. First, French pirates had long tried to siphon silver from the Americas by waylaying Spanish galleons as they rode the Gulf Stream up the southeastern coast of North America before turning east toward Spain. With good reason, Spanish administrators feared that Fort Caroline would entrench the threat of piracy. Second, Spain worried that France would take a broader interest in the Americas, perhaps eventually planting colonies in all of North America. Finally, many Spanish Catholics saw Protestantism as a loathsome contagion, to be expunged from Europe and barred from the Americas.

These interlocking concerns prompted Spain to found a permanent colony in Florida under the direction of a focused and unforgiving man named Pedro Menéndez de Avilés. In 1565 Menéndez established a settlement on the coast called Saint Augustine (still the United States' oldest continuously occupied, non-Indian settlement). Next he and 500 soldiers slogged through the rain and marsh until they found Fort Caroline. In battle and through later executions, the attackers killed Ribault and about 500 of his Huguenots. Flush with victory, Menéndez established several more outposts on Florida's Atlantic and Gulf coasts, and in 1570 even encouraged a short-lived Jesuit mission just miles from where English colonists would establish Jamestown a generation later. As for the Huguenots, the calamity at Fort Caroline dashed hope that the New World would be their haven. Most had to resign themselves to intensifying persecution in France.

The English Reformation >> While the Reformation racked northern Europe, King Henry VIII of England labored at a goal more worldly than those of Luther and Calvin. He wanted a son, a male heir to continue the Tudor dynasty. When his wife, Catherine of Aragon, gave birth to a daughter, Mary, Henry petitioned the Pope to have his marriage annulled in the hope that a new wife would give him a son. This move enraged the king of Spain, who also happened to be Catherine's nephew. He persuaded the pope to refuse Henry's request. Defiantly, England's

king proceeded with the divorce nonetheless and quickly married his mistress, Anne Boleyn. He then went further, making himself, not the pope, the head of the Church of England. Henry was an audacious but practical man, and he had little interest in promoting reformist doctrine. Apart from discarding the Pope, the Church of England remained essentially Catholic in its teachings and rituals.

England's Protestants gained ground during the six-year reign of Henry's son Edward VI but then found themselves persecuted when Edward's Catholic half-sister Mary became queen in 1553. Five years later the situation turned again, when Elizabeth I (Anne Boleyn's daughter) took the throne, proclaiming herself the defender of Protestantism. Elizabeth was no radical Calvinist, however. A vocal minority of her subjects were reformers of that stripe, calling for the English church to purge itself of bishops, elaborate ceremonies, and other Catholic "impurities." Because of the austerity and zeal of such Calvinist radicals, their opponents proclaimed them "Puritans."

Radical Protestants might annoy Elizabeth as she pursued her careful, moderate policies, but radical Catholics frightened her. She had reason to worry that Spain might use English Catholics to undermine her rule. More ominously, Elizabeth's advisors cautioned that Catholic Ireland to the west would be an ideal base from which Spain or France could launch an invasion of England. Beginning in 1565 the queen encouraged a number of her elite subjects to sponsor private ventures for subduing the native Irish and settling loyal English Protestants on their land. As events fell out, this Irish venture proved to be a prelude to England's bolder attempt to found colonies across the Atlantic.

ENGLAND'S ENTRY INTO AMERICA

Among the gentlemen eager to win fame and fortune were Humphrey Gilbert and Walter Raleigh, two adventurers with conquistador appetites for more and more. The pair were like most of the English who went to Ireland, ardent Protestants who viewed the native Catholic inhabitants as superstitious, pagan savages: "They blaspheme, they murder, commit whoredome," complained one Englishman, "hold no wedlocke, ravish, steal. . . ." Thus the English found it easy enough to justify their conquest. They proclaimed it their duty to teach the Irish the discipline of hard work, the rule of law, and the truth of

King Henry VIII of England labored at a goal more worldly than those of Luther and Calvin. He wanted a son.

Protestant Christianity. And, while the Irish were learning these civilized, English ways, they would not be allowed to buy land or hold office or serve on juries or give testimony in courts or learn a trade or bear arms.

When the Irish rebelled at that program of "liberation," the English ruthlessly repressed them, slaughtering not only combatants but civilians as well. Most English in Ireland, like most Spaniards in America, believed that native peoples who resisted civilization and proper Christianity should be subdued at any cost. No scruples stopped Humphrey Gilbert, in an insurgent country, from planting the path to his camp with the severed heads of Irish rebels.

The struggle to colonize and subdue Ireland would serve as a rough model for later English efforts at expansion. The approach was essentially military, like that of the conquistadors. It also set the ominous precedent that Englishmen could treat "savage" peoples with a level of brutal cruelty that would have been inappropriate in wars between "civilized" Europeans. Finding "neither reputation, or profytt" in Ireland, Gilbert, Raleigh, and other West County gentry took their ambition and their Irish education to North America.

The Ambitions of Gilbert, Raleigh, and Wingina

>> In 1578 Gilbert got his chance for glory when Elizabeth granted him a royal patent—the first English colonial **charter**—to explore, occupy, and govern any territory in America " not actually possessed of any Christian prince or people." The vague, wildly unrealistic charter ignored the Indian possession of North America and made Gilbert proprietor of all the land lying between Florida and Labrador. In many ways his dreams looked backward. Gilbert hoped to set up a kind of medieval kingdom of his own, where loyal tenant farmers would work the lands of manors, paying rent to feudal lords. Yet his vision also looked forward to a utopian society. He planned to encourage England's poor to emigrate

> { **charter** document issued by a sovereign ruler, legislature, or other authority creating a public or private corporation

What do you think happened to the Roanoke colonists?

No scruples stopped Humphrey Gilbert, in an **insurgent** country, from planting the path to his camp with the **severed heads** of Irish rebels.

by providing them free land and a government "to be chosen by consent of the people." Elizabeth had high hopes for her haughty champion, but a fierce storm got the better of his ship, and the Atlantic swallowed him before he ever set foot in his American dominions.

Meanwhile Gilbert's stepbrother Walter Raleigh had been laying the groundwork for a British American empire. Raleigh enlisted the talents of Richard Hakluyt, a clergyman, to write an eloquent plea for the English settlement of America, titled *A Discourse Concerning Westerne Planting*. North America's temperate and fertile lands, Hakluyt argued, would not only grow profitable crops, they would also make an excellent base from which to harry the Spanish, search for a Northwest Passage to Asia, and spread Protestantism. Finally, Hakluyt predicted that because the "Spaniardes have executed most outragious and more then Turkishe cruelties in all the west Indies," that Indians would greet Englishmen as liberators.

By the summer of 1584 Raleigh had dispatched an exploratory voyage to the Outer Banks of present-day North Carolina. Expedition

>> John White's sensitive watercolor *Indian Elder or Chief* may well be of Wingina. The portrayal includes the copper ornament worn hanging from his neck, indicating high social status and the presence of an active trade network, since copper is not found on the island. Just as Raleigh had to gauge his strategy in dealing with the Indians, Wingina had to decide how to treat the strange newcomers from across the Atlantic.

EUROPEAN EXPLORATION: FIFTEENTH AND SIXTEENTH CENTURIES

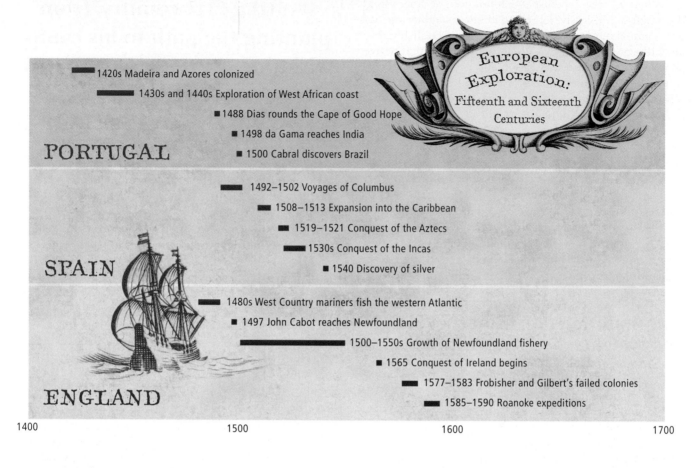

European Exploration: Fifteenth and Sixteenth Centuries

PORTUGAL
- 1420s Madeira and Azores colonized
- 1430s and 1440s Exploration of West African coast
- 1488 Dias rounds the Cape of Good Hope
- 1498 da Gama reaches India
- 1500 Cabral discovers Brazil

SPAIN
- 1492–1502 Voyages of Columbus
- 1508–1513 Expansion into the Caribbean
- 1519–1521 Conquest of the Aztecs
- 1530s Conquest of the Incas
- 1540 Discovery of silver

ENGLAND
- 1480s West Country mariners fish the western Atlantic
- 1497 John Cabot reaches Newfoundland
- 1500–1550s Growth of Newfoundland fishery
- 1565 Conquest of Ireland begins
- 1577–1583 Frobisher and Gilbert's failed colonies
- 1585–1590 Roanoke expeditions

1400   1500   1600   1700

leaders made friendly contact with a people known as the Roanoke and ruled by a "weroance," or chief, named Wingina. The enthusiastic Hakluyt envisioned a colony that would become the Mexico of England, full of plantations producing sugar and silk and mountains yielding gold. Elizabeth knighted Raleigh and allowed him to name the new land "Virginia," after his virgin queen.

But Raleigh was not the only one with grand plans. Almost certainly Wingina had encountered or at least heard of Europeans before 1584. Like most coastal groups in the region, his people would have obtained prized European tools and commodities through indirect trade or by scouring wrecked ships. Eager to fortify his own and his people's power, Wingina recognized that friendly relations with the English would give him access to their trade and influence. Perhaps he believed he would act as patron to the newcomers. After all, they knew little of the region, spoke no Indian languages, and even lacked the skills necessary to survive in the area without native assistance. In short, Wingina seems to have welcomed the English because he believed that they could be useful and that they could be controlled. It was a tragic if understandable

miscalculation—one that Indian leaders would make again and again in colonial America.

Raleigh apparently aimed to establish on Roanoke a mining camp and a military garrison. In a stroke of genius, he included in the company of 108 men a scientist, Thomas Hariot, to study the country's natural resources, and an artist, John White, to make drawings of the Virginia Indians. *A Briefe and True Reporte of the New Found Land of Virginia* (1588), written by Hariot and illustrated by White, served as one of the principal sources about North America and its Indian inhabitants for more than a century. Far less inspired was Raleigh's choice to lead the expedition—two veterans of the Irish campaigns, Sir Richard Grenville and Ralph Lane. Even his fellow conquistadors in Ireland considered Lane proud and greedy. As for Grenville, he was given to breaking wineglasses between his teeth and then swallowing the shards to show that he could stand the sight of blood, even his own.

The bullying ways of both men quickly alienated the natives of Roanoke. Wingina found the newcomers disrespectful, haughty, and cruel: when a local stole a cup, the English tried to teach everyone a lesson by torching his village and destroying its corn stores. As suspicions and resentments mounted on each side, Wingina tried to regain control of the situation the following summer by meeting with Lane to improve relations. But the meeting was a trap. Lane's men opened fire at the Indian envoys, killed Wingina, and hacked the head from his body. All that averted a massive counterattack was the arrival of England's preeminent privateer, Sir Francis Drake, fresh from freebooting up and down the Caribbean. The settlement's 102 survivors piled onto Drake's ships and put an ocean between themselves and the avenging Roanokes.

A Second Roanoke — and Croatoan >>

Undaunted, Raleigh organized a second expedition to plant a colony farther north, in Chesapeake Bay. He recruited 119 men, women, and children, members of the English middle class, and granted each person an estate of 500 acres. He also appointed as governor the artist John White, who brought along a suit of armor for ceremonial occasions.

White deplored Lane's treachery toward Wingina and hated the senseless violence that had characterized the entire endeavor. The artist had spent his time on Roanoke closely observing native peoples, their material cultures, and their customs. His sensitive watercolors, especially those featuring women and children, indicate a genuine respect and affection. White believed that under prudent, moral leaders an English colony could indeed coexist peacefully with American Indians.

Despite his best intentions, everything went wrong. In July of 1587 the expedition's pilot insisted on leaving the colonists at Roanoke Island rather than the Chesapeake. Understandably, the Roanokes took no pleasure in seeing the English return. Sensing that the situation on Roanoke could quickly become desperate, the colonists sent White home to fetch reinforcements.

He returned to England in 1588 just as the massive Spanish navy, the Armada, was preparing an assault on England. Elizabeth enlisted every seaworthy ship and able-bodied sailor to stave off invasion. The Armada was defeated, but White was unable to return to Roanoke Island until 1590. There, he found only an empty fort and a few cottages in a clearing. The sole clue to the colony's fate was an inscription carved on a post: CROATOAN. It was the name of a nearby island off Cape Hatteras.

Had the Roanoke colonists fled to Croatoan for safety? Had they moved to the mainland and joined Indian communities? Had they been killed by Wingina's people? The fate of the "lost colony" remains a mystery, though later rumors suggest that the missing colonists merged with native societies in the interior. His dream of a tolerant, cooperative colony dashed, White sailed back to England, leaving behind the little cluster of cottages, which would soon be overgrown with vines, and his suit of armor, which was already "almost eaten through with rust."

All the world lay before them. Or so it had seemed to the young men from England's West Country who dreamed of gold and glory, conquest and colonization. True, they lived on the fringe of the civilized world in the fifteenth and sixteenth centuries. China remained the distant, exotic kingdom of power and wealth, supplying silks and spices and other luxurious goods. Islamic empires stood astride the land routes from Europe to the east. Nations on the western edge of Europe thus took to the seas. Portugal sent slave and gold traders to Africa, as well as merchants to trade with the civilizations of the Indies. Spanish conquerors such as Cortés toppled Indian empires and brought home mountains of silver. But England's West County sea dogs—would-be conquistadors—met only with frustration. In 1600, more than a century after Columbus's first crossing, not a single English settlement existed in the Americas.

What was left of the freebooting West Country world? Raleigh, his ambition still afire, sailed to South America in quest of a rich city named El Dorado. In 1603, however, Elizabeth's death brought to the English throne her cousin James I, the founder of the Stuart dynasty. The new king arrested the old queen's favorite for treason and imprisoned him for 15 years in the Tower of London. Set free in 1618 at the age of 64, Raleigh returned to South America, his lust for El Dorado undiminished. Along the way he plundered some Spanish silver ships, defying King James's orders. It was a fatal mistake, for England had made peace with Spain. Raleigh lost his head.

James I did not want to harass the king of Spain; he wanted to imitate him. The Stuarts were even more determined than the Tudors had been to enlarge the sphere of royal power. There would be no room in America for a warrior nobility of conquistadors, no room for a feudal fiefdom ruled by the likes of Raleigh or Gilbert. Instead, there would be profitable plantations and colonies managed by loyal, efficient bureaucrats. America would strengthen English monarchs, paving their path to greater power, just

> White believed that under **prudent, moral leaders** an English colony could indeed **coexist peacefully** with American Indians. Despite his best **intentions**, everything went **wrong**.

as the dominions of Mexico and Peru had enlarged the authority of the Spanish Crown. America would be the making of kings and queens.

Or would it? For some Europeans, weary of freebooting conquistadors and sea rovers, the security that Crown rule and centralized states promoted in Western Europe would be enough. But others, men and women who were often desperate and sometimes idealistic, would cast their eyes west across the Atlantic and want more.

CHAPTER SUMMARY

During the late fifteenth century, Europeans and Africans made their first contact with the Americas, where native cultures were numerous and diverse.

- During the fourteenth and early fifteenth centuries, Western Europeans were on the fringes of an international economy drawn together by Chinese goods such as spices, ceramics, and silks.
- A combination of technological advances, the rise of new trade networks and techniques, and increased political centralization made Europe's expansion overseas possible.
- Led by Portugal, European expansion began with a push southward along the West African coast, in pursuit of spices, ivory, and gold. As sugar plantations were established in the islands of the eastern Atlantic, a slave trade in Africans became a part of this expansive commerce.

- Spain took the lead in exploring and colonizing the Americas, consolidating a vast and profitable empire of its own in the place of Aztec and Inca empires. Divisions within Indian empires and the devastating effects of European diseases made Spanish conquest possible.
- The conquistadors who led the Spanish occupation were soon replaced by an elaborate, centralized royal bureaucracy, which regulated most aspects of economic and social life. The discovery of silver provided Spain with immense wealth, while leading to sharply increased mortality among the native population.
- Spanish conquistadors also explored much of the present day southeastern and southwestern United States. They found no empires, silver mines, or rich empires and were thwarted by the Indian peoples they encountered.
- The Protestant Reformation was inaugurated by Martin Luther in 1517 and carried on by John Calvin, whose more activist theology spread from his headquarters in Geneva outward to England, Scotland, the Netherlands, and the Huguenots in France.
- England, apprehensive of Spain's power, did not turn its attention to exploration and colonization until the 1570s and 1580s. By the time it did, European rivalries were heightened by splits arising out of the Protestant Reformation.
- England's merchants and gentry lent support to colonizing ventures, although early efforts, such as those at Roanoke, failed.

Significant Events

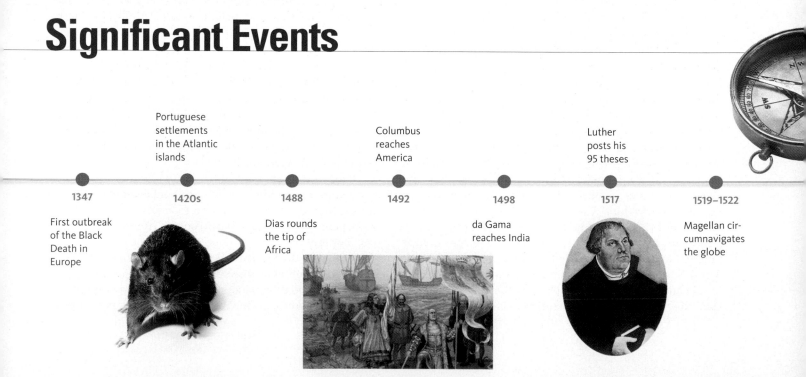

| 1347 | 1420s | 1488 | 1492 | 1498 | 1517 | 1519–1522 |

Portuguese settlements in the Atlantic islands — 1420s

Columbus reaches America — 1492

Luther posts his 95 theses — 1517

First outbreak of the Black Death in Europe — 1347

Dias rounds the tip of Africa — 1488

da Gama reaches India — 1498

Magellan circumnavigates the globe — 1519–1522

Additional Reading

For a description of the entrepreneurs, mariners, and ordinary folk who participated in the era of exploration and discovery, see Kenneth R. Andrews, *Trade, Plunder, and Settlement: Maritime Enterprise and the Genesis of the British Empire, 1480–1630* (1985). For Portugal's initial expansion, see Malyn Newitt, *A History of Portuguese Overseas Expansion, 1400–1668* (2004). John Thornton's *Africa and Africans in the Making of the Atlantic World 1400–1680* (1992) is a detailed analysis of West Africa's role in the changing international economy. For sugar as an engine of expansion, see Philip D. Curtin, *The Rise and Fall of the Plantation Complex: Essays in Atlantic History* (2nd ed., 1998). The demographic catastrophe that followed contact is explored in Noble David Cook, *Born to Die: Disease and New World Conquests* (1998). For a contemporary classic that puts European expansion in global perspective, see Jared Diamond, *Guns, Germs, and Steel: The Fates of Human Societies* (1998).

For Spain in the Caribbean, see Carl Ortwin Sauer, *The Early Spanish Main* (1966). For a scholarly overview of Indians in central Mexico after Cortés, rooted in native language sources, see James Lockhart, *The Nahuas after Conquest: A Social and Cultural History of the Indians of Central Mexico, Sixteenth through Eighteenth Centuries* (1992).

For a magisterial narrative of Spain's activities in North America, see David J. Weber, *The Spanish Frontier in North America* (1992). Rolena Adorno and Patrick Charles Pautz's translation of *The Narrative of Cabeza de Vaca* (2003) is unsurpassed, the castaways' ordeal is splendidly retold by Andrés Reséndez in *A Land So Strange* (2007). Coronado's sojourn is the subject of the exacting work by Richard Flint and Shirley Cushing Flint, *Documents of the Coronado Expedition, 1539–1542* (2005). For the Southeast, see Charles Hudson, *Knights of Spain, Warriors of the Sun: Hernando de Soto and the South's Ancient Chiefdoms* (1997).

For a good introduction to the Reformation in England, see Patrick Collinson, *The Birthpangs of Protestant England* (1988) and Christopher Haigh, *English Revolutions* (1993); Eamon Duffy's *The Voices of Morebath* (2001) offers a vivid depiction of how the Reformation transformed the lives of ordinary people. For early English attempts at colonization, in both Ireland and the Americas, consult the works of Nicholas Canny in the Bibliography, as well as David Beers Quinn, *Set Fair for Roanoke* (1985) and Karen Kupperman, *Roanoake* (1984).

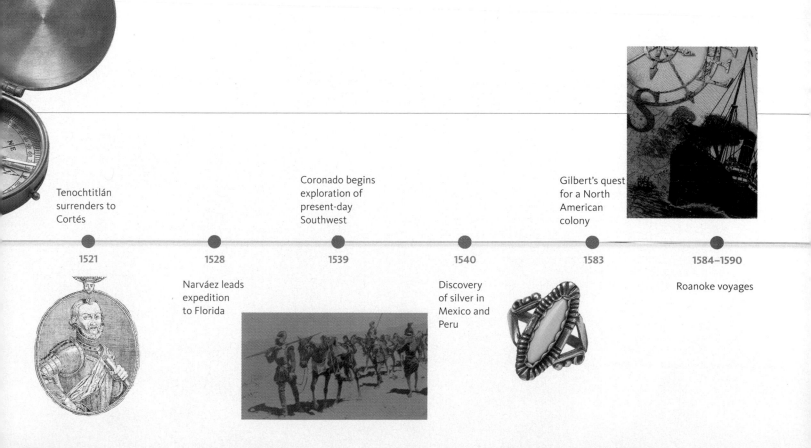

| 1521 | 1528 | 1539 | 1540 | 1583 | 1584–1590 |

Tenochtitlán surrenders to Cortés

Narváez leads expedition to Florida

Coronado begins exploration of present-day Southwest

Discovery of silver in Mexico and Peru

Gilbert's quest for a North American colony

Roanoke voyages

Colonization

This Native American drawing on a canyon wall in present-day Arizona represents the progress of the Spanish into the Southwest. The horses, prominently featured, gave the invaders an initial advantage. "The most essential thing in new lands is horses," one of Coronado's men emphasized. "They instill the greatest fear in the enemy and make the Indians respect the leaders of the army." Many Indian peoples soon put the horse to their own uses, however, and even outshone the Spanish in their riding skills.

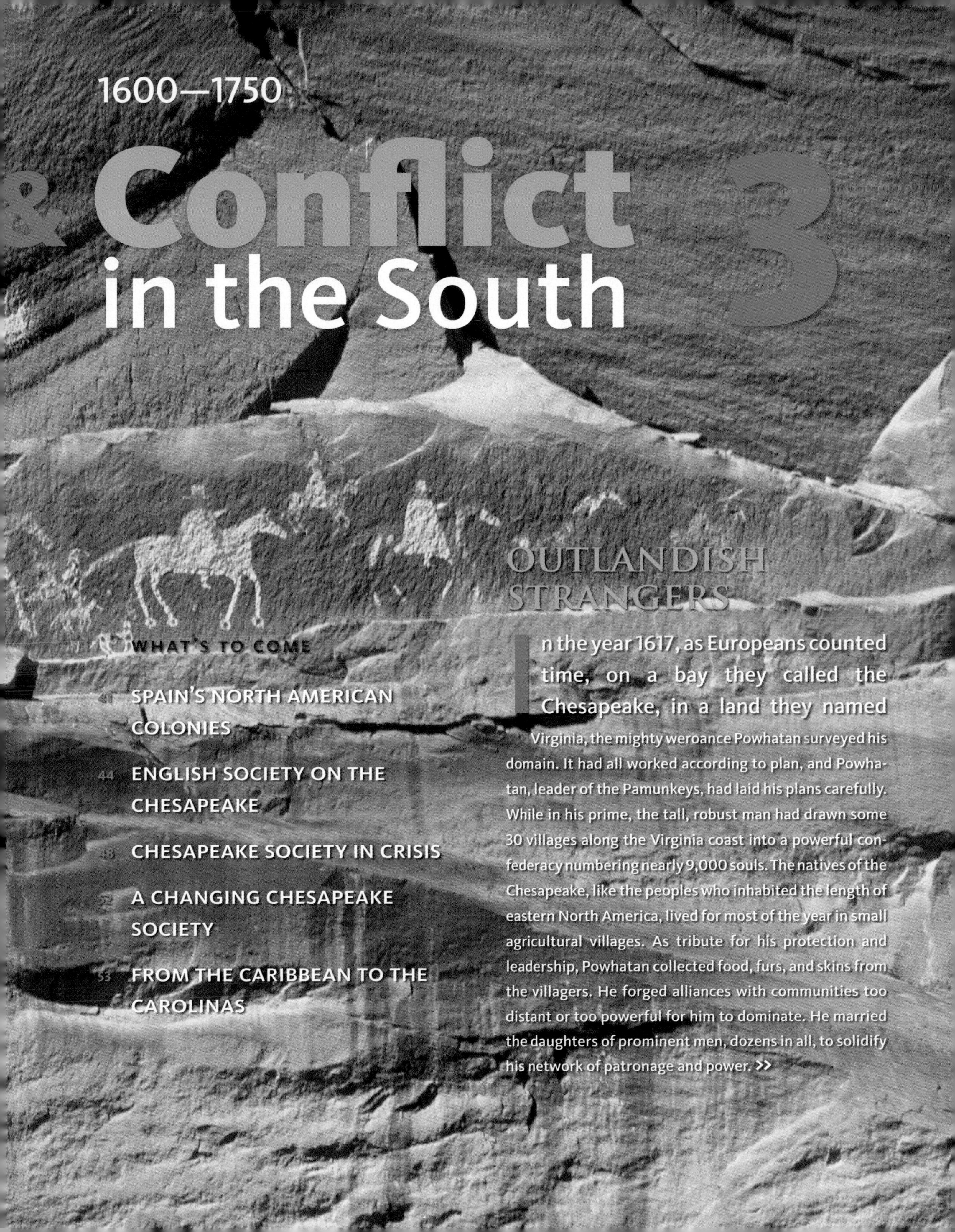

& Conflict in the South

3

OUTLANDISH STRANGERS

WHAT'S TO COME

SPAIN'S NORTH AMERICAN COLONIES

44 **ENGLISH SOCIETY ON THE CHESAPEAKE**

48 **CHESAPEAKE SOCIETY IN CRISIS**

52 **A CHANGING CHESAPEAKE SOCIETY**

53 **FROM THE CARIBBEAN TO THE CAROLINAS**

In the year 1617, as Europeans counted time, on a bay they called the Chesapeake, in a land they named Virginia, the mighty weroance Powhatan surveyed his domain. It had all worked according to plan, and Powhatan, leader of the Pamunkeys, had laid his plans carefully. While in his prime, the tall, robust man had drawn some 30 villages along the Virginia coast into a powerful confederacy numbering nearly 9,000 souls. The natives of the Chesapeake, like the peoples who inhabited the length of eastern North America, lived for most of the year in small agricultural villages. As tribute for his protection and leadership, Powhatan collected food, furs, and skins from the villagers. He forged alliances with communities too distant or too powerful for him to dominate. He married the daughters of prominent men, dozens in all, to solidify his network of patronage and power. »

After 1607 Powhatan was forced to take into account yet another group. The English, as this new people called themselves, came by sea, crammed into three ships. They were 100 men and 4 boys, all clad in heavy, outlandish clothing, many dressed in gaudy colors. The ships followed a river deep into Powhatan's territory and built a fort on a swampy, mosquito-infested site that they called Jamestown.

Powhatan was not frightened. He knew of these strangers from across the waters. Even amid the bounty of the Chesapeake they failed to feed themselves. With bows and arrows, spears and nets, Indian men brought in an abundance of meat and fish. Fields tended by Indian women yielded generous crops of corn, beans, squash, and melon, and edible nuts and fruits grew wild. Still the English starved, and not just during the first few months of their settlement but for several years afterward. Powhatan could understand why the English refused to grow food. Cultivating crops was women's work—like building houses; or making clothing, pottery, and baskets; or caring for children. And the English settlement included no women until two arrived in the fall of 1608. Yet even after more women came, the English still starved, and they expected—no, they demanded—that Powhatan's people feed them.

And yet these hapless folk put on such airs. They boasted about the power of their god—they had only one—and denounced the Indians' "devil-worship" of "false gods." They crowed endlessly about the power of their king, James I, who expected Powhatan to become his vassal. Inconceivable—that Powhatan should willingly bow before this King James, the ruler of so small and savage a race! When the Indians made war, they killed the male warriors of rival communities but adopted their women and children. But when Powhatan's people withheld food or defended their land from these invaders, the English retaliated by murdering Indian women and children. Worse, the English could not even keep order among themselves. Too many of them wanted to lead, and they squabbled constantly.

The temptation to wipe out the helpless, troublesome, arrogant tribe of English—or simply to let them starve to death—had been almost overwhelming. But Powhatan allowed the English to survive. Like Wingina before him, he decided that even these barbaric people had their uses. English labor, English trading goods, and, most important, English guns would help quell resistance within his confederacy and subdue his Indian rivals to the west. In 1614 Powhatan cemented his claim on the English and their weapons with the marriage between his favorite child, Pocahontas, and an ambitious Englishman, John Rolfe.

By 1617 events had vindicated Powhatan's strategy of tolerating the English. His chiefdom flourished, ready to be passed on to his brother. Powhatan's people still outnumbered the English, who seldom starved outright now but continued to fight among themselves and sicken and die. Only one thing had changed in the Chesapeake by 1617: the English were clearing woodland along the rivers and planting tobacco.

That was the doing of Powhatan's son-in-law, Rolfe, a man as strange as the rest of the newcomers, all of them eager to store up wealth and worldly goods. Rolfe had been obsessed with finding a crop that could be grown in Virginia and then sold for gain across the sea. When he succeeded by growing tobacco, other English followed his lead. Odder still, not women but men tended the tobacco fields. Here was more evidence of English inferiority. Men wasted long hours laboring when they might supply their needs with far less effort.

In 1617 Powhatan, ruler of the Pamunkeys, surveyed his domain, and sometime in that year, he died. He had lived long enough to see the tobacco fields lining the riverbanks, straddling the charred stumps of felled trees. But perhaps he went to his grave believing that he had done what Wingina had failed to do: bend the English to his purposes. He died before those stinking tobacco weeds spread over the length of his land and sent his hardwon dominion up in smoke. «

Would you have opposed slavery if you had lived in the seventeenth century?

Then & Now

SEEING WHAT WE WANT TO SEE

Pocahontas, daughter of the mighty weroance Powhatan and wife of English colonist John Rolfe, has long fascinated non-natives. In the first image from 1616 she is represented as a high-status English lady. The second image, from the 1995 Disney film, portrays her as a gorgeous and innocent child of nature. Now as then, we see in her what we want to.

Wingina and Powhattan were not the only native leaders that dreamed of turning Europeans to their advantage. Across North America, the fleeting if destructive encounters of the sixteenth century gave way to sustained colonialism in the seventeenth. As Europeans began to colonize the edges of North America in earnest, Indian peoples struggled not only to survive and adapt to new realities but also, when possible, to profit from the rapid changes swirling around them.

Those often dramatic changes reflected upheavals underway all across the globe. The tobacco John Rolfe had begun to cultivate was only one of several plantation **monoculture**s that Europeans began to establish in their far-flung colonies. Sugar, already flourishing in the Atlantic islands off the coast of West Africa, was gaining a foothold in the islands of the Caribbean. Rice, long a staple in Asia and grown also in Africa, made its way into South Carolina toward the end of the seventeenth century. Because these crops were grown most efficiently on plantations and required intensive labor, African slavery spread during these years, fueled by an expanding international slave trade. Europeans, Africans, and Indians were all, in different ways, caught up in the wrenching transformations.

> **monoculture** growth of a single crop to the virtual exclusion of all others, either on a farm or more generally within a region.

SPAIN'S NORTH AMERICAN COLONIES

Just as Spain had been the first European power to explore North America's interior, so too it led the way in establishing lasting colonies north of Mexico. But while France and especially England eventually established large colonial populations on territory suited to European-style agriculture, Spain confined its northern ventures to the ecologically challenging regions of the upper Rio Grande and coastal Florida. Because economic opportunities and good farmland was abundant elsewhere in Spanish America, few Spaniards migrated to distant and difficult northern outposts. Even so, Spain's colonial endeavors had tremendous implications for North America's native peoples and for the geopolitics of the continent as a whole.

The Founding of a "New" Mexico >> By the 1590s Coronado's dismal expedition a half-century earlier had been all but forgotten. Again, rumors spread in Mexico about great riches in the North. New Spain's viceroy began casting about for a leader to establish a "new" Mexico as magnificent and profitable as its namesake. He chose Juan de Oñate, son of one of New Spain's richest miners and husband to Isabel de Tolosa Cortés Moctezuma, granddaughter of Hernán Cortés and great-granddaughter of Moctezuma. Ignorant of

⌃ Like many other Pueblo peoples, the founders of Acoma built their village atop a sandstone mesa to gain protection from enemies. Constructed in the twelfth century C.E., Acoma may be the oldest continuously occupied settlement in the present-day United States.

northern geography and overestimating New Mexico's riches, Oñate proposed to sail ships up the Pacific to Pueblo country, so that twice a year he could resupply his would-be colony and export its expected treasures.

The magnitude of his misconceptions came into focus in 1598, when he led 500 colonists, soldiers, and slaves to the Upper Rio Grande. Oñate found modest villages, no ocean, and no significant mineral wealth. Even so, he had come with women and children, with livestock and tools, with artisans and tradesmen, with seeds and books and bibles. He had come to stay. Eager to avoid the violence of earlier encounters, Tewa-speaking Pueblos evacuated a village for the newcomers to use. Many native leaders pledged Oñate their allegiance, Pueblo artisans labored on irrigation systems and other public works for the Spaniards, and Indian women (traditionally the builders in Pueblo society) constructed the region's first Catholic Church.

The colonizers mistook this cautious courtesy for subservience. Oñate's oldest nephew, Juan de Zaldívar, was bolder and cruder than most. At Acoma Pueblo, known today as "Sky City" because of its position high atop a majestic mesa, he brazenly seized several sacred turkeys to kill and eat, answering Indian protests with insults. Outraged, Acoma's men fell upon Zaldívar, killing him and several companions. Fueled by grief and rage, Zaldivar's younger brother Vicente laid siege to Acoma Pueblo, killed perhaps 800 of its residents, and made slaves of several hundred more. The savagery of the Acoma siege and similar repressive measures educated all of the region's native communities about the risks of resistance.

But it was easier to instill terror than grow rich. Desperate to salvage their enterprise, Oñate and key followers toiled on long, fruitless expeditions in search of gold, silver, and cities. Vicente de Zaldívar, the headstrong conqueror of Acoma, tried to domesticate bison as had been done with cattle, rather than search for them on the plains. But the bison—"stubborn animals, brave beyond praise"—quickly broke free of the cottonwood coral his men constructed. Most Spaniards turned to the less hazardous pursuit of farming and husbandry to support their families. Others despaired of securing a living in arid New Mexico and fled back into New Spain.

In 1606, royal authorities recalled Oñate and brought him up on charges of mismanagement and abusing Indians. Meanwhile Spain nearly abandoned "worthless" New Mexico, except that the Franciscans insisted it would be a crime to forsake the thousands of Indians they claimed to have baptized since 1598. Spain's New Mexican outpost continued to struggle along.

The Mystery of the Sawed-Off Foot

Estevan Arrellano, the director of New Mexico's Juan de Oñate Monument Visitor's Center, couldn't understand it. One January morning in 1998 Arrellano had arrived at work to find that someone had sawed off the right foot of a new bronze statue of Oñate, the man who founded New Mexico's first Spanish colony in 1598. The vandals soon released a statement. "We took the liberty of removing Oñate's right foot on behalf of our brothers and sisters of Acoma Pueblo," they wrote.

Anyone familiar with the region's brutal colonial history understood the connection. In response to an uprising at Acoma Pueblo,

Oñate had destroyed the village, condemned its women and children to slavery, and ordered that every Acoma man twenty-five and older have his right foot chopped off. Thus, an explanation for the vandalized statue, which Arrellano had to have repaired. "Give me a break," he complained. "It was 400 years ago. It's O.K. to hold a grudge, but for 400 years?"

In fact, monuments to and celebrations of the "distant" past often provoke passionate disagreements in the present. Some Anglo New Mexicans resent the fact that more is not done to memorialize Stephen W. Kearny and other military figures that seized New Mexico for the United States in 1846. New Mexico recently sent a statue of Popé, the leader of the Pueblo Revolt, to represent the state in the Hall of Statues in the U.S. Capitol, despite the protests of some Hispanics that Popé and his followers had massacred Spanish men, women, and children. And, although many Hispanic New Mexicans want to celebrate Oñate as a way to insist on their own centrality to New Mexico's history, many native peoples insist that celebrations of conquistadors implicitly denigrate the suffering and even the humanity of their own ancestors.

As long as history is relevant to contemporary politics, economics, and culture, partisans will continue to fight over the past with memorials, petitions, marches, statues, and even electric saws.

<< Artist Jacques Le Moyne recorded this scene of Florida Indians holding council in the 1560s. Observers from Jean Ribaut's French expedition can be seen in the foreground.

The Growth of Spanish Florida >>

Franciscans became key actors in Spanish North America. Members of a medieval religious order founded by St. Francis of Assisi, Franciscan monks owned no personal property, remained **celibate**, and survived by begging for alms or accepting donations

{ **celibate** abstaining from sexual intercourse; also unmarried.

from wealthy patrons. Franciscans accompanied Columbus on his second voyage, and they began ministering to the Indians of central Mexico soon after Tenochtitlán fell. By the 1570s, Spanish authorities started secularizing central Mexico's missions, transforming them into self-supporting parishes. Franciscans went on to become powerful figures in colonial New Mexico, while Jesuits established several missions in present-day Arizona.

For strategic reasons, the Crown needed the Franciscans even more in Florida than in New Mexico's distant outposts. As long as pirates or rival colonies on the Atlantic seaboard threatened Spanish shipping, the king had to control Florida. Pedro Menéndez de Avilés did much to secure the peninsula in the 1560s when he destroyed France's Fort Caroline and established several posts on the coast (see Chapter 2). By 1600, however, Menéndez was dead and only St. Augustine endured, with a population of perhaps 500. Spanish Florida needed something more to survive.

To extend his influence the king first offered the peninsula's many native peoples trade privileges and regular diplomatic presents. In return, native leaders promised to support the Spanish in war, and tax their people on behalf of the king. Once these alliances were in place, Indian communities were made to accept Franciscan missions and a few resident soldiers, a policy critical to molding and monitoring native villages. By 1675, 40 missions were ministering to as many as 26,000 baptized Indians. The

bishop of Cuba toured Florida and spoke enthusiastically of converts who embraced "with devotion the mysteries of our holy faith." Florida's mission system and network of Indian alliances convinced Spanish authorities that they could maintain their grip on this crucial peninsula.

Popé and the Pueblo Revolt >>

As the seventeenth century progressed, New Mexico also seemed to stabilize. Enough Spanish colonists remained to establish a separate town, El Villa Real de Santa Fe, in 1610. Santa Fe (the second-oldest European town in the United States after St. Augustine) became the hub of Spanish life in New Mexico. Many families settled elsewhere on the Rio Grande, on well-watered lands near Pueblo villages. Economic and political life revolved around a dozen prominent families. By 1675 New Mexico had a diverse colonial population of perhaps 2,500, including Spaniards, Africans, Mexican Indians, mestizos (persons of mixed Spanish-Indian heritage), and mulattos (of Spanish-African heritage).

This population also included large numbers of Indian captives. Occasionally captives came to Spanish households through war, as after the siege of Acoma. In addition, Spaniards purchased enslaved women and children from other Indians and regularly launched slave raids against so-called enemy Indians such as Utes, Apaches, and Navajos. By 1680 half of all New Mexican households included at least one Indian captive. Depending on age, gender, and the master's disposition, such captives could be treated affectionately as low-status family members or terrorized and abused as disposable human property.

The colonists also extracted labor from Pueblo Indians. Officially Pueblo households had to surrender three bushels of corn and one processed hide or large cotton blanket each year. Pueblos also sometimes labored on public works, and elite Spaniards often exploited their privileges by insisting on more tribute and labor than legally allowed. Still, the populous Pueblos could have satisfied Spanish demands with little difficulty except for other changes in their world. First and most importantly, colonialism meant epidemics. Beginning in the 1620s smallpox killed 70 percent of the population within a generation. Whereas New Mexico boasted about 100 native villages at contact, by 1680 only 30 remained inhabited. Infestations of locusts, severe droughts, and crop failures compounded the crisis. A distraught Franciscan reported starving native men, women, and children "lying

SPANISH MISSIONS IN NORTH AMERICA, CA. 1675

From St. Augustine, Spanish missionaries spread into Guale Indian villages in present-day Georgia and westward among the Indians of Timucua, Apalachee, and Apalachicola. In New Mexico, missions radiated outward from the Rio Grande, as distant as Hopi villages in the west.

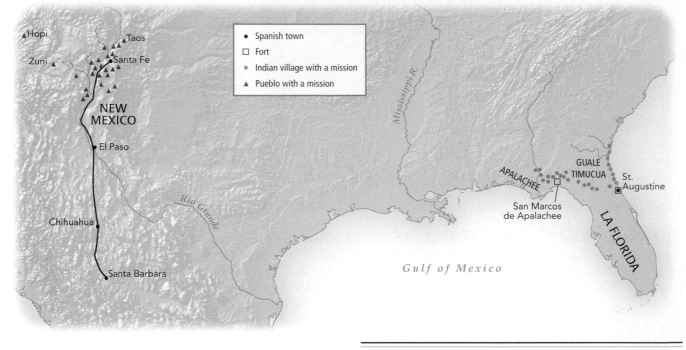

dead along the roads, in the ravines, and in their hovels." Mounted Utes, Apaches, and Navajos, embittered by New Mexican slaving and barred from their customary trade in the pueblos, launched punishing raids against the most vulnerable Pueblo villages.

In their deepening misery Pueblos turned to religion—their own. Since 1598, the Franciscans had worked tirelessly to suppress the dances, idols, and ceremonies that long mediated Pueblo relationships with the divine. By the 1670s Pueblo elders were arguing that the calamities of the past decades could be reversed only by rejecting Christianity and returning to the old faith. Franciscans and civil authorities scrambled to extinguish the revival movement, arresting Pueblo leaders, executing two and whipping 43 others in front of large crowds.

One of the 43, a prominent Tewa man known to history as Popé, nursed his wounds in Taos and called for a war against the Spaniards to purify the land. Many individuals and some entire villages refused to participate. But on August 10, 1680, Indians from across New Mexico rose up and began killing Spaniards, pursuing astonished survivors all the way to Santa Fe. Within weeks the desperate Spanish governor, wounded by an arrow in the face and a gunshot to the chest, gathered the remainder of the colonial population and fled south out of New Mexico. The most successful pan-Indian uprising in North American history, the Pueblo Revolt sent shock waves throughout Spanish America and left the Catholic devout agonizing over what they had done to provoke God's wrath.

ENGLISH SOCIETY ON THE CHESAPEAKE

By 1700, then, Spain viewed its situation in the Americas very differently than it had 100 years earlier. The Pueblo Revolt had checked its power at the northern reach of its American possessions. Equally disturbing was the progress of Spain's European rivals in the Americas during the seventeenth century. During the sixteenth, both France and England had envied Spain's American conquests and wealth but did little to compete, beyond preying on Spanish ships and fishing for cod. During the seventeenth century, this would change.

In fact, even by 1600 other European kingdoms were beginning to view overseas colonies as essential to a nation's power and prosperity. They did so in part because of an economic model known as **mercantilism,** which guided Europe's commercial expansion for 200 years. The primary objective of mercantilism was to enrich the nation by fostering a favorable balance of trade. Once the value of exports exceeded the cost of imports, its advocates argued, gold and silver would flow into home ports.

mercantilism European economic doctrine calling for strict regulation of the economy in order to ensure a balance of exports over imports and increase the amount of gold and silver in a nation's treasury.

If a nation could make do without any imports from other countries, so much the better. It was here that the idea of colonies entered the mercantilist scheme. Colonial producers would supply raw materials that the mother country could not produce, while colonial consumers swelled demand for the finished goods and financial services that the mother country could provide. That logic led England's King James I to approve a private venture to colonize the Chesapeake Bay, a sprawling inlet of the Atlantic Ocean fed by over 100 rivers and streams.

Key: c

Who were the first Europeans to try to colonize the chesapeake Region?

a. the Dutch

b. the English

c. the Spanish

expedition dispatched by the Virginia Company founded Jamestown.

Making the first of many mistakes, Jamestown's 104 men and boys pitched their fort on a swampy inland peninsula in order to prevent a surprise attack from the Spanish. Weakened by bouts of the disease and beset by dysentery, typhoid, and yellow fever, however, they died by the scores.

Even before sickness took its toll, many of Jamestown's colonists had little taste for labor. The gentlemen of the expedition expected to lead rather than to work, while most of the other early settlers were gentlemen's servants and craftworkers who knew nothing about growing crops. Many colonists suffered from malnutrition, which heightened their susceptibility to disease. Only 60 of Jamestown's 500 inhabitants lived through the winter of 1609–1610, known as the "starving time." Desperate colonists unearthed and ate corpses; one settler even butchered his wife. Others imitated their predecessors on Roanoke, bullying Indians for food. Martial law failed to turn the situation around, and skirmishes with native peoples became more brutal and frequent as rows of tobacco plants steadily invaded tribal lands.

The Virginia Company

>> In 1606, the king granted a charter to a number of English merchants, gentlemen, and aristocrats, incorporating them as the Virginia Company of London. The members of the new **joint stock company** sold stock in their venture to English investors, as well as awarding a share to those willing to settle in Virginia at their own expense. With the proceeds from the sale of stock, the company planned to send to Virginia hundreds of poor and unemployed people as well as scores of skilled craftworkers. These laborers were to serve the company for seven years in return for their passage, pooling their efforts to produce any commodities that would return a profit to stockholders. If gold and silver could not be found, perhaps North America would yield other valuable commodities—furs, pitch, tar, or lumber. In the spring of 1607—nearly a decade after Oñate had launched Spain's colonies in New Mexico—the first

joint stock company business in which capital is held in transferable shares of stock by joint owners. The joint stock company was an innovation that allowed investors to share and spread the risks of overseas investment.

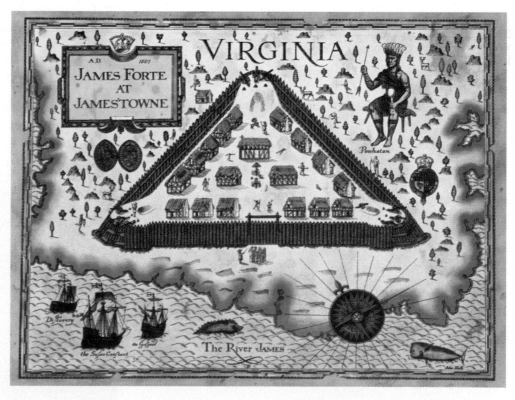

>> In Jamestown's early years, its military orientation was clear. The fort's heavy palisades and its strategic location upriver and some distance inland underscore the colonists' concern for defense—as does the imposing figure of Powhatan, seated at the right.

Reform and a Boom in Tobacco >> Deter-

mined to salvage their investment, Virginia Company managers in 1618 set in place sweeping reforms. To attract more capital and colonists, the company established a "headright" system for granting land to individuals. Those already settled in the colony received 100 acres apiece. New settlers each received 50 acres, and anyone who paid the passage of other immigrants to Virginia—either family members or servants—received 50 acres per "head." The company also abolished martial law, allowing the planters to elect a representative assembly. Along with a governor and an advisory council appointed by the company, the House of Burgesses had the authority to make laws for the colony. It met for the first time in 1619, beginning what would become a strong tradition of representative government in the English colonies.

The new measures met with immediate success. The free and unfree laborers who poured into Virginia during the 1620s made up the first wave of an English migration to the Chesapeake that numbered between 130,000 and 150,000 over the seventeenth century. Drawn from the ranks of ordinary English working people, the immigrants were largely men, outnumbering women by six to one. Most were young, ranging in age from 15 to 24. Because of their youth, most lacked skills or wealth. Some of those who came to the Chesapeake as free immigrants prospered as Virginia's tobacco economy took off. When in the 1620s demand soared and prices peaked in European markets, colonists with an eye for profit planted every inch of their farms in tobacco and reaped windfalls.

Indentured servants accounted for three-quarters of all immigrants to Virginia. For most, the crossing was simply the last of many moves made in the hope of finding work. Although England's population had been rising since the middle of the fifteenth century, the demand for farm laborers was falling because many landowners were converting croplands into pastures for sheep. The search for work pushed young men and women out of their villages, sending them through the countryside and then into the cities. Down and out in London, Bristol, or Liverpool, some decided to make their next move across the Atlantic and signed **indentures.** Pamphlets promoting immigration promised land and quick riches once servants had finished their terms of four to seven years.

indentures contract signed between two parties, binding one to serve the other for a specified period of time.

Even the most skeptical immigrants were shocked at what they found. The death rate in Virginia during the 1620s was higher than that of England during times of epidemic disease. The life expectancy for Chesapeake men who reached the age of 20 was a mere 48 years; for women it was lower still. Servants fared worst of all, because malnutrition, overwork, and abuse made them vulnerable to disease. As masters scrambled to make quick profits, they extracted the maximum amount of work before death carried off their laborers. An estimated 40 percent of servants did not survive to the end of their indentured terms.

War with the Confederacy >> The expand-

ing cultivation of tobacco also claimed many lives by putting unbearable pressure on Indian land. After Powhatan's death in 1617, leadership of the confederacy passed to Opechancanough, who watched, year after year, as the tobacco mania grew. In March 1622 he coordinated a sweeping attack on white settlements that killed about a quarter of Virginia's colonial population. English retaliation over the next decade cut down an entire generation of young Indian men, drove the remaining Powhatans to the west, and won the colonists hundreds of thousands more acres for tobacco.

News of the ongoing Indian war jolted English investors into determining the true state of their Virginia venture. It came to light that, despite the tobacco boom, the Virginia Company was plunging toward bankruptcy. Nor was that the worst news. Stockholders discovered that more than 3,000 immigrants had not survived the brutal conditions of Chesapeake life. An investigation by James I revealed the grisly truth, causing the king to dissolve the Virginia Company and take control of the colony himself in 1624. Henceforth Virginia would be governed as a royal colony.

As the tobacco boom broke in the 1630s and 1640s, Virginians began producing more corn and cattle. Nutrition and overall health improved as a result. More and more poor colonists began surviving their indenture and establishing modest farms of their own. For women who survived servitude, prospects were even better. With wives at a premium, single women stood a good chance of improving their status by marriage. Even so, high mortality rates still fractured families: one out of every four children born in the Chesapeake did not survive to maturity, and among those children who reached their 18th birthday, one-third had lost both parents to death.

By 1650 Virginia could boast about 15,000 colonists, with more arriving every year. But Virginians looking to

WITNESS
The Indian War of 1622

"They came unarmed into our houses . . . yea in some places sat down at Breakfast with our people at their tables, [and] immediately with [our people's] own tools and weapons, either laid down, or standing in their houses, they basely and barbarously murdered, not sparing either age or sex, man, woman, or child . . ."

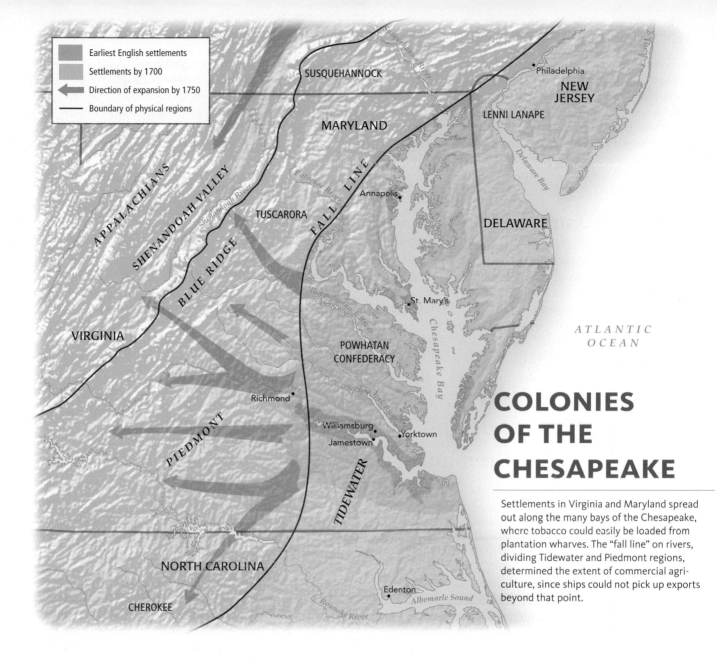

COLONIES OF THE CHESAPEAKE

Settlements in Virginia and Maryland spread out along the many bays of the Chesapeake, where tobacco could easily be loaded from plantation wharves. The "fall line" on rivers, dividing Tidewater and Piedmont regions, determined the extent of commercial agriculture, since ships could not pick up exports beyond that point.

Map legend:
- Earliest English settlements
- Settlements by 1700
- Direction of expansion by 1750
- Boundary of physical regions

expand into more northerly bays of the Chesapeake found their way blocked by a newer English colony.

The Founding of Maryland and the Renewal of Indian Wars >>

Unlike Virginia, established by a private corporation and later converted into a royal colony, Maryland was founded in 1632 by a single aristocratic family, the Calverts. They held absolute authority to dispose of 10 million acres of land, administer justice, and establish a civil government. All these powers they exercised, granting estates, or "manors," to their friends and dividing other holdings into smaller farms for ordinary immigrants. From all these "tenants"— that is, every settler in the colony—the family collected "quitrents" every year, fees for use of the land. The Calverts appointed a governor and a council to oversee their own interests while allowing the largest landowners

to dispense local justice in manorial courts and make laws for the entire colony in a representative assembly.

Virginians liked nothing about Maryland. To begin with, the Calvert family was Catholic and had extended complete religious freedom to all Christians, making Maryland a haven for Catholics. Worse still, the Marylanders were a source of economic competition. Two thousand inhabitants had settled on Calvert holdings by 1640, virtually all of them planting tobacco on land coveted by the Virginians.

Another obstacle to Virginia's expansion was the remnant of the Powhatan confederacy. Hounded for corn and supplies (most colonial fields grew tobacco rather than food), and constantly pressured by the expanding plantation economy, Virginia's native peoples became desperate and angry enough to risk yet another war. Aged Opechancanough sent a new generation of Indians into battle in 1644 against the encroaching Virginia planters. Though his warriors killed several hundred English and brought the frontier to a standstill, Opechancanough was eventually captured and summarily shot through the head. The Powhattan confederacy died with him. Virginia's Indians would never again be in a position to go on the offense against the colony. Over the next decades and centuries, many Indians fled the region altogether. But whole communities remained, quietly determined to continue their lives and traditions in their homeland.

Changes in English Policy in the Chesapeake >> Throughout the 1630s and 1640s colonial affairs drew little concern from royal officials. England itself had become engulfed first by a political crisis and then by a civil war.

Outraged at the contempt that King Charles I had shown toward Parliament, disaffected elites and radical Puritans overthrew the king and executed him in 1649. When the "republic" of Oliver Cromwell turned out to be something closer to a military dictatorship, most English were happy to see their throne restored in 1660 to Charles II, the son of the beheaded king. The new monarch was determined that not only his subjects at home but also his American colonies abroad would contribute to England's prosperity. His colonial policy was reflected in a series of regulations passed in the 1660s and 1670s known as the Navigation Acts.

The acts severely restricted colonial trade with Britain's imperial rivals. In this sense they were mercantilistic, designed to ensure that England alone would profit from colonial production and trade. Chesapeake planters chafed under the Navigation Acts. They were used to conducting their affairs as they pleased—and they were often pleased to trade with the Dutch. Unhappily, the new restrictions came just as tobacco prices were dropping. In the effort to consolidate its empire, England had unintentionally worsened the economic and social difficulties of Chesapeake society.

CHESAPEAKE SOCIETY IN CRISIS

By the 1660s, overproduction was depressing tobacco prices, and wealthy planters reacted by putting even more prime coastal land into production. Newly freed servants had either to become tenants or try to establish farms to the west in Indian country. Meanwhile, export duties on tobacco paid under the Navigation Acts helped plunge many small planters into crushing debt, and some were forced back into servitude. By 1676 one-quarter of Virginia's free white men remained landless and frustrated.

As the discontent of the poor mounted, so did the worries of big planters. The assembly of the colony lengthened terms of servitude, hoping to limit the number of servants entering the free population. It curbed the political rights of landless men, hoping to stifle opposition by depriving them of the vote. But these measures only set off a spate of mutinies among servants and protests over rising taxes among small planters.

Bacon's Rebellion and Coode's Rebellion >> Tensions came to a head in 1676. The immediate spark to rebellion was renewed fighting between desperate Indians and the expanding colonial population. Virginia's royal governor, William Berkeley, favored building forts to guard against Indians, but frontier farmers opposed his plan as expensive and an ineffective way to defend their scattered plantations. When they clamored for an expedition to punish the Indians, Nathaniel Bacon stepped forward to lead it.

Wealthy and well connected, Bacon had arrived recently from England, expecting to receive every favor from the governor—including permission to trade with the Indians from his frontier plantation. But Berkeley and a few select friends already held a monopoly on the Indian trade. When they declined to include Bacon, he took up the cause of his poorer frontier neighbors. Other recent, well-to-do immigrants who resented being excluded from Berkeley's circle of power and patronage also joined the cause.

In the summer of 1676, Bacon marched into Jamestown with a body of armed men and bullied the assembly into approving his expedition to kill Indians. While Bacon carried out that grisly business, slaughtering friendly as well as hostile natives, Berkeley rallied his supporters and declared Bacon a rebel. Bacon retaliated by turning his forces against those led by the governor. Both sides sought allies by offering freedom to servants and slaves willing to join their ranks. Many were willing: for months the followers of Bacon and Berkeley plundered one another's plantations. In September 1676 Bacon reduced Jamestown itself to a mound of ashes. Only his death from dysentery snuffed out the rebellion.

Political upheaval also shook Maryland, where colonists had long resented the sway of the Calvert family. As proprietors, the Calverts and their favorites monopolized political offices, just as Berkeley's circle had in Virginia. Well-to-do planters wanted a share of the Calverts' power.

By 1676 one-quarter of Virginia's free white men remained landless and frustrated.

Smaller farmers, like those in Virginia, wanted a less expensive and more representative government. Compounding the tensions were religious differences: the Calverts and their friends were Catholic, but other colonists, including Maryland's most successful planters, were Protestant.

The unrest peaked in July 1689. A former member of the assembly, John Coode, gathered an army, captured the proprietary governor, and then took grievances to authorities in England. There Coode received a sympathetic hearing. The Calverts' charter was revoked and not restored until 1715, by which time the family had become Protestant.

After the rebellions rich planters in both Chesapeake colonies fought among themselves less and cooperated more. In Virginia older leaders and newer arrivals divided the spoils of political office. In Maryland Protestants and Catholics shared power and privilege. Those arrangements ensured that no future Bacon or Coode would mobilize restless gentlemen against the government. By acting together in legislative assemblies, the planter elite managed to curb the power of royal and proprietary governors for decades.

But the greater unity among the Chesapeake's leading families did little to ease that region's most fundamental problem—the sharp inequality of white society. The gulf between rich and poor planters, which had been etched ever more deeply by the troubled tobacco economy, persisted long after the rebellions of Bacon and Coode. All that saved white society in the Chesapeake from renewed crisis and conflict was the growth of African slavery.

From Servitude to Slavery >> Like the
tobacco plants that spread across Powhatan's land, a labor system based on African slavery was an on-the-ground innovation. Both early promoters and planters preferred paying for English servants to importing alien African slaves. Black slaves, because they served for life, were more expensive than white workers, who served only for several years. Because neither white nor black immigrants lived long, cheaper servant labor was the logical choice. The black population of the Chesapeake remained small for most of the seventeenth century, constituting just 5 percent of all inhabitants in 1675.

Africans had arrived in Virginia by 1619, most likely via the Dutch, who dominated the slave trade until the middle of the eighteenth century. The lives of those newcomers resembled the lot of white servants, with whom they shared harsh work routines and living conditions. White and black bound laborers socialized with one another and formed sexual liaisons. They conspired to steal from their masters and ran away together; if caught, they endured similar punishments. There was more common ground: many of the first black settlers did not arrive directly from Africa but came from the Caribbean, where some had learned English and had adopted Christian beliefs. And not all were slaves: some were indentured servants. A handful were free.

A number of changes after 1680 caused planters to invest more heavily in slaves than in servants. First, as death rates in the Chesapeake began to drop, slaves became a more profitable investment. Although they were more expensive to buy than servants, planters could now expect to get many years of work from their bondspeople. Equally important, masters would have title to the children that slaves were now living long enough to have. At the same time, the influx of white servants was falling off just as the pool of available black labor was expanding. When the Royal African Company lost its monopoly on the English slave trade in 1698, other merchants entered the market. The number of Africans sold by British dealers swelled to 20,000 annually.

Africa and the Atlantic Slave Trade >>
From 1492 to 1820, enslaved African migrants outnumbered European migrants to the new world by nearly five to one. Put differently, before the twentieth-century, African workers did most of the heavy lifting in the economies of the Americas.

For a century after Columbus's arrival, the traffic in slaves to the Americas had numbered a few thousand annually. But as sugar cultivation steadily prospered after 1600, slave imports rose to 19,000 a year during the seventeenth century and mushroomed to 60,000 a year in the eighteenth century. All told, as many as 21 million people were captured in West and Central Africa between 1700 and 1850: some 9 million among them entered the Americas as slaves, but millions died before or during the Atlantic crossing, and as many as 7 million remained slaves in Africa. Although slavery became indispensible to its economy, British North America played a relatively small role in the Atlantic slave trade. Nine-tenths of all Africans brought to the New World landed in Brazil or the Caribbean islands.

The rapid growth of the trade transformed not only the Americas but also Africa. Slavery became more widespread within African society, and slave trading more central to its domestic and international commerce. Most important, the African merchants and political leaders most deeply invested in the slave trade used their profits for political advantage—to build new chiefdoms and states such as Dahomey, Asante, and the Lunda Empire. Their ambitions and the greed of European slave dealers drew an increasingly large number of Africans, particularly people living in the interior, into slavery's web. By the late seventeenth century, Africans being sold into slavery were no longer only those who had put themselves at risk by committing crimes, running into debt, or voicing unpopular political and religious views. The larger number were instead captives taken by soldiers or kidnappers in raids launched specifically to acquire prisoners for the slave trade, or else desperate refugees captured while fleeing war, famine, and disease. During the decades after

But the trade soon came to revolve around a commodity dearer still. As did most peoples throughout history, southeastern Indians sometimes made slaves of their enemies. Carolina's traders vastly expanded this existing slave culture by turning captives into prized commodities. Convinced that local Indians were physically weaker than Africans and more likely to rebel or flee, colonial traders bought slaves from Indian allies and then exported them to other mainland colonies or to the Caribbean. They found eager native partners in this business. Contact with Europe had unleashed phenomenal changes in interior North America. Epidemics ruined one people and gave advantage to another, new commercial opportunities sparked fierce wars over hunting and trading territories, and many thousands of Indian families became displaced and had to rebuild their lives somewhere new. The chaos, conflict, and

> The chaos, conflict, and movements gave enterprising Indians ample opportunity to enslave weak neighbors and stock Carolina's slave pens.

movement gave enterprising Indians ample opportunity to enslave weak neighbors and stock Carolina's slave pens.

To ensure a steady supply of slaves, Carolinian merchants courted a variety of Indian allies during the late seventeenth and early eighteenth centuries and encouraged them to raid mission Indians in Spanish Florida. By 1700 Florida's Indian peoples were in sharp decline, and Charles Town's slave traders turned to the large and powerful Creek, Choctaw, Chickasaw, and Cherokee confederacies of the interior, encouraging them to raid one another. Before long the slave wars had a momentum all their own, extending as far west as the Mississippi River. Even native peoples who deplored the violence and despised the English felt compelled to participate, lest they too become victims.

The trade became central to Carolina's economy, and colonists high and low sought to profit from it. In 1702 Governor James Moore, one of the colony's chief slave traders, launched an audacious raid against Spanish St. Augustine and Florida's missions, returning with hundreds of Indian captives. His campaign inspired still more raids, and over the next few years Creeks, Yamasees, and Englishmen laid waste to 29 Spanish missions, shattering thousands of lives and destroying Spain's precarious system of Indian alliances. By 1706 Spanish authority was once again confined to St. Augustine and its immediate vicinity. Within another 10 years most of Florida had been depopulated of Indians.

It seemed a double victory from Charles Town's perspective. The English had bested a European rival for the Crown, and had reaped enormous profits besides. The fragmentary evidence suggests that Carolinians had purchased or captured between 30,000 and 50,000 Indian slaves before 1715. Indeed, before that date South Carolina exported more slaves than it imported from Africa or the Caribbean. But in 1715 Carolina's merchants finally paid a price for the wars that they had cynically fomented for over 40 years.

With Florida virtually exhausted of slaves, the Yamasees grew nervous. Convinced that Carolina would soon turn on them as it had on other one-time allies, the Yamasees struck first. They attacked traders, posts, and plantations on the outskirts of Charles Town, killing hundreds of colonists and dragging scores more to Florida to sell as slaves in St. Augustine. Panicked authorities turned to other Indian peoples in the region but found most had either joined the Yamasee or were too hostile and suspicious to help. Though it lasted only a few months, the Yamasee War finally put an end to the destructive regional slave trade. Animal skins again dominated regional commerce. The powerful southern confederacies grew wary of aligning too closely with any single European power and henceforth sought to play colonies and empires off each other. It was a strategy that would bring them relative peace and prosperity for generations.

White, Red, and Black: The Search for Order >> As for South Carolina, the Yamasee War set the colony back 20 years. In its aftermath, settlers invested more and more of their resources in African slaves and in the cultivation of rice, a crop that eventually made South Carolina's planters the richest cohort in mainland North America. Unfortunately, South Carolina's swampy coast, so perfectly suited to growing rice, was less suited for human habitation. Weakened by chronic malaria, settlers died in epic numbers from yellow fever, smallpox, and respiratory infections. The European population grew slowly, through immigration rather than natural increase, and numbered only 10,000 by 1730.

Early South Carolinians had little in common but the harsh conditions of frontier existence. Most colonists lived on isolated plantations; early deaths fragmented families and neighborhoods. Immigration after 1700 further intensified the colony's ethnic and religious diversity, adding Swiss and German Lutherans, Scots-Irish Presbyterians, Welsh Baptists, and Spanish Jews. The colony's only courts were in Charles Town; churches and clergy of any denomination were scarce. On those rare occasions when early Carolinians came together, they gathered at Charles Town to escape the pestilential air of their plantations, to

<< Mulberry Plantation in South Carolina was first carved from coastal swamps in 1714. This painting, done half a century later, shows the Great House visible in the distance, flanked by slave quarters. African slaves skilled in rice cultivation oversaw the arduous task of properly planting and irrigating the crop.

sue one another for debt and haggle over prices, or to fight over religious differences and proprietary politics.

Finally, in 1729, the Crown formally established royal government; by 1730 economic recovery had done much to ease the strife. Even more important in bringing greater political stability, the European colonists of South Carolina came to realize that they must unite if they were to counter the Spanish in Florida and the French and their Indian allies on the Gulf Coast.

The growing African population gave European Carolinians another reason to maintain a united front. During the first decades of settlement, frontier conditions and the scarcity of labor had forced masters to allow enslaved Africans greater freedom within bondage. European and African laborers shared chores on small farms. On stock-raising plantations, called "cowpens," African cowboys ranged freely over the countryside. African contributions to the defense of the colony also reinforced racial interdependence and muted European domination. Whenever threats arose—during the Yamasee War, for example—Africans were enlisted in the militia.

European Carolinians depended on African labor even more after turning to rice as their cash crop. In fact, planters began to import slaves in larger numbers partly because of West African skill in rice cultivation. But Europeans harbored deepening fears of the African workers whose labor built planter fortunes. As early as 1708 African men and women had become a majority in the colony, and by 1730 they outnumbered European settlers by two to one. As their colony began to prosper, European Carolinians put into effect strict slave codes like those in the Caribbean that converted their colony into an armed camp and snuffed out the marginal freedoms that African settlers once enjoyed.

The Founding of Georgia >> After 1730 Carolinians could take comfort not only in newfound prosperity and new political harmony but also in the founding of a new colony on their southern border. South Carolinians liked Georgia a great deal more than the Virginians had

liked Maryland, because the colony formed a buffer between British North America and Spanish Florida in much the same way that Yamasees and Shawnees had, before the war.

Enhancing the military security of South Carolina was only one reason for the founding of Georgia. More important to General James Oglethorpe and other idealistic English gentlemen was the aim of aiding the "worthy poor" by providing them with land, employment, and a new start. They envisioned a colony of hardworking small farmers who would produce silk and wine, sparing England the need to import those commodities. That dream seemed within reach when George II made Oglethorpe and his friends the trustees of the new colony in 1732, granting them a charter for 21 years. At the end of that time Georgia would revert to royal control.

Trustees paid the paupers' passage and provided each with 50 acres of land, tools, and a year's worth of supplies.

The trustees did not, as legend has it, empty England's debtors' prisons to populate Georgia. They freed few debtors but recruited from every country in Europe paupers who seemed willing to work hard—and who professed Protestantism. Trustees paid the paupers' passage and provided each with 50 acres of land, tools, and a year's worth of supplies. Settlers who could pay their own way were encouraged to come by being granted larger tracts of land. Much to the trustees' dismay, that generous offer was taken up not only by many hoped-for Protestants but also by several hundred Ashkenazim (German Jews) and Sephardim (Spanish and Portuguese Jews), who established a thriving community in early Savannah.

The trustees were determined to ensure that Georgia became a small farmers' utopia. Rather than selling land, the trustees gave it away, but none of the colony's settlers could own more than 500 acres. The trustees also outlawed slavery and hard liquor in order to cultivate habits of industry and sustain equality among whites. This design for a virtuous and egalitarian utopia was greeted with little enthusiasm by Georgians. They pressed for a free market in land and argued that the colony could never prosper until the trustees revoked their ban on slavery. Because the trustees had provided for no elective assembly, settlers could express their discontent only by moving to South Carolina—which many did during the early decades. As mounting opposition threatened to depopulate the colony, the trustees caved in. They revoked their restrictions on land, slavery, and liquor a few years before the king assumed control of the colony in 1752. Under royal control, Georgia continued to develop an ethnically and religiously diverse society, akin to that of South Carolina. Similarly, its economy was based on rice cultivation and the Indian trade.

Empire . . . utopia . . . independence. . . . For more than a century after the founding of Oñate's colony on the upper Rio Grande in 1598, those dreams inspired residents of New Mexico, Florida, the Chesapeake, the English Caribbean, the Carolinas, and Georgia. Each of these regions served as staging grounds where kings and commoners, free and unfree, men and women, Native American, European, and African played out their hopes. Their acts were as often filled with desperation as with hope, for conditions were often harsh as the plantation monocultures of sugar and rice spread across the globe.

The dream of an expanding empire faltered for the Spanish, who found few riches in the Southwest and eventually found rebellion. The dream of empire failed, too, when James I and Charles I, England's early Stuart kings, found their power checked by Parliament. And the dream foundered fatally for Indians—for Powhatan's successors, who were unable to resist old-world diseases and land-hungry tobacco planters, and for Westos, Shawnees, and the many Indian peoples of Florida who sought to survive, accommodate, or exploit colonialism, but fell to ruin in the end.

English lords had dreamed of establishing feudal utopias in America. But proprietors such as the Calvert family in Maryland and Cooper in the Carolinas found themselves hounded by frontier planters and farmers who sought economic and political power. Georgia's trustees struggled in vain to nurture their dream of a utopia for the poor. The dream of a Spanish Catholic utopia brought by missionaries to the American Southwest dimmed with native resistance and rebellion.

The dream of independence proved the most deceptive of all, especially for the inhabitants of England's colonies. Just a bare majority of the European servant immigrants to the Chesapeake survived to enjoy freedom. The rest were struck down by disease or worn down at the hands of tobacco barons eager for profit. Not only in the Chesapeake but also in the Caribbean and the Carolinas, real independence eluded the English planters. Poorer folk—dependent on richer settlers for land and leadership—deferred to them at church and on election days and depended on them to buy crops or to extend credit. Even the richest planters were dependent on the English and Scottish merchants who supplied them with credit and marketed their crops, as well as on the English officials who made colonial policy.

And everywhere in the American Southeast and Southwest, the lingering dreams of Europeans were realized only through the labor of the least free members of colonial America. That stubborn reality would haunt all Americans who continued to dream of freedom and independence.

Significant Events

Formation of Powhatan's paramount chiefdom

English establish Jamestown

Tobacco boom in Virginia; epidemics in New Mexico reduce Pueblo population by nearly 70 percent

Parliament passes the first of the Navigation Acts

LATE 1500s   1598   1607   1610   1620s   1632   1660

Oñate colonizes New Mexico

Founding of Santa Fe in New Mexico

Calvert founds Maryland

CHAPTER SUMMARY

During the seventeenth century, Spain and England moved to colonize critical regions of southern North America.

- Native peoples everywhere in the American South resisted colonization, despite losses from warfare, disease, and enslavement.
- Spanish colonies in New Mexico and Florida grew slowly and faced a variety of threats. By the late seventeenth century Spanish New Mexico had been lost to the Pueblo Revolt, and Florida's delicate mission system was under siege from English Carolina and its Indian allies.
- Thriving monocultures were established in all of England's southern colonies—tobacco in the Chesapeake, rice in the Carolinas, and sugar in the Caribbean.
- Despite a period of intense enslavement of native peoples, African slavery emerged as the dominant labor system throughout these regions.
- Instability and conflict characterized both Spanish and English colonies in the South for most of the first century of their existence.

Additional Reading

David J. Weber's *Spanish Frontier in North America* (1992) remains by far the best overview of Spain's colonies north of Mexico. For the Southwest more specifically, see also Ramón Gutiérrez, *When Jesus Came, The Corn Mothers Went Away* (1991), John L. Kessell's *Spain in the Southwest* (2002), and James F. Brooks' pathbreaking monograph *Captives and Cousins* (2002). For Spain in the Southeast, see Paul E. Hoffman's *Florida's Frontiers* (2002).

For enduring treatments of early Virginia, see Edmund S. Morgan, *American Slavery, American Freedom* (1975), and Rhys Isaac, *The Transformation of Virginia* (1982). For a more recent account, pivoting on ideas about gender, see Kathleen Brown, *Good Wives, Nasty Wenches, and Anxious Patriarchs* (1996). Karen Kupperman offers an excellent overview of relations between whites and Indians not only in the early South but throughout British North America in *Settling with the Indians* (1980). For native Virginia, see also Helen C. Rountree, *Pocahontas's People* (1990).

In recent years there has been a surge in scholarship on African slavery in the New World. For a new and magisterial overview, see David Brion Davis, *Inhuman Bondage* (2006). For British North America, see Ira Berlin, *Many Thousands Gone* (1998), and Philip D. Morgan, *Slave Counterpoint* (1998). The classic account of the British Caribbean remains Richard Dunn's *Sugar and Slaves* (1972).

The Chesapeake has always drawn more notice from early American historians than South Carolina has, but in recent years some important studies have redressed that neglect. The best overview of that colony's development remains Robert Weir, *Colonial South Carolina* (1982). The complexities of Carolina's slave wars are explored in Alan Gallay, *The Indian Slave Trade* (2002). For fine explorations of more specialized topics, see Peter A. Colclanis, *The Shadow of a Dream* (1989), and Timothy Silver, *A New Face on the Countryside* (1990).

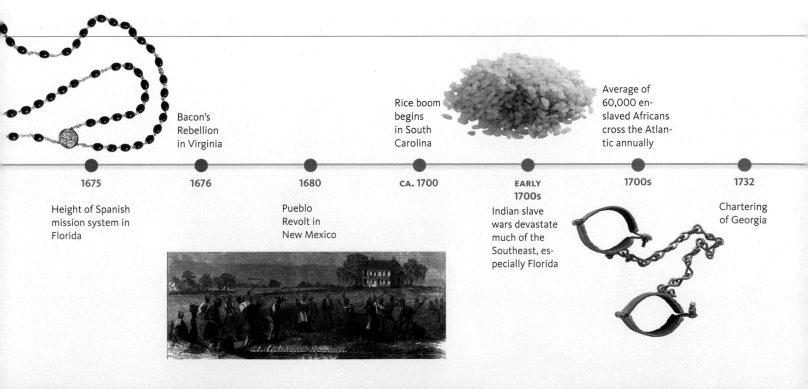

1675	1676	1680	CA. 1700	EARLY 1700s	1700s	1732
Height of Spanish mission system in Florida	Bacon's Rebellion in Virginia	Pueblo Revolt in New Mexico	Rice boom begins in South Carolina	Indian slave wars devastate much of the Southeast, especially Florida	Average of 60,000 enslaved Africans cross the Atlantic annually	Chartering of Georgia

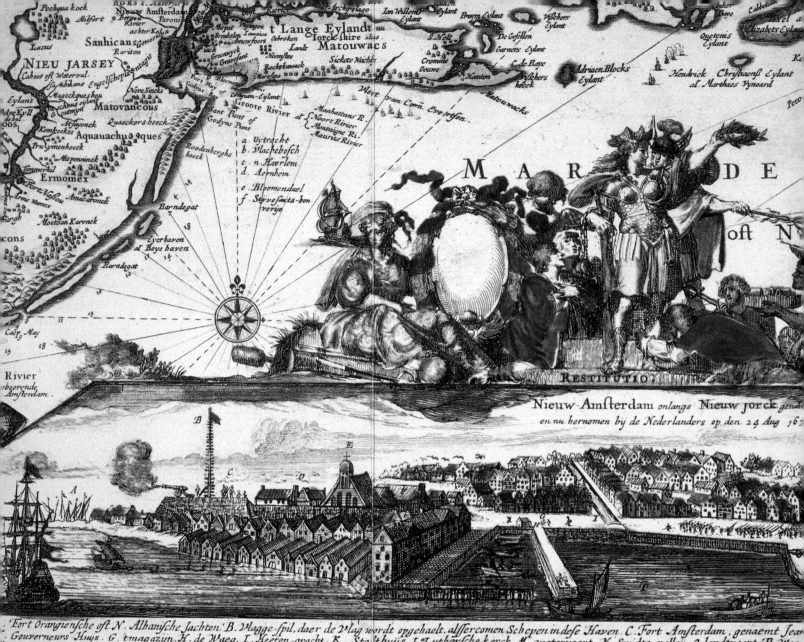

4

1600—1700

Colonization &

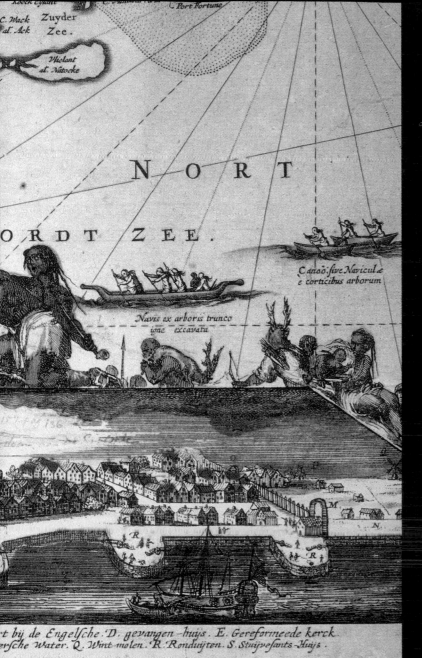

By 1673 when this map of New Amsterdam was engraved, the town had grown considerably from its origins as a fort and fur trading outpost. (Compare the engraving from 1626, on page 62.) Behind the oldest part of the town (at left), a palisade fence still stands as a wall protecting against Indian attacks. The English renamed the city New York and the street running along the palisade was transformed centuries later into a financial center. It retains its original name: Wall Street.

WHAT'S TO COME

62 **FRANCE IN NORTH AMERICA**

65 **THE FOUNDING OF NEW ENGLAND**

68 **STABILITY AND ORDER IN EARLY NEW ENGLAND**

73 **THE MID-ATLANTIC COLONIES**

76 **ADJUSTMENT TO EMPIRE**

BEARS ON FLOATING ISLANDS

They came to her one night while she slept. Into her dreams drifted a small island, and on the island were tall trees and living creatures, one of them wearing the fur of a white rabbit. When she told of her vision, no one took her seriously, not even the shamans and conjurers whose business it was to interpret dreams. No one, that is, until two days later, when the island appeared to all, floating toward shore. On it, as she had seen, were tall trees, and on their branches—bears. Or creatures that looked so much like bears that the men grabbed their weapons and raced to the beach, eager for the good hunt sent by the gods. They were disappointed. The island was not an island at all but a strange wooden ship planted with the trunks of trees. And the bears were not bears at all but a strange sort of men whose bodies were covered with hair. Strangest among them, as she had somehow known, was a man dressed all in white. He commanded great respect among the bearlike men as their "shaman," or priest. ≫

Conflict IN THE North

In that way, foretold by the dreams of a young woman, the Micmac Indians in 1869 recounted their people's first encounter with Europeans more than two centuries earlier. Uncannily, the traditions of other northern tribes record similar dreams predicting the European arrival: "large canoes with great white wings like those of a giant bird," filled with pale bearded men bearing "long black tubes."

However Micmacs and other northern Indians first imagined and idealized Europeans, they quickly came to see them as fully human. Traders might bring seemingly wondrous goods, goods that could transform the way labor, commerce, politics, and war functioned in native communities. Yet the traders themselves hardly seemed magical. They could be by turns gen-erous and miserly, brave and frightful, confident and confused, kind and cruel.

Moreover it soon became clear that these newcomers hailed from different nations, spoke different lan-guages, and often had different goals. English colonists, it seemed, were every day more numerous and wanted nothing so much as land. The French, in contrast, were relatively few and seemed to care for nothing so much as trade—unless it was their Christian God brought with them from across the waters. Strange to say, the Europe-ans argued over their deity as they did over so many other things. The Eng-lish, the French, and the Dutch were all rivals, and the Micmacs and others who encountered these new peoples studied them closely, and began to make alliances.

Everywhere they went, the new-comers provoked dramatic changes. Thousands of English migrants founded villages and towns throughout the sev-enteenth century. They not only took up land but also brought animals and plants that changed the way Indians lived. The Dutch, Europe's most pow-erful commercial nation, planted only a handful of trading settlements along the Hudson River, but they encour-aged the Iroquois confederacy to push into rival Indian territories in a quest for furs to trade. Even the French, who claimed to want little more than beaver pelts, brought profound, sometimes cataclysmic changes—changes that would upend the world that natives knew when Europeans were but bears on floating islands. «

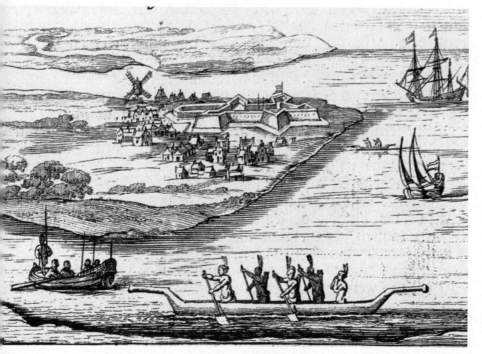

⌃ New Amsterdam (later New York City) in about 1626.
The Dutch who settled here were most interested in obtaining furs from Indians like those paddling the canoe in the foreground. In truth, however, most Dutch in Europe had far more interest in competing with the Portuguese for commerce with the Far East than vying with the English for the North American fur trade.

FRANCE IN NORTH AMERICA

Jacques Cartier first explored the land the French would call Canada in 1535, sailing through the Gulf of St. Lawrence. But not until 1605 did the French plant a perma-nent colony, at Port Royal in Acadia (Nova Scotia). Three years later, Samuel de Cham-plain established Québec farther up the St. Lawrence valley, to pursue the fur trade with less competition from rival Europeans. Champlain aligned himself with local Mon-tagnais, Algonquins, and, especially, the mighty Hurons—a confederacy of farmers 20,000 strong whose towns near the Geor-gian Bay straddled a vast trading network.

The Origins of New France »

The Hurons, Montagnais, and Algonquins had reason to embrace Champlain. Like Europeans elsewhere in North America, the Frenchman came with wondrous textiles, glass, copper, and ironware. At first the Indians treated such things as exotic commodities rather than utilitarian items. Copper kettles, for instance, might be cut into strips for jewelry. But before long, metal tools began transforming native life. The new knives made it far easier to butcher animals; trees could be felled and buildings put up far more easily with iron axes rather than stone; cooking was more efficient with brass kettles that could be placed directly on the fire; flint strike-a-lights eliminated the need to carry hot coals in bounded shells; beads, cloth, needles, and thread allowed for a new level of creative and visual expression; and, because they traveled farther and truer than stone, metal arrowheads made hunters and warriors more deadly than ever before.

For native peoples, all exchanges of goods were bound up in complex social relations. Thus the Montagnais, Algonquins, and Hurons wanted Champlain as a friend as well as a merchant. They persuaded him to accompany them on a campaign against their mutual enemies the Mohawks, one of the five confederated tribes of the Iroquois. Champlain proved his worth in 1609 when he and his Indian companions confronted two hundred Mohawk warriors in what is now upstate New York. The Frenchman strode to the front as the battle was about to begin, raised his musket, and shot dead two Mohawk chiefs. Chaplain's allies let out a joyous cry, for few if any of the warriors had ever seen a gun fired in combat. They drove the remaining Mohawks from the field. It was not the last time European newcomers would alter the balance of power in North America.

The Montagnais, Algonquins, and Hurons became eager trading partners over the next generation. In return for European goods, they provided tens of thousands of otter, raccoon, and especially beaver pelts. The latter went to make fashionable European hats, whereas mink and marten skins were sent to adorn the robes of high-ranking European officials and churchmen. Some of the French derided New France as nothing more than a *comptoir,* a storehouse for the skins of dead animals. Yet Champlain wanted more. He struggled to bring more permanent settlers to Canada and, above all, he looked to bind his native allies firmly to the colonial project. To that end, Champlain recruited certain French men and boys to live with Indian families, to learn their language and customs.

Along with these *couriers de bois,* or "runners in the woods," French authorities engaged Jesuits, members of the Society of Jesus, to establish missions among the Indians. The Jesuits were fired with the passions of the **Counter-Reformation** in Europe, a movement by devout

BACKSTORY
The Power of Dreams

While tracking enemy Iroquois in 1609, Hurons pestered their French ally Champlain about whether or not he had dreamed of victory. Champlain thought this was savage superstition, but that night he dreamed of "Iroquois drowning before our eyes." The Hurons rejoiced, and savored victory two days later.

{ **Counter-Reformation** reform movement within the Roman Catholic Church in response to the Protestant Reformation, seeking to reform and reinvigorate the Church.

Catholics to correct those abuses that had prompted the Protestant Reformation. At first France's Indian allies tolerated Jesuit missionaries but listened to them little. By the 1630s, however, Champlain began insisting that trading partners allow Jesuits to live among them. More importantly, Christianized Indians got better prices for furs than did their unconverted counterparts. Such policies helped the French pursue what they saw as interlocked economic, strategic, and religious objectives.

Among Champlain's allies the Huron proved to be the most reluctant to accept European customs and religion. Converts remained relatively few into the 1640s, and the debate over Huron cultural identity increasingly left the confederacy fragmented and vulnerable to enemies.

New Netherlands, the Iroquois, and the Beaver Wars >>

If Canada was merely a *comptoir,* it was a profitable one, and the rival Dutch noticed. By around 1600 the Netherlands possessed the greatest manufacturing capacity in the world and had become the key economic power in Europe. Because they enjoyed prosperity and religious freedom at home few Dutch folk had any desire to plant colonies abroad. But they did want to tap into the wealth flowing out of North America and therefore laid claim to a number of sites around the Connecticut, Delaware, and Hudson Rivers (the last named for the Englishman Henry Hudson, who first explored it for the Dutch in 1609). Most of New Netherlands' few settlers clustered in the village of New Amsterdam on Manhattan Island at the mouth of the Hudson.

More importantly for the geopolitics of the continent, the Dutch West India Company established a trading outpost 150 miles upriver known as Fort Orange (present-day Albany). By 1630 the powerful Mohawks came to dominate that fort's commerce. Ever since their encounter with Champlain's musket the Mohawks and the other four members of the **Iroquois League**—the Oneidas, Onondagas, Cayugas, and Senecas— had suffered from their lack of direct access to European

{ **Iroquois League** Indian confederacy consisting of the Mohawks, Oneidas, Onondagas, Cayugas, and Senecas (a sixth nation, the Tuscaroras, would join in 1712). The League exerted enormous influence throughout colonial eastern North America.

⌃ This undated French engraving depicts something often overlooked or trivialized by European observers: native women's work. Two Iroquois women grind corn into meal while a swaddled infant rests in a backboard.

tools and weapons. At Fort Orange, the Iroquois finally found that access. As the beaver population, always fragile, collapsed within Iroquois territory, the league used its new weapons to go on the offensive against its northern enemies. To maintain their trading position, they began preying upon Huron convoys on their way to Quebec and then selling the plundered pelts to the Dutch.

Just as this old rivalry revived, a smallpox epidemic plunged the region into catastrophe. Waves of the disease took a nightmarish toll, especially in Indian agricultural communities with densely populated towns. Between 1634 and 1640 the disease killed more than 10,000 Hurons, reducing their total population by half and precipitating a spate of conversions to Christianity that divided the community all the more. The Iroquois likewise suffered greatly, but, unlike the Hurons, reacted by waging war in an effort to obtain captives that could formally replace dead kin.

A second transformative event was the dramatic expansion of the region's arms trade. Reluctant at first to deal in guns, the Dutch at

≪ The Hurons who became infected with smallpox in the 1630s would have experienced fevers, aches, and vomiting before the telltale spots emerged on their skin. Agonizing pustules would have soon covered them from head to toe, as in this modern photograph, and sometimes the pustules merged into oozing sheets that caused large sections of the victims' skin to peel away from their bodies. The disease claimed millions of lives in the Americas after 1492.

Fort Orange relaxed their policy by the late 1630s in order to obtain more furs. Soon the Iroquois had many times more muskets than the Hurons, whom the French had refused to arm so long as they remained unconverted.

Reeling from disease and internal division, the Hurons saw their world collapsing. In 1648, well-armed Iroquois warriors destroyed three Huron towns. The Hurons made the wrenching decision to burn their remaining towns and abandon their lands for good. Perhaps 2,000 became Iroquois, either as war captives or humble refugees. Others merged with neighboring peoples, while thousands more fled and starved or died of exposure in the harsh winter of 1649–1650.

So began the Beaver Wars, a series of conflicts that transformed the colonial north at least as much as the Indian slave wars had the south. Seeking new hunting grounds and new captives to replenish their diminishing population, Iroquois raiders attacked peoples near and far. After the Hurons, they scattered the nearby Petuns, Eries, and Neutrals—peoples who, like the Hurons, were Iroquoian speakers and could be integrated into Iroquois communities with relative ease. Warriors next moved against non-Iroquoian groups, including Delawares and Shawnees in the Ohio Valley, and even extended their raids south to the Carolinas. To the North they attacked Algonquins in the Canadian Shield, and Abenakis and others in New England.

The Lure of the Mississippi ≫ The Beaver
Wars continued in fits and starts for the rest of the seventeenth century, provoking a massive refugee crisis as families fled their traditional territories and tried to rebuild their lives. The wars also very nearly ruined New France. About three hundred Frenchmen were killed or captured, cutting the colony's meager population in half by 1666. French authorities scrambled to find reliable new partners in the fur trade and became less reluctant to trade guns to Indian allies. In the end, the scope of the conflict and the far-flung movement of refugees led the French to take a more expansive view of the continent and their place in it.

That expansive view was encouraged by the discovery of the Mississippi River. By the 1660s, French traders, priests, and officers were making inroads among refugee villages in the Western Great Lakes, a region the French referred to as the *pays d'en haut*, or "upper country." As they did so, they began exploring the greatest watercourse in North America.

pays d'en haut in the seventeenth century, the lands referred to by the French as the "upper country," the land upriver from Montreal as French fur traders passed into the Great Lakes beyond the southern shores of Lake Ontario.

The Mississippi travels nearly 2,500 miles from its source in present-day Minnesota to the Gulf of Mexico, carrying water from several major rivers and dominating a drainage area larger than the Indian subcontinent in Asia. As the French began exploring in earnest, it dawned on them that the Mississippi Valley could be the strategic key to success in North America. French officials courted Indian peoples along the river and its tributaries, employing their hardwon insights into native diplomatic culture along the way. The region's peoples—the Illinois, Shawnees, Quapaws, and others—expressed keen interest in French trade, as well as fear and hatred of their common Iroquois enemies. When René Robert Cavelier, Sieur de La Salle became the first European to descend the river to the Gulf in 1682, he encountered the Natchez, Chickasaws, and others who had not seen Europeans since De Soto and his maniacal march nearly a century and a half before. Other Frenchmen erected trading posts and simple missions, even making contact and tentative alliances with Osages, Arkansas, Ottos, Pawnees, and others west of the great river.

By the early eighteenth century New France had helped broker an uneasy peace between the Iroquois and Indian nations to the west, extended its influence over a vast area, and fortified its colonial core along the St. Lawrence River. In 1700 the colony had scores of simple missions and three modest cities—Quebec, Montreal, and Trois-Rivières—containing a population of about 15,000. Most immigrants to New France eventually returned to Europe, and short-sighted French monarchs insisted that Canada remain Catholic, off limits to France's most obvious emigrants, the Protestant Huguenots. But even with its small colonial population, New France emerged as a powerful player in North America. The French had reason to hope that their strategic and economic alliances with native peoples could help contain the Spanish to the west and limit English expansion from the east.

THE FOUNDING OF NEW ENGLAND

At first, the English regarded the northern part of North America as a place in which only the mad French could see possibility. English fisherfolk who strayed from Newfoundland to the coast of Acadia and New England carried home descriptions of the long, lonely coast, rockbound and rugged. Long winters of numbing cold melted into short summers of steamy heat. There were no minerals to mine, no crops suitable for export, no huge native populations to enslave. The Chesapeake, with its temperate climate and long growing season, seemed a much likelier spot.

But by 1620, worsening conditions at home had instilled in some English men and women the mixture of desperation and idealism needed to settle an uninviting, unknown world. Religious differences among English Protestants became a matter of sharper controversy during the seventeenth century. Along with the religious crisis came mounting political tensions and continuing problems of unemployment and recession. Times were bad—so bad that the anticipation of worse times to come swept English men and women to the shores of New England.

The Puritan Movement >> The colonization of New England started with a king who chose his enemies unwisely. James I, shortly after succeeding Elizabeth I in 1603, vowed to purge England of all radical Protestant reformers. The radicals James had in mind were the **Puritans,** most of whom were either Presbyterians or Congregationalists. Although both groups of Puritan reformers embraced Calvin's ideas, they differed on the best form of church organization. Individual **Presbyterian** churches (or congregations) were guided by higher governing bodies of ministers and laypersons. Those in the **Congregationalist** churches, in contrast, believed that each congregation should conduct its own affairs independently, answering to no other authority.

Puritans reformers within the Church of England during the sixteenth century, who ultimately formed the Congregationalist and Presbyterian churches. Puritans strove to reform English religion, society, and politics by restricting church membership to the pious and godly and by enlisting the state to enforce a strict moral code.

Presbyterians members of a Protestant denomination that originated in sixteenth-century Britain as part of the Puritan movement. Presbyterians embraced Calvinist beliefs and favored a more hierarchical church organization in which individual congregations were guided by presbyteries and synods comprising both laymen and ministers.

Like all Christians, Protestant and Catholic, the Puritans believed that God was all-knowing and all-powerful. And, like all Calvinists, the Puritans emphasized that idea of divine sovereignty known as **predestination.** At the center of their thinking was the belief that God had ordained the outcome of history, including the eternal fate of every human being. The Puritans found comfort in their belief in predestination because it provided their lives with meaning and purpose. They felt assured that a sovereign God was directing the fate of individuals, nations, and all of creation. The Puritans strove to play their parts in that divine drama of history and to discover in their performances some signs of personal salvation.

Congregationalists members of a Protestant denomination that originated in sixteenth-century Britain as part of the Puritan movement. Congregationalists held that each individual congregation should conduct its own religious affairs, answering to no higher authority.

The divine plan, as the Puritans understood it, called for reforming both church and society along the lines laid down by John Calvin. It seemed to the Puritans that England's government hampered rather than promoted

predestination basis of Calvinist theology and a belief that holds that God has ordained the outcome of all human history before the beginning of time, including the eternal fate of every human being.

religious purity and social order. It tolerated drunkenness, theatergoing, gambling, extravagance, public swearing, and Sabbath-breaking. It permitted popular recreations rooted in pagan custom and superstition—sports such as bear baiting and maypole dancing and festivals such as the celebration of Christmas and saints' days.

Even worse, the state had not done enough to purify the English church of the "corruptions" of Roman Catholicism. The Church of England counted as its members everyone in the nation, saint and sinner alike. To the Puritans, belonging to a church was no birthright. They wished to limit membership and the privileges of baptism and communion to godly men and women. The Puritans also deplored the hierarchy of bishops and archbishops in the Church of England, as well as its elaborate ceremonies in which priests wore ornate vestments. Too many Anglican clergy were "dumb dogges" in Puritan eyes, too poorly educated to instruct churchgoers in the truths of Scripture or to deliver a decent sermon.

Because English monarchs refused to take stronger measures to reform church and society, the Puritans became their outspoken critics. Elizabeth I had tolerated this opposition, but James I would not endure it and intended to rid England of these radicals. With some of the Puritans, known as the Separatists, he seemed to succeed.

The Pilgrim Settlement at Plymouth Colony >> The Separatists were devout Congregationalists who concluded that the Church of England was too corrupt to be reformed. They abandoned Anglican worship and met secretly in small congregations. From their first appearance in England during the 1570s, the Separatists suffered persecution from the government—fines, imprisonment, and, in a few cases, execution. Always a tiny minority within the Puritan movement, the Separatists were people from humble backgrounds: craftworkers and farmers without influence to challenge the state. By 1608 some had become so discouraged that they migrated to Holland, where the Dutch government permitted complete freedom of religion. But when their children began to adopt Dutch customs and other religions, some Separatists decided to move again, this time to Virginia.

It can only be imagined what fate would have befallen the unworldly Separatists had they actually settled in the Chesapeake during the tobacco boom. But a series of mistakes—including an error in charting the course

> **They had arrived too late to plant crops and had failed to bring an adequate supply of food. By the spring of 1621, half the immigrants had died.**

of their ship, the *Mayflower*—brought the little band far to the North, to a region Captain John Smith had earlier dubbed "New England." In November 1620, some 88 Separatist "Pilgrims" set anchor at a place they called Plymouth on the coast of present-day southeastern Massachusetts. They were sick with scurvy, weak from malnutrition, and shaken by a shipboard mutiny, and neither the site nor the season invited settlement. As one of their leaders, William Bradford, later remembered:

> For summer being done, all things stand upon them with a weatherbeaten face, and the whole country, full of woods and thickets represented a savage hue. If they looked behind them, there was the mighty ocean which they had passed and was now as a main bar and gulf to separate them from all the civil parts of the world.

For some, the shock was too great. Dorothy Bradford, William's wife, is said to have fallen overboard from the *Mayflower* as it lay anchored off Plymouth. It is more likely that she jumped to her death.

Few Pilgrims could have foreseen founding the first permanent European settlement in New England, and many did not live long enough to enjoy the distinction. They had arrived too late to plant crops and had failed to bring an adequate supply of food. By the spring of 1621, half the immigrants had died. English merchants who had financed the *Mayflower* voyage failed to send supplies to the struggling settlement. Plymouth might have become another doomed colony except that the Pilgrims received better treatment from native inhabitants than they did from their English backers.

Do you think that the Puritans were committed to religious freedom?

trade goods and assistance against native enemies, Masasoit, their chief, agreed to help the starving colonists. At first, the peoples communicated through a remarkable Wampanoag named Squanto, who had been kidnapped by English sailors before the epidemic. Taken to Europe, Squanto learned English and returned to America in time to act as a mediator between Masasoit and the newcomers. The Pilgrims accepted Wampanoag hospitality and instruction, and invited native leaders to a feast in honor of their first successful harvest in 1621 (the genesis of the "First Thanksgiving" story).

The Pilgrims set up a government for their colony, the framework of which was the Mayflower Compact, drawn up on board ship before landing. That agreement provided for a governor and several assistants to advise him, all to be elected annually by Plymouth's adult males. In the eyes of English law, the Plymouth settlers had no clear basis for their land claims or their government, for they had neither a royal charter nor approval from the Crown. But English authorities, distracted by problems closer to home, left the tiny colony of farmers alone.

Though they understood it only dimly, the Pilgrims were, in one historian's memorable phrase, the "beneficiaries of catastrophe." Only four years before their arrival, coastal New England had been devastated by a massive epidemic, possibly the plague. Losses varied locally, but overall the native coastal population may have been reduced by as much as 90 percent. Abandoned villages lay in ruins up and down the coast, including the village of Patuxet, where the Pilgrims established Plymouth. Years later visitors would still marvel at heaps of unburied human remains dating from the epidemic.

The Wampanoags dominated the lands around Plymouth. Still reeling from loss in 1620 and eager to obtain

The Puritan Settlement at Massachusetts Bay

>> Among the Crown's distractions were two groups of Puritans more numerous and influential than the Pilgrims. They included both the Presbyterians and the majority of Congregationalists who, unlike the Pilgrim Separatists, still considered the Church of England capable of being reformed. But the 1620s brought these Puritans only fresh discouragements. In 1625 Charles I inherited his father's throne and all his enemies. When Parliament attempted to limit the king's power, Charles simply dissolved it, in 1629, and proceeded to rule without it. When Puritans pressed for reform, the king began to move against them.

This persecution swelled a second wave of Puritan migration that also drew from the ranks of Congregationalists. Unlike the humble Separatists, these emigrants included merchants, landed gentlemen, and lawyers who organized the Massachusetts Bay Company in 1629. Those able Puritan leaders aimed to build a better society in America, an example to the rest of the world. Unlike the Separatists, they had a strong sense of mission and destiny. They were not abandoning the English church, they insisted, but merely regrouping across the Atlantic for another assault on corruption.

Despite the company's Puritan leanings, it somehow obtained a royal charter confirming its title to most of present-day Massachusetts and New Hampshire. Advance parties in 1629 established the town of Salem on the coast well north of Plymouth. In 1630 the company's first governor, a tough-minded and visionary lawyer named John Winthrop, sailed from England with a dozen other company stockholders and a fleet of men and women to establish the town of Boston. The newcomers intended to build a godly "city on a hill" that would serve as an example to the world.

Once established in the Bay Colony, Winthrop and the other stockholders transformed the charter for their trading company into the framework of government for a colony. The company's governor became the colony's chief executive, and the company's other officers became the governor's assistants. The charter provided for annual elections of the governor and his assistants by company stockholders, known as the freemen. But to create a broad base of support for the new government, Winthrop and his assistants expanded the freemanship in 1631 to include every adult male church member.

The governor, his assistants, and the freemen together made up the General Court of the colony, which passed all laws, levied taxes, established courts, and made war and peace. In 1634 the whole body of the freemen stopped meeting and instead each town elected representatives or deputies to the General Court. Ten years later, the deputies formed themselves into the lower house of the Bay Colony legislature, and the assistants formed the upper house. By refashioning a company charter into a civil constitution, Massachusetts Bay Puritans were well on the way to shaping society, church, and state to their liking.

Contrary to expectations, New England proved more hospitable to the English than did the Chesapeake. The

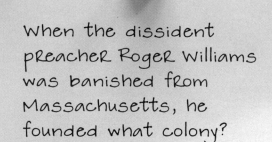

When the dissident preacher Roger Williams was banished from Massachusetts, he founded what colony?

a. Connecticut

b. Rhode Island

c. Vermont

d. Massachusetts

Key: b

character of the migration itself gave New England settlers an advantage, for most arrived in family groups—not as young, single, indentured servants of the sort whose discontents unsettled Virginia society. The heads of New England's first households were typically free men—farmers, artisans, and merchants. Most were skilled and literate. Since husbands usually migrated with their wives and children, the ratio of men to women within the population was fairly evenly balanced.

Most of the immigrants, some 21,000, came in a cluster between 1630 and 1642. Thereafter new arrivals tapered off because of the outbreak of the English Civil War (page 00). This relatively rapid colonization fostered solidarity, because immigrants shared a common past of persecution and a strong desire to create an ordered society modeled on Scripture.

STABILITY AND ORDER IN EARLY NEW ENGLAND

Puritan emigrants and their descendants thrived in New England's bracing but healthy climate. The first generation of colonists lived to an average age of 70, nearly twice as long as Virginians and 10 years longer than men and women living in England. With 90 percent of all offspring reaching adulthood, the typical family consisted of seven or eight children who came to maturity. Because of low death rates and high birthrates, the number of New Englanders doubled about every 27 years—while the populations of Europe and the Chesapeake barely reproduced themselves. By 1700, New England and the Chesapeake both had populations of approximately 100,000. But, whereas the southern population grew because of continuing immigration and the importation of slaves, New England's expanded primarily through natural increase.

Early immigrants to the Bay Colony carved out an arc of villages around Massachusetts Bay. Within a decade settlers pressed into Connecticut, Rhode Island, and New Hampshire. Connecticut and Rhode Island received separate charters from Charles II in the 1660s, guaranteeing their residents the rights to land and government. New

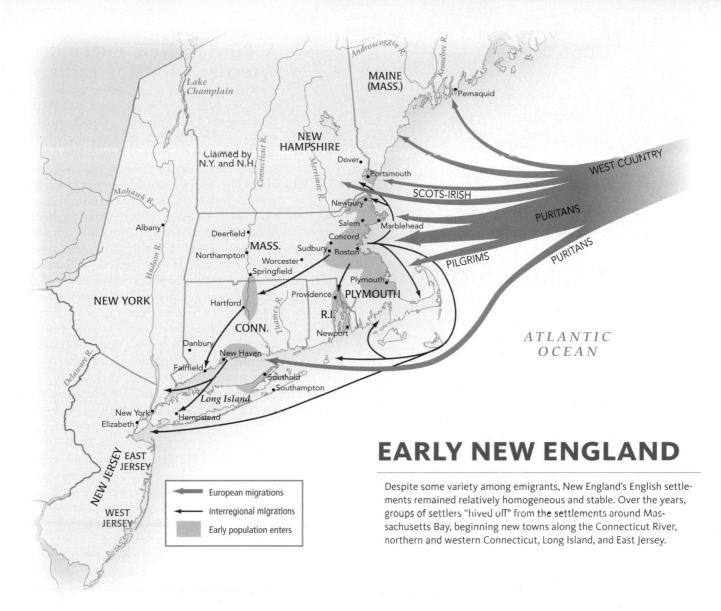

EARLY NEW ENGLAND

Despite some variety among emigrants, New England's English settlements remained relatively homogeneous and stable. Over the years, groups of settlers "hived off" from the settlements around Massachusetts Bay, beginning new towns along the Connecticut River, northern and western Connecticut, Long Island, and East Jersey.

Hampshire, at first part of Massachusetts, became a separate colony in 1679, whereas the handful of hardy souls living along the coast of present-day Maine still accepted the Massachusetts Bay Colony's authority.

Early New Englanders established most of their settlements with an eye to stability and order. Unlike the Virginians, who scattered across the Chesapeake to isolated plantations, most New Englanders established tightly knit communities like those they had left behind in England. Each family received a lot for a house along with about 150 acres of land in nearby fields. Farmers left many of their acres uncultivated as a legacy for future generations, for most had only the labor of their own families to work their land. While the Chesapeake abounded with servants, tenant farmers, and slaves, almost every adult male in rural New England owned property. With little hope of prospering through commercial agriculture, New England farmers also had no incentive to import large numbers of servants and slaves or to create large plantations.

Strong family institutions contributed to New England's order and stability. While the early deaths of parents regularly splintered Chesapeake families, two adult generations were often on hand to encourage order within New England households. Husbands and fathers exacted submission from wives and strict obedience from children. Land gave New England's long-lived fathers great authority over even their grown children; sons and daughters relied on paternal legacies of farms in order to marry and establish their own families.

Whereas churches were few and far between in seventeenth-century Virginia, they constituted the center of community life in colonial New England. Individual congregations ran their own affairs and regulated their own membership. Those wishing to join had to convince ministers and church members that they had experienced

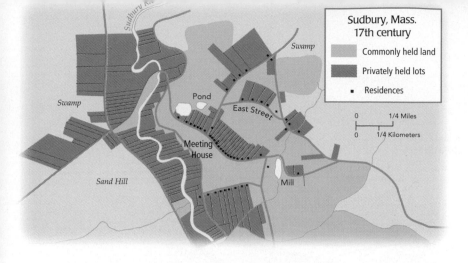

SUDBURY, MASSACHUSETTS

Sudbury, Mass.
17th century

Commonly held land

Privately held lots

■ Residences

0   1/4 Miles

0   1/4 Kilometers

Everyday life in New England centered in small towns such as Sudbury, west of Boston. Families lived in houses clustered around the meeting house, in contrast to the decentralized plantations of the south. The privately held farm lots were mixed together as well, so that neighbors worked and lived in close contact with one another.

a genuine spiritual rebirth or "conversion." Most New Englanders sought and won membership. As majority institutions supported by public taxes, churches had the reach and the resources to oversee public morality, often censuring or expelling wayward neighbors. Still, ministers enjoyed less public power in New England than in the old country. New England's ministers did not serve as officers in the civil government, and the Congregational churches owned no property. In contrast, Catholic and Anglican church officials wielded real temporal power in European states, and the churches held extensive tracts of land.

Is There a God?

"Many times Satan has troubled me . . . by atheism how I could know whether there was a God; I never saw any miracles to confirm me, and those which I read of how did I know but they were feigned? That there is a God my reason would soon tell me by the wondrous works that I see, the vast frame of the heaven and the earth . . ."

A Puritan New Englander Wrestles with Her Faith >>

Finally, New Englanders governed themselves more democratically than did their counterparts in England. Communities throughout the region held regular town meetings of all resident white men. The town fathers generally set the meeting's agenda and offered advice, but the unanimous consent of townsmen determined all decisions. Colony governments in early New England also evolved into representative and responsive institutions. Typically the central government of each colony, such as the General Court of Massachusetts Bay, consisted of a governor and a bicameral legislature, including an upper house, or council, and a lower house, or assembly. All officials were elected annually by the freemen—white adult men entitled to vote in colony elections. Voting qualifications varied, but the number of men enfranchised made up a much broader segment of society than that in seventeenth-century England.

Communities in Conflict >>
Although most New Englanders called themselves Puritans and Congregationalists, the very fervency of their convictions often led them to disagree about how to carry out the teachings of the Bible and the ideas of John Calvin. During the first decades of colonization, such disagreements led to the founding of breakaway colonies. In 1636 Thomas Hooker, the minister of Cambridge, Massachusetts, led part of his congregation to establish the first English settlement in Connecticut. Somewhat more liberal than other Bay Puritans, Hooker favored more lenient standards for church membership. He also opposed the Bay's policy of limiting voting in colony elections to church members. In contrast, New Haven (a separate colony until it became part of Connecticut in 1662) was begun in 1638 by strict Congregationalists who found Massachusetts too liberal.

While Connecticut and New Haven emerged from voluntary migration, enforced exile filled Rhode Island with men and women whose radical ideas unsettled the rest of Massachusetts. Roger Williams, Rhode Island's founder, had come to New England in 1631, serving as a respected minister of Salem. But soon Williams announced that he was a Separatist, like the Pilgrims of Plymouth. He encouraged the Bay Colony to break all ties to the corrupt Church of England. He also urged a more complete **separation of Church and State** than most New Englanders were prepared to accept, and later in his career he endorsed full religious toleration. Finally, Williams denounced the Bay's charter—the legal document that justified Massachusetts's existence—on the grounds that the king had no right to grant land that he had not purchased from the Indians. When Williams boldly suggested that Massachusetts actually inform the king of his mistake, angry authorities prepared to deport him. Instead Williams fled the colony in the dead of winter to live with the Indians. In 1636, he became the founder and first citizen of Providence, later to be part of Rhode Island.

Another charismatic heretic from Massachusetts arrived soon after. Anne Hutchinson, a skilled midwife and the spouse of a wealthy merchant, came to Boston in 1634. Enthusiasm for her minister, John Cotton, started her on a course of explaining his sermons to gatherings of her neighbors—and then to elaborating ideas of her own. The fact that a woman would do such things made the authorities uneasy; they became positively alarmed when they learned that Hutchinson embraced controversial positions on doctrine. Soon a majority of the Bay's ministers accused the popular Hutchinson of holding heretical views. She in turn denounced her detractors, and the controversy escalated. In 1638 the Bay Colony government expelled Hutchinson and her followers for sedition. She settled briefly in Rhode Island before moving on to Long Island, where she died in an Indian attack.

{ **separation of Church and State** principle that religious institutions and their representatives should exercise no civil or judicial powers and that civil governments should give no official sanction, privileges, or financial support to any religious denomination or organization.

Goodwives and Witches >> If Anne Hutchinson had been a man, her ideas would still have been deemed heretical. However, if she had been a man, she might have found other ways to express her intelligence and magnetism. But life in colonial New England offered women, especially married women, little scope for their talents.

Most adult women were hardworking farm wives who cared for large households of children. Between marriage and middle age, most New England wives were pregnant except when breast-feeding. When they were not nursing or minding children, mothers were producing and preparing much of what was consumed and worn by their families. They planted vegetable gardens and pruned fruit trees, salted beef and pork and pressed cider, milked cows and churned butter, kept bees and tended poultry, cooked and baked, washed and ironed, spun, wove, and sewed. While husbands and sons engaged in farm work that changed with the seasons, took trips to taverns and mills, and went off to hunt or fish, housebound wives and daughters were locked into a humdrum routine with little time for themselves.

Women suffered legal disadvantages as well. In contrast to New Mexico and Florida with their Spanish civil law traditions, English common law and colonial legal codes accorded married women virtually no control over property. Wives could not sue or be sued, they could not make contracts, and they surrendered to their husbands any property that they possessed before marriage. Divorce was almost impossible to obtain until the late eighteenth century. Only widows and a few single women had the same property rights as men, but they could not vote in colony elections.

The one arena in which women could attain something approaching equal standing with men was the churches. Puritan women could not become ministers, but after the 1660s they made up the majority of church members. In some churches membership enabled them to vote for ministerial candidates and to voice opinions about admitting and disciplining members. Puritan doctrine itself rejected the medieval Catholic suspicion of women as "a necessary evil," seeing them instead as "a necessary good." Even so, the Puritan ideal of the virtuous woman was a chaste, submissive "helpmeet," a wife and mother who served God by serving men.

Communities sometimes responded to assertive women with accusations of witchcraft. Like most early modern Europeans, New Englanders believed in wizards and witches, men and women who were said to acquire supernatural powers by signing a compact with Satan. A total of 344 New Englanders were charged with witchcraft during the first colonial century, with the notorious Salem Village episode of 1692 producing the largest outpouring of accusations and 20 executions. More than three-quarters of all accused witches were women, usually middle-aged and older, and most of those accused were regarded as unduly independent. Before they were charged with witchcraft, many had been suspected of heretical religious beliefs, others of sexual impropriety. Still others had inherited or stood to inherit property.

> Like most early modern Europeans, New Englanders believed in wizards and witches, men and women who were said to acquire supernatural powers by signing a compact with Satan.

The People in the Way >> Whatever their political battles, doctrinal disputes, and inequalities, New Englanders were all participants in a colonial project that

depended on taking land from other people. At the time of first contact, perhaps 100,000 Algonquian men and women lived in the area reaching from the Kennebec River in Maine to Cape Cod. Like the Puritans, they relied on fishing in spring and summer, hunting year round, and cultivating and harvesting corn and other crops in spring and fall. To an even greater degree than among the colonists, Indian political authority was local. Within each village, a single leader known as the "sachem" or "sagamore" directed economic life, administered justice, and negotiated with other tribes and English settlers. As with New England's town fathers, a sachem's power depended on keeping the trust and consent of his people.

Thus, the newcomers had more in common with their hosts than they cared to admit. But English expansion in the region had to come at someone's expense, and colonists obtained Indian lands in one of three ways. Sometimes they purchased it. Sales varied—they might be free and fair, fraudulent, subtly coerced, or forced through intimidation and violence. Second, colonists eagerly expanded into lands emptied by epidemics. The English often saw God's hand in such events. "Without this remarkable and terrible stroke of God upon the natives," wrote one New Englander after a smallpox epidemic, "[we] would with much more difficulty have found room" to settle.

Third and finally, colonists commonly encouraged and participated in regional wars to obtain native lands. This proved easy enough to do, because, like Europeans, the Indians of New England quarreled frequently with neighboring nations. The antagonism among the English, Spanish, Dutch, and French was matched by the hostilities among the Abenakis, Pawtuckets, Massachusetts, Narragansetts, and Wampanoags of the north Atlantic coast. Epidemics only intensified existing rivalries, because they opened up new opportunities for stronger neighbors to press their advantage.

The English began by aligning with Masasoit and his Wampanoags against other coastal peoples in New England. In 1637 colonial forces joined the Narragansetts in a campaign against the formidable Pequots, who controlled coveted territory in Connecticut. The colonists shocked even their Indian allies when they set fire to the main Pequot village, killing hundreds of men, women, and children. Plymouth's William Bradford recalled that "it was a fearful sight to see them thus frying in the fire, and the streams of blood quenching the same, and horrible was the stink and scent thereof; but the victory seemed a sweet sacrifice, and they gave the praise thereof to God, who had wrought so wonderfully for them." Several years later the colonists turned against their former allies, joining forces with the Mohegans to intimidate the Narragansetts into ceding much of their territory. Only a few colonists objected to those ruthless policies, among them Roger Williams. "God Land," he warned one Connecticut leader, "will be . . . as great a God with us English as God Gold was with the Spainards."

Metacom's War >> Throughout these wars, the colonists more or less nurtured their original alliance with Masasoit and his Wampanoags. Indeed, certain colonists tried to bring the two societies closer together. While the impulse to convert was not nearly as strong in New England as in New Spain or New France, a few Englishmen worked tirelessly to bring the word of their God to Indians.

Puritan minister John Eliot began preaching in Algonquian in the 1640s. Over the next two decades he oversaw a project to publish the scriptures in Algonquian using the Latin alphabet. He also trained scores of native ministers (many of whom became literate), and established seven villages or "praying towns" for Christian Indians. Eliot was not alone. Harvard College defined its mission as "the education of English & Indian youth of this Country" and in 1655 established an Indian college and dormitory on campus. None of these efforts embodied respect for Indian culture or religion. But some New Englanders, at least, wanted to assimilate Indians rather than drive them away.

And yet the colony always grasped for more land. Over time the Puritan-Wampanoag partnership had become a relationship of subordination and suspicion. Rumors of potential native rebellion led colonial authorities to conduct humiliating interrogations and put in place severe rules and restrictions. The colonists' cows and pigs invaded and destroyed Indian fields, provoking innumerable conflicts. When Indians tried to adapt by raising their own cows and pigs, colonial authorities barred them from using common pasture or selling meat in Boston. At the same time, as many as half the dwindling Wampanoags had

Squanto's Advice

"Contrary to what American myth has long held, it is quite unlikely that alewives or other fish were used as fertilizer in Indian fields, notwithstanding the legendary role of the Pilgrims' friend Squanto in teaching colonists this practice. Squanto probably learned the technique while being held captive in Europe . . ."

—William Cronon, *Changes in the Land: Indians, Colonists, and the Ecology of New England*

followed Eliot into the praying towns, threatening tribal unity in a time of mounting crisis.

By 1675 such pressures convinced Masasoit's son and heir, Metacom, whom the English called King Philip, that his nation could be preserved only by chancing war. Complaining that the English were plotting to kill him and other sachems and replace them with Christian Indians more willing to sell land, Metacom rallied most of southern New England's native peoples and laid waste to more than two dozen towns in Plymouth Colony. By the spring of 1676, Metacom's warriors were raiding settlements within 20 miles of Boston. The offensive threatened New England's very existence.

But its momentum could not be sustained. Faced with shortages of food and ammunition, Metacom asked assistance from the Abenakis of Maine and the Mahicans of New York. Both refused. In the summer of 1676 Metacom died in battle; colonial forces brought his severed head to Boston and his hands to Plymouth as trophies. His desperate gamble exhausted native military power in southern New England and virtually destroyed the Wampanoags as a coherent people.

In proportion to population, "King Philip's War" inflicted twice the casualties on New England that the United States as a whole would suffer in the American Civil War. But in the end the region's surviving Indians, Christian or not, found themselves consigned to quiet and often desperate lives on the margins of colonial life.

THE MID-ATLANTIC COLONIES

The inhabitants of the mid-Atlantic colonies—New York, New Jersey, Pennsylvania, and Delaware—enjoyed more secure lives than did most southern colonials. But they lacked the common bonds that lent stability to early New England. Instead, throughout the mid-Atlantic region a variety of ethnic and religious groups vied for wealth from farming and the fur trade and contended bitterly against governments that commanded little popular support.

English Rule in New York >> By the 1660s, the Dutch experiment on the mid-Atlantic coast was faltering. While Fort Orange continued to secure furs for the Dutch West India Company, the colonial population remained small and fractious. The company made matters worse by appointing corrupt, dictatorial governors who ruled without an elective assembly. It also provided little protection for outlying Dutch settlements; when it did attack neighboring Indian nations, it did so savagely, triggering terrible retaliations. By the time the company went bankrupt in 1654, it had virtually abandoned its American colony.

In proportion to population, "King Philip's War" inflicted twice the casualties on New England that the United States as a whole would suffer in the American Civil War.

Taking advantage of the disarray in New Netherlands, Charles II ignored Dutch claims in North America and granted his brother, James, the Duke of York, a proprietary charter there. The charter granted James all of New Netherlands to Delaware Bay as well as Maine, Martha's Vineyard, and Nantucket Island. In 1664 James sent an invading fleet, whose mere arrival caused the Dutch to surrender.

New York's dizzying diversity would make it difficult to govern. The Duke inherited 9,000 or so colonists: Dutch, Belgians, French, English, Portuguese, Swedes, Finns, and Africans—some enslaved, others free. The colony's ethnic diversity ensured a variety of religions. Although the Dutch Reformed church predominated, other early New Netherlanders included Lutherans, **Quakers**, and Catholics. There were Jews as well, refugees from Portuguese Brazil, who were required by law to live in a ghetto in New Amsterdam. The Dutch resented English rule, and only after a generation of intermarriage and acculturation did that resentment fade. James also failed to win friends among New Englanders who had come to Long Island seeking autonomy and cheap land during the 1640s. He grudgingly gave in to their demand for an elective assembly in 1683 but rejected its first act, the Charter of Liberties, which would have guaranteed basic political rights. The chronic political strife discouraged prospective settlers. By 1698 the colony numbered only 18,000 inhabitants, and New York City, the former New Amsterdam, was an overgrown village of a few thousand.

> **Quakers** Protestant sect, also known as the Society of Friends, founded in mid-seventeenth century England. The Quakers believed that the Holy Spirit dwelt within each human being and that religious conviction was the source of their egalitarian social practices, which included allowing women to speak in churches and to preach in public gatherings.

The Founding of New Jersey >> Confusion attended New Jersey's beginnings. The lands lying west of the Hudson and east of the Delaware River had been part of the Duke of York's proprietary grant. But in 1664 he gave about 5 million of these acres to Lord Berkeley and

Sir George Carteret, two of his favorites who were already involved in the proprietary colonies of the Carolinas. New Jersey's new owners guaranteed settlers land, religious freedom, and a representative assembly in exchange for a small quitrent, an annual fee for the use of the land. The proprietors' terms promptly drew Puritan settlers from New Haven, Connecticut. At the same time, unaware that James had already given New Jersey to Berkeley and Carteret, New York's Governor Richard Nicolls granted Long Island Puritans land there.

More complications ensued when Berkeley and Carteret decided to divide New Jersey into east and west and sell both halves to Quaker investors—a prospect that outraged New Jersey's Puritans. Although some English Quakers migrated to West Jersey, the investors quickly decided that two Jerseys were less desirable than one Pennsylvania and resold both East and West Jersey to speculators. In the end the Jerseys became a patchwork of religious and ethnic groups. Settlers who shared a common religion or national origin formed communities and established small family farms. When the Crown finally reunited east and west as a single royal colony in 1702, New Jersey was overshadowed by settlements not only to the north but now, also, to the south and west.

> The **Quakers** behaved in ways and believed in ideas that most people regarded as **odd.** They dressed in a deliberately **plain** and **severe** manner. They **refused** to swear **oaths** or to make **war.** They allowed **women** public roles of religious **leadership.**

Quaker Odysseys >>

Religious and political idealism similar to that of the Puritans inspired the colonization of Pennsylvania, making it an oddity among the mid-Atlantic colonies. The oddity began with an improbable founder, William Penn. Young Penn devoted his early years to disappointing his distinguished father, Sir William Penn, an admiral in the Royal Navy. Several years after being expelled from college, young Penn finally chose a career that may have made the admiral yearn for mere disappointment: he undertook a lifelong commitment to put into practice Quaker teachings. By the 1670s he had emerged as an acknowledged leader of the Society of Friends, as the Quakers formally called themselves.

The Quakers behaved in ways and believed in ideas that most people regarded as odd. They dressed in a deliberately plain and severe manner. They withheld from their social superiors the customary marks of respect, such as bowing, kneeling, and removing their hats. They refused to swear oaths or to make war. They allowed women

public roles of religious leadership. That pattern of behavior reflected their egalitarian ideals, the belief that all men and women shared equally in the "Light Within." Some 40,000 English merchants, artisans, and farmers embraced Quakerism by 1660, and many suffered fines, imprisonment, and corporal punishment.

Since the English upper class has always prized eccentricity among its members, it is not surprising that Penn, despite his Quakerism, remained a favorite of Charles II. More surprising is that the king's favor took the extravagant form of presenting Penn in 1681 with all the land between New Jersey and Maryland. Perhaps the king was repaying Penn for the large sum that his father had lent the Stuarts. Or perhaps the king was hoping to export England's Quakers to an American colony governed by his trusted personal friend.

Penn envisioned that his proprietary colony would provide a refuge for Quakers while producing quitrents for himself. To publicize his colony, he distributed pamphlets praising its attractions throughout the British Isles and Europe. The response was overwhelming: by 1700 its population stood at 21,000. The only early migration of equal magnitude was the Puritan colonization of New England.

Patterns of Growth >>

Perhaps half of Pennsylvania's settlers arrived as indentured servants, while the families of free farmers and artisans made up the rest. The majority were Quakers from Britain, Holland, and Germany, but the colonists also included Catholics, Lutherans, Baptists, Anglicans, and Presbyterians. In 1682 when Penn purchased and annexed the Three Lower Counties (later the colony of Delaware), his colony included the 1,000 or so Dutch, Swedes, and Finns living there.

Quakers from other colonies—West Jersey, Maryland, and New England—also flocked to the new homeland. Those experienced settlers brought skills and connections that contributed to Pennsylvania's rapid economic growth. Farmers sowed their rich lands into a sea of wheat, which merchants exported to the Caribbean. The center of the colony's trade was Philadelphia, a superb natural harbor situated at the confluence of the Delaware and Schuylkill rivers.

In contrast to New England's landscape of villages, the Pennsylvania countryside beyond Philadelphia was

⌃ The tidy, productive farmsteads of the Pennsylvania countryside were the basis of that colony's prosperity during the eighteenth century. Their produce fueled the growth of Philadelphia and sustained the expansion of sugar plantations on England's Caribbean islands.

dotted with dispersed farmsteads. Commercial agriculture required larger farms, which kept settlers at greater distances from one another. As a result, the county rather than the town became the basic unit of local government in Pennsylvania.

Another reason that farmers did not need to cluster their homes within a central village was that they were at peace with the coastal Indians, the Lenni Lenapes (also called Delawares by the English). Thanks to two Quaker beliefs—a commitment to pacifism and the conviction that the Indians rightfully owned their land—peace prevailed between native inhabitants and newcomers. Before Penn sold any land to colonists, he purchased it from the Indians. He also prohibited the sale of alcohol to the tribe, strictly regulated the fur trade, and learned the language of the Lenni Lenapes. "Not a language spoken in Europe," he remarked, "hath words of more sweetness in Accent and Emphasis than theirs."

"Our Wilderness flourishes as a Garden," Penn declared late in 1683, and in fact, his colony lived up to its promises. New arrivals readily acquired good land on liberal terms, while Penn's Frame of Government instituted a representative assembly and guaranteed all inhabitants the basic English civil liberties and complete freedom of worship.

Quakers and Politics ≫ Even so, Penn's colony suffered constant political strife. Rich investors whom he had rewarded with large tracts of land and trade monopolies dominated the council, which held the sole power to initiate legislation. That power and Penn's own claims as proprietor set the stage for controversy. Members of the representative assembly battled for the right to initiate legislation. Farmers opposed Penn's efforts to collect quitrents. The Three Lower Counties agitated for separation, their inhabitants feeling no loyalty to Penn or Quakerism.

Even after 1714, France, England and, to a lesser extent, Spain waged a kind of cold war for a quarter of a century, jockeying for position and influence. Western European monarchs had come to realize that confrontations in North America's vast and distant interior could affect their wars closer to home. In this global chess game, the British had the advantage of numbers: nearly 400,000 subjects in the colonies in 1720, compared with only about 25,000 French spread along a thin line of fishing stations and fur-trading posts, and a meager 5,000 or so Spaniards in New Mexico, Texas, and Florida. But by a considerable margin, native peoples still represented the majority population in North America. Moreover, they still controlled more than 90 percent of its territory. If events in North America could effect the balance of power in Europe, then French and Spanish administrators could still believe that their Indian alliances might yet help them prevail against each other, and, especially, against Britain's booming colonies.

CHAPTER SUMMARY

While the French colonized Canada, the Protestant Reformation in England spurred the colonization of New England and Pennsylvania.

- During the seventeenth century, the French slowly established a fur trade, agricultural communities, and religious institutions in Canada while building Indian alliances throughout the Mississippi drainage.
- Competition over the fur trade in New France and New Netherlands contributed to a devastating series of wars between Iroquois, Hurons, and dozens of other Indian groups.
- Over the same period, English Puritans planted more populous settlements between Maine and Long Island.
- The migration of family groups and a rough equality of wealth lent stability to early New England society, reinforced by the settlers' shared commitment to Puritanism and a strong tradition of self-government.
- The mid-Atlantic colonies also enjoyed a rapid growth of people and wealth, but political wrangling as well as ethnic and religious diversity made for a higher level of social conflict.
- Whereas New Englanders attempted to subdue native peoples, colonists in the mid-Atlantic enjoyed more harmonious relations with the region's original inhabitants, thanks in part to William Penn's Quaker principles.
- The efforts of the later Stuart kings to centralize England's empire ended with the Glorious Revolution in 1688, which greatly reduced tensions between the colonies and the parent country.

Significant Events

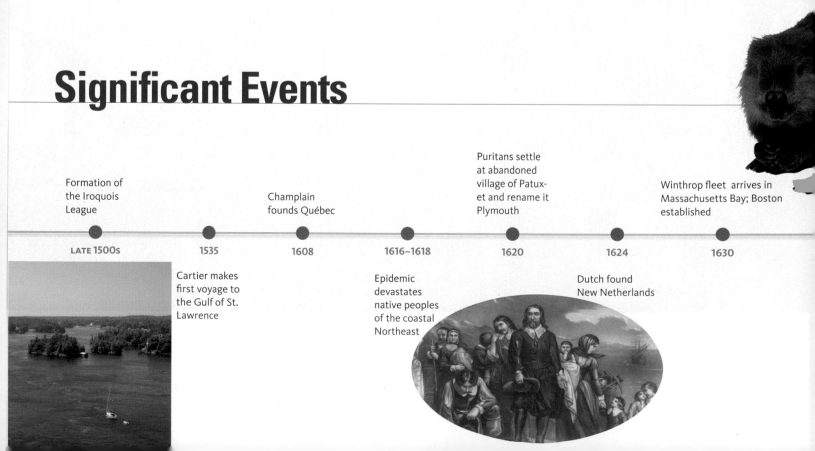

Formation of the Iroquois League

LATE 1500s

Cartier makes first voyage to the Gulf of St. Lawrence

1535

Champlain founds Québec

1608

Epidemic devastates native peoples of the coastal Northeast

1616–1618

Puritans settle at abandoned village of Patuxet and rename it Plymouth

1620

Dutch found New Netherlands

1624

Winthrop fleet arrives in Massachusetts Bay; Boston established

1630

Additional Reading

For introductions to French and Indian encounters, see Olive Patricia Dickason, *Canada's First Nations* (1992) and Bruce G. Trigger, *Natives and Newcomers* (1995). Colin G. Calloway's *One Vast Winter Count* (2003) masterfully synthesizes the history of natives and Europeans in early North America west of the Appalachians, and Daniel K. Richter does the same for Eastern North America in *Facing East from Indian Country* (2001). For a recent history of Dutch America, see Jaap Jacobs, *New Netherland* (2005). Daniel K. Richter's *Ordeal of the Longhouse* (1992) presents a powerful portrait of the Iroquois before, during, and after the Beaver Wars. To understand the appeal of Puritanism, the best book to read is Charles Cohen, *God's Caress* (1986). To learn more about how English influences shaped the evolution of Puritanism in New England, read Stephen Foster's masterly study, *The Long Argument* (1991). And to learn more about the diversity of religious and supernatural views in New England, consult Philip Gura, *A Glimpse of Sion's Glory* (1984), and David Hall, *Worlds of Wonder, Days of Judgment* (1989).

For the everyday lives of northern colonists in New England and New York, rely on Virginia DeJohn Anderson's *New England's Generation* (1991), and Joyce Goodfriend's *Before the Melting Pot* (1991). The best assessment of British imperial policy in the late seventeenth century is Richard R. Johnson, *Adjustment to Empire* (1981). For the complex interplay among English colonialism, environmental change, and Indian power in the Northeast, see William Cronon's classic *Changes in the Land* (1983). The event and memory of "King Philip's War" is the subject of Jill Lepore's *The Name of War* (1998).

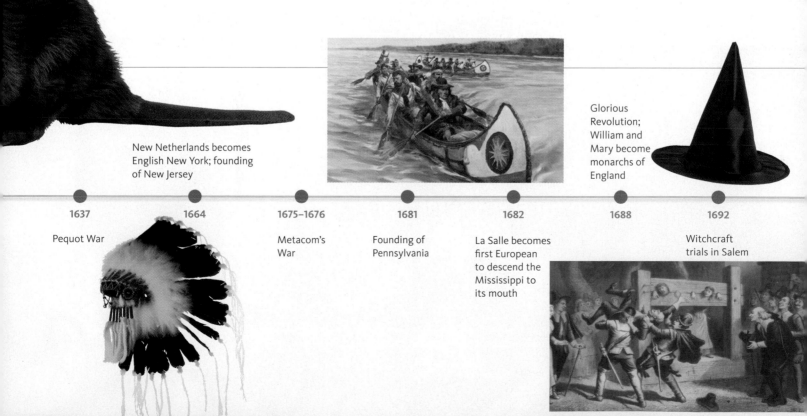

New Netherlands becomes English New York; founding of New Jersey

Glorious Revolution; William and Mary become monarchs of England

| 1637 | 1664 | 1675–1676 | 1681 | 1682 | 1688 | 1692 |

Pequot War

Metacom's War

Founding of Pennsylvania

La Salle becomes first European to descend the Mississippi to its mouth

Witchcraft trials in Salem

THE Mosaic OF
Eighteenth-Cen

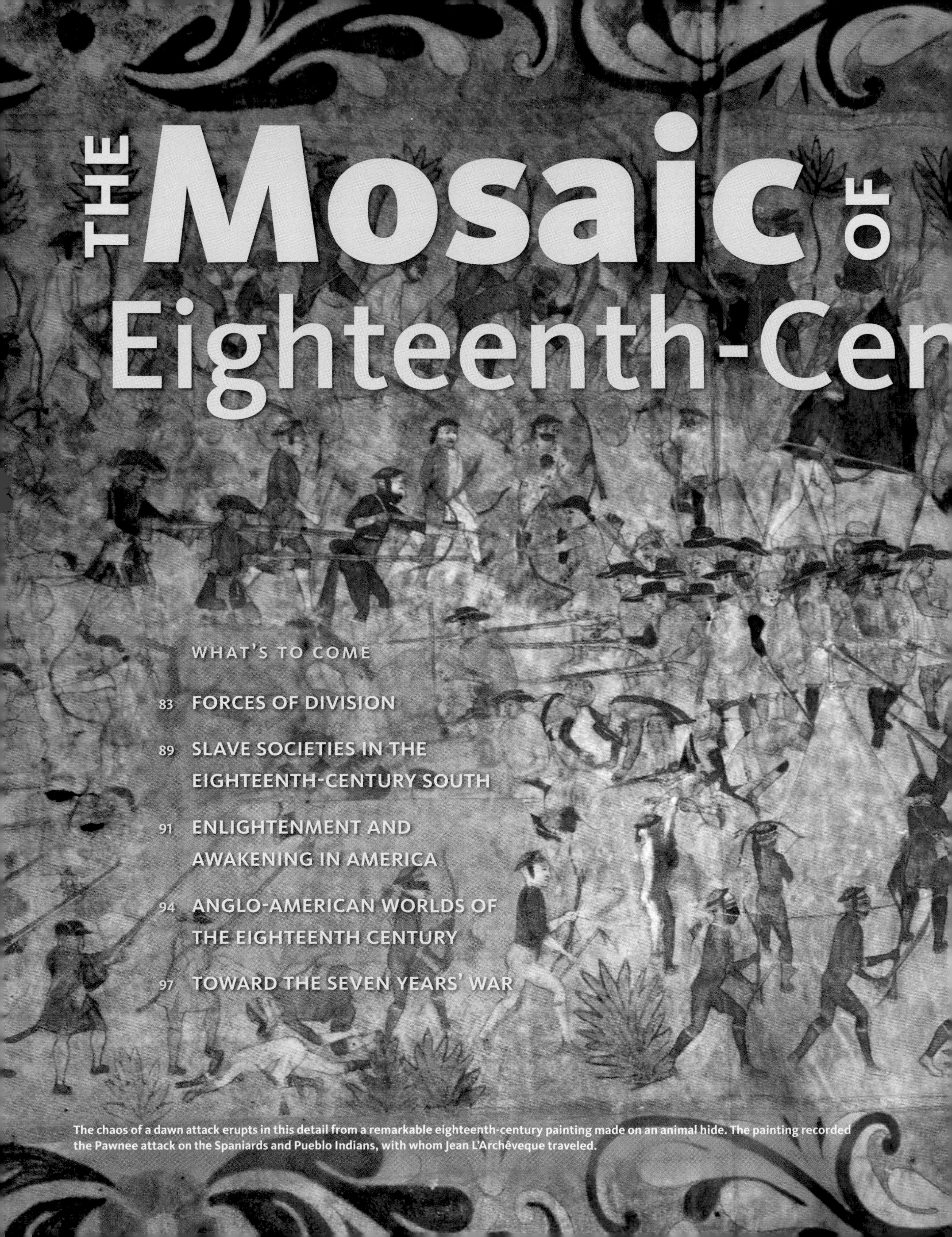

WHAT'S TO COME

83 **FORCES OF DIVISION**

89 **SLAVE SOCIETIES IN THE
EIGHTEENTH-CENTURY SOUTH**

91 **ENLIGHTENMENT AND
AWAKENING IN AMERICA**

94 **ANGLO-AMERICAN WORLDS OF
THE EIGHTEENTH CENTURY**

97 **TOWARD THE SEVEN YEARS' WAR**

The chaos of a dawn attack erupts in this detail from a remarkable eighteenth-century painting made on an animal hide. The painting recorded the Pawnee attack on the Spaniards and Pueblo Indians, with whom Jean L'Archêveque traveled.

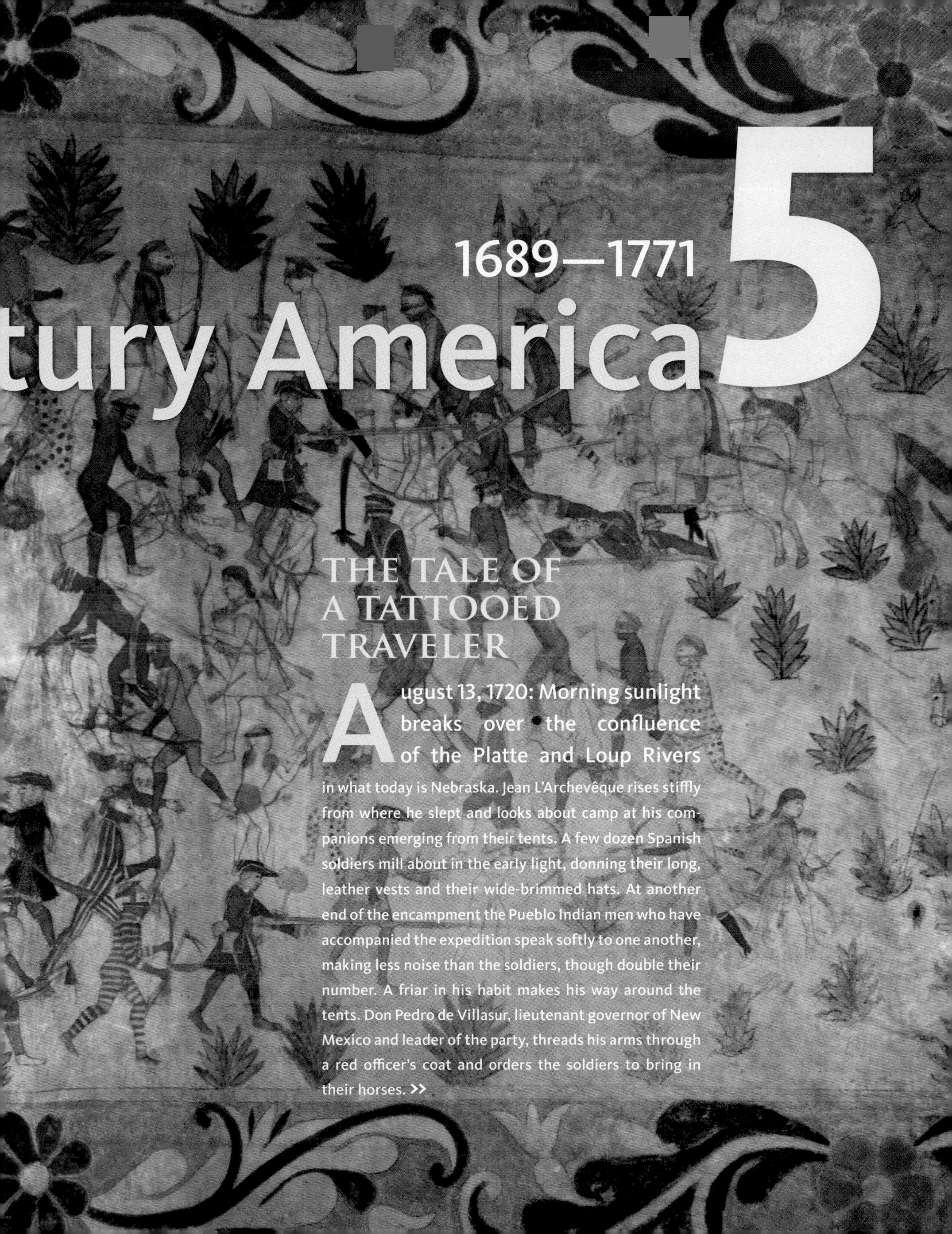

tury America 5

THE TALE OF A TATTOOED TRAVELER

August 13, 1720: Morning sunlight breaks over the confluence of the Platte and Loup Rivers in what today is Nebraska. Jean L'Archevêque rises stiffly from where he slept and looks about camp at his companions emerging from their tents. A few dozen Spanish soldiers mill about in the early light, donning their long, leather vests and their wide-brimmed hats. At another end of the encampment the Pueblo Indian men who have accompanied the expedition speak softly to one another, making less noise than the soldiers, though double their number. A friar in his habit makes his way around the tents. Don Pedro de Villasur, lieutenant governor of New Mexico and leader of the party, threads his arms through a red officer's coat and orders the soldiers to bring in their horses. >>

Most of these men had known L'Archevêque for years—had come to appreciate his sly humor and grown accustomed to his thick accent. But on this morning, as they set about the king's business in an alien land some 600 miles from their homes and families, there must have been something unnerving about the dark, swirling tattoos that covered the Frenchman's face. They had been put there years earlier by a steady Indian hand, in the aftermath of a Texas expedition that had ended in calamity. One had only to look at L'Archevêque to be reminded that things sometimes go badly for both kings and their servants.

It was a tangled path that led the Frenchman to spend that summer morning in the company of Spaniards and Pueblo Indians. Born in 1672 in Bayonne, France, L'Archevêque was only a boy when he boarded ship to the French Caribbean, fleeing his family's financial troubles. Soon the eager 12-year old indentured himself to a wealthy merchant, and in 1684 master and servant enlisted in a colonization scheme led by the French explorer René Robert Cavelier, Sieur de La Salle.

Three years earlier La Salle had been the first to navigate the immense Mississippi River from the Great Lakes to the Gulf of Mexico. Yet, try as he might, La Salle could not find the mouth of the Mississippi when he approached this time from the Gulf of Mexico. Instead he landed on the coast of present-day Texas and embarked on a months-long search for Indian allies. As the months stretched into years, the expedition lost its ships to pirates, desertion, and the sea. Meanwhile, his 300 colonists sickened, starved, and died. In 1687 some of the disgruntled survivors hatched a plan to be rid of him. Young L'Archevêque played a part, distracting the great explorer while an accomplice blew his head apart with a musket shot.

The murder hardly improved L'Archevêque's situation. He and a few desperate companions soon found themselves unhappy guests among Caddo Indians in east Texas. These were the people who tattooed the young man's face, inserting a dye made from walnuts into countless tiny cuts. But in 1690, Spanish explorers stumbled across L'Archevêque and a companion, ransomed the grateful pair from the Caddos, and took them to Mexico City to be questioned.

L'Archevêque had become a pawn in a high-stakes game. News of La Salle's stillborn colony convinced Spanish officials to build missions among the Indians of Texas, in order to prevent France from using the region as a base for threatening New Spain. The project began haltingly, but by the early 1720s ten missions were in place, four presidios (military garrisons), and one civilian settlement—San Antonio. Spain also expanded its power in the North by reconquering New Mexico. Popé's Pueblo Revolt of 1680 had driven out the Spanish (see Chapter 3), but the alliance among the diverse Pueblo villages collapsed within a dozen years. When Spanish colonists returned in 1692, they met only fragmented resistance.

It was in reconquered New Mexico that L'Archevêque found his first real home since boyhood. Sent north perhaps because he could speak both French and Indian languages, L'Archevêque quickly became a fixture in Santa Fe, prospering, marrying well, and gaining the trust of his neighbors. But the lands beyond Santa Fe remained unstable. By 1719, with Spain and France at war in Europe, New Mexico's governor heard that the French had built two large towns to the north where they dispensed weapons to Pawnees and mocked the Spanish. Enraged, the governor ordered his lieutenant Villasur to take L'Archevêque and a group of Indian and Spanish fighters to confront the French—hence the long trek to the Platte River the following summer, where the men awoke at daybreak on August 13 to do the king's business.

But things sometimes go badly for kings and their servants. Moments after ordering his men to bring in their horses, Villasur heard screams and saw dozens of painted Pawnee warriors rush the camp. The lieutenant governor was one of the first to die; L'Archevêque fell soon after. In the end only 13 Spaniards and 40 Pueblo warriors escaped to bring the news back to Santa Fe, where residents long remembered the ambush as one of the great calamities of their history. «

That a merchant's boy from Bayonne, France, could be shipwrecked, recruited to murder, and tattooed in Texas, imprisoned in Mexico and Spain, made respectable on the Upper Rio Grande, and finally buried alongside Spanish and Indian companions somewhere in Nebraska, testifies in a very personal way to the unpredictable changes unleashed by contact between European and American civilizations. Despite their grand ambitions, colonial newcomers often found their plans upended and their lives reordered by the very same forces reworking native life across the North.

As L'Archevêque's adventures illustrate, Spain contended with France for power and influence in Indian lands along the Mississippi and farther west. But France also found itself in conflict with the English in the backcountry beyond the Appalachian Mountains. The rivalries had their beginnings in Europe and flared regularly throughout the late seventeenth century and into the eighteenth. In 1689 England joined the Netherlands and the League of Augsburg (several German-speaking states) in a war against France. While the main struggle raged in Europe, French and English colonials, joined by their Indian allies, skirmished in what was known as King William's War. Peace returned in 1697, but only until the Anglo-French struggle resumed with Queen Anne's War, from 1702–1713.

For a quarter of a century thereafter the two nations waged a kind of cold war, competing for advantage. At stake was not so much control over people or even territory as control over trade. In North America, France and England vied for access to the sugar islands of the Caribbean, a monopoly on supplying manufactured goods to New Spain, and dominance of the fur trade. The British had the advantage of numbers: nearly 400,000 subjects in the colonies in 1720, the year of L'Archevêque's death, compared with only about 25,000 French spread along a thin line of fishing stations and fur trading posts. Yet the French steadily strengthened their chain of forts, stretching from the mouth of the Mississippi north through the Illinois country and into Canada. The forts helped channel the flow of furs from the Great Lakes and the Mississippi River valley into Canada, thus keeping them out of the clutches of English traders. And the forts neatly encircled England's colonies, confining their settlement to the eastern seaboard.

FORCES OF DIVISION

British colonials from Maine to the Carolinas despised the French and resented their empire of fish and furs. But the English were preoccupied with their own affairs and too divided to unify against them. Indeed, England's mainland colonies were split not only by ethnic and regional differences but also by racial and religious prejudices.

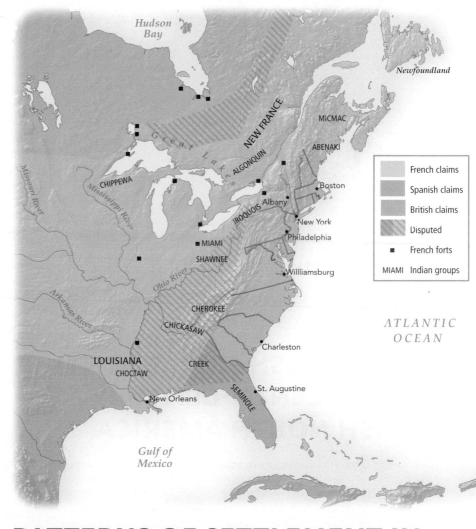

PATTERNS OF SETTLEMENT IN THE EIGHTEENTH CENTURY

The French, English, and Indian nations all jockeyed for power and position across North America. The French expanded their fur trade through the interior while English settlement at midcentury began to press the barrier of the Appalachians. But native peoples still controlled the vast majority of the continent and often held the balance of power in inter-imperial struggles.

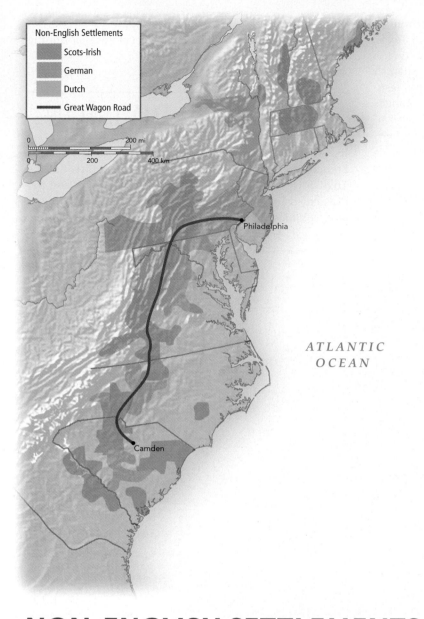

Non-English Settlements
- Scots-Irish
- German
- Dutch
- ▬ Great Wagon Road

0   200 mi
0   200   400 km

Philadelphia

ATLANTIC OCEAN

Camden

NON-ENGLISH SETTLEMENTS IN EIGHTEENTH-CENTURY BRITISH NORTH AMERICA

Many non-English settlers spilled into the backcountry: the Scots-Irish and the Germans followed the Great Wagon Road through the western parts of the middle colonies and southern colonies, while the Dutch and other Germans moved up the Hudson River valley.

Year after year small wooden ships brought a bewildering variety of immigrants to American seaports, aggravating those divisions. Colonials were also separated by vast distances, poor transportation, and slow communications. The frontier districts distrusted seaboard communities and the eastern seaboard disdained the backcountry.

Immigration and Natural Increase

>> One of the largest immigrant groups—250,000 black men, women, and children—had come to the colonies from Africa not by choice but in chains. White arrivals included many English immigrants but also a quarter of a million Scots-Irish, the descendants of seventeenth-century Scots who had regretted settling in northern Ireland; perhaps 135,000 Germans; and a sprinkling of Swiss, Swedes, Highland Scots, and Spanish Jews. Most non-English white immigrants were fleeing lives torn by famine, warfare, and religious persecution. Many had paid for passage by signing indentures to work as servants in America.

The immigrants and slaves who arrived in the colonies between 1700 and 1775 swelled a population that was already growing dramatically from natural increase. The birthrate in eighteenth-century America was triple what it is today. Most women bore between five and eight children, and most children survived to maturity. This astonishing surge was merely one part of a more general global population explosion in the second half of the eighteenth century. China's population of 150 million in 1700 had doubled to more than 313 million by the end of the century. Europe's total rose from about 118 million to 187 million over the same period

The population explosion in the British colonies, fed by the importation of slaves, immigration, and natural increase, made it hard for colonials to share any common identity. Far from fostering political unity, almost every aspect of social development set Americans at odds with one another. And that process of division and disunity was reflected in the outpouring of new settlers into the backcountry.

The Settlement of the Backcountry

>> To white immigrants from Europe, weary of war or worn by want, the seaboard's established communities must have seemed havens of order and stability. But by the beginning of the eighteenth century, even the children of longtime settlers could not acquire land along the coast. In older New England towns, three and four generations were putting pressure on a limited supply of land, while wasteful farming practices had depleted the soil of its fertility. Farther south, earlier settlers had already snatched up the

⌃ This cartoon supported the Paxton Boys by branding Quakers as treacherously sympathetic to frontier Indians. One Quaker, on the left, eagerly supplies Indians with tomahawks, while on the right another makes sexual advances to an Indian woman. Meanwhile, Benjamin Franklin, center, offers a sack of money to buy off hostile Indians.

farmland of Philadelphia's outlying counties, the prime Chesapeake tobacco property, and low-country rice swamps.

With older rural communities offering few opportunities to either native-born or newly arrived white families, both groups were forced to create new communities on the frontier. The peopling of New England's frontier—Maine, New Hampshire, and Vermont—was left mainly to the descendants of old Yankee families. Better opportunities for new immigrants to acquire land at cheaper prices lay south of New York. By the 1720s German and Scots-Irish immigrants as well as native-born settlers were pouring into western Pennsylvania. Some settled permanently, but others streamed southward into the backcountry of Virginia and the Carolinas, where they encountered native-born southerners pressing westward.

Backcountry settlers endured greater isolation than other colonials did. From many farms it was a day's ride to the nearest courthouse; taverns and churches were often as distant. Isolation hindered the formation of strong social bonds, as did the mobility of backcountry settlers. Many families pulled up stakes three or four times before settling permanently. Houses reflected that transience: most families crowded into one-room shacks walled with mud, turf, or crude logs.

The backcountry meant economic isolation as well. Large portions of the interior were cut off from water transport because they were located above the fall line, where rivers flowing to the Atlantic became unnavigable.

By 1755 several crude wagon roads linked western Pennsylvania and Virginia to towns further east, including Philadelphia, but transporting crops and driving livestock overland proved prohibitively expensive. Cut off from outside markets, farmers grew only enough to feed their households. Most backcountry inhabitants could not afford to invest in a slave or even a servant. Those conditions made the frontier, more than anywhere else in America, a society of equals.

Social Conflict on the Frontier >> Despite the discomforts of frontier life, cheap land lured many families to the West. Benjamin Franklin, Pennsylvania's most successful entrepreneur, inventor, and politician, had observed the hordes of Scots-Irish and German immigrants lingering in Philadelphia just long enough to scrape together the purchase price of a frontier farm. From Franklin's point of view, the backcountry performed a valuable service by siphoning off surplus people from congested eastern settlements. But he knew, too, that the opened frontier caused friction, especially between the eastern seaboard and the backcountry.

In Pennsylvania, Franklin himself mediated one such contest between East and West. In 1763 a band of Scots-Irish farmers known as "the Paxton Boys" protested the government's inadequate protection of frontier settlers by killing a number of Indians. Then the Paxton Boys took their protests and their guns to Philadelphia, marching as far as Lancaster before Franklin intervened and promised redress of their grievances.

Strife between East and West was even deadlier and more enduring in North and South Carolina. In both colonies legislatures dominated by coastal planters refused to grant inland settlers equitable political representation or even basic legal institutions. In response to those injustices, two protest movements emerged in the Carolina interior, each known as the Regulation.

Farmers in the South Carolina backcountry organized their Regulation in the 1760s, after that colony's assembly refused to set up courts in the backcountry. Westerners were desperate for protection from outlaws who stole livestock, kidnapped and raped women, and tortured and murdered men. In the absence of courts the Regulators acted as vigilantes, meting out grisly frontier justice. Regulator threats to march on Charleston finally panicked eastern political leaders into extending the court system westward.

Western North Carolinians organized their Regulation to protest not the absence of a legal system but the corruption of local government. Lawyers and merchants, backed by wealthy eastern planters, moved into the western parts of that colony and used local offices to exploit frontier settlers, charging exorbitant fees for legal services, imposing high taxes, and manipulating debt laws. Western farmers responded to these abuses by seizing county courts and finally squared off against an eastern militia led by the governor. Easterners crushed these Regulators at the Battle of Alamance in 1771 and left frontier North Carolinians with an enduring hostility to the seaboard.

Ethnic differences heightened sectional tensions between East and West. While people of English descent predominated along the Atlantic coast, Germans, Scots-Irish, and other white minorities were concentrated in the interior. Many English colonials regarded these new immigrants as culturally inferior. Charles Woodmason, an Anglican missionary in the Carolina backcountry, lamented the arrival of "5 or 6000 Ignorant, mean, worthless, beggarly Irish Presbyterians" who "delighted in a low, lazy, sluttish, heathenish, hellish life." As for German immigrants, by 1751 Franklin was warning that the Pennsylvania English would be overrun by "the Palatine Boors."

Boundary Disputes and Tenant Wars »

The settlement of the frontier also triggered disputes between colonies over their boundaries. The most serious of these border wars pitted New York against farmers from New England who had settled in present-day Vermont: Ethan Allen and the Green Mountain Boys. In the 1760s New York, backed by the Crown, claimed land that Allen and his friends had already purchased from New Hampshire. When New York tried to extend its rule over Vermont, Allen led a successful guerrilla resistance, harassing Yorker settlers and officials, and setting up a competing judicial system in the Green Mountains.

The spread of settlement also set the stage for mass revolts by tenants in areas where proprietors controlled vast amounts of land. In eastern New Jersey, proprietors insisted that squatters pay quitrents on land that had become increasingly valuable. When the squatters, many of them migrants from New England, refused to pay rents, the proprietors began evictions, touching off riots in the 1740s. Tenant unrest also raged in New York's Hudson River valley, where about 30 manors around New York City and Albany dominated the region. The estates encompassed some 2 million acres and were worked by several thousand tenants. Newcomers from New England, however, demanded to own land and preached their ideas to Dutch and German tenants. Armed insurrection exploded in 1757 and again, more violently, in 1766. Tenants refused to pay rents, formed mobs, and stormed the homes of landlords.

Eighteenth-Century Seaports » While most

Americans on the move settled on the frontier, others swelled the populations of colonial cities. By present-day standards such cities were small, harboring from 8,000 to 22,000 citizens by 1750. The scale of seaports remained intimate, too: all of New York City was clustered at the southern tip of Manhattan Island, and the length of Boston or Charleston could be walked in less than half an hour.

All major colonial cities were seaports, their waterfronts fringed with wharves and shipyards. A jumble of shops, taverns, and homes crowded their streets; the spires of churches studded their skylines. By the 1750s, the grandest and most populous was Philadelphia, which boasted straight, neatly paved streets, flagstone sidewalks, and three-story brick buildings. Older cities such as Boston and New York had a more medieval aspect: most of their dwellings and shops were wooden structures with tiny windows and low ceilings, rising no higher than two stories to steeply pitched roofs. The narrow cobblestone streets of Boston and New York also challenged pedestrians, who competed for space with livestock being driven to the butcher, roaming

Was the most critical sectional division in eighteenth-century America between North and South or between East and West?

herds of swine and packs of dogs, clattering carts, carriages, and horses.

Commerce, the lifeblood of seaport economies, was managed by merchants who tapped the wealth of surrounding regions. Traders in New York and Philadelphia shipped the Hudson and Delaware valleys' surplus of grain and livestock to the West Indies. Boston's merchants sent fish to the Caribbean and Catholic Europe, masts to England, and rum to West Africa. Charlestonians exported indigo to English dyemakers and rice to southern Europe. Other merchants specialized in the import trade, selling luxuries and manufactured goods produced in England—fine fabrics, ceramics, tea, and farming implements. Wealth brought many merchants political power: they dominated city governments and shared power in colonial assemblies with lawyers and the largest farmers and planters.

Skilled craftworkers or **artisans** made up the middling classes of colonial cities. The households of master craftworkers usually included a few younger and less skilled journeymen working in other artisans' shops. Unskilled boy apprentices not only worked but also lived under the watchful eye of their masters. Some artisans specialized in the maritime trades as shipbuilders, blacksmiths, and sailmakers. Others, such as butchers, millers, and distillers, processed and packed raw

{ **artisan** skilled craftworker, such as a blacksmith, a cooper, a miller, or a tailor.

ESTIMATED POPULATION OF COLONIAL CITIES, 1720–1770

Although Boston's population remained stable after 1740, it was surpassed owing to the sharp growth of New York and, especially, Philadelphia.

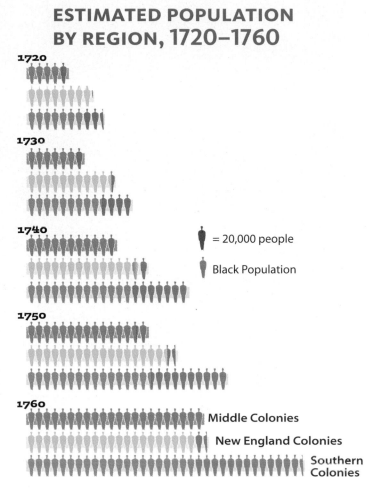

ESTIMATED POPULATION BY REGION, 1720–1760

1720

1730

1740

= 20,000 people

Black Population

1750

1760

Middle Colonies

New England Colonies

Southern Colonies

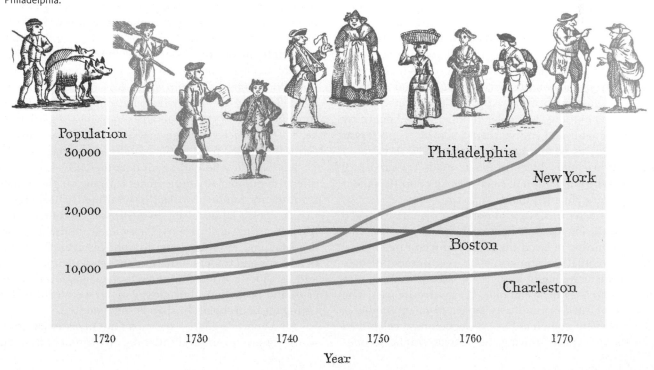

The South East Prospect of The City of Philadelphia By Peter Cooper *Painter*

1 The Draw Bridge	7 John Wilpain	13 Jo. Carpenter Store	19 Abr. Bickh
2 Buds Building	8 Capt Anthonys	14 Sam Carpenter Store	20 Thomas Masters
3 Edw Shipen	9 George Painter	15 S Carpenter Dweling Ho	21 Sam Perry
4 Ant Morris Brew House	10 Ins. Shipen	16 Sam Brunkley	22 Bank Meeting Hous
5 Capt Vinerigs	11 W Fisbourn Store	17 Quak Meeting Houd	23 Tho. Chalky
6 Jonathan Dickinson	12 The Scales	18 The Court House	24 Penny Pott House

ʌ In the mid-eighteenth century, Philadelphia became the largest city in the colonies and the second largest in all the British empire. Its busy harbor served not only as a commercial hub but also as the disembarkation point for thousands of immigrants.

materials for export. Still others served the basic needs of city dwellers—the men and, occasionally, women who baked bread, mended shoes, combed and powdered wigs, and tended shops and taverns.

On the lowest rung of a seaport's social hierarchy were free and bound workers. Free laborers were mainly young white men and women—journeymen artisans, sailors, fishermen, domestic workers, seamstresses, and prostitutes. The ranks of unfree workers included apprentices and indentured servants doing menial labor in shops and on the docks. Black men and women also made up a substantial part of the bound labor force of colonial seaports. While the vast majority of African slaves were sold to southern plantations, a smaller number were bought by urban merchants and craftworkers. Laboring as porters at the docks, as assistants in craft shops, or as servants in wealthy households, black residents made up almost 20 percent of the population in New York City and 10 percent in Boston and Philadelphia.

The character of slavery in northern seaports changed decisively during the mid-eighteenth century. When wars raging in Europe reduced the supply of white indentured servants, colonial cities imported a larger number of Africans. Those newcomers brought to urban black culture a new awareness of a common West African past. The influence of African traditions appeared most vividly in an annual event known as "Negro election day," celebrated in northern seaports. During the festival, similar to ones held in West Africa, some black men and women paraded in their masters' clothes or mounted on their horses. An election followed, to choose black "kings," "governors," and "judges," who then "held court" and settled minor disputes among white and black members of the community. "Negro election day" did not challenge the established racial order with its temporary reversal of roles, but it did allow the black community of seaports to honor their own leaders.

The availability of domestic workers, both black and white, made for leisured lives among women from wealthy white families. Even those city women who could not afford household help spent less time on domestic work than did farming wives and daughters. Although some housewives grew vegetables in backyard gardens or kept a few chickens, large markets stocked by outlying farmers supplied most of the food for urban families.

For women who had to support themselves, seaports offered a number of employments. Young single women from poorer families worked in wealthier households as maids, cooks, laundresses, seamstresses, or nurses. The highest-paying occupations for women, midwifery and dressmaking, required long apprenticeships. The wives of artisans and traders sometimes assisted their husbands and, as widows, often continued to manage groceries, taverns, and printshops, but most women were confined to caring for households, husbands, and children.

All seaport dwellers—perhaps 1 out of every 20 Americans—enjoyed a more stimulating environment than did other colonials. The wealthiest could attend an occasional ball or concert; those living in New York or Charleston might even see a play performed by touring English actors. The middling classes could converse with other tradespeople at private social clubs and fraternal societies. Men of every class found diversion in drink and cockfighting.

But city dwellers paid a price for their pleasures. Commerce was riddled with risk: ships sank and wars disrupted trade. When such disasters struck, the lower classes suffered most. The ups and downs of seaport economies, combined with the influx of immigrants, swelled the ranks of the poor in all cities by the mid–eighteenth century. Furthermore, epidemics and catastrophic fires occurred with greater frequency and produced higher mortality rates in congested seaports than in the countryside.

Social Conflict in Seaports >> The swelling of seaport populations, like the westward movement of whites, often churned up trouble. English, Scots-Irish, Germans, Swiss, Dutch, French, and Spanish jostled uneasily against one another in the close quarters of Philadelphia and New York. To make matters worse, religious differences heightened ethnic divisions. Jewish funerals in New York, for example, drew crowds of hostile and curious Protestants, who heckled the mourners.

Class resentment also stirred unrest. Some merchant families flaunted their wealth, building imposing town mansions. During hard times, expensive coaches and full warehouses became targets of mob vandalism. Crowds also gathered to intimidate and punish other groups who provoked popular hostility—unresponsive politicians,

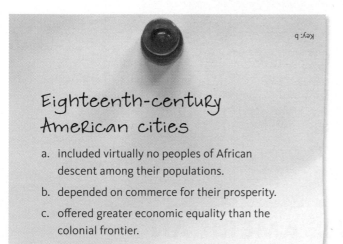

Key: b

Eighteenth-century American cities

a. included virtually no peoples of African descent among their populations.

b. depended on commerce for their prosperity.

c. offered greater economic equality than the colonial frontier.

d. awarded their highest political offices to artisans.

⌃ *The Old Plantation* affords a rare glimpse of life in the slave quarters. At this festive gathering, both men and women dance to the music of a molo (a stringed instrument similar to a banjo) and drums.

prostitutes, and "press gangs." Impressment, attempts to force colonials to serve in the British navy, triggered some of the most violent urban riots.

SLAVE SOCIETIES IN THE EIGHTEENTH-CENTURY SOUTH

Far starker than the inequalities and divisions among seaport dwellers were those between white and black in the South. By 1775 one out of every five Americans was of African ancestry, and over 90 percent of all black Americans lived in the South, most along the seaboard. Here, on tobacco and rice plantations, slaves fashioned a distinctive African American society and culture. But they were able to build stable families and communities only late in the eighteenth century, and against enormous odds.

Whether a slave was auctioned off to the Chesapeake or to the Lower South shaped his or her future in important ways. Slaves in the low country of South Carolina and Georgia lived on large plantations with as many as 50 other black workers, about half of whom were African-born. They had infrequent contact with either their masters or the rest of the sparse white population. And their work was arduous, for rice required constant cultivation. Black laborers tended young plants and hoed fields in the sweltering summer heat; during winter and early spring, they built dams and canals to regulate the flow of water into the rice fields. But the use of the "**task system**" rather than gang labor widened the

task system way of organizing slave labor. Masters and overseers of rice and indigo plantations generally assigned individual slaves a daily task, and after its completion, slaves could spend the rest of the day engaged in pursuits of their own choosing.

window of freedom within slavery. When a slave had completed his assigned task for the day, one planter explained, "his master feels no right to call upon him."

Many Chesapeake slaves, like those in the Lower South, were African-born, but most lived on smaller plantations with fewer than 20 fellow slaves. Less densely concentrated than in the low country, Chesapeake slaves also had more contact with whites. Unlike Carolina's absentee owners, who left white overseers and black drivers to run their plantations, Chesapeake masters actively managed their estates and subjected their slaves to closer scrutiny.

The Slave Family and Community >>

After the middle of the eighteenth century, a number of changes fostered the growth of black families and the vitality of slave communities. As slave importations began to taper off, the rate of natural reproduction among blacks started to climb. As the proportion of new

Africans dropped and the number of native-born black Americans grew, the ratio of men to women in the slave community became more equal. Those changes and the appearance of larger plantations, even in the Chesapeake, created more opportunities for black men and women to find partners and form families. Elaborate kinship networks gradually developed, often extending over several plantations in a single neighborhood.

Even so, black families remained vulnerable. If a planter fell on hard times, members of black families might be sold off to different buyers to meet his debts. When a master died, black families might be divided among surviving heirs. Even under the best circumstances, fathers might be hired out to other planters for long periods or sent to work in distant quarters.

Black families struggling with terrible uncertainties were sustained by the distinctive African American culture evolving in the slave community. The high percentage of native Africans among the eighteenth-century American

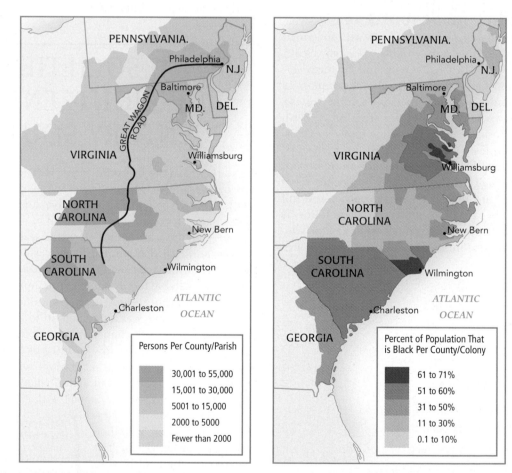

THE DISTRIBUTION OF THE AMERICAN POPULATION, 1775

The African American population expanded dramatically during the eighteenth century, especially in the southern colonies. While the high volume of slave imports accounted for most of the growth in the first half of the century, natural increase was responsible for the rising black population during later decades.

black population made it easier for slaves to retain the ways of their lost homeland. Christianity won few converts, in part because white masters feared that baptizing slaves might make them more rebellious but also because African Americans preferred their traditional religions. African influence appeared as well in the slaves' agricultural skills and practices, folktales, music, and dances.

Slavery and Colonial Society in French Louisiana >>

The experience of Africans unfolded differently in the lower Mississippi valley, France's southernmost outpost in eighteenth-century North America. Louisiana's earliest colonial settlements were begun by a few thousand French soldiers, joined by indentured servants, free settlers straggling down from Canada, and immigrants from France and Germany. When they founded New Orleans in 1718, the colonists immediately clamored for bound laborers, hoping to create prosperous plantations in the surrounding Mississippi Delta. French authorities agreed to their demands, and the Company of the Indies, which managed France's slave trade, brought nearly 6,000 slaves, overwhelmingly men, directly from Africa to Louisiana.

Instead of proving the formula for economic success, the flood of Africans challenged French control. In 1729, with blacks already making up a majority of the population, some newly arrived slaves joined forces with the Natchez Indians who feared the expansion of white settlement. Their rebellion, the Natchez Revolt, left 200 French planters dead—more than 10 percent of the European population of Louisiana. The French retaliated in a devastating counterattack, enlisting both the Choctaw Indians and other enslaved blacks, who were promised freedom in return for their support.

The planters' costly victory persuaded French authorities to stop importing slaves into the colony. As a result, Louisiana did not develop a plantation economy until the end of the eighteenth century, when the cotton boom began. In the meantime, blacks continued to make up a majority of all Louisianans, and by the middle of the eighteenth century, nearly all were native-born. The vast majority were slaves, but their work routines—tending cattle, cutting timber, producing naval stores, working on boats—afforded them greater freedom of movement than most slaves enjoyed elsewhere in the American South. But the greatest prize—liberty—was awarded those black men who served in the French militia, defending the colony from the English and Indians as well as capturing slave runaways.

Slave Resistance in Eighteenth-Century British North America >>

British North America had no similar group of black soldiers, but it also had no shortage of African Americans who resisted captivity. Among newly arrived Africans, collective attempts at escape were most common. Groups of slaves, often made up of newcomers from the same tribe, fled inland and formed "**Maroon**" communities of runaways. These efforts were usually unsuccessful because the Maroon settlements were large enough to be easily detected.

> **"Maroon" communities** groups of escaped slaves, often newly arrived Africans, who fled to the frontiers of colonial settlements in the American South, the Caribbean, and South America.

More acculturated blacks adopted subtler ways of subverting slavery. Domestics and field hands alike faked illness, feigned stupidity and laziness, broke tools, pilfered from storehouses, hid in the woods for weeks at a time, or simply took off to visit neighboring plantations. Other slaves, usually escaping bondage as solitary individuals, found new lives as craftworkers, dock laborers, or sailors in the relative anonymity of colonial seaports.

Less frequently, black rebellion took direct and violent form. Whites in communities with large numbers of blacks lived in dread of arson, poisoning, and insurrection. Four slave conspiracies were reported in Virginia before 1750. In South Carolina, more than two decades of abortive uprisings and insurrection scares culminated in the Stono Rebellion of 1739, the largest slave revolt of the colonial period. Nearly 100 African Americans, led by a slave named Jemmy, seized arms from a store in the coastal district of Stono and killed several white neighbors before they were caught and killed by the white militia.

> Whites in communities with large numbers of blacks lived in dread of arson, poisoning, and insurrection.

ENLIGHTENMENT AND AWAKENING IN AMERICA

The differences among eighteenth-century colonials resulted in more than clashes between regions, races, classes, and ethnic groups. Those differences also made for diversity in the ways that Americans thought and believed. City dwellers were more attuned to European culture than were people living in small villages or on the frontier. White males from well-to-do families of English ancestry were far more likely to receive college educations than were those from poorer or immigrant households. White women of every class and background were excluded from higher education, and slaves received no formal education at all. Where they lived, how well they lived, whether they were male or female, native-born or immigrant, slave or free—all these variables fostered among colonials distinctive worldviews, differing attitudes and assumptions about the individual's relationship to nature, society, and God.

The Enlightenment in America >> The diversity of colonials' inner lives became even more pronounced during the eighteenth century because of the **Enlightenment**, an intellectual movement that started in Europe during the seventeenth century. The leading figures of the Enlightenment stressed the power of

Enlightenment intellectual movement that flourished in Europe from the mid-1600s through the eighteenth century and stressed the power of human reason to promote social progress by discovering the laws that governed both nature and society.

human reason to promote progress by revealing the laws that governed both nature and society. In the American colonies the Enlightenment influenced some curious artisans in major seaports as well as wealthy merchants, lawyers, and landowners with the leisure and education to read the latest books from Europe.

Like many devotees of the Enlightenment, Benjamin Franklin was most impressed by its emphasis on useful knowledge and experimentation. He pondered air currents and then invented a stove that heated houses more efficiently. He toyed with electricity and then invented lightning rods to protect buildings in thunderstorms. Other amateur colonial scientists constructed simple telescopes, classified animal species native to North America, or sought to explain epidemics in terms of natural causes.

Some clergy educated at American colleges (six had been established by 1763) were influenced by the Enlightenment, adopting a more liberal theology that stressed the reasonableness of Christian beliefs. By the middle of the eighteenth century this "rational Christianity" commanded a small following among colonials, usually Anglicans or liberal Congregationalists. Their God was not the Calvinists' awesome deity but a benevolent creator who offered salvation to all, not just to a small, predestined elite. They believed that God's greatest gift to humanity was reason, which enabled all human beings to follow the moral teachings of Jesus. They muted the Calvinist emphasis on human sinfulness and the need for a soul-shattering conversion.

Enlightenment philosophy and rational Christianity did not affect the outlook of most colonials. By the middle of the eighteenth century, over half of all white men (and a smaller percentage of white women) were literate. But the great majority of Americans still looked for ultimate truth in biblical revelation rather than human reason and explained the workings of the world in terms of divine providence rather than natural law.

Widespread attachment to traditional Christian beliefs was strengthened by the hundreds of new churches built during the first half of the eighteenth century. Church attendance ran highest in the northern colonies, where some 80 percent

---

AFTER THE FACT

Enlightened Witchcraft?

Despite the influence of the Enlightenment and the effects of the **Great Awakening**, beliefs in witchcraft and magic persisted among many ordinary colonials and even some educated elites throughout the eighteenth century. A telling bit of evidence comes from the medical records left by one Joseph Stafford, a prominent justice of the peace and physician in rural Rhode Island. Stafford not only practiced medicine but as a "Student of Astronomy and Astrology" also cast horoscopes and told his neighbors' fortunes. One curious slip of paper, tucked into one of his medical texts, reveals Stafford's thoughts about a patient: ". . . God bless and prosper Susan[n]a and deliver her from the false accusations brought against Her who was delivered by God's blessing from their craft and suptiltey [subtlety]."

Great Awakening term used to describe periods of intense religious piety and commitment among Americans that fueled the expansion of Protestant churches.

What does the doctor mean? Although the note's purpose is unclear, Susanna may have sought Stafford's help either because she feared being bewitched or even because she stood accused of practicing witchcraft. Whatever her motives, even more intriguing is that Stafford, a well-educated community leader, saw no contradiction in practicing medicine, making use of magic, and asking God's blessing.

⌃ From John Brooke, *The Refiner's Fire* (1994)

of the population turned out for public worship on the Sabbath. In the South, because of the greater distances involved and the shortage of clergy, about half of all colonials regularly attended Sunday services.

The First Great Awakening >> The Great Awakening also deepened the influence of older forms of Protestant Christianity, and specifically Calvinism, throughout British America. Participation in this religious revival was the only experience that a large number of people everywhere in the colonies had in common.

The first stirrings of revival appeared in the 1730s among Presbyterians and Congregationalists in the middle colonies and New England. Many ministers in these churches preached an "evangelical" message, emphasizing the need for individuals to experience "a new birth" through religious conversion. Among them was the Reverend Jonathan Edwards of Northampton, Massachusetts. Edwards's Calvinist preaching combined moving descriptions of God's grace with terrifying portrayals of eternal damnation. "The God that holds you over the pit of hell, much as one holds a spider or some loathsome insect over the fire, abhors you and is dreadfully provoked," he declaimed to one congregation; ". . . there is no other reason to be given, why you have not dropped into hell since you arise in the morning, but that God's hand has held you up."

These local revivals of the 1730s were mere tremors compared to the earthquake of religious enthusiasm that shook the colonies with the arrival in the fall of 1739 of George Whitefield. This handsome, cross-eyed "boy preacher" from England electrified crowds from Georgia to New Hampshire during his two-year tour of the colonies. He and his many imitators among colonial ministers turned the church into a theater, enlivening sermons with dramatic gestures, flowing tears, and gruesome depictions of hell.

The Aftermath of the Great Awakening >> Whitefield also aroused a storm of controversy. Many "awakened" church members now openly criticized their ministers as cold, unconverted, and uninspiring. To supply the missing fire, some laymen—"and even Women and Common Negroes"—took to "exhorting" any audience willing to listen. The most popular ministers became "**itinerants**," traveling like Whitefield from one town to another. Throughout the colonies, the more moderate clergy questioned the unrestrained emotionalism and the disorder that attended the gatherings of lay exhorters and itinerants.

{ **itinerant** traveling preacher attached to no settled congregation

Although Americans had been fighting over religion well before the Great Awakening, the new revivals left colonials even more divided. The largest single group of churchgoers in the northern colonies remained within the Congregational and Presbyterian denominations. But both these groups split into factions that either supported or condemned the revivals. Quakers and Anglicans shunned the revivals. By contrast, the most radical converts joined forces with the warmest champions of the Awakening, the Baptists.

While northern churches splintered and bickered, the fires of revivalism spread to the South and its backcountry. From the mid-1740s until the 1770s, scores of new Presbyterian and Baptist churches were formed, sparking conflict. Ardent Presbyterians in the Carolina backcountry disrupted Anglican worship by loosing packs of dogs in local chapels. In northern Virginia, Anglicans took the offensive against the Baptists, whose strict moral code sounded a silent reproach to the hard-drinking, high-stepping, horse-racing, slaveholding gentry. County officials, prodded by resentful Anglican parsons, harassed, fined, and imprisoned Baptist ministers.

And so a diverse lot of Americans found themselves continually at odds with one another. Because of differences in religion and education, colonials quarreled over whether rational Christianity enlightened the world or emotional revivalists destroyed its order. Because of ethnic and racial tensions, Spanish Jews found themselves persecuted, and African Americans searched for ways to resist their white masters. Because of westward expansion, Carolina Regulators waged war against coastal planters, while colonial legislatures from Massachusetts to Virginia quarreled over western boundaries.

Benjamin Franklin surely understood the depth of those divisions. He had brooded over the boatloads of non-

English newcomers. He had lived in two booming seaports and felt the explosive force of the frontier. He personified the Enlightenment—and he had heard George Whitefield himself preach from the steps of the Philadelphia courthouse. On the other hand, the majority of colonials were of English descent. And these free, white Americans liked being English. That much they had in common.

ANGLO-AMERICAN WORLDS OF THE EIGHTEENTH CENTURY

Most Americans prided themselves on being English. When colonials named their towns and counties, they named them after places in their parent country. When colonials established governments, they turned to England for their political models. They frequently claimed "the liberties of freeborn Englishmen" as their birthright. Even in diet, dress, furniture, architecture, and literature, colonists adopted English standards of taste.

Yet American society had developed in ways significantly different from that of Great Britain.[1] Some

---

[1] When England and Scotland were unified in 1707, the nation as a whole became known officially as Great Britain; its citizens, as British.

differences made colonials feel inferior, ashamed of their simplicity when compared with London's sophistication. But they also came to appreciate the greater equality of colonial society and the more representative character of colonial governments. If it was good to be English, it was better still to be English in America.

English Economic and Social Development >> The differences between England and America began with their economies. Large financial institutions such as the Bank of England and influential corporations like the East India Company were driving England's commercial development. New textile factories and mines were deepening its industrial development. Although most English men and women worked at agriculture, it, too, had become a business. Members of the gentry rented their estates to tenants, members of the rural middle class. In turn, these tenants hired workers from the swollen ranks of England's landless to perform the farm labor. In contrast, most colonial farmers owned their land, and most family farms were a few hundred acres. The scale of commerce and manufacturing was equally modest.

England's more developed economy fostered the growth of cities, especially London, a teeming colossus of 675,000 inhabitants in 1750. In comparison, 90 percent of

ʌ Coffeehouses such as this establishment in London were favorite gathering places for eighteenth-century Americans visiting Britain. Here merchants and mariners, ministers and students, lobbyists and tourists warmed themselves, read newspapers, and exchanged gossip about commerce, politics, and social life.

all eighteenth-century colonials lived in towns with populations of less than 2,000.

Despite this contrast between urban and rural, England's more advanced economy drew the colonies and the parent country together as a consumer revolution transformed the everyday lives of people on both sides of the Atlantic. By the beginning of the eighteenth century, small manufacturers throughout England had begun to produce an enticing array of consumer goods—fine textiles and hats, ceramics and glassware, carpets and furniture. Americans proved as eager as Britons to acquire these commodities—so eager that the per capita consumption of imported manufactures among colonials rose 120 percent between 1750 and 1773. In both England and its colonies, the spare and simple material life of earlier centuries was giving way to a new order in which even people of ordinary means owned a wider variety of things.

Inequality in England and America >>

The opportunities for great wealth provided by England's more developed economy created deep class distinctions, as did the inherited privileges of its aristocracy. The members of the upper class, the landed aristocracy and gentry, made up less than 2 percent of England's population but owned 70 percent of its land. By right of birth, English aristocrats claimed membership in the House of Lords; by custom, certain powerful gentry families dominated the other branch of Parliament, the House of Commons. England's titled gentlemen shared power and wealth and often family ties with the rich men of the city—major merchants, successful lawyers, and lucky financiers. They too exerted political influence through the House of Commons. The colonies had their own prominent families but no titled ruling class holding political privilege by hereditary right. And even the wealthiest colonial families lived in far less magnificence than their English counterparts.

If England's upper classes lived more splendidly, its lower classes were larger and worse off than those in the colonies. Less than a third of England's inhabitants belonged to the "middling sort" of traders, professionals, artisans, and tenant farmers. More than two-thirds struggled for survival at the bottom of society. In contrast, the colonial middle class counted for nearly three-quarters of the white population. With land cheap, labor scarce, and wages for both urban and rural workers 100 percent higher in America than in England, it was much easier for colonials to accumulate savings and then buy farms of their own.

Colonials were both fascinated and repelled by English society. They gushed over the grandeur of aristocratic estates and imported suits of livery for their servants and tea services for their wives. They exported their sons to Britain for college educations at Oxford and Cambridge, medical school at Edinburgh, and legal training at London's Inns of Court.

⌃ This portrait of John Stuart, the third Earl of Bute (1713–1792), wearing the ceremonial robes of the House of Lords, illustrates the opulence of Britain's ruling class in the eighteenth century.

But colonials recognized that England's ruling classes purchased their luxury and leisure at the cost of the rest of the nation. In his autobiography, Benjamin Franklin painted a devastating portrait of the degraded lives of his fellow workers in a London printshop, who drowned their disappointments by drinking throughout the workday. Like Franklin, many colonials believed that gross inequalities of wealth would endanger liberty. They regarded the idle among England's rich and poor alike as ominous signs of a degenerate nation.

Politics in England and America >>

Colonials were also of two minds about England's government. While they praised the English constitution as the basis of all liberties, they were alarmed by the actual workings of English politics. In theory, England's "**balanced constitution**" was designed to give every order of English society some voice in the workings of government.

balanced constitution view that England's constitution gave every part of English society some voice in the workings of its government.

Whereas the Crown represented the monarchy and the House of Lords the aristocracy, the House of Commons represented the democracy, the people of England. In fact, the monarch's executive ministers had become dominant by creating support for their policies in Parliament through patronage—or, put more bluntly, bribery.

Over the course of the eighteenth century, a large executive bureaucracy had evolved in order to enforce laws, collect taxes, and wage the nearly constant wars in Europe and America. The power to appoint all military and treasury officials, customs and tax collectors, judges and justices of the peace lay with the monarch and his or her ministers. By the middle of the eighteenth century, almost half of all members of Parliament held such Crown offices or government contracts. Royal patronage was also used to manipulate parliamentary elections. The executive branch used money or liquor to bribe local voters into selecting their candidates. The small size of England's electorate fostered executive influence. Perhaps one-fourth of all adult males could vote, and many electoral districts were not adjusted to keep pace with population growth and resettlement. The notorious "rotten boroughs" each elected a member of Parliament to represent fewer than 500 easily bribable voters, while some large cities like Manchester and Leeds, newly populous because of industrial growth, had no representation in Parliament at all.

Americans liked to think that their colonial governments mirrored the ideal English constitution. In terms of formal structure, there were similarities. Most colonies had a royal governor who represented the monarch in America and a bicameral (two-house) legislature made up of a lower house (the assembly) and an upper house (or council). The democratically elected assembly, like the House of Commons, stood for popular interests, while the council, some of whose members were elected and others appointed, more roughly approximated the House of Lords.

But these formal similarities masked real differences between English and colonial governments. On the face of it, royal governors had much more power than the English Crown. Unlike kings and queens, royal governors could veto laws passed by assemblies; they could dissolve those bodies at will; they could create courts and dismiss judges. However, governors who asserted such powers found

that their assemblies protested that popular liberty was being endangered. In most showdowns royal governors had to give way, for they lacked the government offices and contracts that bought loyalty. The colonial legislatures possessed additional leverage, since all of them retained the sole authority to levy taxes.

Even if the governors had enjoyed greater patronage powers, their efforts to influence colonial legislatures would have been frustrated by the sheer size of the American electorate. There were too many voters in America to bribe. Over half and possibly as many as 70 percent of all white adult colonial men were enfranchised. Property requirements were the same in America as in England, but widespread ownership of land in the colonies allowed most men to meet the qualifications easily.

The colonial electorate was also more watchful. Representatives were required to reside in the districts that they served, and a few even received binding instructions from their constituents about how to vote. Representation was also apportioned according to population far more equitably than in England. Since they were so closely tied to their constituents' wishes, colonial legislators were far less likely than members of Parliament to be swayed by executive pressure.

The Imperial System before 1760 »

Most Americans were as pleased with their inexpensive and representative colonial governments as they were

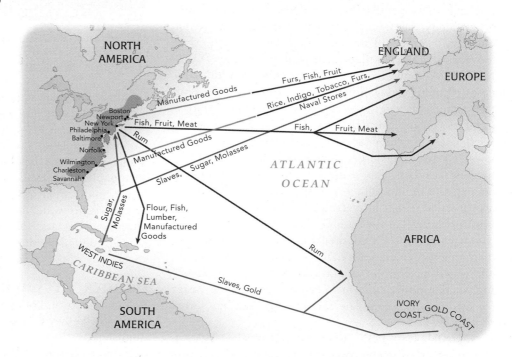

OVERSEAS TRADE NETWORKS

Commercial ties to Spain and Portugal, Africa, and the Caribbean sustained the growth of both seaports and commercial farming regions on the British North American mainland and enabled colonials to purchase an increasing volume of finished goods from England.

Meanwhile, the English thought about their colonies little, understood them less, and wished neither to think about them more nor to understand them better.

horrified by the conduct of politics in England. Meanwhile, the English thought about their colonies little, understood them less, and wished neither to think about them more nor to understand them better.

That indifference contributed to England's haphazard administration of its colonies. The Board of Trade and Plantations, created in 1696, gathered commercial information, reviewed laws and petitions from colonial assemblies, and exchanged letters and instructions with royal governors. But the Board of Trade was only an advisory body.

Real authority over the colonies was divided among an array of other agencies. The Treasury oversaw customs and gathered other royal revenues; the Admiralty Board enforced regulations of trade; the War Office orchestrated colonial defense. In practice, none of these departments spent much time on colonial affairs. But these departments spent most of their hours handling more pressing responsibilities. Most British officials in America seemed equally indifferent.

But the branch of England's government most indifferent to America was Parliament. Aside from passing an occasional law to regulate trade, restrict manufacturing, or direct monetary policy, Parliament made no effort to assert its authority in America. Its members assumed that Parliament's sovereignty extended over the entire empire, and nothing had occurred to make them think otherwise.

For the colonies, this chaotic and inefficient system of colonial administration worked well enough. The very weakness of imperial oversight left Americans with a

great deal of freedom. Even England's regulation of trade rested lightly on the shoulders of most Americans. Southern planters were obliged to send their rice, indigo, and tobacco to Britain only, but they enjoyed favorable credit terms and knowledgeable marketing from English merchants. Colonials were prohibited from finishing iron products and exporting hats and textiles, but they had scant interest in developing domestic industries. Americans were required to import all manufactured goods through England, but by doing so, they acquired high-quality goods at low prices. At little sacrifice, most Americans obeyed imperial regulations. Only sugar, molasses, and tea were routinely smuggled.

Following this policy of **benign neglect** the British empire muddled on to the satisfaction of most people on both sides of the Atlantic. Economic growth and political **autonomy** allowed most Americans to like being English despite their misgivings about their parent nation. The beauty of it was that

benign neglect policy also known as "salutary neglect," pursued by the British empire in governing its American colonies until the end of the Seven Years' War.

autonomy condition of being independent or, in the case of a political structure, the right to self-government

Americans could be English in America, enjoying greater economic opportunity and political equality. If imperial arrangements had remained as they were in 1754, the empire might have muddled on indefinitely.

TOWARD THE SEVEN YEARS' WAR

Three decades after L'Archevêque, the tattooed Frenchman, perished in an imperial skirmish on the Great Plains, two events served as clues of how the competition for power and influence might play out in North America. One was a skirmish much like the one that killed L'Archevêque. The other was a council that brought delegates from seven colonies to Albany, New York, to meet with representatives of the Iroquois Confederacy. Both events took place in the summer of 1754.

The British asked for the council meeting with the Iroquois because France had recently completed a new line of forts stretching from Lake Erie down to the Ohio River. The forts stood directly in the way of the English traders and settlers filtering into the Ohio River Valley. Colonial governors, impressed by the threat, wanted to make sure that they could count on the support of the Iroquois, if yet another war broke out between Britain and France.

The Iroquois had generally remained neutral in this European rivalry, and with good reason. If Britain drove France from North America, English settlers would no doubt spill out onto Indian lands at an even greater rate.

And without competition from French traders, English traders would likely raise the prices of the goods they sold. In the end the Iroquois gave only vague promises of loyalty.

The most prominent delegate to this Albany Congress, as the meeting became known, was Benjamin Franklin. Franklin had larger aims than negotiations with the Iroquois. He presented the other colonial delegates with a plan for colonial cooperation, in which a federal council made up of representatives from each colony would assume responsibility for a united colonial defense. The Albany delegates were alarmed enough by the wavering Iroquois and the threatening French to accept the idea. But when they brought the proposal home to their respective legislatures, not a single one approved the Albany Plan of Union.

While the Albany Congress was debating in July 1754, a second event—the skirmish—occurred some 400 miles to the west, beyond the Appalachian Mountains. There, a young Virginian who dreamed of military glory led a company of Virginia militia in an expedition against Fort Duquesne, the newly built French stronghold at the forks of the Ohio River. The militia's leader wanted more than anything to become an officer in the regular British army, but events did not go the way George Washington hoped. A French counterattack forced him to surrender his own makeshift Fort Necessity, thrown together in the woods, and retreat back to Virginia. The disaster dashed any dreams of martial glory. Washington had no future as a soldier.

The French victorious; the British colonies disunited—two telltales in the wind. In the end, though, they were poor predictors of the way events would play out. By the beginning of 1755 the British had determined to renew their war against France. They intended to limit the fighting to the North American backwoods, but those hopes did not last long. By the time the conflict ended seven years later, the contest between France and England had spread across the globe, with battles fought in the Caribbean, in Africa, in India, and even in the Philippines against France's eventual ally, Spain. The war also decided the question of European sovereignty over North America.

Furthermore, despite outward appearances, British colonials did not prove to be hopelessly disunited. The Albany Congress demonstrated that at least a few Americans such as Franklin had seen beyond the diversity of a divided colonial world to the possibility of political union, however strange the idea first seemed. The backcountry war that spread across four continents would also alter the basic relationship between colonials and their parent nation. With this change, an increasing number of Americans began to see in themselves a likeness that was not English.

Significant Events

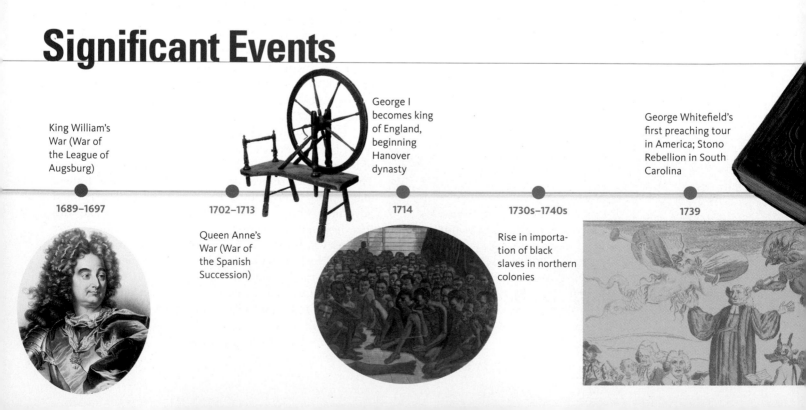

King William's War (War of the League of Augsburg)

1689–1697

Queen Anne's War (War of the Spanish Succession)

1702–1713

George I becomes king of England, beginning Hanover dynasty

1714

Rise in importation of black slaves in northern colonies

1730s–1740s

George Whitefield's first preaching tour in America; Stono Rebellion in South Carolina

1739

CHAPTER SUMMARY

Over the course of the eighteenth century, British North Americans grew increasingly diverse, which made the prospect of any future colonial political union appear remote.

▌ Differences became more pronounced among whites because of the immigration of larger numbers of non-English settlers, the spread of settlement to the back-country, and the growth of major seaports.

▌ Although disorder was not uncommon either on the frontier or in cities, the most serious social and political conflict drew its strength from sectional controversies between East and West.

▌ The South became more embattled, too, as a result of the massive importation of slaves directly from Africa during the first half of the eighteenth century and a rising tide of black resistance to slavery.

▌ After about 1750 the growth of a native-born population strengthened black communal and family life.

▌ Religious conflict among colonials was intensified by the spread of Enlightenment ideas and the influence of the first Great Awakening.

▌ Despite their many differences, a majority of white colonials took pride in their common English ancestry and in belonging to a powerful empire.

Additional Reading

Understanding the effects of ethnic and racial diversity is essential to appreciating the dynamism of eighteenth-century colonial society. Some vivid accounts include Bernard Bailyn, *Voyagers to the West* (1986), and Bernard Bailyn and Philip Morgan, eds., *Strangers within the Realm* (1991). Philip Morgan's *Slave Counterpoint* (1998) offers a state-of-the-art overview of African American cultures in the early South. For mounting class, ethnic, and racial tensions in American seaports, consult Jill Lepore, *New York Burning* (2005), and Gary Nash, *The Urban Crucible* (1979).

Nancy Shoemaker, *A Strange Likeness* (2004) and James M. Merrell, *Into the American Woods* (1999), are two compelling accounts of how Indians and white Americans came to perceive one another as different peoples. For the expansion of colonial settlement into the eighteenth-century backcountry, begin with Eric Hinderaker and Peter C. Mancall, *At the Edge of Empire* (2003), and Rachel Klein, *The Unification of a Slave State* (1990). Among the best studies of religion in eighteenth-century society are Rhys Isaac, *The Transformation of Virginia, 1740–1790* (1982); Patricia Bonomi, *Under the Cope of Heaven* (1986); and George Marsden, *Jonathan Edwards* (2003).

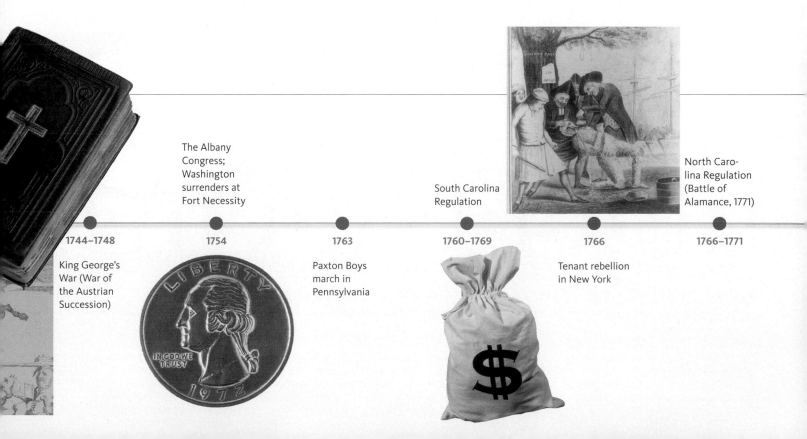

The Albany Congress; Washington surrenders at Fort Necessity

South Carolina Regulation

North Carolina Regulation (Battle of Alamance, 1771)

1744–1748 **1754** **1763** **1760–1769** **1766** **1766–1771**

King George's War (War of the Austrian Succession)

Paxton Boys march in Pennsylvania

Tenant rebellion in New York

6

1754–1776

TOWARD THE WAR FOR American Independence

When the Stamp Act was repealed in 1766, Paul Revere constructed an obelisk to stand under Boston's Liberty Tree. The large monument was framed in wood and covered with drawings executed on oiled, semitransparent paper. Inside was space for 300 lanterns to illuminate the drawings at night. On the far left panel, a threatened Indian represents America being menaced by British officials, including the evil Lord Bute, portrayed as a flying devil carrying the Stamp Act in one claw. In the second panel, the Indian points to his retreating foes, as the Goddess Liberty blows her trumpet. Alas, the oiled paper caught fire, and the obelisk burned down shortly after its construction.

The Repeal of the ——— Stamp-Act 1766

Our FAITH approv'd, our LIBERTY restor'd
Our Hearts bend grateful to our sov'reign Lord
Hail darling Monarch! by this act endear'd
Our firm affections are thy best reward
Sh'd Britains self, against her self divide
And hostile Armies frown on either Side
Sh'd Hosts rebellious shake our Brunswicks Throne
And as they dar'd thy Parent, dare the Son
To this Asylum stretch thine happy Wing
And well contend, who best shall love our KING

Paul Revere Sculp

born SONS, in BOSTON New England
t for a short Season (4th And has her LIBERTY restor'd by the Royal hand of GEORGE the Third

WHAT'S TO COME

102 **THE SEVEN YEARS' WAR**

104 **THE IMPERIAL CRISIS**

114 **TOWARD THE REVOLUTION**

THE JOYS OF BEING ENGLISH

Americans liked being English. They had liked being English from the beginning of colonial settlement, but they liked it more than ever for a few years after 1759. One wonderful day during those years—September 16, 1762—Bostonians turned out to celebrate belonging to the British empire. Soldiers mustered on the Common; bells pealed from the steeples of local churches; the charge of guns fired from the battery resounded through towns; strains of orchestra music from an outdoor concert floated through the city's crowded streets and narrow alleys. When darkness fell and bonfires illuminated the city, Bostonians consumed "a vast quantity of liquor," drinking "loyal healths" to their young king, George III, and in celebration of Britain's victory in the Seven Years' War. »

WN OF BOSTON IN NEW-ENGLAND AND BRITTISH SHIPS

<< Like a swarm of angry bees, British troops disembark on one of Boston's long wharves in 1768. American colonials who had cheered the triumphs of British soldiers only a few years earlier now complained bitterly about the presence of a standing army designed to intimidate them.

III became England's new king. In February of 1763, when the Treaty of Paris formally ended the war, Britain became the largest and most powerful empire in the Western world. Americans were among His Majesty's proudest subjects.

Thirteen years after the celebration of 1762, Boston was a different place. Pride in belonging to the empire had shriveled to shrill charges that England conspired to enslave its colonies. Massachusetts led the way, drawing other colonies deep into resistance. Bostonians initiated many of the petitions and resolves against British authority. When words did not work, they ignited riots, harassed British officials, baited British troops, and destroyed British property. In 1775, they were laying plans for rebellion against the British empire.<<

When the great news of that triumph reached the North American mainland in the fall of 1762, similar celebrations broke out all over the colonies. But the party in America had begun long before, with a string of British victories in French Canada in the glorious year of 1759. It continued through 1760 when all of Canada fell to Anglo-American forces and George

A generation of Americans had loved being English, boasted of their rights as Britons, and celebrated their membership in the all-conquering empire. Ironically, that very pride drove colonials into rebellion, for the men who ran the British empire after 1763 would not allow Americans to be English. Even before the Seven Years' War, some colonials saw that diverging paths of social and political development made them different from the English. After the Seven Years' War, events demonstrated to even more colonials that they were not considered the political equals of the English who lived in England. As their disillusionment with the empire deepened, British North Americans from Massachusetts to Georgia slowly discovered a new identity as Americans and declared their independence from being English.

THE SEVEN YEARS' WAR

The Seven Years' War, which actually lasted nine, pitted Britain and its ally, Prussia, against France, in league with Austria and Spain. The battle raged from 1754 until 1763, ranging over the continent of Europe, the coast of West Africa, India, the Philippines, the Caribbean, and North America.

The Years of Defeat >> The war started when the contest over the Ohio River valley among the English, the French, and the Indians led to George Washington's surrender at Fort Necessity in 1754 (page 98). That episode

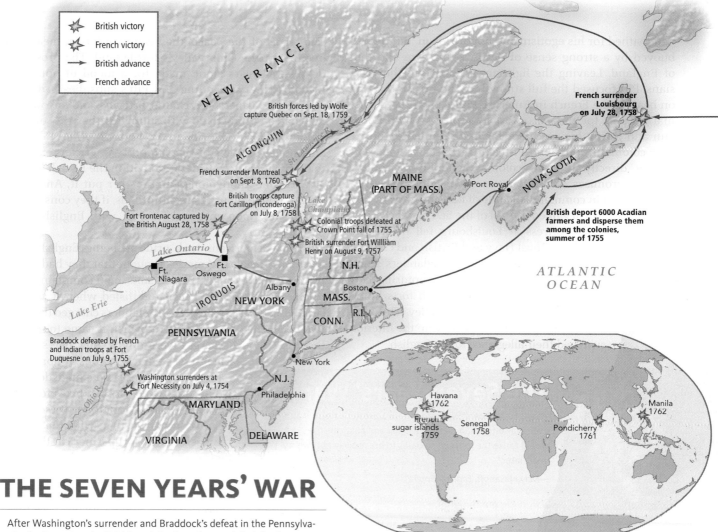

British victory
French victory
British advance
French advance

NEW FRANCE

British forces led by Wolfe capture Quebec on Sept. 18, 1759

ALGONQUIN

French surrender Montreal on Sept. 8, 1760

British troops capture Fort Carillon (Ticonderoga) on July 8, 1758

Fort Frontenac captured by the British August 28, 1758

Lake Ontario

Colonial troops defeated at Crown Point fall of 1755

British surrender Fort William Henry on August 9, 1757

French surrender Louisbourg on July 28, 1758

MAINE (PART OF MASS.)

Port Royal   NOVA SCOTIA

British deport 6000 Acadian farmers and disperse them among the colonies, summer of 1755

ATLANTIC OCEAN

Ft. Niagara   Ft. Oswego

N.H.

IROQUOIS   Albany

NEW YORK   MASS.   Boston

CONN.   R.I.

PENNSYLVANIA

Braddock defeated by French and Indian troops at Fort Duquesne on July 9, 1755

New York

Washington surrenders at Fort Necessity on July 4, 1754

N.J.

Philadelphia

MARYLAND

VIRGINIA   DELAWARE

Havana 1762

French sugar islands 1759   Senegal 1758   Pondicherry 1761   Manila 1762

THE SEVEN YEARS' WAR

After Washington's surrender and Braddock's defeat in the Pennsylvanian backcountry, the British and the French waged their final contest for supremacy in North America in northern New York and Canada. But the rivalry for empire between France and Britain was worldwide, with naval superiority providing the needed edge to Britain. The British navy isolated French forces in India, winning a victory at Pondicherry, while English offensives captured the French sugar islands in the Caribbean and French trading posts along the West African coast. When Spain entered the war on the side of France, British fleets captured both Havana and the strategic port of Manila in the Philippines.

stiffened Britain's resolve to assert its own claims to the Ohio country. In the summer of 1755, as two British regiments led by Major General Edward Braddock approached the French outpost at Fort Duquesne on the forks of the Ohio, they were ambushed and cut to pieces by a party of French and Indians. Washington led the mortally wounded Braddock and the remnants of his army in a retreat. During the summer of Braddock's defeat, New Englanders fared somewhat better against French forces in Nova Scotia and deported 6,000 farmers from that region. The Acadians, as they were known, had their land confiscated, and they were dispersed throughout the colonies.

There followed two disastrous years for Britain and its allies. When England and France formally declared war in May 1756, John Campbell, the Earl of Loudoun, was sent to direct the war in North America. American soldiers

and colonial assemblies alike hated Lord Loudoun. They balked at his efforts to take command over colonial troops and dragged their heels at his demands for men and supplies. Meanwhile, the French strengthened their position in Canada by appointing a new commanding general, Louis Joseph, the marquis de Montcalm. Montcalm drove southward, capturing key British forts and threatening the security of both New York and New England. While he prospered in America, the British were also taking a beating from the French in Europe and in India.

During the years when the French seemed unstoppable, the British looked for help from the strongest tribes of the interior—the Iroquois in the North, the Creek, Choctaw, and Cherokee in the South. Instead, most tribes adopted neutrality or joined the French. As France seemed certain to carry the continent, Indian attacks on English frontier settlements increased.

The Years of Victory >> British fortunes took
a sharp turn for the better when a veteran English politician, William Pitt, came out of retirement to direct the war. Pitt was an odd character, subject to bouts of depression

Grenville made other modest proposals, all approved by Parliament. There was the Currency Act of 1764, which prohibited the colonies from making their paper money legal tender. That prevented Americans from paying their debts to British traders in currency that had fallen to less than its face value. There was the Quartering Act of 1765, which obliged any colony in which troops were stationed to provide them with suitable accommodations. That contributed to the cost of keeping British forces in America. Finally, in March of 1765, Parliament passed the Stamp Act.

taxes duty on trade (known as external taxation) or a duty on items circulating within a nation or a colony (known as internal taxation) intended primarily to raise a revenue rather than to regulate the flow of commerce.

The Stamp Act placed **taxes** on legal documents, customs papers, newspapers, almanacs, college diplomas, playing cards, and dice. After November 1, 1765, all these items had to bear a stamp signifying that their possessor had paid the tax. Violators of the Stamp Act, like those disobeying the Sugar Act, were to be tried without juries in admiralty courts. The English had been paying a similar tax for nearly a century, so it seemed to Grenville and Parliament that colonials could have no objections.

Every packet boat from London that brought news of Parliament's passing another one of Grenville's measures dampened postwar optimism. For all of the differences between the colonies and England, Americans still shared certain firm beliefs about why the British constitution, British customs, and British history all served to protect liberty and the rights of the empire's free-born citizens. For that reason the new measures, which seemed like

↑ One Pennsylvania newspaper showed what it thought of the Stamp Act.

common sense to Grenville and Parliament, did not make sense at all to Americans.

The Beginning of Colonial Resistance »

Like other Britons, colonials in America accepted a maxim laid down by the English philosopher John Locke: property guaranteed liberty. Property, in this view, was not merely real estate, or wealth, or material possessions. It was the source of strength for every individual, providing the freedom to think and act independently. Protecting the individual's right or property was the main responsibility of government, because if personal property was not sacred, then neither was personal liberty.

It followed from this close connection between property, power, and liberty that no people should be taxed without their consent or that of their elected representatives. The power to tax was the power to destroy by depriving a person of property. Yet both the Sugar Act and the Stamp Act were taxes passed by members of Parliament, none of whom had been elected by colonials.

Like the English, colonials also prized the right of trial by jury as one of their basic constitutional liberties. Yet both the Sugar Act and the Stamp Act would prosecute offenders in the admiralty courts, thus depriving colonials of the freedom claimed by all other English men and women.

The concern for protecting individual liberties was only one of the convictions shaping the colonies' response to Britain's new policies. Equally important was their deep suspicion of power itself, a preoccupation that colonials shared with a minority of radical English thinkers. These radicals were known by a variety of names—the "Country Party," the "Commonwealthmen," and "the **Opposition**." They drew their inspiration from the ancient tradition of classical republicanism, which held that representative government safeguarded liberty more reliably than did either monarchy or oligarchy. Underlying that judgment was the belief that human beings were driven by passion and insatiable ambition. One person, or even a few people, could not be entrusted with governing, because they would inevitably become corrupted by power and turn into tyrants. Even in representative governments, the people were obliged to watch those in power at all times: the price of liberty was eternal vigilance.

Opposition diverse group of political thinkers and writers in Great Britain, also known as the Country Party and the Commonwealthmen, who elaborated the tradition of classical republicanism from the late seventeenth century through the eighteenth century.

The Opposition believed that the people of England were not watching their rulers closely enough. During the first half of the eighteenth century, they argued, the entire executive branch of England's government—monarchs and their ministers—had been corrupted by their appetite for power. Proof of their ambition was the executive bureaucracy of civil officials and standing armies that steadily grew larger, interfered more with citizens' lives, and drained increasing amounts of money from taxpayers. Even more alarming, in the Opposition's view, the executive branch's bribery of members of Parliament was corrupting the representative branch of England's government. They warned that a sinister conspiracy originating in the executive branch of government threatened English liberty.

Opposition thinkers commanded little attention in England, where they were dismissed as a discontented radical fringe. But they were revered by political leaders in the American colonies. The Opposition's view of politics confirmed colonial anxieties about England, doubts that ran deeper after 1763. Parliament's attempt to tax the colonies and the quartering of a standing army on the frontier confirmed all too well the Opposition's portrayal of how powerful rulers turned themselves into tyrants and reduced the people whom they ruled to slaves.

In sum, Grenville's new measures led some colonials to suspect that ambitious men ruling England might be conspiring against American liberties. At the very least, the new measures implied that colonials were not the political equals of the English living in England. They were not entitled to taxation by consent or to trial by jury. The heady dreams of the role that the colonies would play in the British empire evaporated, leaving behind the bitter dregs of disappointment. And after the passage of the Stamp Act, dismay mushroomed into militant protest.

Britain's determination to centralize its empire after 1763 was a disaster of timing, not just psychologically but also economically. By then, the colonies were in the throes of a recession. The boom produced in America by government spending during the war had collapsed once subsidies were withdrawn. Colonial merchants were left with full stocks of imported goods gathering dust on their shelves. Farmers lost the brisk and profitable market of the army.

Colonial response to the Sugar Act reflected the painful postwar readjustments. New England merchants led the opposition, objecting to the Sugar Act principally on economic grounds. But with the passage of the Stamp Act, the terms of the imperial debate widened. The Stamp Act hit all colonials, not just New England merchants. It took money from the pockets of anyone who made a will, filed a deed, traded out of a colonial port,

Key: a

Thomas Paine is best described as

a. a radical republican.

b. a Quaker advocate of pacifism.

c. an early English socialist.

d. a defender of monarchy.

bought a newspaper, consulted an almanac, graduated from college, took a chance at dice, or played cards. More important, the Stamp Act served notice that Parliament claimed the authority to tax the colonies directly and for the sole purpose of raising revenue.

Riots and Resolves >>

That unprecedented assertion provoked an unprecedented development: the first display of colonial unity. During the spring and summer of 1765, American assemblies passed resolves denying that Parliament could tax the colonies. That right belonged to colonial assemblies alone, they argued, by the law of nature and by the liberties guaranteed in colonial charters and in the British constitution.

Virginia's assembly, the House of Burgesses, took the lead in protesting the Stamp Act, prodded by Patrick Henry, a young lawyer from western Virginia. The Burgesses passed Henry's resolutions upholding their exclusive right to tax Virginians. They stopped short of adopting those resolves that called for outright resistance. When news of Virginia's stand spread to the rest of the colonies, other assemblies followed suit, affirming that the sole right to tax Americans resided in their elected representatives. But some colonial newspapers deliberately printed a different story—that the Burgesses had approved all of Henry's resolves, including one that sanctioned disobedience to any parliamentary tax. That prompted a few assemblies to endorse resistance. In October 1765 delegates from nine colonies convened in New York, where they prepared a joint statement of the American position and petitioned

WITNESS

Fleeing the Stamp Act Mob

"I had been [gone] but a few minutes before the hellish crew fell upon my house with the rage of devils and in a moment with axes split down the doors and entered my son being in the great entry heard them cry damn him he is upstairs we'll have him . . . they began to take the slate and boards from the roof and were prevented only by the approaching daylight from a total demolition of the building."

⚘ The Stamp Act riots had their roots in raucous demonstrations by "people out of doors," as such crowds were known during the eighteenth century. One annual celebration, the anti-Catholic "Pope's Day," was held every year in Boston. In this engraving, boys dressed as devil's imps accompany a cart bearing an effigy of the pope. In the 1760s, effigies of tax collectors and royal officials appeared instead.

Repeal of the Stamp Act »

Meanwhile, the repeal of the Stamp Act was already in the works back in England. The man who came—unintentionally—to America's relief was George III. The young king was industrious and devoted to the empire, but he was also immature and not overendowed with intellect. Insecurity made him an irksome master, and he ran through ministers rapidly. By the end of 1765, George had replaced Grenville with a new first minister who had opposed the Stamp Act from the outset, the Marquis of Rockingham. He received support from London merchants, who were beginning to feel the pinch of the American nonimportation campaign, and secured repeal of the Stamp Act in March 1766.

the king and Parliament to repeal both the Sugar Act and the Stamp Act.

Meanwhile, colonial leaders turned to the press to arouse popular opposition. Disposed by the writings of the English Opposition to think of politics in conspiratorial terms, they warned that Grenville and the king's other ministers schemed to deprive the colonies of their liberties by unlawfully taxing their property. The Stamp Act was only the first step in a sinister plan to enslave Americans. Whether or not fears of a dark ministerial conspiracy haunted most colonials in 1765, many resisted the Stamp Act. The merchants of Boston, New York, and Philadelphia agreed to stop importing English goods in order to pressure British traders to lobby for repeal. In every colony, organizations emerged to ensure that the Stamp Act, if not repealed, would never be enforced.

The new resistance groups, which styled themselves the "Sons of Liberty," consisted of traders, lawyers, and prosperous artisans. With great success, they organized the lower classes of seaports in opposition to the Stamp Act. The sailors, dockworkers, poor artisans, apprentices, and servants who poured into the streets resembled mobs that had been organized from time to time earlier in the century. Previous riots against houses of prostitution, merchants who hoarded goods, or supporters of smallpox inoculation had not been spontaneous, uncontrolled outbursts. Crowds chose their targets and their tactics carefully and then carried out the communal will with little violence.

In every colonial city, the mobs of 1765 burnt the stamp distributors in effigy, insulted them on the streets, demolished their offices, and attacked their homes. By the first of November, the day that the Stamp Act took effect, most of the stamp distributors had resigned.

The Stamp Act controversy demonstrated to many colonials that they shared the same assumptions about the meaning of representation. To counter objections to the Stamp Act, Grenville and his supporters had claimed that Americans were represented in Parliament, even though they had elected none of its members. Americans were virtually represented, he insisted, for each member of Parliament stood for the interests of the whole empire, not just those of the particular constituency that had elected him.

virtual representation
view that representation is not linked to election but rather to common interests. During the imperial crisis, the British argued that Americans were virtually represented in Parliament, even though colonials elected none of its members.

actual representation
view that the people can be represented only by a person whom they have actually elected to office.

But most colonials could see no virtue in the theory of **virtual representation**. After all, the circumstances and interests of colonials, living an ocean apart, were so different from those of Britons. The newly recognized consensus among Americans was that colonials could be truly represented only by those whom they had elected. Their view, known as **actual representation**, emphasized that elected officials were directly accountable to their constituents.

Americans also had discovered that they agreed about the extent of Parliament's authority over the colonies: it did not include the right to tax. Colonials conceded Parliament's right to legislate and to regulate trade for the good of the whole empire. But taxation, in their view, was the free gift of the people through their representatives—who were not sitting in Parliament.

Members of Parliament brushed aside colonial petitions and resolves, all but ignoring these constitutional arguments. To make its authority clear, Parliament accompanied the repeal of the Stamp Act with a Declaratory Act, asserting that it had the power to make laws for the colonies "in all cases whatsoever." In fact, the Declaratory Act clarified nothing: did Parliament understand the power of legislation to include the power of taxation?

The Townshend Acts >>

In the summer of 1766 George III—again inadvertently—gave the colonies what should have been an advantage by changing ministers again. The king replaced Rockingham with William Pitt, who enjoyed great favor among colonials for his leadership during the Seven Years' War and for his opposition to the Stamp Act. Almost alone among British politicians, Pitt had grasped and approved the colonists' constitutional objections to taxation.

If the man who believed that Americans were "the sons not the bastards of England" had been well enough to govern, matters between Great Britain and the colonies might have turned out differently. But almost immediately after Pitt took office, his health collapsed, and power passed into the hands of Charles Townshend, the chancellor of the exchequer. Townshend's two main concerns were to strengthen the authority of Parliament and royal officials in the colonies at the expense of American assemblies and to raise more revenue at the expense of American taxpayers. In 1767 he persuaded Parliament to tax the lead, paint, paper, glass, and tea that Americans imported from Britain.

Townshend used several strategies to limit the power of colonial assemblies. First, he instructed

<< This 1766 porcelain of Lord Chatham and America attests to the popularity of William Pitt, Earl of Chatham, among Americans who resisted the Stamp Act. The artist's representation of "America" as a black woman kneeling in gratitude echoes the colonists' association of taxation with slavery.

the royal governors to take a firmer hand. To set the example, he singled out for punishment the New York legislature, which was refusing to comply with provisions of the Quartering Act of 1765. The New York assembly held that the cost of quartering the troops constituted a form of indirect taxation. But Parliament backed Townshend, suspending the New York assembly in 1767 until it agreed to obey the Quartering Act.

Townshend also dipped into the revenue from his new tariffs in order to support royal officials. That freed them from the influence of colonial assemblies, which had previously funded the salaries of governors, customs collectors, and judges. Townshend's policies enlarged the number of those bureaucrats. To ensure more effective enforcement of all the duties on imports, he created an American Board of Customs Commissioners, who appointed a small army of new customs collectors. He also established three new vice-admiralty courts in Boston, New York, and Charleston to bring smugglers to justice.

> In Townshend's **efforts** to **centralize** imperial administration, Americans saw **new evidence** that they were **not** being **treated** like the English.

The Resistance Organizes >>

In Townshend's efforts to centralize imperial administration, Americans saw new evidence that they were not being treated like the English. Newspapers and pamphlets took up the cry against taxation. The most widely read publication, "A Letter from a Farmer in Pennsylvania," was the work of John Dickinson, who urged Americans to protest the Townshend duties with a show of superior virtue—hard work, thrift, simplicity, and home manufacturing. By consuming fewer imported English luxuries, Dickinson argued, Americans would advance the cause of repeal. The Townshend Acts also shaped the destiny of Samuel Adams, a leader in the Massachusetts assembly and a consummate political organizer and agitator. First his enemies and later his friends claimed that Adams had decided on independence for America as early as 1768. In that year he persuaded the assembly to send to other colonial legislatures a circular letter condemning the acts and calling for a united American resistance.

As John Dickinson and Samuel Adams whipped up public outrage against the Townshend Acts, the Sons of Liberty again organized the opposition in the streets. Customs officials, like the stamp distributors before them, they were fundamentally at odds. And the call to arms at Lexington and Concord made retreat impossible.

On that point Paine was clear. It was the destiny of Americans to be republicans, not monarchists. It was the destiny of Americans to be independent, not subject to British dominion. It was the destiny of Americans to be American, not English. That, according to Thomas Paine, was common sense.

CHAPTER SUMMARY

Resistance to British authority grew slowly but steadily in the American colonies during the period following the Seven Years' War.

- The new measures passed by Parliament in the early 1760s—the Proclamation of 1763, the Sugar Act, the Stamp Act, the Currency Act, and the Quartering Act—were all designed to bind the colonies more closely to the empire.

- These new measures deflated American expectations of a more equal status in the empire and also violated what Americans understood to be their constitutional and political liberties—the right to consent to taxation, the right to trial by jury, and the freedom from standing armies.

- Although Parliament repealed the Stamp Act, it reasserted its authority to tax Americans by passing the Townshend Act in 1767. With the passage of the Coercive Acts in 1774, many Americans concluded that all British actions in the past decade were part of a deliberate plot to enslave Americans by depriving them of property and liberty.

- When the First Continental Congress convened in September 1774, delegates resisted both radical demands to mobilize for war and conservative appeals to reach an accommodation.

- The First Continental Congress denied Parliament any authority in the colonies except the right to regulate trade; it also drew up the Continental Association, an agreement to cease all trade with Britain until the Coercive Acts were repealed.

- When General Thomas Gage sent troops from Boston in April 1775 to seize arms being stored at Concord, the first battle of the Revolution took place.

Significant Events

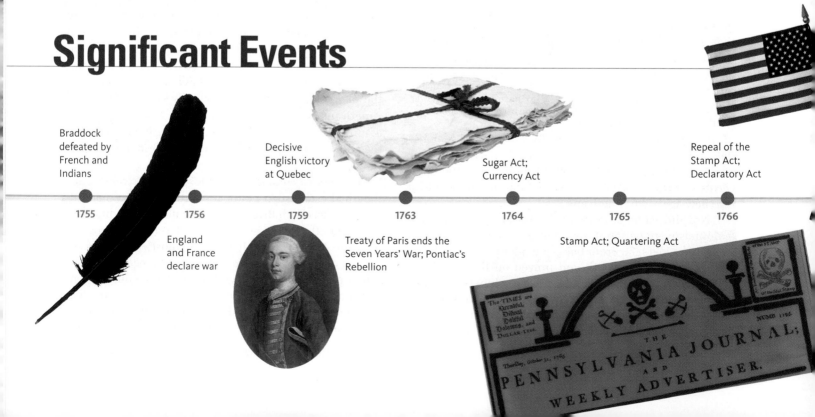

Braddock defeated by French and Indians

1755

1756

England and France declare war

Decisive English victory at Quebec

1759

Treaty of Paris ends the Seven Years' War; Pontiac's Rebellion

1763

Sugar Act; Currency Act

1764

Stamp Act; Quartering Act

1765

Repeal of the Stamp Act; Declaratory Act

1766

Additional Reading

For comprehensive overviews of the entire revolutionary era, consult Edward Countryman, *The American Revolution* (1985), and Edmund S. Morgan, *Birth of the Republic* (1956). Fred Anderson, *Crucible of War* (2000), offers a magisterial account of the Seven Years' War, and Gregory Evans Dowd, *War Under Heaven* (2002), explores the implications of that conflict for American Indians. *The Stamp Act Crisis* (1953) by Edmund S. Morgan and Helen M. Morgan remains the clearest and most vivid portrayal of the issues, events, and people involved in that defining moment of the imperial crisis. For lively coverage of American resistance after the Stamp Act, see Pauline Maier, *From Resistance to Revolution* (1972), and to understand that struggle as lived and recalled by a Boston artisan, read Alfred F. Young's engaging book, *The Shoemaker and the Tea Party* (1999). Two important interpretations of how the logic of resistance took shape among colonials in Massachusetts and Virginia are Robert Gross, *The Minutemen and Their World* (1976), and Timothy Breen, *Tobacco Culture* (1985). A more recent study by Breen, *The Marketplace Revolution* (2005), sheds new light on the role of a transatlantic consumer culture in fueling tensions within the British empire.

Bernard Bailyn, *The Ideological Origins of the American Revolution* (1967), remains the classic study of the English Opposition's influence on the evolution of republican political thought in the American colonies. Many fine biographies chronicle the careers of eighteenth-century Americans who led—or opposed—the resistance to Britain and also shed light on the times in which they lived. Of particular interest are Pauline Maier, *The Old Revolutionaries* (1980); Bernard Bailyn, *The Ordeal of Thomas Hutchinson* (1974); and two recent biographies of Thomas Paine (both published in 2006) by Harvey Kaye and Craig Nelson.

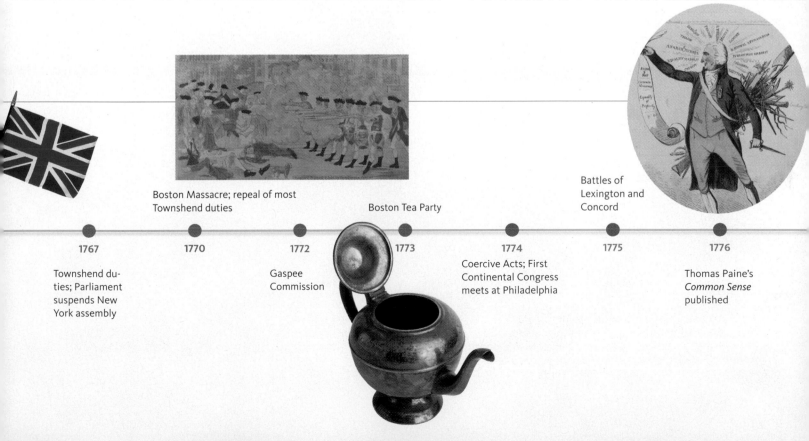

Boston Massacre; repeal of most Townshend duties

Boston Tea Party

Battles of Lexington and Concord

1767

Townshend duties; Parliament suspends New York assembly

1770

1772

Gaspee Commission

1773

1774

Coercive Acts; First Continental Congress meets at Philadelphia

1775

1776

Thomas Paine's *Common Sense* published

BOSTON

CH

On June 17, 1775, thousands of colonials flocked to the rooftops and upper windows of their Boston homes to witness the British attack on Breed's Hill across the water on nearby Charlestown peninsula. As the British artillery sent shells into the peninsula, houses there caught fire and burst into flames. Then the redcoats, unloaded from their ships, launched their assault on the hill.

American
AND THE Revolution

1775—1783

WHAT'S TO COME

122 **THE DECISION FOR INDEPENDENCE**

124 **THE FIGHTING IN THE NORTH**

128 **THE TURNING POINT**

131 **THE STRUGGLE IN THE SOUTH**

134 **THE WORLD TURNED UPSIDE DOWN**

From a high place somewhere in the city—Beacon Hill, perhaps, or Copse Hill General Thomas Gage looked down on Boston. Through a spyglass his gaze traveled over the church belfries and steeples, the roofs of brick and white frame houses. Finally he fixed his sights on a figure far in the distance across the Charles River. The man was perched atop a crude fortification on Breed's Hill, an elevation lying just below Bunker Hill on the Charlestown peninsula. Gage took the measure of his enemy: an older man, past middle age, a sword swinging beneath his homespun coat, a broad-brimmed hat shading his eyes. As he passed the spyglass to his ally, an American loyalist, Gage asked Abijah Willard if he knew the man on the fort. Willard peered across the Charles and identified his own brother-in-law, Colonel William Prescott. A veteran of the Seven Years' War, Prescott was now a leader in the rebel army laying siege to Boston. »

"Will he fight?" Gage wondered aloud.

"I cannot answer for his men," Willard replied, "but Prescott will fight you to the gates of hell."

Fight they did on June 17, 1775, both William Prescott and his men. The evening before, three regiments had followed the colonel from Cambridge to Breed's Hill—soldiers drawn from the thousands of militia who had surrounded British-occupied Boston after the bloodshed at Lexington and Concord. Through the night, they dug trenches and built up high earthen walls atop the hill. At the first light of day, a British warship spotted the new rebel outpost and opened fire. By noon barges were ferrying British troops under Major General William Howe across the half mile of river that separated Boston from Charlestown. The 1,600 raw rebel troops tensed at the sight of scarlet-coated soldiers streaming ashore, glittering bayonets grasped at the ready. The rebels were farmers and artisans, not professional soldiers, and they were frightened out of their wits.

But Prescott and his men held their ground. The British charged Breed's Hill twice, and Howe watched in horror as streams of fire felled his troops. Finally, during the third British frontal assault, the rebels ran out of ammunition and were forced to withdraw. Redcoats poured into the rebel fort, bayoneting its handful of remaining defenders. By nightfall the British had taken Breed's Hill and the rest of the Charlestown peninsula. They had bought a dark triumph at the cost of 228 dead and 800 wounded.

The cost came high in loyalties as well. The fighting on Breed's Hill fed the hatred of Britain that had been building since April. Throughout America, preparations for war intensified: militia in every colony mustered; communities stockpiled arms and ammunition. Around Charlestown civilian refugees fled the countryside, abandoning homes and shops set afire by the British shelling of Breed's Hill. "The roads filled with frightened women and children, some in carts with their tattered furniture, others on foot fleeing into the woods," recalled Hannah Winthrop, one of their number. ≪

The bloody, indecisive fight on the Charlestown peninsula known as the Battle of Bunker Hill actually took place on Breed's Hill. And the exchange between Thomas Gage and Abijah Willard that is said to have preceded the battle may not have taken place at all. But the story has persisted in the folklore of the American Revolution. Whether it really happened or not, the conversation between Gage and Willard raised the question that both sides wanted answered: were Americans willing to fight for independence from British rule? It was one thing, after all, to oppose the British ministry's policy of taxation. It was another to support a rebellion for which the ultimate price of failure was hanging for treason. And it was another matter entirely for men to wait nervously atop a hill as the seasoned troops of their own "mother country" marched toward them with the intent to kill.

Indeed, the question "will they fight?" was revolutionary shorthand for a host of other questions concerning how ordinary Americans would react to the tug of loyalties between long-established colonial governments and a long-revered parent nation and monarch. For slaves, the question revolved around their allegiance to masters who spoke of liberty or to their masters' enemies who promised liberation. For those who led the rebels, it was a question of strengthening the resolve of the undecided, coordinating resistance, instilling discipline—translating the will to fight into the ability to do so. And for those who believed the rebellion was a madness whipped up by artful politicians, it was a question of whether to remain silent or risk speaking out, whether to take up arms for the king or flee. All these questions were raised, of necessity, by the act of revolution. But the barrel of a rifle shortened them to a single, pointed question: will you fight?

THE DECISION FOR INDEPENDENCE

The delegates to the Second Continental Congress gathered at Philadelphia on May 10, 1775, just one month after the battles at Lexington and Concord. They had to determine whether independence or reconciliation offered the best way to protect the liberties of their colonies. Yet during the spring and summer of 1775, even strong advocates of independence did not openly seek a separation from Britain. If independence was to be achieved, radicals needed to forge greater agreement among Americans. Moderates and conservatives harbored deep misgivings about independence: they had to be brought along slowly.

The Second Continental Congress >>

To bring them along, Congress adopted the "Olive Branch Petition" in July 1775, which affirmed American loyalty to George III and asked the king to disavow the policies of his principal ministers. At the same time, Congress issued a declaration denying that the colonies aimed at independence. Yet, less than a month earlier, Congress had authorized the creation of a rebel military force, the **Continental Army**, and had issued paper money to pay for the troops.

> **Continental Army** main rebel military force, created by the Second Continental Congress in July 1775 and commanded by George Washington.

A Congress that sued for peace while preparing for war was a puzzle that British politicians did not even try to understand, least of all Lord George Germain. A tough-minded statesman charged with colonial affairs, he was determined to subdue the rebellion by force. George III proved just as stubborn: he refused to receive the Olive Branch Petition. By the end of that year Parliament had shut down all trade with the colonies and had ordered the Royal Navy to seize colonial merchant ships on the high seas. In November 1775 Virginia's royal governor, Lord Dunmore, offered freedom to any slaves who would join the British. During January of the next year, he ordered the shelling of Norfolk, Virginia, reducing that town to smoldering rubble.

British belligerence withered the cause of reconciliation within Congress and the colonies. Support for independence gained more momentum from the overwhelming reception of *Common Sense* in January 1776. On June 7 Virginia's Richard Henry Lee offered the motion "that these United Colonies are, and of right ought to be, free and independent States . . . and that all political connection between them and the State of Great Britain is, and ought to be, totally dissolved."

The Declaration >>

Congress postponed a final vote on Lee's motion until July. Some opposition still lingered among delegates from the middle colonies, and a committee appointed to write a declaration of independence needed time to complete its work. That committee included some of the leading delegates in Congress: John Adams, Benjamin Franklin, Connecticut's Roger Sherman, and New York's Robert Livingston. But the man who did most of the drafting was a young planter and lawyer from western Virginia.

Thomas Jefferson was just 33 years old in the summer of 1776 when he withdrew to his lodgings on the outskirts of Philadelphia, pulled a portable writing desk onto his lap, and wrote the statement that would explain American independence to a "candid world." In the document's brief opening section, Jefferson set forth a general justification of revolution that invoked the "self-evident truths" of human equality and "unalienable rights" to "life, liberty, and the pursuit of happiness." These natural rights had been "endowed" to all persons "by their Creator," the Declaration pointed out; thus there was no need to appeal to the narrower claim of the "rights of Englishmen."

While the first part of the Declaration served notice that Americans no longer considered themselves English, its second and longer section denied England any authority in the colonies. In its detailed history of American grievances against the British empire, the Declaration referred only once to Parliament. Instead, it blamed George III for a "long train of abuses and usurpations" designed to achieve "absolute despotism." Congress adopted the Declaration of Independence on July 4, 1776.

American Loyalists >>

But the sentiment for independence was not universal. Those who would not back the rebellion, supporters of the king and Parliament, numbered perhaps one-fifth of the population in 1775. While they proclaimed themselves "**loyalists**," their rebel opponents dubbed them "tories." That division made the Revolution a conflict pitting Americans against one another as well as the British.

> **loyalists** supporters of the king and Parliament and known to the rebels as "tories."

Predictably, the king and Parliament commanded the strongest support in colonies that had been wracked by internal strife earlier in the eighteenth century. In New York, New Jersey, Pennsylvania, and the Carolinas, not only did memories of old struggles sharpen worries of future upheaval, but old enemies often took different sides in the Revolution. To win support against Carolina's rebels, whose ranks included most wealthy coastal planters, western loyalist leaders played on

Key: a

Many loyalists feared that declaring independence from Britain would

a. lead to civil war in the former American colonies.

b. discourage immigration from Britain.

c. result in a pan-Indian uprising.

d. encourage the growth of antislavery sentiment on both sides of the Atlantic.

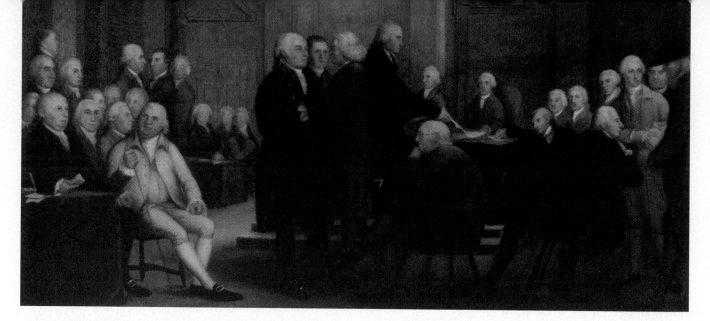

⌃ This painting, which commemorated the signing of the Declaration of Independence, shows Benjamin Franklin (seated center), weighing the consequences of the action he and his colleagues are about to undertake. John Hancock, the president of the Congress, is reported to have remarked, "We must be unanimous; there must be no pulling different ways; we must all hang together." Franklin is said to have rejoined, "Yes, we must indeed all hang together, or most assuredly, we shall all hang separately."

ordinary settlers' resentments of privileged easterners. Grievances dating back to the 1760s also influenced the revolutionary allegiances of former land rioters of New York and New Jersey. If their old landlord opponents opted for the rebel cause, the tenants took up loyalism.

Other influences also fostered allegiance to Britain. Government officials who owed their jobs to the empire, major city merchants who depended on British trade, and Anglicans living outside the South retained strong ties to the parent country. Loyalists were also disproportionately represented among recent emigrants from the British Isles.

Many who took up the king's cause had not lacked sympathy for the resistance. Loyalist leaders like Joseph Galloway and Daniel Leonard had opposed the Stamp Act in 1765 and disapproved of imperial policy thereafter. It was not until the crisis reached a fever pitch in 1774 that more colonials cast their lot with the king. Worse than British taxation, in their view, was the radicalism of American resistance—the dumping of tea into Boston harbor, the forming of the Association, and the defying of royal authority.

Such acts of defiance touched what was for loyalists the rawest nerve: a deep-seated fear of the divisions and instability of colonial society. Without the British around to maintain order, they warned, differences among Americans would result in civil war. It would take the passage of less than a century for such fears to be borne out by events—the Union divided and the North and South locked in a fratricidal war.

Although a substantial minority, loyalists never became numerous enough anywhere to pose a serious threat to the Revolution. A more formidable threat was posed by the British army. And the greatest threat of all was posed by those very Americans who claimed that they wanted independence. For the question remained: would they fight?

THE FIGHTING IN THE NORTH

In the summer of 1775 Americans who wished to remain neutral probably outnumbered either loyalists or rebels. From the standpoint of mere survival, staying neutral made more sense than fighting for independence. Even the most ardent advocates of American rights had reason to harbor doubts, given the odds against the rebel colonists defeating the armed forces of the British empire.

Perhaps no friend of American liberty saw more clearly how slim the chances of a rebel victory were than George Washington. Yet June of 1775 found him, then 43 years old, attending the deliberations of the Second Continental Congress and dressed—a bit conspicuously—in his officer's uniform. Washington was the most celebrated American veteran of the Seven Years' War who remained young enough to lead a campaign. Better still, as a southerner he could bring his region into what thus far had remained mostly New England's fight. Congress readily appointed him commander in chief of the newly created Continental Army.

The Two Armies at Bay >> Thus did Washington find himself, only a month later, looking to bring order to the rebel forces around Boston. He knew he

faced a formidable foe, for the king's troops were seasoned professionals. An aristocratic officer corps drilled and disciplined rank-and-file soldiers, men drawn mainly from the bottom of British society, into a savage fighting machine. At the height of the campaign in America, reinforcements brought the number of British troops to 50,000, strengthened by some 30,000 Hessian mercenaries from Germany and the support of half the ships in the British navy, the largest in the world.

Washington was more modest about the army under his command, and he had much to be modest about. At first Congress recruited his fighting force of 16,600 rebel "regulars," the Continental Army, from the ranks of local New England militia bands. Although enlistments swelled briefly during the patriotic enthusiasm of 1775, for the rest of the war Washington's Continentals suffered chronic shortages of men and supplies. Most men preferred to fight instead as members of local militia units, the "irregular" troops who turned out to support the regular army whenever British forces came close to their neighborhoods.

The general reluctance to join the Continental Army created a host of difficulties for its commander and for Congress. Washington could not create an effective fighting force out of militias that mustered occasionally or men who enlisted for short stints in the Continental Army. But his desire for a professional military establishment clashed with the preferences of most republican leaders. They feared standing armies and idealized "citizen-soldiers"—men of selfless civic virtue who volunteered whenever needed—as the backbone of the common defense.

Only the dwindling number of volunteers gradually overcame republican fears of standing armies. In September 1776 Congress set terms in the Continental Army at a minimum of three years or for the duration of the war and assigned each state to raise a certain number of troops. They offered every man who enlisted in the army a cash bounty and a yearly clothing issue; enlistees for the duration were offered 100 acres of land as well. Still the problem of recruitment persisted. Less than a year later, Congress recommended that the states adopt a draft, but Congress had no authority to compel the states to meet their troop quotas.

Even in the summer of 1775, before enlistments fell off, Washington was worried. As his Continentals laid siege to British-occupied Boston, most officers provided no real leadership, and the men under their command shirked their duties. They slipped away from camp at night; they left sentry duty before

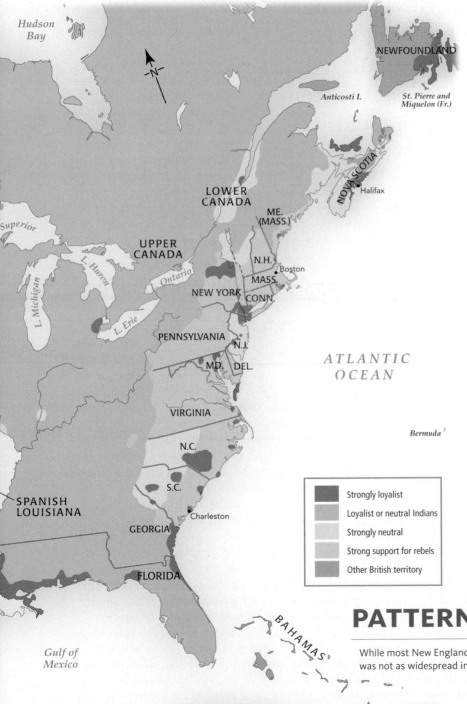

Strongly loyalist

Loyalist or neutral Indians

Strongly neutral

Strong support for rebels

Other British territory

PATTERNS OF ALLEGIANCE

While most New Englanders rallied behind the rebel cause, support for the Revolution was not as widespread in the middle colonies and southern colonies.

being relieved; they took potshots at the British; they tolerated filthy conditions in their camps.

While Washington strove to impose discipline on his Continentals, he also attempted, without success, to rid himself of "the Women of the Army." When American men went off to fight, their wives usually stayed at home. To women then fell the sole responsibility for running farms and businesses, raising children, and keeping households together. They helped to supply the troops by sewing clothing, making blankets, and saving rags and lead weights for bandages and bullets. Other women on the home front organized relief for the widows and orphans of soldiers and protests against merchants who hoarded scarce commodities.

But the wives of poor men who joined the army were often left with no means to support their families. Thousands of such women—1 for every 15 soldiers— drifted after the troops. In return for half-rations, they cooked and washed for the soldiers; and after battles, they nursed the wounded, buried the dead, and scavenged the field for clothing and equipment.

> **When the British landed, the handful of rebel defenders at Kip's Bay fled—straight into the towering wrath of Washington, who happened on the scene during the rout.**

Laying Strategies >>
At the same time that he tried to discipline the Continentals, Washington designed a defensive strategy to compensate for their weakness. To avoid exposing raw rebel troops on "open ground against their Superiors in number and Discipline," he planned to fight the British from strong fortifications. With that aim in mind, in March 1776, Washington barricaded his army on Dorchester Heights, an elevation commanding Boston harbor from the south. That maneuver, which allowed American artillery to fire on enemy warships, confirmed a decision already made by the British to evacuate their entire army from Boston and sail for Halifax, Nova Scotia.

Britain had hoped to reclaim its colonies with a strategy of strangling the resistance in Massachusetts. But by the spring of 1776 they saw clearly that more was required than a show of force against New England. Instead the situation called for Britain to wage a conventional war in America, capturing major cities and crushing the Continental forces in a decisive battle. Military victory, the British believed, would enable them to restore political control and reestablish imperial authority.

The first target was New York City. General William Howe and Lord George Germain, the British officials now charged with overseeing the war, chose that seaport for its central location and—they hoped—its large loyalist population. Howe's army intended to move from New York City up the Hudson River, meeting with British troops under General Sir Guy Carleton coming south from Canada. Either the British drive would lure Washington into a major engagement, crushing the Continentals or, if unopposed, the British offensive would cut America in two, smothering resistance to the south by isolating New England.

Unfortunately for the British, the strategy was sounder than the men placed in charge of executing it. Concern for preserving manpower addicted General Howe to caution, when daring more would have carried the day. Howe's brother, Admiral Lord Richard Howe, the head of naval operations in America, also stopped short of pressing the British advantage, owing to his personal desire for reconciliation. The reluctance of the Howe brothers to fight became the formula for British frustration in the two years that followed.

The Campaigns in New York and New Jersey >>
By mid-August of 1776, 32,000 British troops, including 8000 **Hessians**—the largest expeditionary force of the eighteenth century—faced Washington's army of 23,000, which had marched from Boston to take up positions on Long Island. At dawn on August 22 the Howe brothers launched their offense, pushing the rebel army back across the East River to Manhattan. After lingering on Long Island for a month, the Howes again lurched into action, ferrying their forces to Kip's Bay, just a few miles south of Harlem. When the British landed, the handful of rebel defenders at Kip's Bay fled—straight into the towering wrath of Washington, who happened on the scene during the rout. For once the general lost his habitual self-restraint, flogged both officers and men with his riding crop, and came close to being captured himself. But the Howes remained reluctant to hit hard, occupying New York City but letting Washington's army escape from Manhattan to Westchester County.

Hessians German soldiers who fought with the British Army during the American Revolution.

Throughout the fall of 1776 General Howe's forces followed as Washington's fled southward across New Jersey. On December 7, the British nipping at their heels, the rebels crossed the Delaware River into Pennsylvania. There Howe stopped, pulling back most of his army to winter in New York City and leaving the Hessians to hold the

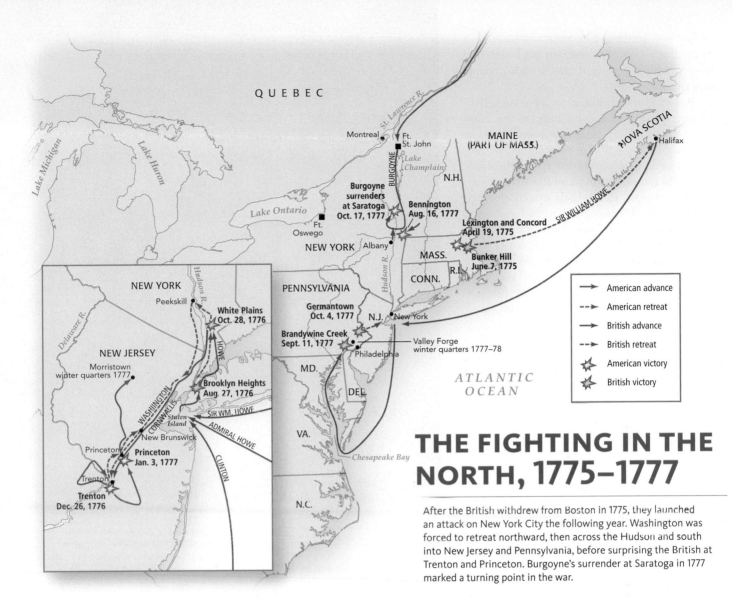

THE FIGHTING IN THE NORTH, 1775–1777

After the British withdrew from Boston in 1775, they launched an attack on New York City the following year. Washington was forced to retreat northward, then across the Hudson and south into New Jersey and Pennsylvania, before surprising the British at Trenton and Princeton. Burgoyne's surrender at Saratoga in 1777 marked a turning point in the war.

British line of advance along the New Jersey side of the Delaware River.

Although the retreat through New York and New Jersey had shriveled rebel strength to only 3,000 men, Washington decided that the campaign of 1776 was not over. On a snowy Christmas night, the Continentals floated back across the Delaware, picked their way over roads sleeted with ice, and finally slid into Hessian-held Trenton at eight in the morning. One thousand German soldiers, still recovering from their spirited Christmas celebration and caught completely by surprise, quickly surrendered. Washington's luck held on January 3, 1777, when the Continentals defeated British troops on the outskirts of Princeton, New Jersey.

During the winter of 1776–1777 the British lost more than battles: they alienated the very civilians whose loyalties they had hoped to ensure. In New York City the presence of the main body of the British army brought shortages of food and housing and caused constant friction between soldiers and city dwellers. In the New Jersey countryside still held by the Hessians, the situation was more desperate. Forced to live

off the land, the Germans aroused resentment among local farmers by seizing "hay, oats, Indian corn, cattle, and horses, which were never or but very seldom paid for," as one loyalist admitted. The Hessians ransacked and destroyed homes and churches; they kidnapped and raped young women.

Many neutrals and loyalists who had had enough of the king's soldiers now took their allegiance elsewhere. Bands of **militia** on Long Island, along the Hudson River, and all over New Jersey rallied to support the Continentals.

> **militia** local defense band of civilians comprising men between the ages of 16 and 65 whose military training consisted only of occasional gatherings known as musters.

Capturing Philadelphia >> By the summer of 1777 General Howe had decided to goad the Americans into battle by capturing Philadelphia. In early August the redcoats disembarked on the Maryland shore and headed for Philadelphia. Washington engaged Howe twice—in September at Brandywine Creek and in October in an

early dawn attack at Germantown—but both times the rebels were beaten back. He had been unable to prevent the British occupation of Philadelphia.

But in Philadelphia, as in New York, British occupation created hostility as the flood of troops jacked up prices for food, fuel, and housing. Philadelphians complained of redcoats looting their shops, trampling their gardens, and harassing them on the streets.

Even worse, the British march through Maryland and Pennsylvania had outraged civilians, who fled before the army and then returned to find their homes and barns bare, their crops and livestock gone. Everywhere Howe's men went in the middle states, they left in their wake Americans with compelling reasons to support the rebels. Worst of all, just days after Howe marched his occupying army into Philadelphia in the fall of 1777, another British commander in North America surrendered his entire army to rebel forces at Saratoga, New York.

Disaster for the British at Saratoga >>
The calamity that befell the British at Saratoga was the doing of a glorymongering general, John "Gentleman Johnny" Burgoyne. After his superior officer, Sir Guy Carleton, bungled a drive into New York in 1776, Burgoyne won approval to command another attack from Canada. The following summer he set out from Quebec with a force of 9,500 redcoats, 2,000 women and children, and a baggage train that included the commander's silver dining service, his dress uniforms, and numerous cases of champagne. As Burgoyne's entourage lumbered southward, a handful of Continentals and a horde of New England militia assembled several miles below Saratoga at Bemis Heights under the command of General Horatio Gates.

On September 19 Gates's rebel scouts, nested high in the trees, spied the glittering bayonets of Burgoyne's approaching force. Benedict Arnold, a brave young officer, led several thousand rebels into battle at a clearing at Freeman's Farm. At the end of the day British reinforcements finally pushed the rebels back from a battlefield piled high with the bodies of soldiers from both sides. Burgoyne tried to flee to Canada but got no farther than Saratoga, where he surrendered his army to Gates on October 17.

Saratoga changed everything. With Burgoyne's surrender, the rebels succeeded in convincing France that, with a little help, the Americans might well reap the fruits of victory.

⌃ At the Battle of Princeton, British troops bayoneted the rebel general Hugh Mercer, an assault later memorialized in this painting by George Washington Parke Custis, the adopted step-grandson of George Washington. This rendering focuses attention not only on Mercer's courage but also on the savagery of the redcoats, both of which helped the rebels gain civilian support.

THE TURNING POINT

France had been waiting for revenge against Britain ever since its humiliating defeat in the Seven Years' War. And for some years, a scheme for evening the score had been taking shape in the mind of the French foreign minister, Charles Gravier de Vergennes. He reckoned that France might turn discontented colonials into willing allies against Britain.

The American Revolution as a Global War >>
Vergennes wanted to make certain that the rift between Britain and its colonies would not be reconciled and that the rebels in America stood a fighting chance. Although France had been secretly supplying the Continen-

tal Army with guns and ammunition since the spring of 1776, Vergennes would go no further than covert assistance.

Congress approached their former French enemies with equal caution. Would France, the leading Catholic monarchy in Europe, make common cause with the republican rebels? A few years earlier American colonials had fought against the French in Canada; only recently they had renounced a king, and for centuries they had overwhelmingly adhered to Protestantism.

But the string of defeats dealt the Continental Army during 1776 convinced Congress that they needed the French. In November Congress appointed a three-member commission to negotiate not only aid from France but also a formal alliance. Its senior member was Benjamin Franklin, who enchanted all of Paris when he arrived sporting a simple fur cap and a pair of spectacles. Hailing Franklin as a homespun sage, Parisians stamped his face on everything from the top of snuffboxes to the bottom of chamber pots.

Still, Franklin understood that mere popularity could not produce the alliance sought by Congress. It was only news that Britain had surrendered an entire army at Saratoga that convinced Vergennes that the rebels could actually win. In February 1778 France signed a treaty of commerce and friendship and a treaty of alliance, which Congress approved in May. Under the terms of the treaties, both parties agreed to accept nothing short of independence for America. The alliance left the British no choice other than to declare war on France. Less than a year later Spain joined France, hoping to recover territory lost to England in earlier wars.

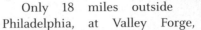

>> The French public's infatuation with Benjamin Franklin knew no bounds. They particularly delighted in his rustic dress and styled him a representative of "frontier" America. He appears in this guise on a snuffbox along with two revered French philosophers, Voltaire and Rousseau.

Only 18 miles outside Philadelphia, at Valley Forge, Washington and his Continentals were assessing their own situation. Some 11,000 rebel soldiers had passed a harrowing winter in that isolated spot, starving for want of food, freezing for lack of clothing, huddling in miserable huts, and hating the British who lay 18 miles away in Philadelphia. The army also cursed their fellow citizens, for its misery resulted from congressional disorganization and civilian indifference. Congress lacked both money to pay and maintain the army and an efficient system for dispensing provisions to the troops. Most farmers and merchants preferred to supply the British, who could pay handsomely, than to do business with financially strapped Congress. What little did reach the army often was food too rancid to eat or clothing too rotten to wear. Perhaps 2,500 perished at Valley Forge, the victims of cold, hunger, and disease.

Why did civilians who supported the rebel cause allow the army to suffer? Probably because by the winter of 1777, the Continentals came mainly from social classes that received little consideration at any time. The respectable, propertied farmers and artisans who had laid siege to Boston in 1775 had stopped enlisting. Serving in their stead were single men in their teens and early twenties, some who joined the army out of desperation, others who were drafted, still others who were hired as substitutes for the more affluent. The landless sons of farmers, unemployed laborers, drifters, petty criminals, vagrants, indentured servants, slaves, even captured British and Hessian soldiers—all men with no other means and no other choice—were swept into the Continental Army. The social composition of the rebel rank and file had come to resemble that of the British army. It is the great irony of the Revolution: a war to protect liberty and property was waged by those Americans who were poorest and least free.

The beginning of spring in 1778 brought a reprieve. Supplies arrived at Valley Forge, and so did a fellow calling himself Baron von Steuben, a penniless Prussian soldier of fortune. Although Washington's men had shown spirit and resilience ever since Trenton, they still lacked discipline and training. Those defects and more von Steuben began to remedy. Barking orders and spewing curses in German and French, the baron (and his translators)

Winding Down the War in the North

Would the American colonies have won their independence without the military assistance of France?

>> The Revolution widened into a global war after 1778. Preparing to fight France and Spain dictated a new British strategy in America. No longer could the British concentrate on crushing the Continental Army; instead they would disperse their forces to fend off challenges all over the world. In May Sir Henry Clinton replaced William Howe as commander in chief and received orders to withdraw from Philadelphia to New York City.

drilled the rebel regiments to march in formation and to handle their bayonets like proper Prussian soldiers. By the summer of 1778, morale had rebounded.

Spoiling for action after their long winter, Washington's army, now numbering nearly 13,500, harassed Clinton's army as it marched overland from Philadelphia to New York. On June 28 at Monmouth Courthouse, a long, confused battle ended in a draw. After both armies retired for the night, Clinton's forces slipped away to safety in New York City. Washington pursued, but he lacked the numbers to launch an all-out assault on New York City.

During the two hard winters that followed, resentments mounted among the rank and file over spoiled food, inadequate clothing, and arrears in pay. The army retaliated with **mutinies**. Between 1779 and 1780 officers managed to quell uprisings in three New England regiments. But in

mutiny refusal of rank-and-file soldiers to follow the commands of their superior officers.

January 1781 both the Pennsylvania and the New Jersey lines mutinied outright and marched on Philadelphia, where Congress had reconvened. Order returned only after Congress promised back pay and provisions and Washington put two ringleaders in front of a firing squad.

War in the West

War in the West >> The battles between Washington's Continentals and the British made the war in the West seem, by comparison, a sideshow of attacks and counterattacks that settled little. American fighters such as George Rogers Clark, captured outposts such as Kaskaskia and Vincennes, without materially affecting the outcome of the war. Yet the conflict sparked a tremendous upheaval in the West, both from the dislocations of war and from the disease that spread in war's wake.

The disruptions were so widespread because the "War for Independence" had also become a war involving the imperial powers of Britain, France, and Spain. Those European powers and the United States pressed Indian tribes to become allies and attacked them when they did not. Caught in the crossfire, some Indian nations were pushed to the brink of their own civil war, splitting into pro-American or British factions.

Indians understood that the pressures of war always threatened to deprive them of their homelands. "You are drawing so close to us that we can almost hear the noise of your axes felling our Trees," one Shawnee told the Americans. Thousands fled the raids and counter-raids, while whole villages relocated. Hundreds made their way even beyond the Mississippi, to seek shelter in territory claimed by Spain.

The political instability was vastly compounded by a smallpox epidemic that broke out first among American troops besieging Quebec in 1775. The disease soon spread to Washington's troops in New England and then south along the coast; it eventually reached

THE SMALLPOX PANDEMIC, 1775–1782

Smallpox spread across North America beginning late in 1775 as American forces attacked the city of Quebec in Canada. The routes of transmission give only a rough idea of the disease's impact, as it moved down the eastern seaboard and around the Gulf of Mexico, and then penetrated the interior, where the scattered surviving data make the pandemic harder to track. But the ravages of smallpox, combined with the disruptions sparked by the western raids of the Revolutionary War, placed severe stress on Indian peoples all across the continent.

New Orleans and leapt to Mexico City by the autumn of 1779. From New Orleans it spread via fur traders up the Mississippi River and across the central plains, and from New Spain northward as well. By the time the pandemic burned out in 1782, it had felled over 130,000. By contrast, the Revolutionary War caused the deaths of some 8,000 soldiers while fighting in battle and another 13,000 from disease, including the mortality from smallpox.

The Home Front in the North >> By 1779

most northern civilians along the eastern seaboard gained a respite from the war. But disease and military demands disrupted family economies throughout the countryside. The seasons of intense fighting drew men off into military service just when their labor was most needed on family farms. Wives and daughters were left to assume the work of husbands and sons while coping with loneliness, anxiety, and grief. Often enough, the disruptions, flight, and loss of family members left lasting scars. Two years after she fled before Burgoyne's advance into upstate New York, Ann Eliza Bleecker confessed to a friend, "I muse so long on the dead until I am unfit for the company of the living."

Despite these hardships, many women vigorously supported the revolutionary cause in a variety of ways. The Daughters of Liberty joined in harassing those who opposed the rebel cause. One outspoken loyalist found himself surrounded by angry women who stripped off his shirt, covered him with molasses, and plastered him with flower petals. In more genteel fashion, groups of well-to-do women collected not only money but medicines, food, and pewter to melt for bullets.

THE STRUGGLE IN THE SOUTH

By the autumn of 1778, the British had come to believe that their most vital aim was to regain their colonies in the mainland South. The Chesapeake and the Carolinas were more profitable to the empire and more strategically important, being so much closer to rich British sugar islands in the West Indies. Inspired by this new "southern strategy," Clinton dispatched forces to the Caribbean and Florida. In addition, the British laid plans for a new offensive drive into the Carolinas and Virginia.

English politicians and generals believed that the war could be won in the South. Loyalists were numerous, they believed, especially in the backcountry, where resentment of the seaboard, a rebel stronghold, would breed readiness among frontier folk to take up arms for the king at the first show of British force. And southern rebels—especially the vulnerable planters along the coast—could not afford to turn their guns away from their slaves. So, at least, the British theorized. All that was needed, they concluded, was for the British army to establish a beachhead in the South and then, in league with loyalists, drive northward, pacifying the population while pressing up the coast.

The Siege of Charleston >> The southern

strategy worked well for a short time in a small place. In November 1778 Clinton sent 3,500 troops to Savannah, Georgia. The resistance in the tiny colony quickly collapsed, and a large number of loyalists turned out to help the British. Encouraged by that success, the British moved on to South Carolina.

During the last days of 1779, an expedition under Clinton himself set sail from New York City. Landing off the Georgia coast, his troops mucked through the swamps to the peninsula lying between the Ashley and the Cooper rivers. At the tip of that neck of land stood Charleston, and the British began to lay siege. By then, an unseasonably warm spring had set in, making the area a heaven for mosquitoes and a hell for human beings. Sweltering and swatting, redcoats weighted down in their woolen uniforms inched their siegeworks toward the city. By early May Clinton's army had closed in, and British shelling was setting fire to houses within the city. On May 12 Charleston surrendered.

Clinton sailed back to New York at the end of June 1780, leaving behind 8,300 redcoats to carry the British offensive northward to Virginia. The man charged with leading that campaign was his ambitious and able subordinate Charles, Lord Cornwallis.

The Partisan Struggle in the South >>

Cornwallis's task in the Carolinas was complicated by

the bitter animosity between rebels and loyalists there. Many Carolinians had taken sides years before Clinton's conquest of Charleston. In the summer and fall of 1775 the supporters of Congress and the new South Carolina revolutionary government mobbed, tortured, and imprisoned supporters of the king in the backcountry. These attacks only hardened loyalist resolve: roving bands seized ammunition, broke their leaders out of jail, and besieged rebel outposts. But within a matter of months, a combined force of rebel militias from the coast and the frontier managed to defeat loyalist forces in the backcountry.

With the fall of Charleston in 1780, the loyalist movement on the frontier returned to life. Out of loyalist vengefulness and rebel desperation issued the brutal civil war that seared the southern backcountry after 1780. Neighbors and even family members fought and killed each other as members of roaming rebel and tory militias. The intensity of **partisan warfare** in the backcountry produced unprecedented destruction. All of society, observed one minister, "seems to be at an end. Every person keeps close on his own plantation. Robberies and murders are often committed on the public roads. . . . Poverty, want, and hardship appear in almost every countenance."

partisan warfare armed clashes among political rivals, typically involving guerilla fighting and the violent intimidation of civilians by militias.

Cornwallis, when confronted with the chaos, erred fatally. He did nothing to stop his loyalist allies or his own troops from mistreating civilians. A Carolina loyalist admitted that "the lower sort of People, who were in many parts originally attached to the British Government, have suffered so severely . . . that Great Britain has now a hundred enemies, where it had one before."

A growing number of civilians outraged by the king's men cast their lot with the rebels. That upsurge of popular support enabled Francis Marion, the "Swamp Fox," and his band of white and black raiders to cut British lines of communication between Charleston and the interior. It mobilized the "over-the-mountain men," a rebel militia in western Carolina, who claimed victory at the Battle of King's Mountain in October 1780. By the end of 1780, these successes had persuaded most civilians that only the rebels could restore order.

If rebel fortunes prospered in the partisan struggle, they faltered in the conventional warfare being waged at the same time in the South. In August 1780 the Continentals commanded by Horatio Gates lost a major engagement to the British force at Camden, South Carolina. In the fall of 1780 Congress replaced Gates with Washington's candidate for the southern command, Nathanael Greene, an energetic, 38-year-old Rhode Islander and a veteran of the northern campaigns.

Greene Takes Command >> Greene bore out Washington's confidence by grasping the military situation in the South. He understood the needs of his 1,400 hungry, ragged, and demoralized troops and instructed von Steuben to lobby Virginia for food and clothing. He understood the importance of the rebel militias and sent Lieutenant Colonel Henry "Lighthorse Harry" Lee to assist Marion's raids. He understood the weariness of southern

WITNESS
Partisan War in the Backcountry

"I was invited by some of my comrades to go and see some of the prisoners. We went to where six were standing together. Some discussion was taking place, I heard some of our men cry out, "Remember Buford," [a rebel] soldier killed by loyalists and the prisoners were immediately hewed to pieces with broadswords."

Legend:
→ American forces
⭐ American victory
⭐ British victory
x Major skirmishes of the partisan conflict in the backcountry

THE FIGHTING IN THE SOUTH, 1780–1781

In December 1780 Nathanael Greene made the crucial decision to split his army, sending Daniel Morgan west, where he defeated the pursuing Banastre Tarleton at Cowpens. Meanwhile, Greene regrouped and replenished at Cheraw, keeping Cornwallis off balance with a raid (dotted line) toward Charleston and the coast. Then, with Cornwallis in hot pursuit, Greene and Morgan rejoined at Salisbury, retreating into Virginia. Cornwallis was worn down in this vain pursuit and lost three-quarters of the troops he began with before finally abandoning the Carolina campaign.

civilians and prevented his men from plundering the countryside.

Above all, Greene understood that his forces could never hold the field against the whole British army. That led him to break the first rule of conventional warfare: he divided his army. In December 1780 he dispatched to western South Carolina a detachment of 600 men under the command of Brigadier General Daniel Morgan of Virginia.

Back at the British camp, Cornwallis worried that Morgan and his rebels, if left unchecked, might rally the entire backcountry against the British. On the other hand, Cornwallis reckoned that he could not commit his entire army to the pursuit of Morgan's men, for then Greene and his troops might retake Charleston. The only solution, unconventional to be sure, was for Cornwallis to divide his army. That he did, sending Lieutenant Colonel Banastre Tarleton and 1,100 men west after Morgan. Cornwallis had played right into Greene's hands: the rebel troops might be able to defeat a British army split into two pieces. For two weeks Morgan led Tarleton's troops on a breakneck chase across the Carolina countryside. In January 1781 at an open meadow called Cowpens, Morgan routed Tarleton's force.

Now Cornwallis took up the chase. Morgan and Greene joined forces and agreed to keep going north until the British army wore out. Cornwallis finally stopped at Hillsboro, North Carolina, but few local loyalists responded to his call for reinforcements. To ensure that loyalist ranks remained thin, Greene decided to make a show of force near the tiny village of Guilford Courthouse. On a brisk March day the two sides joined battle, each sustaining severe casualties before Greene was forced to retreat. But the high cost of victory convinced Cornwallis that he could not put down the rebellion in the Carolinas.

Although Nathanael Greene's command provided the Continentals with effective leadership in the South, it was the resilience of rebel militias that thwarted the British offensive in the Carolinas. Many Continental Army officers complained about the militia's lack of discipline, its habit of melting away when homesickness set in or harvest approached, and its record of cowardice under fire in conventional engagements. But when set the task of ambushing supply trains and dispatch riders, harrying bands of local loyalists, or making forays against isolated British outposts, the militia came through. Many southern civilians refused to join the British or to provide the redcoats with food and information because they knew that once the British army left their neighborhoods, the rebel militia would always be back. The Continental Army in the South lost many conventional battles, but the militia kept the British from restoring political control over the backcountry.

African Americans in the Age of Revolution >> The British also lost in the Carolinas because they did not seek greater support from those southerners who would have fought for liberty with the British: African American slaves.

Black Americans, virtually all in bondage, made up one-third of the population between Delaware and Georgia. Since the beginning of the resistance to Britain, white southerners had worried that the watchwords of liberty and equality would spread to the slave quarters. Gripped by the fear of slave rebellion, southern revolutionaries began to take precautions. Marylanders disarmed black inhabitants and issued extra guns to the white militia. Charlestonians hanged and then burned the body of Thomas Jeremiah, a free black who was convicted of spreading the word to others that the British "were coming to help the poor Negroes."

Southern whites fully expected the British to turn slave rebelliousness to their strategic advantage. As early as 1775, Virginia's royal governor, Lord Dunmore, confirmed white fears by offering to free any slave who joined the British. When Clinton invaded the South in 1779, he renewed that offer. According to Janet Schaw, an Englishwoman visiting her brother's North Carolina plantation, the neighbors had heard that loyalists were "promising every Negro that would murder his master and family he should have his Master's plantation" and that "the Negroes have got it amongst them and believe it to be true."

But in Britain there was overwhelming opposition to organizing support among African Americans. British leaders dismissed Dunmore's ambitious scheme to raise a black army of 10,000 and another plan to create a sanctuary for black loyalists on the southeastern coast. Turning slaves against masters, they recognized, was not the way to conciliate southern whites.

Even so, southern fears of insurrection made the rebels reluctant to enlist black Americans as soldiers. At first, Congress barred African Americans from the Continental Army. But as the rebels became more desperate for manpower, policy changed. Northern states actively encouraged black enlistments, and in the Upper South, some states allowed free men of color to join the army or permitted slaves to substitute for their masters.

Slaves themselves sought freedom from whichever side seemed most likely to grant it. Perhaps 10,000 slaves took up Dunmore's offer in 1775 and deserted their masters, and thousands more flocked to Clinton's forces after the fall of Charleston.

For many runaways the hope of liberation proved an illusion. Although some served the British army as laborers, spies, and soldiers, many died of disease in army camps (upward of 27,000 by one estimate) or were sold back into slavery in the West Indies. About 5,000 black soldiers served in the revolutionary army in the hope of gaining freedom. In addition, the number of runaways to the North soared during the Revolution. In total, perhaps 100,000 men and women—nearly a fifth of the total slave population—attempted to escape bondage. Their odysseys to freedom took some to far-flung destinations: loyalist communities in Nova Scotia, a settlement established by the British in Sierra Leone on the West African coast, even the Botany Bay penal colony in Australia.

THE WORLD TURNED UPSIDE DOWN

Despite his losses in the Carolinas, Cornwallis still believed that he could score a decisive victory against the Continental Army. The theater he chose for that showdown

was the Chesapeake. During the spring of 1781, he and his army joined forces along the Virginia coast with the hero of Saratoga and newly turned loyalist, Benedict Arnold. Embarrassed by debt and disgusted by Congress's shabby treatment of the Continental Army, Arnold had started exchanging rebel secrets for British money in 1779 before defecting outright in 1780. By June of 1781 Arnold and Cornwallis were fortifying a site on the tip of the peninsula formed by the York and the James rivers, a place called Yorktown.

Meanwhile, Washington and his French ally, the comte de Rochambeau, met in Connecticut to plan a major attack. Rochambeau urged a coordinated land-sea assault on the Virginia coast. Washington insisted instead on a full-scale offensive against New York City. Just when the rebel commander was about to have his way, word arrived that a French fleet under the comte de Grasse was sailing for the Chesapeake to blockade Cornwallis by sea. Washington's Continentals headed south.

Surrender at Yorktown >> By the end of September, 7,800 Frenchmen, 5,700 Continentals, and 3,200 militia had sandwiched Yorktown between the devil of an allied army and the deep blue sea of French warships. "If you cannot relieve me very soon," Cornwallis wrote to Clinton, "you must expect to hear the worst." The British navy did arrive—but seven days after Cornwallis surrendered to the rebels on October 19, 1781.

It need not have ended at Yorktown, but timing made all the difference. At the end of 1781 and early in 1782, the

<< On September 30, 1780, a wagon bearing this two-faced effigy was drawn through the streets of Philadelphia. The effigy represents Benedict Arnold, who sits between a gallows and the devil. Note the similarities between this piece of street theater and the demonstrations mounted on Pope's Day several decades earlier, shown on page 110.

British army received setbacks in the other theaters of the war: India, the West Indies, and Florida. The French and the Spanish were everywhere in Europe as well, gathering in the English Channel, planning a major offensive against Gibraltar. The cost of the fighting was already enormous. British leaders recognized that the rest of the empire was at stake and set about cutting their losses in America.

The Treaty of Paris, signed on September 3, 1783, was a diplomatic triumph for the American negotiators: Benjamin Franklin, John Adams, and John Jay. They dangled before Britain the possibility that a generous settlement might weaken American ties to France. The British jumped at the bait. They recognized the independence of the United States and agreed to ample boundaries for the new nation: the Mississippi River on the west, the 31st parallel on the south, and the present border of Canada on the north. American negotiators then persuaded a skeptical France to approve the treaty by arguing that, as allies, they were bound to present a united front to the British. When the French finally persuaded Spain, the third member of the alliance, to reduce its demands on Britain for territorial concessions, the treaty became an accomplished fact. The Spanish settled for Florida and Minorca, an island in the Mediterranean.

Those present at Yorktown on that clear autumn afternoon in 1781 watched as the British second-in-command to Cornwallis (who had sent word that he was "indisposed") surrendered his superior's sword. He offered the sword first, in a face-saving gesture, to the French commander Rochambeau, who politely refused and pointed to Washington. But the American commander in chief, out of a mixture of military protocol, nationalistic pride, and perhaps even wit, pointed to his second-in-command, Benjamin Lincoln.

Some witnesses recalled that British musicians arrayed on the Yorktown green played "The World Turned Upside Down." Their recollections may have been faulty, but the story has persisted as part of the folklore of the American Revolution. The world had, it seemed, turned upside down with the coming of American independence. The colonial rebels shocked the British with their answer to the question: would they fight?

The answer had been yes—but on their own terms. By 1777 most propertied Americans avoided fighting in the Continental Army. Yet whenever the war reached their homes, farms, and businesses, many Americans gave their allegiance to the new nation by turning out with rifles or supplying homespun clothing, food, or ammunition. They rallied around Washington in New Jersey, Gates in upstate New York, Greene in the Carolinas. Middle-class American men fought, some from idealism, others out of self-interest, but always on their own terms, as members of the militia. These citizen-soldiers turned the world upside down by defeating professional armies.

Of course, the militia did not bear the brunt of the fighting. That responsibility fell to the Continental Army, which by 1777 drew its strength from the poorest ranks of American society. Yet even the Continentals, for all their desperation, managed to fight on their own terms. Some asserted their rights by raising mutinies, until Congress redressed their grievances. All of them; as the Baron von Steuben observed, behaved differently than European soldiers did. Americans followed orders only if the logic of commands was explained to them. The Continentals, held in

Some witnesses recalled that British musicians arrayed on the Yorktown green played "The World Turned Upside Down."

contempt by most Americans, turned the world upside down by sensing their power and asserting their measure of personal independence.

Americans of African descent dared as much and more in their quests for liberty. Whether they chose to escape slavery by fighting for the British or the Continentals or by striking out on their own as runaways, their defiance, too, turned the world upside down. Among the tens of thousands of slaves who would not be mastered was one Henry Washington, a native of Africa who became the slave of George Washington in 1763. But Henry Washington made his own declaration of independence in 1776, slipping behind British lines and serving as a corporal in a black unit. Thereafter, like thousands of former slaves, he sought to build a new life elsewhere in the Atlantic world, settling first in Nova Scotia and finally in Sierra Leone. By 1800 he headed a community of former slaves who were exiled to the outskirts of that colony for their determined efforts to win republican self-government from Sierra Leone's white British rulers. Like Thomas Paine, Henry Washington believed that freedom was his only country.

In all those ways, a revolutionary generation turned the world upside down. They were a diverse lot— descended from Indians, Europeans, and Africans, driven by desperation or idealism or greed—but joined, even if they did not recognize it, by their common struggle to break free from the rule of monarchs or masters. What now awaited them in the world of the new United States?

CHAPTER SUMMARY

The American Revolution brought independence to Britain's former colonies after an armed struggle that began in 1775 and concluded with the Treaty of Paris in 1783.

- When the Second Continental Congress convened in the spring of 1775, many of the delegates still hoped for reconciliation— even as they approved the creation of the Continental Army.
- The Second Continental Congress adopted the Declaration of Independence on July 4, 1776, hoping that they could count on a majority of Americans to support the Revolution.
- The British scored a string of victories in the North throughout 1776 and 1777, capturing both New York and Philadelphia.
- The British suffered a disastrous defeat at the Battle of Saratoga in early 1778, which prompted France to openly ally with the American rebels soon thereafter.
- By 1780 Britain aimed to win the war by claiming the South and captured both Savannah, Georgia, and Charleston, South Carolina.
- The Continental Army in the South, led by Nathanael Greene, foiled the British strategy, and Cornwallis surrendered to Washington after the Battle of Yorktown in 1781.
- Except for the first year of fighting, the rank and file of the Continental Army was drawn from the poorest Americans, whose needs for food, clothing, and shelter were neglected by the Continental Congress.

Significant Events

Second Continental Congress convenes at Philadelphia; Congress creates the Continental Army; Battle of Bunker Hill

British summer drive to occupy Philadelphia; battles of Brandywine Creek, Germantown; Burgoyne surrenders at Saratoga; Continental Army encamps for winter at Valley Forge

1775

1776

1777

Publication of *Common Sense*; British troops evacuate Boston; Declaration of Independence; British occupy New York City, forcing Washington to retreat through New Jersey into Pennsylvania; Washington counterattacks at Battle of Trenton

Additional Reading

The outstanding military histories of the American Revolution are Don Higginbotham, *The War for American Independence* (1971), and Robert Middlekauff, *The Glorious Cause, 1763 to 1789* (1982). Both provide a wealth of detail about battles, contending armies, and the role of militias and civilian populations in the fighting. For a compelling treatment of the lives of soldiers in the Continental Army, read Caroline Cox, *A Proper Sense of Honor* (2004), and to become better acquainted with their commander-in-chief, turn to *His Excellency: George Washington* (2004) by Joseph Ellis. Colin Calloway, *The American Revolution in Indian Country* (1995), offers a fine summary of the role of American Indians in that conflict, and for a broader historical perspective on the strategies of Indian nations during the decades surrounding the Revolution, see Gregory Evans Dowd, *A Spirited Resistance* (1992). Benjamin Franklin's efforts to secure an alliance with France come in for lively chronicling by Stacy Schiff in *A Great Improvisation* (2005), and the best introductions to the influence of the American Revolution within the wider Atlantic world are Lester Langley, *The Americas in the Age of Revolution, 1750–1850* (1996), and a collection of essays edited by Eliga Gould and Peter Onuf, *Empire and Nation* (2004). Impressive interpretations of the war's impact on American society include Charles Royster, *A Revolutionary People at War* (1979), and John Shy, *A People Numerous and Armed* (1976). Sylvia Frey offers a thoughtful history of African Americans during this era in *Water from the Rock* (1991), and Cassandra Pybus, *Epic Journeys of Freedom* (2006), recounts the experiences of runaway slaves who seized on the wartime crisis to gain liberty. The role of women in revolutionary America receives excellent coverage in Carol Berkin, *Revolutionary Mothers* (2005), and in Mary Beth Norton's classic study, *Liberty's Daughters* (1980).

British occupy Charleston; partisan warfare of Marion, Sumter; rebel victory at King's Mountain, South Carolina; Nathanael Greene takes southern command

Treaty of Paris

1778   **1780**   **1781**   **1783**

France allies with rebel Americans; France and Britain declare war; British shift focus to the South; Savannah falls

Engagements at Cowpens, Guilford Courthouse; Cornwallis surrenders at Yorktown

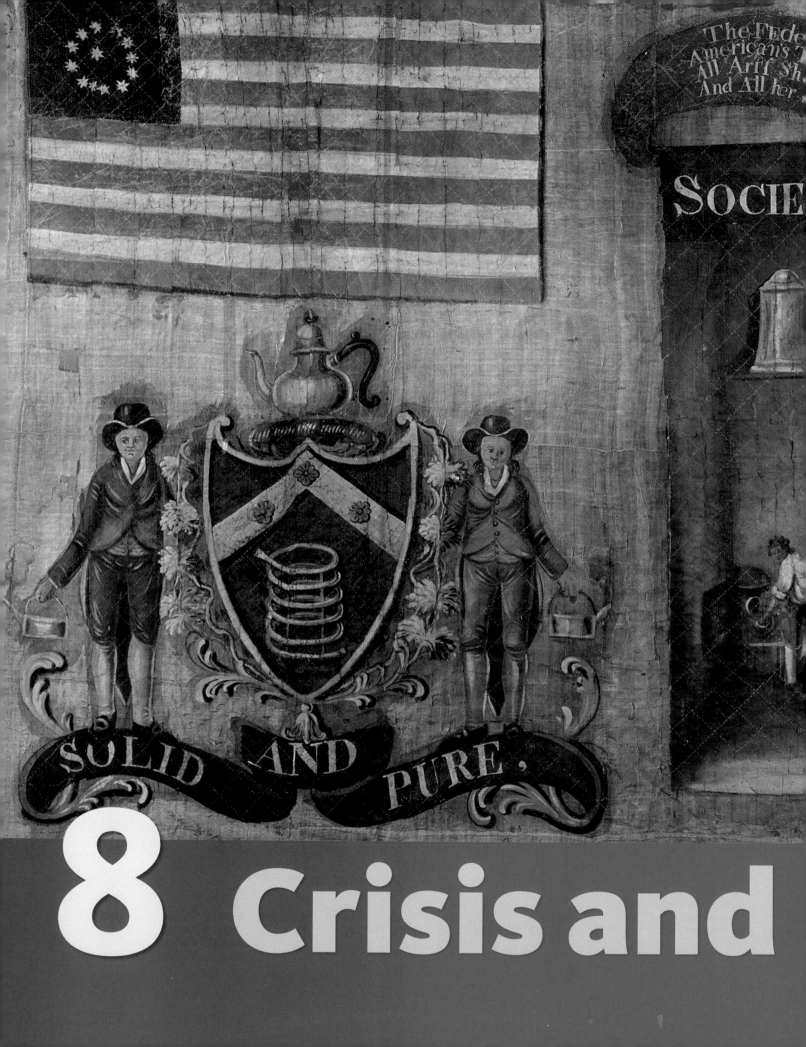

The Fede
American's
All Artif. Sh
And All her.

SOCIE

SOLID AND PURE.

8 Crisis and

WHAT'S TO COME

140 **REPUBLICAN EXPERIMENTS**

142 **THE TEMPTATIONS OF PEACE**

148 **REPUBLICAN SOCIETY**

151 **FROM CONFEDERATION TO CONSTITUTION**

"THESE UNITED STATES"

"**I** am not "a Virginian, but an American,"
Patrick Henry declared in the Virginia
House of Burgesses. Mosts likely he
was lying. Certainly no one listening took him seriously,
for the newly independent colonists did not identify
themselves as members of a nation. They would have said,
as did Thomas Jefferson, "Virginia, Sir, is my country." Or
as John Adams wrote to another native son, "Massachusetts is our country." Jefferson and Adams were men of
wide political vision and experience: both were leaders
in the Continental Congress and more inclined than most
to think nationally. But like other members of the revolutionary generation, they identified deeply with their
home states and even more deeply with their home counties and towns. **»**

The Revolution instilled in many humble folk a new sense of pride and
potential. Typical of such people was the New York Society of Pewter-
ers; their banner celebrates "The Federal Plan Most Solid & Secure /
Americans Their Freedom Will Ensure / All Art Shall Flourish in Columbia's Land / And All her Sons Join as One Social Band."

1776—1789

Constitution

It followed that allegiance to the states, not the Union, determined the shape of the first republican political experiments.

For a decade after independence, the revolutionaries were less committed to creating an American nation than to organizing 13 separate state republics. The Declaration of Independence referred explicitly not to the United States but to these United States. It envisioned not one republic so much as a federation of 13.

Only when peace was restored during the decade of the 1780s were Americans forced to face some unanswered questions raised by their revolution. The Declaration proclaimed that these "free and independent states" had "full power to levy war, conclude peace, contract alliances, establish commerce." Did that mean that New Jersey could sign a trade agreement with France, excluding the other states? If the United States were to be more than a loose federation, how could it assert power on a national scale? Similarly, American borderlands to the west presented problems. If these territories were settled by Americans, would they eventually join the United States? Go their own ways as independent nations? Become new colonies of Spain or England?

Such problems were more than political; they were rooted in social realities. For a political union to succeed, the inhabitants of 13 separate states had to start thinking of themselves as Americans. When it came right down to it, what united a Vermont farmer working his rocky fields and a South Carolina gentleman presiding over a vast rice plantation? What bonds existed between a Kentuckian rafting the Ohio River and a Salem merchant sailing to China for porcelain?

And in a society in which all citizens were said to be "created equal," social inequalities had to be confronted. How could women participate in the Revolution's bid for freedom if they were not free to vote or to hold property? How would free or enslaved African Americans live in a republic based on equality? How could black Americans feel a bond with white Americans when so often the only existing bonds had been forged with chains? **‹‹**

To such questions there were no final answers in 1781. There was ferment, excitement, and experimentation as 13 states each sought to create their governments anew; as Americans—or rather, Virginians and New Yorkers and Georgians and citizens of other countries—began to imagine how the revolutionary virtue of equality might transform their societies. But as the decade progressed, the sense of crisis deepened.

REPUBLICAN EXPERIMENTS

After independence was declared in July 1776, many of America's best political minds turned to draw up **constitutions** for their individual states. In truth, the state constitu-

constitution framework of government establishing the contract between rulers and ruled.

tions were crucial republican experiments, the first efforts at establishing a government of and by the people. All the revolutionaries agreed that the people—not a king or a few privileged aristocrats—should rule. Yet they were equally certain that republican governments were best suited to small territories. They believed that the new United States was too sprawling and its people too diverse to be safely consolidated into a single national republic. They feared, too, that the government of a large republic would inevitably grow indifferent to popular concerns, being distant from many of its citizens. Without being under the watchful eye of the people, representatives would become less accountable to the electorate and turn tyrannical. A federation of small state republics, they reasoned, would stand a far better chance of enduring.

The State Constitutions ›› The new state constitutions retained the basic form of their old colonial governments, most providing for a governor and a bicameral legislature. But most states dramatically changed the balance of power among the different branches of government.

From the republican perspective in 1776, the greatest problem of any government lay in curbing executive power. What had driven Americans into rebellion was the abuse of authority by the king and his appointed officials. To ensure that the executive could never again threaten popular liberty, the new states either accorded almost no power to their governors or abolished that office entirely. The governors had no authority to convene or dissolve the legislature. They could not veto the

↑ Americans responded to independence with rituals of "killing the king," as did this New York crowd in 1776, which is pulling down a statue of George III. Americans also expressed their mistrust of monarchs by establishing state governments with weak executive branches.

legislatures' laws, grant land, or erect courts. Most important, governors had few powers to appoint other state officials. All these limits were designed to deprive the executive of any patronage or other form of influence over the legislature.

What the state governors lost, the legislatures gained. To ensure that those powerful legislatures truly represented the will of the people, the new state constitutions called for annual elections and required candidates for the legislature to live in the district they represented. Many states even asserted the right of voters to instruct the men elected to office how to vote on specific issues. Although no state granted universal manhood suffrage, most reduced the amount of property required of qualified voters. Finally, state supreme courts were also either elected by the legislatures or appointed by an elected governor.

With all power vested in popular assemblies, a majority of voters within a state could do whatever they wanted, unchecked by governors or courts—which opened the door for legislatures to turn as tyrannical as governors. But the revolutionaries brushed that prospect aside: republican theory assured them that the people possessed a generous share of civic virtue, the capacity for selfless pursuit of the general welfare.

In an equally momentous change, the revolutionaries insisted on written state constitutions. Whenever government appeared to exceed the limits of its authority, Americans wanted to have at hand the written contract between rulers and ruled. When eighteenth-century Englishmen used the word constitution, they meant the existing arrangement of government—not an actual document but a collection of parliamentary laws, customs, and precedents. But Americans believed that a constitution should be a written code that stood apart from and above government, a yardstick against which the people measured the performance of their rulers. After all, they reasoned, if Britain's constitution had been written down, available for all to consult, would American rights have been violated?

From Congress to Confederation >>

While Americans lavished attention on their state constitutions, the national government nearly languished during the decade after 1776. With the coming of independence, the Second Continental Congress conducted the common business of the federated states. It created and maintained the Continental Army, issued currency, and negotiated with foreign powers.

But while Congress acted as a central government by common consent, it lacked any legal basis for its authority. To redress that need, in July 1776 Congress appointed a committee to draft a constitution for a national government. The urgent business of waging the war made for delay, but Congress approved the first national constitution in November 1777. It took four more years—until February 1781—for all of the states to ratify these Articles of Confederation.

The Articles of Confederation provided for a government by a national legislature—essentially a continuation of the Second Continental Congress. That body had the authority to declare war and make peace, conduct diplomacy, regulate Indian affairs, appoint military and naval officers, and requisition men from the states. In affairs of finance it could coin money and issue paper currency. Extensive as these responsibilities were, Congress could not levy taxes or even regulate trade. The crucial power of the purse rested entirely with the states, as did the final power to make and execute laws. Even worse, the national government had no distinct executive branch. Congressional committees, constantly changing in their membership,

Should the electoral college be abolished?

>> As the stumps dotting the landscape indicate, western farmers first sought to "improve" their acreage by felling trees. But their dwellings were far less substantial than those depicted in this idealized sketch of an "American New Cleared Farm." And although some Indians guided parties of whites into the West, as shown in the foreground, more often they resisted white encroachment. For that reason, dogs, here perched placidly in canoes, were trained to alert their white masters to the approach of Indians.

not only had to make laws but had to administer and enforce them as well.

Those weaknesses appear more evident in hindsight. For Congress in 1777 it was no easy task to frame a new government in the midst of a war. And most American leaders in the 1770s had given little thought to federalism, the means by which political power could be divided among the states and the national government. In any case, creating a strong national government would have antagonized many Americans, who after all had just rebelled against the distant, centralized authority of Britain's king and Parliament.

Guided by republican political theory and by their colonial experience, American revolutionaries created a loose confederation of 13 independent state republics under a nearly powerless national government. They succeeded so well that the United States almost failed to survive its first decade of independence. The problem was that lessons from the colonial past were not always useful guides to postwar realities. Only when events forced Americans to think nationally did they begin to consider the possibility of reinventing "these United States"—this time under the yoke of a truly federal republic.

THE TEMPTATIONS OF PEACE

The surrender of Cornwallis at Yorktown in 1781 marked the end of military crisis in America. But as the threat from Britain receded, so did the source of American unity. The many differences among Americans, most of which lay submerged during the struggle for independence, surfaced in full force. Those domestic divisions, combined with challenges to the new nation from Britain and Spain, created conflicts that neither the states nor the national government proved equal to handling.

The Temptations of the West >> The greatest opportunities and the greatest problems for postwar Americans awaited in the rapidly expanding West. With the boundary of the new United States now set at the Mississippi River, more settlers spilled across the

Appalachians, planting farmsteads and towns throughout Ohio, Kentucky, and Tennessee. By 1790 places that had been almost uninhabited by whites in 1760 held more than 2.25 million people, one-third of the nation's population.

After the Revolution, as before, western settlement fostered intense conflict. American claims that its territory stretched all the way to the Mississippi were by no means taken for granted by European and Indian powers. The West also confronted Americans with questions about their own national identity. Would the newly settled territories enter the nation as states on an equal footing with the original 13 states? Would they be ruled as dependent colonies? The fate of the West, in other words, constituted a crucial test of whether "these" United States could grow and still remain united.

Foreign Intrigues >> Both the British from their base in Canada and the Spanish in Florida and Louisiana hoped to chisel away at American borders. Their considerable success in the 1780s exposed the weakness of Confederation diplomacy.

Before the ink was dry on the Treaty of Paris, Britain's ministers were secretly instructing Canadians to maintain their forts and trading posts inside the United States' northwestern frontier. They reckoned—correctly—that with the Continental Army disbanded, the Confederation could not force the British to withdraw.

The British also made mischief along the Confederation's northern borders, mainly with Vermont. For decades, Ethan Allen and his Green Mountain Boys had waged a war of nerves with neighboring New York, which claimed Vermont as part of its territory. After the Revolution the British tried to woo Vermont into their empire as a province of Canada, a flirtation which pressured Congress into granting Vermont statehood in 1791.

The loyalty of the southwestern frontier was even less certain. By 1790 more than 100,000 settlers had poured through the Cumberland Gap to reach Kentucky and Tennessee. But the commercial possibilities of the region depended entirely on access to the Mississippi and the port of New Orleans, since it was far too costly to ship southwestern produce over the rough trails east across the Appalachians. And the Mississippi route was still dominated by the Spanish, who controlled Louisiana as well as forts along western Mississippi shores as far north as St. Louis. The Spanish, seeing their opportunity, closed the Mississippi to American navigation in 1784. That action prompted serious talk among southwesterners about seceding from the United States and joining Spain's empire.

The Spanish also tried to strengthen their hold on North America by making common cause with the Indians. Of particular concern to both groups was protecting Spanish Florida from the encroachment of American settlers filtering south from Georgia. Florida's governor complained that those backwoods folk were "distinguished from savages only in their color, language, and the superiority of their depraved cunning and untrustworthiness." So Spanish colonial officials responded eagerly to the overtures of Alexander McGillivray, a young Indian leader whose mother was of French-Creek descent and whose father was a Scots trader. His efforts brought about a treaty of alliance between the Creeks and the Spanish in 1784, quickly followed by similar alliances with the Choctaws and the Chickasaws.

Disputes among the States

>> As if foreign intrigues were not divisive enough, the states continued to argue among themselves over western land claims. The old royal charters for some colonies had extended their boundaries all the way to the Mississippi and beyond. (See the map, below.) But the charters were often vague, granting both Massachusetts and Virginia, for example, undisputed possession of present-day Wisconsin. In contrast, other charters limited state boundaries to within a few hundred miles of the Atlantic coast. "Landed" states like Virginia wanted to secure control over the large territory granted by their charters. "Landless" states (which included

landed states and landless states some of the 13 colonies that became the United States had originally been granted land whose western boundaries were vague or overlapped the land granted to other colonies. During the Confederation period, the so-called "landless" states had boundaries that were firmly drawn on all sides, such as Maryland, New Jersey, and Massachusetts. "Landed" states possessed grants whose western boundaries were not fixed.

Maryland, Delaware, Pennsylvania, Rhode Island, and New Jersey) called on Congress to restrict the boundaries of landed states and to convert western lands into a domain administered by the Confederation.

The landless states lost the opening round of the contest over ownership of the West. The Articles of Confederation acknowledged the

WESTERN LAND CLAIMS, 1782–1802

The Confederation's settlement of conflicting western land claims was an achievement essential to the consolidation of political union. Some states asserted that their original charters extended their western borders to the Mississippi River. A few states, like Virginia, claimed western borders on the Pacific Ocean.

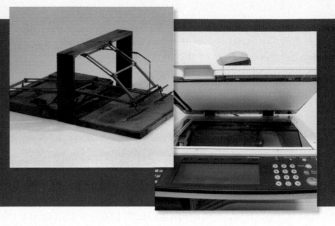

BUT HOW MANY DOTS PER INCH?

This polygraph machine represented the state-of-the-art in duplicating technology when it was patented in 1803. It could produce four copies of a handwritten page, its pens exactly following the motion of the penman's hand. Among the satisfied owners of this predecessor to the purring photocopier was Thomas Jefferson.

old charter claims of the landed states. Then Maryland, one of the smallest landless states, retaliated by refusing to ratify the Articles. Since every state had to approve the Articles before they were formally accepted, the fate of the United States hung in the balance. One by one the landed states relented. The last holdout, Virginia, in January 1781 ceded its charter rights to land north of the Ohio River.

The More Democratic West >> An even

greater source of contention concerned the sort of men westerners elected to political office. The state legislatures of the 1780s were both larger and more democratic in their membership than the old colonial assemblies were. Before the Revolution no more than a fifth of the men serving in the assemblies were middle-class farmers or artisans; government was almost exclusively the domain of the wealthiest merchants, lawyers, and planters. After the Revolution twice as many state legislators were men of moderate wealth. The shift was more marked in the North, where middle-class men predominated among representatives. But in every state, some men of modest means, humble background, and little formal education attained political power.

State legislatures became more democratic in membership mainly because as backcountry districts grew, so did the number of their representatives. Since western districts tended to be less developed economically and culturally, their leading men were less rich and cultivated than the seaboard elite.

But many eastern republican gentlemen, while endorsing government by popular consent, doubted whether ordinary people were fit to rule. The problem, they contended, was that the new western legislators concerned themselves only with the narrow interests of their constituents, not with the good of the whole state. As Ezra Stiles, the president of Yale College, observed, the new breed of politicians were those with "the all-prevailing popular talent of coaxing and flattering," who "whenever a bill is read in the legislature . . . instantly thinks how it will affect his constituents." And if state legislatures could not rise above petty bickering and narrow self-interest, how long would

it be before civic virtue and a concern for the general welfare simply withered away?

The Northwest Territory >> Such fears of

"democratic excess" also influenced policy when Congress debated what to do with the **Northwest Territory**. Carved out of the land ceded by the states to the national government, the Northwest Territory comprised the present-day states of Ohio, Indiana, Illinois, Michigan, and Wisconsin. With so many white settlers moving into these lands, Congress dealt with the issue of expansion by adopting three ordinances.

northwest territory
present-day states of Ohio, Indiana, Illinois, Michigan, and Wisconsin.

The first, drafted by Thomas Jefferson in 1784, divided the Northwest Territory into 10 states, each to be admitted to the Union on equal terms as soon as its population equaled that in any of the existing states. In the meantime, Jefferson provided for democratic self-government of the territory by all free adult males. A second ordinance of 1785 set up an efficient mechanism for dividing and selling public lands. The Northwest Territory was surveyed into townships of six miles square. Each township then was divided into 36 lots of one square mile, or 640 acres.

Congress waited in vain for buyers to flock to the land offices it established. The cost of even a single lot—$640—was too steep for most farmers. Disappointed by the shortage of buyers and desperate for money, Congress finally accepted a proposition submitted by a private company of land speculators that offered to buy some 6 million acres in present-day southeastern Ohio. That several members of Congress numbered among the company's stockholders no doubt added to enthusiasm for the deal.

The transaction concluded, Congress calmed the speculators' worries that incoming settlers might enjoy too much self-government by scrapping Jefferson's democratic design and substituting the Northwest Ordinance of 1787. That ordinance provided for a period in which Congress held sway in the territory through its appointees—a governor, a secretary, and three judges. When the population reached 5,000 free adult males, a legislature was to be established, although its laws required the governor's approval. A representative could sit in Congress but had no vote. When the population reached 60,000, the inhabitants might apply for statehood, and the whole Northwest Territory was to be divided into not less than three or more than five states. The ordinance also guaranteed basic rights—freedom of religion and trial by jury—and provided for the support of public education.

With the Northwest Ordinance in place, Congress had succeeded in extending republican government to the West and incorporating the frontier into the new nation. The Republic now had an orderly way to expand its federation of states in a way that minimized the tensions between the genteel East and the democratic West that had plagued the colonies and the Confederation throughout much of the eighteenth century. Yet ironically, the new ordinance served to heighten tensions in a different way. By limiting the spread of slavery in the northern states, Congress deepened the critical social and economic differences between the North and South, evident already in the 1780s.

The consequences of the new territorial system were also significant for hundreds of thousands of the continent's other inhabitants. In the short term, the ordinance ignored completely the rights of the Shawnee, Chippewa, and other Indian peoples who lived in the region. In the long term, the system "laid the blueprint," as one historian noted, for bringing new lands into the United States. The ordinance thus accelerated the pressures on Indian lands and aggravated the social and geographic dislocations already set in motion by disease and the western conflicts of the Revolutionary War.

Slavery and Sectionalism >> When white Americans declared their independence, they owned nearly half a million black Americans. African Americans of the revolutionary generation, most of them enslaved, constituted 20 percent of the total population of the

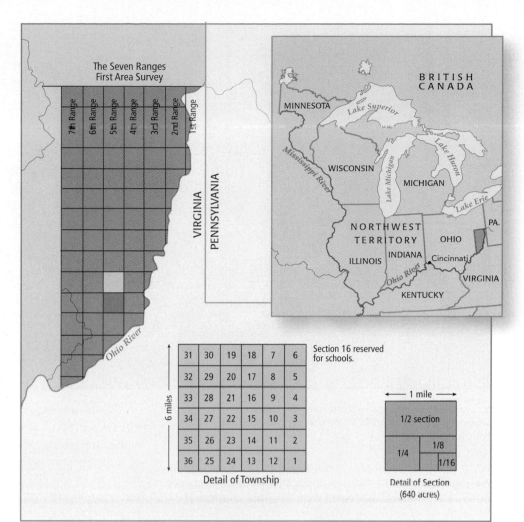

THE ORDINANCE OF 1785

Surveyors entered the Northwest Territory in September of 1785, imposing on the land regular grids of six square miles to define new townships, as shown on this range map of a portion of Ohio. Farmers purchased blocks of land within townships, each one mile square, from the federal government or from land speculators.

colonies in 1775, and nearly 90 percent of them lived in the South. Yet few political leaders directly confronted the issue of whether slavery should be permitted to exist in a truly republican society.

When political discussion did stray toward the subject of slavery, southerners—especially ardent republicans—bristled defensively. Theirs was a difficult position, riddled with contradictions. On the one hand, they had condemned parliamentary taxation as tantamount to political "slavery" and had rebelled, declaring that all men were "created equal." On the other hand, enslaved African Americans formed the basis of the South's plantation economy. To surrender slavery, southerners believed, would be to usher in economic ruin.

Some planters in the Upper South resolved the dilemma by freeing their slaves. Such decisions were made easier

⌃ *Negro Methodists Holding a Meeting in a Philadelphia Alley* evokes the vibrancy of black religious life in the city that became a haven for free African Americans.

by changing economic conditions in the Chesapeake. As planters shifted from tobacco toward wheat, a crop demanding a good deal less labor, Virginia and Maryland liberalized their manumission statutes, laws providing for freeing slaves. Between 1776 and 1789, most southern states also joined the North in prohibiting the importation of slaves, and a few antislavery societies appeared in the Upper South. But no southern state legally abolished slavery. Masters defended their right to hold human property in the name of republicanism.

Eighteenth-century republicans regarded property as crucial, for it provided a man and his family with security, status, and wealth. More important, it provided a measure of independence: to be able to act freely, without fear or favor of others. People without property were dangerous, republicans believed, because the poor could never be politically independent. Southern defenders of slavery thus argued that free, propertyless black people would pose a political threat to the liberty of propertied white citizens. Subordinating the human rights of blacks to the property rights of whites, southern republicans reached the paradoxical conclusion that their freedom depended on keeping African Americans in bondage.

The North followed a different course. Because its economy depended far less on slave labor, black emancipation did not run counter to powerful economic interests. Antislavery societies, the first founded by the Quakers in 1775, spread throughout the northern states during the next quarter century. Over the same period the legislatures of most northern states provided for the immediate or gradual abolition of slavery. Freedom for most northern African Americans came slowly, but by 1830 there were fewer than 3,000 slaves out of a total northern black population of 125,000.

The Revolution, which had been fought for liberty and equality, did little to change the status of most black Americans. By 1800 more enslaved African Americans lived in the United States than had lived there in 1776. Slavery continued to grow in the Lower South as the rice culture of the Carolinas and Georgia expanded and as the new cotton culture spread westward.

Still, a larger number of slaves than ever before became free during the war and in the decades following, whether through military service, successful escape, manumission, or gradual emancipation. All these developments fostered the growth of free black communities, especially in the Upper South and in northern cities. By 1810 free African Americans made up 10 percent of the total population of Maryland and Virginia. The composition of the postwar free community changed as well. Before independence most free blacks had been either mulattoes—the offspring of interracial unions—or former slaves too sick or aged to have value as laborers. In contrast, the free population of the 1780s were darker skinned, younger, and healthier. This group injected new vitality into black communal life, organizing independent schools, churches, and mutual benefit societies for the growing number of "free people of color."

> **peculiar institution** euphemism for slavery, perhaps revealing in its use. Peculiar also suggests the contradiction with the ideals of the Declaration of Independence, that "all men are created equal."

After the Revolution slavery ceased to be a national institution. It became the "**peculiar institution**" of a single region, the American South.

Wartime Economic Disruption >> With

the outbreak of the Revolution, Americans had suffered an immediate loss of the manufactured goods, markets, and credit that Britain had formerly supplied. Matters did not improve with the coming of peace. France and Britain flooded the new states with their manufactures, and postwar Americans, eager for luxuries, indulged in a most unrepublican spending spree. The flurry of buying left some American merchants and consumers as deeply in debt as their governments. When loans from private citizens and foreign creditors such as France had proved insufficient to finance the fighting, both Congress and the states had printed paper money—a whopping total of $400 million. The paper currency was backed only by the government's promise to redeem the bills with money from future taxes, since legislatures balked at the unpopular alternative of levying taxes during the war. For the bills to be redeemed, the United States had to survive, so by the end of 1776, when Continental forces sustained a series of defeats, paper money started to depreciate dramatically. By 1781 it was virtually without value, and Americans coined the expression "not worth a Continental."

The printing of paper money, combined with a wartime shortage of goods, triggered an inflationary spiral of scarcer and scarcer goods costing more and more worthless dollars. In this spiral, creditors were gouged by debtors, who paid them back with depreciated currency. At the same time, soaring prices for food and manufactured goods eroded the buying power of wage earners and small farmers. And the end of the war brought on demands for prompt repayment from the new nation's foreign creditors as well as from soldiers seeking backpay and pensions.

The Contagion of Liberty

Jupiter Hammon (b. 1711), a slave in New York, produced the first printed work by a person of African descent in North America—a poem published in 1761. But he is remembered as much for some comments he made in a religious pamphlet of 1787: "That liberty is a great thing we may know from our own feelings, and we may likewise judge so from the conduct of the white people in the late war. . . . I must say that I have hoped God would open their eyes, when they were so much engaged for liberty, to think of the state of the poor blacks. . . ."

Congress could do nothing. With no power to regulate trade, it could neither dam the stream of imported goods rushing into the states nor stanch the flow of gold and silver to Europe to pay for these items. With no power to prohibit the states from issuing paper money, it could not halt depreciation. With no power to regulate wages or prices, it could not curb inflation. With no power to tax, it could not reduce the public debt. Efforts to grant Congress greater powers met with determined resistance from the states.

Within states, too, economic problems aroused discord. Some major merchants and large commercial farmers had profited handsomely during the war by selling supplies to the American, British, and French armies at high prices. Eager to protect their windfall, they lobbied state legislatures for an end to inflationary monetary policies. That meant passing high taxes to pay wartime debts, a paper currency that was backed by gold and silver, and an active policy to encourage foreign trade.

Less affluent men fought back, pressing legislatures for programs that met their needs. Western farmers, often in debt, urged the states to print more paper money and to pass laws lowering taxes and postponing the foreclosure of mortgages. Artisans opposed merchants by calling for protection from low-priced foreign imports that competed with the goods they produced. They set themselves against farmers as well by demanding price regulation of the farm products they consumed. In the continuing struggle, the state legislatures became the battleground of competing economic factions.

As the 1780s wore on, conflicts mounted. As long as the individual states remained sovereign, the Confederation was crippled—unable to conduct foreign affairs effectively, unable to set coherent economic policy, unable to deal with discontent in the West. Equally dismaying was the discovery that many Americans, instead of being selflessly concerned for the public good, selfishly pursued their private interests.

rose dramatically, and some of these new institutions were devoted to educating women. Not only did the number of schools for women increase, but these schools also offered a solid academic curriculum. By 1850— for the first time in American history—there were as many literate women as there were men.

The Revolution also prompted some states to reform their marriage laws, making divorce somewhat easier, although it remained extremely rare. But although women won greater freedom to divorce, married women still could not sue or be sued, make wills or contracts, or buy and sell property. Any wages that they earned went to their husbands; so did all personal property that wives brought into a marriage; so did the rents and profits of any real estate they owned. Despite the high ideals of "republican motherhood," most women remained confined to the "domestic sphere" of the home and deprived of the most basic legal and political rights.

The Attack on Aristocracy >> Why wasn't the American Revolution more revolutionary? Independence secured the full political equality of white men who owned property, but women were still deprived of political rights, African Americans of human rights. Why did the revolutionaries stop short of extending equality to the most unequal groups in American society—and with so little sense that they were being inconsistent?

In part, the lack of concern was rooted in republican ideas themselves. Republican ideology viewed property as the key to independence and power. Lacking property, women and black Americans were easily consigned to the custody of husbands and masters. Then, too, prejudice played its part: the perception of women and blacks as naturally inferior beings.

But revolutionary leaders also failed to press for greater equality because they conceived their crusade in terms of eliminating the evils of a European past dominated by kings and aristocrats. They believed that the great obstacle to equality was monarchy—kings and queens who bestowed hereditary honors and political office on favored individuals and granted legal privileges and monopolies to favored churches and businesses. These artificial inequalities posed the real threat to liberty, most republicans concluded. In other words, the men of the Revolution were intent on attaining equality by leveling off the top of society. It did not occur to most republicans that the cause of equality could also be served by raising up the bottom—by attacking the laws and prejudices that kept African Americans enslaved and women dependent.

The most significant reform of the republican campaign against artificial privilege was the dismantling of state-supported churches. Most states had a religious establishment. In New York and the South, it was the Anglican Church; in New England, the Congregational Church. Since the 1740s, dissenters who did not worship at state churches had protested laws that taxed all citizens to support the clergy of established denominations. After the Revolution, as more dissenters became voters, state legislators gradually abolished state support for Anglican and Congregational churches.

AFTER THE FACT
Skirting the Issue

Only months after Cornwallis surrendered at Yorktown, this cartoon appeared to razz him. Military defeat has unmanned the British, the poet gloats, and produced a "horrid revolution" in gender roles. While Cornwallis has "turned nurse," other British generals take up women's work—housekeeping ("thumping a cushion"), caring for children, and spinning. Meanwhile, British women like Cornwallis's mistress shoulder muskets and clamor to become soldiers.

CORNWALLIS turned NURSE, and his MISTRESS a SOLDIER.

A Prisoner from Virginia's coast, | Like Hercules, renown'd of old,
Cornwallis has return'd, fir; | The diftaff is his calling ;
Toolong, toolong he rul'd the roaft | And while he hears his miftrefs
And for our ruin burn'd, fir. | fcold, [ing.
Before he was, in wretched plight, | He keeps her brat from bawl-
By armed men furrounded, | Behold him here and fhed a tear,
He fhow'd himfelf a man of might | Sir Henry and Knyphaufen ;
And every thing confounded. | And Arnold too may quake with
Butwhen they thunder'dat his door | fear,
He prov'd by this difafter, | Whom Satan has his claws on.
His race was run, his battles done | Each valiant chief fhall fee with
And Wafhington his mafter. | grief,
His miftrefs in a paffion cry'd, | Their horrid revolution ;
She could have acted bolder ; | Cornwallis forc'd to fpin for
So put his fword upon her fide, | bread,
His mufquet on her fhoulder. | Burgoyne to thump a cufhion.

The cartoon lampoons the British, but we might as easily note that it reveals American anxieties about the war's effect on gender roles. A few American women—mainly poor free whites and servants and runaway slaves—disguised themselves as men and enlisted in the Continental Army. Other "camp followers" (cooks, washerwomen, and nurses) occasionally manned artillery or stood watch for their husbands or other loved ones. Even more women managed family farms and businesses, while their husbands were off fighting, and might be called on to brandish muskets, axes, and pitchforks to defend their communities against marauding loyalists. Abigail Adams made no idle boast when she wrote to her absent spouse that "If our men are all drawn of[f] and we should be attacked, you would find a Race of Amazons in America." Was that a promise or a threat? In a war that produced new freedoms and opportunities for women, did even the victorious male rebels fear meeting the fate of Cornwallis in the cartoon?

<< "Cornwallis Turned Nurse, and His Mistress a Soldier," appeared in *The Continental Almanac for 1782.*

Not only in religious life but in all aspects of their culture, Americans rejected inequalities associated with a monarchical past. In that spirit reformers attacked the Society of Cincinnati, a group organized by former officers of the Continental Army in 1783. The society, which was merely a social club for veterans, was forced to disband for its policy of passing on its membership rights to eldest sons. In this way, critics charged, the Society of Cincinnati was creating artificial distinctions and perpetuating a hereditary warrior nobility.

Today many of the republican efforts at reform seem misdirected. While only a handful of revolutionaries worked for the education of women and the emancipation of slaves, enormous zeal went into fighting threats from a monarchical past that had never existed in America. Yet the threat from kings and aristocrats was real to the revolutionaries—and indeed remained real in many parts of Europe. Their determination to sweep away every shred of formal privilege ensured that these forms of inequality never took root in America.

FROM CONFEDERATION TO CONSTITUTION

While Americans from many walks of life sought to realize the republican commitment to equality, Congress wrestled with the problem of preserving the nation itself. With the new republic slowly rending itself to pieces, some political leaders concluded that neither the Confederation nor the state legislatures were able to remedy the basic difficulties facing the nation. But how could the states be convinced to surrender their sovereign powers? The answer came in the wake of two events—one foreign, one domestic—that lent momentum to the cause of strengthening the central government.

The Jay-Gardoqui Treaty >> The international episode that threatened to leave the Confederation in shambles was a debate over a proposed treaty with Spain. In 1785 southwesterners still could not legally navigate the Mississippi and still were threatening to secede from the union and annex their territory to Spain's American empire. To shore up southwestern loyalties, Congress instructed its secretary of foreign affairs, John Jay, to negotiate an agreement with Spain preserving American rights to navigate on the Mississippi River. But the Spanish emissary, Don Diego de Gardoqui, sweet-talked Jay into accepting a treaty by which the United States would give up all rights to the Mississippi for 25 years. In return, Spain agreed to grant trading privileges to American merchants.

That autumn 2,000 farmers rose in armed rebellion, led by Captain Daniel Shays, a veteran of the Revolution.

Jay, a New Yorker, knew more than a few northern merchants who were eager to open new markets. But when the proposed treaty became public knowledge, southwesterners denounced it as nothing short of betrayal. The treaty was never ratified, but the hostility stirred up during the debate revealed the strength of sectional feelings. Only a decade later, when the Senate ratified a treaty negotiated with Spain by Thomas Pinckney in 1796, did Americans gain full access to the Mississippi.

Shays's Rebellion >> On the heels of this humiliation by Spain came an internal conflict that challenged the notion that individual states could maintain order in their own territories. The trouble erupted in western Massachusetts, where many small farmers were close to ruin. Yet they still had to pay mortgages on their farms, still had other debts, and were perpetually short of money. In 1786 the lower house of the Massachusetts legislature obliged the farmers with a package of relief measures. But creditors in eastern Massachusetts, determined to safeguard their own investments, persuaded the upper house to defeat the measures.

In the summer of 1786 western farmers responded, demanding that the upper house of the legislature be abolished and that the relief measures go into effect. That autumn 2,000 farmers rose in armed rebellion, led by Captain Daniel Shays, a veteran of the Revolution. They closed the county courts to halt creditors from foreclosing on their farms and marched on the federal arsenal at Springfield. The state militia quelled the uprising by February 1787, but the insurrection left many in Massachusetts and the rest of the country thoroughly shaken.

Daniel Shays's rebels were no impoverished rabble. They were reputable members of western communities who wanted their property protected and believed that government existed to provide that protection. The Massachusetts state legislature had been unable to safeguard the property of farmers from the inroads of recession or to protect the property of creditors from the armed debtors who closed the courts. It had failed, in other words, to fulfill the most basic aim of republican government.

Other states with discontented debtors feared what the example of western Massachusetts might mean for the future of the Confederation itself. But by 1786 Shays's Rebellion supplied only the sharpest jolt to a movement for reform that was already under way. Even before the rebellion, a group of Virginians had proposed a meeting of the states to adopt a uniform system of commercial regulations. Once assembled at Annapolis in September 1786, the delegates from five states agreed to a more ambitious undertaking. They called for a second, broader meeting in Philadelphia, which Congress approved, for the "express purpose of revising the Articles of Confederation."

Framing a Federal Constitution >> It was
the wettest spring anyone could remember. The 55 men who traveled over muddy roads to Philadelphia in May 1787 arrived drenched and bespattered. Fortunately, most of the travelers were men in their 30s and 40s, young enough to survive a good soaking. Since most were gentlemen of some means—planters, merchants, and lawyers with powdered wigs and prosperous paunches—they could recover from the rigors of their journey in the best accommodations offered by America's largest city.

The delegates came from all the states except Rhode Island. The rest of New England supplied shrewd backroom politicians—Roger Sherman and Oliver Ellsworth from Connecticut and Rufus King and Elbridge Gerry, Massachusetts men who had learned a trick or two from Sam Adams. The middle states marshaled much of the intellectual might: two Philadelphia lawyers, John Dickinson and James Wilson; one Philadelphia financier, Robert Morris; and the aristocratic Gouverneur Morris. From New York there was Alexander Hamilton, the mercurial and ambitious young protégé of Washington. South Carolina provided fiery orators Charles Pinckney and John Rutledge.

It was "an assembly of the demigods," gushed Thomas Jefferson, who, along with John Adams, was serving as a diplomat in Europe when the convention met. In fact, the only delegate who looked even remotely divine was the convention's presiding deity. Towering a full half foot taller than most of his colleagues, George Washington displayed his usual self-possession from a chair elevated on the speaker's platform where the delegates met, in the Pennsylvania State House. At first glance, the delegate of least commanding presence was Washington's fellow Virginian, James Madison. Short and slightly built, the 36-year-old

Madison had no profession except hypochondria. But he was an astute politician and a brilliant political thinker who, more than anyone else, shaped the framing of the federal Constitution.

The delegates from 12 different states had two things in common. They were all men of considerable political experience, and they all recognized the need for a stronger national union. So when the Virginia delegation introduced Madison's outline for a new central government, the convention was ready to listen.

The Virginia and New Jersey Plans >>
What Madison had in mind was a truly national republic, not a confederation of independent states. His "Virginia Plan" proposed a central government with three branches: legislative, executive, and judicial. Furthermore, the legislative branch, Congress, would possess the power to veto all state legislation. In place of the Confederation's single assembly, Madison substituted a bicameral legislature, with a lower house elected directly by the people and an upper house chosen by the lower from nominations made by state legislatures. Representatives to both houses would be apportioned according to population—a change from practice under the Articles, in which each state had a single vote in Congress. Madison also revised the structure of government that had existed under the Articles by adding an executive, who would be elected by Congress, and an independent federal judiciary.

After two weeks of debate over the Virginia Plan, William Paterson, a lawyer from New Jersey, presented a less radical counterproposal. While his "New Jersey Plan" increased Congress's power to tax and to regulate trade, it kept the national government as a unicameral assembly, with each state receiving one vote in Congress under the policy of equal representation. The delegates took just four days to reject Paterson's plan. Most endorsed Madison's design for a stronger central government.

Even so, the issue of apportioning representation continued to divide the delegates. While smaller states pressed for each state's having an equal vote in Congress, larger states backed Madison's provision for basing representation on population. Underlying the dispute over representation was an even deeper rivalry between southern and northern states. While northern and southern populations were nearly equal in the 1780s, and the South's population

^ James Madison, the scholar and statesman whose ideas and political skill shaped the Constitution.

was growing more rapidly, the northern states were more numerous. Giving the states equal votes would put the South at a disadvantage. Southerners feared being outvoted in Congress by the northern states and felt that only proportional representation would protect the interests of their section.

That division turned into a deadlock as the wet spring burned off into a blazing summer. The stifling heat was made even worse because the windows remained shut, to keep any news of the proceedings from drifting out onto the Philadelphia streets.

The Deadlock Broken

>> Finally, as the heat wave broke, so did the political stalemate. On July 2 a committee headed by Benjamin Franklin suggested a compromise. States would be equally represented in the upper house of Congress, each state legislature appointing two senators to six-year terms. That satisfied the smaller states. In the lower house of Congress, which alone could initiate money bills, representation was to be apportioned according to population. Every 30,000 inhabitants would entitle a state to send one representative for a two-year term. A slave was to count as three-fifths of a free person in the calculation of population, and the slave trade was to continue until 1808. That satisfied the larger states and the South.

By the end of August the convention was prepared to approve the final draft of the Constitution. The delegates agreed that the executive, now called the president, would be chosen every four years. Direct election seemed out of the question—after all, how could citizens in South Carolina know anything about a presidential candidate who happened to live in distant Massachusetts, or vice versa? But if each state chose presidential electors, either by popular election or by having the state legislature name them, those eminent men would likely have been involved in national politics, have known the candidates personally, and be prepared to vote wisely. Thus the Electoral College was established, with each state's total number of senators and representatives determining its share of electoral votes.

An array of other powers ensured that the executive would remain independent and strong: the president would have command over the armed forces, authority to conduct diplomatic relations, responsibility to nominate judges and officials in the executive branch, and the power to veto congressional legislation. Just as the executive branch was made independent, so too the federal judiciary was separated from the other two branches of government. Madison believed that this clear **separation of powers** was essential to a balanced republican government.

> ## Charged only with revising the Articles, the delegates had instead written a completely new frame of government.

Madison's only real defeat came when the convention refused to give Congress veto power over state legislation. Still, the new bicameral national legislature enjoyed much broader authority than Congress had under the Confederation, including the power to tax and to regulate commerce. The Constitution also limited the powers of state legislatures, prohibiting them from levying duties on trade, coining money or issuing paper currency, and conducting foreign relations. The Constitution and the acts passed by Congress were declared the supreme law of the land, taking precedence over any legislation passed by the states. And changing the Constitution would not be easy. Amendments could be proposed only by a two-thirds vote of both houses of Congress or in a convention requested by two-thirds of the state legislatures. Ratification of amendments required approval by three-quarters of the states.

> **separation of powers** principle that each branch of government—the legislature (Congress), the executive (the President), and the judiciary (the Supreme Court)—should wield distinct powers independent from interference or infringement by other branches of government.

On September 17, 1787, 39 of the 42 delegates remaining in Philadelphia signed the Constitution. Charged only with revising the Articles, the delegates had instead written a completely new frame of government. And to speed up ratification, the convention decided that the Constitution would go into effect after only nine states had approved it. They further declared that the people themselves—not the state legislatures—would pass judgment on the Constitution in special ratifying conventions. To serve final notice that the new central government was a republic of the people and not merely another confederation of states, Gouverneur Morris of Pennsylvania hit on a happy turn of phrase to introduce the Constitution. "We the People," the document begins, "in order to form a more perfect union . . ."

Ratification

>> With grave misgivings on the part of many, the states called for conventions to decide whether to ratify the new Constitution. Those with the gravest misgivings—the Anti-Federalists, as they came to be called—voiced familiar republican fears. Older and less cosmopolitan than their **Federalist** opponents, the Anti-Federalists drew on their memories of the struggle with England to frame their criticisms of the Constitution.

> **federalism** governing principle established by the Constitution in which the national government and the states divide power.

Expanding the power of the central government at the expense of the states, they warned, would lead to corrupt and arbitrary rule by new aristocrats. Extending a republic over a large territory, they cautioned, would separate national legislators from the interests and close oversight of their constituents.

Madison responded to these objections in The Federalist Papers, a series of 85 essays written with Alexander Hamilton and John Jay during the winter of 1787–1788. He countered Anti-Federalist concerns over the centralization of power by pointing out that each separate branch of the national government would keep the others within the limits of their legal authority. That mechanism of **checks and balances** would prevent the executive from oppressing the people while preventing the people from oppressing themselves.

checks and balances mechanism by which each branch of government—executive, legislative, and judicial—keeps the others within the bounds of their constitutional authority.

To answer Anti-Federalist objections to a national republic, Madison drew on the ideas of an English philosopher, David Hume. In his famous 10th essay in *The Federalist Papers*, Madison argued that in a great republic "the Society becomes broken into a greater variety of interests, of pursuits, of passions, which check each other." The larger the territory, the more likely it was to contain multiple political interests and parties, so that no single faction could dominate. Instead, each would cancel out the others.

The one Anti-Federalist criticism Madison could not get around was the absence of a national bill of rights. Opponents insisted on an explicit statement of rights to prevent the freedoms of individuals and minorities from being violated by the federal government. Madison finally promised to place a bill of rights before Congress immediately after the Constitution was ratified.

Throughout the early months of 1788, Anti-Federalists continued their opposition. But they lacked the articulate and influential leadership that rallied behind the Constitution and commanded greater access to the public press. In the end, too, Anti-Federalist fears of centralized power proved less compelling than Federalist prophecies of the chaos that would follow if the Constitution were not adopted.

By the end of July 1788 all but two states had voted in favor of ratification. The last holdout, Rhode Island, finally came aboard in May 1790, after Madison had carried through on his pledge to submit a bill of rights to the new Congress. Indeed, these 10 amendments—ratified by enough states to become part of the Constitution by the end of 1791—proved to be the Anti-Federalists' most impressive legacy. The bill of rights set the most basic terms for defining personal liberty in the United States. Among the rights guaranteed were freedom of religion, the press, and speech, as well as the right to assemble and petition and the right to bear arms. The amendments also established clear procedural safeguards, including the right to a trial by jury and protection against illegal searches and seizures. They prohibited excessive bail, cruel and unusual punishment, and the quartering of troops in private homes.

Within the life span of a single generation, Americans had declared their independence twice. In many ways the political freedom claimed from Britain in 1776 was less remarkable than the intellectual freedom from the Old World that Americans achieved by agreeing to the Constitution. The Constitution represented a triumph of the imagination—a challenge to many beliefs long cherished by western Europe's republican thinkers.

Revolutionary ideals had been deeply influenced by the conflicts of British politics, in particular the Opposition's warnings about the dangers of executive power. Those concerns at first committed the revolutionaries to making legislatures supreme. In the end, though, Americans ratified a constitution that provided for an independent executive and a balanced government. The Opposition's fears of distant, centralized power had at first prompted the revolutionaries to embrace state sovereignty. But in the Constitution Americans established a national government with authority independent of the states. Finally, the common sense among all of western Europe's republican theorists—that large national republics were an impossibility—was rejected by Americans, making the United States an impossibility that still endures.

> [T]he common sense among all of western Europe's republican theorists—that large national republics were an impossibility—was rejected by Americans, making the United States an impossibility that still endures.

What, then, became of the last tenet of the old republican creed—the belief that civic virtue would sustain popular liberty? The hard lessons of the war and the crises of the 1780s withered confidence in the capacity of Americans to sacrifice their private interests for the public welfare. Many came to share Washington's sober view that "the few . . . who act upon Principles of disinterestedness are, comparatively speaking, no more than a drop in the Ocean." The Constitution reflected the new recognition that interest rather than virtue shaped the behavior of most people most of the time and that the clash of diverse interest groups would remain a constant of public life.

Yet Madison and many other Federalists did not believe that the competition between private interests would somehow result in policies fostering public welfare. That goal would be met instead by the new national government acting as "a disinterested and dispassionate umpire in disputes between different passions and interests in the State." The Federalists looked to the national government to fulfill that role because they trusted that a large republic, with its millions of citizens, would yield more of that scarce resource—disinterested gentlemen dedicated to serving the public good. Such gentlemen, in Madison's words, "whose enlightened views and virtuous sentiments render them superior to local prejudices," would fill the small number of national offices.

Not all the old revolutionaries agreed. Anti-Federalists drawn from the ranks of ordinary Americans still believed that common people were more virtuous and gentlemen more interested than the Federalists allowed. "These lawyers and men of learning, and moneyed men, that talk so finely," complained one Anti-Federalist, would "get all the power and all of the money into their own hands, and then they will swallow up all us little folks." Instead of being dominated by enlightened gentlemen, the national government should be composed of representatives from every social class and occupational group.

The narrow majorities by which the Constitution was ratified reflected the continuing influence of such sentiments, as well as fear that the states were surrendering too much power. That fear made Patrick Henry so ardent an Anti-Federalist that he refused to attend the Constitutional Convention in 1787, saying that he "smelt a rat." "I am not a Virginian, but an American," Henry had once declared. Most likely he was lying. Or perhaps Patrick Henry, a southerner and a slaveholder, could see his way clear to being an "American" only as long as sovereignty remained firmly in the hands of the individual states. Henry's convictions, 70 years hence, would rise again to haunt the Union.

RATIFICATION OF THE CONSTITUTION

State	Date	Vote For	Vote Against
Delaware	December 8, 1787	30	9
Pennsylvania	December 12, 1787	46	23
New Jersey	December 18, 1787	38	0
Georgia	January 3, 1788	26	0
Connecticut	January 9, 1788	128	40
Massachusetts	February 6, 1788	187	168
Maryland	April 26, 1788	63	11
South Carolina	May 23, 1788	149	73
New Hampshire	June 21, 1788	57	47
Virginia	June 25, 1788	89	79
New York	July 26, 1788	30	27
North Carolina	November 21, 1788	194	77
Rhode Island	May 29, 1790	34	32

CHAPTER SUMMARY

Leading Americans would give more thought to federalism, the organization of a United States, as the events of the postrevolutionary period revealed the weaknesses of the state and national governments.

▌ For a decade after independence, the revolutionaries were less committed to creating a single national republic than to organizing 13 separate state republics, each dominated by popularly elected legislatures.

▌ The Articles of Confederation provided for a government by a national legislature but left the crucial power of the purse, as well as all final power to make and execute laws, entirely to the states.

▌ Many conflicts in the new republic were occasioned by westward expansion, which created both international difficulties with Britain and Spain and internal tensions over the democratization of state legislatures.

▌ In the wake of the Revolution, ordinary Americans struggled to define republican society: workers began to organize; some women claimed a right to greater political, legal, and educational opportunities; and religious dissenters called for disestablishment.

▌ In the mid-1780s the political crisis of the Confederation came to a head, prompted by the controversy over the Jay-Gardoqui Treaty and Shays's Rebellion.

▌ The Constitutional Convention of 1787 produced an entirely new frame of government that established a truly national republic and provided for a separation of powers among a judiciary, a bicameral legislature, and a strong executive.

▌ The Anti-Federalists, opponents of the Constitution, softened their objections when promised a bill of rights after ratification, which was incorporated into the Constitution by 1791.

Significant Events

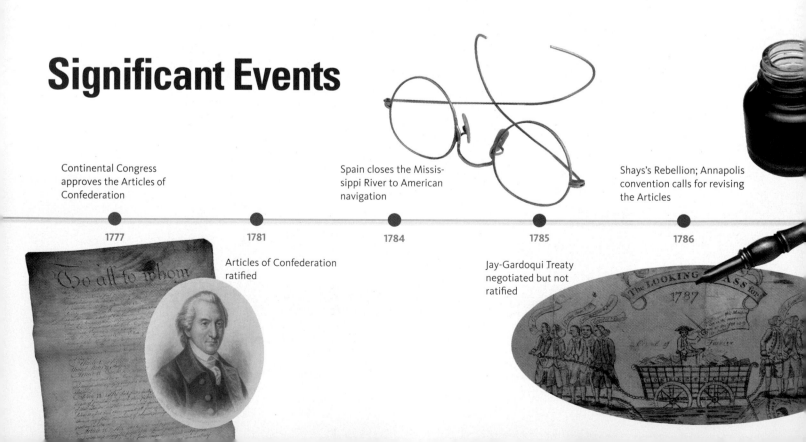

Continental Congress approves the Articles of Confederation

Spain closes the Mississippi River to American navigation

Shays's Rebellion; Annapolis convention calls for revising the Articles

1777　　**1781**　　**1784**　　**1785**　　**1786**

Articles of Confederation ratified

Jay-Gardoqui Treaty negotiated but not ratified

Additional Reading

The work of Gordon Wood is indispensable for understanding the transformation of American politics and culture during the 1780s and thereafter; see especially *The Creation of the American Republic* (1969) and *The Radicalism of the American Revolution* (1992). Other good accounts of the Confederation period and the framing of the Constitution include two books by Forrest MacDonald, *E Pluribus Unum* (1965) and *Novus Ordo Seclorum* (1985), and a collection of essays edited by Alfred Young, *Beyond the American Revolution* (1993). To understand the arguments in favor of the Constitution, consult Garry Wills, *Explaining America* (1981), and to appreciate the contributions of its opponents, read Saul Cornell, *The Other Founders* (1999) and the classic writings of Cecilia Kenyon collected in *Men of Little Faith* (2003). The proceedings of the Constitutional Convention receive vivid coverage in Christopher Collier and James Lincoln Collier, *Decision in Philadelphia* (1987) and Clinton-Rossiter, *1787: The Grand Convention* (1973).

To explore the meaning of republicanism for American women, see two fine studies by Linda Kerber, *Women of the Republic* (1980) and *No Constitutional Right to Be Ladies* (1998), as well as Rosemarie Zagarri's superb biography of Mercy Otis Warren, *A Woman's Dilemma* (1995). For a vivid sense of how the 1780s transformed local society and politics in one Massachusetts county, read John Brooke, *The Heart of the Commonwealth* (1991), and for a fascinating tale of how the Revolution made one ordinary man's life extraordinary, enjoy Alan Taylor, *William Cooper's Town* (1995). The best accounts of how the Revolution's legacy affected the lives of African Americans in the North include Shane White, *Somewhat More Independent* (1991), and Joan Pope Melish, *Disowning Slavery* (1998).

Publication of *The Federalist Papers*

Bill of Rights adopted

1787   1787–1788   1788   1791

Congress adopts the Northwest Ordinance; Constitutional Convention

New Hampshire becomes ninth state to ratify Constitution

The Early

"I FELT MYSELF MAD WITH PASSION"

One spring evening in 1794 General John Neville was riding home from Pittsburgh with his wife and granddaughter. As they went up a hill, his wife's saddle started to slip, so Neville dismounted. As he adjusted the strap, he heard the clip-clop of an approaching horse. A rider galloped up and in a gruff voice asked, "Are you Neville the excise officer?" »

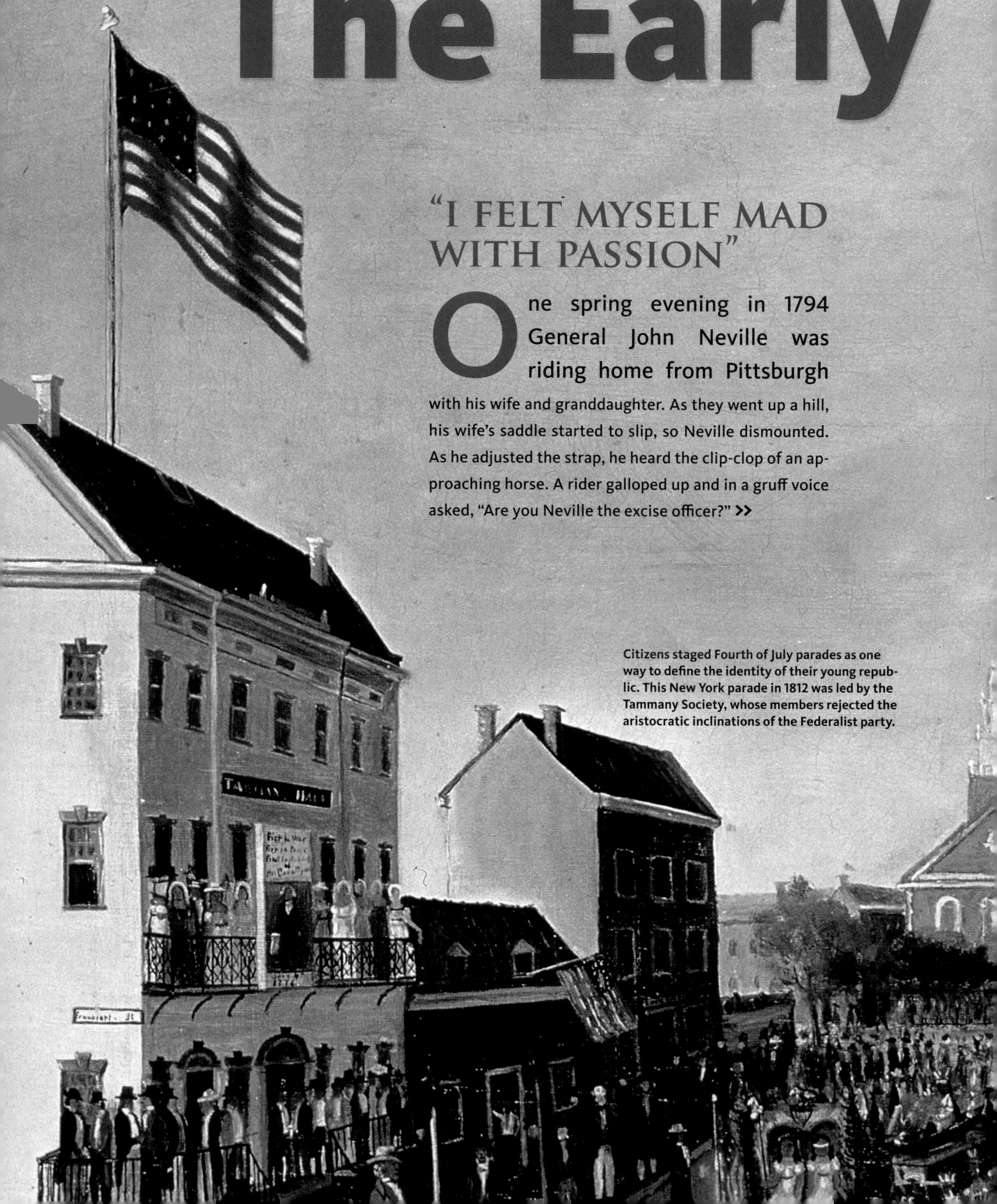

Citizens staged Fourth of July parades as one way to define the identity of their young republic. This New York parade in 1812 was led by the Tammany Society, whose members rejected the aristocratic inclinations of the Federalist party.

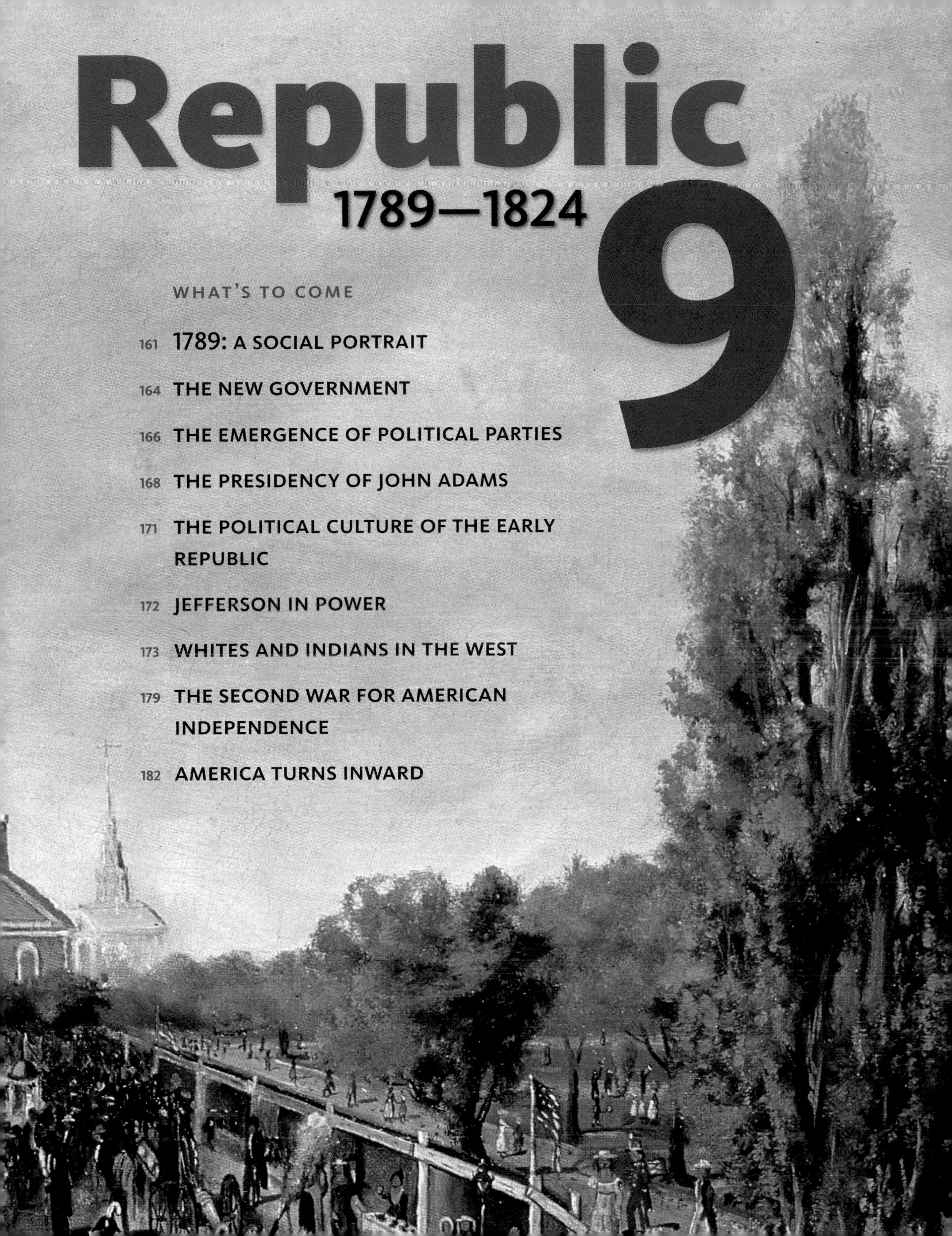

Republic
1789—1824

9

WHAT'S TO COME

161 **1789: A SOCIAL PORTRAIT**

164 **THE NEW GOVERNMENT**

166 **THE EMERGENCE OF POLITICAL PARTIES**

168 **THE PRESIDENCY OF JOHN ADAMS**

171 **THE POLITICAL CULTURE OF THE EARLY REPUBLIC**

172 **JEFFERSON IN POWER**

173 **WHITES AND INDIANS IN THE WEST**

179 **THE SECOND WAR FOR AMERICAN INDEPENDENCE**

182 **AMERICA TURNS INWARD**

"Yes," Neville replied, without turning around.

"Then I must give you a whipping!" cried the rider and leapt from his horse. He grabbed Neville by the hair and lunged at his throat. Breaking free, Neville finally managed to knock the man down: he recognized his attacker as Jacob Long, a local farmer. After Long fled, Neville resumed his journey, badly shaken.

John Neville was not accustomed to such treatment. As one of the wealthiest men in the area, he expected respect from those of lower social rank. And he had received it—until becoming embroiled in a controversy over the new "whiskey tax" on distilled spirits. In a frontier district like western Pennsylvania, farmers regularly distilled their grain into whiskey for barter and sale. Not surprisingly, the **excise tax**, passed by Congress in

excise tax internal tax placed on the production or sale of a commodity, usually a luxury item or nonessential.

1791, was notoriously unpopular. Still, Neville had accepted an appointment to be one of the tax's regional inspectors. For three years he had endured threats as he enforced the law, but this roadside assault showed that popular hostility was rising.

As spring turned to summer, the grain ripened, and so did the people's anger. In mid-July, a federal marshal arrived to serve summonses to a number of farmer-distillers who had

This will make the 'quite   on our bill at grog.

come friend bum I'll take thee to thy master.

for these art our old friend the long nosed pentioner.

AN EXCISEMAN.

⚄ In this antigovernment cartoon, a devil's imp with horns and barbed tail offers to escort a tax collector—the Exciseman—to his master. Like the Stamp Act riots of the Revolutionary period, protesters in western Pennsylvania against the excise tax ritually hanged tax collectors in effigy (*left*).

not paid taxes. One, William Miller, squinted at the paper and was amazed to find the government ordering him to appear in court—hundreds of miles away in Philadelphia—in little more than a month. Even worse, the papers claimed he owed $250.

And there, next to this unknown federal marshal, stood the unyielding John Neville.

"I felt myself mad with passion," recalled Miller. "I thought $250 would ruin me; and . . . I felt my blood boil at seeing General Neville along to pilot the sheriff to my very door." Word of the marshal's presence brought 30 or 40 laborers swarming from a nearby field. Armed with muskets and pitchforks, they forced Neville and the marshal to beat a hasty retreat.

Next morning, the local militia company marched to Neville's estate. A battle ensued, and the general, aided by his slaves, beat back the attackers. A larger group, numbering 500 to 700, returned the following day to find Neville fled and his home garrisoned by a group of soldiers from nearby Fort Pitt. The mob burned down most of the outbuildings and,

after the soldiers surrendered, torched Neville's elegantly furnished home.

Throughout the region that summer, marauding bands roamed the countryside, burning homes and attacking tax collectors. While the greatest unrest flared in western Pennsylvania, farmers in the western districts of several other states also defied federal officials and refused to pay the tax, thus launching a full-scale "Whiskey Rebellion" in the summer of 1794.

Alexander Hamilton, a principal architect of the strong federal government established by the Constitution, knew a challenge to authority when he saw one: "Shall there be a government, or no government?" So did an alarmed George Washington, now president and commander-in-chief of the new republic, who led an army of 13,000 men—larger than that he had commanded at Yorktown against the British—into the Pennsylvania countryside.

That show of force cowed the Pennsylvania protesters, snuffing out the Whiskey Rebellion. But the riots and rebellion deepened fears for the future of the new republic. As Benjamin Franklin remarked in 1788, Americans were skilled at overthrowing governments, but only time would tell whether they were any good at sustaining them. By 1794 Franklin's warning seemed prophetic. ◀◀

Federalists such as Washington and Hamilton—supporters of a powerful national government—had high hopes for their newly created republic. Stretching over some 840,000 square miles in 1789, it was approximately four times the size of France, five times the size of Spain, ten times the size of Great Britain. Yet the founders of the republic knew how risky it was to unite such a vast territory. Yankee merchants living along Boston wharves had economic interests and cultural traditions distinct from those of backcountry farmers who raised hogs, tended a few acres of corn, and distilled whiskey. Even among farmers, there was a world of difference between a South Carolina planter who shipped tons of rice to European markets and a New Hampshire family whose stony fields yielded barely enough to survive. Could the new government established by the Constitution provide a framework strong enough to unite such a socially diverse nation? Within a decade national political leaders split into two sharply opposed political parties, drawing ordinary men and women into civic life.

Social and political divisions within the nation were sharpened by currents of global change, both across the Atlantic and westward across the continent. After 1789 an increasingly bloody revolution in France sharpened old rivalries, and as Europe plunged into war, Americans were torn in their loyalties. Britain also determined to make Americans fight for their independence once again, while in the west, Spain and later France pressured white settlers beyond the Appalachians. Indian nations, buffeted by disease and dislocation, sought to unite in a confederacy west of the Appalachian Mountains.

In short, the early republic was a fragile creation, buffeted by changes beyond its borders and struggling to create a stable government at home. During the nation's first three decades, its survival depended on balancing the interests of a socially and economically diverse population.

> In short, the early republic was a **fragile** creation, buffeted by **changes** beyond its borders and struggling to create a **stable** government at home.

1789: A SOCIAL PORTRAIT

When the Constitution went into effect, the United States stretched from the Atlantic Ocean to the Mississippi River. The first federal census, compiled in 1790, counted approximately 4 million people, divided about evenly between the northern and southern states. Only about 100,000 settlers lived beyond the Appalachians in the Tennessee and Kentucky territories, which were soon to become states.

Within the Republic's boundaries were two major groups that lacked effective political influence: African Americans and Indians. In 1790 black Americans numbered 750,000, almost one-fifth the total population. More than 90 percent lived in the southern states from Maryland to Georgia; most were slaves who worked on tobacco and rice plantations, but there were free blacks as well. The census did not count the number of Indians living east of the Mississippi. North of the Ohio, the powerful Miami Confederacy discouraged settlement, while to the south, five strong, well-organized tribes—the Creeks, Cherokees, Chickasaws, Choctaws, and Seminoles—dominated the region from the Appalachians to the Mississippi River.

That composition would change as the white population continued to double about every 22 years. Immigration contributed only a small part to this astonishing growth. On average, fewer than 10,000 Europeans arrived annually between 1790 and 1820. The primary cause was natural increase, since, on average, American white women gave birth to nearly eight children each. As a result, the United States had an unusually youthful population: in 1790 almost half of all white Americans were under 16 years old. The age at first marriage was about 25 for men, 24 for women—and three or four years younger in newly settled areas—which contributed to the high birthrate.

This youthful, growing population remained overwhelmingly rural. Only 24 towns and cities boasted 2,500 or more residents, and 19 out of 20 Americans lived outside them. In fact, more than 80 percent of American families in 1800 were engaged in agriculture. In such a rural environment the movement of people, goods, and information was slow. Few individuals used the expensive postal system, and most roads were still little more than dirt paths hacked through the forest. In 1790 the country had 92 newspapers, but they were published mostly in towns and cities along major avenues of transportation.

Life in isolated regions contrasted markedly with that in bustling urban centers like New York and Philadelphia. But the most basic division in American society was not between the cities and the countryside, important as that was. What would divide Americans most broadly over the coming decades was the contrast between semisubsistence and commercial ways of life. Semisubsistence farmers lived on the produce of their own land and labor. Americans in the commercial economy were tied more closely to the larger markets of a far-flung world.

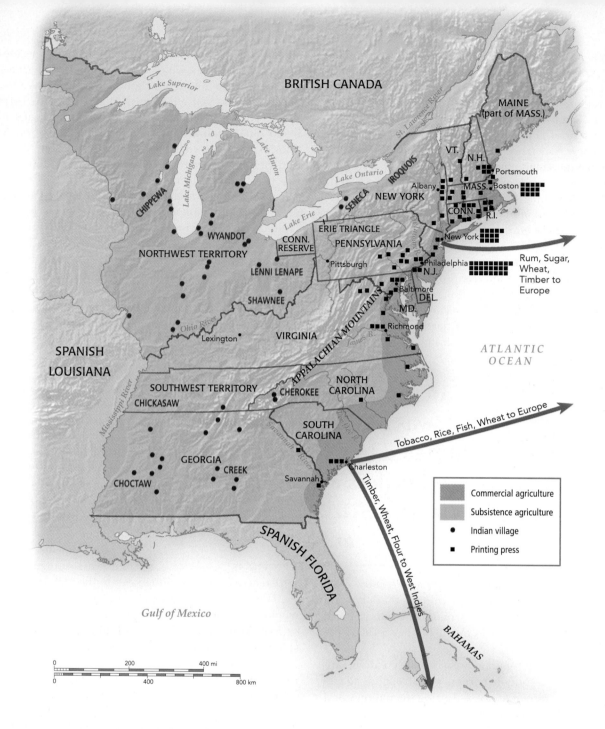

SEMISUBSISTANCE & COMMERCIAL AMERICA, 1790

To prosper, a commercial economy demanded relatively cheap transportation to move goods. Thus in 1790, American commerce was confined largely to settled areas along the coast and to navigable rivers below the fall line. Because commerce depended on an efficient flow of information and goods, newspapers flourished in these areas.

Semisubsistence and Commercial Economies >>

Most rural white Americans in the interior of the northern states and the backcountry of the South lived off the produce of their own land. Wealth in those areas, although not distributed equally, was spread fairly broadly. And subsistence remained the goal of most white families. "The great effort was for every farmer to produce anything he required within his own family," one European visitor noted. In such an economy women played a key role. Wives and daughters had to be skilled in making articles such as candles, soap, clothing, and hats, since the cost of buying such items was steep.

With labor scarce and expensive, farmers also depended on their neighbors to help clear fields, build homes, and harvest crops. If a farm family produced a small surplus, it usually exchanged it locally rather than selling it for cash in a distant market. In this barter economy, money was seldom seen and was used primarily to pay taxes and purchase imported goods.

Indian economies were also based primarily on subsistence. In the division of labor women raised crops, while men fished or hunted—not only for meat but also for skins to make clothing. Because Indians followed game more seasonally than did white settlers, they moved their villages to several different locations over the course of a year. But both whites and Indians in a **semisubsistence economy** moved periodically to new fields after they had exhausted the old ones. Indians exhausted agricultural lands less quickly because they planted beans, corn, and squash in the same field, a technique that better conserved soil nutrients.

> **semisubsistence economy** economy in which individuals and families produce most of what they need to live on.

Despite the image of both the independent "noble savage" and the self-reliant yeoman farmer, virtually no one in the backcountry operated within a truly self-sufficient economy. Although farmers tried to grow most of the food their families ate, they normally bought salt, sugar, and coffee, and they often traded with their neighbors for food and other items. In addition, necessities such as iron, glass, lead, and gunpowder had to be purchased, and many farmers hired artisans to make shoes and weave cloth. Similarly, Indians were enmeshed in the wider world of European commerce, exchanging furs for iron tools or clothing and ornamental materials.

Outside the backcountry, Americans were tied much more closely to a **commercial economy**. Here, merchants, artisans, and even farmers did not subsist on what they produced but instead sold goods or services in a wider market and lived on their earnings. Cities and towns, of course, played a key part in the commercial economy. But so did the agricultural regions near the seaboard and along navigable rivers.

> **commercial economy** economy in which individuals are involved in a network of markets and commercial transactions. Such economies are often urban, where goods and services are exchanged for money and credit; agricultural areas are also commercial when crops and livestock are sold in markets rather than consumed by those who grew or raised them.

For commerce to flourish, goods had to move from producers to market cheaply enough to reap profits. Water offered the only cost-effective transportation over any distance; indeed, it cost as much to ship goods a mere 30 miles over primitive roads as to ship by boat 3,000 miles across the Atlantic to London. Cost-effective transportation was available to the planters of the Tidewater South, and city merchants used their access to the sea to establish trading ties to the West Indies and Europe. But urban artisans and workers were also linked to this market economy, as were many farm families in the Hudson valley, southeastern Pennsylvania, and southern New England.

In commercial economies, wealth was less equally distributed. By 1790, the richest 10 percent of Americans living in cities and in the plantation districts of the Tidewater South owned about 50 percent of the wealth. In the backcountry the top 10 percent was likely to own 25 to 35 percent of the wealth.

The Constitution and Commerce >> In many ways the fight over ratification of the Constitution represented a struggle between the commercial and the subsistence-oriented elements of American society. Urban merchants and workers as well as commercial farmers and planters generally rallied behind the Constitution. They took a broader, more cosmopolitan view of the nation's future, and they had a more favorable view of government power.

Americans who remained a part of the semisubsistence **barter economy** tended to oppose the Constitution. More provincial in outlook, they feared concentrated power, were suspicious of cities and commercial institutions, opposed aristocracy and special privilege, and in general just wanted to be left alone.

> **barter economy** networks of trade based on the mutual exchange of goods and services with little or no use of coin or currency.

And so in 1789 the United States embarked on its new national course, with two rival visions of the direction that the fledgling Republic should take. Which vision would prevail—a question that was as much social as it was political—increasingly divided the generation of revolutionary leaders in the early republic.

BACKSTORY
Forbidding George

Even in his own day, Washington had a reputation for being aloof. Gouverneur Morris, a colleague, bet Alexander Hamilton that he could approach Washington, slap him on the back and say, "My dear general, I am very happy to see you look so well." When Morris tried, Washington fixed him with an icy stare, removed Morris's arm from his shoulder, and left him to retreat into the crowd. In a republic whose future was uncertain, Washington insisted on the dignity of his office.

THE NEW GOVERNMENT

Whatever the Republic was to become, Americans agreed that George Washington personified it. When the first Electoral College cast its votes, Washington was unanimously elected, the only president in history so honored. John Adams became vice president. Loyalty to the new Republic, with its untried form of government and diversity of peoples and interests, rested to a great degree on the trust and respect Americans gave Washington.

⚞ Washington's trip from Virginia to New York City to assume the presidency was a triumphant procession, as Americans enthusiastically greeted him with cheers and even flowers strewn along his path.

Washington Organizes the Government ≫

George Washington realized that as the first occupant of the executive office, everything he did was fraught with significance. "I walk on untrodden ground," he commented. "There is scarcely any part of my conduct which may not hereafter be drawn into precedent."

The Constitution made no mention of a cabinet. Yet the drafters of the Constitution, aware of the experience of the Continental Congress under the Articles of Confederation, clearly assumed that the president would have some system of advisers. Congress authorized the creation of four departments—War, Treasury, State, and Attorney General—whose heads were to be appointed with the consent of the Senate. Washington's most important choices were Alexander Hamilton as secretary of the treasury and Thomas Jefferson to head the State Department. Washington gradually excluded Adams from cabinet discussions,

and any meaningful role for the vice president, whose duties were largely undefined by the Constitution, soon disappeared.

The Constitution created a federal Supreme Court but beyond that was silent about the court system. The Judiciary Act of 1789 set the size of the Supreme Court at 6 members; it also established 13 federal district courts and 3 circuit courts of appeal. Supreme Court justices spent much of their time serving on these circuit courts, a distasteful duty whose long hours "riding the circuit" caused one justice to grumble that Congress had made him a "traveling postboy." The Judiciary Act made it clear that federal courts had the right to review decisions of the state courts and specified cases over which the Supreme Court would have original jurisdiction. Washington appointed John Jay of New York, a staunch Federalist, as the first chief justice.

Hamilton's Financial Program ≫

When Congress called on Alexander Hamilton to prepare a report on the nation's finances, the new secretary of the treasury undertook the assignment eagerly. A brilliant thinker and an ambitious politician, he did not intend to be a minor figure in the new administration. Convinced that human nature was fundamentally selfish, Hamilton was determined to link the interests of the wealthy with those of the new government. He also intended to use federal power to encourage manufacturing and commerce in order to make the United States economically strong and independent of Europe.

Neither goal could be achieved until the federal government solved its two most pressing financial problems: revenue and credit. Without revenue it could not be effective. Without credit—the faith of merchants and other nations that the government would repay its debts—it would lack the ability to borrow. Hamilton proposed that all $52 million of the federal debt, much of it generated by the Revolutionary War, be paid in full (or funded). He also recommended that the federal government assume responsibility for the remaining $25 million in debts that individual states owed—a policy of "assumption." He intended with these twin policies to put the new federal government on a sound financial footing and enhance its power by increasing its need for revenue and making the wealthy look to the national government, not the states. Hamilton also proposed a series of excise taxes, including a controversial 25 percent levy on whiskey, to help meet government expenses.

After heated debate, Congress deadlocked over funding and assumption. Finally, at a dinner with Hamilton, Jefferson and James Madison of Virginia agreed to support his proposal if, after 10 years in Philadelphia, the permanent seat of government would be located in the South, on the Potomac River between Virginia and Maryland. Aided by

HAMILTON'S FINANCIAL SYSTEM

Under Hamilton's financial system, more than 80 percent of federal revenues went to pay the interest on the national debt. Note that most of the revenue came from tariff duties (customs).

Debt
$75.6 Million

Foreign Debt $11.7

State Debt $21.5

Domestic Debt $42.4

Excise and Other $1.2

Customs $4.4

Revenue
$5.6 Million

Other $1.0

Interest on Debt $4.6

Annual Expenditures
$5.6 Million

this understanding, funding and assumption passed Congress. In 1791 Congress also approved a 20-year charter for the first Bank of the United States. The bank would hold government deposits and issue banknotes that would be received in payment of all debts owed the federal government. Congress proved less receptive to the rest of Hamilton's program, although a limited tariff to encourage manufacturing and several excise taxes, including the one on whiskey, won approval.

The passage of Hamilton's program caused a permanent rupture among supporters of the Constitution. Madison, who had collaborated closely with Hamilton in the 1780s, broke with his former ally over funding and assumption. Jefferson finally went over to the opposition when Hamilton announced plans for a national bank. Eventually the two warring factions organized themselves into political parties: the Republicans, led by Jefferson and Madison, and the Federalists, led by Hamilton and Adams.[1] But the division emerged slowly over several years.

Hamilton's program promoted the commercial sector at the expense of semisubsistence farmers. Thus it rekindled many of the concerns that had surfaced during the struggle over ratification of the Constitution. The ideology of the Revolution had stressed that republics inevitably contained groups who sought power in order to destroy popular liberties and overthrow the republic. To some Americans, Hamilton's program seemed a clear threat to establish a privileged and powerful financial aristocracy— perhaps even a monarchy.

Who, after all, would benefit from the funding proposal? During and after the Revolution, the value of notes issued by the Continental Congress dropped sharply. Speculators had bought up most of these notes for a fraction of their face value from small farmers and workers. If the government finally paid back the debt, speculators would profit accordingly. Equally disturbing, members of Congress had been purchasing the notes before the adoption of Hamilton's program. Nearly half the members of the House owned U.S. securities, a dangerous mimicking of Britain, where the Bank of England's loans to many members of Parliament gave it great political influence.

Fears were heightened because Americans had little experience with banks: only three existed in the country when the Bank of the United States was chartered. One member of Congress expressed a common attitude when he said that he would no more be caught entering a bank than a house of prostitution. Then, too, banks and commerce were a part of the urban environment that rural Americans so distrusted. Although Hamilton's opponents admitted that a certain amount of commerce was necessary, they believed that it should remain subordinate. Hamilton's program, in contrast, encouraged manufacturing and urbanization, developments that history suggested were incompatible with liberty and equality.

After Congress approved the bank bill, Washington hesitated to sign it. When he consulted his cabinet, Jefferson stressed that the Constitution did not specifically authorize Congress to charter a bank. Both he and Madison upheld the idea of strict construction—that the Constitution should be interpreted narrowly and the federal government restricted to powers expressly delegated to it. Otherwise, the federal government would be the judge

1 The Republican party of the 1790s, sometimes referred to as the Jeffersonian Republicans, is not to be confused with the modern-day Republican party, which originated in the 1850s.

>> Alexander Hamilton took a leading role both in the Washington administration and in the formation of the republic's first political parties. Though short of stature, he cut a dashing figure with his erect bearing, strutting manner, meticulous dress, and carefully powdered hair.

of its own powers, and there would be no safeguard against the abuse of power.

Hamilton countered that the Constitution contained implied as well as enumerated powers. He particularly emphasized the clause that permitted Congress to make all laws "necessary and proper" to carry out its duties. A bank would be useful in carrying out the enumerated powers of regulating commerce and maintaining the public credit; Congress thus had a right to decide whether to establish one. In the end Washington accepted Hamilton's arguments and signed the bill.

Economically Hamilton's program was a success. The government's credit was restored, and the national bank ended the inflation of the previous two decades and created a sound currency. In addition, Hamilton's theory of implied powers and broad construction gave the nation the flexibility necessary to respond to unanticipated crises.

THE EMERGENCE OF POLITICAL PARTIES

Members of the Revolutionary generation fervently hoped that political parties would not take root in the United States. "If I could not go to heaven but with a party, I would not go at all," remarked Jefferson. Influenced by radical English republican thought, American critics condemned parties as narrow interest groups that placed selfishness and party loyalty above a concern for the public good. Despite Americans' distrust of such institutions, however, the United States became the first nation to establish truly popular parties.

Social conditions encouraged the rise of parties. Because property ownership was widespread, the nation had a broad **suffrage**. During the American Revolution legislatures lowered property requirements in many states, increasing the number of voters still further. If party members hoped to

suffrage right to vote }

hold office, they had to offer a program attractive to the broader voting public. When parties acted as representatives of economic and social interest groups, they became one means by which a large electorate could make its feelings known. In addition, the United States had the highest literacy rate in the world and the largest number of newspapers, further encouraging political interest and participation. Finally, the fact that well-known patriots of the Revolution headed both the Federalists and the Republicans helped defuse the charge that either party was hostile to the Revolution or the Constitution.

Americans and the French Revolution >> While domestic issues first split the supporters of the Constitution, it was a crisis in Europe that pushed the nation toward political parties. Americans had hoped that their revolution would spark similar movements for liberty on the European continent, and in fact the American Revolution was only one of a series of revolutions in the late eighteenth century that shook the Western world, the most important of which began in France in 1789. There a rising population and the collapse of government finances sparked a challenge to royal authority that became a mass revolution. The French revolutionary ideals of "liberty, equality, and fraternity" eventually spilled across Europe.

Americans first hailed the Revolution. Many rejoiced to learn that the Bastille prison had been stormed and that a new National Assembly had abolished feudal privileges and adopted the Declaration of the Rights of Man. But by 1793, American enthusiasm for the Revolution had cooled after radical elements instituted a reign of terror, executing the king and queen and many of the nobility. The French republic even outlawed Christianity and substituted the worship of Reason. Finally in 1793 republican France and monarchical England went to war. Americans were deeply divided over whether the United States should continue its old alliance with France or support Great Britain.

Hamilton and his allies viewed the French Revolution as sheer anarchy. French radicals seemed to be destroying the very institutions that held civilization together: the church, social classes, property, law and order. The United States, Hamilton argued, should renounce the 1778 treaty of alliance with France and side with Britain. By contrast, Jefferson and his followers supported the treaty and regarded France as a sister republic. They believed that despite deplorable excesses, its revolution was spreading the doctrine of liberty.

Washington's Neutral Course >> Washington, for his part, was convinced that in order to prosper, the United States must remain independent of European quarrels and wars. Thus he issued a proclamation of American neutrality and tempered Jefferson's efforts to support France.

Under international law, neutrals could trade with belligerents—nations at war—as long as the trade had existed before the outbreak of hostilities and did not involve war supplies. But both France and Great Britain refused to respect the rights of neutrals in the midst of their desperate struggle. They began intercepting American ships and confiscating cargoes. In addition, Britain, which badly needed manpower to maintain its powerful navy, impressed into service American sailors it suspected of being British subjects. Britain also continued to maintain the western forts it had promised to evacuate in 1783, and it closed the West Indies, a traditional source of trade, to American ships.

Recognizing that the United States was not strong enough to challenge Britain militarily, Washington sent John Jay to negotiate the differences between the two countries. Although Jay did persuade the British to withdraw their troops from the Northwest, he could gain no other concessions. Disappointed, Washington nonetheless submitted Jay's Treaty to the Senate. After a bitter debate, the Senate narrowly ratified it in June of 1795.

The Federalists and the Republicans Organize >> Thus events in Europe contributed directly to the rise of parties in the United States by stimulating fears over the course of American development. By the mid-1790s both sides were organizing on a national basis. Hamilton took the lead in coordinating the Federalist party, which grew out of the voting bloc in Congress that had enacted his economic program. Increasingly, Washington drew closer to Federalist advisers and policies and became the symbol of the party, although he clung to the vision of a nonpartisan administration.

The guiding genius of the opposition movement was Hamilton's onetime colleague James Madison. Jefferson, who resigned as secretary of state at the end of 1793, became the symbolic head of the party, much as Washington reluctantly headed the Federalists. But it was Madison who orchestrated the Republican strategy and lined up their voting bloc

in the House. The disputes over Jay's Treaty and over the whiskey tax in 1794 and 1795 gave the Republicans popular issues, and they began organizing on the state and local levels. Republican leaders had to be careful to distinguish between opposing the administration and opposing the Constitution. And they had to overcome the ingrained idea that an opposition party was seditious.

As more and more members of Congress allied themselves with one faction or the other, voting became increasingly partisan. By 1796 even minor matters were decided by partisan votes. Gradually, party organization filtered downward to local communities.

The 1796 Election >> As long as Washington remained head of the Federalists, they enjoyed a huge advantage. But in 1796 the weary president, stung by the abuse heaped on him by the opposition press, announced that he would not accept a third term. In doing so, he set a two-term precedent that future presidents followed until Franklin Roosevelt. In his Farewell Address Washington warned against the dangers of parties and urged

Man or God and How to Tell the Difference

E very nation makes its own myths, alongside or intermixed with its history—and historians often analyze the objects of this mythmaking. Unlike most members of the American pantheon, Washington attained exalted status during his lifetime. Merely by retiring to private life at the end of the Revolutionary War, he vaulted in the public esteem from a victorious general to a republican saint. Washington had become a self-denying patriot who shunned the temptation to seize political power by exploiting his military glory. Only when chosen as president under the new Constitution did he come out of retirement.

Like most of the founders, Washington took care to ensure that his fame would endure. In retirement he sat patiently for a steady stream of visiting artists, among them the French sculptor Jean Antoine Houdon, who cast this bust from a life mask in 1785. Even to reproduce Washington in this classical style (note the Greco-Roman clothing) elevates him to the pantheon of Greek and Roman republicans so admired by Enlightenment thinkers. But despite his strivings for immortality, Washington resisted becoming a republican deity. At the conclusion of two terms in office he retired again to Mount Vernon.

a return to the earlier nonpartisan system. That vision, however, had become obsolete: parties were an effective way of expressing the interests of different social and economic groups within the nation. When the Republicans chose Thomas Jefferson to oppose John Adams, the possibility of a constitutional system without parties ended.

The framers of the Constitution did not anticipate that political parties would run competing candidates for both the presidency and the vice presidency. Thus they provided that, of the candidates running for president, the one with the most electoral votes would win and the one with the second highest number would become vice president. But Hamilton strongly disliked both Adams and Jefferson. Ever the intriguer, he tried to manipulate the electoral vote so that the Federalist vice presidential candidate, Thomas Pinckney of South Carolina, would be elected president. In the ensuing confusion, Adams won with 71 electoral votes, and his rival, Jefferson, gained the vice presidency with 68 votes.

Federalist and Republican Ideologies >>

The fault line between Federalists and Republicans reflected basic divisions in American life. Geographically, the Federalists were strongest in New England, with its commercial ties to Great Britain and its powerful tradition of hierarchy and order. Moving farther south, the party became progressively weaker. Of the southernmost states, the Federalists enjoyed significant strength only in aristocratic South Carolina. The Republicans won solid support in semisubsistence areas such as the West, where farmers were only weakly involved with commerce. The middle states were closely contested, although the most cosmopolitan and commercially oriented elements remained the core of Federalist strength.

In other ways, each party looked both forward and backward: toward certain traditions of the past as well as toward newer social currents that would shape America in the nineteenth century.

Most Federalists viewed themselves as a kind of natural aristocracy making a last desperate stand against the excesses of democracy. They clung to the notion that the upper class should rule over its social and economic inferiors. In supporting the established social order, most Federalists opposed unbridled individualism. In their view, government should regulate individual behavior for the good of society and protect property from the violent and unruly.

Yet the Federalists were remarkably forward-looking in their economic ideas. They sensed that the United States would become a major economic and military power only by government encouragement of economic development.

The Republicans, in contrast, looked backward to the traditional Revolutionary fear that government power threatened liberty. The Treasury, they warned, was corrupting Congress, the army would enslave the people, and interpreting the Constitution broadly would make the federal government all-powerful. Nor did Republican economic ideals anticipate future American development. For the followers of Madison and Jefferson, agriculture—not commerce or manufacturing—was the foundation of American liberty and virtue. Republicans also failed to appreciate the role of financial institutions in promoting economic growth, condemning speculators, bank directors, and holders of the public debt.

Yet the Jeffersonians were more farsighted in matters of equality and personal liberty. Their faith in the people put them in tune with the emerging egalitarian temper of society. They embraced the virtues of individualism, hoping to reduce government to the bare essentials. And they looked to the West—the land of small farms and a more equal society—as the means to preserve opportunity and American values.

THE PRESIDENCY OF JOHN ADAMS

As president, John Adams became the head of the Federalists, although in many ways he was out of step with his party. Unlike Hamilton, Adams felt no pressing need to aid the wealthy, nor was he fully committed to Hamilton's commercial-industrial vision. As a revolutionary leader who in the 1780s had served as American minister to England, Adams also opposed any alliance with Britain.

Increasingly Adams and Hamilton clashed over policies and party leadership. Part of the problem stemmed from personalities. Adams was so thin-skinned that it was difficult for anyone to get along with him, and Hamilton's intrigues in the 1796 election had not improved relations between the two men. Although Hamilton had resigned from the Treasury Department in 1795, key members of Adams's cabinet regularly turned to the former secretary for advice. Indeed, they opposed Adams so often that the frustrated president sometimes dealt with them, according to Jefferson, "by dashing and trampling his wig on the floor."

The Naval War with France >> Adams

began his term trying to balance relations with both Great Britain and France. Because the terms of Jay's Treaty were so favorable to the British, the French in retaliation set their navy and privateers to raiding American shipping. To resolve the conflict, Adams dispatched three envoys to France in 1797, but the French foreign minister demanded a bribe before negotiations could even begin. The American representatives refused, and when news of these discussions became public, it became known as the XYZ Affair.

In the public's outrage over French bribery, Federalist leaders saw a chance to retain power by going to war.

In the public's outrage over French bribery, Federalist leaders saw a chance to retain power by going to war. In 1798 Congress repudiated the French alliance of 1778 and enlarged the army and navy. Republicans suspected that the real purpose of the army was not to fight the French army—none existed in North America—but to crush the opposition party and establish a military despotism. All that remained was for Adams to whip up popular feeling and lead the nation into war.

But Adams feared he would become a scapegoat if his policies failed. Furthermore, he distrusted standing armies and preferred the navy as the nation's primary defense. So an unofficial naval war broke out between the United States and France as ships in each navy raided the fleets of the other, while Britain continued to impress American sailors and seize ships suspected of trading with France.

Suppression at Home >> Meanwhile, Federalist leaders attempted to suppress disloyalty at home. In the summer of 1798 Congress passed several measures known together as the Alien and Sedition Acts. The Alien Act authorized the president to arrest and deport aliens suspected of "treasonable" leanings. Although never used, the act directly threatened immigrants who had not yet become citizens, many of whom were prominent Jeffersonians. To limit the number of immigrant voters—again, most of them Republicans—Congress increased the period of residence required to become a **naturalized** citizen from 5 to 14 years. But the most controversial law was the Sedition Act, which established heavy fines and even imprisonment for writing, speaking, or publishing anything of "a false, scandalous and malicious" nature against the government or any officer of the government.

{ **naturalization** act of granting full citizenship to someone born outside the country.

Because of the partisan way it was enforced, the Sedition Act quickly became a symbol of tyranny. Federalists convicted and imprisoned a number of prominent Republican editors, and several Republican papers ceased publication. In all, 25 people were arrested under the law and 10 convicted and imprisoned.

The crisis over the Sedition Act forced Republicans to develop a broader conception of freedom of the press. Previously, most Americans had agreed that newspapers should not be restrained before publication but that they could be punished afterward for sedition. Jefferson and others now argued that the American government was uniquely based on the free expression of public opinion, and thus criticism of the government was not a sign of criminal intent. Only overtly seditious acts, not opinions, should be subject to prosecution. The courts eventually endorsed this view, adopting a new, more absolute view of freedom of speech guaranteed by the First Amendment.

The Republican-controlled legislatures of Virginia and Kentucky each responded to the crisis of 1798 by passing a set of resolutions. Madison secretly wrote those for Virginia, and Jefferson those for Kentucky. These resolutions proclaimed that the Constitution was a compact among sovereign states that delegated strictly limited powers to the federal government. When the government exceeded those limits and threatened the liberties of citizens, states had the right to interpose their authority.

But Jefferson and Madison were not ready to rend a union that had so recently been forged. The two men intended for the Virginia and Kentucky resolutions only to rally public opinion to the Republican cause. They opposed any effort to resist federal authority by force.

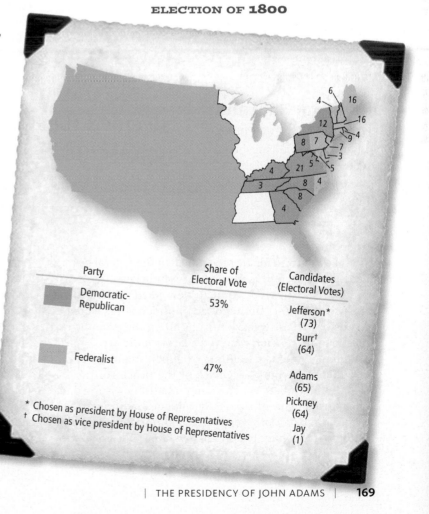

ELECTION OF 1800

Party	Share of Electoral Vote	Candidates (Electoral Votes)
Democratic-Republican	53%	Jefferson* (73)
		Burr† (64)
Federalist	47%	Adams (65)
		Pickney (64)
		Jay (1)

* Chosen as president by House of Representatives
† Chosen as vice president by House of Representatives

The Election of 1800 >>

With a naval war raging on the high seas and the Alien and Sedition Acts sparking debate at home, Adams shocked his party by negotiating a peace treaty with France. It was a courageous act, for Adams not only split his party in two but also ruined his own chances for reelection by driving Hamilton's pro-British wing of the party into open opposition. But the nation benefited, as peace returned.

With the Federalist party split, Republican prospects in 1800 were bright. Again the party chose Jefferson to run against Adams, along with Aaron Burr for vice president. Sweeping to victory, the Republicans won the presidency, as well as control of both houses of Congress for the first time. Yet the election again demonstrated the fragility of the fledgling political system. Jefferson and Burr received an equal number of votes, but the Constitution did not distinguish between the votes for president and vice president. With the election tied, the decision lay with the House of Representatives, where each state was allotted one vote. Because Burr refused to step aside for Jefferson, the election remained deadlocked for almost a week, until the Federalists decided that Jefferson represented the lesser of two evils. They allowed his election on the 36th ballot. In 1804 the Twelfth Amendment corrected the problem, specifying that electors were to vote separately for president and vice president.

John Marshall and Judicial Review >>

Having lost both the presidency and control of Congress in 1800, the Federalists took steps to shore up their power before Jefferson took office. They did so by expanding the size of the federal court system, the one branch of the federal government that they still controlled. The Judiciary Act of 1801 created 6 circuit courts and 16 new judgeships. Federalists justified these "midnight appointments" (executed by Adams in the last weeks of his term) on the grounds that the expanding nation required a larger judiciary.

Among Adams's last-minute appointments was that of William Marbury as justice of the peace for the District of Columbia. When James Madison assumed the office of secretary of state under the new administration, he found a batch of undelivered commissions, including Marbury's. Wishing to appoint loyal Republicans to these posts, Jefferson instructed Madison not to hand over the commissions, whereupon Marbury sued. The case of *Marbury v. Madison* went directly to the Supreme Court in 1803.

Chief Justice John Marshall, a Federalist and one of Adams's late-term appointments, actually ruled in favor of Madison—but in a way that strengthened the power of the federal courts. Marshall affirmed the right of the Supreme Court to review statutes and interpret the meaning of the Constitution. "It is emphatically the province of and duty of the judicial department to say what the law is," he wrote in upholding the doctrine of **judicial review**. In Marshall's view, the Court "must of necessity expound and interpret" the Constitution and the laws when one statute conflicted with another or when a law violated the framework of the Constitution.

judicial review doctrine set out by Chief Justice John Marshall in *Marbury v. Madison*, that the judicial branch of the federal government possesses the power to determine whether the laws of Congress or the actions of the executive branch violate the Constitution.

Marshall and his colleagues later asserted the power of the Court to review the constitutionality not only of federal but also of state laws. In fact, during his long tenure as Chief Justice (over 30 years), John Marshall extended judicial review to all acts of government.

As John Adams left office, he looked back with mixed feelings on the 12 years that the Federalist party had held power. Under Washington's firm leadership and his own, his party had made the Constitution a workable instrument of government. The Federalists had proved that a republican form of government was compatible with stability and order. They had established economic policies that brought a return of prosperity. Washington had established the principle of American neutrality in foreign affairs, which became an accepted ideal by both parties for decades to come.

But most Federalists took no solace in such reflections, because the forces of history seemed to be running against them. In the election of 1800 they stood as the champions of order and hierarchy, of government by the wellborn, of a society in which social betters guided their respectful inferiors. They had waged one last desperate battle to save their disintegrating world—and had lost. Power had fallen into the hands of the ignorant rabble, led by that demagogue Thomas Jefferson.

> Because Burr **refused** to **step aside** for Jefferson, the election remained **deadlocked** for almost a **week**, until the Federalists decided that Jefferson represented the **lesser** of two evils.

THE POLITICAL CULTURE OF THE EARLY REPUBLIC

Such extreme views poisoned the political atmosphere of the early republic. Two distinct parties had emerged during the 1790s, but both longed to reestablish a one-party system. Neither Federalists nor Republicans could accept the novel idea that political parties might peacefully resolve differences among competing social, geographic, and economic interests. Instead, each party regarded its opponents as a dangerous faction of ambitious men striving to increase their wealth and power at the expense of republican liberty.

What resulted was a political culture marked by verbal and, at times, physical violence. Republicans accused Washington and Hamilton of being British agents and monarchists; Federalists denounced Jefferson as an atheist and his partisans as a pack of "blood-drinking cannibals." The leading Republican newspaper editor in Philadelphia plunged into a street brawl with his Federalist rival; two members of Congress slugged it out on the floor of the House of Representatives. Mobs threatened the leaders of both parties, and at the height of the crisis of 1798–1799, Adams smuggled guns into his home for protection.

Popular Participation in Political Festivals >>

The deepening divisions among national leaders also encouraged ordinary Americans to take an interest in politics. Beginning in the 1790s and for decades thereafter, activists in cities and villages everywhere in the new republic organized grand festivals to celebrate American patriotism and the glories of the Republicans or the Federalists. That grassroots movement democratized the conduct of politics by educating men and women, white and black, voters and nonvoters alike, about the issues of the day. In doing so, such activities encouraged strong partisan loyalties.

Holidays such as the Fourth of July or Washington's Birthday became prime occasions for local party leaders to rally their fellow-citizens. They hosted celebrations that began with parades in which marchers, hoisting banners to identify their particular trade, militia company, or social club, processed through the main street to a church, meeting hall, or public square. There the assembled throng of marchers and onlookers sang patriotic songs, recited prayers, and listened to the reading of the Declaration of Independence, all capped by a rousing sermon or political oration. Then the party started: in the North, taverns and hotels hosted community banquets; in the South, the crowds flocked to outdoor barbecues. Everywhere the feasts ended with many toasts to the glories of republican liberty and, of course, to the superiority of Federalists or Republicans.

⚠ In 1821 these "victuallers"—suppliers of food—marched along the streets of Philadelphia in a typical celebration. The butchers wear traditional white frocks as they march ahead of a two-story float. In the thriving market economy butchers displayed civic pride as they hauled over 86,000 pounds of beef, pork, lamb, and other foods to the market in 100 carts.

These local celebrations not only made an impact on those who were able to attend the festivities but also reached a wider audience through newspaper accounts. During the 1790s and beyond, the number of local or regional newspapers in the new republic mushroomed, but their coverage was far from objective. Most editors were either staunch Federalists or ardent Republicans who could be counted on to publish glowing accounts of the festivities sponsored by their party and to instruct a much wider audience about party policies and values.

These political festivals and newspaper accounts aimed to woo the loyalty of white adult males who held enough property to vote. But they also sought the support of the white women who joined in the crowds and even took part in parades. In one New Jersey village, the folks lining the parade route cheered as "16 young ladies uniformed in white with garlands in their hats" marched past, playing a patriotic anthem on their flutes. Federalists and Republicans alike encouraged women's involvement on these occasions, hoping that displays of approval from "the American Fair" would encourage husbands and male admirers to support their parties.

African-American Celebrations >>

African Americans, too, were drawn to political festivals, but unlike white women, they discovered that party organizers were determined to keep them away. In the years after 1800, bullies often drove black men and women from Fourth of July celebrations with taunts, threats, and assaults. James

Forten, a leading citizen of Philadelphia's African American community, complained that because of the hostility of drunken whites, "black people, upon certain days of public jubilee, dare not to be seen" on the streets after noon.

The growing free black population of northern cities countered that opposition by organizing celebrations to express their own political convictions. They established annual holidays to celebrate the abolition of the slave trade in Britain and the United States as well as the successful slave revolt in the Caribbean that resulted in the founding of Haiti in 1804 (see p. 254). Those acts of defiance—the spectacle of blacks marching down the main streets with banners flying and bands of music playing, and of black audiences cheering orators who publicly condemned slavery—only inflamed racial hatred and opposition among many whites.

But African Americans continued to press for full citizenship by persuading sympathetic white printers to publish poetry, slave narratives, and pamphlets composed by black authors. The strategy of those writings was to refute racist notions by drawing attention to the intelligence, virtue, and patriotism of black American women and men, both free and enslaved. Typical was the autobiography of Venture Smith, the first slave narrative published in the United States (1798), which followed his captivity as a young boy in West Africa through his lifelong struggle in New England to purchase his own freedom and that of his wife and children. Hard-working and thrifty, resourceful and determined to better himself and his family, Venture Smith's story invited white readers to conclude that he was as true a republican and a self-made man as Benjamin Franklin.

> Those acts of defiance—the spectacle of blacks marching down the main streets with banners flying and bands of music playing, and of black audiences cheering orators who publicly condemned slavery—only inflamed racial hatred and opposition among many whites.

JEFFERSON IN POWER

The growing political engagement of ordinary white Americans played an important role in electing Thomas Jefferson to the presidency. He later referred to his election as "the Revolution of 1800," asserting that it "was as real a revolution in the principles of our government as that of 1776 was in its form." That claim exaggerates: Jefferson's presidency did little to enhance political rights or social opportunities of white women or African Americans. Even so, during the following two decades Republicans did set the United States on a more democratic course. And in their dealings with Britain and France, as well as with the Indian tribes of the West, Republican administrations defined, for better and worse, a fuller sense of American nationality.

The New Capital City >> Thomas Jefferson

was the first president to be inaugurated in the new capital, Washington, D.C. In 1791 George Washington had commissioned Pierre Charles L'Enfant, a French architect and engineer who had served in the American Revolution, to draw up plans for the new seat of government. L'Enfant designed a city with broad avenues, statues and fountains, parks and plazas, and a central mall. Because the Federalists believed that government was the paramount power in a nation, they had intended that the city would be a new Rome—a cultural, intellectual, and commercial center of the Republic.

The new city fell far short of this grandiose dream. It was located in a swampy river bottom near the head of the Potomac, and the surrounding hills rendered the spot oppressively hot and muggy during the summer. The streets were filled with tree stumps and became seas of mud after a rain. Much of the District was wooded, and virtually all of it remained unoccupied. When the government moved to its new residence in 1800, the Senate chamber, where Jefferson took the oath of office, was the only part of the Capitol that had been completed.

This isolated and unimpressive capital reflected the new president's attitude toward government. Distrustful of centralized power of any kind, Jefferson deliberately set out to remake the national government into one of limited scope that touched few people's daily lives. The states rather than the federal government were "the most competent administrators for our domestic concerns," he asserted in his inaugural address. Ever the individualist, he recommended a government that left people "free to regulate their own pursuits of industry and improvement."

Jefferson's Philosophy

>> Jefferson was a product of the Enlightenment, with its faith in the power of human reason to improve society and decipher the universe. He considered "the will of the majority" to be "the only sure guardian of the rights of man," which he defined as "life, liberty, and the pursuit of happiness." Although he conceded that the masses might err, he was confident they would soon return to correct principles. His faith in human virtue exceeded that of most of the founding generation, yet in good republican fashion, he feared those in power, even if they had been elected by the people. Government seemed to Jefferson a necessary evil at best.

To Jefferson, agriculture was a morally superior way of life. "Those who labour in the earth are the chosen people of God, if ever he had a chosen people," he wrote in *Notes on the State of Virginia* (1787). Jefferson praised rural life for nourishing the honesty, independence, and virtue so essential in a republic.

Although Jefferson asserted that "the tree of liberty must be refreshed from time to time by the blood of patriots and tyrants," his reputation as a radical was undeserved. While he wanted to extend the suffrage to a greater number of Americans, he clung to the traditional republican idea that voters should own property and thus be economically independent. One of the largest slaveholders in the country, he increasingly muffled his once-bold condemnation of slavery, and in the last years of his life he reproached critics of the institution who sought to prevent it from expanding westward.

Slaveholding aristocrat and apostle of democracy, lofty theorist and pragmatic politician, Jefferson was a complex, at times contradictory, personality. But like most politicians, he was flexible in his approach to problems and tried to balance means and ends. And like most leaders, he quickly discovered that he confronted very different problems in power than he had in opposition.

Jefferson's Economic Policies

>> The new president quickly proceeded to cut spending and to reduce the size of the government. He also abolished the internal taxes enacted by the Federalists,

> Slaveholding aristocrat and apostle of democracy, lofty theorist and pragmatic politician, Jefferson was a complex, at times contradictory, personality.

including the controversial excise on whiskey, and thus was able to get rid of all tax collectors and inspectors. Land sales and the tariff duties would supply the funds needed to run the scaled-down government.

The most serious spending cuts were made in the military branches. Jefferson slashed the army budget in half, decreasing the army to 3,000 men. In a national emergency, he reasoned, the militia could defend the country. Jefferson reduced the navy even more, halting work on powerful frigates authorized during the naval war with France.

By such steps, Jefferson made significant progress toward paying off Hamilton's national debt. Still, he did not entirely dismantle the Federalists' economic program. Funding and assumption could not be reversed—the nation's honor was pledged to paying these debts, and Jefferson understood the importance of maintaining the nation's credit. More surprising, Jefferson argued that the national bank should be left to run its course until 1811, when its charter would expire. In reality, he expanded the bank's operations and, in words reminiscent of Hamilton, advocated tying banks and members of the business class to the government by rewarding those who supported the Republican party. In effect, practical politics had triumphed over agrarian economics.

WHITES AND INDIANS IN THE WEST

For all his pragmatism, Jefferson still viewed the lands stretching from the Appalachians to the Pacific through the perspective of his agrarian ideals. America's vast spaces provided enough land to last for a thousand generations, he predicted in his inaugural address, enough to transform the United States into "an empire of liberty."

The Miami Confederacy Resists

>> That optimistic vision contrasted sharply with the views of most Federalists, who feared the West as a threat to social order and stability. In the 1790s they had good reason to fear. British troops refused to leave their forts in the Northwest, and Indian nations still controlled most of the region. Recognizing that fact, the United States conceded that Indian nations had the right to negotiate as sovereign powers. North of the Ohio, leaders of the Miami Confederacy, composed of eight tribes, stoutly refused to sell their homelands without "the united voice of the confederacy."

In response the Washington administration sent 1,500 soldiers in 1790 under General Josiah Harmar to force the Indians to leave by burning their homes and fields. The Miami Confederacy, led by Blue Jacket and Little Turtle, roundly defeated the whites. Harmar was courtmartialed, the nation embarrassed, and a second expedition organized the following year under General Arthur St. Clair. This force of over 2,000 was again routed by Little Turtle, whose warriors killed 600 and wounded another 300. The defeat was the worst in the history of Indian wars undertaken by the United States. (In contrast, Custer's defeat in 1876 counted 264 fatalities.)

President Washington dispatched yet another army of 2,000 to the Ohio Valley, commanded by "Mad Anthony" Wayne, an accomplished general. At the Battle of Fallen Timbers in August 1794, Wayne won a decisive victory, breaking the Indians' hold on the Northwest. In the Treaty of Greenville (1795), the tribes **ceded** the southern two-thirds of the area between Lake Erie and the Ohio River, opening it up to white families. Federalists were still not eager to see the land settled. Although they allowed the sale of federal land, they kept the price high, with a required purchase of

cede to give up possession of

at least 640 acres—more than four times the size of most American farms.

Once in power, Jefferson and the Republicans encouraged settlement by reducing the minimum tract that buyers could purchase (to 320 acres) and by offering land on credit. Sales boomed. By 1820 more than 2 million whites lived in a region they had first entered only 50 years earlier. From Jefferson's perspective, western expansion was a blessing economically, socially, and even politically, because most of the new westerners were Republican.

Doubling the Size of the Nation >> With

Spain's colonial empire weakening, Americans were confident that before long they would gain control of Florida and the rest of the Mississippi, either through purchase or by military occupation. Spain had already agreed, in Pinckney's Treaty (see page 000), to allow Americans to navigate the lower Mississippi River. But in 1802 Spain suddenly retracted this right. More alarming, word came

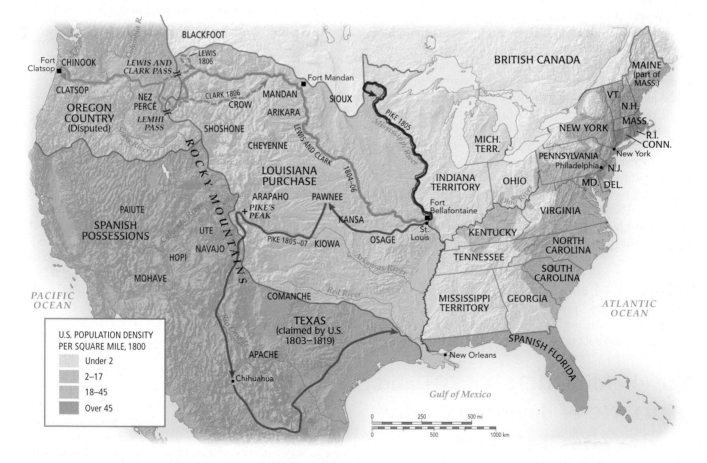

EXPLORATION AND EXPANSION: THE LOUISIANA PURCHASE

The vast, largely uncharted Louisiana Purchase lay well beyond the most densely populated areas of the United States. The Lewis and Clark expedition, along with Lieutenant Zebulon Pike's exploration of the upper Mississippi River and the Southwest, opened the way for westward expansion.

that France was about to take control of Louisiana—the territory lying between the Mississippi River and the Rocky Mountains—after a secret agreement with Spain. Under the leadership of Napoleon Bonaparte, France had become the most powerful nation on the European continent, with the military might to protect its new colony and to block American expansion.

Jefferson dispatched James Monroe to Paris to join Robert Livingston, the American minister, in negotiating the purchase of New Orleans and West Florida from the French and thus securing control of the Mississippi. The timing was fortunate: With war looming again in Europe, Napoleon lost interest in Louisiana. He needed money, and in April 1803 he offered to sell not just New Orleans but all of Louisiana to the United States. This proposal flabbergasted Livingston and Monroe. Their instructions said nothing about acquiring all of Louisiana, and they had not been authorized to spend what the French demanded. But here was an opportunity to expand dramatically the boundaries of the United States. Pressed for an immediate answer, Livingston and Monroe took a deep breath and, after haggling over a few details, agreed to purchase Louisiana for approximately $15 million. In one fell swoop, the American negotiators had doubled the country's size by adding some 830,000 square miles.

While Jefferson was pleased at the prospect of acquiring so much territory, he found the legality of the act troubling. The Constitution, after all, did not authorize the acquisition of territory by treaty. In the end, the president sent the treaty to the Senate for ratification, noting privately, "The less we say about constitutional difficulties the better." Once again pragmatism triumphed over theory.

Even before the Louisiana Purchase was completed, Congress secretly funded an expedition up the Missouri River to the Pacific. Leading that party were Meriwether Lewis, Jefferson's secretary, and William Clark, a younger brother of George Rogers Clark. Jefferson instructed them to make detailed observations of the soil, climate, rivers, minerals, and plant and animal life. They were also to investigate the practicability of an overland route to the Pacific and engage in diplomacy with the Indians along the way. By pushing onward to the Pacific, Lewis and Clark would strengthen the American title to Oregon, which several nations claimed but none effectively occupied.

In the spring of 1804 Lewis and Clark left St. Louis and headed up the Missouri River with 48 men. They laboriously hauled their boats upstream to present-day North Dakota, where they spent the winter with the Mandan Indians. The next spring, they headed west again. Only with great difficulty did the expedition pass the rugged mountains ahead of the winter snows and then float down first the Snake and then the Columbia River to the Pacific.

The western country Lewis and Clark traversed had been shaken by momentous changes over the previous quarter of a century. The trade routes across the plains and through the mountains circulated goods in greater quantities than ever before. Horses and guns in particular upset older Indian ways, making tribes more mobile and more dangerous. Lewis and Clark's expedition spotted Spanish horse gear from Mexico in villages along the upper Missouri River, guns from French traders to the northeast, and British teapots along the Columbia River. Most disruptive to these western lands was smallpox, which had made its way along the same trade routes ever since the pandemic of the 1780s (see Chapter 7). The disease decimated Indian populations and forced many tribes to resettle.

After a bleak winter in Oregon, the expedition returned home over the Rockies in 1806. It brought back thousands of plant and animal specimens and produced a remarkably accurate map of its journey. Lewis and Clark had crossed a continent disrupted by change. In the century to come the changes would only accelerate.

Pressure on Indian Lands and Culture >>

East of the Mississippi, white settlers continued to flood into the backcountry. Jefferson endorsed the policy that Indian tribes either would have to assimilate into American culture by becoming farmers and abandoning their seminomadic hunting or would have to move

⌃ Tents ringed the central area of a camp meeting where benches faced the preachers' platform. What does this illustration of an 1837 camp meeting suggest about gender relations and religious experience?

west. Jefferson defended these alternatives as in the best interests of the Indians, because he believed that otherwise they faced extermination. But he also recognized that by becoming farmers they would need less land. He encouraged the policy of selling goods on credit in order to lure Indians into debt. "When these debts get beyond what the individuals can pay," the president observed, "they become willing to lop them off by a cession of lands."

Between 1800 and 1810 whites pressed Indians into ceding more than 100 million acres in the Ohio River valley. The loss of so much land devastated Indian cultures and transformed their environment by reducing hunting grounds and making game and food scarce. "Stop your people from killing our game," the Shawnees complained in 1802 to federal Indian agents. "They would be angry if we were to kill a cow or hog of theirs, the little game that remains is very dear to us." Tribes also became dependent on white trade to obtain blankets, guns, metal utensils, alcohol, and decorative beads. To pay for these goods with furs, Indians often overtrapped, which forced them to invade the lands of neighboring tribes, provoking wars.

The strain produced by white expansion led to alcoholism, growing violence among tribe members, family disintegration, and the collapse of the clan system designed to regulate relations among different villages. The question of how to deal with white culture became a matter of anguished debate. While some Native Americans attempted to take up farming and accommodate to white ways, for most the course of assimilation proved unappealing and fraught with risk.

White Frontier Society >> Whites faced their
own problems on the frontier. In the first wave of settlement came backwoods families who cleared a few acres of forest by girdling the trees, removing the brush, and planting corn between the dead trunks. Such settlers were mostly squatters without legal title to their land. As a region filled up, these pioneers usually sold their improvements and headed west again.

Taking their place, typically, were young single men from the East, who married and started families. These pioneers, too, engaged in semisubsistence agriculture, save for the lucky few whose prime locations allowed them to transport their crops down the Ohio and Mississippi rivers to New Orleans for shipment to distant markets. But

> Key: d
>
> The Shawnee Indian leader Tecumseh tried to thwart the westward expansion of white settlement by
>
> a. forging alliances among the Indian nations of the Old Northwest.
> b. forging alliances among northern and southern Indian nations located between the Appalachians and the Mississippi.
> c. forging an alliance with the British during the War of 1812.
> d. all of these

many frontier families struggled, moving several times but never managing to rise from the ranks of squatters or tenant farmers to become independent landowners. Fledgling western communities lacked schools, churches, and courts, and inhabitants often lived miles distant from even their nearest neighbors.

The Beginnings of the Second Great Awakening >> This
hardscrabble frontier proved the perfect tinder for sparking a series of dramatic religious revivals in the decades surrounding 1800. What lit the fire were missionary efforts by major Protestant churches—particularly the Baptists and the Methodists—who sent their ministers to travel the countryside on horseback and to preach wherever they could gather a crowd. Often those religious meetings took place outdoors and drew eager hearers from as far as 100 miles away, who camped for several days in makeshift tents to listen to sermons and to share in praying and singing hymns.

Thus was born a new form of Protestant worship, the camp meeting, which drew national notice after a mammoth gathering at Cane Ridge, Kentucky, in August of 1801. At a time when the largest city in the state had only 2,000 people, more than 10,000 men, women, and children, white and black, flocked there to hear dozens of ministers preaching the gospel. Many in the crowd were overwhelmed by powerful religious feelings, some shrieking and shaking over guilt for their sins, others laughing and dancing from their high hopes of eternal salvation.

Some Protestant ministers denounced the "revival" at Cane Ridge and elsewhere as yet another instance of the ignorance and savagery of westerners. Other ministers were more optimistic: they

Was there any strategy that Indian nations between the Appalachians and the Mississippi could have adopted to halt white expansion?

THE INDIAN RESPONSE TO WHITE ENCROACHMENT

With land cessions and white western migration placing increased pressure on Indian cultures after 1790, news of the Prophet's revival fell on eager ears. It spread especially quickly northward along the shores of Lake Michigan and westward along Lake Superior and the interior of Wisconsin. Following the Battle of Tippecanoe, Tecumseh eclipsed the Prophet as the major leader of Indian resistance, but his trips south to forge political alliances met with success.

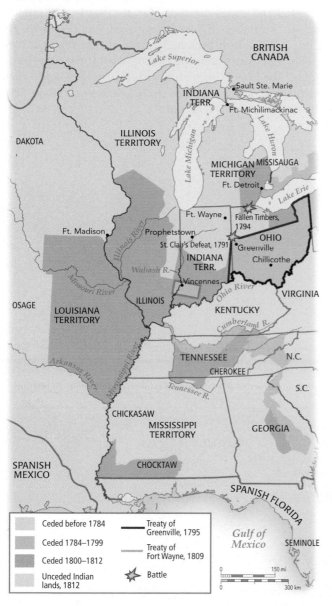

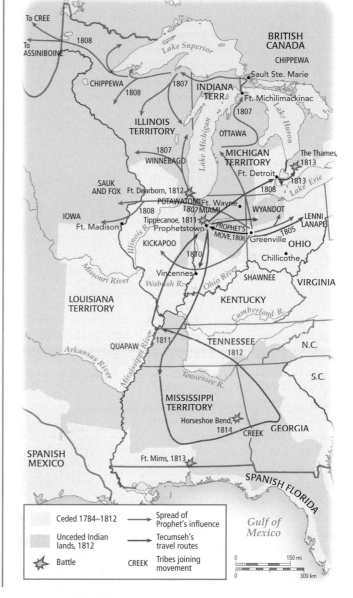

saw frontier camp meetings as the first sign of a Protestant Christian renewal that would sweep the new republic. Their hopes set the stage for what would come to be called the Second Great Awakening, a wave of religious revivals that swept throughout the nation after 1800 (see Chapter 12).

The Prophet, Tecumseh, and the Pan-Indian Movement >> Native peoples also turned to religion to meet the challenges of the early national frontier.

Indeed, in traditional Indian religions, they found the resource to revitalize their cultures by severing all ties with the white world. During the 1790s a revival led by Handsome Lake took hold among the Iroquois, following the loss of most of the Iroquois lands and the collapse of their military power in western New York. Later Lalawethika, also known as the Prophet, sparked a religious renewal among the Shawnees. The Prophet's early life was bleak: he was a poor hunter and as a child accidentally blinded himself in the right eye with an arrow; the ridicule of his fellow tribe members drove him to alcoholism.

Suddenly, in April 1805 he lapsed into a trance so deep that he was given up for dead. When he revived, he spoke of being reborn. From this vision and others, he outlined a new creed for the Shawnees.

Taking a new name—Tenskwatawa (Open Door)—he urged the Shawnees to renounce whiskey and white goods and return to their old ways of hunting with bows and arrows, eating customary foods such as corn and beans, and wearing traditional garb. The Shawnee could revitalize their culture, the Prophet insisted, by condemning intertribal violence, embracing monogamous marriage, and rejecting the idea of private instead of communal property. Except for guns, which could be used in self-defense, his followers were to discard all items made by whites. Intermarriage with white settlers was forbidden.

Setting up headquarters in 1808 at the newly built village of Prophetstown in Indiana, Tenskwatawa led a wider revival among the tribes of the Northwest. Just as thousands of white settlers traveled to Methodist or Baptist camp meetings in the woods, where preachers denounced the evils of liquor and called for a return to a purer way of life, so thousands of Indians from northern tribes traveled to the Prophet's village for inspiration. Many were concerned about the threatened loss of Indian lands.

Whereas Tenskwatawa's strategy of revitalization was primarily religious, his older brother Tecumseh turned to political and military solutions. William Henry Harrison described Tecumseh as "one of those uncommon geniuses which spring up occasionally to produce revolutions and overturn the established order of things." Tall and athletic, an accomplished hunter and warrior, Tecumseh traveled throughout the Northwest, urging tribes to forget ancient rivalries and unite to protect their lands. Just as Indian nations in the past had adopted the strategy of uniting in a confederacy, Tecumseh's alliance brought together the Wyandot, Chippewa, Sauk and Fox, Winnebago, Potawatomi, and other tribes on an even larger scale.

But the campaign for Pan-Indian unity ran into serious obstacles. Often, Tecumseh was asking tribes to unite with their traditional enemies in a common cause. When he headed south in 1811, he encountered greater resistance. Most southern tribes were more prosperous, were more acculturated, and felt less immediate pressure on their land from whites. His southern mission ended largely in failure.

To compound Tecumseh's problems, while he was away a force of Americans under Governor Harrison defeated the Prophet's forces at the Battle of Tippecanoe in November 1811 and destroyed Prophetstown. As a result, Tecumseh became convinced that the best way to contain white expansion was to play off the Americans against the British, who still held forts in the Great Lakes region. Indeed, by 1811, the United States and Great Britain were on the brink of war.

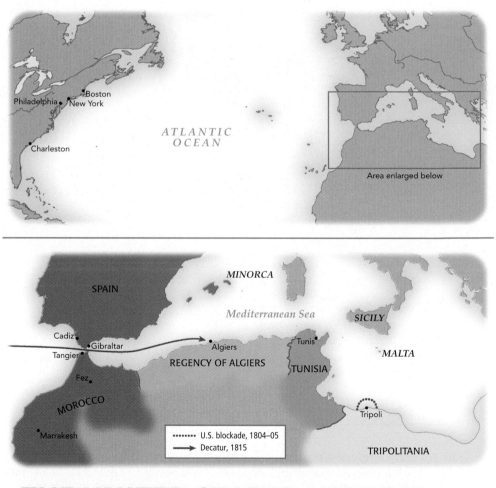

THE UNITED STATES AND THE BARBARY STATES, 1801–1815

The young United States, like many European powers, found its trading vessels challenged by the Barbary states of Morocco, Algiers, Tunisia, and Tripoli. When the pasha of Tripoli declared war on the United States in 1801, Jefferson dispatched a force that blockaded Tripoli to bring the war to an end in 1805. Tribute paid to the other Barbary States continued until 1816, after a new naval force, led by Captain Stephen Decatur, forced the ruler of Algiers to end the practice.

∧ Corsairs, light, maneuverable ships sailing out of Barbary ports such as Tripoli (shown here), were well fitted for their purpose. As one historian noted: "Like stinging insects, their light, rapid vessels were designed to strike at unarmed or lightly armed merchantmen, while being able to flee very speedily at the mere approach of a warship."

THE SECOND WAR FOR AMERICAN INDEPENDENCE

As Tecumseh worked to achieve a Pan-Indian alliance, Jefferson encountered his own difficulties in trying to achieve American political unity. The president hoped to woo all but the most extreme Federalists into the Republican camp. His reelection in 1804 showed how much progress he had made, as he defeated Federalist Charles Cotesworth Pinckney and carried 15 of 17 states. With the Republicans controlling three-quarters of the seats in Congress, one-party rule seemed at hand.

But events across the Atlantic complicated the efforts to unite Americans. Only two weeks after Napoleon agreed to sell Louisiana to the United States, war broke out between France and Great Britain. As in the 1790s the United States found itself caught between the world's two greatest powers. Jefferson insisted that the nation should remain neutral in a European war. But the policies he proposed to maintain neutrality sparked sharp divisions in American society and momentarily revived the two-party system.

In the past, Jefferson had not shrunk from the use of force in dealing with foreign nations—most notably the Barbary states of North Africa—Algiers, Morocco, Tripoli, and Tunis. During the seventeenth and eighteenth centuries their corsairs plundered the cargo of enemy ships and enslaved the crews. European nations found it convenient to pay tributes to the Barbary states so their ships could sail unmolested. But both Jefferson and John Adams disliked that idea. The "policy of Christendom" of paying trib-ute, complained Adams, "has made Cowards of all their Sailors before the Standard of Mahomet [Mohammed]."

By the time John Adams became president, he had subdued his outrage and agreed to tributes. But when Tripoli increased its demands in 1801, President Jefferson sent a squadron of American ships to force a settlement. In 1803 Tripoli captured the *U.S.S. Philadelphia*. Only the following year did Lieutenant Stephen Decatur repair the situation by sneaking into Tripoli's harbor and burning the vessel. The American blockade that followed forced Tripoli to give up its demands for tribute. Even so, the United States continued paying tribute to the other Barbary states until 1816.

The Embargo >> Jefferson was willing to fight the Barbary States, but he drew back from declaring war against Britain or France. Between 1803 and 1807, Britain seized more than 500 American ships; France more than 300. The British navy also impressed into service thousands of sailors, some of who were deserters from England's fleet but others who were native-born Americans. Despite such harrassment, Jefferson pursued a program of "peaceable coercion" designed to protect neutral rights without war. His proposed **embargo** not only prohibited American ships from trading with foreign

> **embargo** government act prohibiting trade with a foreign country or countries, usually to exert economic pressure.

ports but also stopped the export of all American goods. The president was confident that American exports were so essential to the two belligerents that they would quickly agree to respect American neutral rights. In December 1807 Congress passed the Embargo Act.

Jefferson had seriously miscalculated. France did not depend on American trade and so managed well enough, while British ships quickly took over the carrying trade as American vessels lay idle. Under the embargo, both American imports and exports plunged. As the center of American shipping, New England port cities protested the loudest, and their merchants smuggled behind officials' backs.

Madison and the Young Republicans »

Following Washington's example, Jefferson did not seek a third term. A caucus of Republican members of Congress selected James Madison to run against Federalist Charles Cotesworth Pinckney. Madison triumphed easily, although in discontented New England, the Federalists picked up 24 seats in Congress.

Few men have assumed the presidency with more experience than James Madison, yet his tenure as president proved disappointing. Despite his intellectual brilliance, he lacked the force of leadership and the inner strength to impose his will on less capable men.

With a president reluctant to fight for what he wanted, leadership passed to Congress. The elections of 1810 swept in a new generation of Republicans, led by the magnetic 34-year-old Henry Clay of Kentucky, who gained the rare distinction of being elected Speaker in his first term. These younger Republicans were more nationalistic than the generation led by Jefferson and Madison. They sought an ambitious program of economic development and were aggressive expansionists, especially those from frontier districts. Their willingness to go to war earned them the name of War Hawks. Though they numbered fewer than

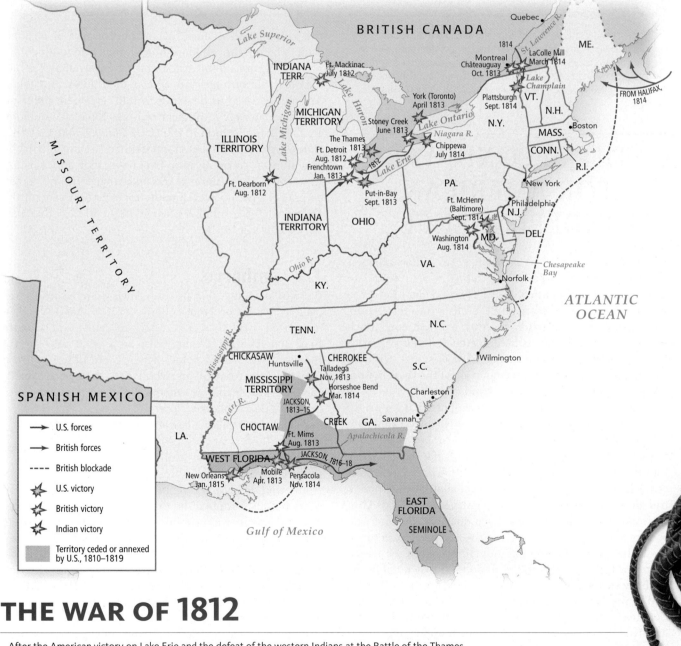

THE WAR OF 1812

After the American victory on Lake Erie and the defeat of the western Indians at the Battle of the Thames, the British adopted a three-pronged strategy to invade the United States, climaxing with an attempt on New Orleans. But they met their match in Andrew Jackson, whose troops marched to New Orleans after fighting a series of battles against the Creeks and forcing them to cede a massive tract of land.

30 in Congress, they quickly became the driving force in the Republican party.

The Decision for War >> During Jefferson's final week in office in early 1809, Congress repealed the Embargo Act. The following year Congress authorized trade with France and England but decreed that if one of the two belligerents agreed to stop interfering with American shipping, trade with the other would be prohibited.

Given these circumstances, Napoleon outmaneuvered the British by announcing that he would put aside the French trade regulations. Madison took the French emperor at his word and reimposed a ban on trade with England. French raiders continued to seize American ships, but American anger focused on the British, who then seized many more ships and continued to impress American sailors. Finally, on June 16, 1812, the British ministry suspended the searches and seizures of American ships.

The concession came too late. Two days earlier, unaware of the change in policy, Congress granted Madison's request for a declaration of war against Britain. The vote was mostly along party lines, with every Federalist voting against war. By contrast, members of Congress from the South and the West clamored most strongly for war. Their constituents were consumed with a desire to seize additional territory in Canada or in Florida (owned by Britain's ally Spain). In addition, they accused the British of stirring up hostility among the Indian tribes.

Perhaps most important, the War Hawks were convinced that Britain had never truly accepted the verdict of the American Revolution. To them, American independence—and with it republicanism—hung in the balance. For Americans hungering to be accepted in the community of nations, nothing rankled more than still being treated by the British as colonials.

With Britain preoccupied by Napoleon, the War Hawks expected an easy victory. In truth, the United States was totally unprepared for war. Crippled by Jefferson's cutbacks, the navy was unable to lift the British blockade of the American coast, which bottled up the country's merchant marine and most of its navy. As for the U.S. army, it was small and poorly led. When Congress moved to increase its size to 75,000, even the most hawkish states failed to meet their quotas. Congress was also reluctant to levy taxes to finance the war.

A three-pronged American invasion of Canada from Detroit, Niagara, and Lake Champlain failed dismally in 1812. Americans fared better the following year, as both sides raced to build a navy on the strategically located Lake Erie. Led by Commander Oliver Hazard Perry, American forces won a decisive victory at Put-In Bay in 1813.

As the United States struggled to organize its forces, Tecumseh sensed that his longawaited opportunity had come to drive Americans out of the western territories. "Here is a chance . . . such as will never occur again," he told a war council, "for us Indians of North America to form ourselves into one great combination." Allying with the British, Tecumseh traveled south in the fall to talk again with his Creek allies. To coordinate an Indian offensive for the following summer, he left a bundle of red sticks with eager Creek soldiers. They were to remove one stick each day from the bundle and attack when the sticks had run out.

Some of the older Creeks were more acculturated and preferred an American alliance. But about 2,000 younger "Red Stick" Creeks launched a series of attacks, climaxed by the destruction of Fort Mims along the Alabama River in August 1813. Once again, the Indians' lack of unity was a serious handicap, as warriors from the Cherokee, Choctaw, and Chickasaw tribes, traditional Creek enemies, allied with the Americans. At the Battle of Horseshoe Bend in March 1814, General Andrew Jackson and his Tennessee militia soundly defeated the Red Stick Creeks. Jackson promptly dictated a peace treaty under which the Creeks ceded 22 million acres of land in the Mississippi Territory. They and the other southern tribes still retained significant landholdings, but Indian military power had been broken in the South, east of the Mississippi.

Farther north, in October 1813, American forces under General William Henry Harrison defeated the British and their Indian allies at the Battle of the Thames. In the midst of heavy fighting Tecumseh was killed. With him died any hope of a Pan-Indian movement.

The British Invasion >> As long as the war against Napoleon continued, the British were unwilling to divert army units to North America. But in 1814 Napoleon was at last defeated. Free to concentrate on America, the British devised a coordinated strategy to invade the United States in the northern, central, and southern parts of the country. The main army headed south from Montreal but was checked when Americans destroyed the British fleet on Lake Champlain.

Meanwhile, a smaller British force captured Washington and burned several public buildings, including the

WITNESS

Impressed by the British Navy

"I had a protection [i.e., passport] from the Customhouse in Salem, which I showed to captain Elliot: he swore that I was an Englishman, tore my protection to pieces before my eyes, and threw it overboard, and ordered me to go to work—I told him I did not belong to his flag, and I would do no work under it. He then ordered my legs to be put in irons, and the next morning ordered the master of arms to . . . give me two dozen lashes. . . ."

Capitol and the president's home. To cover the scars of this destruction, the executive mansion was painted with whitewash and became known as the White House. The burning of the capital was a humiliating event: President Madison and his wife, Dolley, were forced to flee. But the defeat had little military significance. The principal British objective was Baltimore, where for 25 hours their fleet bombarded Fort McHenry in the city's harbor. When Francis Scott Key saw the American flag still flying above the fort at dawn, he hurriedly composed the verses of "The Star Spangled Banner," which was eventually adopted as the national anthem.

The third British target was New Orleans, where a formidable army of 7,500 British troops was opposed by a hastily assembled force commanded by Major General Andrew Jackson. The Americans included regular soldiers; frontiersmen from Kentucky and Tennessee; citizens of New Orleans, including several companies of free African Americans; Choctaw Indians; and a group of pirates. Jackson's outnumbered and ill-equipped forces won a stunning victory, which made the general an overnight hero.

In December 1814, while Jackson was organizing the defense of New Orleans, New England Federalists met in Hartford to map strategy against the war. Angry as they were, the delegates still rejected calls for secession. Instead they proposed a series of amendments to the Constitution that showed their displeasure with the government's economic policies and their resentment of the South's national political power.

To the convention's dismay, its representatives arrived in Washington to present their demands just as news of Andrew Jackson's victory was being trumpeted on the streets. The celebrations badly undercut the Hartford Convention, as did news from across the Atlantic that American negotiators in Ghent, Belgium, had signed a treaty ending the war. Hostilities had ceased, technically, on Christmas Eve 1814, two weeks before the Battle of New Orleans. Both sides were relieved to end the conflict, even though the Treaty of Ghent left unresolved the issues of impressment, neutral rights or trade.

AMERICA TURNS INWARD

The return of peace hard on the heels of Jackson's victory sparked a new confidence in many Americans. The new nationalism sounded the death knell of the Federalist party, for even talk of secession at the Hartford Convention had tainted the party with disunion and treason. In the 1816 election Madison's secretary of state, James Monroe,

⌃ After Andrew Jackson's victory at New Orleans, the Hartford Convention looked to many like a traitorous leap into the arms of the British king.

Free states and territories

Slave states and territories

Closed to slavery in Missouri Compromise

Open to slavery in Missouri Compromise

THE MISSOURI COMPROMISE AND THE UNION'S BOUNDARIES IN 1820

resoundingly defeated Federalist Rufus King of New York. Four years later Monroe ran for reelection unopposed.

Monroe's Presidency >> The major domestic challenge that Monroe faced was the renewal of sectional rivalries in 1819, when the Missouri Territory applied for admission as a slave state. Before the controversy over Missouri erupted, slavery had not been a major issue in American politics. Congress had debated the institution when it prohibited the African slave trade in 1808, the earliest year this step could be taken under the Constitution. But lacking any specific federal legislation to stop it, slavery had crossed the Mississippi River into the Louisiana Purchase. Louisiana entered the Union in 1812 as a slave state, and in 1818 Missouri, which had about 10,000 slaves in its population, asked permission to come in too.

In 1818 the Union contained 11 free and 11 slave states. As the federal government became stronger and more active, both the North and the South worried about maintaining their political power. The North's greater population gave it a majority in the House of Representatives, 105 to 81. The Senate, of course, was evenly balanced, because each state had two senators regardless of population. But Maine, which previously had been part of Massachusetts, requested admission as a free state. That would upset the balance unless Missouri came in as a slave state.

Representative James Tallmadge of New York disturbed this delicate state of affairs when in 1819 he introduced an amendment that would establish a program of gradual emancipation in Missouri. For the first time Congress directly debated the morality of slavery, often bitterly. The House approved the Tallmadge amendment, but

the Senate refused to accept it, and the two houses deadlocked.

When Congress reconvened in 1820, Henry Clay of Kentucky promoted what came to be known as the Missouri Compromise. Under its terms Missouri was admitted as a slave state and Maine as a free state. In addition, slavery was forever prohibited in the remainder of the Louisiana Purchase north of 36°30' (the southern boundary of Missouri). Clay's proposal, the first of several sectional compromises he would engineer in his long career, won congressional approval and Monroe signed the measure, ending the crisis. But southern fears for the security of slavery and northern fears about its spread remained.

Monroe's greatest achievements were diplomatic, accomplished largely by his talented secretary of state, John Quincy Adams, the son of President John Adams. An experienced diplomat, Adams thought of the Republic in continental terms and was intent on promoting expansion to the Pacific. Such a vision required dealing with Spain, which had never recognized the legality of the Louisiana Purchase. In addition, between 1810 and 1813 the United States had occupied and unilaterally annexed Spanish West Florida.

But Spain was preoccupied with events farther south in the Americas. In the first quarter of the nineteenth century, its colonies one after another revolted and established themselves as independent nations. These revolutions increased the pressure on the Spanish minister to America, Luis de Onís, to come to terms with the United States. So, too, did Andrew Jackson, who marched into East Florida and captured several Spanish forts in 1818. Jackson had exceeded his instructions, but Adams understood the additional pressure this aggression put on Onís and refused to disavow it.

Fearful that the United States might next invade Texas or other Spanish territory, Spain agreed to the Transcontinental Treaty in February 1819. Its terms set the boundary between American and Spanish territory all the way to the Pacific. Spain not only gave up its claims to the Pacific Northwest but also ceded Florida. In order to obtain the line to the Pacific, the United States abandoned its contention that Texas was part of the Louisiana Purchase.

More importantly, the United States also came to terms with Great Britain. Following the War of 1812, the British abandoned their connections with the western Indian tribes and no longer attempted to block American expansion to the Rocky Mountains. In a growing spirit of cooperation, the countries agreed in 1818 to the 49th parallel as the northern boundary of the Louisiana Purchase and also to joint control of the Oregon Territory for 10 years, subject to renewal.

In his annual message to Congress, on December 2, 1823. Monroe also announced that the United States would not interfere with already established European colonies in the Western Hemisphere. But any intervention in the new republics of Latin America, he warned, would be considered a hostile act: "The American continents . . . are henceforth not to be considered as subjects for future colonization by any European powers." The essence of this policy was the concept of two worlds, one old and one new, each refraining from interfering in the other's affairs. American public opinion hailed Monroe's statement and then promptly forgot it. Only years later would it be referred to as the Monroe Doctrine.

The three decades after 1789 demonstrated how profoundly events in the wider world could affect life within the United States, shaping its politics, its boundaries, its economy—its future.

The French Revolution contributed to splintering the once-united leaders of the American Revolution into two rival parties. The wars that followed, between France and England, deepened the divisions between Federalists and Republicans and prompted both parties to mobilize the political loyalties of ordinary white American men and women. Napoleon's ambitions to conquer Europe handed Jefferson the Louisiana Territory, while British efforts to reclaim its American empire tempted some New Englanders to secede from the Union and encouraged Tecumseh's hopes of mounting a pan-Indian resistance on the frontier. The Haitian Revolution in the Caribbean prompted free blacks in northern cities to protest racial inequalities and slavery within the United States.

But by the 1820s, most white Americans paid less attention to events abroad than to expanding across the vast North American continent. Jefferson had dreamed of an "empire of liberty," delighting in expansion as the means to preserve a nation of small farmers. But younger, more

nationalistic Republicans had a different vision of expansion. They spoke of internal improvements, protective tariffs to foster American industries, roads and canals to link farmers with towns, cities, and wider markets. These new Republicans were not aristocratic, like the Federalists of old. Still, their dream of a national, commercial republic resembled Franklin's and Hamilton's more than Jefferson's. They had seen how handsomely American merchants and commercial farmers profited when European wars swelled demand for American wheat and cotton. They looked to profit from speculation in land, the growth of commercial agriculture, and new methods of industrial manufacturing. If they represented the rising generation, what would be the fate of Crèvecoeur's semisubsistence farm communities? The answer was not yet clear.

CHAPTER SUMMARY

Basic social divisions between the commercial and semi-subsistence regions shaped the politics of the new United States. Between 1789 and the 1820s, the first parties emerged and, along with them, a more popular and participatory political culture. Over the same decades, Indian confederacies mounted a sustained resistance to westward expansion, while events in Europe deepened divisions among Federalists and Republicans and threatened the very existence of the fledgling American republic.

- The first party to organize in the 1790s was the Federalists, led by Alexander Hamilton and George Washington.
- Divisions over Hamilton's policies as secretary of the treasury led to the formation of the Republicans, led by James Madison and Thomas Jefferson.
- The commercially minded Federalists believed in order and hierarchy, supported loose construction of the Constitution, and wanted a powerful central government to promote economic growth.

Significant Events

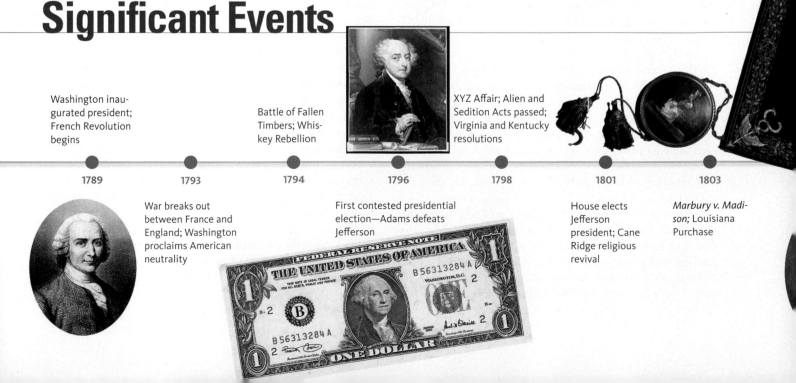

Washington inaugurated president; French Revolution begins

Battle of Fallen Timbers; Whiskey Rebellion

XYZ Affair; Alien and Sedition Acts passed; Virginia and Kentucky resolutions

1789   1793   1794   1796   1798   1801   1803

War breaks out between France and England; Washington proclaims American neutrality

First contested presidential election—Adams defeats Jefferson

House elects Jefferson president; Cane Ridge religious revival

Marbury v. Madison; Louisiana Purchase

- The Republican party, with its sympathy for agrarian ideals, endorsed strict construction of the Constitution, wanted a less active federal government, and harbored a strong fear of aristocracy.
- The French Revolution, the XYZ Affair, the naval war, and the Alien and Sedition Acts also deepened the partisan division between Federalists and Republicans during the 1790s. The Federalists demonstrated that the new government could be a more active force in American society, but their controversial domestic and foreign policies, internal divisions, and open hostility to the masses eventually led to their downfall.
- Before becoming president, Jefferson advocated the principles of agrarianism, limited government, and strict construction of the Constitution. But once in power, he failed to dismantle Hamilton's economic program and promoted western expansion by acquiring Louisiana from France.
- Chief Justice John Marshall proclaimed that the courts were to interpret the meaning of the Constitution (judicial review), a move that helped the judiciary emerge as an equal branch of government.
- Lewis and Clark produced the first reliable information and maps of the Louisiana territory. The lands they passed through had been transformed over the previous 25 years by disease, dislocation, and the arrival of horses and guns.
- The Shawnee prophet Tenskwatawa and his brother Tecumseh organized the most important Indian resistance to the expansion of the new republic, but the movement collapsed with the death of Tecumseh during the War of 1812.
- France and Britain both interfered with neutral rights, and the United States went to war against Britain in 1812.
- In the years after 1815 there was a surge in American nationalism, reflected and reinforced by Britain's recognition of American sovereignty and the Monroe Doctrine's prohibition of European intervention in the Western Hemisphere. But the Missouri crisis was an early indication of growing sectional rivalries.

Additional Reading

Two good overviews of early national politics are Stanley Elkins and Eric McKitrick's *The Age of Federalism* (1993) and James Roger Sharp, *American Politics in the Early Republic* (1993). For a fuller understanding of Federalist political thought, consult Linda Kerber, *Federalists in Dissent* (1970), and David Hackett Fischer, *The Revolution of American Conservatism* (1965); for the Republicans, read Lance Banning, *The Jeffersonian Persuasion* (1978), and Drew R. McCoy, *The Elusive Republic* (1980). Another approach to understanding the politics of this period is to read about the lives of leading political figures: among the best are Joseph Ellis's biographies of John Adams (*Passionate Sage,* 1993) and Thomas Jefferson (*American Sphinx,* rev. ed., 1998) and two biographies of Alexander Hamilton by Ron Chernow and Gerald Stourzh (all cited in the full bibliography). To become better acquainted with the popular political culture of the early republic, consult *Beyond the Founders* (2004), a superb collection of essays edited by Jeffrey Pasley, Andrew W. Robertson, and David Waldstreicher. For an engaging narrative about the political influence exerted by white women, see Catherine Allgor, *Parlor Politics* (2000), and for rich descriptions of the social and political interactions among whites, African Americans, and Indians in the new republic, see Joshua Rothman, *Notorious in the Neighborhood* (2003), and John Wood Sweet, *Bodies Politic* (2003). To gain a fuller understanding of the lives of both Indians and western frontier settlers, rely on Gregory Evans Dowd, *A Spirited Resistance* (1993); Roger Kennedy, *Mr. Jefferson's Lost Cause* (2003); John Mack Faragher's *Sugar Creek* (1986); Adam Rothman, *Slave Country* (2005); Alan Taylor, *William Cooper's Town* (1995); and R. David Edmunds, *The Shawnee Prophet* (1983) and *Tecumseh and the Quest for Indian Leadership* (1984).

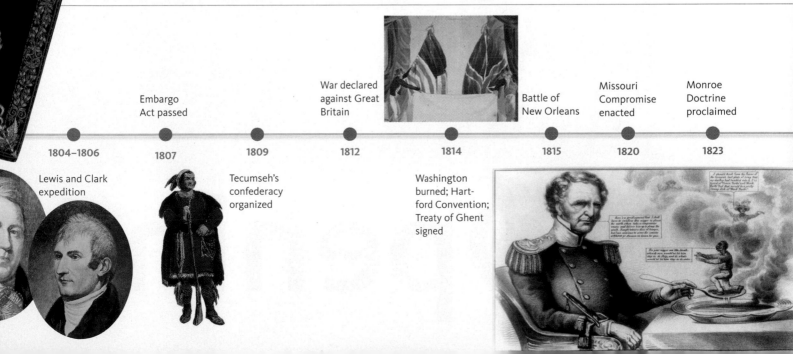

| 1804–1806 | 1807 | 1809 | 1812 | 1814 | 1815 | 1820 | 1823 |

Lewis and Clark expedition

Embargo Act passed

Tecumseh's confederacy organized

War declared against Great Britain

Washington burned; Hartford Convention; Treaty of Ghent signed

Battle of New Orleans

Missouri Compromise enacted

Monroe Doctrine proclaimed

10

THE Opening

The Erie Canal was pivotal in transforming many inland settlements from semisubsistence economies into commercial ones. Mary Keys painted this watercolor of Lockport, New York, along the canal. A team of three horses pulls the canal boat as the respectably clothed passengers enjoy the scenery.

Lockport on Erie Canal   New York.   Painted by

Keys. 1842

WHAT'S TO COME

189   THE MARKET REVOLUTION

193   A RESTLESS TEMPER

194   THE RISE OF FACTORIES

199   SOCIAL STRUCTURES OF
      THE MARKET SOCIETY

201   PROSPERITY AND ANXIETY

FROM BOOM TO BUST WITH ONE-DAY CLOCKS

In the years before the Civil War, the name of Chauncey Jerome could be found traced in neat, sharp letters in a thousand different places across the globe: everywhere from the fireplace mantels of southern planters to the log cabins of Illinois farmers, and even in Chinese trading houses. For Chauncey Jerome was a New England clockmaker whose clever and inexpensive machines had conquered the markets of the world. »

OF America 1815—1850

As a boy Jerome had apprenticed himself to a carpenter, but after serving in the War of 1812 he decided to try clock-making. For years he eked out a living peddling his products from farmhouse to farmhouse, until 1824, when his career took off thanks to a "very showy" bronze looking-glass clock. Between 1827 and 1837 Jerome's factory produced more clocks than any other in the country. But when the Panic of 1837 struck, Jerome had to scramble to avoid financial ruin.

Looking for a new opportunity, he set out to produce an inexpensive brass "one-day" clock—so called because its winding mechanism kept it running that long. Traditionally, the works of these clocks were made of wood, and the wheels and teeth had to be painstakingly cut by hand. Jerome's brass version proved more accurate and cheaper to boot. Costs came down further when he began to use interchangeable parts and combined his operations for making cases and movements within a single factory in New Haven, Connecticut. By systematically organizing the production process, Jerome brought the price of a good clock within the reach of ordinary people. So popular were the new models that desperate competitors began attaching Jerome labels to their own inferior imitations.

Disaster loomed again in 1855 when Jerome took on several unreli-

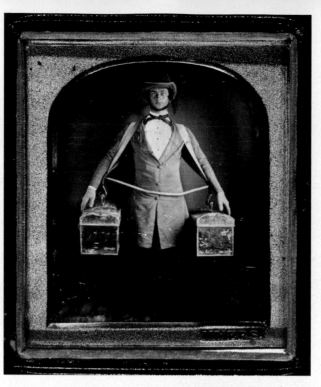

« Peddlers like this one helped spread the market economy to every corner of the United States. Early in his career, Chauncey Jerome himself peddled his clocks from farmhouse to farmhouse.

able partners. Within a few years his business faltered, then failed. At the age of 62, the once-prominent business leader found himself working again in a clock factory as an ordinary mechanic. He lived his last years in poverty.

Chauncey Jerome's life spanned the transition from the master-apprentice system of production to the beginnings of mechanization and the rise of the factory system. By 1850 the notion of independent American farmers living mainly on what they themselves produced had become a dream of the past. In its place stood a commercial republic in which a full-blown national market encompassed most settled areas of the country.

The concept of the market is crucial here. Americans tied themselves to one another eagerly, even aggressively, through the mechanism of the free market. They sold cotton or wheat and bought manufactured cloth or brass one-day clocks. They

borrowed money not merely to buy a house or farm but also to speculate and profit. They relied, even in many rural villages, on cash and paper money instead of bartering for goods and services. American life moved from less to more specialized forms of labor. It moved from subsistence-oriented to more commercially oriented outlooks and from face-to-face local dealings to impersonal, distant transactions. It shifted from the mechanically simple to the technologically complex and from less dense patterns of settlement on farms to more complex arrangements in cities and towns. Such were the changes Chauncey Jerome witnessed—indeed, changes he helped to bring about himself, with his clocks that divided the working days of Americans into more disciplined, orderly segments.

As these changes took place, Jerome sensed that society had taken on a different tone—that the marketplace and its ethos had become dominant. "It is all money and business, business and money which make the man now-a-days," he complained. "Success is every thing...." The United States, according to one foreign traveler, had become "one gigantic workshop, over the entrance of which there is the blazing inscription 'No admission here except on business.'" «

THE MARKET REVOLUTION

The national market economy began to develop following the War of 1812. As the United States entered a period of unprecedented economic expansion, the economy became varied enough to grow without relying on international trade. Before the war, if European nations suddenly stopped purchasing American commodities like tobacco and timber, the domestic economy faltered. Since so many Americans remained rural and primarily self-sufficient, they could not absorb any increase in goods produced by American manufacturers.

But the War of 1812 marked an important turning point in the creation and expansion of a domestic market. First the embargo and then the war itself stimulated manufacturing, particularly in textiles. In addition, war had also bottled up capital in Europe. When peace was restored, this capital flowed into the United States to take advantage of new investment opportunities. Finally, the war experience led the federal government to adopt policies designed to spur economic expansion.

The New Nationalism >>
After the war with Britain, leadership passed to a new generation of the Republic—younger men such as Henry Clay, John C. Calhoun, and John Quincy Adams. Each was an ardent nationalist eager to use federal power to promote development. Increasingly dominant within the Republican party, they advocated the "New Nationalism," a set of economic policies designed to help all regions prosper and bind the nation more tightly together.

Even James Madison saw the need for increased federal activity, given the problems the government experienced during the war. The national bank had closed its doors in 1811 when its charter expired, and the result had been financial chaos. With Madison's approval, Congress in 1816 chartered the Second Bank of the United States for a period of 20 years. Madison also agreed to a mildly protective tariff to aid young American industries by raising the price of competing foreign goods. Finally, Madison supported federal aid for internal improvements such as roads, canals, and bridges, since the war had demonstrated how cumbersome it was to move troops or supplies overland.

Did the Market Revolution benefit most Americans?

The Cotton Trade >>
The most important spur to American economic development after 1815 was the growing cotton trade. Cotton production was limited until 1793, when Eli Whitney invented the cotton gin, a mechanical device that removed sticky seeds from the lint. With a slave now able to clean 50 pounds of cotton a day (compared with only 1 pound by hand), and with prices high on the world market, cotton production in the Lower South soared. By 1840 the South produced more than 60 percent of the world supply, and cotton accounted for almost two-thirds of all American exports.

As for the North, its factories increasingly made money by turning raw cotton into cloth, while northern merchants reaped profits from shipping the cotton and then reshipping the textiles. Planters used the income they earned to purchase foodstuffs from the West and goods and services from the Northeast.

The Transportation Revolution >>
For a market economy to become truly national, a transportation network linking various parts of the nation was essential. The economy had not become self-sustaining earlier partly because the only way to transport goods cheaply was by water. Thus trade was limited largely to coastal and international markets, for even on rivers, bulky goods moved easily in only one direction: downstream.

After 1815, all that changed. From 1825 to 1855—the span of a single generation—the cost of transportation on land fell 95 percent, while its speed increased fivefold. As a result, new regions were drawn quickly into the market.

Canals attracted considerable investment capital, especially after the success of the Erie Canal. Built between 1818 and 1825, the canal stretched 364 miles from Albany on the Hudson River to Buffalo on Lake Erie. Its construction by the state was an act of faith, for in 1816 the United States had only 100 miles of canals, none longer than 28 miles. But within a few years of opening, the Erie Canal paid for itself. It reduced the cost of shipping a ton of goods from Buffalo to New York City from more than 19 cents a mile to less than 3 cents. Where the canal's busy traffic passed, settlers flocked, and towns like Rochester and Lockport sprang up and thrived by moving goods and serving markets. The steady flow of goods eastward gave New York City the dominant position in the scramble for control of western trade.

TRAVEL TIMES, 1800 AND 1830

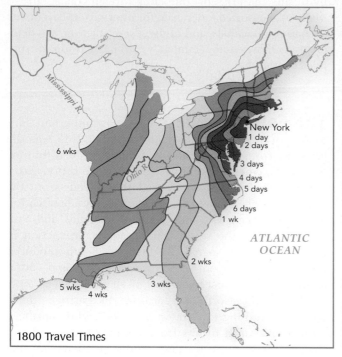

1800 Travel Times

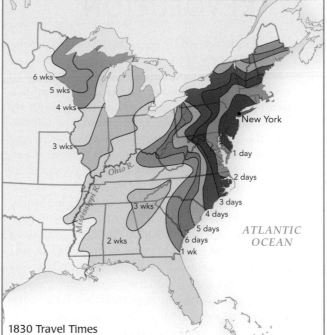

1830 Travel Times

New York's commercial rivals, like Philadelphia and Baltimore, were soon frantically trying to build their own canals to the West. Western states such as Ohio and Indiana, convinced that their prosperity depended on cheap transportation, constructed canals to link interior regions with the Great Lakes. By 1840 the nation had completed more than 3,300 miles of canals at a cost of about $125 million. Almost half of that amount came from state governments.

Because of its vast expanse, the United States depended particularly on river transportation. But shipping goods downstream from Pittsburgh to New Orleans took 6 weeks, and the return journey required 17 weeks or more. Steamboats reduced the time of an upstream trip from New Orleans to Louisville from 90 to 8 days while cutting costs by 90 percent.

Robert Fulton in 1807 demonstrated the commercial possibilities of propelling a boat with steam when his ship, the Clermont, traveled from New York City to Albany on the Hudson River. But steamboats had the greatest effect on transportation on western rivers, where the flat-bottomed boats could haul heavy loads even in low water.

The first significant railroads appeared in the 1830s, largely as feeder lines to canals. Soon enough, cities and towns saw that their future depended on having good rail links. The country had only 13 miles of track in 1830, but 10 years later railroad and canal mileage were almost exactly equal (3,325 miles). By 1850, the nation had a total of 8,879 miles.

Railroad rates were usually higher, but railroads were twice as fast as steamboats, offered more direct routes, and could operate year-round. Although railroads increasingly dominated the transportation system after 1850, canals and steamboats were initially the key to creating a national market.

Revolution in Communications >> What rail and steam engines did for transportation, Samuel F. B. Morse's telegraph did for communications. Morse in 1837 patented a device that sent electrical pulses over a wire, and before long, telegraph lines fanned out in all directions, linking various parts of the country in instantaneous communication. The new form of communication sped business information, helped link the trans-

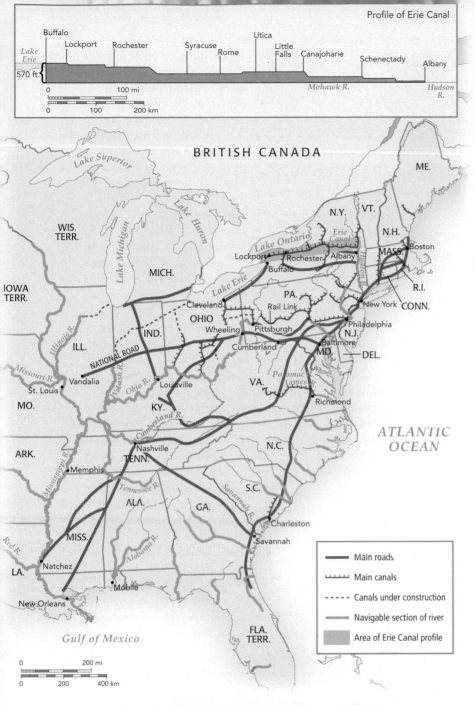

Profile of Erie Canal

Buffalo, Lockport, Rochester, Syracuse, Rome, Utica, Little Falls, Canajoharie, Schenectady, Albany

Lake Erie 570 ft.

Mohawk R. *Hudson R.*

THE TRANSPORTATION NETWORK OF A MARKET ECONOMY, 1840

Canals played their most important role in the Northeast, where they linked eastern cities to western rivers and the Great Lakes. Steamboats were most crucial in the extensive river systems of the South and the West.

portation network, and enabled newspapers to provide readers with up-to-date news.

Indeed, the invention of the telegraph and the perfection of a power press in 1847 by Robert Hoe and his son Richard revolutionized journalism. The mechanical press sharply increased the speed with which sheets could be printed over the old hand method and brought newspapers within economic reach of ordinary families. Hoe's press had a similar impact on book publishing, since thousands of copies could be printed at affordable prices.

The Postal System >>

A national market economy depended on mass communications to transmit commercial information and bring into contact producers and sellers separated by great distances. Although postage was relatively expensive, the American postal system subsidized the distribution of newspapers and helped spread other forms of commercial information. Indeed, in the years before the Civil War, the postal system employed more laborers than did any other enterprise in the country. Although the system's primary purpose was to promote commerce, the system had a profound social impact by accustoming people to long-range and even impersonal communication.

When traveling in the United States in 1831, the French commentator Alexis de Tocqueville was amazed at the scope of the postal system. "There is an astonishing circulation of letters and newspapers among these savage woods," he reported from the Michigan frontier. Although the British and French post offices handled a greater volume of mail, the American system was much more extensive.

Agriculture in the Market Economy >>

The new forms of transportation had a remarkable effect on farm families: they became linked ever more tightly to a national market system. Given cheap transportation, farmers increased their output in order to sell the surplus at distant markets. In this shift toward commercial agriculture, farmers began cultivating more acres, working longer hours, and adopting scientific farming methods, including crop rotation and the use of manures as fertilizer. Instead of bartering goods with neighbors, they more often paid cash or depended on banks to extend them credit. Instead of marketing crops themselves, they began to rely on regional merchants. Like southern planters, western wheat farmers increasingly sold in a world market.

As transportation and market networks connected more areas of the nation, they encouraged regional specialization. The South increasingly concentrated on staple crops for export, and the West grew foodstuffs, particularly grain. Eastern farmers, unable to compete with the wheat yields of western farms, shifted to producing fruits, vegetables, and dairy products for rapidly growing urban areas. The cities of the East no longer looked primarily to the sea for their trade; they looked to southern and western markets. That, indeed, was a revolution in markets.

John Marshall and the Promotion of Enterprise

>> A national market system also needed a climate favorable to investment. Under the leadership of Chief Justice John Marshall, the Supreme Court became the branch of the federal government most aggressive in protecting the new forms of business central to the growing market economy.

Marshall, who presided over the Court from 1801 to 1835, convinced his colleagues to uphold the sanctity of private property and the power of the federal government to promote economic growth. In the case of *McCulloch v. Maryland* (1819) the Court upheld the constitutionality of the Second Bank of the United States. Just as Alexander Hamilton had argued in the debate over the first national bank, Marshall emphasized that the Constitution gave Congress the power to make all "necessary and proper" laws to carry out its delegated powers. If Congress believed that a bank would help it meet its responsibilities, such as maintaining the public credit and regulating the currency, then the bank was constitutional. By upholding Hamilton's doctrine of implied powers, Marshall enlarged federal power to an extraordinary degree.

He also encouraged a more freewheeling commerce in *Gibbons v. Ogden* (1824), which gave Marshall a chance to define the greatest power of the federal government in peacetime, the right to regulate interstate commerce. In striking down a steamboat monopoly granted by the state of New York, the chief justice gave the term *commerce* the broadest possible definition, declaring that it covered all commercial dealings and that Congress's power over interstate commerce could be "exercised to its utmost extent." The result was increased business competition throughout society.

At the heart of most commercial agreements were private contracts, made between individuals or companies. Marshall took an active role in defining contract law, which was then in its infancy. The case of *Fletcher v. Peck* (1810) showed how far he

New York City owed its rise to prosperity and preeminence during the first half of the nineteenth century mainly to

a. its thriving trade with Great Britain and other European countries.

b. its great restaurants and awesome club scene.

c. the construction of the Erie Canal in the 1820s.

d. the completion of a network of railroads linking it to Chicago and San Francisco in the 1840s.

Key: c

was willing to go to protect private property. The justices unanimously struck down a Georgia law that struck down a land grant to a group of speculators that had bribed the legislature to get it. A grant was a contract, Marshall declared, and since the Constitution forbade states to impair "the obligation of contracts," the legislature could not interfere with the grant once it had been made. Although the framers of the Constitution probably meant contracts to refer only to agreements between private parties, Marshall made no distinction between public and private agreements, thereby greatly expanding the meaning of the contract clause.

The most celebrated decision Marshall wrote on the contract clause was in *Dartmouth College v. Woodward*, decided in 1819. This case arose out of the attempt by New Hampshire to alter the college's charter of 1769. The Court overturned the state law on the grounds that state charters were also contracts and could not be altered by later legislatures. By this ruling Marshall intended to protect **corporations**, which conducted business under charters granted by individual states.

corporation Business entity that has been granted a charter granting it legal rights, privileges, and liabilities distinct from the individual members that are a part of it.

Thus the Marshall Court sought to encourage economic risk-taking by protecting property and contracts, by limiting state interference, and by creating a climate of business confidence.

BACKSTORY
I'll Wait for the Airplane to Be Invented

While ideal for shipping goods, canal boats did little to delight their many passengers. Boats on the Erie Canal crept along at the stately pace of four miles an hour, prompting the writer Nathaniel Hawthorne to grouse about the "overpowering tedium" of his journeys. It was enough to make any traveler long for a nap—but, as one woman passenger complained, the boats' sleeping quarters were so "crowded we had not a breath of air." Those who kept on deck often diverted themselves with fiddle music and singing.

‹‹ Europeans were shocked that Americans bolted their food or gorged themselves on anything within reach, as this English drawing indicates.

A RESTLESS TEMPER

Between 1815 and 1850, the nation reverberated with almost explosive energy. An emphasis on speed affected nearly every aspect of American life. Steamboat captains risked boiler explosions for the honor of having the fastest boat on the river, prompting the visiting English novelist Charles Dickens to comment that traveling under these conditions seemed like taking up "lodgings on the first floor of a powder mill." American technology emphasized speed over longevity. Unlike European railroads, American railroads were lightweight, were hastily constructed, and paid little heed to the safety or comfort of passengers. Americans ate so quickly that one disgruntled European insisted food was "pitch-forked down."

Population Growth ›› If the economic hallmark of this new order was the growth of a national market, there were social factors that also contributed to American restlessness. The American population continued to double about every 22 years—more than twice the rate of Great Britain. The census, which stood at fewer than 4 million in 1790, surpassed 23 million in 1850. Although the birthrate peaked in 1800, it declined only slowly before 1840.

From 1790 to 1820 natural increase accounted for virtually all of the country's population growth. But immigration, which had been disrupted by the Napoleonic Wars in Europe, revived after 1815. In the 1830s some 600,000 immigrants arrived, more than double the number in the quarter century after 1790.

The Restless Movement West ››
The vast areas of land opened for settlement absorbed much of the burgeoning population. As settlers streamed west, speculation in western lands reached frenzied proportions. Whereas only 68,000 acres of the public domain had been sold during the year 1800, sales peaked in 1818, at a staggering 3.5 million acres.

The Panic of 1819 sent sales and prices crashing, and in the depression that followed many farmers lost their farms. Congress reacted by abolishing credit sales of federal land and demanding payment in cash, but it tempered this policy by lowering the price of the cheapest lands to $1.25 an acre and reducing the minimum tract to 80 acres.

Even so, speculators purchased most of the public lands sold, since there was no limit on the amount of acreage an individual or a land company could buy. These land speculators played a leading role in settlement of the West. To hasten sales, they usually sold land partially on credit— a vital aid to poorer farmers. They also provided loans to purchase needed tools and supplies. Many farmers became speculators themselves, buying up property in the neighborhood and selling it to latecomers at a tidy profit.

Given such rapid settlement, geographic mobility became one of the most striking characteristics of the American people. The 1850 census revealed that nearly half of all native-born free Americans lived outside the state where they had been born. The typical American "has no root in the soil," visiting Frenchman Michel Chevalier observed, but "is always in the mood to move on, always ready to start in the first steamer that comes along from the place where he had just now landed."

It was the search for opportunity, more than anything else, that accounted for such restlessness. In 1851, a new railroad line bypassed the village of Auburn, Illinois. Despite the village's handsome location, residents quickly abandoned it in order to live in the new town that sprang up around the depot, even though that land was swampier. A neighboring farmer purchased the old village and plowed up the streets, and Auburn reverted to a cornfield.

Urbanization ›› Even with the growth of a national market, the United States remained a rural nation. Nevertheless, the four decades after 1820 witnessed the fastest rate of urbanization in American history. As a result, the ratio of farmers to city dwellers steadily dropped, from 15

THE RISE OF FACTORIES

It was an isolated life, growing up in rural, hilly Vermont. But stories of the textile factories that had sprung up in Lowell and other towns in Massachusetts reached even small villages, such as Barnard. Fifteen-year-old Mary Paul was working there as a domestic servant when, in 1845, two friends helped her find her first job at the Lowell mills. "I am in need of clothes which I cannot get about here," she explained to her farm-bound father. After four years she returned home, but now found "countryfied" life too confining, and before long she left her rural hometown— this time for good.

Mary Paul was one of thousands of rural Americans whose lives were fundamentally altered by the economic transformations of the young republic. The changes in her lifestyle and her working habits demonstrated that the new factories and industries needed more than technological innovation to run smoothly. Equally crucial, labor needed to be reorganized.

Technological Advances >> Before 1815 manufacturing had been done in homes or shops by skilled artisans. As master craftworkers, they imparted the knowledge of their trades to apprentices and **journeymen**. In addition, women often worked in their homes part-time

to 1 in 1800 to 5.5 to 1 in 1850. Improved transportation, the declining productivity of many eastern farms, the beginnings of industrialization, and the influx of immigrants all stimulated the growth of cities.

The most heavily urbanized area of the country was the Northeast, where in 1860 more than a third of the population lived in cities.[1] Important urban centers such as St. Louis and Cincinnati arose in the West. The South, with only 10 percent of its population living in cities, was the least urbanized region.

1 The Northeast included New England and the mid-Atlantic states (New York, Pennsylvania, and New Jersey). The South comprised the slave states plus the District of Columbia.

⌃ St. Louis, a major urban center that developed in the West, depended on the steamboat to sustain its commerce, as this 1859 illustration makes clear.

⚶ This traffic jam in New York City conveys the rapid pace and impatient quality of American life in the first half of the nineteenth century. "In the streets all is hurry and bustle," one European visitor to the city reported. "Carts, instead of being drawn by horses at a walking pace, are often met at a gallop, and always in a brisk trot. . . . The whole population seen in the streets seem to enjoy this bustle and add to it by their own rapid pace, as if they were all going to some place of appointment, and were hurrying on under the apprehension of being too late."

under the putting-out system, making finished articles from raw material supplied by merchant capitalists. After 1815 this older form of manufacturing began to give way to factories with machinery tended by unskilled or semiskilled laborers.

> **journeyman** Person who has served an apprenticeship in a trade or craft and who is a qualified worker employed by another person.

From England came many of the earliest technological innovations. But Americans often improved on the British machines. "Everything new is quickly introduced here," one visitor commented in 1820. "There is no clinging to old ways; the moment an American hears the word 'invention' he pricks up his ears." From 1790 to 1860 the United States Patent Office granted more patents than England and France combined.

The first machines required highly skilled workers both to build and to repair them. Eli Whitney had a better idea. Having won a contract to produce 10,000 rifles for the government, he developed machinery that would mass-produce parts that were interchangeable from rifle to rifle. Such parts had to be manufactured to rigid specifications, but once the process was perfected, these parts allowed a worker to assemble a rifle quickly with only a few tools. Simeon North applied the same principle to the production of clocks, and Chauncey Jerome followed North's example and soon surpassed him.

Textile Factories >> The factory system originated in the Northeast, where capital, water power, and transportation facilities were available. As in England, the production of cloth was the first manufacturing process to use the new technology on a large scale. Eventually all the processes of manufacturing fabrics were brought together in a single location, and machines did virtually all the work.

In 1820 a group of wealthy Boston merchants known as the Boston Associates set up operations at Lowell, Massachusetts, which soon became the nation's most famous center of textile manufacturing. Its founders intended to avoid the misery that surrounded English factories by combining **paternalism** with high profits. Instead of relying primarily on child labor or a permanent working class, the Lowell mills employed daughters of New England farm families. Female workers lived in company boardinghouses under the watchful eye of a matron. To its many visitors, Lowell presented an impressive sight, with huge factories and well-kept houses. Female workers were encouraged to attend lectures and use the library; they even published their own magazine, *the Lowell Offering.*

> **paternalism** Attitude or policy of treating individuals or groups in a fatherly manner, by providing for their needs without granting them rights of responsibilities.

The reality of factory life, however, involved strict work rules and long hours of tedious, repetitive work.

At Lowell, for example, workers could be fined for lateness or misconduct, such as talking on the job, and the women's morals in the boardinghouses were strictly guarded. Work typically began at 7 A.M. (earlier in the summer) and continued until 7 at night, six days a week. With only 30 minutes for the noon meal, many workers had to run to the boardinghouse and back to avoid being late. Winter was the "lighting up" season, when work began before daylight and ended after dark. The only light after sunset came from whale oil lamps that filled the long rooms with smoke.

Although the labor was hard, the female operators earned from $2.40 to $3.20 a week, wages considered good by the standards of the time. (Domestic servants and seamstresses were paid less than a dollar a week.) The average "mill girl" was between 16 and 30 years old. Most were not working to support their families back home on the farm; instead, they wanted to accumulate some money for perhaps the first time in their lives and sample some of life's pleasures. "I must . . . have something of my own before many more years have passed," Sally Rice wrote in rejecting her parents' request that she return home to Somerset, Vermont. "And where is that something coming from if I go home and earn nothing?"

Like Rice, few women in the mills intended to work permanently. The majority stayed no more than five years before getting married. The sense of sisterhood that united women in the boardinghouses made it easier for farm daughters to adjust to the stress and regimen the factory imposed on them.

As competition in the textile industry intensified, factory managers tried to raise productivity. In the mid-1830s the mills began to increase the workloads and speed up the machinery. Even these changes failed to maintain previous profits, and on several occasions factories cut wages. The ever-quickening pace of work finally provoked resistance among the women in the mills. Several times in the 1830s wage cuts sparked strikes in which a minority of workers walked out. In the 1840s workers' protests focused on the demand for a 10-hour day.

As the mills expanded, a smaller proportion of the workers lived in company boardinghouses, and moral

↑ Mill workers, Lowell. "I am in need of clothes which I cannot get about here," Mary Paul had told her father in rural Vermont. Indeed, these workers wear the textiles they themselves helped produce in factories like Lowell's, each pattern slightly different.

regulations were relaxed. But the greatest change was a shift in the workforce from native-born females to Irish immigrants, including men and children. The Irish, who made up only 8 percent of the Lowell work-force in 1845, amounted to almost half by 1860. Desperately poor and eager for any work, they did not view their situation as temporary. Wages continued to decline, and a permanent working class took shape.

Lowell and the Environment >> Lowell
was a city built on water power. Early settlers had used the power of the Merrimack River to run mills, but never on the scale of the textile factories. As the market spread, Americans came to link progress with the fullest use of the environment's natural resources.

By 1836, Lowell had seven canals, with a supporting network of locks and dams, to govern the Merrimack's flow and distribute water to the city's 26 mills. As more and more mills were built, both at Lowell and other sites, the Boston Associates erected dams at several points along the river to store water and divert it into power canals for factories. At Lawrence, they constructed the largest dam in the world at the time, a 32-foot-high granite structure that spanned 1,600 feet across the river. But even dammed, the Merrimack's waters proved insufficient. So the Associates gained control of over 100 square miles of New Hampshire lakes that fed the river system. Damming these lakes provided a regular flow of water, especially in the drier summer months.

By regulating the river's waters, the Associates made the Merrimack valley the nation's greatest industrial center in the first half of the nineteenth century. But not all who lived there benefited. By raising water levels, the dams flooded farmlands, blocked the transportation of logs downstream, and damaged mills upstream by reducing the current. The dams also devastated the fish population by preventing upstream spawning, while factories routinely dumped their wastes into the river to be carried downstream, eventually contaminating water supplies. Epidemics of typhoid, cholera, and dysentery increased, so that by midcentury Lowell had a reputation as a particularly unhealthy city.

DEVELOPMENT OF THE LOWELL MILLS

As more mills were built at Lowell, the demand increased for water to power them. By 1859 the mills drew water from lakes 80 to 100 miles upstream, including Winnipesauke, Squam, and Newfound. The map at left shows the affected watersheds. In the city of Lowell (*right*), a system of canals was enlarged over several decades. In the painting (done in 1845), the machine shop can be seen at left, with a row of mills alongside a canal. Rail links tied Lowell and Boston together.

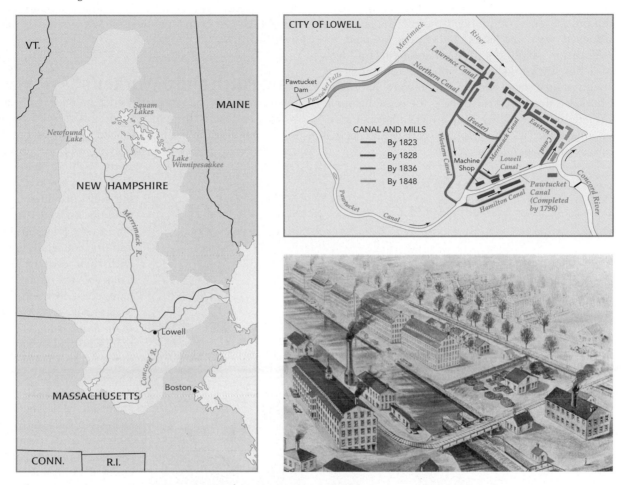

Industrial Work >> The creation of an industrial labor force that was accustomed to working in factories did not occur easily. Previously, artisans had worked within the home. Apprentices were considered part of the family, and masters were responsible not only for teaching their apprentices a trade but also for providing them some education and for supervising their moral behavior. Journeymen knew that if they perfected their skill, they could become respected master artisans with their own shops. And skilled artisans worked not by the clock, at a steady pace, but rather in bursts of intense labor alternating with greater leisure.

The factory changed that. Factory goods were not so finished or elegant as those done by hand, and pride in artisanship gave way to rates of productivity. At the same time, workers were required to discard old habits, because industrialism demanded a worker who was sober, dependable, and self-disciplined. Absenteeism, lateness, and drunkenness hurt productivity and disrupted the regular factory routine. Thus industrialization not only produced a fundamental change in the way work was organized but also transformed the very nature of work.

With the loss of personal freedom also came the loss of standing in the community. The master-apprentice relationship gave way to factories' sharp separation of workers from management. Few workers rose through the ranks to supervisory positions, and even fewer could set up their own businesses, as many artisans dreamed. Even well-paid workers sensed their decline in status.

The Labor Movement >> In this newly emerging economic order, workers sometimes organized to protect their rights and traditional ways of life. Craftworkers such as carpenters, printers, and tailors formed unions, and in 1834 individual unions came together in the National Trades' Union.

Union leaders argued that labor was degraded in America: workers endured long hours, low pay, and low status. Unlike most American social thinkers of the day, they accepted the idea of conflict between different classes. They did not believe that the interests of workers and employers could be reconciled, and they blamed the plight of labor on monopolies, especially banking and paper money, and on machines and the factory system.

If the unions' rhetoric sounded radical, the solutions they proposed were moderate. Reformers agitated for public education, abolition of imprisonment for debt, political action by workers, and effective unions as the means to guarantee social equality and restore labor to its former honored position. Proclaiming the republican virtues of freedom and equality, they attacked special privilege, denounced the lack of equal opportunity, and decried workers' loss of independence.

nized workers' right to strike, but these gains had little immediate impact.

Workers were united in resenting the industrial system and their loss of status, but they were divided by ethnic and racial antagonisms, gender, conflicting religious perspectives, occupational differences, party loyalties, and disagreements over tactics. For them, the factory and industrialism were not agents of opportunity but reminders of their loss of independence and a measure of control over their lives.

Sam Patch and a Worker's "Art" >> Some

fought against the loss of independence in unusual ways. The waterfalls that served as a magnet for capitalists building mills also attracted their workers. Such cascades were places to visit during off-hours to picnic, swim, fish, or laze about. And for those with nerve, the falls provided a place to show off skills in a different way. Every mill town had its waterfall jumpers, with their own techniques to survive the plunge (knees bent, chest thrust forward). No jumper won more fame than Sam Patch, a young man who had begun working at the Pawtucket mills at the age of seven.

Patch gained wider attention when he jumped at Passaic Falls, New Jersey, where a mill owner was opening a private park that charged admission, in order to keep away "the lazy, idle, rascally" and lower-class riffraff. Workers who resented this undemocratic practice rejoiced when Patch spoiled the park's opening by leaping 70 feet into the foaming water. Thousands of ordinary folk cheered him from outside the park. Eventually Patch's daring led him to the biggest challenge of all: Niagara Falls. Twice he leapt more than 80 feet into the cascade's churning waters. But he drowned a month later when he dared Genesee Falls in another mill town along the Erie Canal—Rochester, New York. Still, his fame persisted for decades. Leaping waterfalls was "an art which I have knowledge of and courage to perform," he once declared defiantly. In a market economy where skilled "arts" were being replaced by machine labor, Sam Patch's acts were a defiant protest against the changing times.

⌃ Waterfalls at mill towns, like this one in Pawtucket, Rhode Island, were places to swim, fish, and relax, as the people do in the foreground. Jumpers like Sam Patch leaped off the Pawtucket bridge and also off the roof of a nearby building into the foamy froth.

The labor movement gathered some momentum in the decade before the Panic of 1837, but in the depression that followed, labor's strength collapsed. During hard times, few workers were willing to strike or engage in collective action. Nor did skilled craftworkers, who spearheaded the union movement, feel a particularly strong bond with semiskilled factory workers and unskilled laborers. More than a decade of agitation did finally win the 10-hour day for some workers by the 1850s, and the courts also recog-

SOCIAL STRUCTURES OF THE MARKET SOCIETY

Thousands of miles beyond Lowell's factory gates a different class of Americans roamed, who at first appeared unconnected to the bustle of urban markets. These were the legendary mountain men, who flourished from the mid-1820s through the mid-1840s. Traveling across the Great Plains, along upland streams, and over the passes of the Rockies, outdoorsmen such as Jim Bridger, Jedediah Smith, and James Walker wore buckskin hunting shirts, let their hair grow to their shoulders, and stuck pistols and tomahawks in their belts. Wild and exotic, the mountain men became romantic symbols of the American quest for individual freedom.

Yet these wanderers, too, were tied to the emerging market society. The mountain men hunted beaver pelts and shipped them east, to be turned into fancy hats for gentlemen. The fur trade was not a sporting event but a business, dominated by organizations such as John Jacob Astor's American Fur Company, and the trapper was the agent of an economic structure that stretched from the mountains to eastern cities and even to Europe. Most of these men went into the wilderness not to flee civilization but to make money. Of those who survived the fur trade, most returned and took up respectable new careers as shopkeepers, traders, ranchers, politicians, and even bankers. They, like farmers, were expectant capitalists for whom the West was a land of opportunity.

The revolution in markets, in other words, affected Americans from all walks of life: mountain men as well as merchants, laborers as well as farmers. Equally critical, it restructured American society as a whole.

Economic Specialization >> To begin with, the spread of the market produced greater specialization. Transportation networks made it possible for farmers to concentrate on producing certain crops, while factories could focus on making a single item such as cloth or shoes. Within factories, the division of labor meant that the process of manufacturing an item became more specialized, broken down into less skilled tasks.

This process evolved at different rates. Textiles and milling were completely mechanized, while other sectors of the economy, such as shoes and men's clothing, depended little on machinery. Moreover, large factories were the exception rather than the rule. Still, the tendency was toward more technology, greater efficiency, and increasing specialization.

Specialization had consequences at home as well as in the workplace. The average eighteenth-century American woman produced items such as thread, cloth, clothing, and candles in the home for family use. As factories spread, however, household manufacturing all but disappeared, and women lost many of the economic functions they had previously performed in the family unit. Again, textiles are a striking example. Between 1815 and 1860, the price of cotton cloth fell from 18 to 2 cents a yard, and because it was also smoother and more brightly colored than homespun, most women purchased cloth rather than making it themselves. Similarly, the development of ready-made men's clothing reduced the amount of sewing women did, especially in urban centers.

Materialism >> European visitors were struck during these years by how much Americans were preoccupied with material goods. The new generation did not invent materialism, but the spread of the market after 1815 made it much more evident. "I know of no country, indeed," Tocqueville commented, "where the love of money has taken stronger hold on the affections of men."

In a nation that had no legally recognized aristocracy, no established church, and class lines that were only informally drawn, wealth became the most obvious symbol of status. Materialism reflected more than a desire for goods and physical comfort. It represented a quest for respect and recognition. The esteem of the founding generation for intellectual achievement was mostly lost in the scramble for wealth that seemed to consume the new generation.

Wealth and the Emerging Middle Class >> In the years after 1815 a new middle class took shape in American society. A small class of shopkeepers, professionals, and master artisans had existed earlier, but the creation of a national market economy greatly expanded its size and influence. As specialization

> "I know of no country, indeed," Tocqueville commented, "where the love of money has taken stronger hold on the affections of men."

increased, office work and selling were more often physically separated from the production and handling of merchandise. Businesspeople, professionals, storekeepers, clerks, office workers, and supervisors began to think of themselves as a distinct social group. Members of the growing middle class had access to more education and enjoyed greater social mobility. They were paid not only more but differently. A manual worker might earn $300 a year, paid as wages computed on an hourly basis. Professionals received a yearly salary and might make $1,000 a year or more.

Middle-class neighborhoods, segregated along income and occupational lines, also began to develop in towns and cities. In larger cities improved transportation enabled middle-class residents to move to surrounding suburbs and commute to work. Leisure also became segregated, as separate working-class and middle-class social organizations and institutions emerged.

As middle-class Americans accumulated greater wealth, they were able to consume more. Thus material goods became emblems of success and status—as clockmaker Chauncey Jerome sadly discovered when his business failed and his wealth vanished. Indeed, this materialistic ethos was most apparent in the middle class, as they strove to set themselves apart from other groups in society.

Furthermore, as American society became more specialized after 1815, greater extremes of wealth appeared. As the new markets created fortunes for the few, the factory system lowered the wages of workers by dividing labor into smaller, less skilled tasks. At the upper end of the social scale, wealth was most highly concentrated in large eastern cities and in the cotton kingdom of the South. Still, throughout the nation the tendency was for the rich to get richer and own a larger share of the community's total wealth. By 1860, 5 percent of American families owned more than 50 percent of the nation's wealth. In villages where the market revolution had not penetrated, wealth tended to be less concentrated.

In a market society, the rich were able to build up their assets because those with capital were in a position to increase it dramatically by taking advantage of new investment opportunities. Although a few men, such as Cornelius Vanderbilt and John Jacob Astor, vaulted from the bottom ranks of society to the top, most of the nation's richest individuals came from wealthy families.

Social Mobility >> The existence of great fortunes is not necessarily inconsistent with the idea of social mobility or property accumulation.

social mobility Movement of individuals from one social class to another.

⌃ Thomas Hicks's painting, *Calculating*, captures the spirit of the United States as the market revolution unfolded. Americans, one foreign visitor reported, were a "guessing, reckoning, expecting and calculating people." During this period the phrase "I calculate" came to mean "I think." The man carefully going over his figures wears a beaver hat, the end product of the fur trade, and many mountain men ended up as calculating businessmen.

Although the gap between the rich and the poor widened after 1820, even the incomes of most poor Americans rose, because the total amount of wealth produced in America had become much larger. From about 1825 to 1860 the average per capita income almost doubled, to $300. Voicing the popular belief, a New York judge proclaimed, "In this favored land of liberty, the road to advancement is open to all."

Social mobility existed in these years, but not as much as contemporaries boasted. Most laborers—or more often their sons—did manage to move up the social ladder, but only a rung or two. Few unskilled workers rose higher than to a semiskilled occupation. Even the children of skilled workers normally did not escape the laboring classes to enter the middle-class ranks of clerks, managers, or lawyers. For most workers improved status came in the form of a savings account or home ownership, which gave them some security during economic downswings and in old age.

A New Sensitivity to Time >> It was no accident that Chauncey Jerome's clocks spread throughout the nation along with the market economy. The new methods of doing business involved a new and stricter sense of time. Factory life necessitated a more regimented

schedule, where work began at the sound of a bell, workers kept machines going at a constant pace, and the day was divided into hours and even minutes.

Clocks began to invade private as well as public space. With mass production ordinary families could now afford clocks, and even farmers became more sensitive to time as they were integrated into the market.

PROSPERITY AND ANXIETY

As Americans watched their nation's frontiers expand and its market economy grow, many began to view history in terms of continuous improvement. The path of commerce, however, was not steadily upward. Rather, it advanced in a series of wrenching **boom-bust cycles**: accelerating growth, followed by a crash, and then depression.

The country remained extraordinarily prosperous from 1815 until 1819, only to sink into a depression that lasted from 1819 to 1823. During the next cycle, the economy expanded slowly during the 1820s, followed by almost frenzied speculation in the 1830s. Then came the inevitable contraction in 1837, and the country suffered an even more severe depression from 1839 to 1843. The third cycle followed the same pattern: gradual economic growth during the 1840s, frantic expansion in the 1850s, and a third depression, which began in 1857 and lasted until the Civil War. In each of these "panics," thousands of workers were thrown out of work, overextended farmers lost their farms, and many businesses closed their doors.

> **boom-bust cycle** Periods of expansion and recession or depression that an economy goes through. Also referred to as *business cycle*.

This mock banknote illustrates the anxieties often felt in times of "bust," when the value of currencies plummeted and it was difficult to tell whether the banks that issued paper money were solvent.

In such an environment, prosperity and personal success seemed all too fleeting. Because Americans believed the good times would not last—that the bubble would burst and another "panic" set in—their optimism was often tinged by insecurity and anxiety. They knew too many individuals like Chauncey Jerome, who had been rich and then lost all their wealth in a downturn.

The Panic of 1819 >>

The initial shock of this boom-and-bust psychology came with the Panic of 1819, the first major depression in the nation's history. From 1815 to 1818 cotton had commanded truly fabulous prices on the Liverpool market. In this heady prosperity, the federal government extended liberal credit for land purchases, and the new national bank encouraged merchants and farmers to borrow in order to catch the rising tide.

But in 1819 the price of cotton collapsed and took the rest of the economy with it. Once the inflationary bubble burst, land values, which had been driven to new heights by the speculative fever, plummeted 50 to 75 percent almost overnight. As the economy went slack, so did the demand for western foodstuffs and eastern manufactured goods and services, pushing the nation into a severe depression. Because the market economy had spread to new areas, the downturn affected not only city folk but rural Americans as well. New cotton planters in the Southwest, who were most vulnerable to the ups and downs of the world market, were especially hard hit.

As depression spread in the years following 1819, most Americans could not guess that the ups and downs of the boom-and-bust cycle would continue through the next three decades, their swings made sharper by the growing networks of the market economy both nationally and internationally. But the interconnections between buyers and sellers did feed both prosperity and panic. Farmers and factories specialized in order to sell goods to distant buyers. Canals and railroads widened the network, speeding products, information, and profits. And as markets tied distant lands more tightly together, international events contributed to the business cycles.

It was the Liverpool market in England, in fact, that bid the price of American cotton to its high at over 32 cents. Then in 1816 and 1817 English textile manufacturers, looking for cheaper cotton, began to import more cotton from India, plummeting the price of New Orleans cotton to 14 cents. Broader changes also hurt American markets. The French and the British had been at war with one another for decades—more than 100 years, if the imperial wars of the seventeenth and eighteenth centuries were counted. In 1814 and 1815 the major powers of Europe hammered out a peace at the Congress of Vienna, one that lasted, with only minor interruptions, until the coming of World War I in 1914. When Europe had been at war, American farmers had found a ready market abroad. With thousands of European soldiers returning to their usual work as farmers, demand for American goods dropped.

The stresses of the panic of 1819 shook the political system at home too. As the depression deepened and hardship spread, Americans viewed government policies as at least partly to blame. The postwar nationalism, after all, had been based on the belief that government should stimulate economic development through a national bank and protective tariff, by improving transportation, and by opening up new lands. As Americans struggled to make sense of their new economic order, they looked to take more direct control of the government that was so actively shaping their lives. During the 1820s, the popular response to the market and the Panic of 1819 produced a strikingly new kind of politics in the Republic.

CHAPTER SUMMARY

By uniting the country in a single market, the market revolution transformed the United States during the quarter century after 1815.

▪ The federal government promoted the creation of a market through a protective tariff, a national bank, and internal improvements.

▪ The development of new forms of transportation, including canals, steamboats, and eventually railroads, allowed goods to be transported cheaply on land.

▪ The Supreme Court adopted a pro-business stance that encouraged investment and risk-taking.

▪ Economic expansion generated greater national wealth, but it also brought social and intellectual change.

▪ Americans pursued opportunity, embraced a new concept of progress, viewed change as normal, developed a strong materialist ethic, and considered wealth the primary means to determine status.

▪ Entrepreneurs reorganized their operations to increase production and sell in a wider market.

▪ The earliest factories were built to serve the textile industry, and the first laborers in them were young women from rural families.

▪ Factory work imposed on workers a new discipline based on time and strict routine.

▪ Workers' declining status led them to form unions and resort to strikes, but the depression that began in 1837 destroyed these organizations.

▪ The market revolution distributed wealth much more unevenly and left Americans feeling alternatively buoyant and anxious about their social and economic status.

▪ Social mobility existed, but it was more limited than popular belief claimed.

▪ The economy lurched up and down in a boom-bust cycle.

▪ In hard times, Americans looked to the government to relieve economic distress.

Significant Events

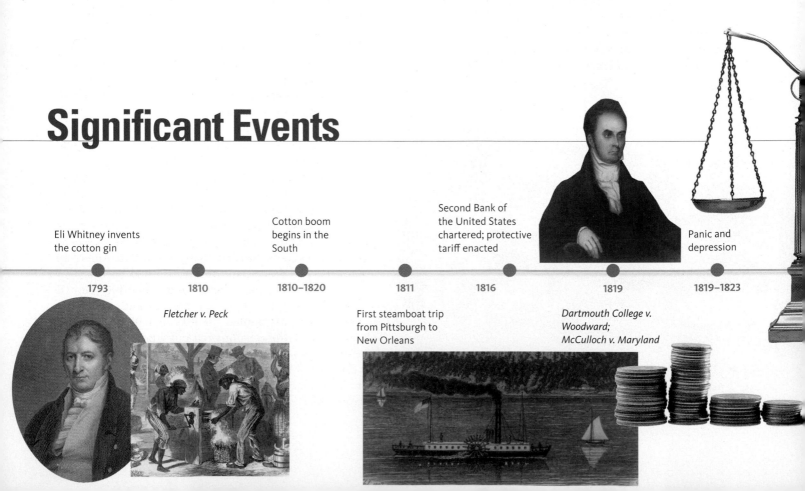

Eli Whitney invents the cotton gin
1793

Fletcher v. Peck
1810

Cotton boom begins in the South
1810–1820

First steamboat trip from Pittsburgh to New Orleans
1811

Second Bank of the United States chartered; protective tariff enacted
1816

Dartmouth College v. Woodward; McCulloch v. Maryland
1819

Panic and depression
1819–1823

Additional Reading

For a provocative overview of the economic changes during this period and their impact on society and culture, consult Charles Sellers, *The Market Revolution* (1991). Then dip into two fine anthologies of essays: Melvin Stokes and Stephen Conway, eds., *The Market Revolution in America* (1996), and Scott C. Martin, ed., *Cultural Change and the Market Revolution in America, 1789–1860* (2005). The best recent book on the transportation revolution is John Larson, *Internal Improvements* (2001), and for a fascinating study of the role played by the postal system in linking Americans, see Richard John, *Spreading the News* (1995). There are many fine studies of urban social classes during the first half of the nineteenth century, and among the best are Sean Wilentz, *Chants Democratic* (1984), which traces the formation of New York City's working class, and Stuart Blumin, *The Emergence of the Middle Class* (1989). To understand the market economy's affect on rural society,

read John Mack Faragher's vivid account of the transformation of a farming community in frontier Illinois, *Sugar Creek* (1986), and Robert Shalhope, *A Tale of New England* (2003), which traces the fortunes of a Vermont farmer and his family.

There is also no shortage of excellent books exploring the relationship between the market revolution and antebellum American culture. Begin with Karen Halttunen's classic study of middle-class culture, *Confidence Men and Painted Women* (1982), and a more recent study, Thomas Augst, *The Clerk's Tale* (2003), and then turn to Paul Johnson's lively exploration of working-class culture, *Sam Patch, the Famous Jumper* (2003). To celebrate any occasion, treat yourself to Stephen Nissenbaum, *The Battle for Christmas* (1996). And to console yourself in between celebrations, turn to Scott Sandage, *Born Losers: A History of Failure in America* (2005).

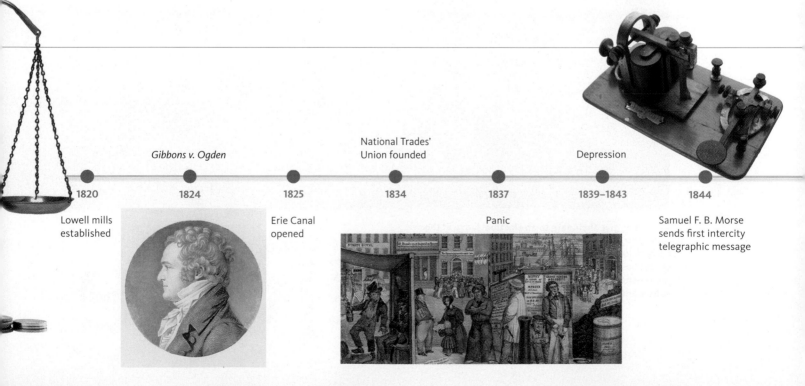

Gibbons v. Ogden

National Trades' Union founded

Depression

| 1820 | 1824 | 1825 | 1834 | 1837 | 1839–1843 | 1844 |

Lowell mills established

Erie Canal opened

Panic

Samuel F. B. Morse sends first intercity telegraphic message

11

As citizens give their oath to an election judge at this county election, party workers dispense free drinks, offer party tickets (center, below the banner), and keep a tally of who has voted (the man sitting on the steps). Drinking is prominently featured: one groggy voter has to be held up as he stands in line.

THE Rise

1824—1840

WHAT'S TO COME

207 EQUALITY AND OPPORTUNITY

207 THE NEW POLITICAL CULTURE
OF DEMOCRACY

210 JACKSON'S RISE TO POWER

211 DEMOCRACY AND RACE

215 THE NULLIFICATION CRISIS

216 THE BANK WAR

219 VAN BUREN AND DEPRESSION

220 THE JACKSONIAN PARTY SYSTEM

"WANTED: CURLING TONGS, COLOGNE, AND SILK-STOCKINGS . . ."

The notice, printed in a local newspaper, made the rounds in the rural Pearl River district of Mississippi. A traveler, the advertisement announced, had lost a suitcase while fording the Tallahala River. The contents included "6 ruffled shirts, 6 cambric handkerchiefs, 1 hair-brush, 1 toothbrush, 1 nail-brush . . ." ❯❯

OF Democracy

As the list went on, the popular reaction would inevitably shift from amusement to disdain: "1 pair curling tongs . . . 1 bottle Cologne, 1 [bottle] rose-water, 4 pairs silk stockings, and 2 pairs kid gloves." The howls of derision that filled the air could only have increased on learning that anyone finding said trunk was requested to contact the owner—Mr. Powhatan Ellis of Natchez.

Powhatan Ellis was no ordinary backcountry traveler. Born into a genteel Virginia family, Ellis had moved in 1816 to the raw Southwest to enlarge his fortune. With his cultivated tastes and careful dress, he upheld the tradition of the gentleman politician. In Virginia he would have commanded respect: indeed, in Mississippi he had been appointed district judge and U.S. senator. But for the voters along the Pearl River, the advertisement for his trunk of ruffled shirts, hair oils, and fancy "skunkwater" proved to be the political kiss of death. His opponents branded him an aristocrat and a dandy, and his support among the piney woods farmers evaporated faster than a morning mist along Old Muddy on a sweltering summer's day.

No one was more satisfied with this outcome than the resourceful Franklin E. Plummer, one of Ellis's political enemies. For in truth, while the unfortunate Powhatan Ellis had lost a trunk fording a stream, he had not placed the advertisement trying to locate it. That was the handiwork of Plummer, who well understood the new playing field of American politics in the 1820s. Born in New England, Plummer had made his way as a young man to the new state of Mississippi, where he set himself up as an attorney, complete with a law library of three books, and was quickly elected to the legislature.

Plummer's ambition soon extended beyond the state capital, and in 1830 he announced his candidacy for Congress. In his campaign, he portrayed himself as the champion of the people battling the aristocrats of Natchez. Contrasting his humble background with that of his wealthy opponent, Plummer proclaimed: "We are taught that the highway to office, distinction and honor, is as free to the meritorious poor man, as to the rich; to the man who has risen from obscurity by his own individual exertions, as to him who has inherited a high and elevated standing in society, founded on the patrimony of his ancestors." Taking as his slogan "Plummer for the People, and the People for Plummer," he was easily elected.

As long as Plummer maintained his image as one of the people, he remained invincible. But as a candidate for the U.S. Senate, his touch deserted him. Borrowing money from a Natchez bank, he purchased a stylish coach, put his servant in a uniform, and campaigned across the state. Aghast at such aristocratic pretensions, his followers promptly abandoned him. He died in 1852 in obscurity and poverty. Ah, Plummer! Even the trustiest tribune of the People may succumb to the temptations of power and commerce. «

⌃ By 1840 the new style of democratic politics was in full swing. This rally in Knoxville, Tennessee, uses a camp meeting-style platform in the woods to rally supporters. The makeup of this audience underscores another feature of Jacksonian democracy; the vote went only to adult white males.

In fact, Franklin Plummer was being pulled two ways by the forces transforming American society. The growth of commerce opened up opportunities for more and more Americans during the quarter century after 1815. Through his connections with bankers and the well-to-do, Plummer saw the opportunity to accumulate wealth and to gain status and respect.

Yet at the same time that new markets were producing a more **stratified**, unequal society, the nation's politics were becoming more democratic. The new political system that developed after 1820 differed from that of the early Republic. Just as national markets linked the regions of America economically, the new system of national politics with its mass electioneering techniques involved more voters than ever before. Plummer's world reflected that more egalitarian **political culture**. But the relationship between the new equalities of politics and the new opportunities of the market was an uneasy one.

> **stratified** layered; in this case according to class or social station.
>
> **political culture** patterns, habits, institutions, and traits associated with a political system.

carried the future King Louis-Philippe of France on a trip down the Mississippi made their republican feelings plain when the keelboat ran aground. "You kings down there!" bellowed the captain. "Show yourselves and do a man's work, and help us three-spots pull off this bar!" The ideology of the Revolution made it clear that, in the American deck of cards at least, "three-spots" counted as much as jacks, kings, and queens. Kings were not allowed to forget that—and neither was Franklin Plummer.

By equality, Americans did not mean equality of wealth or property. "I know of no country where profounder contempt is expressed for the theory of permanent equality of property," Alexis de Tocqueville wrote. Nor did equality mean that all citizens had equal talent or capacity. In the end, what Americans upheld was equality of opportunity, not equality of condition. "True republicanism requires that every man shall have an equal chance—that every man shall be free to become as unequal as he can," one American commented. In an economy that could go bust as well as boom, Americans agreed that one primary objective of government was to safeguard opportunity. Thus the new politics of democracy walked hand in hand with the new opportunities of the market.

EQUALITY AND OPPORTUNITY

Middle- and upper-class Europeans who visited the United States during these decades were especially sensitive to the egalitarian quality of American life. To begin with, they discovered that only one class of seats was available on stagecoaches and railcars. These were filled according to the rough-and-ready rule of first come, first served. In steamboat dining rooms or at country taverns, everyone ate at a common table, sharing food from the same serving plates. As one upper-class gentleman complained: "The rich and the poor, the educated and the ignorant, the polite and the vulgar, all herd on the cabin floor, feed at the same table, sit in each others laps, as it were." Indeed, the democratic "manners" of Americans seemed positively shocking. In Europe social inferiors would speak only if spoken to. But Americans felt free to strike up a conversation or to shake hands with anyone, including total strangers.

Americans were proud of such democratic behavior, which they viewed as a valued heritage of the Revolution. The keelboaters who

⌃ As this nattily dressed butcher suggests, clothes were not much help in sorting out social status in America. Although the clothing of the upper class was often made of finer material, by the 1820s less prosperous Americans wore similar styles. "The washerwoman's Sunday attire is now as nearly like that of the merchant's wife as it can be," commented one astonished observer.

THE NEW POLITICAL CULTURE OF DEMOCRACY

The stately James Monroe, with his powdered hair and buckled shoes and breeches, was not part of the new politics. But in 1824 as he neared the end of his second term, a host of new leaders in the Republican party looked to succeed him. The Republican congressional caucus finally settled on William H. Crawford of Georgia as the party's presidential nominee. Condemning "King Caucus" as undemocratic, three other Republicans, all ardent nationalists, refused to withdraw from the race: Secretary of State John Quincy Adams; John C. Calhoun, Monroe's secretary of war; and Henry Clay, the Speaker of the House.

None of these men bargained on the sudden emergence of another Republican

ELECTION OF 1824

Candidate (No parties)	Electoral Vote (%)	Popular Vote (%)
Andrew Jackson	99 (38)	153,544 (43)
John Quincy Adams	84 (32)	108,740 (31)
William Harris Crawford	41 (16)	46,618 (13)
Henry Clay	37 (14)	47,136 (13)
Nonvoting territories		
Not U.S. territory		

More significant, the election of 1824 shattered the old party system. Henry Clay and John Quincy Adams began to organize a new party, known as the National Republicans to distinguish it from Jefferson's old party. For the next decade the political system continued to evolve. By the mid-1830s, the National Republicans gave way to the Whigs, a political party that also drew members from another party that flourished briefly, the Anti-Masons.* The Democrats as the other major party came together under the leadership of Andrew Jackson. Once established, this second party system dominated the nation's politics until the 1850s.

Social Sources of the New Politics >>

Why was it that a new style and new system of politics emerged in the 1820s? Part of the answer lay in the Panic of 1819. During the depression that followed, many Americans became convinced that government policy had aggravated, if not actually produced, hard times. Consequently, they decided that the government had a responsibility to relieve distress and promote prosperity.

The connection made between government policy and economic well-being stimulated rising popular interest in politics during the 1820s. Agitation mounted, especially at the state level, for government to enact debtor relief and provide other forms of assistance. Elections became the means through which the majority expressed its policy preferences, by voting for candidates pledged to specific programs. The older idea that representatives should be independent, voting their best judgment, gave way to the notion that representatives were to carry out the will of the people, as expressed in the results of elections.

With more citizens championing the "will of the people," pressure mounted to open up the political process. Most states eliminated property

candidate, Andrew Jackson, the hero of the Battle of New Orleans. Because of his limited experience, no one took Jackson's candidacy seriously at first, including Jackson himself. But soon the general's supporters and rivals began receiving reports of his popularity. Savvy politicians flocked to his standard, but it was the people who first made Jackson a serious candidate.

The Election of 1824 >>
Calhoun eventually dropped out of the race, but none of the four remaining candidates received a majority of the popular vote. Still, Jackson led the field and also finished first in the Electoral College. Under the terms of the Twelfth Amendment, the House was to select a president from the top three candidates. Henry Clay, who finished fourth and was therefore eliminated, met privately with Adams and then rallied the votes in the House needed to put Adams over the top.

Two days later, Adams announced that Clay would be his secretary of state, the usual stepping-stone to the presidency. Jackson and his supporters promptly charged that there had been a "corrupt bargain" between Adams and Clay. Before Adams had even assumed office, the 1828 race was under way.

*The Anti-Masons had led a campaign against the Freemasons or Masons, a fraternal order whose members shared the Enlightenment belief in the power of reason but whose secret meetings and rituals seemed aristocratic and undemocratic to many Americans.

OPINION

Did the period between the American Revolution and the 1830s bring about a significant democratization in American politics?

∧ Democratic reforms of the 1820s and 1830s brought a new sort of politician to prominence, one whose life was devoted to party service and whose living often depended on public office. This cartoon from 1834 shows the downside of the new situation. Andrew Jackson sports the wings, horns, and tail of a devil as he dangles the rewards of various political offices above a clamoring group of eager job-seekers.

qualifications for voting in favor of white manhood suffrage, under which all adult white males were allowed to vote. Similarly, property requirements for office holders were reduced or dropped.

Presidential elections became more democratic as well. By 1832 South Carolina was the only state where the legislature rather than the voters still chose presidential electors. Parties began to hold conventions as a more democratic method of nominating candidates and approving a platform. And because a presidential candidate had to carry a number of states in different sections of the country, the backing of a national party, with effective state and local organizations, became essential.

The democratic winds of change affected European societies and eventually other areas of the world as well. In no other major country, however, were these reforms achieved as early and with as little resistance as in the United States. Suffrage provides a good example. In Britain, in response to growing demonstrations and the cautionary example of the French monarchy's overthrow in 1830, Parliament approved the Reform Bill of 1832, which enfranchised a number of property holders and gave Britain the broadest electorate in Europe. Yet in fact, only about 15 percent of the adult males in Britain enjoyed the

right of suffrage after the bill's passage. Even Britain's second Reform Act (1867) enfranchised only about one-third of the adult males. Likewise, virtually all the Latin American republics established in the 1820s and 1830s imposed property requirements on voting or forbade certain occupational groups, such as servants and peasants, to vote.

As the new reforms went into effect in the United States, voter turnout soared. Whereas in the 1824 presidential election, only 27 percent of eligible voters had bothered to go to the polls, in 1840, 78 percent cast ballots, probably the highest turnout in American history.

All these developments favored the emergence of a new type of politician: one whose life was devoted to party service and whose living often depended on public office. As the number of state internal improvement projects increased during the 1820s, so did the number of government jobs that could support party workers. No longer was politics primarily the province of the wealthy, who spent only part of their time on public affairs. Instead, political leaders were more likely to come from the middle ranks of society, especially outside the South. As Franklin Plummer demonstrated, a successful politician now had to mingle with the masses and voice their feelings— requirements that put the wealthy elite at a disadvantage.

Politics became mass entertainment, with campaign hoopla frequently overshadowing issues. Parades, massive rallies, and barbecues were used to rouse voters, and treating to drinks became an almost universal campaign tactic. ("The way to men's hearts is down their throats," quipped one Kentucky vote-getter.) Although politicians talked often about principles, political parties were pragmatic organizations, intent on gaining and holding power.

The Jacksonian era has been called the Age of the Common Man, but such democratic tendencies had distinct limits. Women and slaves were not allowed to vote, nor could free African Americans (except in a few states) or Indians. Nor did the parties always deal effectively with (or even address) basic problems in society. Despite such limitations, however, popular political parties provided an essential mechanism for peacefully resolving differences among competing interest groups, regions, and social classes.

Key: a, b, d

Dramatic changes in American politics between the Revolution and the Civil War included (circle all correct answers):

a. the rise of a group of professional politicians.

b. the expansion of voting rights for white men.

c. the extension of voting rights to white women.

d. political candidates celebrating the "common man" and touting their own humble origins.

great secretary of state, had hardly a political bone in his body. Cold and tactless, he could build no popular support for the ambitious and often farsighted programs he proposed. His proposals that government promote not only manufacturing and agriculture but also the arts, literature, and science left his opponents aghast.

Nor would Adams take any steps to gain reelection. Henry Clay finally undertook to organize the National Republicans, but with a reluctant candidate he labored under serious handicaps. The new style of politics came into its own nationally only when Andrew Jackson swept to power at the head of a new party, the Democrats. During the campaign, he remained vague about his position on many issues, and the 1828 race descended into a series of personal attacks, splattering mud on all involved. But Jackson emerged victorious, with enormous majorities behind him in the South.

JACKSON'S RISE TO POWER

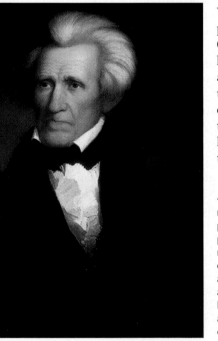

When he assumed the presidency in 1825, John Quincy Adams might have worked to create a mass-based party. On the state level, the new democratic style of politics was already making headway. But Adams, a talented diplomat and a

<< Jackson's stubborn determination shines through in this portrait painted in 1835. "His passions are terrible," Jefferson noted. "When I was President of the Senate, he was Senator, and he could never speak on account of the rashness of his feelings. I have seen him attempt it repeatedly, and as often choke with rage."

President of the People >> The election of 1828 marked the beginning of politics as Americans have practiced it ever since, with two disciplined national parties actively competing for votes, emphasizing personalities over issues, and resorting to mass electioneering techniques. Yet in terms of public policy, the meaning of the election was anything but clear. The people had voted for Jackson as a national hero without any real sense of what he would do with his newly won power.

The first president from west of the Appalachians, Jackson was a man of action, and though he had a quick mind, he had little use for learning. His troops had nicknamed him Old Hickory out of respect for his toughness, but that strength sometimes became arrogance, and he could be vindictive and a bully. Over the course of his turbulent career he had fought several duels, one of which left a bullet embedded for the rest of his life within inches of his heart. For all his flaws, however, Jackson was a shrewd politician. He knew how to manipulate men and could be affable or abusive as the occasion demanded. He also displayed a keen sense of public opinion, reading the shifting national mood better than any of his contemporaries.

spoils system practice of rewarding loyal party members with jobs in government.

As the nation's chief executive, Jackson defended the **spoils system**, under which government jobs were awarded to political supporters.

Replacing officials regularly was a democratic reform, he insisted: the practice would guard against insensitive bureaucrats who presumed that they held their positions by right. The cabinet, he believed, existed more to carry out his will than to offer counsel. Throughout his term he insisted on his way—and usually got it.

The Political Agenda in the Market Economy >> Jackson took office at a time when the market economy was expanding throughout America and the nation's population was spreading geographically. The three major problems his administration faced were directly caused by the resulting growing pains.

First, the demand for new lands put continuing pressure on Indians, whose valuable cornfields and hunting grounds could produce marketable commodities like cotton and wheat. Second, as the economies of the North, South, and West became more specialized, their rival interests forced a confrontation over the tariff. And finally, the booming economy focused attention on the role of credit and banking in society and on the new commercial attitudes that were a central part of the developing market economy. The president attacked all three issues in his characteristically combative style.

DEMOCRACY AND RACE

As a planter, Jackson benefited from the international demand for cotton that was drawing new lands into the market. He had gone off to the Tennessee frontier in 1788, a rowdy, ambitious young man who could afford to purchase only one slave. Caught up in the speculative mania of the frontier, he became a prominent land speculator, established himself as a planter, and by the time he became president, owned nearly 100 slaves. His popularity derived not only from defeating the British but also from opening extensive tracts of valuable Indian lands to white settlement.

Even so, in 1820 an estimated 125,000 Indians remained east of the Mississippi River. In the Southwest the Choctaws, Creeks, Cherokees, Chickasaws, and Seminoles retained millions of acres of prime agricultural land in the heart of the cotton kingdom. Led by Georgia, southern states demanded that the federal government clear these titles.

As white pressure for removal intensified, a shift in the attitude toward Indians and toward race in general occurred. In the past whites most often had attributed cultural differences among whites, blacks, and Indians to the environment. Increasingly after 1815 the dominant white culture stressed "innate" racial differences that could never be erased. A growing number of Americans began to argue that the Indian was a permanently inferior savage who blocked progress.

Accommodate or Resist? >> The clamor among southern whites for removal placed the southwestern tribes in a difficult situation. Understandably, they rejected the idea of abandoning their lands. They diverged, however, over how to respond. Among the Cherokees, mixed-bloods led by John Ross argued that a program of accommodation—of adopting white ways—would best stave off removal. After a bitter struggle Ross prevailed, and in 1827 the Cherokees adopted a written constitution modeled after that of the United States. They also enacted the death penalty for any member who sold tribal lands to whites without consent of the governing general council. Developing their own alphabet, they published a bilingual newspaper, the *Cherokee Phoenix*.

The division between traditionalists and those favoring accommodation reflected the fact that Indians too had been drawn into a web of market relationships. As more Cherokee families began to sell their surplus crops, they ceased to share property communally as in the past. Cherokee society became more stratified and unequal, just as white society had, and economic elites dominated the tribal government. Nor were the Cherokees untouched by the cotton boom. Some tribal leaders, particularly half-bloods who could deal easily with white culture, became wealthy planters who owned many black slaves and thousands of acres of cotton land. Largely of mixed ancestry, slaveholders were the driving force behind acculturation.

As cotton cultivation expanded among the Cherokees, slavery became harsher and a primary means of determining status, just as in southern white society. The general council passed several laws forbidding intermarriage with blacks and excluding blacks and mulattoes from voting or holding office. Ironically, at the same time that white racial attitudes toward Indians were deteriorating, the Cherokees' view of African Americans drew closer to that of white society.

Trail of Tears >> As western land fever increased and racial attitudes hardened,

Jackson prodded Congress to provide funds for Indian removal. At the same time, the Georgia legislature declared Cherokee laws null and void and decreed that tribal members would be tried in state courts. In 1830 Congress finally passed a removal bill.

But the Cherokees brought suit in federal court against Georgia's actions. In 1832 in the case of *Worcester v. Georgia*, the Supreme Court, in an opinion written by Chief Justice John Marshall, ruled that Georgia had no right to extend its laws over Cherokee territory. Pronouncing Marshall's decision "stillborn," Jackson ignored the Court's edict and went ahead with plans for removal.

Although Jackson assured Indians that they could be removed only voluntarily, he paid no heed when state governments harassed tribes into surrendering lands. Under the threat of coercion, the Choctaws, Chickasaws, and Creeks reluctantly agreed to move to tracts in present-day Oklahoma. In the process, land-hungry schemers cheated tribal members out of as much as 90 percent of their land allotments.

The Cherokees held out longest, but to no avail. In order to deal with more pliant leaders of the tribe, Georgia authorities kidnapped Chief John Ross, who had led the resistance to relocation, and threw him into jail. Ross was finally released but not allowed to negotiate the treaty, which stipulated that the Cherokees leave their lands no later than 1838. When that time came, most refused to go. In response, President Martin Van Buren had the U.S. Army round up resistant members and force them, at bayonet point, to join the westward march. Of the 15,000 who traveled this Trail of Tears, approximately one-quarter died along the way of exposure, disease, and exhaustion.

Some Indians chose resistance. In the Old Northwest a group of the Sauk and Fox led by Black Hawk recrossed the Mississippi into Illinois in 1832 and were crushed by federal troops and the militia. More successful was the resistance of a minority of Seminoles led by Osceola. Despite Osceola's death, the Seminoles held out until 1842 in the Florida Everglades before being subdued and removed. In the end, only a small number of southern tribe members were able to escape removal.

In his farewell address in 1837, Jackson defended his policy by piously asserting that the eastern tribes had been finally "placed beyond the reach of injury or oppression, and that [the] paternal care of the General Government will hereafter watch over them and protect them." Indians, however, knew the bitter truth of the matter. Without effective political power, they were at the mercy of the pressures of the marketplace and the hardening racial attitudes of white Americans.

Free Blacks in the North

>> Unlike with Indian removal, the rising discrimination against free African Americans did not depend directly on presidential action. Still, it was Jackson's Democratic party, which was in the vanguard of promoting white equality, that was also the most strongly proslavery and the most hostile to black rights. The intensifying racism that accompanied the emergence of democracy in American life bore down with particular force on free African Americans.

Before the Civil War, the free black population remained small: about 171,000 in 1840. Although those numbers amounted to less than 2 percent of the North's population, most states enacted laws to keep African Americans in an inferior position. (For a discussion of free African Americans in the South, see Chapter 13.)

Most black northerners lacked meaningful political rights. Black men could vote on equal terms with whites in only five New England states. New York imposed a property requirement only on black voters, which disfranchised the vast majority. Moreover, in New Jersey, Pennsylvania, and Connecticut, African American men lost the right to vote after having previously enjoyed that privilege.

Blacks in the North were also denied basic civil rights that whites enjoyed. Five states forbade them to testify against whites, and either law or custom kept African Americans from juries everywhere except in Massachusetts. In addition, several western states passed black exclusion laws prohibiting free African Americans from immigrating into the state. These laws were seldom enforced, but they were available to harass the free black population.

BACKSTORY

Great White Father?

Although he made his political reputation as an Indian hater, Andrew Jackson adopted a Creek Indian boy—a child orphaned when Jackson's troops killed his parents. "He is a savage," Jackson wrote to his wife, "but one that fortune has thrown in my hands." The boy, who kept his Indian name, Lyncoya, died of tuberculosis at 16.

INDIAN REMOVAL

During Jackson's presidency, the federal government concluded nearly 70 treaties with Indian tribes in the Old Northwest as well as in the South. Under their terms, the United States acquired approximately 100 million acres of Indian land.

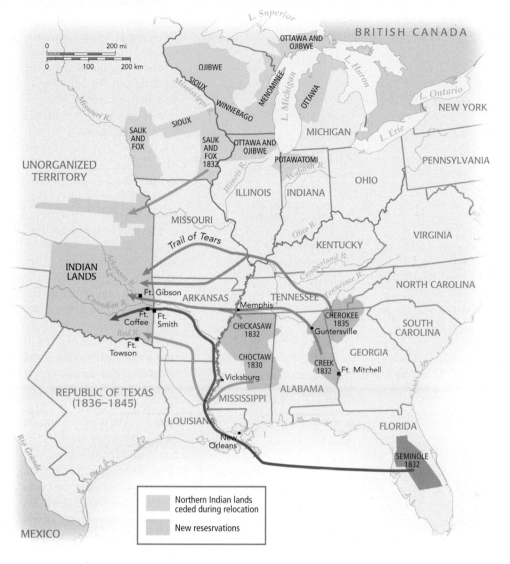

Legend:
- Northern Indian lands ceded during relocation
- New reservations

Discrimination pushed African American males into the lowest-paying and most unskilled jobs: servants, sailors, waiters, and common laborers. African American women normally continued working after marriage, mostly as servants, cooks, laundresses, and seamstresses, since their wages were critical to the family's survival. Blacks were willing strikebreakers, because white workers, fearing economic competition and loss of status, were overtly hostile and excluded them from trade unions. A number of antiblack riots erupted in northern cities during these years. Driven into abject poverty, free blacks in the North suffered from inadequate diet, were more susceptible to disease, and in 1850 had a life expectancy 8 to 10 years less than that of whites.

The African American Community

>> Free blacks had long suffered from such oppression and injustice. Between the Revolution and the War of 1812, they had responded by founding schools, churches, and mutual aid societies to sustain their communities. Typically, black leaders strove to strike a moderate tone in their published writings, praising whites who embraced the antislavery cause, emphasizing the achievements of black men and women, and even calling for a gradual rather than an immediate abolition of slavery. But by the 1820s, many African American leaders in the North turned to more confrontational tactics, advocating militant resistance to slavery and condemning the racism and inequalities that blighted the lives of free blacks everywhere in the United States. Among the most outspoken of this new generation of black leaders was David Walker, whose *Appeal to the Colored Citizens of the World* (1829) urged slaves to use violence to end bondage. After 1840, black frustration generated a nationalist movement that

Segregation, or the physical separation of the races, was widely practiced in the free states. African Americans were excluded from public transportation or assigned to separate sections. Throughout the North they could not go into most hotels and restaurants, and if permitted to enter theaters and lecture halls, they sat in the corners and balconies. In white churches, they sat in separate pews and took communion after white members. In virtually every community, black children were excluded from the public schools or forced to attend overcrowded and poorly funded separate schools. Commented one English visitor: "We see, in effect, two nations—one white and another black—growing up together . . . but never mingling on a principle of equality."

THE SPREAD OF WHITE MANHOOD SUFFRAGE

White manhood suffrage became the norm during the Jacksonian era, but in a number of states free black males who had been voting by law or by custom lost the right to vote. After 1821 a $250 property requirement disfranchised about 90 percent of adult black males in New York.

White Male Suffrage
(No Property Qualification)

Before 1800

1800 to 1830

1830 to 1860

Concentration of free blacks
(approximately 2,000 or more per county)

● Free black male vote in 1789
or when admitted to the Union

■ Free black male vote in 1860

1810 Date of the abolition of taxpaying
qualification. States without a
date adopted white male suffrage
when admitted to the Union.

African Americans. That animosity found vent in race riots, which erupted in Pittsburgh, Boston, Cincinnati, and New Haven.

The depth of racism in the culture could be seen in the rise of the minstrel show, the most popular form of entertainment in Jacksonian America. Originating in the 1830s and 1840s, these shows played to packed houses in cities and towns throughout the nation. They featured white actors performing in blackface, whose skits dealt in the broadest of racial stereotypes, ridiculing blacks as physically different and portraying them as buffoons.

Minstrelsy's greatest success came in northern cities. Its basic message was that African Americans could not cope with freedom and therefore did not belong in the North. Slaves were portrayed as happy and contented, whereas free blacks were caricatured either as strutting dandies or as helpless ignoramuses. Drawing its patrons from workers, Irish immigrants, and the poorer elements in society, minstrelsy assured these white champions of democracy that they remained superior.

The unsettling economic, social, and political changes of the Jacksonian era heightened white Americans' fear of failure, which stimulated racism. The popular yet unrealistic expectation was that any white man might become rich. Yet in fact, 20 percent or more of white adult males of this era never accumulated any property. Their lack of success prompted them to relieve personal tensions through increased hostility toward their black neighbors. The power of racism in Jacksonian America stemmed at least in part from the fact that equality remained part of the nation's creed while it steadily receded as a social reality.

emphasized racial unity, self-help, and for some, a renewal of ties with Africa.

Racism Strikes a Deeper Root >> What prompted greater militancy among African Americans after the 1820s was also the growth of an increasingly virulent racism among whites. Ironically, the success of efforts to promote education, religious piety, and temperance within the free black community threatened many lower-class whites and intensified their resentment of

THE NULLIFICATION CRISIS

Indian removal and antiblack discrimination provided one answer to the question of who would be given equality of opportunity in America's new democracy: Indians and African Americans would not. The issue of nullification raised a different, equally pressing question. As the North, South, and West increasingly specialized economically in response to the market revolution, how would a democratic system of government help various regions or interest groups to accommodate their differences?

The Growing Crisis in South Carolina >>

South Carolina had been particularly hard-hit by the depression of 1819. When prosperity returned to the rest of the nation, many of the state's cotton planters still suffered. With lands exhausted from years of cultivation, they could not compete with the fabulous yields of frontier planters in Alabama and Mississippi.

Under these difficult conditions, South Carolinians increasingly blamed federal tariffs for their miseries.

When Congress raised the duty rates in 1824, they assailed the tariff as an unfair tax that raised the prices of goods they imported while it benefited other regions of the nation. Other southern states opposed the 1824 tariff as well, though none so vehemently.

The one southern state in which black inhabitants outnumbered whites, South Carolina had also been growing more sensitive about the institution of slavery. In 1822 Denmark Vesey, a daring and resourceful free black carpenter in Charleston, secretly organized a plan to seize control of the city and raise the standard of black liberty. At the last moment, white officials thwarted the conspiracy and executed Vesey and his chief lieutenants; nevertheless, white South Carolinians were convinced that other conspirators still lurked in their midst. As an additional measure of security, they began to push for stronger constitutional protection of slavery. After all, the constitutional doctrine of broad construction and implied powers had already been used to justify higher protective tariffs. What was to prevent it from being used to end slavery?

When Congress, over the protests of the state's representatives, raised the duty rates still higher in 1828 with the so-called "Tariff of Abominations," South Carolina's legislature published the *South Carolina Exposition and Protest*, which outlined for the first time the theory of nullification. Only later was it revealed that its author was Jackson's own vice president, John C. Calhoun.

Calhoun was the most impressive intellect of his political generation. During the 1820s the South Carolina leader made a slow but steady journey away from nationalism toward an extreme states' rights position. When he was elected Jackson's vice president, South Carolinians assumed that tariff reform would be quickly forthcoming. But Jackson and Calhoun soon quarreled, and Calhoun lost all influence in the administration.

In his theory of nullification, Calhoun argued that the Union was a compact between sovereign states. Thus the people of each state, acting in special conventions, had the right to nullify any federal law that exceeded the powers granted to Congress under the Constitution. In response, Congress could either repeal the law or propose a constitutional amendment expressly giving it the power in question. If the amendment was ratified, the nullifying state could either accept the decision or exercise its ultimate right as a sovereign state and secede from the Union.

In 1830, Senator Daniel Webster of Massachusetts responded that the Union was not a compact of sovereign states. The people, and not the states, he argued, had created the Constitution. "It is the people's constitution, the people's government, made for the people, made by the people, and answerable to the people." Webster also insisted that the federal government did not merely act as the agent of the states but had sovereign powers in those areas where it had been delegated responsibility.

The Nullifiers Nullified >>

When Congress passed another tariff in 1832 that failed to give the state any relief, South Carolina's legislature called for the election of delegates to a popular convention, which overwhelmingly adopted an ordinance in November that declared the tariffs of 1828 and 1832 "null, void, and no law, nor binding upon this state, its officers or citizens" after February 1, 1833.

Jackson, who had spent much of his life defending the nation, was not about to tolerate any defiance of his authority or the federal government's. In his Proclamation on Nullification, issued in December 1832, he insisted that the Union was perpetual and that under the Constitution, no state had the right to secede. To reinforce his announced determination to enforce the tariff laws, Congress passed the Force Bill, reaffirming the president's military powers.

Yet Jackson was also a skillful politician. At the same time that he threatened South Carolina, he urged Congress to reduce the tariff rates. With no other state willing to follow South Carolina's lead, Calhoun reluctantly agreed to a compromise tariff in 1833. South Carolina's convention repealed the nullifying ordinance, and the crisis passed.

Calhoun's doctrine had proved too radical for the rest of the South. Even so, the controversy convinced many southerners that they were becoming a permanent minority. "We are divided into slave-holding and non-slave-holding states," concluded nullifier William Harper, "and this

> "We are divided into slave-holding and non-slave-holding states," concluded nullifier William Harper, "and this is the broad and marked distinction that must separate us at last."

is the broad and marked distinction that must separate us at last." As that feeling of isolation grew, it was not nullification but the threat of secession that ultimately became the South's primary weapon.

THE BANK WAR

Jackson understood well the political ties that bound the nation. He grasped much less firmly the economic and financial connections that linked regions of the country through banks and national markets. His clash with the Second Bank of the United States led to the greatest crisis of his presidency.

The National Bank and the Panic of 1819 >>

Chartered by Congress in 1816 for a 20-year period, the Second Bank of the United States suffered from woeful mismanagement. At first it helped fuel the speculative pressures in the economy. Then it turned about-face and sharply contracted credit by calling in loans when the depression hit in 1819. Critics viewed the Bank's policies not as a consequence but as the cause of the financial downswing. To many Americans, the Bank had already become a monster.

The psychological effects of the Panic of 1819 were almost as momentous as the economic. The shock of the depression made the 1820s a time of soul-searching, during which many uneasy farmers and workers came to view the hard times as punishment for having lost sight of the old virtues of simplicity, frugality, and hard work. For these Americans, banks were a symbol of the commercialization of American society and the rapid passing of a simpler way of life.

In 1823 Nicholas Biddle, a rich 37-year-old Philadelphia businessman, became president of the national bank. Biddle was intelligent and thoroughly familiar with the banking system, but he was also impossibly arrogant and politically dense. He set out to use the bank to regulate the amount of credit available in the economy, and thereby provide the nation with a sound currency.

The government regularly deposited its revenues in the national bank. These revenues were paid largely in bank notes (paper money) issued by state-chartered banks. If Biddle believed that a state bank had issued more notes than was safe, he presented them to that bank and demanded they be redeemed in **specie** (gold or silver). Because banks did not have enough specie reserves to back all the paper money they issued, the only way a state bank could continue to

specie coined money of gold or silver. Also referred to as hard money or hard currency. In contrast, banknotes or notes are paper money or paper currency.

redeem its notes was to call in its loans and reduce the amount of its notes in circulation. This action had the effect of lessening the amount of credit in the economy. On the other hand, if Biddle felt that a bank's credit policies were reasonable, he simply returned the state bank notes to circulation without presenting them for redemption.

Under Biddle's direction the Bank became a financial colossus with enormous power over state banks and over the economy. Yet Biddle used this power responsibly to provide the United States a sound paper currency, which the expanding economy needed.

Although the Bank had strong support in the business community, workers complained that they were often paid in **depreciated** state bank notes that could be redeemed for only a portion of their face value, a practice that cheated them of their full wages. They called for a "hard money" currency of only gold and silver. Hard money advocates viewed bankers and financiers as profiteers who manipulated the paper money system to enrich themselves at the expense of honest, hardworking farmers and laborers.

{ **depreciated** decreased in value owing to market conditions.

The Bank Destroyed

>> Jackson's own experiences left him with a deep distrust of banks and paper money. In 1804 his Tennessee land speculations had brought him to the brink of bankruptcy, from which it took years of painful struggle to free himself. Reflecting on his personal situation, he became convinced that banks and paper money threatened to corrupt the Republic.

As president, Jackson periodically called for reform of the banking system, but Biddle refused even to consider curbing the Bank's powers. Already distracted by the nullification controversy, Jackson warned Biddle not to inject the bank issue into the 1832 campaign. When Biddle went ahead and applied for a renewal of the Bank's charter in 1832, four years early, Jackson was furious. "The Bank is trying to kill me," he stormed, "but I will kill it."

Despite the president's opposition, Congress passed a recharter bill in the summer of 1832. Immediately Jackson vetoed it as unconstitutional (rejecting Marshall's earlier ruling in *McCulloch v. Maryland*). Condemning the Bank as an agent of special privilege, the president pledged to protect "the humble members

of society—the farmer, mechanics, and laborers" against "the advancement of the few at the expense of the many."

When Congress failed to override Jackson's veto, the Bank became a central issue of the 1832 campaign. Jackson's opponent was Henry Clay, a National Republican who eagerly accepted the financial support of Biddle and his bank. Clay went down to defeat, and once reelected, Jackson was determined to move boldly. He believed that as a private corporation the Bank wielded a dangerous influence over government policy and the economy, and he was justly incensed over its interference in the election.

To cripple the Bank, the president simply ordered all the government's federal deposits withdrawn. Since such an act clearly violated federal law, Jackson was forced to

---

The Bank and Bare-Knuckled Boxers

Historians often use political cartoons to interpret the currents of American culture. By their nature cartoons deal in visual symbols; to be accessible to their readers, the symbols cannot be subtle. For present-day viewers, however, some decoding is needed. Both the woman holding the bottle of port and the man standing beside the "Old Monongahela Whiskey" (a cat on his head, no less!) look ridiculous. Yet they send contrasting messages in this cartoon, in which Nicholas Biddle and Andrew Jackson (right) square off as bare-knuckled boxers in the war over the Bank.

The woman's fancy flowered bonnet and ruffled collar suggest an aristocratic fussiness—as does the port, which was an imported, upper-class beverage. The plain frontiersman, in contrast, wears simple buckskin and keeps his whiskey—a drink of the masses—close at hand. Just as Franklin Plummer portrayed his Mississippi opponent as a cologne-scented dandy (see page 206), this cartoonist sees Biddle as the aristocrat doing battle with Jackson, defender of the common folk.

⋀ This Whig cartoon blames the Democratic party for the depression that began during Van Buren's adminis-tration. Barefoot workers go unemployed, and women and children beg and sleep in the streets. Depositors clamor for their money from a bank that has suspended specie payments, while the pawnbroker and liquor store do a thriving business and the sheriff rounds up debtors.

transfer one secretary of the treasury and fire another before he finally found an ally, Roger Taney, willing to take the job and carry out the edict. Taney (pronounced "Taw-ney") gradually withdrew the government's funds while depositing new revenues in selected state banks.

Biddle fought back by deliberately precipitating a brief financial panic in 1833, but Jackson refused to budge. Eventually Biddle had to relent, and Jackson's victory was complete. When the Bank's charter expired in 1836, no national banking system replaced it.

Jackson's Impact on the Presidency ≫

Jackson approached the end of his administration in tri-umph. Indian removal was well on its way to completion, the nullifiers had been confounded, and the "Monster Bank" had been destroyed. In the process, Jackson immea-surably enlarged the power of the presidency. "The Presi-dent is the direct representative of the American people," he lectured the Senate when it opposed him. "He was elected by the people, and is responsible to them." With this declaration, Jackson redefined the character of the

presidential office and its relationship to the people.

Jackson also converted the veto into an effective presidential power. During his two terms in office, he vetoed 12 bills, compared with only 9 for all previous presidents combined. Moreover, where his predecessors had vetoed bills only on strict constitutional grounds, Jackson felt free to block laws simply because he thought them bad policy. The threat of such action became an effective way to shape pend-ing legislation to his liking, a tactic which fundamentally strengthened the power of the president over Congress. The development of the modern presidency began with Andrew Jackson.

"The President is the direct representative of the American people," [Jackson] lectured the Senate when it opposed him.

VAN BUREN AND DEPRESSION

With the controls of the national bank removed, state banks rapidly expanded their activities, including the printing of more money. As the currency expanded, so did the number of banks: from 329 in 1829 to 788 in 1837. A spiraling **inflation** set in as prices rose 50 percent after 1830 and interest rates by half as much.

inflation increase in the overall price of goods and services over an extended period of time; or a similar decrease over time of the purchasing power of money.

As prices soared, so did speculative fever. By 1836 land sales, which had been only $2.6 million four years earlier, approached $25 million. Almost all these lands were bought entirely on credit with bank notes. In July 1836 Jackson issued the Specie Circular, which decreed that the government would accept only specie for the purchase of public land. Land sales plummeted, but the speculative pressures in the economy were already too great.

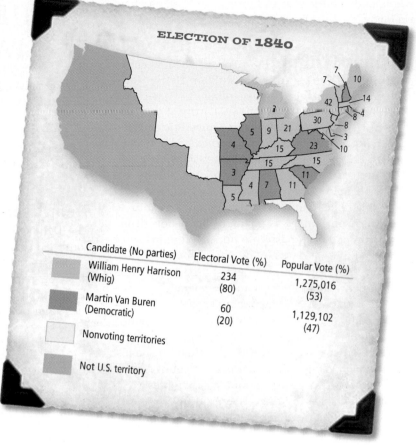

ELECTION OF 1840

Candidate (No parties)	Electoral Vote (%)	Popular Vote (%)
William Henry Harrison (Whig)	234 (80)	1,275,016 (53)
Martin Van Buren (Democratic)	60 (20)	1,129,102 (47)
Nonvoting territories		
Not U.S. territory		

"Van Ruin's" Depression

During Jackson's second term, his opponents had gradually come together in a new party, the Whigs. Led by Henry Clay, they charged that "King Andrew I" had dangerously concentrated power in the presidency. The Whigs also embraced Clay's "American System," designed to spur national economic development through a protective tariff, a national bank, and federal aid for internal improvements. In 1836 the Democrats nominated Martin Van Buren, who triumphed over three Whig sectional candidates.

Van Buren had less than two months in office to savor his triumph before the speculative mania collapsed, and with it the economy. After a brief recovery, the bottom fell out of the international cotton market in 1839, and the country entered a serious depression. It was not until 1843 that the economy revived.

> After a **brief recovery,** the **bottom fell out** of the international **cotton market** in 1839, and the **country** entered a **serious depression.**

Public opinion identified hard times with the policies of the Democratic party. Since he continued to oppose a new national bank, Van Buren instead persuaded Congress in 1840 to create an Independent Treasury to hold the government's funds. Its offices were forbidden to accept paper currency, issue any bank notes, or make any loans. The government's money would be safe, as Van Buren intended, but it would also remain unavailable to banks to make loans and stimulate the economy. Whigs, in contrast, hoped to encourage manufacturing and revive the economy by passing a protective tariff, continuing state internal improvement projects, protecting corporations, and expanding the banking and credit system.

As the depression deepened, thousands of workers were unemployed, and countless businesses failed. Nationally, wages fell 30 to 50 percent. "Business of all kinds is completely at a stand," wrote New York business and civic leader Philip Hone in 1840, "and the whole body politic sick and infirm, and calling aloud for a remedy."

The Whigs Triumph >>

For the 1840 presidential campaign the Whigs turned to William Henry Harrison, who had defeated the Shawnee Indians at Tippecanoe, to oppose Van Buren. In the midst of the worst depression of the century, Whigs employed the democratic electioneering techniques that Jackson's supporters had perfected. They hailed Harrison as a man of the people while painting Van Buren as a dandy and an aristocrat who wore a corset, ate off gold plates with silver spoons, and used cologne. Whig rallies featured hard cider and log cabins to reinforce Harrison's image as a man of the people. Ironically, Harrison had been born into one of Virginia's most aristocratic families and was living in a 16-room mansion in Ohio. But the Whig campaign, by casting the election as a contest between aristocracy and democracy, was perfectly attuned to the prevailing national spirit.

In the campaign of 1840, Whigs also prominently involved women, urging them to become politically informed in order to morally instruct their husbands. Women attended Whig rallies, conducted meetings, made speeches, and wrote campaign pamphlets, activities previously performed solely by men. Democrats were uneasy about this innovation, yet had no choice but to follow suit. Within a few years the presence of women at party rallies was commonplace.

The election produced a record turnout, with nearly four-fifths of the eligible voters going to the polls. Although the popular vote was fairly close (Harrison led by about 150,000 votes out of 2.4 million cast), in the Electoral College he won an easy victory, 234 to 60.

The "log cabin" campaign marked the final transition from the deferential politics of the Federalist era to the egalitarian politics that had emerged in the wake of the Panic of 1819. As the *Democratic Review* conceded after the Whigs' victory in 1840, "We have taught them how to conquer us."

> As the *Democratic Review* conceded after the Whigs' victory in 1840, "We have taught them how to conquer us."

THE JACKSONIAN PARTY SYSTEM

It is easy, given the hoopla of democratic campaigning, to be distracted from the central fact that the new political system was directly shaped by the social and economic strains of an expanding nation. Whigs and Democrats held different attitudes toward the changes brought about by the market, banks, and commerce.

Democrats, Whigs, and the Market >>

The Democrats tended to view society as a continuing conflict between "the people"—farmers, planters, and workers—and a set of greedy aristocrats. They charged that this "paper money aristocracy" of bankers, stock jobbers, and investors manipulated the banking system for their own profit. For Democrats, the Bank War became a battle to restore the old Jeffersonian Republic with its values of simplicity, frugality, hard work, and independence.

Jackson understood the dangers private banks posed to a democratic society. Yet Democrats, in effect, wanted the rewards and goods that the market offered without sacrificing the features of a simple agrarian republic. They wanted the wealth that the market produced without the competitive society, the complex dealings, the dominance of urban centers, and the loss of independence that came with it.

Whigs were more comfortable with the market. They envisioned no conflict between farmers and mechanics on the one hand and businesspeople and bankers on the other. The government's responsibility was to provide a well-regulated economy that guaranteed opportunity for citizens of ability. In such an economy, banks and corporations were not only useful but necessary.

Whigs and Democrats also disagreed over how active government should be. Despite Andrew Jackson's inclination to be a strong president, Democrats as a rule believed in limited government. Government's role in the economy was to promote competition by destroying monopolies and special privileges. In keeping with this philosophy, Democrats also rejected the idea that moral beliefs were the proper sphere of government action. Religion and politics, they believed, should be kept clearly separate, and they generally opposed humanitarian legislation.

The Whigs, in contrast, viewed government power positively. They believed that it should be used to protect individual rights and public liberty, and that it had a special role where individual effort was ineffective. By regulating the economy and competition, the government could ensure equal opportunity. Indeed, for Whigs the concept of government promoting the general welfare went beyond the economy. Northern Whigs in particular also believed that government power should be used to foster the moral welfare of the country. They were much more likely to favor temperance or antislavery legislation and aid to education. Whigs portrayed themselves not only as the party of prosperity, but also as the party of respectability and proper behavior.

The Social Bases of the Two Parties >>

In some ways the social makeup of the two parties was similar. To be competitive Whigs and Democrats both had to have significant support among farmers, the largest group in society, and workers. Neither party could carry an election by appealing exclusively to the rich or the poor.

The Whigs, however, enjoyed disproportionate strength among the business and commercial classes, especially following the Bank War. Whigs appealed to planters who needed credit to finance their cotton and rice trade in the world market, to farmers who were eager to sell their surpluses, and to workers who wished to improve their social position. Democrats attracted farmers isolated from the market or uncomfortable with it, workers alienated from the emerging industrial system, and rising entrepreneurs who wanted to break monopolies and open the economy to newcomers like themselves. The Whigs were strongest in the towns, cities, and rural areas that were fully integrated into the market economy, whereas Democrats dominated areas of semisubsistence farming that were more isolated and languishing economically. Attitude toward the market, rather than economic position, was more important in determining party affiliation.

Religion and ethnic identities also shaped partisanship. As the self-proclaimed "party of respectability," Whigs attracted the support of high-status native-born church groups, including Congregationalists and Unitarians in New England and Presbyterians and Episcopalians elsewhere. The party also attracted immigrant groups that most easily merged into the dominant Anglo-Protestant culture, such as the English, Welsh, and Scots. Democrats, however, recruited more Germans and Irish, whose more lenient observance of the Sabbath and (among Catholics) use of parochial schools generated native-born hostility. Democrats appealed to the lower-status Baptists and

Methodists, particularly in states where they earlier had been subjected to legal disadvantages. Both parties also attracted freethinkers and the unchurched, but the Democrats had the advantage because they resisted demands for temperance and sabbatarian laws, such as the prohibition of Sunday travel. In the few states where they could vote, African Americans were solidly Whig in reaction to the Democratic party's strong racism and hostility to black rights.

In the Americas as well as in Europe, the rise of democratic governance and the spread of market economies evolved roughly in tandem over the same half-century. Andrew Jackson's triumph was only the latest in a series of upheavals stretching back to the American and French Revolutions of the eighteenth century. Latin America, too, experienced democratic revolutions. From 1808 to 1821 Spain's American provinces declared their independence one by one, taking inspiration from the writings of Jefferson and Thomas Paine as well as the French *Declaration of the Rights of Man*. Democracy did not always root itself in the aftermath of these revolutions, but democratic ideology remained a powerful social catalyst.

In the United States, the parallel growth of national markets and democratic institutions exhibited a similarly checkered history. If Jackson championed the cause of the "common people," he also led the movement to displace Indians from their lands. A poor white American might vote for "Old Hickory" at the same time that he took comfort that African Americans could never rise as high as he in an increasingly racist society. Furthermore, the advance of the market created social strains, including the increasing impoverishment of the labor force in the North and the growing gap in society between the richest and the poorest.

Still, Americans had evolved a system of democratic politics to deal with the conflicts that the new order produced. The new national parties, like the new markets, had become essential structures uniting the American nation. They advanced an ideology of equality and opportunity, competed vigorously with one another, and mobilized large numbers of ordinary Americans in the political process. Along with the market, democracy had become an integral part of American life.

> If Jackson championed the cause of the "common people," he also led the movement to displace Indians from their lands.

CHAPTER SUMMARY

Beginning in the 1820s, the United States experienced a democratic revolution that was identified with Andrew Jackson.

- The rise of democracy was stimulated by the Panic of 1819, which caused Americans to look toward both politicians and the government to address their needs.
- The new political culture of democracy included the use of conventions to make nominations, the celebration of the wisdom of the people, the adoption of white manhood suffrage, and the acceptance of political parties as essential for the working of the constitutional system.
- The new politics had distinct limits, however. Women were not given the vote, and racism intensified.
  - The eastern Indian tribes were forced to move to new lands west of the Mississippi River.
  - Free African Americans found themselves subject to increasingly harsh discrimination and exclusion.

- In politics, Andrew Jackson came to personify the new democratic culture. Through his forceful leadership, he significantly expanded the powers of the presidency.
  - Jackson threatened to use force against South Carolina when it tried to nullify the federal tariff using John C. Calhoun's theory of nullification—that is, that a state convention could nullify a federal law.
  - In response, nationalists advanced the idea of the perpetual Union. The compromise of 1833, which gradually lowered the tariff, ended the crisis.
  - Jackson vetoed a bill to recharter the Second Bank of the United States and destroyed the Bank by removing its federal deposits.
  - Under President Martin Van Buren, the nation entered a severe depression.
- Capitalizing on hard times and employing the democratic techniques pioneered by the Democrats, the Whigs gained national power in 1840.
- By 1840 the two parties had developed different ideologies.
  - The Whigs were more comfortable with the mechanisms of the market and linked commerce with progress.
  - The Democrats were uneasy about the market and favored limited government.

Significant Events

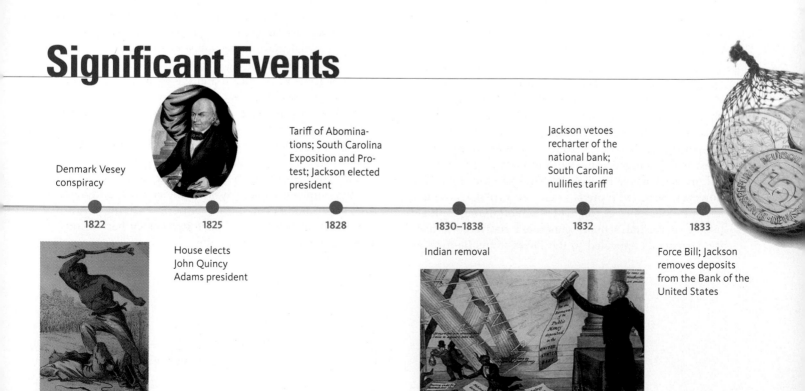

Denmark Vesey conspiracy

1822

BLOW FOR BLOW.

House elects John Quincy Adams president

1825

Tariff of Abominations; South Carolina Exposition and Protest; Jackson elected president

1828

1830–1838

Indian removal

Jackson vetoes recharter of the national bank; South Carolina nullifies tariff

1832

1833

Force Bill; Jackson removes deposits from the Bank of the United States

Additional Reading

The most comprehensive reinterpretation of antebellum political history from Jackson to Lincoln is Sean Wilentz, *The Rise of Democracy* (2005). For a broader perspective on the evolution of American political culture throughout the nineteenth century, see Glenn Altschuler and Stuart Blumin, *Rude Republic* (2000). A good interpretation of Jacksonian politics is Harry Watson, *Liberty and Power* (1990), and important discussions of party ideologies include Marvin Meyers, *The Jacksonian Persuasion* (1957); Daniel Walker Howe, *The Political Culture of American Whigs* (1979); and Lawrence Frederick Kohl, *The Politics*

of Individualism (1988). For the history of the Whig party, the book to read is Michael Holt, *The Rise and Fall of the American Whig Party* (1999).

The best account of the nullification crisis is still William Freehling, *Prelude to the Civil War* (1966), and Robert Remini offers a succinct analysis of the banking controversy in *Andrew Jackson and the Bank War* (1967). Paul Goodman, *Towards a Christian Republic* (1988) is the most valuable study of Anti-Masonry. On Indian removal in the South, see John Ehle, *The Trail of Tears* (1997), and Robert Remini, *Andrew Jackson and His Indian Wars* (2001).

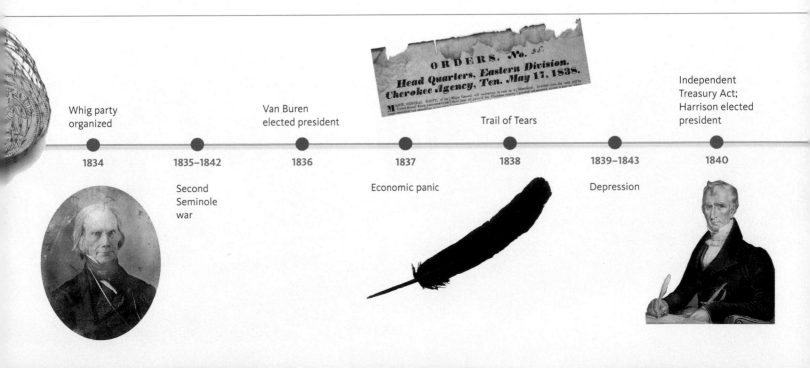

1834	1835–1842	1836	1837	1838	1839–1843	1840
Whig party organized		Van Buren elected president		Trail of Tears		Independent Treasury Act; Harrison elected president
	Second Seminole war		Economic panic		Depression	

The Fires of Perfection

1820—1850

12

WHAT'S TO COME

227 **REVIVALISM AND THE SOCIAL ORDER**

229 **WOMEN'S SPHERE**

231 **AMERICAN ROMANTICISM**

232 **THE AGE OF REFORM**

235 **ABOLITIONISM**

239 **REFORM SHAKES THE PARTY SYSTEM**

THE BEECHERS AND THE KINGDOM OF GOD

In 1826 the Reverend Lyman Beecher was probably the most celebrated minister of the Republic, and the pulpit of Hanover Street Church was his to command. Beecher looked and spoke like a pious farmer, but every Sunday he was transformed when he mounted the pulpit of Boston's most imposing church. From there, he would blaze forth denunciations of dancing, drinking, dueling, or "infidelity," all the while punctuating his sermon with pump-handle strokes of the right hand. »

Bursting with energy and enthusiasm, Methodists head toward a camp meeting in 1819. At a time when the nation had lurched into an economic "panic," the bonds of unity created by this revival and others like it brought a sense of stability and peace amidst widespread change. Such revivals also motivated believers to create a better world around them.

⌃ Lyman Beecher (*center*) with his family in 1855. Five of his six sons, all of whom were ministers, stand in back. In front, daughters Catharine (holding his arm to steady it for the long exposure) and Isabella are on the left; Harriet, the author of *Uncle Tom's Cabin*, is at the far right.

Nor were Beecher's ambitions small. His goal was nothing less than to bring the kingdom of Christ to the nation and the world. Like many ministers, Beecher had studied the final book of the New Testament, the Revelation to John. The Revelation foretold in the latter days of the Earth a glorious millennium—a thousand years of peace and triumph—when the saints would rule and evil would be banished from the world. Beecher was convinced that the long-awaited millennium might well begin in the United States.

Personal experience reinforced this optimism. Born to a sturdy line of New England blacksmiths in 1775, Lyman Beecher entered Yale College during the high tide of postwar nationalism. In the revivals of the Second Great Awakening that came to many colleges in 1802, the young student had been one of those converted.

Much of Beecher's boundless energy went into raising a family of 11 children, every one of whom he prayed would take leading roles in bringing the kingdom of God to America. The family attended two services on Sunday, a weekly prayer meeting, and a monthly "concert of prayer," where the devout met to pray for the conversion of the world.

To usher in the kingdom of God entire communities and even nations would have to be swept with the fire of **millennialism**. Toward that end

> **millennialism** belief in the thousand-year reign of Christ predicted in the New Testament's final book, the Revelation to John.

Beecher joined other Protestant ministers in supporting a host of religious reforms and missionary organizations. Such benevolent associations distributed Bibles, promoted Sunday schools, and ministered to the poor.

Beecher also directed his righteous artillery on a host of evils that seemed to be obstructing God's kingdom. With scorn he attacked elite Unitarians, whose liberal, rational creed rejected the divinity of Jesus. But he also condemned what he viewed as sinful pastimes of the lower class: playing cards, gambling, and drinking. And he denounced Roman Catholic priests and nuns as superstitious, devious agents of "Antichrist."

Beecher's efforts at "moral reform" antagonized many immigrants and other working people who enjoyed liquor or lotteries. They didn't like to be told that they shouldn't buy grog from the booths selling it on Boston Common. Thus, when a blaze broke out in the basement of his church in 1830, local firefighters rushed to Hanover Street—for the pleasure of watching while Beecher's church burned to the ground. ≪

Any fire, real or spiritual, is unpredictable as it spreads from one scrap of tinder to the next. That proved to be the case with reform movements of the 1820s and 1830s, as they moved in diverging, sometimes contradictory ways. What did it mean, after all, to bring in Christ's kingdom? The goals of the early reform societies were moral rather than social. Leaders like Beecher sought to convert individuals and to church the unchurched with the help of religious revivals and benevolent associations. Their conservative aim, as he expressed it, was to restore America to "the moral government of God."

Other Christians, however, began to focus on social issues such as slavery, the inequality of women, and the operation of prisons. To these problems they demanded more radical solutions. Ironically, many of Beecher's children went well beyond his more conservative strategies for hastening the millennium. They spoke out for abolition, women's rights, and education in ways that left their father distinctly uncomfortable. In their activities the Beechers reflected the diversity of the reform impulse itself.

REVIVALISM AND THE SOCIAL ORDER

Society during the Jacksonian era was undergoing deep and rapid change. The revolution in markets brought both economic expansion and periodic depressions, and in such anxious times some reformers sought stability and moral order from the religious community. The bonds of unity created by a revival brought a sense of peace in the midst of a society in change. Revivals could reinforce strength and discipline, too, in an emerging industrial culture that demanded sobriety and regular working habits.

Other reformers, however, sought to check the excesses of Jacksonian America by radically remaking institutions or devising utopian, experimental ways of living and working together. The drive for renewal, in other words, led reformers sometimes to preserve social institutions, other times to overturn them. It led them sometimes to liberate, other times to control. And the conflicting ways in which these dynamics operated could be seen in the electric career of Charles Grandison Finney.

Finney's New Measures and New Theology >> As a young man, in 1821, Finney experienced a soul-shattering conversion that led him to give up his law practice to become an itinerant minister. Between the mid-1820s and the early 1830s he conducted a series of spectacular revivals in the booming port cities along the new Erie Canal, a region that came to be known as the "burned over district," so many religious fires swept through.

Like George Whitefield before him, Finney had an entrancing voice that carried great distances. His success, however, resulted as much from his use of special techniques—"the new measures." Finney held "protracted meetings" night after night to build excitement. Speaking bluntly, he prayed for sinners by name, encouraged women to testify in public gatherings, and placed those struggling with conversion on the "anxious bench" at the front of the church. Such techniques all heightened the emotions of the conversion process. The cries of agonized prayers, the groans, and the uncontrolled crying often resounded through the hall.

Finney's new measures had actually been used during the frontier revivals of the Second Great Awakening (page 000). His contribution was to popularize the techniques and use them systematically. "A revival is not a miracle," he coolly declared, "it is a purely scientific result of the right use of constituted means." Like other **evangelical** revivalists, Finney looked to help individuals to undergo an emotionally wrenching conversion experience and be reborn.

> **evangelical** term that derives from a Greek word meaning the bringing of good news—in this case, the Gospel.

Finney also rejected many religious doctrines of Calvinism, including predestination, which maintained that God had already determined which individuals were destined to be saved or damned, and no human effort could change this decision. By the 1820s such a proposition seemed unreasonable to citizens of a democratic republic. Finney embraced the doctrine of free will, contending that all men and women who wanted to could be saved. To those anxious about their salvation, he thundered, "Do it!"

With salvation within reach of every individual, what might be in store for society at large? "If the church would do her duty," Finney confidently predicted, "the millennium may come in this country in three

The Second Great Awakening

"The wave of popular religious movements that broke upon the United States in the half century after independence did more to Christianize American society than any thing before or since. Nothing makes that point more clearly than the growth of Methodist and Baptist movements among white and black Americans."

—Nathan Hatch, *The Democratization of American Christianity*

In *The Way of Good and Evil* devout Christians are all helped on the path (*right*) to millennial perfection by the virtues of family, religion, education, and hard work. Sinners on the left, however, take the path of disobedience, intemperance, and lying—straight to hell.

Religion and the Market Economy »

Revival audiences responded to the call for reform partly because they were unsettled by the era's rapid social changes. In the North, evangelical religion proved strongest not in isolated backwaters but in frontier areas just entering the market economy. Rochester, New York, a booming flour-milling center on the Erie Canal, epitomized that social environment.

When Charles Finney came to town in the winter of 1830–1831, Rochester was a community in crisis. It had grown in a decade and a half from a village of 300 souls to a commercial city of more than 20,000. That wrenching expansion produced sharp divisions among the town's leaders, a large working class that increasingly lived apart from employers and beyond their moral control, and a rowdy saloon culture catering to canal boatmen and other transients. Finney preached almost daily in Rochester for six months, and, assisted by local ministers, his revivals doubled church membership. Religion helped bring order to what had been a chaotic and fragmented city.

Although revivals such as Finney's Rochester triumph drew converts from all segments of American society, they appealed especially to the middle class. Lawyers, merchants, retailers, and manufacturers all played central roles in the larger market economy and invested in factories and railroads. The market put intense pressure on these upwardly mobile citizens: they viewed success as a reflection of moral character, yet also feared that they would lose their wealth in the next economic downturn.

years." By the 1830s Finney had taken to preaching not merely faith in human progress but something more—human perfectibility. Embracing this new theology of "perfectionism," he boldly asserted that all Christians should "aim at being holy and not rest satisfied until they are as perfect as God."

By preaching an optimistic message of free will and salvation for all, Finney and his eager imitators transformed Protestantism. But not all clergy applauded. For many supporters of the Second Great Awakening, including Lyman Beecher, Finney's new measures went too far, while his theology of perfectionism verged on heresy. "I'll meet you at the State Line," warned Beecher, when Finney considered bringing his methods to Massachusetts, "... and fight you every inch of the way to Boston."

» Revivalist Charles Finney gained fame in New York state's "burned over district," where he led religious revivals in many of the towns along the bustling Erie Canal. As Finney's fame spread, he eventually used a huge tent, 100 feet in diameter, which was able to seat 3,000 worshipers.

A Slave's Conversion Experience

"I stopped, dropped the plow, and started running, but the voice kept on speaking to me saying, 'Fear not, my little one, for behold! I come to bring you a message of truth.' Everything got dark, and I was unable to stand any longer. I began to feel sick, and there was a great roaring. I tried to cry and move but I was unable to do either."

Workers, too, were among the converted. Beyond religious motivations, joining a church reflected a desire to get ahead in the new economy by accepting moral self-discipline. To a striking degree, social mobility and church membership were linked. In Rochester two-thirds of the male workers who were church members improved their occupational status in a decade. In contrast, workers who did not join a church rarely stayed in town more than a few years, and those who stayed were likely to decline in status.

Revivalists such as Finney were interested in saving souls, not money, and their converts were most concerned with their spiritual state. Even so, evangelical Protestantism reinforced values needed to succeed in the new competitive economy. Churchgoers accepted the values of hard work and punctuality, self-control and sobriety. In that sense, religion was one means of fostering social order in a disordered society.

The Rise of African American Churches >>

Independent black churches grew in size and importance as well, as African Americans in urban areas increasingly resented being treated as second-class worshipers. The most important was the African Methodist Episcopal (AME) Church, organized in 1816. Growing fears for the security of slavery caused southern white communities, especially in the Deep South, to suppress independent black churches after 1820. But these evangelical churches continued to grow in the North. By 1856 the AME Church had about 20,000 members.

As a result of the Second Great Awakening, the dominant form of Christianity in America became evangelical Protestantism. Membership in the major Protestant churches—Congregational, Presbyterian, Baptist, and Methodist—soared. By 1840 an estimated half of the adult population was connected to some church, with the Methodists emerging as the largest Protestant denomination

in both the North and the South. Evangelicalism was in harmony with the basic values of early-nineteenth-century Americans. Its emphasis on the ability of everyone to bring about his or her salvation upheld the American belief in individualism. By catering to a mass audience without social distinctions, the revivals reinforced the American belief in democracy and equality. And Finney's invincibly optimistic doctrine of perfectionism matched the spirit of the age.

WOMEN'S SPHERE

Women played a large role in the Second Great Awakening. Indeed, female converts outnumbered males by about three to two. Usually the first convert in a family was a woman, and many men who converted were related to women who had come forward earlier.

Women loomed large in the revivals partly because of changes in their own social universe. Instead of parents arranging the marriages of their children, couples were beginning to wed more often on the basis of affection. Under such conditions, a woman's prospects for marriage became less certain, and in older areas such as New England, the migration of so many young men out of the region compounded this uncertainty. At the same time, marriage remained essential for a woman's economic security. The unpredictability of these social circumstances especially drew women between the ages of 12 and 25 to conversion. Joining a church heightened a young woman's sense of purpose. By establishing respectability and widening her social circle of friends, it also enhanced her chances of marriage.

The Ideal of Domesticity >> The era's changing economic order brought other pressures to bear on wives and mothers. Most men now worked outside the home, while the rise of factories led to a decline in part-time work such as spinning, which women had once performed to supplement family income. Moreover, except on the frontier, home manufacturing was no longer essential, because the family purchased articles that women previously had made, such as cloth, soap, and candles.

This growing separation of the household from the workplace meant that the home took on a new social identity. It was idealized as a place of "**domesticity**," a haven away from the competitive, workaday world, with the mother firmly at its center. If men's sphere was the world of factories, offices, and fields, women's sphere was the home, where they were to dispense love and comfort and teach moral values to husbands and children.

> **domesticity** devotion to home life, and a woman's place at the center of that life.

Women, who were considered morally stronger, were also held to a higher standard of sexual purity. A man's

As business affairs grew increasingly separate from the family in the nineteenth century, the middle-class home became a female domain. A woman's role as a wife and mother was to dispense love and moral guidance to her husband and her children. As this domestic scene makes clear, she was the center of the family, and in a world beset by flux, she was to be an unchanging symbol of morality.

in Europe, so that after 1850 it was culturally dominant. Employment opportunities expanded for women as industrialization accelerated in Europe, yet the social expectation among the middle class was that women would not be employed outside the home. This redefinition of women's roles was more sweeping in Europe because previously, middle-class women had left the task of child rearing largely to hired nurses and governesses. By midcentury, these mothers devoted much more time to domestic duties, including rearing the children. Family size also declined, both in France and in England. The middle class was most numerous in England; indeed, the importance of the middle class in Britain during Queen Victoria's reign gave these ideals the label **Victorianism**.

Victorianism constellation of middle-class values attributed to the proper virtues of Britain's Queen Victoria. The culture's emphasis on "refinement" and "manners" established a social hierarchy offering some sense of stability.

Most American women hardly had time to make the ideal of domesticity the center of their lives. Farmers' wives had to work constantly, while lower-class families could not get by without the wages of female members. Still, most middle-class women tried to live up to the ideal, and many found the effort confining. "The great trial is that I have nothing to do," one complained. "Here I am with abundant leisure and capable, I believe, of accomplishing some good, and yet with no object on which to expend my energies."

Women's socially defined role as guardians of morality helps explain their prevalence among converts. Religious activity was one way that women could exert influence in society, to say nothing of influencing their husbands.

sexual infidelity, although hardly condoned, brought no lasting shame. But a woman who engaged in sexual relations before marriage or was unfaithful afterward was threatened with everlasting disgrace. Under this double standard, women were to be passive and submerge their identities in those of their husbands.

No woman played a more important role in creating the ideal of domesticity than Lyman Beecher's daughter Catharine. Like earlier advocates of "republican motherhood," Catharine Beecher argued that women exercised power as moral guardians of the nation. The proper care of a middle-class household was also a crucial responsibility, and Beecher wrote several books on efficient home management. Catharine Beecher also advocated giving women greater educational opportunities in order to become schoolteachers. The school was an extension of the home, she maintained, and teachers, like mothers, should instill sound moral values in children. Women also exerted their moral authority through benevolent organizations, which fostered close friendships.

The ideal of domesticity was not unique to the United States. The middle class became increasingly important

The Middle-Class Family in Transition »

As the middle-class family adapted to the pressures of competitive society by becoming a haven of moral virtue, it developed a new structure and new set of attitudes closer in spirit to the modern family's. One basic change was the rise of privacy. The family was increasingly seen as a sheltered retreat from the outside world. In addition, the pressures to achieve success led middle-class young adults to delay marriage, since a husband was expected to support his wife.

Did the status of women improve in the United States between the American Revolution and the Civil War?

Smaller family size was a result of delaying marriage as well, since wives began bearing children later. Especially among the urban middle class, women began to use birth control to space children farther apart and minimize the risks of pregnancy. These practices contributed to a decline in the birthrate, from slightly more than 7 children per family in 1800 to 5.4 in 1850— a 25 percent drop. Family size was directly related to the success ethic, since in the newer, market-oriented society children needed extended education and special training in order to succeed and thus were a greater financial burden.

Indeed, more parents showed greater concern about providing their children with advantages in the race for success. Middle-class families were increasingly willing to bear the additional expense of educating their sons longer, and they also frequently equalized inheritances rather than giving priority to the eldest son or favoring sons over daughters.

The term "Second Great Awakening" refers to

a. the renewed interest in democratizing American politics among antebellum Americans.

b. a series of religious revivals in the early nineteenth century which swelled membership in Protestant churches.

c. a resurgence of interest in the ideas of the Enlightenment among antebellum Americans.

d. the widespread recognition after the Panic of 1819 that government policies could affect the national economy.

Key: b

AMERICAN ROMANTICISM

Along with evangelical Protestantism, a second major cultural current shaped social change and the reform movements of the era. That movement, known as **Romanticism**, began in Europe as a reaction against the Enlightenment. The Enlightenment had placed reason at the center of human achievement; Romanticism instead emphasized the importance of emotion and intuition as sources of truth. It gloried in the unlimited potential of the individual, who might soar if freed from the restraints of institutions. In elevating inner feelings and heartfelt convictions, Romanticism reinforced the emotionalism of religious revivals. Philosophically, its influence was strongest among intellectuals who took part in the Transcendental movement and in the dramatic flowering

Romanticism intellectual and artistic movement that arose in the early nineteenth century out of a rejection of the Enlightenment values of reason and balance. Romanticism emphasized the individual's expression of emotion and intuition.

of American literature. And like revivalism, Romanticism offered its own paths toward perfectionism.

The Transcendentalists >> Above all, Romanticism produced individualists. Thus Transcendentalism is difficult to define, because its members resisted being lumped together. It blossomed in the mid-1830s, when a number of Unitarian clergy such as George Ripley and Ralph Waldo Emerson resigned their pulpits, loudly protesting the church's smug, lifeless teachings. The new "Transcendentalist Club" attracted a small following among other discontented Boston intellectuals, including Margaret Fuller, Bronson Alcott, and Orestes Brownson.

Like European Romantics, American Transcendentalists emphasized feeling over reason, seeking a spiritual communion with nature. By transcend they meant to go beyond or to rise above—specifically above reason and beyond the material world. Transcendentalists also shared in Romanticism's glorification of the individual. "Trust thyself. Every heart vibrates to that iron string," Emerson advised. Like the devout at Finney's revivals, who sought to perfect themselves and society, listeners who flocked to Emerson's lectures were infused with the spirit of optimistic reform.

As the currents of Romanticism percolated through American society, the country's literature came of age. In 1820 educated Americans still tended to ape the fashions of England and Europe. But as the population grew, education increased, and the country's literary market

BACKSTORY
An Ecumenical Spirit
Despite his sharp criticism of Charles Finney, Lyman Beecher ultimately sought to unify evangelicals in order to combat Unitarians and Roman Catholics. At a conference held in New Lebanon, New York, in the summer of 1827, the partisans of both men came together, with the Finneyites agreeing not to refer to the Beecherites as "cold," "unconverted," or "dead," and the Beecherites pledging not to call the Finneyites "heretics," "enthusiasts," or "mad."

In the summer of 1858 members of the cultural Saturday Club of Boston made an excursion to the Adirondacks to observe nature. In *Philosopher's Camp*, painted by William J. Stillman, who organized the expedition, a group on the left dissects a fish under the supervision of the famous scientist Louis Agassiz. Alone at the center of the painting stands Ralph Waldo Emerson, in a contemplative mood.

expanded, American writers looked with greater interest at the customs and character of their own society.

In extolling nature, many of America's new Romantic writers betrayed a concern that the advance of civilization, with its market economy and crowded urban centers, might destroy the natural simplicity of the land. For example, Henry David Thoreau used nature as a backdrop to explore the conflict between the unfettered individual and the constraints of society. In 1845 Thoreau built a cabin on the edge of Walden Pond in Concord, living by himself for 16 months to demonstrate the advantages of self-reliance. His experiences became the basis for *Walden* (1854), which eloquently denounced Americans' frantic competition for material goods and wealth. Only in nature, Thoreau argued, could one find true independence, liberty, equality, and happiness. Voicing the anti-institutional impulse of Romanticism, he took individualism to its antisocial extreme.

In contrast to Thoreau, who prized isolation, Walt Whitman embraced American society in its infinite variety. A journalist and laborer in the New York City area, Whitman was inspired by the common people, whose "manners, speech, dress, friendships . . . are unrhymed poetry." In taking their measure in *Leaves of Grass* (1855), he pioneered a new, modern form of poetry, unconcerned with meter and rhyme and filled with frank imagery and sexual references.

More brooding in spirit were Nathaniel Hawthorne and Herman Melville, two intellectuals who did not share the Transcendentalists' sunny optimism. Melville's dark masterpiece, *Moby-Dick* (1851), featured the relentless pursuit of a great white whale by Captain Ahab, a prototype of the ruthless businessman despoiling nature's resources in his ferocious pursuit of success.

But with so many opportunities opening before them, most Americans ignored such searching criticism. They preferred to celebrate, with Emerson, the glories of democracy and the individual's quest for perfection.

THE AGE OF REFORM

Inspired by Romanticism or religion, many antebellum Americans sought to remake society at large. One radical way of reforming the world was by withdrawing from it, to form a utopian community that would demonstrate the possibilities of perfection. Such communities looked to replace the competitive individualism of American society with a purer spiritual unity and group cooperation.

Utopian Communities >> During the early 1840s, for example, Emerson's friend George Ripley organized Brook Farm, a Transcendentalist community near Boston where members could live "a more wholesome and simple life than can be led amidst the pressure of our competitive institutions." Other utopian communities were more directly linked to religious movements and figures, but religious or secular, such communities shared the optimism of perfectionism and millennialism.

The Shakers proved to be one of the most long-lived utopian experiments. Ann Lee, the daughter of an English blacksmith, led a small band of followers to America in 1774. Through a series of religious visions Lee became convinced that God had a dual nature and that her own life would reveal the female side of the divinity, just as Jesus Christ revealed the masculine. The Shaker movement's greatest growth, however, came after Lee's death, when her followers recruited converts at revivals such as Cane Ridge. The new disciples founded about 20 communal settlements based on the teachings of Mother Ann, as she was known. Convinced that the end of the world was at hand and that there was no need to perpetuate the human race, Shakers practiced celibacy. Men and women normally worked apart, ate at separate tables, and had separate living quarters.

Shakers accorded women unusual authority and equality. Community tasks were generally assigned by gender, with women performing household chores and men laboring in the fields. Leadership of the church, however, was split equally between men and women. The sect's members worked hard, lived simply, and impressed outsiders with their cleanliness and order. Lacking any natural increase, membership began to decline after 1850, from a peak of about 6,000 members.

The Oneida Community, founded by John Humphrey Noyes, also set out to alter the relationship between the sexes, though in a rather different way. Noyes, a convert of Charles Finney, took Finney's doctrine of perfection to extremes. While Finney argued that men and women should strive to achieve perfection, Noyes announced that he had actually reached this blessed state. Creating a commune in Putney, Vermont (and moving after 1848 to Oneida, New York), Noyes preached the doctrine of "complex marriage." Commune members were permitted to have sexual relations with multiple partners, but only with the approval of the community and after a searching examination of the couple's motives. Noyes eventually undertook experiments in planned reproduction by selecting "scientific" combinations of parents to produce morally perfect children. He attracted over 200 members to the Oneida Community. But in 1879 an internal dispute drove him from power, and the community splintered.

The Mormon Experience >> The Church of Jesus Christ of Latter-day Saints, whose members are generally known as Mormons, was founded by a young man named Joseph Smith in western New York's "burned over district." In 1827, at the age of only 22, Smith announced that he had discovered a set of golden tablets on which was written the Book of Mormon. Claiming a commission from God to reestablish the true church, Smith gathered a group of devoted followers.

Like Charles Finney's more liberal theology, Mormonism declared that salvation was available to all. Moreover, Mormon culture upheld the middle-class values of hard work, thrift, self-control, and material success. And by teaching that Christ would return to rule the earth, it shared in the hope of a coming millennial kingdom.

Mormonism was an outgrowth less of evangelicalism, however, than of the primitive gospel movement, which sought to reestablish the ancient church. In restoring what Smith called "the ancient order of things," Mormons created a **theocracy** uniting church and state, reestablished biblical priesthoods and titles, and adopted temple rituals. Smith undertook to gather the saints in a "city of Zion," first in Ohio and then in Missouri, in preparation for Christ's return. But his unorthodox teachings provoked bitter persecution wherever he went, and mob violence finally hounded him and his followers out of Missouri in 1839. In response, Smith established a new holy city, Nauvoo, along the Mississippi River in Illinois.

{ **theocracy** system of government dominated by the clergy.

At Nauvoo, Smith introduced the most distinctive features of Mormon theology, including baptism for the dead, eternal marriage, and polygamy, or plural marriage. As a result, Mormonism increasingly diverged from traditional Christianity and became a distinct new religion. Neighboring residents, alarmed by the Mormons' growing political power and reports that church leaders were practicing polygamy, demanded that Nauvoo's charter be revoked and the church suppressed. In 1844 Smith was murdered by an anti-Mormon mob. The Mormons abandoned Nauvoo in 1846, and the following year Brigham Young, Smith's successor, led them westward to Utah.

Socialist Communities >> The hardship and poverty that accompanied the growth of industrial factories inspired utopian communities based on science and reason rather than religion. Robert Owen, a Scottish industrialist, came to the United States in 1824 and founded the community of New Harmony in Indiana. Owen believed that the character of individuals was shaped by their surroundings, and that by changing those surroundings, one could change human character. Unfortunately, most of the 900 or so volunteers who flocked to New Harmony lacked the skills and commitment needed to make the community a success, and bitter factions split the settlement.

<< The Mormon temple at Nauvoo, Illinois, was adorned with this sun stone and other celestial carvings drawn from a dream vision by Joseph Smith. The image resembles some of the astronomical symbols popularized by the Masons, a fraternal order whose secret rituals and symbols were hotly debated in western New York, where Smith grew up.

The experience of New Harmony and other communities demonstrated that the United States was poor soil for socialistic experiments. Wages were too high and land too cheap to interest most Americans in collectivist ventures. And individualism was too strong to create a commitment to cooperative action.

The Temperance Movement >> The most significant reform movements of the period sought not to withdraw from society but to change it directly. One of the most determined of these was the temperance movement.

The origins of the campaign lay in the heavy drinking of the early nineteenth century. Alcohol consumption soared after the Revolution, so that by 1830 the average American consumed four gallons of absolute alcohol a year, the highest level in American history and nearly triple present-day levels. The social costs for such habits were high: broken families, abused and neglected wives and children, sickness and disability, poverty, and crime. The temperance movement undertook to eliminate these problems by curbing drinking.

Led largely by clergy, the movement at first focused on drunkenness and did not oppose moderate drinking. But in 1826 the American Temperance Society was founded, taking voluntary abstinence as its goal. During the next decade approximately 5,000 local temperance societies were founded. As the movement gained momentum, annual per capita consumption of alcohol dropped sharply, so that by 1845 it had fallen below two gallons a year.

The temperance movement was more sustained and more popular than other reforms. It appealed to young and old, to urban and rural residents, to workers and businesspeople. And it was the only reform movement with significant support in the South. Its success came partly for social reasons. Democracy necessitated sober voters; factories required sober workers. But temperance advocates also stressed the suffering that men inflicted on women and children, and thus the movement appealed to women as a means to defend the home and carry out their domestic mission.

Educational Reform >> In 1800 Massachusetts was the only state requiring free public schools supported by community funds. The call for tax-supported education arose first among workers, as a means to restore their deteriorating position in society. But middle-class reformers quickly took control of the movement, looking to uplift common citizens and make them responsible. Reformers appealed to business leaders by arguing that the new economic order needed educated workers.

Under Horace Mann's leadership, Massachusetts adopted a minimum-length school year, provided for training of teachers, and expanded the curriculum to include subjects such as history, geography, and various applied skills. By the 1850s the number of schools, attendance figures, and school budgets had all increased sharply. Still, outside of Massachusetts there were only a few high schools. Moreover, attendance was rarely compulsory, and many poor parents sent their children to work instead of school. School reformers enjoyed their greatest success in the Northeast and the least in the South, where planters opposed paying taxes to educate poorer white children.

Educational opportunities for women also expanded. Teachers such as Catharine Beecher and Emma Hunt Willard established a number of private girls' schools, putting to rest the objection of many male educators that fragile female minds could not absorb large doses of mathematics, physics, or geography. In 1833 Oberlin became the nation's first coeducational college. Four years later Mary Lyon founded Mount Holyoke, the first American college for women.

ANNUAL CONSUMPTION OF DISTILLED SPIRITS, PER CAPITA, 1710–1920

Beginning in 1790, per capita levels of drinking steadily rose, until 1830, when the temperance movement produced a sharp decline over the next two decades.

"FRIENDS" AND NEIGHBORS

Nineteenth-century singles in search of lodgings often rented rooms and took their meals in boardinghouses. Considerably less inviting than the apartments shared by present-day sitcom casts of twenty-somethings, antebellum boardinghouses—with their thin walls, indigestible fare, gossipy denizens, and skinflint keepers—became the butt of countless jokes. They made a tempting target in a culture that prized domesticity.

The Asylum Movement >> After 1820 there was also a dramatic increase in the number of asylums of every sort—orphanages, jails, and hospitals. Advocates of asylums called for isolating and separating the criminal, the insane, the ill, and the dependent from outside society. The goal of care in asylums, which earlier had focused on confinement, shifted to the reform of personal character.

Dorothea Dix, a Boston schoolteacher, took the lead in advocating state-supported asylums for the mentally ill. Her widely read report detailed the horrors to which the mentally ill were subjected, which included being beaten, chained, and kept in cages and closets. In response to her efforts, 28 states maintained mental institutions by 1860.

Like other reform movements, the push for new asylums and better educational facilities reflected overtones of both liberation and control. Asylums freed prisoners and the mentally ill from the harsh punishments of the past, but the new techniques of "rehabilitation" forced prisoners to march in lockstep. Education brought with it the freedom to question and to acquire knowledge, but some reformers hoped that schools would become as

orderly as prisons. Louis Dwight, who advocated solitary confinement for prisoners at night and total silence by day, suggested eagerly that such methods "would greatly promote order, seriousness, and purity in large families, male and female boarding schools, and colleges.

ABOLITIONISM

In the fall of 1834, Lyman Beecher, by then the president of Lane Seminary in Cincinnati, was continuing his efforts to "overturn and overturn" on behalf of the kingdom of God. The school had everything needed by an institution for training ministers to convert the West—everything, that is, except students. In October all but 8 of Lane's 100 students had departed after months of bitter controversy with Beecher and the trustees over the issue of abolition.

Beecher knew the source of his troubles: a scruffy yet magnetic student named Theodore Dwight Weld. Weld had been firing up his classmates over the need to end slavery. Beecher was not surprised, for Weld had been converted by that incendiary Finney. Weld was also a follower of William Lloyd Garrison, whose abolitionist writings had sent shock waves across the entire nation. Indeed, Beecher's troubles at Lane Seminary provided only one example of how the flames of reform could spread along paths not anticipated by those who had kindled them.

The Beginnings of the Abolitionist Movement >> William Lloyd Garrison symbolized the transition from a moderate antislavery movement

⌃ Prison reformers believed that rigid discipline, extensive rules, and (in some programs) solitary confinement were necessary to rehabilitate criminals. Prisoners often had to march lockstep under strict supervision and wear uniforms such as those seen in this photograph from the 1870s.

to the more militant abolitionism of the 1830s. A deeply religious young man, Garrison endorsed the colonization movement, which advocated sending blacks to Africa, and went to Baltimore in 1829 to work for Benjamin Lundy, who edited the leading antislavery newspaper in the country.

It was in Baltimore that Garrison first encountered the opinions of free African Americans, who played a major role in launching the abolitionist movement. To Garrison's surprise, most of them strongly opposed the colonization movement as proslavery and antiblack. "This is our home, and this is our country," a free black convention proclaimed in 1831. "Here we were born, and here we will die." Influenced by such sentiments, Garrison developed views far more radical than Lundy's. Within a year of moving to Baltimore, the young firebrand was convicted of libel and imprisoned.

Once released, Garrison hurried back to Boston, determined to publish a new kind of antislavery journal. On January 1, 1831, the first issue of *The Liberator* appeared, and abolitionism was born. In appearance, the bespectacled Garrison seemed frail, almost mousy, but in print he was abrasive, withering, and uncompromising. "On this subject, I do not wish to think, or speak, or write with moderation," he proclaimed. "I am in earnest—I will not equivocate—I will not excuse—I will not retreat a single inch—AND I WILL BE HEARD." Repudiating gradual emancipation and embracing "immediatism," Garrison insisted that slavery end at once. He denounced colonization as a racist movement and upheld the principle of racial equality. To those who suggested that slaveowners should be compensated for freeing their slaves, Garrison was firm. Southerners ought to be convinced by "moral suasion" to renounce slavery as a sin.

Garrison attracted the most attention, but other abolitionists spoke with equal conviction. Wendell Phillips, from a socially prominent Boston family, held listeners spellbound with his speeches. Lewis Tappan and his brother Arthur, two New York City silk merchants, boldly placed their wealth behind various humanitarian causes, including abolitionism. James G. Birney, an Alabama slaveholder, converted to abolitionism after wrestling with his conscience, and Angelina and Sarah Grimké, the daughters of a South Carolina planter, left their native state to speak against the institution. And there was Angelina's future husband, Theodore Weld, the restless student at Lane Seminary who had fallen so dramatically under Garrison's influence.

To abolitionists, slavery was a moral, not an economic, question. The institution seemed a contradiction of the

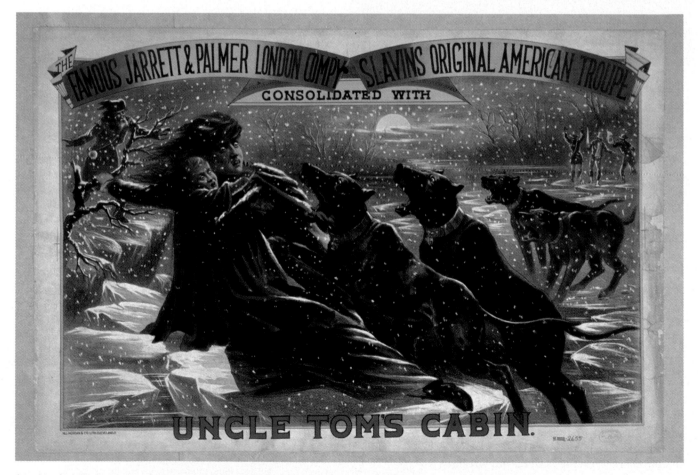

⌃ In this playbill advertising a dramatic production of *Uncle Tom's Cabin*, vicious bloodhounds pursue the light-skinned Eliza, who clutches her child as she frantically leaps to safety across the ice-choked Ohio River.

>> Black abolitionist Frederick Douglass (*second from left at the podium*) was only one of nearly 50 runaway slaves who appeared at an abolitionist convention held in August 1850 in Cazenovia, New York. The question of whether women should be allowed to take active roles in the movement fractured antislavery advocates and sparked women reformers to speak out more strongly for women's rights.

principle of the American Revolution that all human beings had been created with natural rights. Abolitionists condemned slavery because of the breakup of marriages and families by sale, the harsh punishment of the lash, slaves' lack of access to education, and the sexual abuse of black women. But most of all, abolitionists denounced slavery as outrageously contrary to Christian teaching. Abolitionism forced the churches to face the question of slavery head-on, and in the 1840s the Methodist and Baptist churches each split into northern and southern organizations over the issue.

The Spread of Abolitionism >> After helping organize the New England Anti-Slavery Society in 1832, Garrison joined with Lewis Tappan and Theodore Weld the following year to establish a national organization, the American Anti-Slavery Society. During the years before the Civil War, perhaps 200,000 northerners belonged to an abolitionist society.

Abolitionists were concentrated in the East, especially New England, and in areas that had been settled by New Englanders, such as western New York and northern Ohio. The movement was not strong in cities or among businesspeople and workers. Most abolitionists were young, generally in their 20s and 30s when the movement began, and had grown up in rural areas and small towns in middle-class families. Intensely religious, many had been profoundly affected by the revivals of the Second Great Awakening.

Theodore Weld was cut from this mold. After enrolling in Lane Seminary in 1833, he promoted immediate abolitionism among his fellow students. Unlike some abolitionists, who opposed slavery but disdained blacks as inferior, Lane students mingled freely with Cincinnati's free black population. In the summer of 1834, Beecher and Lane's trustees forbade any discussion of slavery on campus and ordered students to return to their studies. All but a handful left the school and enrolled at Oberlin College, where Charles Finney was professor of theology.

Free African Americans, who made up the majority of subscribers to Garrison's *Liberator*, provided important support and leadership for the movement. Frederick Douglass assumed the greatest prominence. Having escaped from slavery in Maryland, he became an eloquent critic of its evils. Other important black abolitionists included Martin Delany, William Wells Brown, William Still, and Sojourner Truth. Most black Americans endorsed peaceful means to end slavery, but David Walker in his *Appeal to the Colored Citizens of the World* (1829) urged blacks to resist bondage with violence.

A network of antislavery sympathizers developed in the North to convey runaway slaves to Canada and freedom. While not as extensive or as tightly organized as contemporaries claimed, the Underground Railroad hid fugitives and transported them northward from one station to the next. Free African Americans, who were more readily trusted by wary slaves, played a leading role in the Underground Railroad. One of its most famous conductors was Harriet Tubman, an escaped slave who repeatedly returned to the South and eventually escorted more than 200 slaves to freedom.

Opponents and Divisions >> The drive for immediate abolition faced massive obstacles. With slavery increasingly important to the South's economic life, the abolitionist cause encountered extreme hostility there. And in the North, where racism was equally entrenched, abolitionism provoked bitter resistance. Even abolitionists like Garrison treated blacks paternalistically, contending that they should occupy a subordinate place in the antislavery movement.

On occasion, northern resistance turned violent. An anti-abolitionist mob burned down the headquarters of the American Anti-Slavery Society in Philadelphia, and in 1837 in Alton, Illinois, Elijah Lovejoy was murdered when he tried to protect his printing press from an angry crowd. The leaders of these mobs were not from the bottom of society but, as one of their victims noted, were "gentlemen of property and standing." Prominent leaders in the community, they reacted vigorously to the threat that abolitionists posed to their power and prosperity and to the established order.

But abolitionists were also hindered by divisions among reformers. At Oberlin College Finney, too, ended up opposing Theodore Weld's fervent abolitionism. Within another decade, Lyman Beecher would see his daughter Harriet Beecher Stowe write the most successful piece of antislavery literature in the nation's history, *Uncle Tom's Cabin* (page 236). Even the abolitionists themselves splintered. More conservative reformers wanted to work within established institutions, using churches and political action to end slavery. But for Garrison and his followers, the mob violence demonstrated that slavery was only part of a deeper national disease, whose cure required the overthrow of American institutions and values.

By the end of the decade, Garrison had worked out a program for the total reform of society. He embraced perfectionism, denounced the clergy, and urged members to leave the churches. Condemning the Constitution as pro-slavery—"a covenant with death and an agreement with hell"—he argued that no person of conscience could participate in the corrupt political system. This platform was radical enough on all counts, but the final straw for Garrison's opponents was his endorsement of women's rights as an inseparable part of abolitionism.

⚡ Elizabeth Cady Stanton, one of the instigators and guiding spirits at the Seneca Falls convention, photographed with two of her children about that time.

The Women's Rights Movement >> Women faced many disadvantages in American society. They were kept out of most jobs, denied political rights, and given only limited access to education beyond the elementary grades. When a woman married, her husband became the legal representative of the marriage and gained complete control of her property. Any unmarried woman was made the ward of a male relative.

When abolitionists divided over the issue of female participation, women found it easy to identify with the situation of slaves, since both were victims of male tyranny. Sarah and Angelina Grimké took up the cause of women's rights after they were criticized for speaking to audiences that included men as well as women. Sarah, who had wanted to be a lawyer, responded with *Letters on the Condition of Women and the Equality of the Sexes* (1838), a pioneering feminist tract that argued that women deserved the same rights as men. Abby Kelly, another abolitionist, remarked that women "have good cause to be grateful to the slave," because in "striving to strike his irons off, we found most surely, that we were manacled ourselves."

Two abolitionists, Elizabeth Cady Stanton and Lucretia Mott, launched the women's rights movement after they were forced to sit behind a curtain at a world antislavery convention in London. In 1848 Stanton and Mott organized a conference in Seneca Falls, New York, that attracted about a hundred supporters. The meeting issued a Declaration of Sentiments, modeled after the Declaration of Independence, that began, "All men and women are created equal." The Seneca Falls convention called for educational and professional opportunities for women, control by women of their property, recognition of legal equality, and repeal of laws awarding the father custody of the children in divorce. The most controversial proposal, and the only resolution that did not pass unanimously, was one demanding the right to vote.

Before 1860, several states gave women greater control over their property, and a few made divorce easier or granted women the right to sue in courts. But disappointments and defeats outweighed these early victories. It was in the longer term that success lay. The Seneca Falls convention set the agenda for the women's rights movement for the remainder of the century and many its leaders had already taken their places at the forefront of the movement. They included Stanton, Susan B. Anthony, Lucy Stone, and—as Lyman Beecher by now must have expected—one of his daughters, Isabella Beecher Hooker.

The Schism of 1840 >> It was Garrison's position on women's rights that finally split the antislavery movement. The showdown came in 1840 when delegates to the American Anti-Slavery Society convention debated whether women could hold office in the organization. Garrison carried the day. His opponents, led by Lewis Tappan, resigned to found the rival American and Foreign Anti-Slavery Society.

The schism of 1840 lessened the influence of abolitionism as a reform movement. Although abolitionism heightened moral concern about slavery, it failed to convert the North to its program, and its supporters remained a tiny minority. For all the considerable courage of its leaders, they lacked a realistic, long-range plan for eliminating so deeply entrenched an institution.

REFORM SHAKES THE PARTY SYSTEM

Abolitionism demonstrated the serious limitations of moral suasion and individual conversions as a solution to deeply rooted social problems. In America's democratic society, politics and government coercion promised a more effective means to impose a new moral vision on the nation. As a result, reformers increasingly entered the political arena to achieve their goals.

Politicians did not particularly welcome the new interest. Because the Whig and Democratic parties both drew on evangelical and nonevangelical voters, heated moral debates over the harmful effects of drink or the evils of slavery threatened to detach regular party members from their old loyalties and disrupt party unity.

As the focus of reform shifted toward the political arena, women lost influence. As major participants in the benevolent organizations of the 1820s and 1830s, they had used their efforts on behalf of "moral suasion." But since women could not vote, they felt excluded when the temperance and abolitionist movements turned to electoral action to accomplish their goals. By the 1840s female reformers increasingly demanded the right to vote as the means to reform society.

The Maine Law >>
The poltical parties could resist the women's suffrage movement because most of its advocates lacked the right to vote. Less easily put off were temperance reformers. Although drinking had significantly declined in American society by 1840, it had hardly been eliminated. After 1845 the arrival of large numbers of German and Irish immigrants, who were accustomed to consuming alcohol, made voluntary prohibition even more remote. In response, temperance advocates proposed state laws that would outlaw the manufacture and sale of alcoholic beverages.

The issue of prohibition cut across party lines, with Whigs and Democrats on both sides of the question. When party leaders tried to dodge the issue, the temperance movement adopted the strategy of endorsing the legislative candidates who pledged to support a prohibitory law. To win additional recruits, temperance leaders took up techniques used in political campaigns, including house-to-house canvasses, parades and processions, bands and singing, banners, picnics, and mass rallies.

The movement's first major triumph came in 1851. The Maine Law, as it was known, authorized search and seizure of private property in that state and provided stiff penalties for selling liquor. In the next few years a number of states enacted similar laws, although most were struck down by the courts or later repealed.

Even though prohibition was temporarily defeated, the issue badly disrupted the unity of the Whig and Democratic parties and brought to the polls a large number of new voters, including many "wets" who wanted to preserve their right to drink. By dissolving the ties between so many voters and their parties, the temperance issue played a major role in the eventual collapse of the Jacksonian party system in the 1850s.

Abolitionism and the Party System >>
Abolition was the most divisive issue to come out of the benevolent movement. In 1835 abolitionists distributed over a million pamphlets through the post office to southern whites. A wave of excitement swept the South when the first batches arrived. Former senator Robert Hayne led a Charleston mob that burned sacks of U.S. mail containing abolitionist literature, and postmasters in other southern cities refused to deliver the material. When the Jackson administration acquiesced in this censorship, abolitionists protested that their civil rights had been violated. In reaction, the number of antislavery societies in the North nearly tripled.

With access to the mails impaired, abolitionists began flooding Congress with petitions against slavery. Asserting that Congress had no power over the institution, angry southern representatives persuaded the House to adopt the so-called gag rule in 1836. It tabled without consideration any petition dealing with slavery. Claiming that the right of petition was also under attack by slavery's champions, abolitionists gained new supporters. In 1844 the House finally repealed the controversial rule.

Many abolitionists outside Garrison's extreme circle were increasingly convinced that an antislavery third party offered a more effective means of attacking slavery. In 1840 these political abolitionists founded the Liberty party and nominated for president James Birney, a former slaveholder who had converted to abolitionism. Birney received only 7,000 votes, but the Liberty party was the seed from which a stronger antislavery political movement would grow. In the next two decades, abolitionism's greatest importance would be in the political arena rather than as a voluntary reform organization.

> In 1835 **abolitionists** distributed over **a million pamphlets** through the post office to **southern whites.**

The ferment of reform from 1820 to 1850 reflected a multitude of attempts to deal with transformations working through not just the United States but also Europe. Americans crowded the docks of New York City eagerly awaiting the latest installment of Charles Dickens's novels from England, tales often set amid urban slums and dingy factories. European middle classes embraced the home as a domestic refuge, as did their counterparts in America. The "benevolent empire" of American reform organizations drew inspiration from similar British campaigns. Robert Owen launched his utopian reforms in New Lanark, Scotland, before his ideas were tried out at New Harmony, Indiana.

Abolition was potentially the most dangerous of these trans-Atlantic reforms because slavery was so deeply and profitably intertwined with the industrial system. Slave labor produced cotton for the textile factories of New England, Great Britain, and Europe; plantation economies supplied the sugar, rice, tea, and coffee that were a part of European and American diets. Revolutionary France had abolished slavery in 1794, but Napoleon reinstated it, along with the slave trade. Great Britain outlawed the trade in 1808 (as did the United States) and then freed nearly 800,000 slaves in its colonies in 1834.

As late as 1840, however, the abolition movement lacked the power to threaten the political system. But the growing northern concern about slavery highlighted differences between the two sections. Despite the strength of evangelicalism in the South, the reform impulse spawned by the revivals found little support there, discredited as it was by its association with abolitionism. The party system confronted the difficult challenge of holding together sections that, although sharing much, were also diverging in important ways. Increasingly the South appeared to be a unique society with its own distinctive way of life.

CHAPTER SUMMARY

The Jacksonian era produced the greatest number of significant reform movements in American history.

▌ The movements grew out of the revivals of the Second Great Awakening, which emphasized emotion and preached the doctrines of good works and salvation available to all.

▌ Evangelical Protestantism also endorsed the ideals of perfectionism and millennialism.

▌ The revival theology helped people adjust to the pressures in their daily lives created by the new market economy.

Significant Events

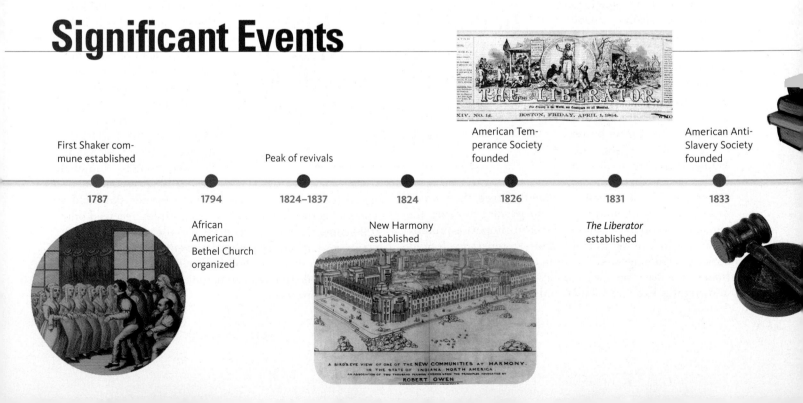

First Shaker commune established — 1787

African American Bethel Church organized — 1794

Peak of revivals — 1824–1837

New Harmony established — 1824

American Temperance Society founded — 1826

The Liberator established — 1831

American Anti-Slavery Society founded — 1833

- Romanticism, which emphasized the unlimited potential of each individual, also strengthened reform.
- Women's role in society was now defined by the ideal of domesticity—that women's lives should center on the home and the family.
- Middle-class women turned to religion and reform as ways to shape society.
- Utopian communities sought to establish a model society for the rest of the world to follow.
- Humanitarian movements combated a variety of social evils.
  - Crusades for temperance, educational reform, and the establishment of asylums all gained significant support.
  - Abolitionism precipitated both strong support and violent opposition, and the movement itself split in 1840.
- Temperance, abolitionism, and women's rights movements all turned to political action to accomplish their goals.
- Although it survived, the party system was seriously weakened by these reform movements.

Additional Reading

Good introductions to antebellum evangelical religion and reform include Robert Abzug, *Cosmos Crumbling* (1994); Charles Hambrick-Stowe, *Charles G. Finney and the Spirit of American Evangelicalism* (1996); and Bertram Wyatt-Brown, *Lewis Tappan and the Evangelical War Against Slavery* (1971). For suggestive analyses of the relationship between antebellum evangelicalism and the sweeping changes in economic and political life, consult Richard Carwardine, *Evangelicals and Politics in Antebellum America* (1997); Candy Gunther Brown, *The Word in the World* (2004); and Paul Johnson and Sean Wilentz, *The Kingdom of Matthias* (1994). The best studies of the role of women in evangelical churches and reform societies are Anne Boylan, *The Origins of Women's Activism* (1988); Lori Ginzberg, *Women and the Work of Benevolence* (1990); and Nancy Hewitt, *Women's Activism and Social Change* (1984). To understand the link between reformist activism and the early women's rights movement, begin with Lori Ginzberg, *Untidy Origins* (2005), and Nancy Isenberg, *Sex and Citizenship in the United States* (1998).

Despite the dominant influence of evangelical Protestants, both Roman Catholics and Mormons attracted a growing number of adherents during the antebellum period. For a fascinating account of the origins and rise of Mormonism, see John Brooke, *The Refiner's Fire* (1996), and for a compelling account of how American Protestants responded to the impressive growth of Roman Catholicism after the 1830s, see Ryan Smith, *Gothic Arches, Latin Crosses* (2006). To explore the reasons why a small but influential minority of nineteenth-century Americans rejected all forms of Christianity in favor of agnosticism or atheism, rely on James Turner, *Without God, Without Creed* (1985).

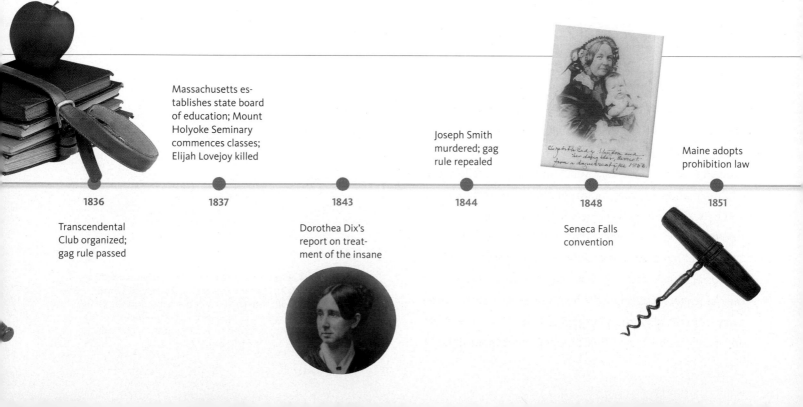

Massachusetts establishes state board of education; Mount Holyoke Seminary commences classes; Elijah Lovejoy killed

Joseph Smith murdered; gag rule repealed

Maine adopts prohibition law

1836   **1837**   **1843**   **1844**   **1848**   **1851**

Transcendental Club organized; gag rule passed

Dorothea Dix's report on treatment of the insane

Seneca Falls convention

13 The Old

WHAT'S TO COME

245 **THE SOCIAL STRUCTURE OF THE COTTON KINGDOM**

249 **CLASS STRUCTURE OF THE WHITE SOUTH**

252 **THE PECULIAR INSTITUTION**

255 **SLAVE CULTURE**

259 **SOUTHERN SOCIETY AND THE DEFENSE OF SLAVERY**

WHERE IS THE REAL SOUTH

The impeccably dressed Colonel Daniel Jordan, master of 261 slaves at Laurel Hill, strolls down his oak-lined lawn to the dock along the Waccamaw River, a day's journey north of Charleston, to board the steamship Nina. On Fridays, it is Colonel Jordan's custom to visit the exclusive Hot and Hot Fish Club, founded by his fellow low-country planters, to play a game of lawn bowling or billiards and be waited on by black servants in livery as he sips an iced mint julep. For Colonel Jordan, this is the South.

Several hundred miles to the west another steamboat, the *Fashion*, makes its way along the Alabama River. One of the passengers is upset by the boat's slow pace. He has been away from his plantation in the Red River country of Texas and is eager to get back. "Time's money, time's money!" he »

A seller of chicken legs and rolls at the Richmond railway station in 1860. Modern viewers are likely to note the woman's proud, almost jaunty appearance. But the British traveler who sketched her betrayed the prejudices of his day, describing such vendors as "Negro girls, of the most tawdry dress and of extreme vulgarity . . ."

mutters. "Time's worth more'n money to me now; a hundred percent more, 'cause I left my niggers all alone; not a damn white man within four mile on 'em." When asked what they are doing, since the cotton crop has already been picked, he says, "I set 'em to clairin', but they ain't doin' a damn thing. . . . But I'll make it up, I'll make it up when I get thar, now you'd better believe." For this Red River planter, time is money and cotton is his world— indeed, cotton is what the South is all about. "I am a cotton man, I am, and I don't car who knows it," he proclaims. "I know cotton, I do. I'm dam' if I know anythin' but cotton."

At the other end of the South, the slave Sam Williams works in the intense heat of Buffalo Forge, an iron-making factory in the Shenandoah Valley. As a refiner, Williams heats pig iron in white-hot coals, then slings the ball of glowing metal onto an anvil, where he pounds it with huge, water-powered hammers to remove the impurities. Ambitious and hardworking, he earns extra money (at the same rate paid to whites) for any iron he produces beyond his weekly quota. His wife, Nancy, in charge of the dairy, earns extra money, too. Their savings at the local bank total more

than $150. The income helps them keep their family intact in an unstable environment: they know that their owner is unlikely to sell away slaves who work so hard. For Sam and Nancy Williams, family ties, worship at the local Baptist church, and socializing with their fellow slaves are what make life important.

In the bayous of the Deep South, only a few miles from where the Mississippi Delta meets the Gulf, Octave Johnson hears the dogs coming. For over a year Johnson has been a runaway slave. He fled from a Louisiana plantation when the overseer threatened to whip him for staying in bed. To survive, he hides in the swamps four miles behind the plantation—stealing turkeys, chickens, and pigs and trading with other slaves. As uncertain as this life is, nearly 30 other slaves have joined him over the past year.

When the pack of hounds bursts upon them, the slaves do not flee but kill as many dogs as possible. Then they plunge into the bayou, and as the hounds follow, alligators make short work of another six. ("Alligators [prefer] dog flesh to personal flesh," he explains later.) For Octave Johnson the real South is a matter of weighing one's prospects between the uncertainties

of alligators and the overseer's whip— and deciding when to say no.

Ferdinand Steel and his family are not forced, by the flick of the lash, to rise at five in the morning. They rise because the land demands it. Steel, in his 20s, owns 170 acres of land in Carroll County, Mississippi. His life is one of continuous hard work, caring for the animals and tending the crops. His mother, Eliza, and sister, Julia, have plenty to keep them busy: making soap, fashioning dippers out of gourds, sewing.

The Steel family grows cotton, too, but not with the single-minded devotion of the planter aboard the *Fashion*. Self-sufficiency and family security always come first, and Steel's total crop amounts to only five or six bales. His profit is never enough for him to consider buying even one slave—but the cotton means cash, and cash means that he can buy things he needs in town. Though fiercely independent, Steel and his scattered neighbors help each other raise houses, clear fields, shuck corn, and quilt. They depend on one another and are bound together by blood, religion, obligation, and honor. For small farmers such as Ferdinand Steel, these ties constitute the real South. ≪

The portraits could go on: different people, different Souths, all of them real. Such contrasts underscore the difficulty of trying to define a regional identity. Encompassing in 1860 the 15 slave states plus the District of Columbia, the South was a land of great social and geographic diversity.

Yet despite its many differences of people and geography, the South was bonded by ties so strong, they eventually outpulled those of the nation itself. At the heart of this unity was an agricultural system that took advantage of the region's warm climate and long growing season. Most important, this rural agricultural economy was based on the institution of slavery, which had far-reaching effects on all aspects of southern society. It shaped not only the culture of the slaves themselves but also the lives of their masters and mistresses, and even of farm families and herders in the hills and backwoods, who saw few slaves from day to day. To understand the Old South, then, we must understand how the southern agricultural economy and the institution of slavery affected the social class structure of both white and black southerners.

THE DIVERSE SOUTH

The Old South encompassed a wide variety of social settings. On this map, locate the residences of the five individuals profiled in the chapter introduction.

THE SOCIAL STRUCTURE OF THE COTTON KINGDOM

We have already seen (in Chapter 10) that the spread of cotton stimulated the nation's remarkable economic growth after the War of 1812. Demand spurred by the textile industry sent the price of cotton soaring on the international market, and white southerners scrambled into the fresh lands of the old Southwest to reap the profits to be made in the cotton sweepstakes.

Deep South, Upper South >> As Indian lands were opened to white settlement, word spread of the "black belt" region of central Alabama, where the dark, rich soil was particularly suited to growing cotton, and of the tremendous yields from the soils along the Mississippi River's broad reaches. "The Alabama Feaver rages here with great violence and has carried off vast numbers of our Citizens," a North Carolinian wrote in 1817. A generation later, in the 1830s, immigrants were still "pouring in with a ceaseless tide," but by the 1840s residents were leaving Alabama and Mississippi for even fresher cotton lands along the Red River and up into Texas. By the eve of the Civil War nearly a third of the total cotton crop came from west of the Mississippi River. As Senator James Henry

Hammond of South Carolina boasted in 1858, cotton was king in the Old South: its primary export and the major source of southern wealth.

As cotton transformed the boom country of the Deep South, agriculture in the **Upper South** also adjusted. Scientific agricultural practices reversed the decline in tobacco, which had begun in the 1790s. More important, farmers in the Upper South made wheat and corn their major crops. Because the new crops required less labor, slaveholders in the Upper South sold their surplus slaves to planters in the **Deep South**. There, eager buyers paid as much as $1,500 in the late 1850s for a prime field hand.

> **Upper South** the border states (Delaware, Maryland, Kentucky, and Missouri) and Virginia, North Carolina, Tennessee, and Arkansas.
>
> **Deep South** South Carolina, Georgia, Florida, Alabama, Mississippi, Louisiana, and Texas.

Southern prosperity, however, masked basic problems in the economy. Much of the South's new wealth resulted from migration of its population to more fertile western lands. The amount of prime agricultural land was limited, and once it was settled, the South could not sustain its rate of expansion. Furthermore, the single-crop agriculture practiced by southern farmers (especially in tobacco and corn) rapidly wore out the soil. Wheat production in the Upper South helped to restore soils, but because farmers now plowed fields rather than using the hoe, this shift accelerated soil erosion. In addition, reliance on a single

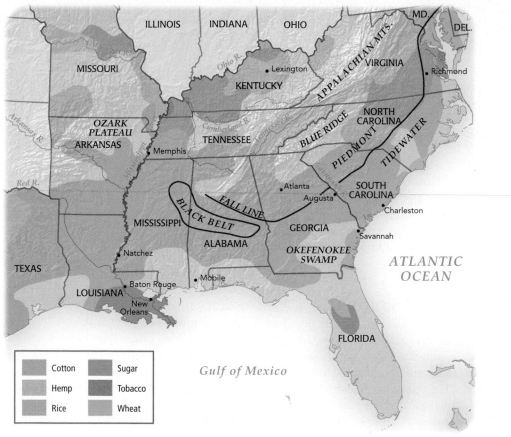

Cotton | Sugar
Hemp | Tobacco
Rice | Wheat

COTTON AND OTHER CROPS OF THE SOUTH

By 1860, the cotton kingdom extended across the Lower South into the Texas prairie and up the Mississippi River valley. Tobacco and hemp were the staple crops of the Upper South, where they competed with corn and wheat. Rice production was concentrated in the swampy coastal region of South Carolina and Georgia as well as the lower tip of Louisiana. The sugar district was in southern Louisiana.

had no public schools outside its few cities. The 1850 census showed that among native-born white citizens, 20 percent were unable to read and write. In the middle states the figure was 3 percent; in New England, only 0.4 percent.

Distribution of Slavery >>

Even more than agrarian ways, slavery set the South apart. Whereas in 1776 slavery had been a national institution, by 1820 it was confined to the states south of Pennsylvania and the Ohio River. The South's "peculiar institution" bound white and black southerners together in a multitude of ways.

Slaves were not evenly distributed throughout the region. More than half lived in the Deep South, where African Americans outnumbered white southerners in both South Carolina and Mississippi by the 1850s. Elsewhere in the Deep South, the black population exceeded 40 percent in all states except Texas. In the Upper South, in contrast, whites greatly outnumbered blacks. Only in Virginia and North Carolina did the slave population top 30 percent.

Geography determined some of this distribution. In areas of fertile soil, flat or rolling countryside, and good transportation, slavery and the plantation system dominated. In the pine barrens, areas isolated by lack of transportation, and hilly and mountainous regions, small family farms and few slaves were the rule.

Almost all enslaved African Americans, male and female, worked in agricultural pursuits, with only about 10 percent living in cities and towns. On large plantations, a few slaves were domestic servants, and others were skilled artisans—blacksmiths, carpenters, or bricklayers—but most toiled in the fields.

Slavery as a Labor System >>

Slavery was, first and foremost, a system to manage and control labor. The plantation system, with its extensive estates and large labor forces, could never have developed without slavery. Slaves represented an enormous capital investment, worth more than all the land in the Old South. Furthermore, slavery remained a highly profitable investment. The average slaveowner spent perhaps $30 to $35 a year to support an adult slave; some expended as little as half that. Even at the higher cost of support, a slaveowner took about 60 percent of the annual wealth produced by a slave's labor.

crop increased toxins and parasites in the soil, making southern agriculture more vulnerable than diversified agriculture was.

Perhaps the most striking environmental consequence of the expansion of southern society was the increase in disease. Epidemic diseases such as malaria, yellow fever, and cholera were brought to the area by Europeans. The clearing of land—which increased runoff, precipitated floods, and produced pools of stagnant water—encouraged their spread, especially in the Lower South.

The Rural South >>

The Old South, then, was expanding, dynamic, and booming economically. But the region remained overwhelmingly rural, with 84 percent of its labor force engaged in agriculture in 1860, compared with 40 percent in the North. Conversely, the South produced only 9 percent of the nation's manufactured goods. Efforts to diversify the South's economy made little headway in the face of the high profits from cotton. With so little industry, few cities developed in the South. North Carolina, Florida, Alabama, Mississippi, Arkansas, and Texas did not contain a single city with a population of 10,000.

As a rural society, the South showed far less interest in education. Most wealthy planters opposed a state-supported school system, because they hired tutors or sent their children to private academies. Georgia in 1860 had only one county with a free school system, and Mississippi

THE SPREAD OF SLAVERY, 1820–1860

Between 1820 and 1860, the slave population of the South shifted south and westward, concentrating especially heavily in coastal South Carolina and Georgia, in the black belt of central Alabama and Mississippi (so named because of its rich soil), and in the Mississippi valley.

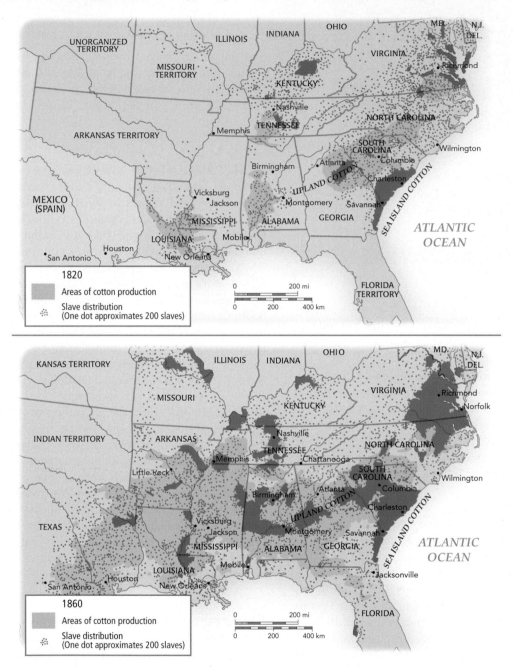

For those who pinched pennies and drove slaves harder, the profits were even greater.

By concentrating wealth and power in the hands of the planter class, slavery shaped the tone of southern society. Planters were not aristocrats in the European sense of having special legal privileges or formal titles of rank. Still, the system encouraged southern planters to think of themselves as a landed gentry upholding the aristocratic values of pride, honor, family, and hospitality.

Public opinion in Europe and in the North grew increasingly hostile to the peculiar institution, causing white southerners to feel like an isolated minority defending an embattled position. Yet they clung tenaciously to slavery, for it was the base on which the South's economic growth and way of life rested. As one Georgian observed on the eve of the Civil War, slavery was "so intimately mingled with our social conditions that it would be impossible to eradicate it."

CLASS STRUCTURE OF THE WHITE SOUTH

Once a year around Christmastime, James Henry Hammond gave a dinner for his neighbors at his South Carolina plantation, Silver Bluff. The richest man for miles around as well as an ambitious politician, the aristocratic Hammond used these dinners to put his neighbors under personal obligation to him as well as to receive the honor and respect he believed his due. In addition Hammond hired his neighbors to perform various tasks and allowed them to use his grist mill and gin their cotton. His less affluent neighbors recognized Hammond's social rank but they, too, displayed a strong personal pride. After their superior ungraciously complained about the inconvenience of these services, only three of his neighbors came to his Christmas dinner in 1837, a snub that enraged him. As Hammond's experience demonstrated, class relations among whites in the Old South were a complex blend of privilege, patronage, and equality.

The Slaveowners >>

In 1860 the region's 15 states had a population of 12 million, of which roughly two-thirds were white, one-third were black slaves, and about 2 percent were free African Americans. Of the 8 million white southerners, only about a quarter either owned slaves or were members of slaveowning families. Moreover, most slaveowners owned only a few slaves. If one uses the census definition of a planter as a person who owned 20 or more slaves, only about 1 out of every 30 white southerners belonged to families of the planter class.

A planter of consequence, however, needed to own at least 50 slaves, and there were only about 10,000 such families—less than 1 percent of the white population. This privileged group made up the aristocracy at the top of the southern class structure. Owners of large numbers of slaves were very rare; only about 2,000 southerners, such as Colonel Daniel Jordan, owned 100 or more slaves. Although limited in size, the planter class nevertheless owned more than half of all slaves and controlled more than 90 percent of the region's total wealth.

Tidewater and Frontier >>

Southern planters shared a commitment to preserve slavery as the source of their wealth and stature. Yet in other ways they were a diverse group. On the one hand, the tobacco and rice planters of the Atlantic Tidewater were part of a settled region and a culture that reached back 150 to 200 years. States such as Mississippi and Arkansas, in contrast, had rawer and more volatile societies, since most non-Indian residents had flooded into the region after 1815.

It was along the Tidewater, especially the bays of the Chesapeake and the South Carolina coast, that the legendary "Old South" was born. Here, masters erected substantial homes, some—especially between Charleston and Columbia—the classic white-pillared mansions in the Greek revival style. An Irish visitor observed that in Maryland and Virginia the great planters lived in "a style which approaches nearer to that of the English country gentleman than what is to be met with anywhere else on the continent." As in England, the local gentry often served as justices of the peace, and the Episcopal church remained the socially accepted road to heaven. Here, too, family names continued to be important in politics.

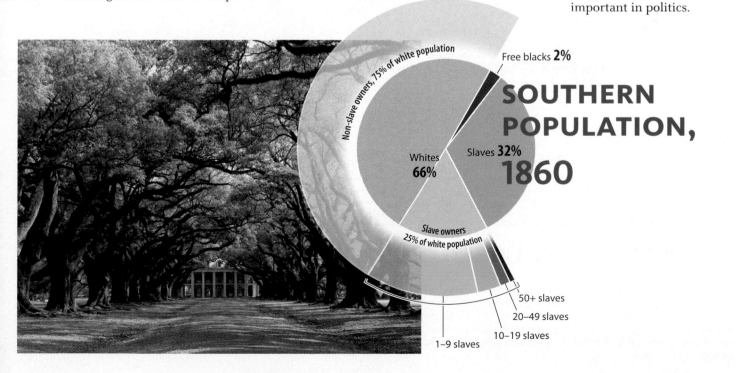

Non-slave owners, 75% of white population

Free blacks **2%**

Whites **66%**

Slaves **32%**

SOUTHERN POPULATION, 1860

Slave owners 25% of white population

1–9 slaves

10–19 slaves

20–49 slaves

50+ slaves

While the newer regions of the South boasted of planters with cultivated manners, as a group the cotton lords were a different breed. Whatever their background, these entrepreneurs had moved west for the reason so many other white Americans had: to make their fortunes. By and large, the cotton gentry were men of ordinary backgrounds who had risen through hard work, aggressive business tactics, and good luck. For them, the cotton boom and the exploitation of enslaved men and women offered the chance to move up in a new society that lacked an entrenched elite.

"Time's money, time's money." For men like the impatient Texan, time was indeed money, slaves were capital, and cotton by the bale signified cash in hand. This business orientation was especially apparent in the cotton kingdom, where planters sought to maximize their profits and constantly reinvested their returns in land and slaves. And while most planters ranked among the richest citizens in America, the homes of the newer cotton gentry were often simple one- or two-story unpainted wooden frame houses. Some were even log cabins. "If you wish to see people worth millions living as [if] they were not worth hundreds," advised one southwestern planter in 1839, "come to the land of cotton and negroes." Practical men, few of the new cotton lords had absorbed the culture and learning of the traditional country gentleman.

The Master at Home >>

Whether supervising a Tidewater plantation or creating a cotton estate on the Texas frontier, the master had to coordinate a complex agricultural operation. He gave daily instructions concerning the work to be done, settled disputes between slaves and the overseer, and generally handed out rewards and penalties. In addition, the owner made the critical decisions for planting, harvesting, and marketing the crops as well as for investments and expenditures.

In performing his duties, the plantation owner was supposed to be the "master" of his crops, his family, and his slaves. Defenders of slavery often held up this paternalistic ideal—the care and guidance of dependent "children"— and maintained that slavery promoted a genuine bond of

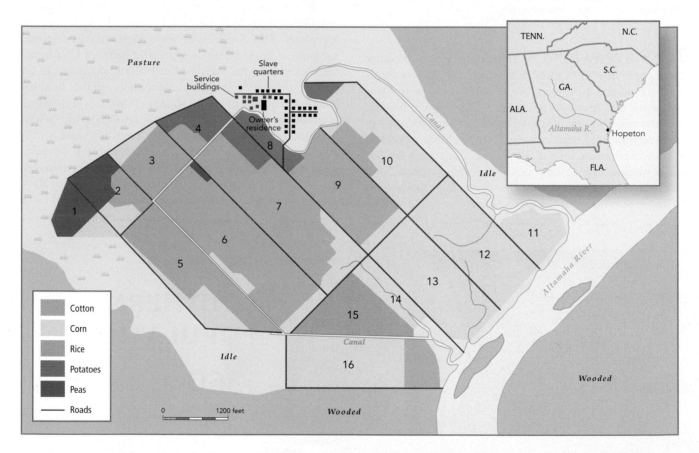

A PLANTATION LAYOUT, HOPETON, GEORGIA

Often covering a thousand acres or more, a plantation was laid out like a small village and contained several fields and usually extensive uncleared woods. Somewhere near the master's "big house" were the quarters— slave cabins clustered along one or more streets. Service buildings might include a smokehouse, stables, a gin house (for cotton) or a rice mill, and an overseer's dwelling. Like most large plantations, Hopeton produced a considerable amount of foodstuffs, but it grew both rice and cotton as staples. Most plantations concentrated on a single cash crop.

affection between the caring master and his loyal slaves. In real life, however, the forces of the market made this paternalistic ideal less evident. Even in the Tidewater, planters were concerned with money and profits. Indeed, some of the most brutal forms of slavery existed on rice plantations. Except for a few domestic servants, owners of large plantations generally had little contact with their slaves. Nor could paternalism mask the reality that slavery everywhere rested on violence, racism, and exploitation.

⌃ Sarah Pierce Vick, the mistress of a plantation near Vicksburg, Mississippi, pauses to speak to one of her slaves, who may be holding feed for her horse. A plantation mistress had many duties and, while enjoying the comforts brought by wealth and status, often found her life more difficult than she had anticipated before marriage.

illegitimate children by slave women suffered no social or legal penalties, even in the case of rape (southern law did not recognize such a crime against slave women), whereas a white woman guilty of adultery lost all social respectability. One planter's wife spoke of "violations of the moral law that made mulattoes as common as blackberries," and another recalled, "I saw slavery . . . teemed with injustice and shame to all womankind and I hated it."

Some women drew a parallel between their situation and that of the slaves. Both were subject to male dominance, and independent-minded women found the subordination of marriage difficult. Susan Dabney Smedes, in her recollection of growing up on an Alabama plantation, recalled that "it was a saying that the mistress of a plantation was the most complete slave on it."

Still, plantation mistresses were unwilling to forgo the material comforts that slavery made possible. Moreover, racism was so pervasive within American society that the few white southern women who privately criticized the institution displayed little empathy for the plight of slaves themselves, including black women. Whatever the burdens of the plantation mistress, they were hardly akin to the bondage of slavery itself.

The Plantation Mistress >> Upper-class southern white women, like those in the North, grew up with the ideal of domesticity, reinforced by the notion of a paternalistic master who was lord of the plantation. But the plantation mistress soon discovered that the daily demands placed on her made that ideal hard to fulfill.

In her youth a genteel lady enjoyed a certain amount of leisure. But once married and the mistress of a plantation, she discovered the magnitude of her responsibilities. Nursing the sick, making clothing, tending the garden, caring for the poultry, and overseeing every aspect of food preparation were all her domain. She also supervised and planned the work of the domestic servants. After taking care of breakfast, one harried Carolina mistress recounted that she "had the [sewing] work cut out, gave orders about dinner, had the horse feed fixed in hot water, had the box filled with cork: . . . now I have to cut out the flannel jackets." Sarah Williams, the New York bride of a North Carolina planter, admitted that her mother-in-law "works harder than any Northern farmer's wife I know."

Unlike female reformers in the North, upper-class southern women did not openly challenge their role, but some found their sphere confining. The greatest unhappiness stemmed from the never-ending task of managing slaves. One southern mistress confessed she was frightened at being "always among people whom I do not understand and whom I must guide, and teach and lead on like children." Yet without the labor of slaves, the lifestyle of these women was an impossibility.

Many women also despised the widespread double standard for sexual behavior. A man who fathered

Yeoman Farmers >> In terms of numbers, yeoman farm families were the backbone of southern society, accounting for well over half the southern white population. These farmers owned no slaves and farmed the traditional 80 to 160 acres, like northern farmers. About 80 percent owned their own land. They settled almost everywhere in the South, except in the rice and sugar districts and valuable river bottomlands of the Deep South, which were monopolized by large slaveowners. Like Ferdinand Steel, most were semisubsistence farmers who raised primarily corn and hogs, along with perhaps a few bales of cotton or some tobacco, which they sold to obtain the cash needed to buy items like sugar, coffee, and salt. Yeoman farmers lacked the wealth of planters, but they had a pride and dignity that earned them the respect of their richer neighbors.

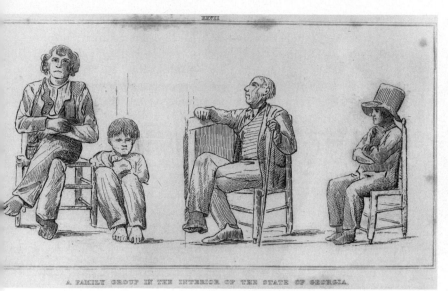

A FAMILY GROUP IN THE INTERIOR OF THE STATE OF GEORGIA.

<< A majority of white southerners were members of non-slaveholding yeoman farm families. Ruggedly independent, these families depended on their own labor and often lived under primitive conditions. Basil Hall, an Englishman traveling through the South in 1827 and 1828, sketched members of this Georgia family with the aid of a camera lucida, an optical device that projected an image from real life onto paper, where it could be traced with accuracy.

Poor Whites >> The poorest white southerners were confined to land that no one else wanted. They lived in rough, windowless log cabins located in the remotest areas and were often squatters without title to the land they were on. The men spent their time hunting and fishing, while women did the domestic work, including what farming they could manage. Circumstances made their poverty difficult to escape. Largely illiterate, they suffered from malnutrition stemming from a monotonous diet of corn, pork, and whiskey, and they were afflicted with malaria and hookworm, diseases that sapped their energy. Other white southerners referred to them scornfully as crackers, white trash, sandhillers, and clay eaters.

The number of poor whites in the Old South is difficult to estimate. There may have been as few as 100,000 or as many as a million; probably they numbered about 500,000, or a little more than 5 percent of the white population.

Because poor whites traded with slaves, exchanging whiskey for stolen goods, contemptuous planters often bought them out simply to rid the neighborhood of them. For their part, poor whites keenly resented planters, but their hostility toward African Americans was even stronger. Poor whites refused to perform any work commonly done by slaves and vehemently opposed ending slavery. Emancipation would remove one of the few symbols of their status—that they were, at least, free.

While southern farmers led more isolated lives than did their northern counterparts, their social activities were not very different. Religion played an important role at camp meetings held in late summer, after the crops were laid by and before harvest time. As in the North, neighbors also met to exchange labor and tools. The men rolled logs to clear fields of dead trees, women met for quilting bees, and adults and children alike would gather to shuck corn. Court sessions, militia musters, political rallies—these, too, were occasions that brought rural folk together.

Since yeoman farmers lacked cheap slave labor, good transportation, and access to credit, they could not compete with planters in the production of staples. In the North urban centers became a market for small farmers to sell their staple crops, but in the South the lack of towns limited this internal market. Thus while southern yeoman farmers were not poor, they suffered from a chronic lack of money and the absence of conveniences that northern farm families enjoyed. Josiah Hinds, who hacked a farm out of the isolated woods of northern Mississippi, worried that his children were growing up "wild." He complained that "education is but little prized by my neighbours," who were satisfied "if the corn and cotton grows to perfection . . . [and] brings a fare price, and hog meat is at hand to boil with the greens."

In some ways, then, the worlds of the yeoman farmers and the upper-class planters were not only different but also in conflict. Still, a hostility between the two classes did not emerge. Yeoman farmers admired planters and hoped that one day they would join the gentry themselves. Furthermore, they accepted slavery as a means of controlling African Americans as members of an inferior social caste based on race. "Now suppose they was free," one poor farmer told Frederick Law Olmsted, a northern visitor. "You see they'd all think themselves as good as we." Racism and fear of black people were sufficient to keep nonslaveholders loyal to southern institutions.

THE PECULIAR INSTITUTION

Slaves were not free. That overwhelming fact must be understood before anything is said about the kindness or the cruelty individual slaves experienced; before any consideration of healthy or unhealthy living conditions; before any discussion of how slave families coped with hardship, rejoiced in shared pleasures, or worshiped in prayer. The lives of slaves were affected day in and day out, in big ways and small, by the basic reality that slaves were not their own masters. The master determined a slave's workload, whether a slave could visit a nearby plantation, and whether a slave family remained intact. Whatever slaves wanted to do, they had always to consider the response of their masters.

When power is distributed as unequally as it was between masters and slaves, every action on the part of the enslaved involves a certain calculation, conscious or unconscious. The consequences of every act, of every expression or gesture, have to be considered. In that sense, the line between freedom and slavery penetrated every corner of a slave's life, and it was an absolute and overwhelming distinction.

One other stark fact reinforced the sharp line between freedom and slavery: slaves were distinguished on the basis of color. While the peculiar institution was an economic system of labor, it was also a **caste system** based on race. The color line of slavery made it easier to defend the institution and win the support of yeoman farmers and poor white southerners, even though in many ways the system held them back. Hence slavery must be understood on many levels: not only as an economic system but also as a racial and cultural one, in terms of not only its outward conditions of life and labor but also the inner demands it made on the soul.

> **caste system** system of social stratification separating individuals by various distinctions, among them hereditary, rank, profession, wealth, and race

Work and Discipline >> The conditions slaves encountered varied widely, depending on the size of the farm or plantation, the crop being grown, the personality of the master, and whether he was an absentee owner. On small farms slaves worked in the fields alongside their owners and had much closer contact with whites. On plantations, in contrast, most slaves dealt primarily with the overseer, who was paid by the size of the harvest he brought in and was therefore often harsh in his approach.

Houseservants and the drivers, who supervised the field hands, received the highest status, and skilled artisans such as carpenters and blacksmiths were also given special recognition. The hardest work was done by the field hands, both men and women.

What role did race play in maintaining the institution of slavery? Could a system of white or Indian slavery have existed as easily?

Some planters organized their slaves in the gang system, in which a white overseer or a black driver supervised gangs of 20 to 25 adults. Although this approach extracted long hours of reasonably hard labor, the slaves had to be constantly supervised, and shirkers were difficult to detect. Other planters preferred the task system, under which each slave was given a specific daily assignment to complete, after which he or she was finished for the day. This system allowed slaves to work at their own pace, gave them an incentive to work carefully, and freed overseers from having to closely supervise the work. But slaves resisted vigorously if masters tried to increase the workload. The task system was most common in the rice fields, whereas the gang system predominated in the cotton districts. Many planters used a combination of the two.

During cultivation and harvest, slaves were in the field 15 to 16 hours a day, eating a noonday meal there and resting before resuming labor. Work was uncommon on Sundays, and frequently only a half day was required on Saturdays. Even so, the routine was taxing. "I am never caught in bed after day light nor is any body else on the place," an Arkansas cotton planter reported, "and we continue in the cotton fields when we can have fair weather till it is so dark we can't see to work."

WITNESS
Resistance and Discipline on a Cotton Plantation

"October 4, 1839. Boy Lewis came in last night [after having run away for five days] gave him the worst whipping I ever gave any young negro. I predict he will not runaway *soon*. Building a jail for him, Dennis, and Ginny Jerry—intend jailing them from Saturday nights 'till Monday mornings . . .'"

Often masters rewarded hard-working slaves, but the threat of punishment was always present. Slaves could be denied passes; their food allowance could be reduced; and if all else failed, they could be sold. The most common instrument of punishment was the whip. The frequency of its use varied from plantation to plantation, but few slaves escaped the lash entirely. "We have to rely more and more on the power of fear," planter James Henry Hammond acknowledged. "We are determined to continue masters, and to do so we have to draw the rein tighter and tighter day by day to be assured that we hold them in complete check."

Slave Maintenance >> Planters generally bought rough, cheap cloth for slave clothing and each year gave adults at most only a couple of outfits and a pair of shoes.

Some planters provided well-built housing, but more commonly slaves lived in cramped, poorly built cabins that were leaky in wet weather, drafty in cold, and furnished with only a few crude chairs or benches and a table, perhaps a mattress filled with corn husks or straw, and a few pots and dishes. In order to keep medical expenses down, slaveowners treated sick slaves themselves and called in a doctor only for serious cases. On average, a slaveowner spent less than a dollar a year on medical care for each slave.

Nevertheless, the United States was the only slave society in the Americas where the slave population increased naturally—indeed, at about the same rate as for the white population. Even so, infant mortality among slaves was more than double that of the white population; for every 1,000 live births among southern slaves, more than 200 died before the age of 5. For those who survived infancy, enslaved African Americans had a life expectancy about 8 years less than that of white Americans. As late as 1860, fewer than two-thirds of slave children survived to the age of 10.

Resistance >>
Given the wide gulf between freedom and slavery, it was only natural that slaves resisted the bondage imposed on them. The most radical form of resistance was rebellion, which occurred repeatedly in slave societies in the Americas. In Latin America, slave revolts were relatively frequent, involving hundreds and even thousands of slaves and pitched battles in which large numbers were killed. The most successful slave revolt occurred in France's sugar-rich colony, Saint Domingue (the western part of the Caribbean island of Hispaniola). There, free blacks who had fought in the American Revolution because of France's alliance with the United States brought back the ideals of freedom and equality. The brutally overworked population of half a million slaves received further encouragement from the example of the French Revolution. Led by Toussaint L'Ouverture, black slaves established Haiti in 1804, the second independent republic in the Western Hemisphere.

Elsewhere, Jamaica averaged one significant revolt every year from 1731 to 1823, while in 1823 thousands rose in Guiana. Jamaica witnessed an uprising of some 20,000 slaves in 1831. These revolts were savagely suppressed. And in Brazil, which had the largest number of slaves outside the United States, the government took 50 years to bring under control a colony of some 20,000 fugitive slaves who had sought refuge in the mountains.

In contrast, slave revolts were rare in the United States. Unlike in Latin America, in the Old South whites outnumbered blacks, the government was much more powerful, a majority of slaves were native-born, and family life was stronger. Slaves recognized the odds against them, and many potential leaders became fugitives instead. What is remarkable is that American slaves revolted at all.

Early in the nineteenth century several well-organized uprisings were barely thwarted. In 1800 Gabriel Prosser, a slave blacksmith, recruited perhaps a couple hundred slaves to march on Richmond and capture the governor. But a few conspirators betrayed the plot, and Prosser and other leaders were captured and executed. Denmark Vesey's conspiracy in Charleston in 1822 met a similar fate (page 000).

The most famous slave revolt, led by a literate slave preacher named Nat Turner, was more spontaneous. Turner, who lived on a farm in southeastern Virginia, was given unusual privileges by his master, whom he described as a kind and trusting man. A religious mystic, Turner became convinced that God had selected him to punish white people through "terror and devastation." One night in 1831 following an eclipse of the sun, he and six other slaves stole out and murdered Turner's master and family. Recruiting some 70 slaves as they went, Turner's band killed 57 white men, women, and children. But the revolt was crushed within 48 hours, and Turner was eventually captured, tried, and executed. Even so, the uprising left white southerners uneasy. Turner had seemed a model slave, yet who could read a slave's true emotions behind the mask of obedience?

Few slaves followed Turner's violent example. But there were more subtle ways of resisting a master's authority. Most dramatically, slaves could run away. With the odds stacked heavily against them, few runaways

> Which American nation took 50 years to suppress a colony of 20,000 escaped slaves established in the mountains?
>
> a. Haiti
> b. United States
> c. Brazil
> d. Cuba
>
> Key: c

BACKSTORY
Dizzy from Thirst
The intense heat of plantation fieldwork could leave slaves so dizzy, they would call out "I see a monkey." Water was provided sometimes in ceramic "monkey pots," other times in a canteen like this one. Note that the canteen has two spouts: guess which was for the overseer and which for the slaves?

escaped safely to freedom except from the border states. More frequently, slaves fled to nearby woods or swamps. Some runaways stayed out only a few days; others, like Octave Johnson, held out for months.

Many slaves resisted by abusing their masters' property. They mishandled animals, broke tools and machinery, misplaced items, and worked carelessly in the fields. Slaves also sought to trick the master by feigning illness or injury and by hiding rocks in the cotton they picked. Slaves complained directly to the owner about an overseer's mistreatment, thereby attempting to drive a wedge between the two.

The most common form of resistance was theft. Slaves raided the master's smokehouse, secretly slaughtered his stock, and killed his poultry. Slaves often distinguished between "stealing" from one another and merely "taking" from white masters. "Dey always done tell us it was wrong to lie and steal," recalled Josephine Howard, a former slave in Texas, "but why did the white folks steal my mammy and her mammy? They lives . . . over in Africy. . . . That's the sinfulles' stealin' there is."

Slaves learned to outwit their masters, one former bondsman testified, by wearing an "impenetrable mask" around whites: "How much of joy, of sorrow, of misery and anguish have they hidden from their tormentors." Frederick Douglass, the most famous fugitive slave, explained that "as the master studies to keep the slave ignorant, the slave is cunning enough to make the master think he succeeds."

SLAVE CULTURE

Trapped in bondage, slaves could at least forge a culture of their own by combining strands from their African past with customs that evolved from their life in America. This slave culture was most distinct on big plantations, where the large slave population lived farther apart from white scrutiny.

The Slave Family >> Maintaining a sense of family was one of the most remarkable achievements of African Americans in bondage, given the obstacles they faced. Southern law did not recognize slave marriages as legally binding, nor did it allow slave parents complete authority over their children. Black women faced the possibility of rape by the master or overseer without legal recourse, and husbands, wives, and children had to live with the fear of being sold and separated. From 1820 to 1860 more than two million slaves were sold in the interstate slave trade. Perhaps 600,000 husbands and wives were separated by such sales.

Still, family ties remained strong, as slave culture demonstrated. The marriage ceremony among slaves varied from a formal religious service to jumping over the broomstick in front of the slave community to nothing more than the master's giving verbal approval. Whatever the ceremony, slaves viewed the ritual as a public affirmation of the couple's commitment to their new duties and responsibilities. Rather than adopting white norms, slaves developed their own moral code concerning sexual relations and marriage. Although young slaves often engaged in premarital sex, they were expected to choose a partner and become part of a stable family. It has been estimated that at least one in five slave women had one or more children before marriage, but

AFTER THE FACT
Steamboat Manifests and Starvation

Historians have for many years combed individual plantation records and the accounts of travelers to judge how well slaves were treated and how long they lived. Such testimony, however, can be impressionistic and inconsistent.

More recently researchers have turned to a different set of data: about 50,000 records collected between 1820 and 1860 from shippers on coastal and inland waterways. To ensure that slaves were not being imported from Africa, merchants were required to record information about slaves traveling on steamboats. The lists include vital data on age, weight, and height.

An analysis of these shipping "manifests" makes clear that slave children in particular faced daunting conditions. On average, they weighed less at birth than white children did and were badly undernourished at least until the age of 6. Slave women were worked hard even during the final months of pregnancy; as a result more than half of all conceptions ended in miscarriage or in the infant's early death. For every 1,000 live births among southern slaves, more than 200 died before the age of 5, and fewer than two-thirds of slave children lived to age 10. Those who did had a life expectancy about 8 years less than that of white Americans.

most of these mothers eventually married. "The negroes had their own ideas of morality, and they held them very strictly," the daughter of a Georgia planter recalled. "They did not consider it wrong for a girl to have a child before she married, but afterwards were very strict upon anything like infidelity on her part."

The traditional nuclear family of father, mother, and children was the rule, not the exception, among slaves. Women did the indoor work such as cooking, washing, and sewing, and men performed outdoor chores, such as gathering firewood, hauling water, and tending the animals and garden plots. The men also hunted and fished to supplement the spare weekly rations. "My old daddy . . . caught rabbits, coons an' possums," recalled Louisa Adams of North Carolina. "He would work all day and hunt at night."

Songs and Stories of Protest and Celebration >>
In the songs they sang, slaves expressed some of their deepest feelings about life. "The songs of the slave represent the sorrows of his heart," commented Frederick Douglass. Surely there was bitterness as well as sorrow when slaves sang:

> We raise the wheat
> They give us the corn
> We bake the bread
> They give us the crust
> We sift the meal
> They give us the husk
> We peel the meat
> They give us the skin
> And that's the way
> They take us in

Yet songs were also central to the celebrations held in the slave quarters: for marriages, Christmas revels, and after harvest time. And a slave on the way to the fields might sing, "Saturday night and Sunday too / Young gals on my mind."

Slaves expressed themselves through stories as well as song. Most often these folktales used animals as symbolic models for the predicaments in which slaves found themselves. In the best known of these, the cunning Brer Rabbit was a weak fellow who used his wits to defeat larger animals like Brer Fox and Brer Bear. Such stories, whether direct or symbolic, taught the young how to survive in a hostile world.

The Lord Calls Us Home >>
Religion stood at the center of slave culture. Slaveowners encouraged a carefully controlled form of religion among slaves. "Church was what they called it," one former slave protested, "but all that preacher talked about was for us slaves to obey our masters and not to lie and steal. Nothing about Jesus was ever said and the overseer stood there to see that the preacher talked as he wanted him to talk." In response, some slaves rejected all religion.

Most, however, sought a Christianity beyond the control of the master. On many plantations they met secretly at night, when they would break into rhythmic singing and dancing, modeled on the ring shout of African religion. Even in regular services, observers noted the greater emotion of black worshipers. "The way in which we worshiped is almost indescribable," one slave preacher recalled. "The singing was accompanied by a certain ecstasy of motion, clapping of hands, tossing of heads, which would continue

>> Lewis Miller of York, Pennsylvania, painted this picture of Virginia slaves dancing in 1853. Dancing and music were important components of slave culture and provided a welcome respite from work under slavery. Declared one runaway slave: "The sternest . . . master cannot frighten us or whip the fun out of us."

without cessation about half an hour." In an environment where slaves, for most of the day, were prevented from expressing their deepest feelings, such meetings provided a satisfying emotional release.

Although secret religious meetings were important, the religious experience of most enslaved African Americans occurred mainly within the regular white-controlled churches of the South. Perhaps a million slaves were included in the southern churches before the Civil War, especially in the Methodist and Baptist churches. Indeed, in some areas, slaves were a majority in local congregations. As a result, most slaves worshiped together with their masters rather than in separate services. At one point during the regular service ministers delivered a special message to the slaves, but they also heard the same sermon as whites, with its emphasis on faith and salvation. The churches were also the one institution in the South where blacks were accorded a measure of equality.

Black members were held to the same standards of conduct, were subject to the same church discipline, and were allowed to testify against whites.

Religion also provided slaves with values to guide them through their lives and give them a sense of self-worth. Slaves learned that God one day would raise the poor and downtrodden to honor and glory. Just as certainly, on the final Day of Judgment, masters would be punished for their sins. "This is one reason why I believe in hell," a former slave declared. "I don't believe a just God is going to take no such man as my former master into His Kingdom."

Again, song played a central role. Slaves sang religious "spirituals" at work and at play as well as in religious services. Seemingly meek and otherworldly, the songs often contained a hidden element of protest. Frederick Douglass disclosed that when slaves sang longingly of "Canaan, sweet Canaan," they were thinking not only of the Bible's Promised Land but of the North and freedom.

Religion, then, served not only to comfort slaves after days of toil and sorrow. It also strengthened the sense of togetherness and common purpose and held out the promise of eventual freedom in this world and the next. Having faith that "some of these days my time will come" was one of the most important ways that slaves coped with bondage and resisted its pressure to rob them of their self-esteem.

The Slave Community >> While slaves managed to preserve a culture of their own, they found it impossible to escape fully from white control. In terms of social hierarchy, the prestige of a slave driver rested ultimately on the authority of the white master, and skilled slaves and house servants often felt superior to other slaves, an attitude masters promoted. Light-skinned slaves sometimes deemed their color a badge of superiority. Fanny Kemble recorded that one woman begged to be relieved of field labor, which she considered degrading, "on 'account of her color.'"

Despite these divisions, the realities of slavery and white racism inevitably drove black people closer together in a common bond and forced them to depend on one another to survive. Excluded from the individualistic society of whites, slaves out of necessity created a community of their own.

Free Black Southerners >> Of the 4 million African Americans living in the South in 1860, only 260,000—about 7 percent—were free. More than 85 percent of them lived in the Upper South. Free black southerners were also much more urban than either the southern white or slave populations. In 1860 almost a third of the free African Americans in the Upper South, and more than half in the Lower South, lived in towns and

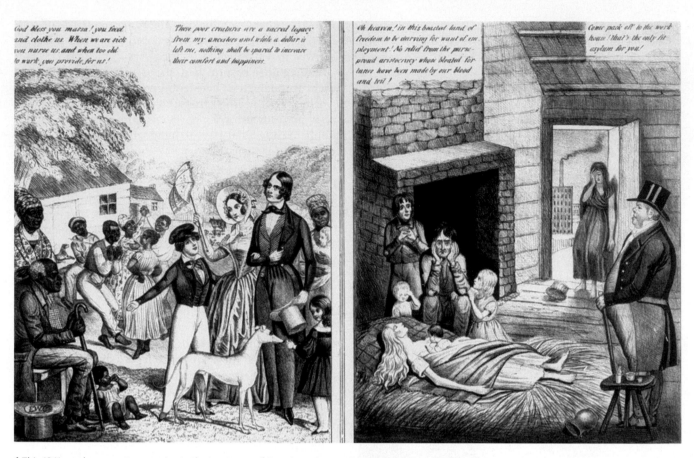

⌃ This 1841 proslavery cartoon contrasts the treatment of American slaves, who are allegedly well fed, well clothed, and well cared for, with the plight of English factory workers. Defenders of slavery made the same comparisons to northern laborers.

cities. As a rule, free African Americans were more literate than slaves, and they were disproportionately female and much more likely to be of mixed ancestry.

Most free black southerners lived in rural areas, although usually not near plantations. A majority eked out a living farming or in low-paying unskilled jobs, but some did well enough to own slaves themselves. In 1830 about 3,600 did, although commonly their "property" was their wives or children, purchased because they could not be emancipated under state laws. A few, however, were full-blown slaveowners.

The boundary sometimes blurred between free and enslaved African Americans. Sally Thomas of Nashville was technically a slave, but in the 1830s and 1840s her owner allowed her to ply her trade as a laundress and keep some of her wages. (She used $350 of these savings to purchase the freedom of one of her sons.) The boundary stretched especially for African Americans working along rivers and the seashore in the fishing trades, as pilots or seamen, or as "watermen" ferrying supplies and stores in small boats. Under such conditions, laborers preserved more freedom and initiative than most agricultural workers.

Along Albemarle Sound in North Carolina, free blacks and slaves flocked from miles around to

"fisherman's courts," a kind of annual hiring fair. Amid an atmosphere of drinking, carousing, cockfighting, and boxing, men who ran commercial fishing operations signed up workers. The crews would then go down to the shore in late February or early March to net vast schools of fish, working around the clock. A single team might haul 100,000 herring onto the beach in four to seven hours. Women and children then headed, gutted, cleaned, and salted the fish. A good "cutter" might head tens of thousands of herring a day. In such settings African Americans, both free and slave, could share news with folk they did not regularly see.

Following Nat Turner's rebellion of 1831, southern legislatures increased the restrictions placed on free African Americans. They were forbidden to enter a new state, had to carry their free papers, could not assemble when they wished, were subject to a nightly curfew, often had to post a bond and be licensed to work, and could not vote, hold office, or testify in court against white people.

Free African Americans occupied an uncertain position in southern society, well above black slaves but distinctly beneath even poorer white southerners. They were victims of a society that had no place for them.

SOUTHERN SOCIETY AND THE DEFENSE OF SLAVERY

While the South was a remarkably diverse region, it was united above all by the institution of slavery. As the South's economy became more dependent on slave-produced staples, slavery became more central to the life of the South, to its culture and its identity.

The Virginia Debate of 1832 >> During the Revolution, the leading critics of slavery were southerners—Jefferson, Washington, Madison, and Patrick Henry among them. But beginning in the 1820s, in the wake of the controversy over admitting Missouri as a slave state, southern leaders became more aggressive in defending slavery. The turning point occurred in the early 1830s, when the South found itself increasingly under attack. It was in 1831 that William Lloyd Garrison began publishing his abolitionist newspaper, *The Liberator*. That was also the year Nat Turner led his revolt, which frightened so many white southerners.

In response to the Turner insurrection, a number of Virginia's western counties, where there were few slaves, petitioned the legislature in 1832 to adopt a program for gradual emancipation. In the end, however, the legislature refused. The debate represented the last significant attempt of white southerners to take action against slavery. Instead, during the 1830s and 1840s southern leaders defended slavery as a good, not just for white but for black people. As John C. Calhoun proclaimed in 1837, "I hold that in the present state of civilization, where two races . . . are brought together, the relation now existing in the slaveholding states between the two is, instead of an evil, a good—a positive good."

The Proslavery Argument >> White southern leaders justified slavery in a variety of ways. Ministers argued that none of the biblical prophets or Christ himself had ever condemned slavery. Defenders of the institution pointed out that classical Greece and Rome also depended on slavery. They even cited John Locke, that giant of the Enlightenment, who had recognized slavery in the constitution he drafted for the colony of Carolina. African Americans belonged to an intellectually and emotionally inferior race, slavery's defenders argued, and therefore lacked the ability to care for themselves.

Proslavery writers sometimes argued that slaves in the South lived better than factory workers in the North. Masters cared for slaves for life, whereas northern workers had no claim on their employer when they were unemployed, old, or no longer able to work. In advancing this argument, white southerners exaggerated the material comforts of slavery and minimized the average worker's living conditions—to say nothing, of course, about the incalculable psychological value of freedom. Still, to many white southerners, slavery seemed a more humane system of labor relations.

Defenders of slavery did not really expect to convert northerners. Their target was more often slaveowners themselves. As Duff Green, a southern editor, explained, "We must satisfy the consciences, we must allay the fears of our own people. We must satisfy them that slavery is of itself right—that it is not a sin against God—that it is not an evil, moral or political. In this way only," he went on, "can we prepare our own people to defend their institutions."

Closing Ranks >> Not all white southerners could quell their doubts. Still, in the decades before the Civil War, few outside the border states contended that slavery was wrong. And southern whites who did oppose slavery found themselves harassed, assaulted, and driven into exile. Southern mobs destroyed the presses of antislavery papers. Southern mails were forcibly closed to abolitionist propaganda. Southerners such as James Birney and Sarah and Angelina Grimké had to leave their native region to carry on the fight against slavery from the free states.

Increasingly, too, slavery entered the national political debate. Before 1836 Andrew Jackson's popularity in the South blocked the formation of a competitive two-party system. The rise of the abolitionist movement in the 1830s, however, left many southerners uneasy, and when the Democrats nominated the northerner Martin Van Buren in 1836, southern Whigs charged that Van Buren could not be counted on to meet the abolitionist threat to slavery. The Whigs made impressive gains in the South in 1836, carrying several states and significantly narrowing the margin between the two parties.

During the Jacksonian era, most southern political battles did not revolve around slavery. Still, southern politicians in both parties had to be careful about being the least bit critical of slavery or southern institutions. They knew quite well that, even if their constituents were not so fanatical as John Calhoun in the defense of the peculiar institution, southern voters overwhelmingly supported slavery.

As the past several chapters have made clear, two remarkable transformations were sweeping the world in the first half of the nineteenth century. The first was a series of political upheavals leading to increased democratic participation in many nation-states. The second, the industrial revolution, applied machine labor and technological innovation to commercial and agricultural economies.

Although it is common to identify the industrial revolution with New England's factories and the North's cities, that revolution transformed the rural South, too. Cotton could not have become king without the demand created by textile factories or without the ability to "gin" the seeds out of cotton by Eli Whitney's invention. Nor could cotton production flourish without industrial advances in transportation, which allowed raw materials to be shipped worldwide. As for democratic change, the suffrage was extended in Britain by the Reform Bill of 1832, and popular uprisings spread across Europe in 1830 and 1848. In the United States white southerners and northerners participated in the democratic reforms of the 1820s and 1830s.

The industrial and democratic revolutions thus transformed the South as well as the North, though in different ways. Increasingly slavery became the focus of disputes between the two sections. The industrial revolution's demand for cotton increased the demand for slave labor and the profits to be gained from it. Yet the spread of democratic ideology worldwide increased pressure to abolish slavery. France and Britain had already done so. In eastern Europe the near-slavery of feudal serfdom was being eliminated as well: in 1848 within the Hapsburg empire; in 1861 in Russia; in 1864 in Romania.

By the mid-1840s the contradictory pressures of the industrial and democratic revolutions were beginning to sharpen, as the United States embarked on a new program of westward expansion that thrust the slavery issue into the center of politics. Americans were forced to debate how much of the newly won territory should be open to slavery; and in doing so, some citizens began to question whether the Union could permanently endure, half slave and half free.

CHAPTER SUMMARY

The Old South was a complex, biracial society that increasingly diverged from the rest of the United States in the years before 1860.

▌ Southerners placed heavy emphasis on agriculture and upheld the superiority of the rural way of life. Few cities and towns developed.

▌ Southern commercial agriculture produced staple crops for sale in northern and European markets: tobacco, sugar, rice, and, above all, cotton.

▌ As southern agriculture expanded into the fresh lands of the Deep South, the slave population moved steadily westward and southward, and the Upper South became more diversified agriculturally.

▌ Slavery played a major role in shaping the class structure of the Old South.

▌ Ownership of slaves brought privilege and status, and the largest slaveowners were extraordinarily wealthy.

▌ Planters on the older eastern seaboard enjoyed a more refined lifestyle than did those on the new cotton frontier.

▌ Most slaveowners, however, owned only a few slaves, and the majority of southern whites were nonslaveowning yeoman farmers.

▌ At the bottom of the white class structure were the poor whites.

▌ Slavery hurt nonslaveholding whites economically, but class tensions were muted in the Old South because of racial fears.

Significant Events

Gabriel Prosser's rebellion

Denmark Vesey conspiracy

Agricultural reform movement in Upper South

1800   1815–1860   1822   1830–1840   1830–1860

Spread of the cotton kingdom

Proslavery argument developed

- The institution of slavery was both a labor system and a social system, regulating relations between the races.
  - Slaves resisted bondage in many ways, ranging from the subtle to the overt. Slave revolts, however, were rare.
  - Slaves developed their own culture, in which the family, religion, and songs played key roles in helping them cope with the pressures of bondage.
  - Slaves' shared experiences created a community based on a common identity and mutual values.
- As slavery increasingly came under attack, white southerners rallied to protect their peculiar institution.
  - They developed a set of arguments defending slavery as a positive good.
  - Both political parties in the South strongly defended the institution and southern rights.
- Many Americans, both North and South, shared the same values: personal independence, social egalitarianism, evangelical Protestantism. But beginning in the mid-1840s with renewed westward expansion, the slavery issue increased sectional tensions.

Additional Reading

The reports of Frederick Law Olmsted, who traveled through the South in the 1850s, make a fascinating jumping-off point for a first look at the region. Much of Olmsted's material is conveniently collected in Lawrence Powell, ed., *The Cotton Kingdom* (1984). A contrasting approach to traveling about is to stay at one plantation, as Erskine Clarke does in his brilliant *Dwelling Place: A Plantation Epic* (2005). Based on meticulous research, this upstairs/downstairs saga profiles the intertwined lives of masters and slaves on a Georgia coastal plantation from 1805–1869. James Oakes, *Slavery and Freedom* (1990), and William W. Freehling, *The Road to Disunion* (1990), are good syntheses that analyze the diversity and the contradictions of the antebellum South.

Although old, Frank Owsley's *Plain Folk of the Old South* (1949), about southern yeoman farmers, is still useful and can be supplemented by Samuel C. Hyde Jr., ed., *Plain Folk of the South Revisited* (1997). The lives of upper-class southern white women and their servants are analyzed in Elizabeth Fox-Genovese, *Within the Plantation Household* (1988), whereas Victoria E. Bynum, *Unruly Women* (1992), deals with white and black women of lower status.

The best exploration of slavery as a labor system remains Kenneth M. Stampp, *The Peculiar Institution* (1956), but the most perceptive treatment of slave culture is Eugene D. Genovese, *Roll, Jordan, Roll* (1974). Charles Joyner, *Down by the Riverside* (1984), sensitively recreates slave culture in the rice districts, and Wilma A. Dunaway, *The African-American Family in Slavery and Emancipation* (2002), focuses on plantations in the mountain South (and in doing so challenges the prevailing view that slaves carved out a modicum of autonomy within bondage). John Hope Franklin and Loren Schweninger, *Runaway Slaves* (1999), details an important aspect of slave resistance. Walter Johnson, *Soul by Soul: Life Inside the Antebellum Slave Market* (1999), provides a concrete and chilling view of the trade that helped sustain the Peculiar Institution. Ira Berlin, *Slaves Without Masters* (1974), is an excellent account of southern free blacks. As for the political and ideological aspects of slavery, consult Drew Faust, *A Sacred Circle* (1977), and William J. Cooper, Jr., *The Politics of Slavery* (1978).

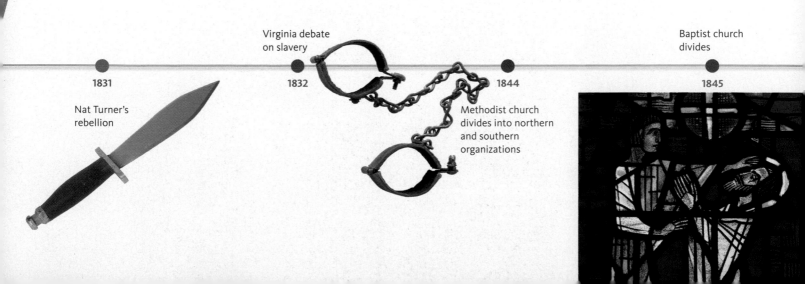

Virginia debate on slavery

Baptist church divides

1831

1832

1844

1845

Nat Turner's rebellion

Methodist church divides into northern and southern organizations

14

Western Expansion
and the Rise of the
Slavery Issue 1820–1850

Indian encampments around Fort Pierre along the Upper Missouri River, 1834.

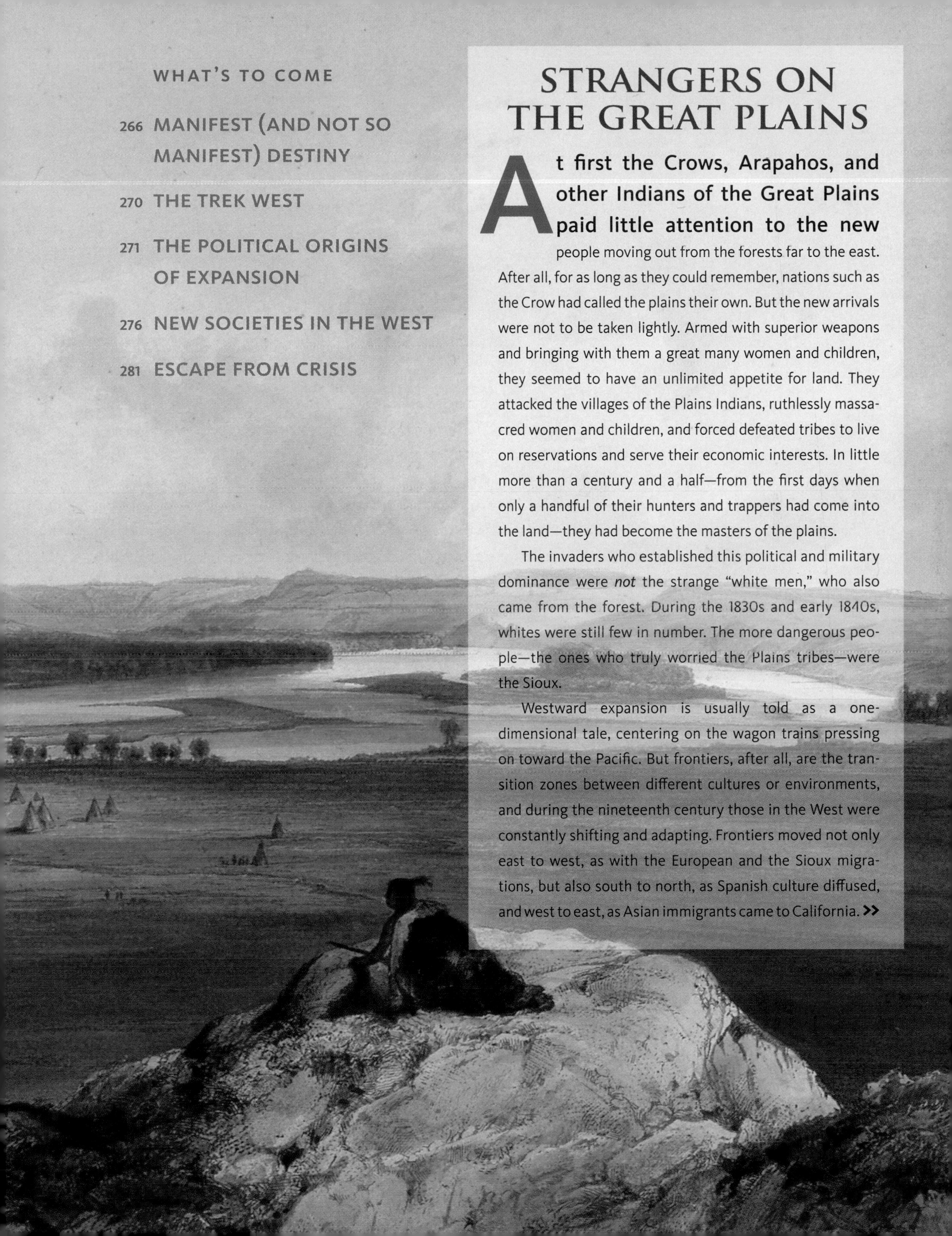

WHAT'S TO COME

266 MANIFEST (AND NOT SO MANIFEST) DESTINY

270 THE TREK WEST

271 THE POLITICAL ORIGINS OF EXPANSION

276 NEW SOCIETIES IN THE WEST

281 ESCAPE FROM CRISIS

STRANGERS ON THE GREAT PLAINS

At first the Crows, Arapahos, and other Indians of the Great Plains paid little attention to the new people moving out from the forests far to the east. After all, for as long as they could remember, nations such as the Crow had called the plains their own. But the new arrivals were not to be taken lightly. Armed with superior weapons and bringing with them a great many women and children, they seemed to have an unlimited appetite for land. They attacked the villages of the Plains Indians, ruthlessly massacred women and children, and forced defeated tribes to live on reservations and serve their economic interests. In little more than a century and a half—from the first days when only a handful of their hunters and trappers had come into the land—they had become the masters of the plains.

The invaders who established this political and military dominance were *not* the strange "white men," who also came from the forest. During the 1830s and early 1840s, whites were still few in number. The more dangerous people—the ones who truly worried the Plains tribes—were the Sioux.

Westward expansion is usually told as a one-dimensional tale, centering on the wagon trains pressing on toward the Pacific. But frontiers, after all, are the transition zones between different cultures or environments, and during the nineteenth century those in the West were constantly shifting and adapting. Frontiers moved not only east to west, as with the European and the Sioux migrations, but also south to north, as Spanish culture diffused, and west to east, as Asian immigrants came to California. **>>**

<< The horse frontier, moving onto the Great Plains from the southwest, and the gun frontier, crossing from the opposite direction in the northeast, contributed to the turbulence of the trans-Mississippi West in the mid-nineteenth century. In 1875 a Kiowa Indian named Koba drew this picture of a Kiowa on horseback. He carries a rifle, and the dots surrounding the figure represent musket balls that have been fired.

Furthermore, frontiers marked not only human but also animal boundaries. Horses, cattle, and pigs, all of which had been imported from Europe, moved across the continent, often in advance of European settlers. These animals transformed the way Indian peoples lived. Frontiers could also be technological, as in the case of trade goods and firearms. Moreover, as we have already seen, disease moved across the continent with disastrous consequences for natives who had not acquired immunity to European microorganisms.

Three frontiers revolutionized the lives of the Sioux: those of the horse, the gun, and disease. The horse frontier spread ahead of European settlement from the southwest, where horses had first been imported by the Spanish. The Spanish, however—unlike English and French traders—generally refused to sell firearms to Indians, so the gun frontier moved in the opposite direction, from northeast to southwest. The two waves met and crossed along the upper Missouri during the first half of the eighteenth century. For the tribes that possessed them, horses provided greater mobility, both for hunting bison and for fighting. Guns, too, conferred obvious advantages, and the arrival of these new elements inaugurated an extremely unsettled era for Plains Indian cultures.

The Sioux were first lured from the forest onto the Minnesota prairie during the early 1700s to hunt beaver, whose pelts could be exchanged with European traders for manufactured goods. Having obtained guns in exchange for furs, the Sioux drove the Omahas, Otos, Cheyennes, and Missouris (who had not yet acquired guns) south and west. But by the 1770s their advantage in firepower had disappeared, and any farther advance was blocked by powerful tribes such as the Mandans and Arikaras. These peoples were primarily horticultural, raising corn, beans, and squash and living in well-fortified towns. They also owned more horses than the Sioux; thus it was easier for them to resist attacks.

But the third frontier, disease, threw the balance of power toward the Sioux after 1779. That year, a continental smallpox pandemic struck the plains via New Mexico (page 130). The horticultural tribes were hit especially hard because they lived in densely populated villages, where the epidemic spread more easily. The Sioux embarked on a second wave of westward expansion in the late eighteenth century, so that by the time Lewis and Clark came through in 1804, they firmly controlled the upper Missouri as far as the Yellowstone River.

The Sioux's nomadic life, centered on the buffalo hunt, enabled them to avoid the worst ravages of disease, especially the smallpox epidemic of 1837, which reduced the plains population by as much as half. Indeed, the Sioux became the largest nation on the plains and was the only one whose high birthrate approximated that of whites. From an estimated 5,000 in 1804, they grew to 25,000 in the 1850s. Their numbers increased Sioux military power as well as the need for new hunting grounds, and during the first half of the nineteenth century they pushed even farther up the Missouri, conquered the plains west of the Black Hills, and won control of the hunting grounds on the Platte River. <<

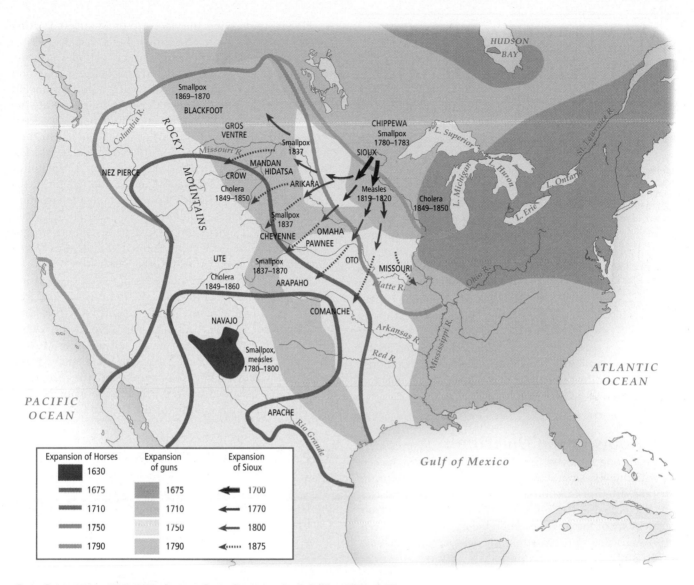

Expansion of Horses
- 1630
- 1675
- 1710
- 1750
- 1790

Expansion of guns
- 1675
- 1710
- 1750
- 1790

Expansion of Sioux
- 1700
- 1770
- 1800
- 1875

Map labels: HUDSON BAY, BLACKFOOT, Smallpox 1869–1870, GROS VENTRE, Smallpox 1837, CHIPPEWA, Smallpox 1780–1783, SIOUX, NEZ PIERCE, MANDAN, HIDATSA, CROW, ARIKARA, Measles 1819–1820, Cholera 1849–1850, L. Superior, L. Michigan, L. Huron, L. Ontario, L. Erie, Columbia R., ROCKY MOUNTAINS, Missouri R., Cholera 1849–1850, Smallpox 1837, CHEYENNE, OMAHA, PAWNEE, OTO, MISSOURI, UTE, Smallpox 1837–1870, Cholera 1849–1860, ARAPAHO, Platte R., Ohio R., St. Lawrence R., NAVAJO, Smallpox, measles 1780–1800, COMANCHE, Arkansas R., Red R., Mississippi R., ATLANTIC OCEAN, PACIFIC OCEAN, APACHE, Rio Grande, Gulf of Mexico

SIOUX EXPANSION AND THE HORSE AND GUN FRONTIERS

In 1710 the horse and gun frontiers had not yet crossed, but by 1750 the two waves began to overlap. The Sioux pushed west during the early eighteenth century thanks to firearms; they were checked from further expansion until the 1770s, when smallpox epidemics again turned the balance in their favor.

These shifting frontiers of animals, disease, firearms, and trade goods disrupted the political and cultural life of the Great Plains. And as white Americans moved westward, their own frontier lines produced similar disruptions, not only between white settlers and Indians but also between Anglo-American and Hispanic cultures. The relations between Indian peoples and Mexico were also in flux, as many tribes across the Plains began attacking Mexico during the 1830s. There would even be a frontier moving west to east, as thousands of Chinese were drawn, along with other immigrants from North and South America, Australia, and Hawaii, to gold fields discovered after 1848. Ironically, perhaps the greatest instability created by the moving frontiers occurred in established American society. As the political system of the United States struggled to incorporate territories, the North and South engaged in a fierce debate over whether the new lands should become slave or free. Just as the Sioux's cultural identity was brought into question by moving frontiers, so, too, was the identity of the American Republic.

MANIFEST (AND NOT SO MANIFEST) DESTINY

"Make way . . . for the young American Buffalo—he has not yet got land enough," roared one U.S. politician in 1844. In the space of a few years, the United States acquired Texas,

Manifest Destiny political doctrine which flourished in the mid-nineteenth century, that the benefits of democracy would spread along with territorial expansion. Yet Manifest Destiny was also racist in its assumption of the inferiority of other peoples and cultures; and it encompassed a purely economic desire to expand the nation's commerce and power.

California, the lower half of the Oregon Territory, and the lands between the Rockies and California: nearly 1.5 million square miles in all. John L. O'Sullivan, a prominent Democratic editor in New York, struck a responsive chord when he declared that it had become the United States' "**manifest destiny** to overspread the continent allotted by Providence for the free development of our yearly multiplying millions." The cry of Manifest Destiny soon echoed in other editorial pages and in the halls of Congress.

The Roots of the Doctrine >>
Many Americans had long believed that their country had a special, even divine, mission, which could be traced back to the Puritans' attempt to build a "city on a hill." Manifest Destiny also contained a political component, inherited from the ideology of the Revolution. In the mid-nineteenth century, Americans spoke of extending democracy, with widespread suffrage among white males, no king or aristocracy, and no established church, "over the whole North American continent."

Americans believed that their social and economic system, too, should spread around the globe. They pointed to its broad ownership of land, individualism, and free play of economic opportunity as superior features of American life. More importantly, Manifest Destiny was about power, especially economic power. American business interests recognized the value of the fine harbors along the Pacific Coast, which promised a lucrative trade with Asia, and they hoped to make those harbors American.

>> With the Star of Empire blazing from her forehead, the Spirit of progress dominates John Gast's painting *Manifest Destiny*. Indians and wild animals retreat in the face of advancing progress, illustrated by Anglo-American settlers and farmers, railroads and other forms of transportation, telegraph lines, schools symbolized by a book, and, in the distance, cities. In reality, the movement of the frontier was hardly one-dimensional, as Hispanic, Indian, Asian, and Anglo-American cultures clashed.

Finally, underlying the doctrine of Manifest Destiny was widespread racism. The same belief in racial superiority that was used to justify Indian removal under Jackson, to uphold slavery in the South, and to excuse segregation in the North also proved useful in defending expansion westward. The United States had a duty to regenerate the backward peoples of America, declared politicians and propagandists. Their reference was not so much to Indians: the forced expulsion of assimilated Cherokees during Indian removal made clear what most American policy makers thought about Indian "regeneration." By the 1840s it was rather the Mexicans who had caught the attention of Manifest Destiny's prophets of progress. The Mexican race "must amalgamate and be lost, in the superior vigor of the Anglo-Saxon race," proclaimed O'Sullivan's *Democratic Review*, "or they must utterly perish."

Before 1845 most Americans assumed that expansion would be achieved without international war. American settlement would expand westward, and when the time was right, neighboring provinces, like ripe fruit, would fall naturally into American hands. Texas, New Mexico, Oregon, and California—areas that were sparsely populated and weakly defended—dominated the American expansionist imagination. With time, Americans became less willing to wait patiently for the fruit to fall.

The Mexican Borderlands >>
The heart of Spain's American empire was Mexico City, where spacious boulevards spread out through the center of the city and the University of Mexico, the oldest university in North America, had been accepting students since 1553, a full 85 years earlier than Harvard. From the Mexican point

<< Town plazas, such as this one in San Felipe, Coahuila (in Mexico), were commercial centers in the Mexican Southwest. Traders from outlying ranchos enjoy refreshments or examine clothing and other goods offered for sale.

of view, the frontier was 1,000 miles to the north, a four-week journey to Texas, another two weeks to New Mexico, and three months by land and sea to the missions of California. Being isolated, these Mexican provinces developed with little metropolitan supervision.

California's settlements were anchored by four coastal *presidios,* or forts, at San Diego, Santa Barbara, Monterey, and San Francisco. Between them lay 21 Catholic missions run by a handful of Franciscans (there were only 36 in 1821). The missions controlled enormous tracts of land on which grazed gigantic herds of cattle, sheep, and horses. The animals and irrigated fields were tended by about 20,000 Indians, who in certain ways lived and worked like slaves.

{ **presidio** Spanish military garrison.

When Mexico won its independence from Spain in 1821, little changed in California at first. But in 1833 the Mexican Congress stripped the Catholic church of its vast landholdings. These lands were turned over to Mexican cattle ranchers, usually in massive grants of 50,000 acres or more. The new *rancheros* ruled their estates much as great planters of the Old South. Labor was provided by Indians, who again were forced to work for little more than room and board. Indeed, the mortality rate of Indian workers was twice that of southern slaves and four times that of the non-native Californians. At this time the Mexican population of California was approximately 4,000. During the 1820s and 1830s Yankee traders set up shop in California in order to buy cattle hides for the growing shoe industry at Lynn and elsewhere. Still, in 1845 the American population in California amounted to only 700.

Spanish settlement of New Mexico was denser than that of California: the province had about 44,000 Spanish-speaking inhabitants in 1827. But as in California, its society was dominated by *ranchero* families that grazed large herds of sheep along the upper Rio Grande valley between El Paso and Taos. A few individuals controlled most of the wealth, while their workers eked out a meager living. Mining of copper and gold was a side industry, and here, too, the profits enriched a small upper class. Spain had long outlawed any commerce with Americans, but after Mexico declared its independence in 1821, yearly caravans from the United States began making the long journey along the Santa Fe Trail. Although this trade flourished over the next two decades, developments in the third Mexican borderland, neighboring Texas, worsened relations between Mexico and the United States.

The Texas Revolution

>> At first, the new government in Mexico encouraged American immigration to Texas, where only about 3,000 Mexicans, mostly ranchers, lived. In 1821 Moses Austin, an American, received a grant from the Spanish government to establish a colony. After his death, his son Stephen took over the project, laying out the little town of San Felipe de Austin along the Brazos River and offering large grants of land at almost no cost.

By 1824 the colony's population exceeded 2,000. Stephen Austin was only the first of a new wave of American land agents, or *empresarios,* who obtained permission from Mexican authorities to settle families in Texas. Ninety percent of the new arrivals came from the South. Many, intending to grow cotton, brought slaves.

Tensions between Mexicans and American immigrants grew with the Texas economy. Most settlers from the States were Protestant. Although the Mexican government did not insist that all new citizens become Catholic, it did officially bar Protestant churches. In 1829 Mexico abolished slavery, then

BACKSTORY

The First Illegal Immigration Crisis

PARE

Alarmed at the rush of Americans into Texas, in 1830 Mexican officials outlawed further immigration. Americans kept coming, despite the new law. Thousands of illegal immigrants poured into Mexican Texas in the next few years and many of these late arrivals were the most ardent advocates of rebellion by 1835.

looked the other way when Texas slaveholders evaded the law. In the early 1830s the Mexican government began to have second thoughts about American settlement and passed laws prohibiting any new immigration. Austin likened the new anti-immigration laws to "trying to stop the Mississippi with a dam of straw." It was an apt metaphor: between 1830 and 1833 illegal American immigrants and their slaves flooded into Mexican Texas, nearly doubling its colonial population.

Admitting that the new regulations had served only to inflame Texans, Mexico repealed them in 1833. But by then colonial ill-will had ballooned along with the population. By mid-decade the American white population of 40,000 was nearly 10 times the number of Mexicans in the territory. Once again Mexico's government talked of abolishing slavery in Texas. Even more disturbing to the American newcomers, in 1834 President Antonio López de Santa Anna and his allies in the Mexican Congress began passing legislation that took power away from

the states and concentrated it in Mexico City. Texans had been struggling for more autonomy, not less. When Santa Anna brutally suppressed an uprising against the central government in the state of Zacatecas, Texans grew all the more nervous. Finally, when conflicts over taxes led Santa Anna to march soldiers north and enforce his new regime, a ragtag Texas army drove back the advance party and then captured Mexican troops in nearby San Antonio. A full-scale rebellion was under way.

The Texas Republic >> As Santa Anna massed

his forces, a provisional government on March 2, 1836, proclaimed Texan independence. The document was signed by a number of prominent **Tejanos**, Mexican residents of Texas. The constitution of the new Republic of Texas borrowed heavily from the U.S. Constitution, except that it explicitly

Tejano Texan of Hispanic descent

^ Throughout the Spanish and Mexican periods, town life in California, New Mexico, and Texas revolved around central plazas and their churches. One of the first structures to be built in Santa Fe, the Mission Church of San Miguel (est. c. 1610) is today the oldest church building in the present-day United States. The painting, executed in 1882 by the German artist Rudolf Cronau, shows San Miguel in some disrepair but still surrounded by Sunday worshippers.

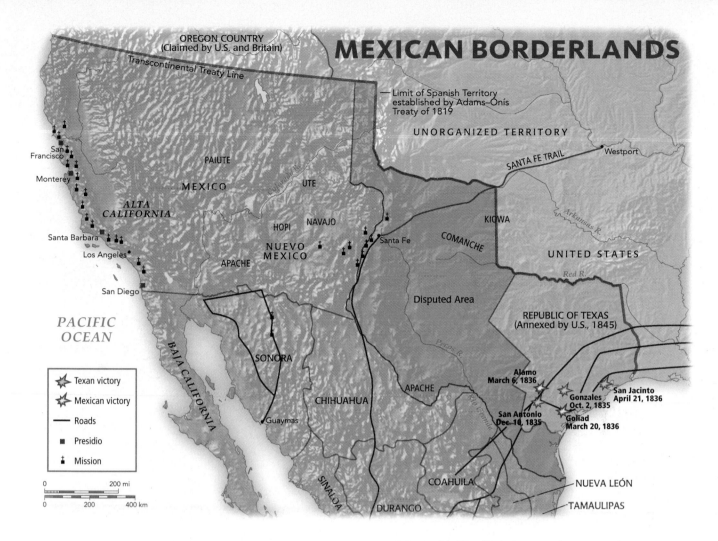

MEXICAN BORDERLANDS

OREGON COUNTRY
(Claimed by U.S. and Britain)
Transcontinental Treaty Line

— Limit of Spanish Territory
established by Adams–Onís
Treaty of 1819

UNORGANIZED TERRITORY

SANTA FE TRAIL

Westport

San Francisco

PAIUTE

Monterey

MEXICO

UTE

ALTA CALIFORNIA

HOPI   NAVAJO

Santa Barbara

NUEVO MEXICO

Santa Fe

KIOWA

COMANCHE

Arkansas R.

Los Angeles

APACHE

UNITED STATES

San Diego

Red R.

PACIFIC OCEAN

Disputed Area

REPUBLIC OF TEXAS
(Annexed by U.S., 1845)

BAJA CALIFORNIA

Pecos R.

SONORA

Guaymas

CHIHUAHUA

APACHE

Alamo
March 6, 1836

Rio Grande

San Antonio
Dec. 10, 1835

Gonzales
Oct. 2, 1835

San Jacinto
April 21, 1836

Goliad
March 20, 1836

COAHUILA

NUEVA LEÓN

SINALOA

DURANGO

TAMAULIPAS

Texan victory
Mexican victory
Roads
Presidio
Mission

0   200 mi
0   200   400 km

prohibited the new Texas Congress from interfering with slavery. Meanwhile, Santa Anna's troops overran a Texan garrison at an old mission in San Antonio, known as the Alamo, and killed all its 187 defenders—including the famous backwoodsman and U.S. congressman, Davy Crockett. The Mexicans, however, paid dearly for the victory, losing more than 1,500 men. The massacre of another force at Goliad after it surrendered further inflamed American resistance.

But anger was one thing; organized resistance another. The commander of the Texas forces was Sam Houston, a former governor of Tennessee. Houston's intellectual ability and talent as a stump speaker thrust him to the forefront of the Texas independence movement. Houston knew his army needed seasoning, so he retreated steadily eastward, buying time in order to forge a disciplined fighting force. By late April he was ready. Reinforced by eager volunteers from the United States, Houston's men surprised the Mexican army camped along the San Jacinto River. Shouting "Remember the Alamo!" they took only 15 minutes to overwhelm the Mexicans (who had been enjoying an afternoon siesta) and capture Santa Anna.

Threatened with execution, the Mexican commander signed treaties recognizing Texan independence and ordering his remaining troops south of the Rio Grande.

Texans would later claim that Santa Anna thereby acknowledged the Rio Grande as Texas's southern boundary. The Mexican Congress repudiated the agreement, especially the claim to the Rio Grande. Houston assumed office in October 1836 as president of the new republic, determined to bring Texas into the American Union as quickly as possible.

Houston assumed that the United States would quickly annex such a vast and inviting territory. But Andrew Jackson worried that any such move would revive sectional tensions and hurt Martin Van Buren's chances in the 1836 presidential election. Only on his last day in office did he extend formal diplomatic recognition to the Texas Republic. Van Buren, distracted by the economic panic that broke out shortly after he entered office, took no action during his term.

Rebuffed, Texans decided to go their own way. In the 10 years following independence, the Lone Star Republic attracted more than 100,000 immigrants by offering free land to settlers. Mexico refused to recognize Texan independence, and the vast majority of its citizens still wished to join the United States, where most of them, after all, had been born. There matters stood when the Whigs and William Henry Harrison won the presidency in 1840.

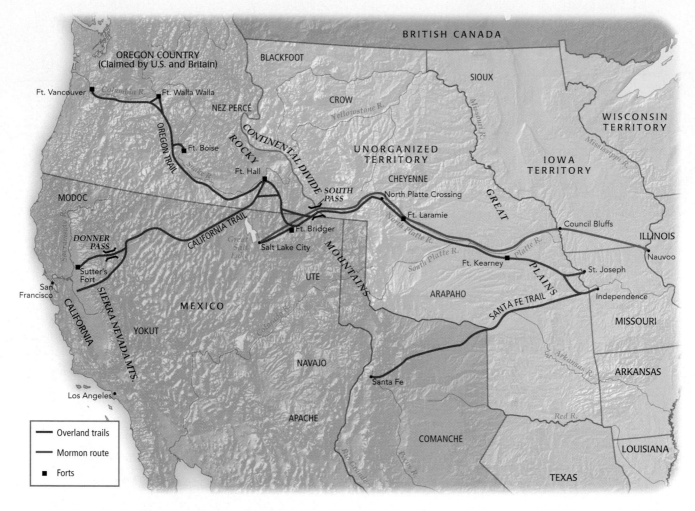

THE OVERLAND TRAIL

Beginning at several different points, the Overland Trail followed the Platte and Sweetwater rivers across the plains to South Pass, where it crossed the Continental Divide. The trail split near Fort Hall. Between 1840 and 1860 more than a quarter of a million emigrants made the trek.

THE TREK WEST

As thousands of white Americans were moving into Texas, and increasingly bringing slaves with them, a much smaller trickle headed toward the Oregon country. Since 1818 the United States and Great Britain had occupied that territory jointly, as far north as latitude 54°40. Although white settlement remained sparse, by 1836 American settlers outnumbered the British in the Willamette valley.

Pushed by the Panic of 1837 and six years of depression and pulled by tales of Oregon's lush, fertile valleys and the healthy, frost-free climate along California's Sacramento River, many American farmers struck out for the West Coast. Missouri was "cleaned" out of money, worried farmer Daniel Waldo, and his wife was even more adamant about heading west: "If you want to stay here another summer

and shake your liver out with the fever and ague, you can do it," she announced to her husband, "but in the spring I am going to take the children and go to Oregon, Indians or no Indians." The wagon trains began rolling west.

The Overland Trail >> Only a few hundred emigrants reached the West in 1841 and 1842, but in 1843 more than 800 followed the Overland Trail across the mountains to Oregon. From then on, they came by the thousands. The migration was primarily a family enterprise, and many couples had only recently married. Most adults were between 20 and 50, since the hard journey discouraged the elderly. Furthermore, a family of four needed about $600 to outfit their journey, an amount that excluded the poor.

Caravans of 20 to 30 wagons were common the first few years, but after 1845 parties traveled in smaller trains of 8 to 10 wagons. Large companies used up the grass quickly, disagreements were more likely, and breakdowns (and hence halts) were more frequent. The trip itself lasted about 6 months.

Women on the Overland Trail >> The journey west often placed a special strain on women. Few wives were as eager as Dan Waldo's to undertake the move. "Poor Ma said only this morning, 'Oh I wish we never had started,'" one daughter reported, "and she looks so sorrowful and dejected." In one study of Oregon-bound parties, three-fourths of the women did not want to head west.

At first, parties divided work by gender, as had been done back home. Women cooked, washed, sewed, and took care of the children, while men drove the wagons, cared for the stock, stood guard, and did the heavy labor. Necessity placed new demands on women, however, and eventually altered their roles. Within a few weeks, they found themselves helping to repair wagons and construct bridges. When men became exhausted, sick, or injured, women stood guard and drove the oxen. The change in work assignments proceeded only in one direction, however, for few men undertook "women's work."

As women strove to maintain a semblance of home on the trail, they often experienced a profound sense of loss. Trains often worked or traveled on the Sabbath, which had been ladies' day back home and an emblem of women's moral authority. Women also felt the lack of close companions to whom they could turn for comfort. One woman, whose husband separated their wagon from the train after a dispute, sadly watched the other wagons pull away: "I felt that indeed I had left all my friends to journey over the dreaded plains without one female acquaintance even for a companion—of course I wept and grieved about it but to no purpose."

Indians and the Trail Experience >> The peoples whose lands were crossed by white wagon trains reacted in a number of ways to the westward tide. The Sioux, who had long been trading with whites, were among those who regularly visited overlanders to trade for blankets, clothes, cows, rifles, and knives. But the European migrants took a heavy toll on the Plains Indians' way of life: emigrant parties scared off game and reduced buffalo herds, overgrazed the grass, and depleted the supply of wood. Having petitioned unsuccessfully in 1846 for government compensation, some Sioux decided to demand payment from the wagon trains crossing their lands. Whether parties paid or not depended on the relative strength of the two groups, but whites complained bitterly of what seemed to them outright robbery.

Their fears aroused by sensational stories, overland parties were wary of Indians, but this menace was greatly exaggerated, especially on the plains. Few wagon trains were attacked by Indians, and less than 4 percent of deaths on the trail were caused by Native Americans. In truth, emigrants more often killed Indians. For overlanders the most aggravating problem posed by native peoples was theft of stock. Many companies received valuable assistance from Indians, who acted as guides, directed them to grass and water, and transported animals and wagons across rivers.

> ## Few wagon trains were attacked by Indians, and less than 4 percent of deaths on the trail were caused by Native Americans.

THE POLITICAL ORIGINS OF EXPANSION

President William Henry Harrison made the gravest mistake of his brief presidential career when he ventured out one raw spring day, bareheaded and without an overcoat, to buy groceries at the Washington markets. He came down with pneumonia and died only one month after his inauguration.

For the first time in the nation's history, a vice president succeeded to the nation's highest office on the death of the president. John Tyler of Virginia had once been a Democrat and a strong supporter of states' rights. But after he quarreled with Jackson during the Nullification controversy, Democrats refused to have anything to do with him, so Tyler joined the Whigs, who nominated him for vice president in 1840 in order to balance the ticket sectionally. During the rollicking campaign that followed, the Whigs sang all too accurately: "And we'll vote for Tyler, therefore, / Without a why or wherefore." Indeed, once in office, Tyler repeatedly vetoed bills passed by Henry Clay and his own party. Disgusted, the Whigs in Congress formally expelled their president from the party.

Tyler's Texas Ploy >> Although shunned by most Whigs and Democrats, Tyler still believed that he might win another four years in the White House if only he latched onto the right popular issue. That issue, he came to believe, was the annexation of Texas. In April 1844 the president sent to the Senate for ratification a treaty he had

secretly negotiated to bring Texas into the Union. He also decided to run for president as an independent.

Meanwhile, the frontrunners for the Whig and Democratic presidential nominations were Clay and Van Buren. Although rivals, they were both moderates who feared that the slavery issue would be injected into the campaign if Texas was annexed as a slave state. Apparently by prearrangement, both men issued letters opposing annexation on the grounds that it threatened the Union and would provoke war with Mexico.

As expected, the Whigs unanimously nominated Clay on a platform that ignored the expansion issue entirely. But Van Buren's Democratic opponents viewed the former president as an ineffective leader who had stumbled through a depression and in 1840 gone down in ignominious defeat. They persuaded the convention to adopt a rule requiring a two-thirds vote to nominate a candidate. That blocked Van Buren's nomination. On the ninth ballot the delegates finally turned to James K. Polk of Tennessee, who favored annexation, as well as the "reoccupation" of Oregon, all the way to its northernmost boundary at 54°40'.

Angered by the convention's outcome, Van Buren's supporters in the Senate joined the Whigs in decisively defeating Tyler's treaty of annexation. Tyler eventually

withdrew from the race, but the Texas issue would not go away. Seeking to shore up his support in the South, Clay announced that he would be glad to see Texas annexed if it would not lead to war. And in the North, a few antislavery Whigs turned to James G. Birney, running on the Liberty party ticket.

In the end, Polk squeaked through by 38,000 votes out of nearly 3 million cast. If just half of Birney's 15,000 ballots in New York had gone to Clay, he would have carried the state and been narrowly elected president. Indignant Whigs charged that by refusing to support Clay, political abolitionists had made the annexation of Texas, and hence the addition of slave territory to the Union, inevitable. And indeed, in the new atmosphere following Polk's victory, Congress approved a joint resolution annexing Texas. On March 3, 1845, his last day in office, Tyler invited Texas to enter the Union.

To the Pacific >> Humorless, calculating, and often deceitful, President Polk pursued his objectives with dogged determination. Embracing a continental vision of the United States, he not only endorsed Tyler's offer of annexation but looked beyond, hoping to gain the three best harbors on the Pacific: Puget Sound, San Francisco, and San Diego. That meant wresting Oregon from Britain and California from Mexico.

Claiming that American title to all of Oregon was "clear and unquestionable," Polk convinced Congress to terminate the joint occupation. His blustering, which was intended to put pressure on Great Britain, gained weight by the fact that American settlers in Oregon outnumbered the British 5,000 to 750. However, Polk hardly wanted war with a nation as powerful as Great Britain. So when the British offered, in June 1846, to divide the Oregon Territory along the 49th parallel, he readily agreed (see map, page 000). The arrangement gave the United States Puget Sound, which had been the president's objective all along.

Provoking a War >> The Oregon settlement left Polk free to deal with Mexico. In 1845 Congress admitted Texas to the Union as a slave state, but Mexico had never formally recognized Texas's independence. Mexico insisted, moreover, that Texas's southern boundary was the Nueces River, not the Rio Grande, 130 miles to the south, as claimed by Texas. In reality, Texas had never controlled the disputed region; the Nueces had always been Texas's boundary when it was a Mexican province; and if taken literally, the Rio Grande border incorporated most of New Mexico, including Santa Fe, Albuquerque, Taos, and other major towns. Few Texans had

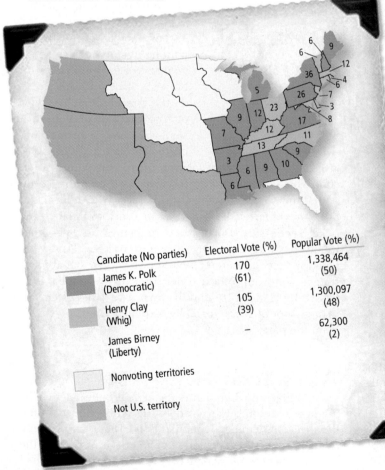

ELECTION OF 1844

Candidate (No parties)	Electoral Vote (%)	Popular Vote (%)
James K. Polk (Democratic)	170 (61)	1,338,464 (50)
Henry Clay (Whig)	105 (39)	1,300,097 (48)
James Birney (Liberty)	—	62,300 (2)
Nonvoting territories		
Not U.S. territory		

ever even been to these places. Indeed, the one time Texas tried to exert authority in the region, New Mexicans had to ride out onto the Plains to save the lost and starving expedition. Nonetheless, Polk was already looking toward the Pacific and he supported the Rio Grande boundary.

As soon as Texas entered the union, Mexico broke off diplomatic relations with the United States, and Polk sent American troops under General Zachary Taylor into the newly acquired state. At the same time, knowing that the unstable Mexican government desperately needed money, he attempted to buy territory to the Pacific. Sending John Slidell of Louisiana to Mexico as his special minister, Polk was prepared to offer up to $32 million in return for clear title to the Rio Grande boundary, the remaining part of New Mexico, and California. But the Mexican public overwhelmingly opposed ceding any more territory to the land-hungry "Yankees," and the government refused to receive the proposal. "Depend upon it," reported Slidell, as he departed from Mexico in March 1846, "we can never get along well with them, until we have given them a good drubbing."

Blocked on the diplomatic front, Polk ordered Taylor, who had already crossed the Nueces with 4,000 troops, to proceed south to the Rio Grande. From the Mexican standpoint, the Americans had invaded their country and occupied their territory. For his part, Polk hoped that, since he could not buy the territory he wanted, that at least Taylor's position on the Rio Grande would provoke the Mexican army into starting a war.

By May 9 Polk and his cabinet had lost patience with the plan and decided to submit a war message to Congress without Mexican provocation. But on that day word arrived that two weeks earlier Mexican forces had crossed the Rio Grande and attacked some of Taylor's troops, killing 11 Americans. The president quickly rewrote his war message, placing the entire blame for the war on Mexico. "Mexico has passed the boundary of the United States, has invaded our territory, and shed American blood upon American soil," he told Congress on May 11. "War exists, and notwithstanding all our efforts to avoid it, exists by the act of Mexico herself." The administration sent a bill to Congress calling for volunteers and requesting money to supply American troops.

Indians and Mexicans >> In battle, Mexican

forces often outnumbered their American enemies. Even so, Mexico suffered from critical disadvantages

---

Hide and Go Seek

Just as native peoples in Eastern North America could tip the balance of power between competing empires in the colonial era, Indians west of the Mississippi continued to exert influence over international events well into the nineteenth century. How can we trace such influence? A few precious sources from the period allow historians to glimpse things from native perspectives. Kiowas, for example, kept pictorial calendars painted on buffalo hides that memorialized two key events each year, one for summer and one for winter. The winter of 1840–1841 was memorialized as "hide-quiver war expedition winter."

What was a "hide quiver"? By the 1840s, young Kiowa warriors preferred quivers made from sleek Mexican leather or panther skin to those made from buffalo hide, which only old men still used. "Hide-quiver war expedition winter" refers to a campaign comprising older men who headed south into Mexico.

Traditionally Kiowas and Comanches left the older men behind to protect women and children and guard their herds of horses and mules. But in the summer of 1840 an historic peace agreement with their traditional Cheyenne and Arapaho enemies provided the Kiowas and Comanches with a newfound sense of security. When winter came, even aged warriors rode off to steal horses and mules from Mexicans. Bearing their dusky, outmoded quivers made of buffalo hide, they accompanied sons and nephews in raids hundreds of miles below the Rio Grande. Attacks such as these increased over the next several years and indirectly helped the United States win its war against Mexico.

---

in the U.S.–Mexican War. Chronic instability in its central government left the nation divided against itself in its moment of crisis. An empty national treasury fueled this instability and made it difficult to mobilize an effective response to the American invasion. Mexico was also at a disadvantage in terms of military technology. While Mexican forces relied on bulky, fixed cannon, the U.S. army employed new light artillery that could be repositioned quickly as battles progressed. Light artillery tipped the balance in several crucial engagements.

Finally, much of Mexico had to fight two wars at once. While Mexico enjoyed formal diplomatic title to most of the present-day American West, Indians still controlled the vast majority of that territory, and Mexico had seen its relations with these Indians collapse in the 15 years before the U.S. invasion. During the late eighteenth century, Comanches, Navajos, Utes, and several different tribes of Apaches had made peace with Spanish authorities, ending decades of destructive war. Spaniards provided Indian leaders with gifts, guaranteed fair trade, and even handed out rations to minimize the animal thefts that could spark conflict.

This expensive and delicate system began to falter once Mexico achieved independence in 1821. Lacking the finances, the political unity, the stability, and the diplomatic resources of Spain, Mexican authorities watched the peace with northern Indians slip away. By the early 1830s, Native men were traveling hundreds of miles to raid Mexican ranches, haciendas, and towns, killing or capturing the people they found there, and stealing or destroying animals and other property. Whenever they were able, Mexicans did the same things to their Indian enemies. American markets helped drive the increasing violence, as Indian or white traders from the United States eagerly purchased horses and mules stolen from Mexico. These traders supplied Indian raiders with arms and ammunition in return. By the eve of the U.S. invasion of Mexico the violence encompassed all or parts of nine Mexican states and had claimed thousands of Mexican and Indian lives.

Thus when American troops invaded northern Mexico they were literally marching in the footsteps of Navajos, Kiowas, Comanches, and Apaches, traversing territory that had already endured more than a decade of war. As Indian peoples pursued their own political, strategic, and economic goals, they made it far easier for the United States to achieve its objectives. Too few northern Mexicans were willing or able to resist the U.S. conquest—impoverished, divided, and exhausted as they were by ongoing Indian raids.

Opposition to the War >>

The war with Mexico posed a dilemma for Whigs. They were convinced (correctly) that Polk had provoked the conflict in order to acquire more territory from Mexico, and many northern Whigs accused the president of seeking to extend slavery. But they remembered, too, that the Federalist Party had doomed itself to extinction by opposing the War of 1812. Throughout the conflict, they strenuously attacked the conduct of "Mr. Polk's War." But they could not bring themselves to cut off funding for it.

Pro-war sentiment was strongest in the Old Southwest and most of the Old Northwest. It was much weaker in the East, where antislavery "Conscience Whigs" were prominent. "If I were a Mexican," Senator Thomas Corwin of Ohio affirmed in the Senate, "I would tell you, . . . 'we will greet you with bloody hands and welcome you to hospitable graves.'" With their party deeply divided over

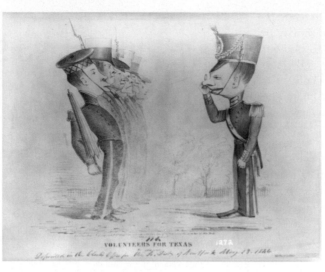

^ The U.S.–Mexican War was a divisive issue even at the outset, when this cartoon was published mocking early recruits. Note that one soldier holds a parasol instead of a rifle and that his prissy commander squints through a monocle.

the issue of the expansion of slavery, Whigs opposed the acquisition of any territory from Mexico.

The Price of Victory >>

Even before any word of hostilities arrived in California, a group of impetuous American settlers around Sacramento launched the "Bear Flag Revolt." In June 1846 they proclaimed California an independent republic. While Mexican Californians under former governor Pio Pico organized a determined resistance, by the following January California was safely in American hands.

Meanwhile, Taylor moved south from the Rio Grande and won several battles. At each town conquered or surrendered he read statements provided in advance by President Polk and the War Department, promising to respect private property and protect the long-suffering residents from Indian attack. Taylor's campaign culminated in a narrow victory over General Antonio López de Santa Anna at Buena Vista in southern Coahuila. Polk had gained the territory he sought to reach the Pacific and wanted an end to the war. But Mexico refused to surrender, so the president ordered an invasion into the heart of the country.

After an American army led by General Winfield Scott captured Mexico City in September 1847, Mexico agreed to terms. The two nations ratified the Treaty of Guadalupe Hidalgo in 1848. The treaty transferred half of Mexico's territory—more than half a million square miles, including Texas —to the United States. In return the United States assumed all the outstanding claims that U.S. citizens had filed against Mexico and gave the Mexicans 15 million dollars.

The war had cost the United States $97 million and 13,000 American lives, mostly as a result of disease. Yet the real cost was even higher. By bringing vast

Was the U.S.–Mexican War justified?

new territories into the Union, the war forced the explosive slavery issue to the center of national politics and threatened to upset the balance of power between North and South. Ralph Waldo Emerson had been prophetic: "The United States will conquer Mexico," he wrote when the war began, "but it will be as the man who swallows the arsenic which brings him down in turn. Mexico will poison us."

The Rise of the Slavery Issue >> When the second party system emerged during the 1820s, Martin Van Buren had championed political parties as one way to forge links between North and South that would strengthen the Union. But the Texas movement increased sectional suspicions, and President Polk did nothing to ease this problem.

Polk was a politician to his bones: constantly maneuvering, promising one thing, doing another, making a pledge, taking it back—using any means to accomplish his ends. Discontent over his double-dealing finally erupted in August 1846, when Polk requested $2 million from Congress, as he vaguely explained, to "facilitate negotiations" with Mexico. It was widely understood that the money was to be used to bribe the Mexican government to cede territory to the United States. On August 8, David Wilmot, an obscure Pennsylvania congressman, startled Democratic leaders by introducing an amendment to the bill that barred slavery from any territory acquired from Mexico. The Wilmot Proviso, as the amendment became known, passed the northern-controlled House of Representatives several times, only to be rejected in the Senate, where the South had more power. As such, it revealed mounting sectional tensions.

Wilmot himself was hardly an abolitionist. Indeed, he hoped to keep not only slaves but all black people out

THE U.S.–MEXICAN WAR

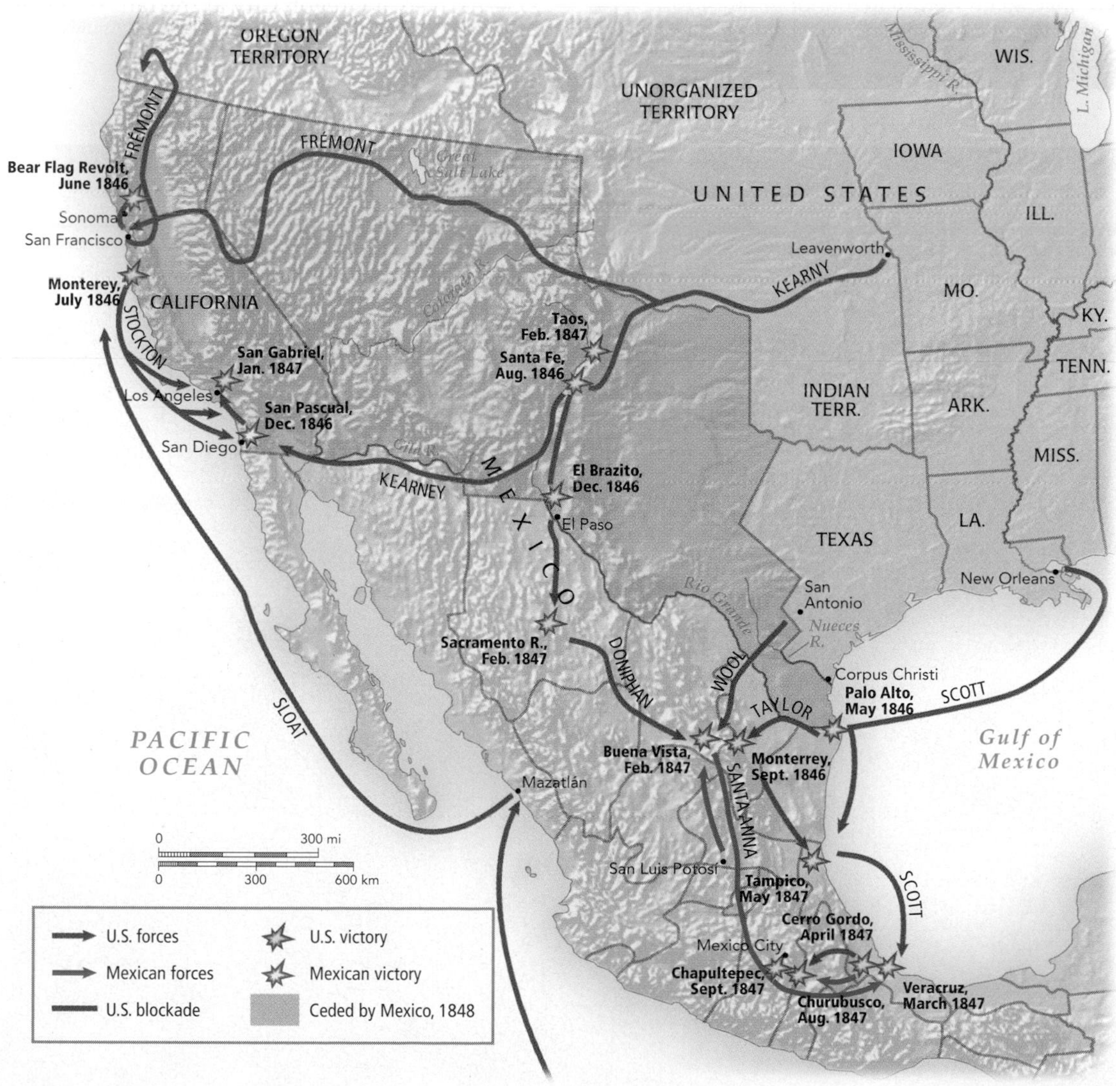

society of the East. With the development of markets and transportation, wealth became concentrated, some families fell to the lower rungs of society, and those who were less successful left, seeking yet another fresh start.

The Gold Rush >>

In January 1848, while constructing a sawmill along the American River, James Marshall noticed gold flecks in the millrace. More discoveries followed, and when the news reached the East, it spread like wildfire. The following spring some 55,000 emigrants jammed the Overland Trail as "forty-niners" on the way to California. Another 25,000 traveled by boat. In only two years, from 1848 to the end of 1849, California's population jumped from 14,000 to 100,000. By 1860 it stood at 380,000.

Among those who joined the rush was William Swain, a 27-year-old farmer in western New York. Bidding goodbye to his wife and daughter in 1849 and set off for the gold fields to make his fortune. On his arrival he entered a partnership and staked a claim along the Feather River, but months of back-breaking work in icy waters led only to the discovery that his claim was "worth nothing." He sold out and joined another company, but early rains soon forced a halt to the work. In October 1850, after less than a year in the diggings, Swain returned home, only a few hundred dollars richer. He counted himself one of the vast

WITNESS
In the Gold Diggings

"We selected a poor spot for a location and staked all on it, and it has proved worth nothing . . . I was in hopes to have sent home a good pile of money before this time, but I am not able to at present . . . I am of the opinion that the gold will soon be gathered from these washings and then will come the hardest part of this gold fever . . . But were I to be unfortunate in all my business here and arrive at last at home without *one cent*, I should ever be glad that I have taken the trip to California."

majority of miners who had seen "their bright daydreams of golden wealth vanish like the dreams of night."

Predictably, mining the miners offered a more reliable road to prosperity. Perhaps half the inhabitants of a mining town were shopkeepers, businesspeople, and professionals who provided services for prospectors. Also conspicuous were gamblers, card sharks, and other outcasts, all bent on separating the miner from his riches.

More than 80 percent of the prospectors who poured into the gold country were Americans, including free blacks. Mexicans, Australians, Argentinians, Hawaiians, Chinese, French, English, and Irish also came. Observers praised the diggings' democratic spirit. Yet such assertions overlooked strongly held nativist prejudices: when frustrated by a lack of success, American miners directed their hostility toward foreigners. The miners ruthlessly exterminated the Indians in the area, sometimes hunting them for sport. Mob violence drove Mexicans out of nearly every camp, and the Chinese were confined to claims abandoned by Americans as unprofitable. The state eventually enacted a foreign miners' tax that fell largely on the Chinese. Free African Americans felt the sting of discrimination as well, both in the camps and in state law. White American miners proclaimed that "colored men were not privileged to work in a country intended only for American citizens."

Only about 5 percent of gold rush emigrants were women or children; given this relative scarcity, men were willing to pay top dollar for women's domestic skills. Women supported themselves by cooking, sewing, and washing, as well as by running hotels and boardinghouses. "A smart woman can do very well in this country," one woman informed a friend in the East. "It is the only country I ever was in where a woman received anything like a just compensation for work." Women went to the mining frontier to be with their husbands, to make money, or to find adventure. But the class most frequently seen in the diggings was prostitutes, who numbered perhaps 20 percent of female Californians in 1850.

Before long, the most easily worked claims had been played out and large corporations moved in heavy equipment to get at hidden ore. Such techniques caused lasting environmental damage. Abandoned prospect holes and diggings pockmarked the gold fields and created piles of debris that heavy rains would wash down the valley, choking streams and ruining lands below. Excavation of hillsides, construction of dams to divert rivers, and the destruction of the forest cover to meet the heavy demand for lumber and firewood caused serious erosion of the soil and spring floods.

In the heyday of the gold Rush mining camps, what percent of miners were Chinese?

a. 2%

b. 5%

c. 10%

d. 20%

Key: d

Instant City: San Francisco >> When the United States assumed control of California, San Francisco had a population of perhaps 200. But thousands of emigrants took the water route west, passing through San Francisco's harbor on their way to the diggings. By 1856 the city's population had jumped to an astonishing 50,000. In a mere 8 years the city had attained the size New York had taken 190 years to reach.

The product of economic self-interest, San Francisco developed in helter-skelter fashion. Residents lived in tents or poorly constructed, half-finished buildings. Land prices soared, speculation was rampant, and commercial forces dominated. To enlarge the commercial district, hills began to be leveled, with the dirt used to fill in the bay (thereby creating more usable land). Since the city government took virtually no role in directing development, almost no land was reserved for public use. Property owners defeated a proposal to widen the streets, prompting the city's leading newspaper to complain, "To sell a few more feet of lots, the streets were compressed like a cheese, into half their width."

The Migration from China >> The gold rush that swelled San Francisco's streets was a global phenomenon. Americans predominated in the mining population, but Latin Americans, Europeans, Australians, and Chinese flocked to California. An amazing assortment of languages could be heard on the city's streets: indeed, in 1860 San Francisco was 50 percent foreign-born.

The most distinctive ethnic group was the Chinese. They had come to Gum San, the land of the golden mountain. Those who arrived in California overwhelmingly hailed from the area of southern China around Canton—and not by accident. Although other provinces also suffered from economic distress, population pressures, social unrest, and political upheaval, Canton had a large European presence, since it was the only port open to outsiders. That situation changed after the first Opium War (1839–1842), when Britain forced China to open other ports to trade. For Cantonese, the sudden loss of their trade monopoly produced widespread economic hardship. At the same time, a series of religious and political revolts in the region led to fighting that devastated the countryside. Many residents concluded that emigration was the only way to survive, and western ships in the harbors of Canton and nearby Hong Kong (a British possession since 1842) made it easier to migrate to California rather than to southeast Asia.

Between 1849 and 1854, some 45,000 Chinese flocked to California. Like other gold seekers, Chinese immigrants were overwhelmingly young and male, and they wanted only to accumulate savings and return home to their families. (Indeed, only 16 Chinese women arrived before 1854.) Generally poor, Chinese immigrants arrived already in debt, having borrowed the price of their steamship ticket; they fell further into debt to Chinese merchants in San Francisco, who loaned them money to purchase needed supplies.

When the Chinese were harassed in the mines, many opened laundries in San Francisco and elsewhere, since little capital was required—soap, scrub board, iron, and ironing board. Other Chinese around San Francisco set up restaurants or worked in the fishing industry. In these early years they found Americans less hostile, as long as they stayed away from the gold fields. As immigration and the competition for jobs increased, however, anti-Chinese sentiment intensified.

Gradually, San Francisco took on the trappings of a more orderly community. The city government established a public school system, erected streetlights, created a municipal water system, and halted further filling in of the bay. Industry was confined to the area south of the city; several new working-class neighborhoods grew up near the downtown section. Fashionable neighborhoods sprouted on several hills, as high rents drove many residents from the developing commercial center, and churches and families became more common. By 1856, the city of the gold rush had been replaced by a new city whose stone and brick buildings gave it a sense of permanence.

The Mormons in Utah >> The makeshift, often chaotic society spawned by the gold rush was a product of largely uncontrolled economic forces. In contrast, the society evolving in the Great Basin of Utah exhibited an entirely different but equally remarkable growth. Salt Lake City became the center of a religious kingdom established by the Church of Jesus Christ of Latter-day Saints.

After Joseph Smith's death in 1844 (page 000), the Mormon Church was led by Brigham Young, who lacked Smith's religious mysticism but was a brilliant organizer. Young decided to move his followers to the Great Basin, an isolated area a thousand miles from the settled parts of the United States. In 1847 the first thousand settlers arrived, the vanguard of thousands more who extended Mormon settlement throughout the valley of the Great Salt Lake and the West. Church officials also held the government positions, and Young had supreme power in legislative, executive, and judicial matters as well as religious affairs. In 1849

the state of Deseret was officially established, with Brigham Young as governor. It applied for admission to the Union.

The most controversial church teaching was the doctrine of polygamy, or plural marriage, which Young sanctioned publicly in 1852. Visitors reported with surprise that few Mormon wives seemed to rebel against the practice. Some plural wives developed close friendships; indeed, in one sample almost a third of plural marriages included at least two sisters. Moreover, because polygamy distinguished Mormonism from other religions, plural wives saw it as an expression of their religious faith. "I want to be assured of *position in God's estimation*," one such wife explained. "If polygamy is the Lord's order, we must carry it out."

The Mormons connected control of water to their sense of mission and respect for hierarchy. The Salt Lake valley, where the Mormons established their holy community, lacked significant rivers or abundant sources of water. Thus success depended on irrigating the region, something never before attempted. When the first Mormons arrived from the East, they began constructing a coordinated series of dams, aqueducts, and ditches, bringing life-giving water to the valleys of the region. Fanning out from their original settlement, they founded colonies throughout the West, all tied to Salt Lake City and joined by ribbons of water. Mormon farmers grew corn, wheat, hay, and an assortment of fruits and vegetables. By 1850, there were more than 16,000 irrigated acres in what would eventually become the state of Utah. The Mormons were the first Anglos to extensively use irrigation in North America.

Manipulation of water reinforced the Mormons' sense of hierarchy and group discipline. Centralized authority in the hands of church officials made possible an overall plan of development, allowed for maximum exploitation of resources, and freed communities from the disputes over water rights that plagued many settlements in the arid West. In a radical departure from American ideals, church leaders insisted that water belonged to the community, not individuals, and vested this authority in the hands of the local bishop. Control of scarce water resources reinforced the power of the church hierarchy over not just the faithful but dissidents as well. Community needs, as interpreted by church leaders, took precedence over individual rights. Thus irrigation did more than make the desert bloom. By checking the Jeffersonian ideal of an independent, self-sufficient farmer, it also made possible a centralized, well-regulated society under the firm control of the church.

Shadows on the Moving Frontier >>
Transformations such as Salt Lake City and San Francisco were truly remarkable. But Americans were not coming into a trackless, unsettled wilderness. As frontier lines crossed, 75,000 Mexicans had to adapt to American rule.

The Treaty of Guadalupe Hidalgo guaranteed Mexicans in the ceded territory "the free enjoyment of their liberty and property." As long as Mexicans continued to be a sizable majority in a given area, their local influence usually remained strong. But wherever Anglos became more numerous, they demanded conformity to American customs. When Mexican Americans remained faithful to their heritage, language, and religion, these cultural differences worked to reinforce Hispanic powerlessness, social isolation, and economic exploitation.

New Mexico had the largest Hispanic population as well as the fewest Anglos in the Mexican cession. As a result, upper-class Mexican Americans maintained their position as ranchers employing large numbers of mixed-blood workers. These ranchers had cultivated American allies during the Santa Fe trade, and their connections grew stronger as American businesspeople entered the territory in the 1850s. Neither group had many qualms about exploiting poorer Hispanics.

In California, the rush of American emigrants quickly overwhelmed Hispanic settlers. Even in 1848, before the discovery of gold, Americans in California outnumbered Mexicans two to one, and by 1860 Hispanics amounted to only 2 percent of the population. At the time of the American conquest, the 200 or so *ranchero* families owned about 14 million acres, but U.S. law required verification of their original land grants by a federal commission. Since the average claim took 17 years to complete and imposed complex procedures and hefty legal fees, many *rancheros* lost large tracts of land to Americans.

Less affluent Mexicans scratched out a bare existence on ranches and farms or in the growing cities and towns. As the Hispanic population in California became primarily urban, women took a larger role in the family. Many men became seasonal workers who were absent part of the year, and thus women became more involved in sustaining the family economically.

Mexican Americans in Texas were also greatly outnumbered: they totaled only 6 percent of the population in 1860. Stigmatized by whites as racial inferiors, they were the poorest group in free society. One response to this dislocation, an option commonly taken by persecuted minorities, was social banditry. An example was the folk hero Juan Cortina. A member of a displaced landed family in southern Texas, Cortina was driven into resistance in the 1850s by American harassment. He began stealing from wealthy Anglos to aid poor Mexican Americans, proclaiming, "To me is entrusted the breaking of the chains of your slavery." Cortina continued to raid Texas border settlements until finally fleeing to Mexico. Cortina and his men demonstrated the depth of frustration and resentment among Hispanics over their abuse at the hands of the new Anglo majority.

ESCAPE FROM CRISIS

With the return of peace, Congress confronted the problem of whether to allow slavery in the newly acquired territories. David Wilmot, in his controversial proviso, had already proposed outlawing slavery throughout the Mexican cession. John C. Calhoun, representing the extreme southern position, countered that slavery was legal in all territories. The federal government had acted as the agent of all the states in acquiring the land, Calhoun argued, and southerners had a right to take their property there, including slaves. Only when the residents of a territory drafted a state constitution could they decide the question of slavery.

Between these extremes were two moderate positions. One proposed extending the Missouri Compromise line of 36°30' to the Pacific, which would have continued the earlier policy of dividing the national domain between the North and the South. The other proposal, championed by Senator Lewis Cass of Michigan and Senator Stephen A. Douglas of Illinois, was to allow the people of the territory rather than Congress to decide the status of slavery. This solution, which became known as **popular sovereignty**, was deliberately ambiguous, since its supporters refused to specify whether the residents could make this decision at any time or only when drafting a state constitution, as Calhoun insisted.

> **popular sovereignty** doctrine, devised by Senator Stephen A. Douglas of Illinois, that a territory could decide by vote whether or not to permit slavery within its boundaries.

When Congress organized the Oregon Territory in 1848, it prohibited slavery there, since even southerners

^ JOHN C. CALHOUN South Carolina's senator insisted that slavery was legal in all territories.

admitted that the region was too far north to grow the South's staple crops. But this seemingly straightforward decision made it impossible to apply the Missouri Compromise line to the other territories. Without Oregon as a part of the package, the bulk of the remaining land would be open to slavery, something at which the North balked. Almost inadvertently, one of the two moderate solutions had been discarded by the summer of 1848.

A Two-Faced Campaign >> In the election of 1848 both major parties tried to avoid the slavery issue. The Democrats nominated Lewis Cass, a supporter of popular sovereignty, while the Whigs bypassed all their prominent leaders and selected General Zachary Taylor, who had taken no position on any public issue and who remained silent throughout the campaign. The Whigs adopted no platform and planned instead to emphasize the general's war record.

But the slavery issue would not go away. A new antislavery coalition, the **Free Soil party**, brought together

Free Soil Party antislavery party formed in 1848 by northern Democrats disillusioned with southern Democratic support for slavery.

} northern Democrats who had rallied to the Wilmot Proviso, Conscience Whigs who disavowed Taylor's nomination because he was a slaveholder, and political abolitionists in the Liberty party. To gain more votes, the Free Soil platform focused on the dangers of extending slavery rather than on the evil of slavery itself. Ironically, the party nominated Martin Van Buren—the man who for years had struggled to keep the slavery issue out of national politics.

Both the Whigs and the Democrats ran different campaigns in the North and the South. To southern audiences, each party promised it would protect slavery in the territories; to northern voters, each claimed it would keep the territories free. In this two-faced, sectional campaign, the Whigs won their second national victory. Taylor held on to the core of Whig voters in both sections. But in the South, where the contest pitted a southern slaveholder against two northerners, Taylor won many more votes than Clay had in 1844. As one southern Democrat complained, "We have lost hundreds of votes, solely on the ground that General Cass was a Northerner and General Taylor a Southern man." Furthermore, Van Buren polled five times as many votes as the Liberty party had four years earlier. Increasingly the two national political parties were being pulled apart along sectional lines.

The Compromise of 1850 >> Once he became president, Taylor could no longer remain silent. The territories gained from Mexico had to be organized; furthermore, by 1849 California had gained enough residents to be admitted as a state. In the Senate the balance of power between North and South stood at 15 states each. California's admission would break the sectional balance.

Called "Old Rough and Ready" by his troops, Taylor was a forthright man of action, but he was politically inexperienced and oversimplified complex problems. Since even Calhoun admitted that entering states had the right to ban slavery, Taylor proposed that the way to end the sectional crisis was to skip the territorial stage by splitting the entire Mexican cession into two huge states, New Mexico and California. Even more shocking to southern Whigs, he proposed to apply the Wilmot Proviso to the entire area, since he was convinced that slavery would never flourish there. When Congress convened in December 1849, Taylor recommended that California and New Mexico be admitted as free states. The president's plan touched off the most serious sectional crisis the Union had yet confronted.

Into this turmoil stepped Henry Clay, now 73 years old and nearing the end of his career. A savvy card player all his life, Clay loved the bargaining, the wheeling and dealing, the late-night trade-offs eased along by a bottle of bourbon that were part of politics. Clay decided that a grand compromise was needed to end all disputes between the North and South and save the Union. Already, Mississippi had summoned a southern convention to meet at Nashville to discuss the crisis, and extremists were pushing for secession.

Clay's compromise, submitted in January 1850, addressed all the major controversies between the two sections. California, he proposed, should be admitted as a free state, which represented the clear wishes of most settlers there. The rest of the Mexican cession would be organized as two territories, New Mexico and Utah, under the doctrine of popular sovereignty. Thus slavery would not be prohibited in these regions. Clay also proposed that Congress abolish the slave trade but not slavery itself in the District of Columbia and that a new, more rigorous fugitive slave law be passed to enable southerners to reclaim runaway slaves. To reinforce the idea that both North and South were yielding ground, Clay combined those provisions that dealt with the Mexican cession (and several others adjusting the Texas–New Mexico border) into a larger package known as the Omnibus Bill.

With the stakes so high, the Senate debated the bill for six months. Clay, wracked by a hacking cough, spent long hours trying to line up the needed votes. But for once, the great card player had misplayed his hand. The Omnibus Bill required that the components of the compromise be approved as a package. Extremists in Congress from both regions, however, combined against the moderates and rejected the bill.

With Clay exhausted and his strategy in shambles, Democrat Stephen A. Douglas assumed leadership of the pro-compromise forces. The sudden death in July of President Taylor, who had threatened to veto Clay's plan, aided the compromise movement. One by one, Douglas submitted

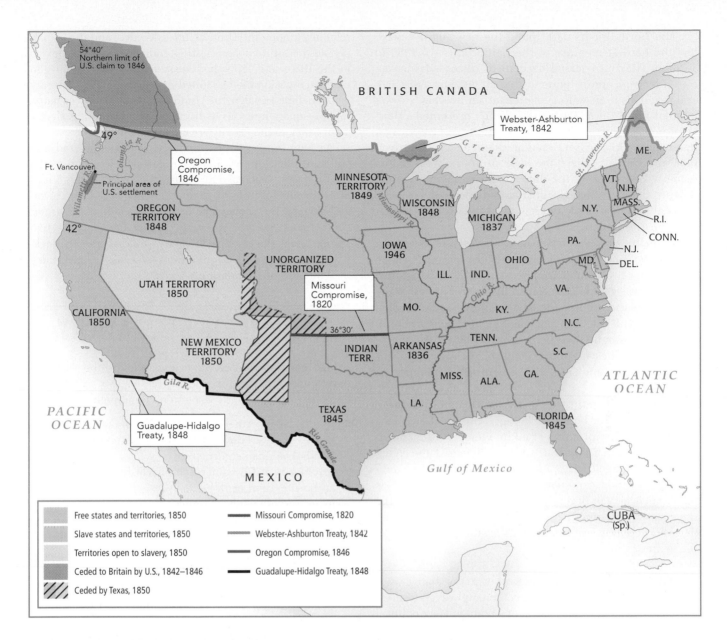

The map legend reads:

- Free states and territories, 1850
- Slave states and territories, 1850
- Territories open to slavery, 1850
- Ceded to Britain by U.S., 1842–1846
- Ceded by Texas, 1850
- Missouri Compromise, 1820
- Webster-Ashburton Treaty, 1842
- Oregon Compromise, 1846
- Guadalupe-Hidalgo Treaty, 1848

Map labels: 54°40' Northern limit of U.S. claim to 1846; 49°; Ft. Vancouver; Principal area of U.S. settlement; Columbia R.; Willamette R.; 42°; OREGON TERRITORY 1848; Oregon Compromise, 1846; BRITISH CANADA; Great Lakes; St. Lawrence R.; Webster-Ashburton Treaty, 1842; ME.; VT.; N.H.; MASS.; R.I.; CONN.; N.Y.; PA.; N.J.; MD.; DEL.; MINNESOTA TERRITORY 1849; WISCONSIN 1848; MICHIGAN 1837; IOWA 1946; Mississippi R.; OHIO; Ohio R.; VA.; UTAH TERRITORY 1850; UNORGANIZED TERRITORY; Missouri Compromise, 1820; ILL.; IND.; CALIFORNIA 1850; MO.; KY.; 36°30'; N.C.; NEW MEXICO TERRITORY 1850; INDIAN TERR.; ARKANSAS 1836; TENN.; S.C.; Gila R.; MISS.; ALA.; GA.; ATLANTIC OCEAN; PACIFIC OCEAN; Guadalupe-Hidalgo Treaty, 1848; I.A.; TEXAS 1845; Rio Grande; FLORIDA 1845; MEXICO; Gulf of Mexico; CUBA (Sp.)

TERRITORIAL GROWTH AND THE COMPROMISE OF 1850

the individual measures for a vote. Northern representatives provided the necessary votes to admit California and abolish the slave trade in the District of Columbia, while southern representatives supplied the edge needed to organize the Utah and New Mexico territories and pass the new fugitive slave law. On the face of it, everyone had compromised. But in truth, only 61 members of Congress, a mere 21 percent of the membership, had not voted against some part of the Compromise.

By September 17 all the separate parts of the Compromise of 1850 had passed and been signed into law by the new president, Millard Fillmore. The Union, it seemed, was safe.

Away from the Brink >> The general public, both North and South, rallied to the Compromise. At the convention of southern states in Nashville, the fire-eaters—the radical proponents of states' rights and secession—found themselves voted down by more moderate voices. Even in the Deep South, coalitions of pro-Compromise Whigs and Democrats soundly defeated secessionists in the state elections that followed. Still, most southerners felt that a firm line had been drawn. With California's admission, they were now outnumbered in the Senate, so it was critical that slaveholders be granted equal legal access to the territories. They announced that any breach of the Compromise of 1850 would justify secession.

The North, for its part, found the new fugitive slave law the hardest measure of the Compromise of 1850 to swallow. The controversial law denied an accused runaway a trial by jury, and it required that all citizens assist federal marshals in its enforcement. Harriet Beecher Stowe's popular novel *Uncle Tom's Cabin* (1852) presented a powerful moral indictment of the law—and of slavery as an institution. Despite sentimental characters, a contrived plot, and clumsy dialect, the book profoundly moved its readers. Emphasizing the duty of Christians toward the downtrodden, it reached a greater audience than any previous abolitionist work and heightened moral opposition to the institution.

In reality, however, fewer than 1,000 slaves a year ran away to the North, many of whom did not succeed. Despite some cases of well-publicized resistance, the 1850 fugitive slave law was generally enforced in the free states. Many northerners did not like the law, but they were unwilling to tamper with the Compromise. Stephen Douglas spoke accurately enough when he boasted in 1851, "The whole country is acquiescing in the compromise measures—everywhere, North and South. Nobody proposes to repeal or disturb them."

And so calm returned. In the lackluster 1852 presidential campaign, both the Whigs and the Democrats endorsed the Compromise. Franklin Pierce, a little-known New Hampshire Democrat, soundly defeated the Whig candidate, Winfield Scott. Even more significant, the antislavery Free Soil candidate received only about half as many votes as Van Buren had four years before. With the slavery issue seemingly losing political force, it appeared that the Republic had weathered the storm unleashed by the Wilmot Proviso.

But the moving frontier had worked many changes during the 1830s and 1840s; and many more upheavals awaited the decade ahead. From a continental point of view, political relations among the United States, Mexico, and the Indian peoples had shifted significantly. Indian attacks on Mexico in the 1820s and 1830s had weakened Mexico's ability to repel an invasion by the United States. And with the treaty of Guadelupe Hidalgo, the United States gained over half a million square miles, as its frontier leaped from the Mississippi valley to the Pacific Ocean.

In between remained territory still unorganized and still controlled by formidable Indian peoples. And as the North became increasingly industrialized and the South more firmly committed to an economy based on cotton and slavery, the movement of Americans into those territories soon revived growing conflict between the two sections over slavery. The disputes would shatter the Jacksonian party system, reignite the slavery issue, and shake the Union to its foundation.

CHAPTER SUMMARY

In the 1840s the United States expanded to the Pacific, a development that required an aggressive war and that led to the rise of the slavery issue in national politics.

- In the 1840s Americans proclaimed that it was the United States' Manifest Destiny to expand across the North American continent.
- Americans in Texas increasingly clashed with Mexican authorities, and in 1835–36 Texans revolted and established an independent republic.
- Americans headed for Oregon and California on the Overland Trail.
  - The journey put special pressures on women as the traditional division of labor by gender broke down.
  - White migration also put pressure on Plains Indians' grazing lands, wood supplies, and freedom of movement.

Significant Events

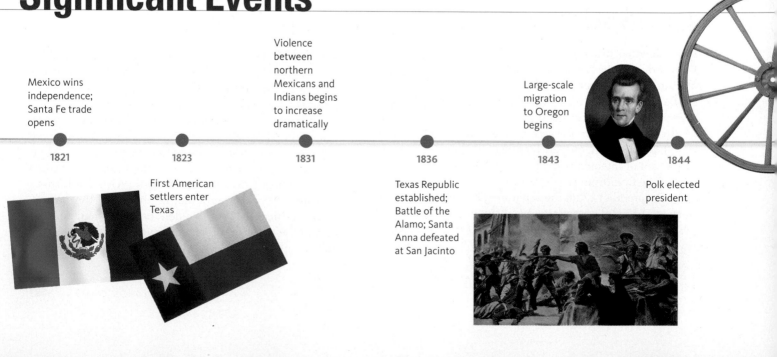

Mexico wins independence; Santa Fe trade opens

1821

First American settlers enter Texas

1823

Violence between northern Mexicans and Indians begins to increase dramatically

1831

1836

Texas Republic established; Battle of the Alamo; Santa Anna defeated at San Jacinto

Large-scale migration to Oregon begins

1843

1844

Polk elected president

- The gold rush spawned a unique society that was overwhelmingly male, highly mobile, and strongly nativist and racist.
  - Led by Brigham Young, the Mormons established a tightly organized, centrally controlled society in the Great Salt Lake basin.
  - Throughout the Southwest the Hispanic population suffered at the hands of the new Anglo majority, as did the Chinese immigrants who flocked to California.
- President James K. Polk entered office with a vision of the United States as a continental nation.
  - He upheld President John Tyler's annexation of Texas and agreed to divide the Oregon country with Britain.
  - Polk instigated a war with Mexico in order to obtain that country's northern territories.
  - Divided, impoverished, and distracted by ongoing wars with Indians, Mexico was forced to surrender more than half a million square miles of territory in the aftermath of the war.
- The U.S.–Mexican War reinjected the slavery issue into American national politics.
  - The Wilmot Proviso sought to prohibit slavery from any territory acquired from Mexico.
  - The struggle over the Proviso eventually disrupted both major parties.
  - Congress momentarily stilled the sectional crisis with the Compromise of 1850.

Additional Reading

For the Sioux, see the enduring article by Richard White, "The Winning of the West: The Expansion of the Western Sioux in the Eighteenth and Nineteenth Centuries," *Journal of American History* (1978), 319–343. David J. Weber, *The Mexican Frontier, 1821–1846* (1982), is a superb study of the Southwest prior to American control. For a more recent account, with a transnational interpretation of the Texas Rebellion, see Andrés Reséndez, *Changing National Identities at the Frontier* (2005). For conflicts between Mexicans and Indians before and during the U.S.–Mexican War, see Brian DeLay, *War of a Thousand Deserts* (2008). For the Overland Trail, see John Mack Faragher, *Women and Men on the Overland Trail* (1979). Leonard J. Arrington and Davis Bitton, *The Mormon Experience* (2nd ed., 1992), is a good survey. Susan Lee Johnson's *Roaring Camp* (2001) explores social interaction during the gold rush. Robert V. Hine and John Mack Faragher, *The American West* (2001), is an excellent synthesis of the region's history.

For two magisterial interpretations of American history in this period, see Sean Wilentz's *The Rise of American Democracy* (2005), and Daniel Walker Howe's *What Hath God Wrought* (2007). Thomas R. Hietala offers a stimulating analysis of the social roots of expansionism in *Manifest Design* (1985). The drive to annex Texas is carefully untangled in William W. Freehling, *The Road to Disunion* (1990). The best discussions of Polk's handling of the Oregon and Texas issues remain Charles G. Sellers Jr., *James K. Polk, Continentalist, 1843–1846* (1966), and David M. Pletcher, *The Diplomacy of Annexation* (1973). Michael F. Holt presents a powerful analysis of the Whig party's difficulties in this decade in *The Rise and Fall of the American Whig Party* (1999). Howard Lamar's classic account *The Far Southwest* (1966) explores political and economic power in the territories after conquest. For more recent work on the region's postwar history, see Samuel Truett and Elliott Young, *Continental Crossroads* (2004). Holman Hamilton, *Prologue to Conflict* (new ed., 2005), is an excellent study of the Compromise of 1850.

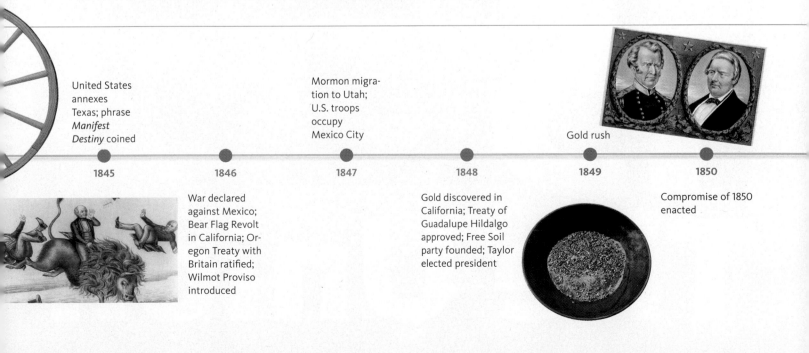

1845 — United States annexes Texas; phrase *Manifest Destiny* coined

1846 — War declared against Mexico; Bear Flag Revolt in California; Oregon Treaty with Britain ratified; Wilmot Proviso introduced

1847 — Mormon migration to Utah; U.S. troops occupy Mexico City

1848 — Gold discovered in California; Treaty of Guadalupe Hildalgo approved; Free Soil party founded; Taylor elected president

1849 — Gold rush

1850 — Compromise of 1850 enacted

During the 1850s Kansas became a battleground over whether slavery would expand into the new territories. Artist John Steuart Curry's mural *Tragic Prelude* places abolitionist John Brown at the center of the conflicts that led to civil war. What elements of the painting make the struggle seem mythic, almost Biblical, in this mural done about 80 years after the event?

15
The Union

WHAT'S TO COME

290 **SECTIONAL CHANGES IN AMERICAN SOCIETY**

295 **THE POLITICAL REALIGNMENT OF THE 1850s**

298 **THE WORSENING CRISIS**

301 **THE ROAD TO WAR**

THE SACKING OF A KANSAS TOWN

Into town they rode, several hundred strong, unshaven, rough-talking, and "armed . . . to the teeth with rifles and revolvers, cutlasses and bowie-knives." At the head of the procession flapped an American flag, alongside another featuring a crouching tiger emblazoned on black and white stripes, followed by banners proclaiming "Southern Rights" and "The Superiority of the White Race." At the rear rolled five artillery pieces. Watching intently from his office window, Josiah Miller, the editor of the Lawrence *Kansas Free State*, predicted, "Well, boys, we're in for it." >>

Broken 1850–1861

For residents of Lawrence, Kansas, the worst seemed at hand. The town had been founded by the New England Emigrant Aid Company, a Yankee association that recruited settlers in an effort to keep Kansas Territory from becoming a slave state. Accepting Senator Stephen Douglas's idea that the people should decide the status of slavery, the town's residents intended to see to it that under popular sovereignty Kansas entered the Union as a free state. Emigrants from the neighboring slave state of Missouri were equally determined that no "abolition tyrants" would control the territory. There had been conflict in Kansas almost immediately: land disputes, horse thievery, shootings on both sides.

In the ensuing turmoil, the federal government seemed to back the proslavery forces. A U.S. district court indicted several of Lawrence's leading citizens for treason, and federal marshal Israel Donaldson called for a posse to help make the arrests. Donaldson's posse, swelled by eager volunteers from across the Missouri border, arrived outside Lawrence on the night of May 20, 1856.

Meanwhile, Lawrence's "committee of safety" had agreed on a policy of non-resistance. Donaldson arrested two men without incident and, finding no one else on his list, dismissed his posse. But Sheriff Samuel Jones, who on his previous visit to Lawrence had been shot, had a score to settle. The irate sheriff took over the band and led the cheering, thoroughly liquored "army" into town at three o'clock in the afternoon. Ignoring the pleas of some leaders, the mob smashed the presses of two newspapers, the *Herald of Freedom* and the *Kansas Free State*. Then the horde unsuccessfully tried to blow up the now-deserted Free State Hotel, which more closely resembled a fort, before finally putting it to the torch. When the mob rode off, it left the residents of Lawrence unharmed but thoroughly terrified.

Retaliation by free state partisans was not long in coming. Hurrying north toward Lawrence, an older man with a grim visage and steely eyes heard the news that the town had been attacked. "Old Man Brown," as everyone called him, was on his way to provide reinforcements. A severe, God-fearing Calvinist, John Brown was also a staunch abolitionist who had once remarked that he believed "God had raised him up on purpose to break the jaws of the wicked." Brooding over the failure of the free-staters to resist the "slave hounds" from Missouri, Brown decided not to push on to Lawrence; instead, he ordered his followers to sharpen their heavy cutlasses. "Caution," he announced, "is nothing but the word of Cowardice."

Three days after the Lawrence raid, Brown headed under cover of dark toward Pottawatomie Creek with a half dozen others, including four of his sons. Announcing that they were "the Northern Army" come to serve justice, they burst into the cabin of James Doyle, a proslavery man from Tennessee. As Brown marched Doyle and his three sons off, Doyle's terrified wife, Mahala, begged him to spare her youngest, and the old man relented. The others were led a hundred yards down the road and hacked to death with broadswords by Owen and Salmon Brown. Old Man Brown then walked up to James Doyle's body and put a bullet through his forehead. Before the night was done, two more cabins had been visited and two more proslavery settlers brutally executed. Not one of the five murdered men owned a single slave or had any connection with the raid on Lawrence.

Brown's action precipitated a new wave of fighting in Kansas, and the news of the tumult further angered residents in both sections of the nation. "Everybody here feels as if we are upon a volcano," remarked one member of Congress in Washington.

The country was indeed atop a smoldering volcano that would finally erupt in the spring of 1861, showering death and destruction across the land. Popular sovereignty, the last remaining moderate solution to the controversy over the expansion of slavery, had failed dismally in Kansas. The violence and disorder in the territory provided a stark reply to Stephen Douglas's proposition: what could be more peaceable, more fair, than the notion of popular sovereignty? **«**

^ "Nobody believes this Republican movement can prove the basis of a permanent party," commented one American in the mid-1850s. But the violence in the Kansas territory over the expansion of slavery dramatically fueled the growth of the new Republican party. By 1860 it was organizing huge marches like this torchlight parade supporting Abraham Lincoln for president.

SECTIONAL CHANGES IN AMERICAN SOCIETY

The road to war was not straight or short. Six years elapsed between the Compromise of 1850 and the crisis in "Bleeding Kansas." Another four would pass before the first shot was fired. And the process of separation involved more than popular fears, ineffective politicians, and an unwillingness to compromise. As we have seen, Americans were bound together by a growing transportation network, by national markets, and by a national political system. Increasingly, however, the changes occurring in American society heightened sectional tensions. As the North continued to industrialize, its society came into conflict with that of the South. The coming of civil war, in other words, involved social and economic changes as well as political ones.

The Growth of a Railroad Economy >>

By the time the Compromise of 1850 produced a lull in the tensions between North and South, the American economy had left behind the depression of the early 1840s and was booming again. Its basic structure, however, was changing. Cotton remained the nation's major export, but it was no longer the driving force for American economic growth. After 1839 this role was taken over by the construction of a vast railroad network covering the eastern half of the continent. By 1850 the United States possessed more than 9,000 miles of track; 10 years later it had over 30,000 miles, more than the rest of the world combined. Much of the new construction during the 1850s occurred west of the Appalachian Mountains—over 2,000 miles in Ohio and Illinois alone.

Because western railroads ran through less settled areas, they depended especially on public aid. State and local governments made loans to rail companies and sometimes exempted them temporarily from taxes. Federal land grants were crucial, too. By mortgaging or selling the land to farmers, the railroad raised construction capital and also stimulated settlement, which increased its business and

profits. By 1860 Congress had allotted about 28 million acres of federal land to 40 different companies.

The effect of the new lines rippled through the economy. Nearby farmers began to specialize in cash crops and market them in distant locations. With the profits they purchased manufactured goods. Before the railroad reached Athens, Tennessee, the surrounding counties produced about 25,000 bushels of wheat, selling at less than 50 cents a bushel. Once the railroad came, farmers near Athens grew 400,000 bushels and sold their crop at a dollar a bushel. Railroads also stimulated the mining and iron industries, which provided the bar and sheet iron needed for tracks, engines and other equipment.

The new rail networks shifted the direction of western trade. In 1840 most northwestern grain was shipped down the Mississippi River to the bustling port of New Orleans. But low water made steamboat travel risky in summer, and ice shut down traffic in winter. Products such as lard, tallow, and cheese quickly spoiled if stored in New Orleans' sweltering warehouses.

With the new rail lines, traffic from the Midwest increasingly flowed west to east. Chicago became the region's hub, connecting the farms of the upper Midwest to New York and other eastern cities. The South's overall share of western trade dropped dramatically. The old political alliance between South and West, based on shared economic interests, was weakened by the new patterns of commerce.

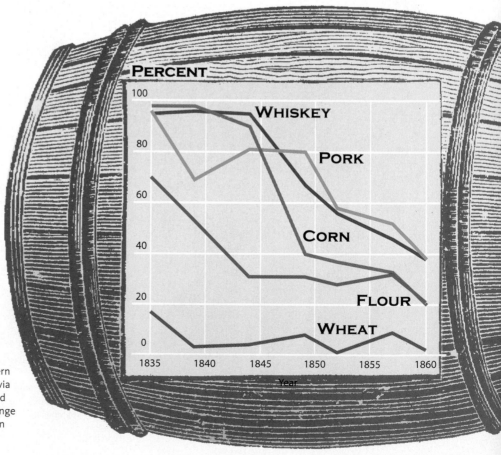

>> PROPORTION OF WESTERN EXPORTS SHIPPED VIA NEW ORLEANS 1835–1860 In 1835 nearly 100 percent of western exports of corn, pork, and whiskey were being shipped via New Orleans. By 1860 only about 40 percent of pork and whiskey and 20 percent of flour and corn were. The change in shipping patterns weakened the political ties between the South and the Old Northwest.

The growing rail network was not the only factor that led farmers in the Northeast and Midwest to become more commercially oriented. Another was the sharp rise in international demand for grain. Farmers responded by specializing in cash crops such as wheat and corn, and investing in equipment to increase productivity. "The power of cotton over the financial affairs of the Union has in the last few years rapidly diminished," the *Democratic Review* remarked in 1849, "and bread stuffs will now become the governing power."

The spreading network of railroads made the split between North and South worse by

a. making it easier for the North to attack the South.

b. reorienting the western trade from the South to the East.

c. allowing abolitionist pamphlets to be shipped to the slave states in large numbers.

d. encouraging white factory workers to move west and take jobs that would have gone to slaves.

Key: b

Western farmers altered the landscape by reducing the annual fires, often set by Indians, that had kept the prairie free from trees. In the fires' absence, trees reappeared on land not in cultivation and, if undisturbed, eventually formed wood lots. The earlier unbroken landscape gave way to independent farms, each fenced in the precise checkerboard pattern established by the Northwest Ordinance. It was an artificial ecosystem of animals, wood lots, and crops whose large, uniform layout made western farms more efficient than the more irregular farms in the East.

Railroads and the Prairie Environment >>

As railroad lines fanned out from Chicago, farmers began to acquire open prairie land in Illinois and then Iowa, putting its deep black soil into production. Commercial agriculture transformed this remarkable treeless environment.

To settlers accustomed to woodlands, the thousands of square miles of grass taller than a person were an awesome sight. In 1838 Edmund Flagg gazed on "the tall grasstops waving in . . . billowy beauty in the breeze; the narrow pathway winding off like a serpent over the rolling surface, disappearing and reappearing till lost in the luxuriant herbage." Tallgrass prairies had their perils too: year-round, storms sent travelers searching for the shelter of trees along river valleys, and stinging insects were thick in the summer.

Normal plows could not penetrate the densely tangled roots of prairie grass, until John Deere invented a sharp-cutting steel plow in 1837 that sliced through the sod without soil sticking to the blade. In addition, Cyrus McCormick refined a mechanical reaper that harvested 14 times more wheat with the same amount of labor. By the 1850s McCormick was selling 1,000 reapers a year and could not keep up with demand, while Deere turned out 10,000 plows annually.

The new commercial farming transformed the landscape and the environment. Indians had grown corn in the region for years, but never in fields as large as those of white farmers, whose surpluses were shipped east. Prairie farmers also introduced new crops that were not part of the earlier ecological system, notably wheat, along with fruits and vegetables. Native grasses were replaced by a small number of plants cultivated as commodities. Domesticated grasses replaced native grasses in pastures for making hay.

Railroads and the Urban Environment >>

Railroads transformed the urban environment as well. Communities soon recognized that their economic survival depended on creating rail links to the countryside and to major urban markets. Large cities feared they would be left behind in the struggle to be the dominant city in the region, and smaller communities saw their very survival at stake in the battle for rail connections.

Communities that obtained rail links found the new technology difficult to adjust to. Merchants in Jacksonville, Illinois, complained about the noise, dirt, and billowing smoke produced by the new locomotives passing through their business district. "The public square was filled with teams [of horses]," one resident recalled, "and whenever the engine steamed into the square making all the noise possible, there was such a stampede." After a few years, the tracks were relocated to the outskirts of town. Increasingly communities kept railroads away from fashionable neighborhoods and shopping areas. As the tracks became a physical marker of social and economic divisions in the town, the notion of living "on the wrong side of the tracks" became a way of defining the urban landscape.

Rising Industrialization >>

The expansion of commercial agriculture, along with the shift from water power to steam, spurred the growth of industry. Out of the 10 leading American industries, 8 processed raw materials produced by agriculture, including flour milling and the manufacture of textiles, shoes, and woolens. (The only exceptions were iron and machinery.)

Most important, the factory system of organizing labor and the technology of interchangeable parts spread to other areas of the economy during the 1850s. Isaac

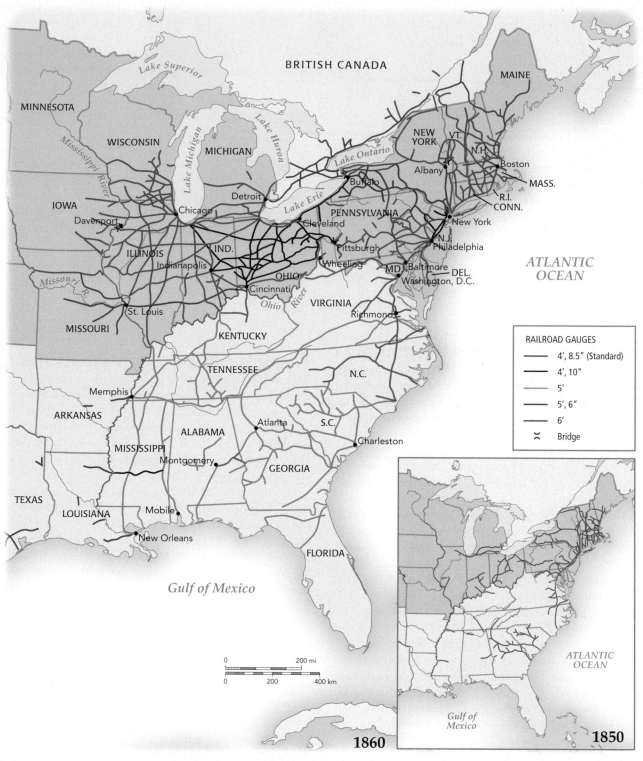

Railroad Gauges legend:
- 4', 8.5" (Standard)
- 4', 10"
- 5'
- 5', 6"
- 6'
- Bridge

1860

1850

GROWTH OF THE RAILROAD NETWORK, 1850–1860

Although a good deal of track mileage was laid during the 1850s, total track mileage is misleading because the United States lacked a fully integrated rail network in 1860. A few trunk-line roads had combined a number of smaller lines into a single system to make shipment of goods easier. The Pennsylvania Railroad, for example, linked Philadelphia and Pittsburgh. But the existence of five major track gauges (or widths) meant that passengers and freight often had to be transferred from one line to the next. And north-south traffic was further disrupted by the lack of bridges over the Ohio River.

^ "Conditions of famine across Ireland led many to buy passage on ships like this one, departing for the United States. New York was the major port of entry for immigrants who surged into the United States during the 1840s and 1850s.

Singer began using interchangeable parts in 1851 to mass-produce sewing machines, which made possible the ready-made clothing industry, while workers who assembled farm implements performed a single step in the process over and over again. By 1860 the United States had nearly a billion dollars invested in manufacturing, almost twice as much as in 1849. And for the first time, less than half the workers in the North were employed in agriculture.

Immigration >> The surge of industry depended on a large factory labor force. Natural increase helped swell the nation's population to more than 30 million by 1860, but only in part, since the birthrate had begun to decline. It was the beginning of mass immigration to America during the mid-1840s that kept population growth soaring.

In the 20 years from 1820 to 1840, about 700,000 newcomers had entered the United States. That figure jumped to 1.7 million in the 1840s, then to 2.6 million in the 1850s. Though even greater numbers arrived after the Civil War, as a percentage of the nation's total population, the wave from 1845 to 1854 was the largest influx of immigrants in American history. The great majority of newcomers were in the prime of life, between 10 and 40 years old. Certainly the booming economy and the lure of freedom drew immigrants, but they were also pushed by deteriorating

conditions in Europe. In Ireland, a potato blight, which first struck in 1845, led to widespread famine. Out of a population of 9 million, as many as a million people perished, while a million and a half more emigrated, two-thirds to the United States.

The Irish tended to be poorer than other immigrant groups of the day. Although the Protestant Scots-Irish continued to emigrate, as so many had during the eighteenth century, the decided majority of the Irish who came after 1845 were Catholic. Because they were poor and unskilled, the Irish congregated in the cities, where the women performed domestic service and took factory jobs and the men did manual labor.

Germans and Scandinavians also had economic reasons for leaving Europe. They included small farmers whose lands had become marginal or who had been displaced by landlords, and skilled workers thrown out of work by industrialization. Some fled political and social oppression and came to live under the free institutions of the United States. Since arriving in America, wrote a Swede who settled in Iowa in 1850, "I have not been compelled to pay a penny for the privilege of living. Neither is my cap worn out from lifting it in the presence of gentlemen."

Unprecedented unrest and upheaval prevailed in Europe in 1848, the so-called year of revolutions. The

Although many Germans and Scandinavians arrived in modest straits, few were truly impoverished, and many could afford to buy a farm or start a business. Unlike the Irish, Germans tended to emigrate as families, and wherever they settled, they formed social, religious, and cultural organizations to maintain their language and customs. Whereas the Scandinavians, Dutch, and English immigrants were Protestant, half or more of the Germans were Catholic.

Factories came more and more to depend on immigrant labor, including children, since newcomers would work for lower wages and were less likely to protest harsh working conditions. The shift to an immigrant workforce could be seen most clearly in the textile industry, where by 1860 over half the workers in New England mills were foreign-born.

The sizable foreign-born population in many American cities severely strained urban resources. Immigrants who could barely make ends meet were forced to live in overcrowded, unheated tenement houses, damp cellars, and even shacks. Urban slums became notorious for crime and drinking, which took a heavy toll on families and the poor. In the eyes of many native-born Americans, immigrants were to blame for driving down factory wages and pushing American workers out of jobs. Overshadowing these complaints was a fear that America might not be able to **assimilate** the new groups, with their unfamiliar languages and customs. These fears precipitated an outburst of political **nativism** in the mid-1850s.

assimilate to absorb a culturally distinct group into the dominant culture.

nativism outlook championing the supremacy of "native" cultural traits and political rights over those of immigrants from different backgrounds.

famine that had driven so many Irish out of their country was part of a larger food shortage caused by a series of poor harvests. In this situation, middle-class reformers, who wanted civil liberty and a more representative government, joined forces with lower-class workers to overthrow several regimes. France, Austria, Hungary, Italy, and Prussia all witnessed popular uprisings. Yet though these revolts gained temporary success, they were all quashed by the forces of the old order. Liberal hopes for a more open, democratic society suffered a severe setback.

In the aftermath of this failure, a number of hard-pressed German workers and farmers as well as disillusioned radicals and reformers emigrated to the United States, the symbol of democratic liberalism in the world. They were joined by the first significant migration from Asia, as thousands of Chinese joined the gold rush to California and other strikes (page 277). This migration was part of a century-long phenomenon, as approximately fifty million Europeans, largely from rural areas, would migrate to the Western Hemisphere.

Southern Complaints ›› With British and northern factories buying cotton in large quantities, southern planters prospered in the 1850s. But instead of

investing in machinery as northern commercial farmers had, white southerners invested in slaves. During the 1850s, the price of prime field hands reached record levels.

Despite southern prosperity, the section's leaders repeatedly complained that the North had used its power over banking and commerce to convert the South into a colony. Storage and shipping charges, insurance, port fees, and commissions, which added some 20 percent to the cost of cotton and other commodities, went into the pockets of northern merchants, shippers, and bankers. The idea that the South was a colony of the North was inaccurate, but southern whites found it a convincing explanation of the North's growing wealth. More important, it reinforced their resistance to federal aid for economic development, which they were convinced would enrich the North at southern expense. This attitude further weakened the South's political alliance with the West, which needed federal aid for transportation.

White southerners also feared that the new tide of immigration would shift the sectional balance of power. Most immigrants shunned the South, not wanting to compete with cheap slave labor. The lack of industry and the limited demand for skilled labor also shunted immigrants northward. As a result, the North surged even further ahead of the South in population, thereby strengthening its control of the House of Representatives and heightening southern concern that the North would rapidly settle the western territories.

THE POLITICAL REALIGNMENT OF THE 1850s

When Franklin Pierce (he pronounced it "Purse") assumed the presidency in 1853, he was only 48 years old, the youngest man yet to be elected president. He was also a supporter of the "Young America" movement of the Democratic party, which enthusiastically looked to spread democracy around the globe and annex additional territory to the United States.

The believers in Young America felt it idle to argue about slavery when the nation could be developing new resources. In 1853 Pierce did manage to conclude the Gadsden Purchase, thereby gaining control of about 45,000 square miles of Mexican desert, which contained the most practical southern route for a transcontinental railroad. He had no success with his major goal, acquiring Cuba, the rich sugar-producing island where slavery had once been important. In any case, he soon had his hands full with the proposals of another Democrat of the Young America stamp, Senator Stephen A. Douglas of Illinois.

The Kansas-Nebraska Act >> Known as the Little Giant, Douglas was ambitious, bursting with energy, and impatient to get things done. As chairman of the Senate's Committee on Territories, he hoped to organize federal lands west of Missouri as part of his program for economic development. And as a citizen of Illinois, he wanted Chicago selected as the eastern terminus of the proposed transcontinental railroad. To do so, the rest of the Louisiana Purchase would have to be organized into territories, since any northern rail route would run through that region.

Under the terms of the Missouri Compromise of 1820, slavery was prohibited in this portion of the Louisiana Purchase (pages 182–183). Douglas had tried once to organize the area while keeping a ban on slavery—only to have his bill voted down by southern opposition in the Senate. In January 1854 he reintroduced the measure. This time, to obtain southern support, he omitted the prohibition on slavery that had been in effect for 34 years.

The bill created two territories: Kansas, directly west of Missouri, and a much larger Nebraska Territory, located west of Iowa and the Minnesota Territory. The Missouri Compromise was explicitly repealed. Instead, popular sovereignty was to determine the status of slavery in both territories, though it was left unclear whether residents of Kansas and Nebraska could prohibit slavery at any time or only at the time of statehood, as southerners insisted. It was widely assumed that Kansas would be a slave state and Nebraska a free state.

The Kansas-Nebraska Act outraged northern Democrats, Whigs, and Free Soilers alike. Critics rejected Douglas's contention that popular sovereignty would keep the territories free. The bill, they charged, was meant to give slaveholders—the "Slave Power"—territory previously consecrated to freedom. Most northern opponents of the bill focused on the expansion of slavery and the political threat of a Slave Power rather than the moral evil of slavery. Indignation swept the North, but the Senate passed the bill easily. The real fight came in the House, where the North held a large majority. President Pierce put intense pressure on his fellow northern Democrats to come along, and finally the bill passed by a narrow margin, 113 to 100. Pierce signed it on May 30, 1854.

The Collapse of the Second American Party System >> The furor over the Kansas-Nebraska Act laid bare the underlying tensions that had developed between the North and the South. These tensions put mounting pressure on the political parties, and in the 1850s the Jacksonian party system collapsed. Voters who had been loyal to one party for years, even decades, began switching allegiances. By the time the process of realignment was completed, a new party system had emerged, divided this time along clearly sectional lines.

In part, the old party system decayed because new problems had replaced the traditional economic issues of

Free states and territories, 1854

Slave states and territories, 1854

Open to slavery by Compromise of 1850

Open to slavery by Kansas-Nebraska Act, 1854

THE KANSAS-NEBRASKA ACT

When the Kansas-Nebraska Act of 1854 opened the remaining portion of the Louisiana Purchase to slavery under the doctrine of popular sovereignty, conflict between the two sections focused on control of Kansas, directly west of the slave state of Missouri.

both Whigs and Democrats. The Whigs alienated many of their traditional Protestant supporters by openly seeking the support of Catholics and recent immigrants. Then, too, the growing agitation for the prohibition of alcohol divided both parties, especially the Whigs. Finally, both the Whigs and the Democrats were increasingly perceived as little more than corrupt engines of plunder. Many voters became disillusioned.

Thus the party system was already weak when the Kansas-Nebraska Act divided the two major parties along sectional lines. In such an unstable atmosphere, independent parties flourished. Antislavery veterans, who had earlier sparked the Liberty and Free Soil parties, united with Whigs and anti-Nebraska Democrats in the new antislavery Republican party. Their calculations were derailed, however, when another new party capitalized on fears aroused by the recent flood of immigrants.

The Know-Nothings >> In 1854 the American party, a secret nativist organization whose members were called Know-Nothings, suddenly emerged as a potent political force. (Its members, sworn to secrecy, had been instructed to answer inquiries by replying, "I know

nothing.") Taking as their slogan "Americans should rule America," Know-Nothings denounced illegal voting by immigrants, the rising crime and disorder in urban areas, and immigrants' heavy drinking. They were also strongly anti-Catholic and were convinced that the church's "undemocratic" hierarchy of bishops and archbishops was conspiring to undermine American democracy. Know-Nothings advocated lengthening the residency period for

BACKSTORY
Anti-Catholic Violence

Between 1834 and 1860 American nativists burned down twenty Catholic churches and convents from Maine to Texas. Anti-Catholic riots broke out in Philadelphia; Charlestown, Massachusetts; and Louisville, Kentucky. Longstanding prejudices among Protestants were inflamed by the best-selling *Awful Disclosures of Maria Monk*, a tell-all that falsely claimed that Montreal nuns had been forced to have sex with priests and that their illegitimate children were baptized, then strangled and buried in the convent basement.

naturalization and ousting from office corrupt politicians who openly bid for foreign and Catholic votes.

The Know-Nothings won a series of remarkable victories in the 1854 elections. Their showing spelled doom for the Whigs, as party members deserted in droves to the Know-Nothings. With perhaps a million voters enrolled in its lodges in every state of the Union, Know-Nothing leaders confidently predicted in 1855 that they would elect the next president.

Yet only a year later—by the end of 1856—the party had collapsed as quickly as it had risen. Inexperienced leaders failed to enact the party's reform platform; but in the end, rising sectional tensions destroyed the party when it adopted a proslavery platform for the elections of 1856. Northern party members then flocked to the other new party, the Republicans. This party, unlike the Know Nothings, had no base in the South. It intended to elect a president by sweeping the free states, which controlled a majority of the electoral votes.

The Republicans and Bleeding Kansas >>

At first, the Republican party made little headway in the North. Although it attracted a variety of Whigs, anti-Nebraska Democrats, and Free Soilers, many moderate Whigs and Democrats viewed the party as too radical.

Those attitudes changed on the heels of the alarming developments in Kansas. Most early settlers migrated to Kansas for the same reason other white Americans headed west: the chance to prosper in a new land. But Douglas's idea of popular sovereignty transformed the new settlement into a referendum on slavery in the territories. A race soon developed between northerners and southerners to settle Kansas first. To the proslavery residents of neighboring Missouri, free state communities like Lawrence seemed ominous threats. "We are playing for a mighty stake," former senator David Rice Atchison of Missouri insisted. "If we win, we carry slavery to the Pacific Ocean; if we fail we lose Missouri, Arkansas and Texas and all the territories; the game must be played boldly."

When the first Kansas elections were held in 1854 and 1855, Missourians poured over the border, seized the polls, and stuffed the ballot boxes. This massive fraud tarnished popular sovereignty at the outset and greatly aroused public opinion in the North. It also provided proslavery forces with a commanding majority in the Kansas legislature, where they enacted a strict legal code designed to intimidate antislavery settlers. This Kansas Code limited such time-honored rights as freedom of speech, impartial juries, and fair elections. Mobilized into action, the free-staters in the fall of 1855 organized a separate government, drafted a state constitution prohibiting slavery, and asked Congress to admit Kansas as a free state. In such a polarized situation, violence quickly broke out between the two factions, which culminated in the raid on Lawrence in May 1856 (see the chapter introduction).

The Caning of Charles Sumner >> Only a few days before the proslavery attack on Lawrence, Republican senator Charles Sumner of Massachusetts delivered a scathing speech, "The Crime against Kansas." Sumner passionately condemned slavery and deliberately insulted the state of South Carolina and one of its senators. Preston S. Brooks, a member of Congress from South Carolina, was outraged that Sumner had insulted his relative and mocked his state.

Several days later, on May 22, Brooks strode into the Senate after it had adjourned, went up to Sumner, who was seated at his desk, and proceeded to beat him over the head with a cane. The cane shattered into three pieces from the violence of the attack, but Brooks, swept up in the emotion of the moment, furiously continued hitting Sumner until the senator collapsed unconscious, drenched in blood.

Northerners were electrified to learn that a senator of the United States had been beaten unconscious in the Senate chamber. What caused them even greater consternation was southern reaction—for in his own region, Preston Brooks was lionized as a hero. Instantly, the Sumner caning breathed life into the fledgling Republican party.

SOUTHERN CHIVALRY — ARGUMENT versus CLUB'S.

⋏ The caning of Senator Charles Sumner of Massachusetts by Representative Preston S. Brooks of South Carolina inflamed public opinion. In this northern cartoon, the fallen Sumner, a martyr to free speech, raises his pen against Brooks's club. Rushing to capitalize on the furor, printmakers did not know what the obscure Brooks looked like and thus had to devise ingenious ways of portraying the incident. In this print, Brooks's face is hidden by his raised arm.

Its claims about "Bleeding Kansas" and the Slave Power now seemed credible.

The Election of 1856 ≫

In the face of the storm over Kansas, the Democrats turned to James Buchanan of Pennsylvania as their presidential nominee. Buchanan's supreme qualification was having the good fortune to have been out of the country as minister to England when the Kansas-Nebraska Act was passed. The American party, split badly by the Kansas issue, nominated former president Millard Fillmore.

The Republicans chose John C. Frémont, a western explorer who had helped liberate California during the Mexican War. The party's platform denounced slavery as a "relic of barbarism" and demanded that Kansas be admitted as a free state. Throughout the summer the party hammered away on Bleeding Sumner and Bleeding Kansas.

A number of basic principles guided the Republican party, one of which was the ideal of free labor. Slavery degraded labor, Republicans argued, and would inevitably drive free labor out of the territories. Condemning the South as a stagnant, hierarchical, and economically backward region, Republicans praised the North as a fluid society of widespread opportunity where enterprising individuals could improve their lot. Stopping the expansion of slavery, in Republican eyes, would preserve this heritage of opportunity and economic independence for white Americans. Republicans also appealed to former Know-Nothings by criticizing the Catholic Church, particularly its political activity, and by being much more favorable to temperance.

Also important was the moral opposition to slavery, strengthened by works like Harriet Beecher Stowe's *Uncle Tom's Cabin.* Republican speakers and editors stressed that slavery was a moral wrong, that it was incompatible with the ideals of the Republic and Christianity. "Never forget," Republican leader Abraham Lincoln declared on one occasion, "that we have before us this whole matter of the right and wrong of slavery in this Union, though the immediate question is as to its spreading out into new Territories and States."

More negatively, Republicans gained support by shifting their attacks from slavery itself to the Slave Power, or the political influence of the planter class. Pointing to the Sumner assault and the incidents in Kansas, Republicans contended that the Slave Power had set out to destroy the liberties of white northerners. Just as the nation's founders had battled against tyranny, aristocracy, and minority rule in the Revolution, so the North confronted the unrepublican Slave Power. "If our government, for the sake of Slavery, is

> Throughout the summer the party hammered away on Bleeding Sumner and Bleeding Kansas.

to be perpetually the representative of a minority," argued the *Cincinnati Commercial,* "it may continue republican in form, but the substance of its republicanism has departed."

In the election, Buchanan all but swept the South (losing only Maryland to Fillmore) and won enough free states to push him over the top. Still, the violence in Kansas and Sumner's caning nearly carried Frémont into the presidency. Had he carried Pennsylvania plus one more free state, he would have been elected. For the first time in American history, an antislavery party based entirely in the North threatened to elect a president and snap the bonds of union.

THE WORSENING CRISIS

James Buchanan was one of the most experienced men ever elected president: he had served in Congress, in the cabinet, and in the foreign service. Moderates in both sections hoped that the new president would thwart Republicans in the North and secessionists of the Deep South, popularly known as "fire-eaters." Throughout his career, however, Buchanan had taken the southern position on sectional matters, and he proved insensitive to the concerns of northern Democrats. Moreover, on March 6, 1857, only two days after Buchanan's inauguration, the Supreme Court rendered one of the most controversial decisions in its history.

The Dred Scott Decision ≫

The owner of a Missouri slave named Dred Scott had taken him to live for several years in Illinois, a free state, and in what is now Minnesota, where slavery had been banned by the Missouri Compromise. Eventually the owner returned with Scott to Missouri. Scott sued for his freedom on the grounds that his residence in a free state and a free territory had made him free, and his case ultimately went to the Supreme Court. Two northern justices joined all five southern members in ruling 7 to 2 that Scott remained a slave. The majority opinion was written by Chief Justice Roger Taney of Maryland.

Wanting to strengthen the judicial protection of slavery, Taney ruled that African Americans could not be and never had been citizens of the United States. Instead, he insisted that they were "regarded as beings of an inferior order" at the time the Constitution was adopted, "so far inferior that they had no rights which the white man was bound to respect." In addition, the Court ruled that the Missouri Compromise was unconstitutional. Congress, it declared, had no power to ban slavery from any territory of the United States.

While southerners rejoiced at this result, Republicans denounced the Court for rejecting their party's main principle, that Congress should prohibit slavery in all territories. "We know the court . . . has often over-ruled its own decisions," Abraham Lincoln observed, "and we shall do what we can to have it over-rule this." For Republicans, the decision foreshadowed the spread of slavery throughout the West and even the nation.

But the decision also was a blow to Douglas's moderate solution of popular sovereignty. If Congress had no power to prohibit slavery in a territory, how could it authorize a territorial legislature to do so? While the Court did not rule on this point, the clear implication of the Dred Scott decision was that popular sovereignty was also unconstitutional. The Court, in effect, had endorsed John C. Calhoun's radical view that slavery was legal in all the territories. In so doing, the Court, which had intended to settle the question of slavery in the territories, instead pushed the political debate toward new extremes.

Although the nation grappled with the Dred Scott decision, an economic depression aggravated sectional conflict. The Panic of 1857 was nowhere near as severe as the depression of 1839–1843. But the psychological results were far-reaching, for the South remained relatively untouched. With the price of cotton and other southern commodities still high, southern secessionists hailed the panic as proof that an independent southern nation could survive economically. Insisting that cotton sustained the international economy, James Henry Hammond, a senator from South Carolina, boasted: "No, you dare not make war on cotton. No power on earth dares to make war on it. Cotton is king."

The Lecompton Constitution >> Although

the Dred Scott decision and economic depression weakened the bonds of the Union, Kansas remained at the center of the political stage. In June 1857, when the territory elected delegates to draft a state constitution, free-staters boycotted the election, giving proslavery forces control of the convention that met in Lecompton. The delegates promptly drafted a constitution that made slavery legal. Even more boldly, they scheduled a referendum in which voters could not vote against either the constitution or slavery. Once again, free-staters boycotted the election, and the Lecompton constitution was approved.

President Buchanan had pledged earlier that there would be a free and fair vote on the Lecompton constitution. But the outcome offered Buchanan the unexpected opportunity to create one additional slave state and thereby satisfy his southern supporters by pushing the Lecompton constitution through Congress. This was too much for Douglas, who broke party ranks and denounced the Lecompton constitution as a fraud. Although the administration prevailed in the Senate without Douglas's support,

the House rejected the constitution. In a compromise, Congress returned the constitution to Kansas for another vote. This time it was decisively defeated, 11,300 to 1788. No doubt remained that as soon as Kansas had sufficient population, it would come into the Union as a free state.

The attempt to force slavery on the people of Kansas drove many conservative northerners into the Republican party. And Douglas now found himself assailed by the southern wing of his party. On top of that, in the summer of 1858, he faced a desperate fight for reelection to the Senate in his race against Republican Abraham Lincoln.

The Lincoln-Douglas Debates >> "He is the strong man of his party . . . and the best stump speaker, with his droll ways and dry jokes, in the West," Douglas commented when he learned of Lincoln's nomination to oppose him. "He is as honest as he is shrewd, and if I beat

POLITICAL DEBATE TACTICS

Campaigners such as Barack Obama and Hillary Clinton routinely jockey for advantage, with the underdog pushing for more debates and greater exposure. In 1858 Abraham Lincoln was much less well known than his opponent, Stephen O. Douglas. Since Douglas commanded a crowd wherever he went, Lincoln followed the senator around, giving his own speeches shortly after Douglas had delivered his. The "Little Giant" was so irritated, he agreed to the famous seven debates, so long as Lincoln agreed not to follow him around.

>> Superb debaters, Douglas (*left*) and Lincoln (*right*) nevertheless had very different speaking styles. The deep-voiced Douglas was constantly on the attack, drawing on his remarkable memory and showering points like buckshot in all directions. Lincoln, who had a high-pitched voice, developed his arguments more carefully and methodically, and he relied on his sense of humor and unmatched ability as a storyteller to drive his points home to the audience.

Born in the slave state of Kentucky, Lincoln had grown up mostly in southern Indiana and central Illinois. Yet his intense ambition lifted him above the backwoods from which he came. He compensated for a lack of schooling through disciplined self-education, and he became a shrewd courtroom lawyer of respectable social standing. Known for his sense of humor, he was nonetheless subject to fits of acute depression.

Lincoln's first love was always politics. A fervent admirer of Henry Clay and his economic program, he became a Whig and then, after the party's collapse, joined the Republicans and became one of their key leaders in Illinois. Lincoln challenged Douglas to discuss the issues of slavery and the sectional controversy in a series of seven debates.

him my victory will be hardly won." Tall (6 feet, 4 inches) and gangly, Lincoln had an awkward manner as he spoke, yet his logic and sincerity carried the audience with him. His sentences had none of the oratorical flourishes common in that day. "If we could first know *where* we are, and *whither* we are tending, we could then better judge *what* to do, and *how* to do it," Lincoln began, in accepting his party's nomination for senator in 1858. He then commented on a proverb from the Bible:

> "A house divided against itself cannot stand."
> I believe this government cannot endure, permanently half *slave* and half *free*.
> I do not expect the Union to be *dissolved*—
> I do not expect the house to *fall*—but I *do* expect it will cease to be divided.
> It will become *all* one thing, or *all* the other.
> Either the *opponents* of slavery, will arrest the further spread of it, and place it where the public mind shall rest in the belief that it is in the course of ultimate extinction; or its *advocates* will push it forward, till it shall become alike lawful in all the States, *old* as well as *new*—*North* as well as *South*.

The message echoed through the hall and across the pages of the national press.

In the campaign, Douglas sought to portray Lincoln as a radical who preached sectional warfare. The nation *could* endure half slave and half free, Douglas declared, as long as states and territories were left alone to regulate their own affairs. Lincoln countered by insisting that the spread of slavery was a blight on the Republic. Even though Douglas had voted against the Lecompton constitution, he could not be counted on to oppose slavery's expansion, for he admitted that he didn't care whether slavery was voted "down or up."

In the debate held at Freeport, Illinois, Lincoln asked Douglas how under the Dred Scott decision the people of a territory could lawfully exclude slavery before statehood. Douglas answered, with what became known as the Freeport Doctrine, that slaveowners would never bring their slaves into an area where slavery was not legally protected. Therefore, Douglas explained, if the people of a territory refused to pass a slave code, slavery would never be established there.

In a close race, the legislature elected Douglas to another term in the Senate.[1] But on the national scene, southern Democrats angrily repudiated him and

1 State legislatures elected senators until 1913, when the Seventeenth Amendment was adopted. Although Lincoln and Douglas both campaigned for the office, Illinois voters actually voted for candidates for the legislature who were pledged to one of the senatorial candidates.

condemned the Freeport Doctrine. And although Lincoln lost, his impressive performance marked him as a possible presidential contender for 1860.

The Beleaguered South >> While northerners increasingly feared that the Slave Power was conspiring to extend slavery into the free states, southerners worried that the "Black Republicans" would hem them in and undermine their political power.

The very factors that brought prosperity during the 1850s stimulated the South's sense of crisis. As the price of slaves rose sharply, the proportion of southerners who owned slaves had dropped almost a third since 1830. At the same time, California and Kansas had been closed to southern slaveholders—unfairly, in their eyes. Finally, Douglas's clever claim that a territory could effectively outlaw slavery using the Freeport Doctrine seemed to negate the Dred Scott decision that slavery was legal in all the territories.

Several possible solutions to the South's internal crisis had failed. Agricultural reform to restore worn-out lands had made significant headway only in Virginia and Maryland. Elsewhere the rewards of a single-crop economy were too great to persuade southern farmers to adopt new methods. Another alternative—bringing industry to the South—had also failed to take root. Finally, private military expeditions in Latin America, which were designed to strengthen the South by adding slave territory to the United States, came to naught.

The South's growing sense of isolation made this crisis more acute. By the 1850s slavery had been abolished throughout most of the Americas, and in the United States the South's political power was steadily shrinking. Only the expansion of slavery and the admission of new slave states held any promise of preserving the South's political power and protecting its way of life. "The truth is," fumed one Alabama politician, ". . . the South is excluded from the common territories of the Union. The right of expansion claimed to be a necessity of her continued existence, is practically and effectively denied the South."

Was the Civil War an "irresistible conflict," as Senator William Seward of New York insisted, or could it have been avoided?

WITNESS
John Brown's Impact
"You can hardly have formed an idea of the intensity of feeling . . . in regard to John Brown . . . The mass of the people . . . have, while condemning Brown's scheme as a criminal attempt to right a great wrong by violent measures, and as equally ill-judged and rash in execution, felt for the man himself a deep sympathy and a fervent admiration. . . . They have felt that . . . he died a real martyr in the cause of freedom."

THE ROAD TO WAR

In 1857 John Brown—the abolitionist firebrand—had returned to the East from Kansas, consumed with the idea of attacking slavery in the South itself. Financed by a number of prominent northern reformers, Brown gathered 21 followers, including 5 free blacks, in hope of fomenting a slave insurrection. On the night of October 16, 1859, his band seized the unguarded federal armory at Harpers Ferry in Virginia. But no slaves rallied to Brown's standard: few lived in the area to begin with. Before long the raiders found themselves surrounded and holed up in the town. Charging with bayonets fixed, federal troops commanded by Colonel Robert E. Lee soon captured Brown and his raiders. On December 2, 1859, Virginia hanged Brown for treason.

Brown's raid at Harpers Ferry was yet another blow weakening the forces of compromise within the nation. Although the invasion itself was a dismal failure, the old man knew how to bear himself with a martyr's dignity. Republicans made haste to denounce Brown's raid, lest they be tarred as radicals, but other northerners were less cautious. Ralph Waldo Emerson described Brown as a "saint, whose martyrdom will make the gallows as glorious as the cross." While only a minority of northerners endorsed Brown, southerners were shocked by such displays of sympathy. "I have always been a fervid Union man," one North Carolina resident wrote, "but I confess the endorsement of the Harpers Ferry outrage has shaken my fidelity and I am willing to take the chances of every probable evil that may arise from disunion, sooner than submit any longer to Northern insolence and Northern outrage."

A Sectional Election >> When Congress convened in December, there were ominous signs everywhere of the growing sectional rift. Intent on destroying Douglas's Freeport Doctrine, southern radicals demanded a congressional slave code to protect slavery in the territories. To northern Democrats, such a platform spelled political

death. As one Indiana Democrat put it, "We cannot carry a single congressional district on that doctrine in the state."

At the Democratic convention in April, southern radicals boldly pressed their demand for a federal slave code. Instead the convention adopted the Douglas platform upholding popular sovereignty, whereupon the delegations from eight southern states walked out. The convention finally reassembled two months later and nominated Douglas. At this point most of the remaining southern Democrats departed and, together with those delegates who had seceded earlier, nominated Vice President John C. Breckinridge of Kentucky on a platform supporting a federal slave code. The last major national party had shattered.

The Republicans turned to Abraham Lincoln, a moderate on slavery who was strong in his home state of Illinois and the other doubtful states that the party had failed to carry in 1856. Republicans also sought to broaden their appeal by adding to their platform several economic planks that endorsed a moderately protective tariff, a homestead bill, and a northern transcontinental railroad.

The election that followed was really two contests in one. In the North, which had a majority of the electoral votes, only Lincoln and Douglas had any chance to carry a state. In the South, the race pitted Breckinridge against John Bell of Tennessee, the candidate of the new Constitutional Union party. Although Lincoln received less than 40 percent of the popular vote and had virtually no support in the South, he won 180 electoral votes, 27 more than needed for election. For the first time, the nation had elected a president who headed a completely sectional party and who was committed to stopping the expansion of slavery.

Secession >> Although the Republicans had not won control of either house of Congress, Lincoln's election struck many southerners as a blow of terrible finality. Lincoln had been lifted into office on the strength of the free states alone. It was not unrealistic, many fire-eaters argued, to believe that he would use federal aid to encourage the border states to free their slaves voluntarily. Once slavery disappeared there, and new states were added, the necessary three-fourths majority would exist to approve a constitutional amendment abolishing slavery. Or perhaps Lincoln might send other John Browns

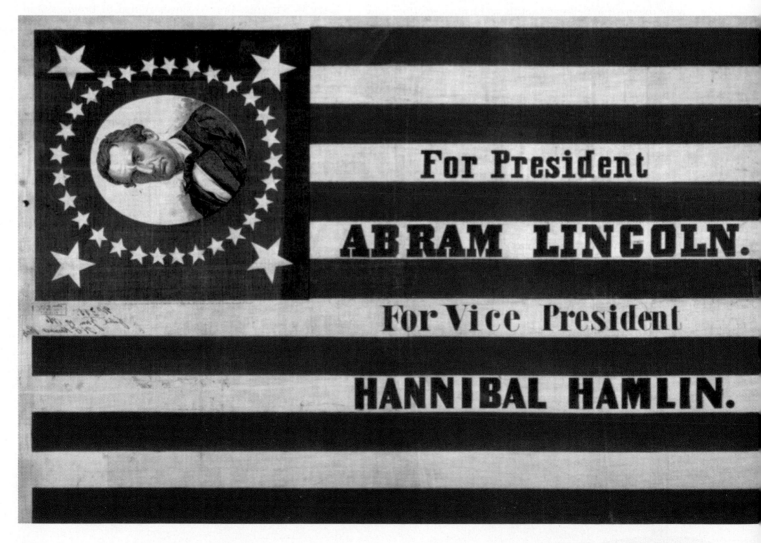

into the South to stir up more slave insurrections. The Montgomery (Alabama) *Mail* accused Republicans of intending "to free the negroes and force amalgamation between them and the children of the poor men of the South."

Secession seemed the only alternative left to protect southern rights. South Carolina, which had challenged federal authority in the nullification crisis of the 1830s, was determined to force the other southern states to act. On December 20, 1860, a popular convention unanimously passed a resolution seceding from the Union. The rest of the Deep South followed, and on February 7, 1861, the states stretching from South Carolina to Texas organized the Confederate States of America and elected Jefferson Davis president.

But the Upper South and the border states declined to secede, hoping that once again Congress could patch together a settlement. Senator John Crittenden of Kentucky proposed extending to California the old Missouri Compromise line of 36° 30'. Slavery would be prohibited north of this line and given federal protection south of it in all territories, including any acquired in the future. Furthermore, Crittenden proposed an "unamendable amendment" to the Constitution, forever safeguarding slavery in states where it already existed.

But the Crittenden Compromise was doomed for the simple reason that the two groups who were required to make concessions—Republicans and secessionists—had no interest in doing so. "We have just carried an election on principles fairly stated to the people," Lincoln wrote in opposing the compromise. "Now we are told in advance, the government shall be broken up, unless we surrender to those we have beaten, before we take the offices. If we surrender, it is the end of us, and of the government."

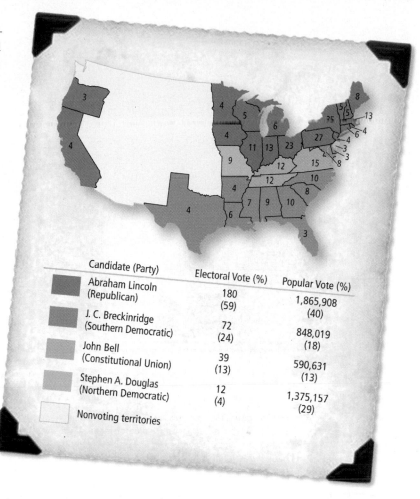

Candidate (Party)	Electoral Vote (%)	Popular Vote (%)
Abraham Lincoln (Republican)	180 (59)	1,865,908 (40)
J. C. Breckinridge (Southern Democratic)	72 (24)	848,019 (18)
John Bell (Constitutional Union)	39 (13)	590,631 (13)
Stephen A. Douglas (Northern Democratic)	12 (4)	1,375,157 (29)
Nonvoting territories		

ELECTION OF 1860

Although Lincoln did not win a majority of the popular vote, he still would have been elected even if the votes for all three of his opponents had been combined, because he won a clear majority in every state he carried except California, Oregon, and New Jersey (whose electoral votes he split with Douglas).

The Outbreak of War

>> As he prepared to become president, Lincoln pondered what to do about secession. In his inaugural address on March 4, he sought to reassure southerners that he did not intend, "directly or indirectly, to interfere with the institution of slavery in the States where it exists." But echoing Andrew Jackson in the nullification crisis, he maintained that "the Union of these states is perpetual," and he announced that he intended to "hold, occupy and possess" federal property and collect customs duties under the tariff. He closed by calling for a restoration of the "bonds of affection" that united all Americans.

The new president hoped for time to work out a solution, but on his first day in office he was given a dispatch from Major Robert Anderson, commander of the federal garrison at Fort Sumter in Charleston harbor. Sumter was one of the few remaining federal outposts in the South. Anderson informed the government that he was almost out of food and that, unless resupplied, he would have to surrender. For a month Lincoln looked for a way out, but he finally sent a relief expedition. As a conciliatory gesture, he notified the governor of South Carolina that supplies were being sent and that if the fleet were allowed to pass, only food, and not men, arms, or ammunition, would be landed.

The burden of decision now shifted to Jefferson Davis. From his point of view, secession was a constitutional right, and the Confederacy was not a bogus but a legitimate government. To allow the United States to hold property and maintain military forces within the Confederacy would destroy its claim of independence. Davis therefore instructed the Confederate commander at Charleston to demand the immediate surrender of Fort Sumter and, if

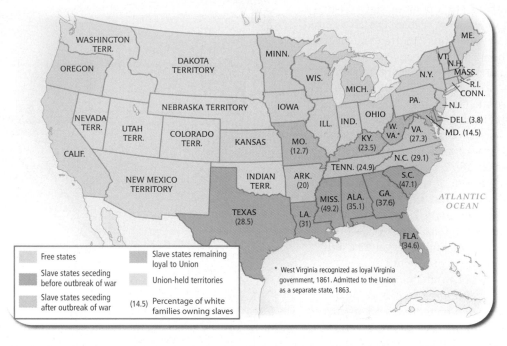

THE PATTERN OF SECESSION

Led by South Carolina, the Deep South seceded between Lincoln's election in November and his inauguration in March. The Upper South did not secede until after the firing on Fort Sumter. The four border slave states never seceded and remained in the Union throughout the war. As the map indicates, secession sentiment was strongest in states where the highest percentage of white families owned slaves.

refused, to open fire. When Anderson declined the ultimatum, Confederate batteries began shelling the fort on April 12 at 4:30 A.M. Some 33 hours later Anderson surrendered. A wave of indignation swept across the North in response. When Lincoln called for 75,000 volunteers to put down the rebellion, four states in the Upper South, led by Virginia, also seceded. Matters had passed beyond compromise.

The Roots of a Divided Nation >> And

so the Union was broken. After 70 years, the forces of sectionalism and separatism had finally outpulled the ties binding "these United States." Why did affairs come to such a pass?

In some ways, the revolution in markets, improving transportation networks, and increasingly sophisticated systems of credit and finance all served to tie the nation together. The cotton planter who rode the steamship *Fashion* along the Alabama River ("Time's money! Time's money!") was wearing ready-made clothes manufactured in New York from southern cotton. Chauncey Jerome's clocks from Connecticut were keeping time not only for commercial planters but also for Lowell mill workers like Mary Paul, who learned to measure her lunch break in

minutes. Farmers in both Tennessee and Iowa were interested in the price of wheat in New York, for it affected the profits that could be made shipping their grain by the new railroad lines. American society had become far more specialized and far more interdependent since the days of Crèvecoeur's self-sufficient farmer of the 1780s.

But a specialized economy had not brought unity. For the North, specialization meant more factories, more cities and towns, and a higher percentage of urban workers. Industry affected midwestern farmers as well, for their steel plows and McCormick reapers allowed them to farm larger holdings and required greater capital investment in the new machinery. For its part, the South was transformed by the industrial revolution too, as textile factories made cotton the booming mainstay of its economy. But for all its growth, the region remained largely a rural society. Its prosperity stemmed from expansion westward into new areas of cotton production, not new forms of production or technology.

Above all, the intensive labor required to produce cotton, rice, and sugar made slavery an inseparable part of the southern way of life—"so intimately mingled with our social conditions," as one Georgian admitted, "that it would be impossible to eradicate it." An increasing number of northerners viewed slavery as evil, not so much out of high-minded sympathy toward slaves but as a labor system that threatened the republican ideals of white American society.

It fell to the political system to try to resolve sectional conflict, through a system of national parties that represented various interest groups and promoted democratic debate. But the political system had critical weaknesses. The American process of electing a president gave the winning candidate a state's entire electoral vote, regardless of the margin of victory. That procedure made a northern sectional party possible, since the Republicans could never have carried an election on the basis of a popular vote alone. In addition, since 1844 the Democratic party had required a two-thirds vote to nominate its presidential candidate. Unintentionally, this requirement made it difficult to pick any truly forceful leader and gave the South a veto over the party's candidate. Yet the South, by itself, could not elect a president.

The nation's republican heritage also contributed to the political system's vulnerability. Ever since the Revolution, when Americans accused the king and Parliament of deliberately plotting to deprive them of their liberties, Americans were on the watch for political conspiracies. For their part, Republicans emphasized the existence of the Slave Power bent on eradicating northern rights. Southerners, on the other hand, accused the Black Republicans of conspiring to destroy southern equality. Each side viewed itself as defending the country's republican tradition from an internal threat.

But in the end, the threat to the Union came not from within but from beyond its borders. As the United States expanded in the 1840s, it incorporated vast new territories, becoming a truly continental republic. And that

AN EMINENT SOUTHERN CLERGYMAN,
During an eloquent discourse, is wonderfully assisted in finding scriptural authority for Secession and Treason, and the divine ordination of Slavery.

forced the Union, in absorbing new lands, to define itself anew. If the American frontier had not swept so quickly toward the Pacific, the nation might have been able to postpone the day of reckoning on slavery until some form of gradual emancipation could be adopted. But the luxury of time was not available. The new territories became the battlegrounds for two contrasting ways of life, with slavery at the center of the debate. Elsewhere in the world the push toward abolition grew louder, whether of serfdom in eastern Europe or of slavery across the globe. Americans who saw the issue in moral terms joined that chorus. They saw no reason why the abolition of slavery should be postponed.

In 1850, supporters and opponents of slavery were still willing to compromise on how "the peculiar institution" could expand into the new territories. But a decade later, many Americans both North and South had come to accept the idea of an irrepressible conflict between two societies, one based on freedom, the other on slavery, in which only one side could ultimately prevail. At stake, it seemed, was control of the nation's future. Four years later, as a weary Abraham Lincoln looked back to the beginning of the conflict, he noted, "Both parties deprecated war, but one of them would make war rather than let the nation survive, and the other would accept war rather than let it perish, and the war came."

CHAPTER SUMMARY

In the 1850s, the slavery issue reemerged in national politics and increasingly disrupted the party system, leading to the outbreak of war in 1861.

▌ Fundamental economic changes heightened sectional tensions in the 1850s.

   ▌ The construction of a vast railroad network reoriented western trade from the South to the East.

   ▌ A tide of new immigrants swelled the North's population (and hence its political power) at the expense of the South, thereby stimulating southern fears.

▌ The old Jacksonian party system was shattered by the nativist movement and by renewed controversy over the expansion of slavery.

   ▌ In the Kansas-Nebraska Act, Senator Stephen A. Douglas tried to defuse the slavery debate by incorporating popular sovereignty (the idea that the people of a territory should decide the status of slavery there). This act effectively repealed the Missouri Compromise.

   ▌ Popular sovereignty failed in the Kansas Territory, where fighting broke out between proslavery and antislavery partisans.

▌ Sectional violence reached a climax in May 1856 with the proslavery attack on Lawrence, Kansas, and the caning of Senator Charles Sumner of Massachusetts by Representative Preston S. Brooks of South Carolina.

▌ Sectional tensions sparked the formation of a new antislavery Republican party, and the party system realigned along sectional lines.

   ▌ The Supreme Court's Dred Scott decision, the Panic of 1857, the congressional struggle over the proslavery Lecompton constitution, and John Brown's attack on Harpers Ferry in 1859 strengthened the two sectional extremes.

▌ In 1860 Abraham Lincoln became the first Republican to be elected president.

   ▌ Following Lincoln's triumph, the seven states of the Deep South seceded.

   ▌ When Lincoln sent supplies to the Union garrison in Fort Sumter in Charleston harbor, Confederate batteries bombarded the fort into submission.

   ▌ The North rallied to Lincoln's decision to use force to restore the Union, and in response the four states of the Upper South seceded.

Significant Events

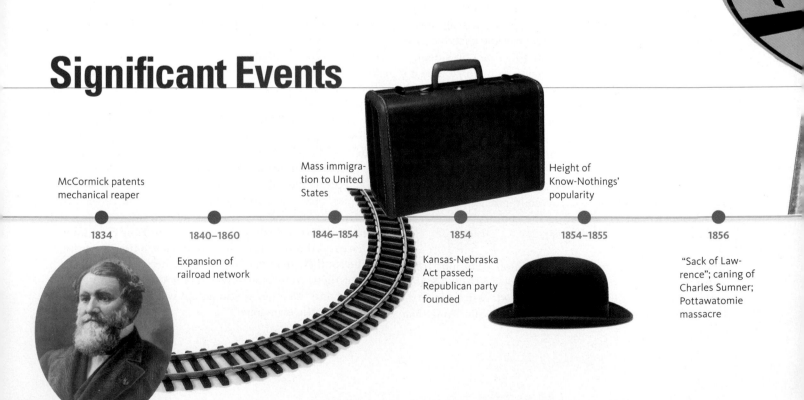

McCormick patents mechanical reaper

1834

Expansion of railroad network

1840–1860

Mass immigration to United States

1846–1854

Kansas-Nebraska Act passed; Republican party founded

1854

Height of Know-Nothings' popularity

1854–1855

"Sack of Lawrence"; caning of Charles Sumner; Pottawatomie massacre

1856

Additional Reading

The problem of the coming of the Civil War has attracted considerable historical attention over the years. David M. Potter, *The Impending Crisis, 1848–1861* (1976), is a superior political treatment of the period. The political aspects of the conflict also take center stage in Michael F. Holt's brief and incisive work, *The Fate of Their Country: Politicians, Slavery Extension, and the Coming of the Civil War* (2004). Holt stresses the self-interest of the political leaders and plays down the larger structural economic and social factors. A contrasting and similarly brief study can be found in Don E. Fehrenbacher, *The South and Three Sectional Crises* (1980).

The heavy immigration during these years is described in Philip D. Taylor, *The Distant Magnet* (1971). Michael F. Holt provides the best treatment of the Know Nothing Party, as well as the more general topic of antebellum political realignment, in *The Political Crisis of the 1850s* (1978).

John McCardell's *The Idea of a Southern Nation* (1979) is a solid, well-written treatment of southern nationalism in this period. The most thorough examination of the blend of factors that produced the Republican party is William E. Gienapp, *The Origins of the Republican Party, 1852–1856* (1987). Eric Foner, in *Free Soil, Free Labor, Free Men* (1970), focuses on the ideas of Republican party leaders. For the turbulent history of Kansas in this period, see James A. Rawley, *Race and Politics* (1969). The critical events of 1857 are the focal point of Kenneth M. Stampp's *America in 1857* (1990). The secession movement has largely been investigated in specific southern states. A particularly good example of this approach is Stephen A. Channing's account of secession in *South Carolina, Crisis of Fear* (1974), although Charles B. Dew provides a regional view by examining the role of the Secession Commissioners appointed by the Confederacy to persuade wavering southerners in *Apostles of Secession* (2001). Kenneth M. Stampp, *And the War Came* (1950), is the best study of northern public opinion during the secession crisis. A sophisticated examination of the war's origins is Gabor S. Boritt, ed., *Why the War Came* (1996). For a discussion of the broader issue of why the South chose secession and fought the Civil War, see Gary W. Gallagher and Alan T. Nolan, eds., *The Myth of the Lost Cause and Civil War History* (2000).

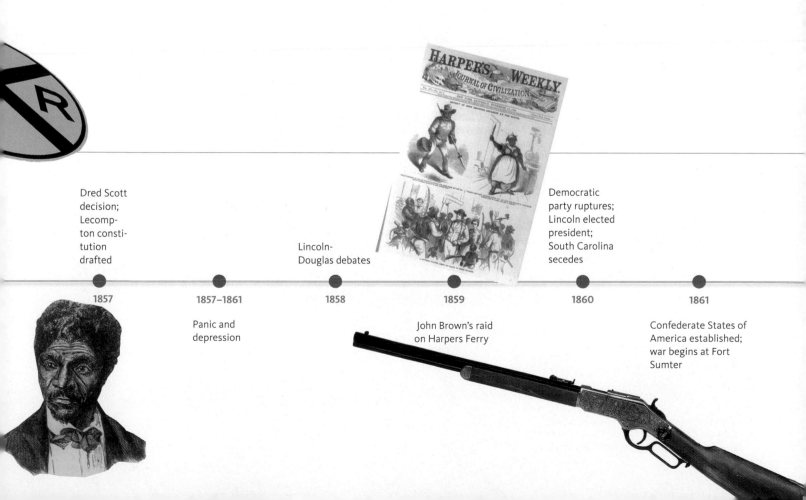

1857 — Dred Scott decision; Lecompton constitution drafted

1857–1861 — Panic and depression

1858 — Lincoln-Douglas debates

1859 — John Brown's raid on Harpers Ferry

1860 — Democratic party ruptures; Lincoln elected president; South Carolina secedes

1861 — Confederate States of America established; war begins at Fort Sumter

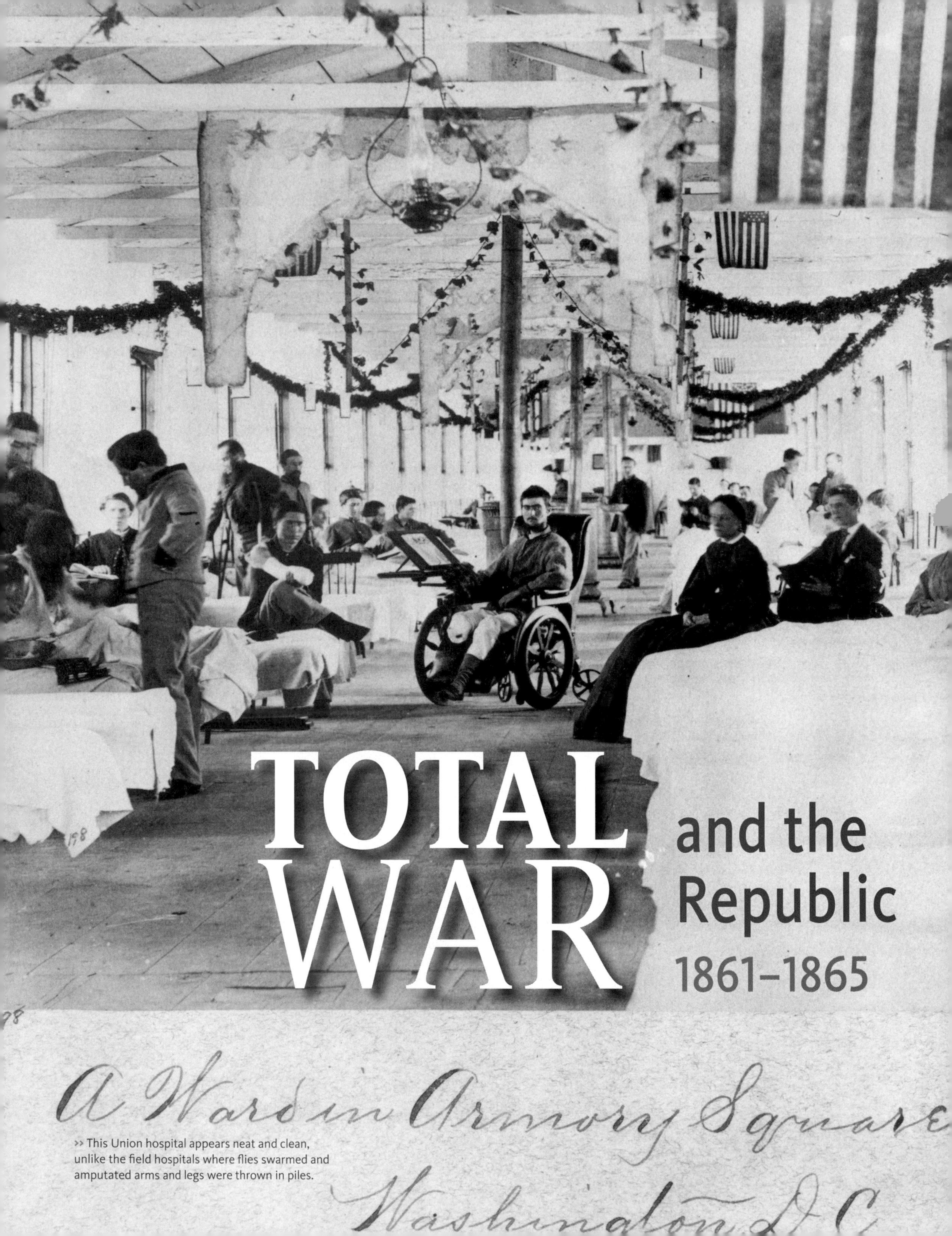

TOTAL WAR

and the Republic 1861–1865

>> This Union hospital appears neat and clean, unlike the field hospitals where flies swarmed and amputated arms and legs were thrown in piles.

A Ward in Armory Square

Washington D C

16

WHAT'S TO COME

311 THE DEMANDS
OF TOTAL WAR

313 OPENING MOVES

317 EMANCIPATION

319 THE CONFEDERATE HOME FRONT

321 THE UNION HOME FRONT

323 GONE TO BE A SOLDIER

325 THE UNION'S TRIUMPH

A ROUT AT BULL RUN

T he war won't last sixty days!" Of that Jim Tinkham was confident. With dreams of a hero's return, Tinkham enlisted for three months in a Massachusetts regiment. Soon he was transferred to Washington as part of the Union army being assembled by General Irvin McDowell to crush the rebellion. Tinkham was elated when in mid-July 1861 he was finally ordered to march toward the Confederates concentrated at Manassas Junction, 25 miles away.[1]

The battle began at dawn on July 21, with McDowell commanding 30,000 troops against General Pierre Beauregard's 22,000. Tinkham did not arrive on the field until early afternoon. As his regiment pushed toward the front, he felt faint at his first sight of the dead and wounded, some mangled horribly. But he was soon caught up in the excitement of battle as he charged up Henry Hill. Suddenly the Confederate ranks broke, and exuberant Union troops shouted: "The war is over!" **>>**

[1] The Union and the Confederacy often gave different names to a battle. The Confederates called the first battle Manassas; the Union, Bull Run.

^ The Civil War was the first conflict whose major battles routinely involved more than 100,000 troops, and casualties soared beyond the scale Americans experienced in the U.S.–Mexican War. The battle of Antietam, fought in 1862, produced almost 23,000 casualties, the bloodiest single day of the war. A group of Confederate soldiers are shown where they fell along the Hagerstown Pike. Said one Union officer of the fighting: "Men, I cannot say fell; they were knocked out of the ranks by dozens."

The arrival of fresh troops, however, enabled the Confederates to regroup. Among the reinforcements who rushed to Henry Hill was 19-year-old Randolph McKim of Baltimore. A student at the University of Virginia, McKim joined the First Maryland Infantry as a private when Abraham Lincoln imposed martial law in his home state. "The cause of the South had become identified with liberty itself," he explained. The arrival of the First Maryland and other reinforcements in the late afternoon turned the tide of battle. The faltering Confederate line held, and Union troops began to withdraw.

But with retreat came confusion. Discipline dissolved and the army degenerated into a stampeding mob. As they fled, terrified troops threw away their equipment, shoved aside officers who tried to stop them, and raced frantically past the wagons and artillery pieces that clogged the road.

All the next day in a drizzling rain, mud-spattered troops straggled into the capital in complete disorder. William Russell, an English reporter, asked one pale officer where they were coming from. "Well, sir, I guess we're all coming out of Virginny as far as we can, and pretty well whipped too," he replied. Joining the stampede was Jim Tinkham, who confessed he would have continued on to Boston if he had not been stopped by a guard in Washington.

The rout at Bull Run sobered the North. Gone were dreams of ending the war with one glorious battle. Gone was the illusion that 75,000 volunteers serving three months would be sufficient. As one perceptive observer noted, "We have undertaken to make war without in the least knowing how." Having cast off his earlier misconceptions, a newly determined Jim Tinkham reenlisted for a three-year hitch.

Still, it was not surprising that both sides underestimated the magnitude of the conflict. Warfare as it had evolved in Europe consisted largely of maneuverings that took relatively few lives, respected private property, and left civilians largely unharmed. The Civil War, on the other hand, was the first war whose major battles routinely involved more than 100,000 troops. So many combatants could be equipped only through the use of factory-produced weaponry, they could be moved and supplied only with the help of railroads, and they could be sustained only through the concerted efforts of civilian society as a whole. The morale of the population, the quality of political leadership, and the use of industrial and economic might were all critical to the outcome. Quite simply, the Civil War was the first total war in history. **<<**

THE DEMANDS OF TOTAL WAR

When the war began, the North had an enormous advantage in manpower and industrial capacity. The Union's population was 2.5 times larger; it contained more railroad track and rolling stock and possessed more than 10 times the industrial capacity.

From a modern perspective, the South's attempt to resist against such odds seems hopeless. Yet this view indicates how much the conception of war has changed. European observers, who knew the strength and resources of the two sides, believed that the Confederacy could never be conquered. Indeed, the South enjoyed definite strategic advantages. To be victorious, it did not need to invade the North—only to defend its own land and prevent the North from destroying its armies. Southern soldiers knew the topography of their home country better, and a friendly population regularly supplied them with intelligence about Union troop movements.

The North, in contrast, had to invade and conquer the Confederacy and destroy the southern will to resist. To do so, it would have to deploy thousands of soldiers to defend long supply lines in enemy territory, a situation that significantly reduced the northern advantage in manpower. Yet by 1865 Union forces had penetrated virtually every part of the 500,000 square miles of the

Resources of the Union and Confederacy, 1861

	Union	Confederacy	Union advantage
Total population	23,300,000	9,100,000*	**2.5 to 1**
White male population (18–45 years)	4,600,000	1,100,000	**4.2 to 1**
Bank deposits	$207,000,000	$47,000,000	**4.4 to 1**
Value of manufactured goods	$1,730,000,000	$156,000,000	**11 to 1**
Railroad mileage	22,000	9,000	**2.4 to 1**
Shipping tonnage	4,600,000	290,000	**16 to 1**
Value of textiles produced	$181,000,000	$10,000,000	**18 to 1**
Value of Firearms produced	$2,290,000	73,000	**31 to 1**
Pig iron production (tons)	951,000	37,000	**26 to 1**
Coal production (tons	13,680,000	650,000	**21 to 1**
Corn and wheat production (bushels)	698,000,000	314,000,000	**2.2 to 1**
Draft animals	5,800,000	2,900,000	**2 to 1**
Cotton production (bales)	43,000	5,344,000	**1 to 124**

*Slaves accounted for 3,300,000, or 40 percent

⌃ RESOURCES OF THE UNION AND THE CONFEDERACY, 1861
(Source: U.S. Census 1860 and E. B. Long, *The Civil War Day by Day* [New York: Doubleday, 1971], p. 723.)

Confederacy and were able to move almost at will. The Civil War demonstrated the capacity of a modern society to overcome the problems of distance and terrain with technology.

Political Leadership

>> To sustain a commitment to total war required effective political leadership. This task fell on Abraham Lincoln and Jefferson Davis, presidents of the rival governments.

Jefferson Davis grew up in Mississippi accustomed to life's advantages. Educated at West Point, he fought in the Mexican War, served as Franklin Pierce's secretary of war, and became one of the South's leading advocates in the Senate. Although he was hardworking and committed, he was quarrelsome, resented criticism, and refused to work with those he disliked. "He cannot brook opposition or criticism," one member of the Confederate Congress testified, "and those who do not bow down before him have no chance of success with him."

Yet for all Davis's personal handicaps, he faced an institutional one even more daunting. The Confederacy had been founded on the ideology of states' rights. Yet to meet the demands of total war, Davis would need to increase the authority of the central government beyond anything the South had ever experienced.

When Lincoln took the oath of office, his national experience consisted of one term in the House of Representatives. But Lincoln was a shrewd judge of character and a superb politician. To achieve a common goal, he willingly overlooked withering criticism and personal slights. He was not easily humbugged, overawed, or flattered and never allowed personal feelings to blind him to his larger objectives. "No man knew better how to summon and dispose of political ability to attain great political ends," commented one associate.

"This is essentially a People's contest," Lincoln asserted at the start of the war, and few presidents have been better able to communicate with the average citizen. He regularly visited Union troops in camp, in the field, and in army hospitals. "The boys liked him," wrote Joseph Twichell, from a Connecticut regiment, "in fact his popularity with the army is and has been universal." Always Lincoln reminded the public that the war was being fought for the ideals of the Revolution and the Republic. It was a test, he remarked in his famous address at Gettysburg, of whether a nation "conceived in Liberty, and dedicated to the proposition that all men are created equal" could "long endure."

He also proved the more effective military leader. Jefferson Davis took his title of commander in chief literally, constantly interfering with his generals, but he failed to formulate an overarching strategy. In contrast, Lincoln clearly grasped the challenge confronting the Union. He accepted General Winfield Scott's proposal to blockade the Confederacy, cut off its supplies, and slowly strangle it into submission. But unlike Scott, he realized that this plan was not enough. The South would also have to be invaded and defeated, not only on an eastern front in Virginia but in the West, where Union control of the Mississippi would divide the Confederacy. Lincoln understood that the Union's superior manpower and matériel would become decisive only when the Confederacy was simultaneously threatened along a broad front. It took time before the president found generals able to execute this novel strategy.

The Border States

>> When the war began, only Delaware of the border slave states was certain to remain in the Union. Lincoln's immediate political challenge was to retain the loyalty of Maryland, Kentucky, and Missouri. Maryland especially was crucial, for if it was lost, Washington itself would have to be abandoned.

Lincoln moved vigorously—even ruthlessly—to secure Maryland. He suppressed pro-Confederate newspapers and suspended the writ of **habeas corpus**, the right under the Constitution of an arrested person either to be charged with a specific crime or to be released. That done, he held without trial prominent Confederate sympathizers. Under these conditions Unionists won a complete victory in the fall state election.

habeas corpus The right of habeus corpus is meant to ensure that the government cannot arbitrarily arrest and imprison a citizen without giving grounds for doing so.

As for Kentucky, which had proclaimed itself neutral, Lincoln forbid Union generals from occupying the state, preferring to wait for Unionist sentiment to assert itself. After Unionists won control of the legislature in the summer election, a Confederate army entered the state, giving Lincoln the opening he needed. He quickly sent in troops, and Kentucky stayed in the Union.

In Missouri, guerrilla warfare raged between Union and Confederate sympathizers throughout the war. But a Union victory in the state in March 1862 kept Missouri within the Union. In Virginia, internal divisions led to the creation of a new border state, as the hilly western counties where slavery was weak refused to support the Confederacy. After adopting a congressionally mandated program of

Was Lincoln justified in suspending *habeas corpus*? Was the Bush administration justified in doing so in the war on terror?

△ UNION CREW ON A NAVY GUNBOAT Traditionally, more African Americans had served on Navy ships than in the army. About 20 percent of this crew appears to be African Americans.

gradual emancipation, West Virginia was formally admitted to the Union in June 1863.

The Union scored an important triumph in holding the border states. The population of all five equaled that of the four states of the Upper South that had joined the Confederacy, and their production of military supplies— food, animals, and minerals—was greater. Furthermore, Maryland and West Virginia contained railroad lines critical to the defense of Washington, while Kentucky and Missouri gave the Union army access to the major river systems of the western theater, down which it launched the first successful invasions of the Confederacy.

OPENING MOVES

After the Confederate victory at Bull Run, Congress authorized a much larger army of long-term volunteers, and Lincoln named 34-year-old George McClellan, a West Point graduate and former railroad executive, to be the new commander. Energetic and ambitious, he spent the next eight months directing the much-needed task of organizing and drilling the Army of the Potomac.

Blockade and Isolate >> Although the U.S. Navy began the war with only 42 ships available to blockade 3,550 miles of Confederate coastline, by the spring of 1862 it had taken control of key islands off the coasts of the Carolinas and Georgia, to use as supply bases. The navy also began building powerful gunboats to operate on the rivers. In April 1862 Flag Officer David G. Farragut ran a gauntlet of Confederate shore batteries to capture New Orleans, the Confederacy's largest port. Memphis, another important river city, fell to Union forces in June.

Although small, fast ships continued to slip through the blockade, southern trade suffered badly. As a countermeasure, the Confederacy converted the wooden *USS Merrimack* (rechristened the *Virginia),* into an ironclad gunboat. In March 1862 a Union ironclad, the *Monitor,* battled it to a standoff, and the Confederates scuttled the *Virginia* when they evacuated Norfolk in May. After that, the Union's naval supremacy was secure.)

The Confederacy looked to diplomacy as another means to lift the blockade. With cotton so vital to European economies, especially Great Britain's, southerners believed Europe would formally recognize the Confederacy and come to its aid. The British government favored the South, but it hesitated to act until Confederate armies demonstrated that

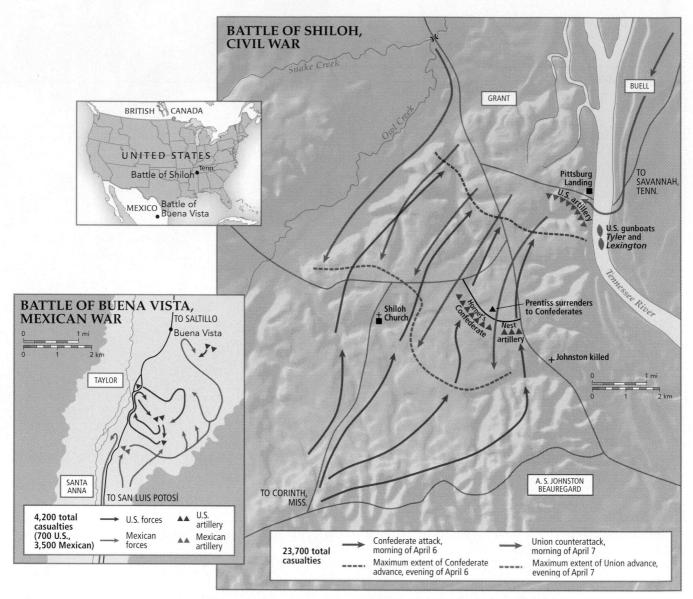

BATTLE OF SHILOH, CIVIL WAR

BRITISH CANADA

UNITED STATES

Battle of Shiloh •Tenn.

MEXICO •Battle of Buena Vista

Snake Creek

Owl Creek

BUELL

GRANT

Pittsburg Landing

U.S. artillery

TO SAVANNAH, TENN.

U.S. gunboats *Tyler* and *Lexington*

Tennessee River

+ Shiloh Church

Hornet's Confederate

Prentiss surrenders to Confederates

Nest artillery

+ Johnston killed

TO CORINTH, MISS.

A. S. JOHNSTON BEAUREGARD

0   1 mi
0   1   2 km

BATTLE OF BUENA VISTA, MEXICAN WAR

TO SALTILLO
Buena Vista

0   1 mi
0   1   2 km

TAYLOR

SANTA ANNA

TO SAN LUIS POTOSÍ

4,200 total casualties (700 U.S., 3,500 Mexican)

→ U.S. forces
→ Mexican forces
▲▲ U.S. artillery
▲▲ Mexican artillery

23,700 total casualties

→ Confederate attack, morning of April 6
---- Maximum extent of Confederate advance, evening of April 6
→ Union counterattack, morning of April 7
---- Maximum extent of Union advance, evening of April 7

THE CHANGING MAGNITUDE OF BATTLE

During the Mexican War at Buena Vista, the American army of 4,800 men was overextended to defend a two-mile line against 15,000 Mexicans. At Shiloh, in contrast, battle lines stretched almost six miles. (The maps are drawn to the same scale.) Against 40,000 Confederates, Grant galloped back and forth, rallying some 35,000 troops organized under five subordinates and coordinating the overnight reinforcement of 25,000 troops. The size of the armies, the complexity of their organization, the length of the battle lines, and the number of casualties all demonstrate the extent to which the magnitude of battle had changed.

they could win the war. Meanwhile, new supplies of cotton from Egypt and India enabled the British textile industry to recover. In the end, Britain and the rest of Europe refused to recognize the Confederacy, and the South was left to stand or fall on its own resources.

Grant in the West >> In the western war theater, the first decisive Union victory was won by a short, shabbily dressed, cigar-chomping general named Ulysses S. Grant. An undistinguished student at West Point, Grant eventually had

resigned his commission. He had failed at everything he tried in civilian life, and when the war broke out, he was a store clerk in Galena, Illinois. Almost 39, he promptly volunteered, and two months later became a brigadier general.

Grant's quiet, self-effacing manner gave little indication of his military ability or iron determination. He had a flair for improvising, was alert to seize any opening, and remained extraordinarily calm and clear-headed in battle. Most important, Grant grasped that hard fighting, not fancy maneuvering, would bring victory. "The art of war is simple," he once explained. "Find out where your enemy is, get at him as soon as you can and strike him as hard as you can, and keep moving on."

Grant realized that rivers were avenues into the interior of the Confederacy, and in February 1862, supported by Union gunboats, he captured Fort Henry on the Tennessee River and Fort Donelson on the Cumberland. These victories forced the Confederates to withdraw from Kentucky and middle Tennessee. Grant continued south with 40,000 men, but he was surprised on April 6 by General Albert Johnston at Shiloh, just north of the Tennessee-Mississippi border. Johnston was killed in the day's fierce fighting, but by nightfall his army had driven the Union troops back to the Tennessee River, where they huddled numbly as a cold rain fell. William Tecumseh Sherman, one of Grant's subordinates, found the general standing under a dripping tree, his coat collar drawn up against the damp, puffing on a cigar. Sherman was

about to suggest retreat, but something in Grant's eyes, lighted by the glow of his stogie, made him hesitate. So he said only, "Well, Grant, we've had the devil's own day, haven't we?" "Yes," the Union commander replied quietly. "Lick 'em tomorrow, though." And he did. With the aid of reinforcements, which he methodically ferried across the river all night, Grant counterattacked the next morning and drove the Confederates from the field.

But victory came at a high price, for Shiloh inflicted more than 23,000 casualties. The Confederacy would not yield easily. "At Shiloh," Grant wrote afterward, "I gave up all idea of saving the Union except by complete conquest."

Eastern Stalemate >> Grant's victories did not silence his critics, who charged that he drank too much. But Lincoln was unmoved. "I can't spare this man. He

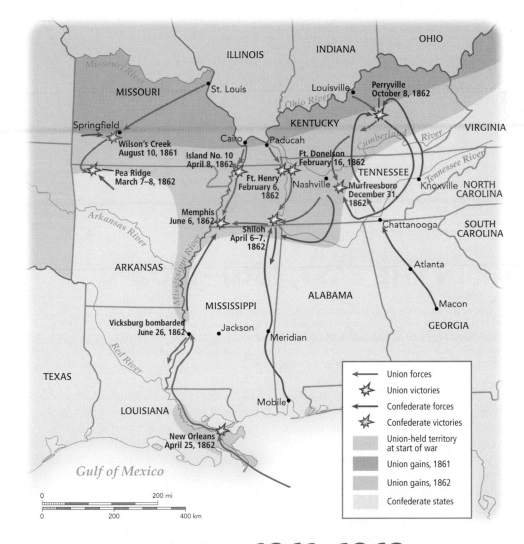

THE WAR IN THE WEST, 1861–1862

Grant's push southward stalled after his costly victory at Shiloh; nevertheless, by the end of 1862 the Union had secured Kentucky and Missouri, as well as most of Confederate Tennessee and the upper and lower stretches of the Mississippi River.

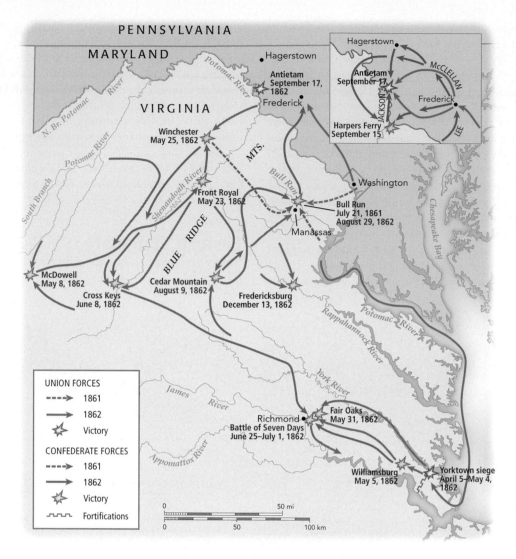

Map labels:

PENNSYLVANIA
MARYLAND
VIRGINIA

Hagerstown
Antietam September 17, 1862
Frederick
Winchester May 25, 1862
Front Royal May 23, 1862
MTS.
Bull Run
Washington
Bull Run July 21, 1861 August 29, 1862
Manassas
McDowell May 8, 1862
Cross Keys June 8, 1862
Cedar Mountain August 9, 1862
Fredericksburg December 13, 1862
BLUE RIDGE
Shenandoah River
Potomac River
N. Br. Potomac River
South Branch
Chesapeake Bay
Rappahannock River
Potomac River
James River
Appomattox River
York River
Richmond
Fair Oaks May 31, 1862
Battle of Seven Days June 25–July 1, 1862
Williamsburg May 5, 1862
Yorktown siege April 5–May 4, 1862

Inset map:
Hagerstown
Antietam September 17
McCLELLAN
JACKSON
Frederick
Harpers Ferry September 15
LEE

Legend:
UNION FORCES
----> 1861
——> 1862
✪ Victory

CONFEDERATE FORCES
----> 1861
——> 1862
✪ Victory
⌐⌐⌐ Fortifications

0   50 mi
0   50   100 km

THE WAR IN THE EAST, 1861–1862

McClellan's campaign against Richmond failed when Joseph Johnston surprised him at Fair Oaks. Taking command of the Army of Northern Virginia, Lee drove back McClellan in the Seven Days' battles, then won a resounding victory over Pope in the second Battle of Bull Run. He followed this up by invading Maryland. McClellan checked his advance at Antietam. The Army of the Potomac's devastating defeat at Fredericksburg ended a year of frustration and failure for the Union in the eastern theater.

fights." That was a quality in short supply in the East, where General McClellan directed operations.

McClellan looked like a general, but beneath his arrogance and bravado lay a self-doubt that rendered him excessively cautious. As the months dragged on and McClellan did nothing but train and plan, Lincoln's frustration grew. "If General McClellan does not want to use the army I would like to *borrow* it," he remarked sarcastically. In the spring of 1862 the general finally transported his 130,000 troops to the Virginia coast and began inching toward Richmond, the Confederate capital. That summer he faced a new and formidable adversary as Robert E. Lee took command of the Army of Northern Virginia. Where McClellan was cautious and defensive, the aristocratic Lee was daring and ever alert to assume the offensive. His first name, one

of his colleagues commented, should have been Audacity: "He will take more chances, and take them quicker than any other general in this country."

In the Seven Days' battles, McClellan successfully parried the attacks of Lee and Thomas "Stonewall" Jackson, a deeply religious Calvinist whose rigorous discipline honed his troops to a hard edge. But McClellan, ever cautious, pulled the Union army back until it was under the protection of Union gunboats. Frustrated, Lincoln ordered the Peninsula campaign abandoned and formed a new army under John Pope. After Lee mauled Pope at the second Battle of Bull Run in August, Lincoln restored McClellan to command.

Now Lee looked to strike a decisive victory for the Confederacy. He invaded the North, hoping to detach Maryland and isolate Washington. By good fortune McClellan learned of Lee's battle plan but even with this advantage managed only to launch a series of badly coordinated assaults near Antietam Creek on September 17. Lee repulsed the attack, though barely. The bloody exchanges horrified both sides for their sheer carnage. Nearly 5,000 soldiers were killed and another 18,000 wounded, making it the bloodiest single day in American history. Soon after McClellan allowed Lee's army to escape back into Virginia, an exasperated Lincoln permanently relieved him of command.

The winter of 1862 was the North's Valley Forge, as morale sank to an all-time low. General Ambrose Burnside, who assumed McClellan's place, took little more than a month to demonstrate his utter incompetence at the Battle of Fredericksburg. The Union's disastrous defeat there prompted Lincoln to put "Fighting Joe" Hooker in charge. In the West, Grant had emerged as the dominant figure, but the Army of the Potomac still lacked a capable commander, the deaths kept mounting, and no end to the war was in sight.

EMANCIPATION

In 1858 Abraham Lincoln had proclaimed that the United States must eventually become either all slave or all free. When the war began, however, the president refused to make emancipation a Union war aim. He feared the social upheaval that such a revolutionary step would cause, and he did not want to alarm the wavering border slave states.

Republican radicals such as Senator Charles Sumner and newspaper editor Horace Greeley pressed Lincoln to adopt a policy of emancipation. Slavery had caused the war, they argued; its destruction would hasten the war's end. Lincoln, however, placed first priority on saving the Union. "My paramount object in this struggle is to save the Union, and is not either to save or to destroy slavery," he wrote Greeley in 1862. "If I could save the Union without freeing any slave I would do it, and if I could save it by freeing all the slaves I would do it, and if I could save it by freeing some and leaving others alone, I would also do that." For the first year of the war, this remained Lincoln's policy.

The Presence of Death

"The Civil War matters to us today because it ended slavery and helped to define the meanings of freedom, citizenship, and equality. It established a newly centralized nation-state and launched it on a trajectory of economic expansion and world influence. But for those Americans who lived in and through the Civil War, the texture of the experience, its warp and woof, was the presence of death."

—Drew Faust,
This Republic of Suffering

The Logic of Events >> As the Union army began to occupy Confederate territory, slaves flocked to the Union lines. In May 1861 the army adopted the policy of declaring runaway slaves "**contraband** of war" and refused to return them to their rebel owners. In the Confiscation Act of August 1861, Congress provided that slaves used for military purposes by the Confederacy would become free if they fell into Union hands. For a year Lincoln accepted that position but would go no further. When two of his generals, acting on their own authority, abolished slavery in their districts, he countermanded their orders.

contraband goods seized by a government during wartime, when the goods were being used by an enemy nation or being shipped to an enemy nation by a neutral nation. The term was also applied during the Civil War to escaped slaves who fled behind Union lines.

By 1862 opinion was clearly shifting. In July Congress passed the Second Confiscation Act, which declared that the slaves of anyone who supported the rebellion would be freed if they came into federal custody. Unlike with the first act, it did not matter whether the slaves had been used for military purposes. Lincoln signed this bill, then proceeded to ignore it. Instead, he encouraged the border states to undertake programs of gradual emancipation, warning them that the war was likely to destroy slavery of its own momentum.

When Lincoln's efforts were rebuffed, on July 22 he presented to his cabinet a proposed proclamation freeing the slaves in the Confederacy. He was increasingly confident that the border states would remain in the Union, and he wanted to strike a blow that would weaken the Confederacy militarily. By making the struggle one of freedom versus slavery, such a proclamation would also undermine Confederate efforts to obtain diplomatic recognition. But Lincoln decided to wait for a Union military victory, so that his act would not seem like one of desperation.

The Emancipation Proclamation >> On September 22, 1862, in the aftermath of the victory at Antietam, Lincoln announced that all slaves within rebel lines would be freed unless the seceded states returned to their allegiance by January 1, 1863. When that day came, the Emancipation Proclamation went into effect. Excluded from its terms were the Union slave states and areas of the Confederacy that were under Union control. In all, about 830,000 of the nation's 4 million slaves were not covered by its provisions. Since Lincoln justified his actions on strictly military grounds, he believed he had no legal right to apply the measure to areas not in rebellion.

After initial criticism of the Proclamation, European public opinion swung toward the Union. Within the Union, popular reaction was mixed. Even so, the Emancipation Proclamation had immense symbolic importance, for it redefined the nature of the war. The North was fighting, not to save the old Union, but to create a new nation. The war had become, in Lincoln's words, "remorseless revolution."

African Americans' Civil War >> Under

the pressure of war, slavery disintegrated. Well before federal troops entered an area, slaves undermined the institution by openly challenging white authority and claiming greater personal freedom. One experienced overseer reported in frustration that the "slaves will do only what pleases them, go out in the morning when it suits them, come in when they please, etc."

Early in the conflict slaves concluded that emancipation would be one consequence of a Union victory.

freedmen or **freedpeople** } former slaves

Perhaps as many as half a million—one-seventh of the total slave population of the Confederacy—fled to Union lines. The ex-slaves, called "freedmen," ended up living in refugee or contraband camps that were overcrowded and disease-ridden and provided only the most basic shelter and food.

Convinced that freed slaves would not work on their own initiative, the U.S. government put some contrabands to work assisting the army. Their wages were well below those paid white citizens for the same work. In the Mississippi valley, where two-thirds of the freedpeople under Union control were located, most were forced to work on plantations leased or owned by loyal planters. They worked for little more than room and board, and the conditions often approximated slavery.

Black Soldiers >> In adopting the policy of eman-

cipation, Lincoln also announced that African Americans would be accepted into the navy and, more controversially, the army. Resistance to accepting black volunteers in the army remained especially strong in the Midwest. Black northerners themselves were divided over whether to enlist, but Frederick Douglass spoke for the vast majority when he argued that once a black man had served in the army, there was "no power on earth which can deny that he has earned the right of citizenship in the United States."

In the end, nearly 200,000 black Americans served in the Union forces, about 10 percent of the Union's total military manpower. Some, including two of Douglass's sons, were free, but most were former slaves who enlisted after escaping to Union lines. As a concession to the racism of white troops, blacks served in segregated units under white officers. Not until June 1864 did Congress grant equal pay to African American soldiers.

Assigned at first to the most undesirable duties, black soldiers successfully lobbied for the chance to fight. They deeply impressed white troops with their courage under fire. "I have been one of those men, who never had much confidence in colored troops fighting," one Union officer admitted, "but these doubts are now all removed, for they fought as bravely as any troops in the Fort." In the end 37,000 African American servicemen gave their lives, a rate of loss about 40 percent higher than that among white soldiers. Black recruits had good reason to fight fiercely: they knew that the freedom of their race hung in the balance, they hoped to win civil rights at home by

⌄ Black men, including runaway slaves, joined the Union army and navy beginning in 1863. As soldiers, former slaves developed a new sense of pride and confidence. At his first roll call, recruit Elijah Marrs recalled, "I felt freedom in my bones."

their performance on the battlefield, they resented racist sneers about their loyalty and ability, and they knew that capture might mean death.

THE CONFEDERATE HOME FRONT

"How shall we subsist this winter?" John Jones wondered in the fall of 1862. A clerk in the War Department in Richmond, Jones found it increasingly difficult to make ends meet. Prices kept going up, essential items were in short supply, and the signs of hardship were everywhere: in the darned and patched clothing, in the absence of meat from the market, in the desperation on people's faces. Coffee was a luxury Jones could no longer afford; he sold his watch to buy fuel. "I cannot afford to have more than an ounce of meat daily for each member of my family of six," he recorded in 1864. ". . . We see neither rats nor mice about the premises now." By the end of the year inflation had taken such a toll that a month's supply of food and fuel was costing him $762, a sum sufficient to have supported his family for a year in peacetime. "This is war, terrible war!"

Nowhere was the effect of war more complete than within the Confederacy. Changes there were especially ironic, since the southern states had seceded in order to preserve their traditional ways. The demands of war fundamentally transformed the southern economy, society, and government.

The New Economy >> With the Union blockade tightening, the production of foodstuffs became crucial. More and more plantations switched from cotton to raising grain and livestock. As a result, cotton production dropped from 4.5 million bales in 1861 to 300,000 in 1864. Even so, food production declined. In the last two years of the war, the shortage was serious.

The Union blockade also made it impossible to rely on European manufactured goods. So the Confederate War Department built and ran factories, took over the region's mines, and regulated private manufacturers so as to increase the production of war goods. Although the Confederacy never became industrially self-sufficient, its accomplishments were impressive. In fact, the Confederacy sustained itself far better in industrial goods than it did in agricultural produce. It was symbolic that when Lee surrendered, his troops had sufficient guns and ammunition to continue, but they had not eaten in two days.

New Opportunities for Southern Women >> Southern white women took an active role in the war. Some gained notoriety as spies; others smuggled military supplies into the South. Women also spent a good deal of time knitting and sewing clothes for soldiers. Perhaps most important, with so many men fighting, women took charge of agricultural production. On plantations the mistress often supervised the slaves as well as the wrenching shift from cotton to foodstuffs. "All this attention to farming is uphill work with me," one South Carolina woman confessed to her army husband.

One such woman was Emily Lyles Harris, the wife of a small slaveowner in upcountry South Carolina. When her husband joined the army in 1862, she was left to care for her seven children as well as supervise the slaves and manage the farm. Despite the disruptions of wartime, she succeeded remarkably, one year producing the largest crop of oats in the neighborhood and always making enough money for her family to live decently. She took little pride, however, in her achievements. "I shall never get used to being left as the head of affairs at home," she confessed. "The burden is very heavy, and there is no one to smile on me as I trudge wearily along in the dark with it." While she pushed on, by 1865 she openly hoped for defeat.

The war also opened up new jobs off the farm. Given the personnel shortage, "government girls" became essential to fill the growing Confederate bureaucracy. At first women were paid half the wages of male coworkers, but by the end of the war they had won equal pay. Women also staffed the new factories springing up in southern cities and towns, undertaking even dangerous work in munitions plants.

∧ "Nannie" McKenzie Semple was one of many southern white women who worked for the Confederate government. Semple's salary, for working as a "Treasury Girl," netted her more than what the average soldier received.

Confederate Finance and Government >>

The most serious domestic problem the Confederate government faced was finance, for which officials at Richmond never developed a satisfactory program. Only in 1863 did the government begin levying a **graduated income tax** (from 1 to 15 percent) and a series of excise taxes. Most controversial, the government resorted to a tax-in-kind on farmers that, after exempting a certain portion, took one-tenth of their crops. Even more unpopular was the policy of impressment, which allowed the army to seize private property for its own use, often with little or no compensation.

graduated income tax tax based on a percentage of an individual's income, the percentage increasing as total income increases.

Above all, the Confederacy financed the war effort simply by printing paper money not backed by specie, some $1.5 billion, which amounted to three times more than the federal government issued. The result was runaway inflation, so that by 1865 a Confederate dollar was worth only 1.7 cents in gold and prices had soared to 92 times their prewar base. Prices were highest in Richmond, where flour sold for $275 a barrel by early 1864 and coats for $350 each.

In politics even more than finance, the Confederacy exercised far greater powers than those of the federal government before 1861. Indeed, Jefferson Davis strove to meet the demands of total war by transforming the South into a centralized, national state. He sought to limit state authority over military units, and in April 1862 the Confederacy passed the first national **conscription** law in American history. The same year, the Confederate Congress authorized Davis to invoke martial law and suspend the writ of habeas corpus.

conscription act of compulsory enrollment for military service, as opposed to a voluntary enlistment.

Critics protested that Davis was destroying states' rights, the driving principle of the Confederacy. Intent on preserving states' traditional powers, Confederate governors obstructed the draft and retained military supplies. When President Davis suspended the writ of habeas corpus, his own vice president, Alexander H. Stephens, accused him of aiming at a dictatorship. Davis used those powers for a limited time and only with the permission of Congress, yet in practice it made little difference whether the writ was suspended or not. With disloyalty a greater problem than in the Union, the Confederate army arrested thousands of civilians.

But the Confederate draft, more than any other measure, produced an outcry. As one Georgia leader complained, "It's a notorious fact if a man has influential friends—or a little money to spare he will never be enrolled." Most controversially, the draft exempted from service one white man on every plantation with 20 or more slaves (later reduced to 15). This law was designed to preserve control of the slave population, but more and more nonslaveholders complained that it was a rich man's war and a poor man's fight.

Hardship and Suffering >>

By the last year of the conflict, food shortages had become so severe that ingenious southerners concocted various substitutes: parched corn in place of coffee, strained blackberries in place of vinegar. Scarcity bred speculation, hoarding, and spiraling prices. The high prices and food shortages led to riots, most seriously in Richmond early in April 1863, when about 300 women and children chanting "Bread!" looted stores.

As always, war corroded the discipline and the order of society. Speculation was rampant, gambling halls were crowded with revelers seeking relief, and many southerners spent money in frenzied haste. Even in the army, theft became common, and in Richmond, the House of Representatives was robbed and Jefferson Davis's favorite horse stolen.

The frantic effort to escape war's grim reality led to a forced gaiety among southern civilians. "The cities are gayer than before the war," one refugee reported, "—parties every night in Richmond, suppers costing ten and twenty thousand dollars." Walking home at night after spending several hours at the bedside of a dying soldier, Judith McGuire passed a house echoing with laughter, music, and dancing. "The revulsion was sickening," she wrote in her diary. "I . . . felt shocked that our own Virginians, at such a time, should remind me of scenes which we were wont to think only belonged to . . . foreign society." The war was a cancer that ate away not only at southern society but at the southern soul itself.

Key: e

The states-rights government of the confederacy allowed its central government to exercise which of the following powers?

a. creation of a graduated income tax

b. establishment of the first national draft law in American history

c. proclamation of martial law

d. suspension of habeas corpus

e. all of these

THE UNION HOME FRONT

Since the war was fought mostly on southern soil, northern civilians rarely felt its effects directly. Yet to be effective, the North's economic resources had to be organized and mobilized.

Government Finances and the Economy >>

To begin with, the North required a comprehensive system to finance its massive campaign. Taxing the populace was one obvious means, and taxes paid for 21 percent of Union war expenses, compared with only 1 percent of the Confederacy's. In August 1861 Congress levied the first federal income tax, of 3 percent on all incomes over $800 a year. When that, along with increased tariff duties, proved insufficient, Congress enacted a comprehensive tax law in 1862 that for the first time brought the tax collector into every northern household.

> **bonds** certificates of debt issued by a government or corporation promising to repay the buyers of the bonds their original investment, plus interest, by a specified date of maturity.

The government also borrowed heavily, through the sale of $2.2 billion in **bonds**. It financed the rest of the war's cost by issuing paper money. In all, the Union printed $431 million in greenbacks (so named because of their color on one side). Congress also instituted a national banking system, allowing nationally chartered banks to issue notes backed by U.S. bonds. By taxing state bank notes out of circulation, Congress for the first time created a uniform national currency.

During the war, the Republican-controlled Congress encouraged economic development. Tariffs to protect industry from foreign competition rose to an average rate of 47 percent, compared to 19 percent in 1860. To encourage development of the West, the Homestead Act of 1862 granted 160 acres of public land—the size of the traditional American family farm—to anyone (including women) who settled and improved the land for five years. In addition, the Land Grant College Act of 1862 donated the proceeds from certain land sales to finance public colleges and universities. This aid was especially crucial in promoting higher education in the West.

A Rich Man's War >>

Over the course of the war the government purchased more than $1 billion worth of goods and services. In response to this heavy demand, the economy boomed and business and agriculture prospered. Since prices rose faster than wages, workers' real income dropped almost 30 percent, which meant that the working class paid a disproportionate share of financing the war.

The Republican belief that government should play a major role in the economy also fostered a cozy relationship between business and politics. In the rush to profit from government contracts, some suppliers succumbed to the temptation to sell inferior goods at inflated prices. Uniforms made of "shoddy"—bits of unused thread and recycled cloth—were fobbed off in such numbers that the word became an adjective describing inferior quality.

Stocks and dividends rose with the economy, speculation during the last two years of the war became particularly feverish, and the fortunes made went toward the purchase of showy luxuries. Like Richmond, Washington became the symbol of this moral decay. Prostitution, drinking, and corruption reached epidemic proportions in the capital, and social festivities became the means to shut out the numbing horror of the casualty lists.

Women and the Workforce >>

Even more than in the South, the war opened new opportunities for northern women. Countless wives ran farms while their husbands were away at war. One traveler in Iowa reported, "I met more women driving teams on the road and saw more at work in the fields than men." The war also stimulated the shift to mechanization: by 1865 three times as many reapers and harvesters were in use as in 1861. Beyond the farm, women filled approximately 100,000 new jobs in industry. As in the South, they also worked as clerks in the expanding government bureaucracy.

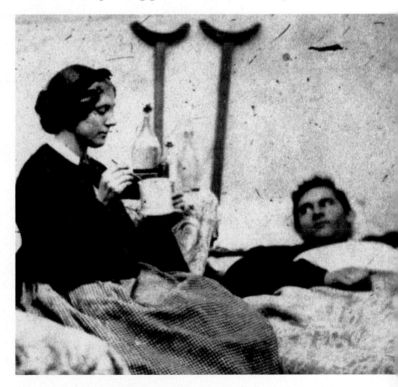

⌃ A nurse tends a wounded Union soldier in a military hospital in Nashville, Tennessee. Despite the opposition of army doctors, hundreds of female volunteers worked in army hospitals for each side.

The war also allowed women to enter and eventually dominate the profession of nursing. "Our women appear to have become almost wild on the subject of hospital nursing," protested one physician, who like many others opposed their presence. Led by Drs. Emily and Elizabeth Blackwell, Dorothea Dix, and Mary Ann Bickerdyke, women fought the bureaucratic inefficiency of the army medical corps. Their service in the hospital wards reduced the hostility to women in medicine.

One nurse was Clara Barton, who later founded the Red Cross. During the battle of Fredericksburg, she worked in a battlefield hospital. She later recalled that as she rose from the side of one soldier, "I wrung the blood from the bottom of my clothing, before I could step, for the weight about my feet." She steeled herself at the sight of amputated arms and legs casually tossed in piles outside the front door as the surgeons cut away. Sleeping in a tent nearby, she drove herself to the brink of exhaustion until the last patients were transferred to permanent hospitals.

Civil Liberties and Dissent >>

In mobilizing the northern war effort, Lincoln did not hesitate to curb dissenters. Shortly after the firing on Fort Sumter, he suspended the writ of habeas corpus in specified areas, which allowed the indefinite detention of anyone suspected of disloyalty or activity against the war. Although the Constitution permitted such suspension in time of rebellion or invasion, Lincoln did so without consulting Congress (unlike President Davis), and he used his power far more broadly, expanding it in 1862 to cover the entire North for cases involving antiwar activities. The president also decreed that those arrested under its provisions could be tried in a military court. Eventually more than 20,000 individuals were arrested, most of whom were never brought to trial.

Democrats attacked Lincoln as a tyrant bent on destroying the Constitution. After the war, the Supreme Court, in *Ex parte Milligan* (1866), struck down the military conviction of a civilian accused of plotting to free Confederate prisoners of war. The Court ruled that as long as the

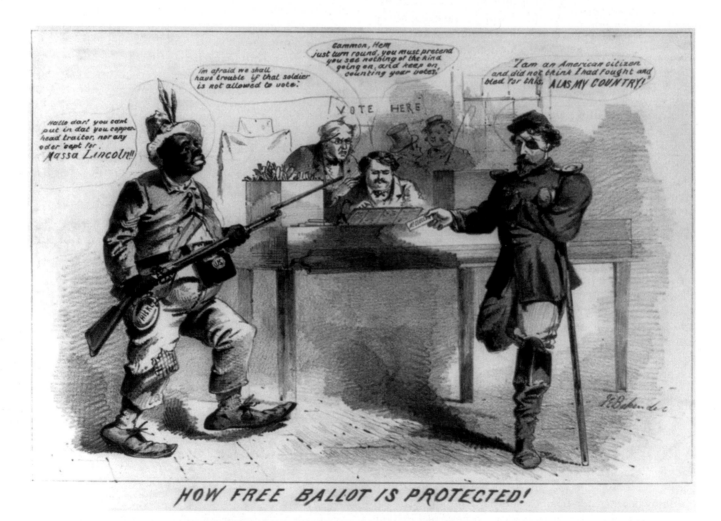

^ This anti-Republican cartoon from Philadelphia expresses the fears of many Copperhead Democrats that the war for Union had been subverted by becoming a war on slavery. A caricatured black soldier tries to prevent a legless Union veteran from voting for General McClellan, Lincoln's opponent in the election of 1864. The election clerk beside the stuffed ballot box is told to "pretend you see nothing" of the ballot stuffing.

^ The average soldier spent 50 days in camp for every day in battle. The dull routine of roll call, drill, and march was complicated by poor sanitation, miserable food, sickness and disease.

regular courts were open, civilians could not be tried by military tribunals.

Republicans labeled those who opposed the war **Copperheads**, conjuring up the image of a venomous snake waiting to strike the Union. Copperheads constituted the extreme peace wing of the Democratic party. They condemned the draft as an attack on individual freedom and an instrument of special privilege. According to the provisions enacted in 1863, a person would be exempt from the present draft by paying a commutation fee of $300, about a year's wages for a worker or an ordinary farmer. Or those drafted could hire a substitute, the cost of which was beyond the reach of all but the wealthy. In July 1863, largely Irish workers in New York City rose in anger against the draft. By the time order was restored four days later, at least 105 people had been killed, the worst loss of life from any riot in American history.

> **Copperhead** derogatory term used by Republicans to label northern Democrats who opposed the war policies of the Lincoln administration and advocated a negotiated peace.

GONE TO BE A SOLDIER

Marcus Spiegel, the son of a rabbi, came to the United States after the German revolution of 1848 failed. Spiegel became a naturalized citizen and was trying to make it in the restaurant business in Ohio when the war began. He considered it his duty to preserve the Union for his children, so he enlisted as a lieutenant and eventually rose to the rank of colonel. Spiegel did not go to war to end slavery and flatly proclaimed that black people were not "worth fighting for." But after seeing slavery first hand, his views changed, and by 1864 he was "in favor of doing away with the institution of Slavery." He assured his wife that "this is no hasty conclusion but a deep conviction." A few weeks later, Spiegel died while fighting in Louisiana.

By war's end about two million men had served the Union cause and another million the Confederate. They were mostly young, with almost 40 percent of entering soldiers 21 years of age or younger. They were not drawn disproportionately from the poor, and in both North and South, farmers and farm laborers accounted for the largest number of recruits.

Discipline >> The near-holiday atmosphere of the war's early months soon gave way to dull routine. Men from rural areas, accustomed to the freedom of the farm, complained about the endless recurrence of reveille, roll call, and drill. "When this war is over," one Rebel promised, "I will whip the man that says 'fall in' to me." Troops in neither army cared for the spit and polish of regular army men. "They keep us very strict here," noted one Illinois soldier. "It is the most like a prison of any place I ever saw."

By modern standards training was minimal and discipline lax in both armies. Troops from rural families found it harder to adjust to army routine than did urban soldiers, especially factory workers, who were more familiar with impersonal organizations and used to greater social control.

Many southerners were "not used to control of any sort," one Rebel noted, "and were not disposed to obey anyone except for good and sufficient reason given." Manifesting strong feelings of equality that clashed with military hierarchy, Yanks and Rebs alike complained about officers' privileges and had no special respect for rank. "The boys recognized no superiors, except in the line of legitimate duty," an Indiana private explained. The Union discontinued the election of lower officers, but this tradition was retained in the Confederate army, further undermining discipline, since those known as strict disciplinarians were eventually defeated.

Camp Life >> On average, soldiers spent 50 days in camp for every day in battle. Camp life was often unhealthy as well as unpleasant. Poor sanitation, miserable food, exposure, and primitive medical care contributed to widespread sickness and disease. It was a common belief that if a fellow went to the hospital, "you might as well say good bye." Conditions were even worse in the Confederate hospitals, for the Union blockade produced a shortage of medical supplies. Twice as many soldiers died from dysentery, typhoid, and other diseases as from wounds.

The boredom of camp life, the horrors of battle, and the influence of an all-male society all corrupted morals. Swearing and heavy drinking were common and gambling was pervasive, especially immediately after payday. Prostitutes flooded the camps of both armies. Yet with death so near, some soldiers also sought solace in religion, especially in Confederate camps. A wave of revivals swept their ranks during the last two winters of the war, producing between 100,000 and 200,000 conversions. Significantly, the first major revivals occurred after the South's twin defeats at Vicksburg and Gettysburg. Then, too, as battle after battle thinned Confederate ranks, the prospect of death loomed increasingly large.

The Changing Face of Battle >> As in all modern wars, technology revolutionized the conditions under which Civil War soldiers fought. Smoothbore muskets, which at first served as the basic infantry weapon, gave way to the rifle, so named because of the grooves etched into the barrel to give a bullet spin. The percussion cap rendered a rifle serviceable in wet weather. More important, the new weapon had an effective range of 400 yards—five times greater than that of the old musket. As a result, soldiers fought each other from greater distances and battles produced many more casualties. Over 100 regiments on both sides suffered more than 50 percent casualties in a single battle.

Under such conditions, the defense became a good deal stronger than the offense. Although larger artillery

At first neither the Union nor the Confederacy possessed adequate field hospitals to treat the war's thousands of casualties. Wounded soldiers lay untended in a drenching rain, or waited so long for assistance, their open wounds teemed with maggots "as though a swarm of bees had settled" on them. Confederate Walter Lenoir had his wounded leg sawn off below the knee and then endured a 20-mile ride in a rude farm wagon, every jolt causing "a pang which felt as if my stump was thrust into liquid fire."

pieces were too inaccurate to effectively support attacking troops, they proved deadly when fired at close range against advancing infantry.

As the haze of gunfire covered the land and the constant spray of bullets mimicked rain pattering through the treetops, soldiers discovered that their romantic notions about war had no place on the battlefield. Men witnessed horrors they had never envisioned as civilians and choked from the stench of decaying flesh. They realized that their efforts to convey to those back home the gruesome truth of combat were inadequate. "No tongue can tell, no mind can conceive, no pen portray the horrible sights I witnessed this morning," a Union soldier wrote after Antietam. And yet they tried.

An Ohio soldier at Antietam (23,000 casualties), two days after the fighting: "The smell was offul . . . there was about 5 or 6,000 dead bodes decaying over the field . . . I could have walked on the boddees all most from one end too the other." A Georgian, the day after Chancellorsville (30,000 casualties): "It looked more like a slaughter pen than anything else. . . . The shrieks and groans of the wounded . . . was heart rending beyond all description." A Maine soldier who fought at Gettysburg (50,000 casualties): "I have Seen . . . men rolling in their own blood, Some Shot in one place, Some another. . . . our dead lay in the road and the Rebels in their hast to leave dragged both their baggage wagons and artillery over them and they lay mangled and torn to pieces so that Even friends could not tell them. You can form no idea of a battle field."

Hardening Attitudes >> Throughout the war, Civil War soldiers continued to speak in terms of the traditional ideals of duty, honor, and patriotism. Nevertheless,

military service profoundly changed them. The early volunteers of 1861 expected to fight a restrained war that upheld their moral code. They admired the courage of the foe and considered it pointless to kill an isolated soldier.

By 1864 the nature of war had been transformed. Soldiers discovered the futility of mass frontal assaults, and under the rain of fire on the battlefield, they sought to kill enemy soldiers any way they could in order to hasten the war's end. At the same time, they became indifferent to death and suffering. Amidst "the daily sight of blood and mangled bodies," combatants began taking personal property from the dead and wounded and even prisoners after a battle.

Increasingly alienated from civilians back home, soldiers on both sides developed a stronger sense of comradeship with their adversaries, based on their belief that only other soldiers could understand what they had gone through and why they acted the way they did. In the face of what Charles Francis Adams, Jr., termed "the carnival of death," soldiers braced themselves with a grim determination to see the war through to the end. Not glorious exploits but endurance became the true measure of heroism. Exclaimed one chastened Georgia soldier, "What a scourge is war."

THE UNION'S TRIUMPH

In the spring of 1863 matters still looked promising for Lee. At the battle of Chancellorsville, he won another brilliant victory. But during the fighting Stonewall Jackson was accidentally shot by his own men, and he died a few days later—a grievous setback for the Confederacy. Determined to take the offensive, Lee invaded Pennsylvania in June with an army of 75,000. Lincoln's newest general, George Gordon Meade, warily shadowed the Confederates. On the first of July, advance parties from the two armies accidentally collided at the town of Gettysburg, and the war's greatest battle ensued.

Reveille rouses drowsy Union soldiers on a wintry morning as a drummer boy warms his hands. Instead of the glory they expected, reveille, roll call, and drill constituted Civil War soldier's usual camp routine. A hired black laborer Is already at work as the troops awaken.

For once it was Lee who had the extended supply lines and was forced to fight on ground chosen by his opponent. After two days of assaults failed to break the Union left or right, Lee made the greatest mistake of his career, sending 14,000 men under General George Pickett in a charge up the center of the Union line. "Pickett's division just seemed to melt away in the blue musketry smoke which now covered the hill," one Confederate officer wrote. "Nothing but stragglers came back." With the loss of more than a third of his troops, Lee was never again able to assume the offensive.

Lincoln Finds His General >>
To the west, Grant had been trying for months to capture Vicksburg, a Rebel stronghold on the Mississippi. In a daring maneuver, he left behind his supply lines and marched inland, feeding his army from the produce of Confederate farms. These were the tactics of total war, and seldom had they been tried before. On July 4, the city surrendered. With the fall of Port Hudson, Louisiana, four days later, the Mississippi was completely in Union hands, thus dividing the Confederacy.

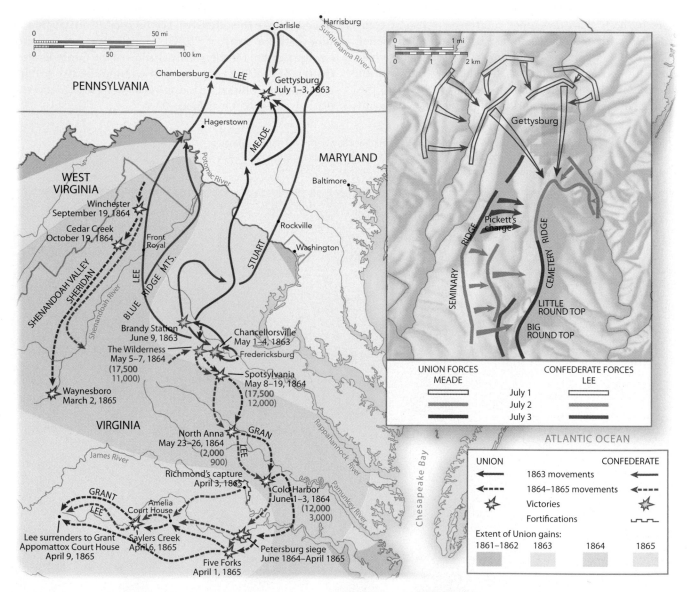

THE WAR IN THE EAST, 1863–1865

Lee won his most brilliant victory at Chancellorsville, then launched a second invasion of the North, which ended in defeat at Gettysburg. In 1864 Grant delivered a series of blows against Lee's outnumbered forces in Virginia. Despite staggering losses, Grant pressed on in a ruthless demonstration of total war. (Note the casualties listed from mid-May to mid-June of 1864; Grant lost nearly 60,000 men, equal to Lee's total strength.) In April 1865, too weak to defend Richmond any longer, Lee surrendered at Appomattox Courthouse.

Grant followed up this victory by rescuing Union forces holed up in Chattanooga. His performance confirmed Lincoln's earlier judgment that "Grant is my man, and I am his the rest of the war." In March 1864 Lincoln brought Grant east and placed him in command of all the Union armies.

Grant recognized that in the past Union forces had "acted independently and without concert, like a balky team, no two ever pulling together." He intended to change that. While he launched a major offensive against Lee in Virginia, William Tecumseh Sherman, who replaced Grant as commander of the western army, would drive a diagonal wedge through the Confederacy from Tennessee across Georgia. Grant instructed Sherman to "get into the interior of the enemy's country so far as you can, inflicting all the damage you can against their war resources."

In May and June 1864 Grant tried to maneuver Lee out of the trenches and into an open battle. But Lee was too weak to win head-on, so he opted for a strategy of attrition, hoping to inflict such heavy losses that the northern will would break. It was a strategy that nearly worked, for Union casualties were staggering. In a month of fierce fighting, the Army of the Potomac lost 60,000 men. Yet at the end of the campaign Grant's reinforced army was larger than when it started, whereas Lee's was significantly weaker.

Unable to break Lee's lines, Grant settled into a siege of Petersburg, which guarded Richmond's last remaining rail

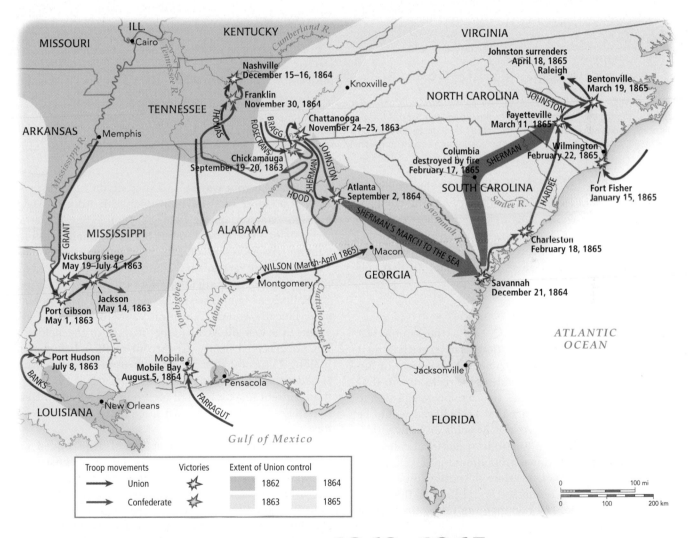

THE WAR IN THE WEST, 1863–1865

The Union continued its war of mobility in the western theater, bringing more Confederate territory under its control. After Grant captured Vicksburg, the entire Mississippi River lay in Union hands. His victories at Lookout Mountain and Missionary Ridge, near Chattanooga, ended the Confederate threat to Tennessee. In 1864 Sherman divided the Confederacy by seizing Atlanta and marching across Georgia; then he turned north. When Joseph Johnston surrendered, several weeks after Lee's capitulation at Appomattox, the war was effectively over.

U.S. Gunboat Cimerone "U.S.TROOPS BURNING "The COLE HOUSE and PLANTATION. OPPOSITE HARRIS Steamer Landing Fro

⌃ General William Sherman demonstrated the tactics of total war in the autumn of 1864. "Destroyed all we could not eat . . . burned their cotton and gins . . . burned and twisted their railroads . . .," wrote one of Sherman's soldiers. This drawing, done by a Union private, depicts a similar destructive raid on a plantation along Virginia's James River in 1862, and by the spring of 1865, Confederate armies were increasingly unable to resist Union might.

link to the south. In the west, meanwhile, the gaunt and grizzled Sherman fought his way by July to the outskirts of Atlanta, which was heavily defended and gave no sign of capitulating. "Our all depends on that army at Atlanta," wrote Mary Chesnut in August, based on her conversations with Confederate leaders in Richmond. "If that fails us, the game is up."

War in the Balance >> As the Union war machine swept more and more northerners south to their death, and with Grant and Sherman bogged down in Virginia and Georgia, Lincoln's chances for reelection in 1864 seemed slim. Yet the president rejected any suggestion to postpone the election, an act that he believed would be to lose democracy itself. At the Republican convention, he made certain that the Republican platform called for adoption of a constitutional amendment abolishing slavery. To balance the ticket, he selected Andrew Johnson, the military governor of Tennessee and a prowar Democrat, as his running mate. The two men ran under the label of the "Union" party.

The Democrats nominated George McClellan, the former Union commander. Their platform called for an armistice and a peace conference. Warned that a cessation of fighting would lead to disunion, McClellan partially repudiated this position, insisting that "the Union is the one condition of peace—we ask no more." In private he made it clear that if elected he intended to restore slavery. Late in August, Lincoln was still gloomy about his prospects, as well as those of the Union itself. But Admiral David Farragut won a dramatic victory at Mobile Bay, and a few weeks later, in early September, Sherman finally captured Atlanta. As Secretary of State Seward gleefully noted, "Sherman and Farragut have knocked the bottom out of the Chicago [Democratic] nominations."

Polling an impressive 55 percent of the popular vote, Lincoln won 212 electoral votes to McClellan's 21. Eighteen states allowed soldiers to vote in the field, and Lincoln received nearly 80 percent of their ballots. One lifelong Democrat described the sentiment in the army: "I had rather stay out here a lifetime (much as I dislike it) than consent to a division of our country." Jefferson Davis remained defiant, but the last hope of a Confederate victory was gone.

Equally important, the election of 1864 ended any doubt that slavery would be abolished in the reconstructed Union. The Emancipation Proclamation had not put an end to the question, for its legal status remained unclear. Lincoln argued that as a war measure, it would have no standing once peace returned; and in any case, it had not freed slaves in the border states or those parts of the Confederacy already under Union control.

In 1864 the Senate approved an amendment to the Constitution that freed all slaves without compensating their owners. The measure passed the House on January 31, 1865. By December, enough states had ratified the Thirteenth Amendment to make it part of the Constitution.

The war's greatest generals, Ulysses S. Grant (*left*) and Robert E. Lee (*right*), confronted each other in the eastern theater during the last year of the war. A member of a distinguished Virginia family, the tall, impeccably dressed Lee was every inch the aristocratic gentleman. Grant, a short, slouched figure with a stubby beard, dressed indifferently, but his determination is readily apparent in this picture, taken at his field headquarters in 1864.

The Twilight of the Confederacy >>

For the Confederacy, the outcome of the 1864 election had a terrible finality. In March 1865 the Confederate Congress authorized recruiting 300,000 slaves for military service. When he signed the bill, Davis announced that freedom would be given to those who volunteered and to their families. That same month he offered through a special envoy to abolish slavery in exchange for British diplomatic recognition. A Mississippi paper denounced this proposal as "a total abandonment of the chief object of this war." The British rejected the offer, and the war ended before any slaves were mustered into the Confederate army, but the demands of total war had forced Confederate leaders to forsake the Old South's most important values and institutions.

In the wake of Lincoln's reelection, the Confederate will to resist rapidly disintegrated. White southerners had never fully united behind the war effort, but the large majority had endured great suffering to uphold it. As Sherman pushed deeper into the Confederacy, however, the war came home to southern civilians as never before. "We haven't got nothing in the house to eat but a little bit o meal," wrote the wife of one Alabama soldier in December 1864. ". . . Try to get off and come home and fix us all up some and then you can go back. . . . If you put off a-coming, 'twont be no use to come, for we'll all . . . [be] in the grave yard." He deserted. In the last months of the fighting, over half the Confederacy's soldiers were absent without leave.

After the fall of Atlanta, Sherman gave a frightening demonstration of the meaning of total war. He imitated Grant's strategy by abandoning his supply lines for an audacious 300-mile march to the sea. The goal was to deprive Lee's army of the supplies it desperately needed to continue and to break the southern will to resist. Or as he bluntly put it, "to whip the Rebels, to humble their pride, to follow them to their recesses, and make them fear and dread us."

WITNESS

A Georgia Plantation Mistress in Sherman's Path

"Oh God, the time of trial has come! . . . To my smokehouse, my dairy, pantry, kitchen, and cellar, like famished wolves they come, breaking locks and whatever is in their way . . . they tore down my garden palings, made a road through my back yard and lot field, driving their stock and riding through, tearing down my fences and desolating my home—wantonly doing it when there was no necessity for it."

CHAPTER SUMMARY

As the first total war in history, the Civil War's outcome depended not just on armies but also on the mobilization of society's human, economic, and intellectual resources.

▮ Confederate president Jefferson Davis's policy of concentrating power in the government at Richmond, along with the resort to a draft and impressment of private property, provoked strong protests from many southerners.

▮ Abraham Lincoln's policies, especially his suspension of the writ of habeas corpus and his interference with civil liberties, were equally controversial.

▮ But Lincoln skillfully handled the delicate situation of the border states in the first year of the war, keeping them in the Union.

▮ Lincoln at first resisted pressure to make emancipation a Union war aim, but he eventually issued the Emancipation Proclamation, which transformed the meaning of the war.

▮ African Americans helped undermine slavery in the Confederacy and made a vital contribution to the Union's military victory.

▮ The war had a powerful impact on the home front.
  ▮ Women confronted new responsibilities and enjoyed new occupational opportunities.
  ▮ In the Confederacy, hardship and suffering became a fact of life.
  ▮ The Confederate government's financial and tax policies and the tightening Union blockade increased this suffering.

▮ Both societies also experienced the ravages of moral decay.

▮ The Civil War changed the nature of warfare.
  ▮ Technology, particularly the use of rifles and rifled artillery, revolutionized tactics and strategy.
  ▮ The Union eventually adopted the strategy of attacking the civilian population of the South.
  ▮ Soldiers in both armies suffered from disease and inadequate medical care, poor food, moral corruption, and the mounting death toll.

▮ The war altered the nation's political institutions, its economy, and its values.

Significant Events

Border states remain in the Union; Battle of Bull Run

1861

1862

Forts Henry and Donelson captured; Battle of Shiloh; New Orleans captured; McClellan's Peninsula campaign fails; Battle of Antietam; Lincoln suspends writ of habeas corpus throughout the Union; Battle of Fredericksburg

Additional Reading

Histories of the Civil War tend to concentrate on either the home front or the military, and on either the Confederacy or the Union. A good single-volume history of the war, up to date in its scholarship and balanced in its judgments, covering all these topics, is James M. McPherson, *Battle Cry of Freedom* (1988). In recent years military historians have devoted more attention to the relationship between society and the military. An interesting example that traces the evolution of the Union's strategy toward southern civilians is Mark Grimsley, *The Hard Hand of War* (1995).

The best biography of Lincoln, based on extensive research, is David Donald, *Lincoln* (1995). William E. Gienapp, *Abraham Lincoln and Civil War America* (2002), is a concise biography that focuses on the presidential years. Much longer, but vividly written, is Doris Kearns Goodwin's *Team of Rivals: The Political Genius of Abraham Lincoln* (2005). Mark E. Neely has written two innovative studies of civil liberties in wartime: *The Fate of Liberty* (1991) examines the Union and *Southern Rights* (1999) deals with the Confederacy. For the South's bid for independence, Emory M. Thomas, *The Confederate Nation, 1861–1865* (1979), is the standard account. The fullest discussion of southern politics is George C. Rable, *The Confederate Republic* (1994). After years of relative neglect, historians have turned their attention to the vital home front. Drew Faust, *Mothers of Invention* (1996), is an imaginative study of slaveholding women in the Confederacy; Daniel Sutherland, *Seasons of War* (1995), and William Blair, *Virginia's Private War* (1998), analyze the experiences of several Virginian counties in the war; and Stephen V. Ash, *When the Yankees Came* (1995), examines southerners under Union occupation. For the northern home front, see J. Matthew Gallman, *The North Fights the Civil War* (1994). Leon Litwack, *Been in the Storm So Long* (1979), is a gracefully written account of African Americans' experiences during the war, and James L. Roark's *Masters without Slaves* (1977) discusses the collapse of the southern slaveholders' world. Gerald F. Linderman, *Embattled Courage* (1987), presents an interesting assessment of soldiers in both armies. Chandra Manning, in *What This Cruel War Was Over* (2007), argues that early on both Union and Confederate soldiers identified slavery as the root of the war and that Union rank-and-file widely believed in emancipation as early as the end of 1861. Two excellent collections of essays that evaluate the war's outcome from various angles are David H. Donald, ed., *Why the North Won the Civil War* (1961), and Gabor S. Boritt, ed., *Why the Confederacy Lost* (1992).

Emancipation Proclamation issued; Union institutes conscription; Confederacy enacts general tax laws, initiates impressment; bread riots in the Confederacy; Battle of Gettysburg; Vicksburg captured; New York City draft riots

Sherman's march through the Carolinas; Lee surrenders; Lincoln assassinated; Thirteenth Amendment ratified

1863

1864

1865

Grant becomes Union general in chief; Grant's Virginia offensive; siege of Petersburg; fall of Atlanta; Lincoln reelected; Sherman's march to the sea

Though a slave, Benjamin Montgomery had been the business manager of the two Davis plantations before the war. He had also operated a store on Hurricane Plantation with his own line of credit in New Orleans. In 1863 Montgomery fled to the North, but when the war was over, he returned to Davis Bend, where the federal government had confiscated the Davis plantations and was leasing plots of the land to black farmers. Montgomery quickly emerged as the leader of the African American community at the Bend. ≪

>> *A Visit from the Old Mistress*, by Winslow Homer, captures the conflicting, often awkward emotions felt by both races after the war.

Then, in 1866, President Andrew Johnson pardoned Joseph Davis and restored his lands. Davis was now over 80 years old and lacked the will and stamina to rebuild, yet unlike many ex-slaveholders, he felt bound by obligations to his former slaves. Convinced that with proper encouragement African Americans could succeed economically in freedom, he sold his land secretly to Benjamin Montgomery. Only when the law prohibiting African Americans from owning land was overturned in 1867 did Davis publicly confirm the sale to his former slave.

For his part, Montgomery undertook to create a model society at Davis Bend based on mutual cooperation. He rented land to black farmers, hired others to work his own fields, sold supplies on credit, and ginned and marketed the crops. To the growing African American community, he preached the gospel of hard work, self-reliance, and education.

Hard work indeed: these black farmers faced the destruction caused by the war, several disastrous floods, insects, droughts, and declining cotton prices. Yet before long, cotton production exceeded that of the prewar years, and in 1870 the black families at Davis Bend produced 2,500 bales. The Montgomerys eventually acquired 5,500 acres, which made them reputedly the third largest planters in the state, and they won national and international awards for the quality of their cotton. Their success demonstrated what African Americans, given a fair chance, might accomplish.

The experiences of Benjamin Montgomery after 1865 were not those of most black southerners, who did not own land or have a powerful white benefactor. Yet all African Americans shared Montgomery's dream of economic independence. As one black veteran noted: "Every colored man will be a slave, and feel himself a slave until he can raise him own bale of cotton and put him own mark upon it and say this is mine!" Blacks could not gain effective freedom simply through a proclamation of emancipation. They also needed economic power, including their own land that no one could unfairly take away.

For nearly two centuries the laws had prevented slaves from possessing such economic power. If these conditions were to be overturned, black Americans needed political power, too. Thus the Republic would have to be reconstructed to give African Americans political power that they had been previously denied.

War, in its blunt way, had roughed out the contours of a solution, but only in broad terms. Clearly, African Americans would no longer be enslaved. The North, with its industrial might, would be the driving force in the nation's economy and retain the dominant political voice. But beyond that, the outlines of a reconstructed Republic remained vague. Would African Americans receive effective power? How would North and South readjust their economic and political relations? These questions lay at the heart of the problem of Reconstruction.

PRESIDENTIAL RECONSTRUCTION

Throughout the war Abraham Lincoln had considered Reconstruction his responsibility. Elected with less than 40 percent of the popular vote in 1860, he was acutely aware that once the states of the Confederacy were restored to the Union, the Republicans would be weakened unless they ceased to be a sectional party. By a generous peace, Lincoln hoped to attract former Whigs in the South, who supported many of the Republicans' economic policies, and build up a southern wing of the party.

Lincoln's 10 Percent Plan >>

Lincoln outlined his program in a Proclamation of **Amnesty** and Reconstruction, issued in December 1863. When a minimum of 10 percent of the qualified voters from 1860 took a **loyalty oath** to the Union, they could organize a state government. The new state constitution had to abolish slavery and provide

> **amnesty** general pardon granted by a government, usually for political crimes.
>
> **loyalty oath** oath of fidelity to the state or to an organization.

for black education, but Lincoln did not insist that high-ranking Confederate leaders be barred from public life.

Lincoln indicated that he would be generous in granting pardons to Confederate leaders and did not rule out compensation for slave property. Moreover, while he privately advocated limited black suffrage in the disloyal southern states, he did not demand social or political equality for black Americans. In Louisiana, Arkansas, and Tennessee he recognized pro-Union governments that allowed only white men to vote.

The Radical Republicans found Lincoln's approach much too lenient. Strongly antislavery, Radical members of Congress had led the struggle to make emancipation a war aim. Now they led the fight to guarantee the rights of former slaves, or freedpeople. The Radicals believed that it was the duty of Congress, not the president, to set the terms under which states would regain their rights in the Union. Though the Radicals often disagreed on other matters, they were united in a determination to readmit southern states only after slavery had been ended, black rights protected, and the power of the planter class destroyed.

Under the direction of Senator Benjamin Wade of Ohio and Representative Henry Winter Davis of Maryland, Congress formulated a much stricter plan of Reconstruction. The Wade-Davis bill required half the white adult males to take an oath of allegiance before drafting a new state constitution, and it restricted political power to the hard-core Unionists. Lincoln vetoed this approach, but as the war drew to a close, he appeared ready to make concessions to the Radicals, such as placing the defeated

>> The mood of white southerners at the end of the war was mixed. Many, like the veteran caricatured here by northern cartoonist Thomas Nast, remained hostile. Others, like Texas captain Samuel Foster, came to believe that the institution of slavery "had been abused, and perhaps for that abuse this terrible war . . . was brought upon us as a punishment."

South temporarily under military rule. Then Booth's bullet found its mark, and Lincoln's final approach to Reconstruction would never be known.

Reconstruction under Andrew Johnson >>

In the wake of defeat, the immediate reaction among white southerners was one of shock, despair, and hopelessness. Some former Confederates were openly antagonistic. A North Carolina innkeeper remarked bitterly that Yankees had stolen his slaves, burned his house, and killed all his sons, leaving him only one privilege: "To hate 'em. I git up at half-past four in the morning, and sit up till twelve at night, to hate 'em." Most Confederate soldiers were less defiant, having had their fill of war. Even among hostile civilians the feeling was widespread that the South must accept northern terms. A South Carolina paper admitted that "the conqueror has the right to make the terms, and we must submit."

This psychological moment was critical. To prevent a resurgence of resistance, the president needed to lay out in unmistakable terms what white southerners had to do to regain their old status in the Union. Perhaps even a clear and firm policy would not have been enough. But with Lincoln's death, the executive power came to rest in far less capable hands.

Andrew Johnson, the new president, had been born in North Carolina and eventually moved to Tennessee, where he worked as a tailor. Barely able to read and write when he married, he rose to political power by portraying himself as the champion of the people against the wealthy planter class. "Some day I will show the stuck-up aristocrats who is running the country," he vowed as he began his political career. Although he accepted emancipation as one consequence of the war, Johnson lacked any concern for the welfare of African Americans. "Damn the negroes," he said during the war, "I am fighting these traitorous aristocrats, their masters." After serving in Congress and as military governor of Tennessee following its occupation

⌃ Ruins in Charleston, South Carolina

by Union forces, Johnson, a Democrat, was tapped by Lincoln in 1864 as his running mate on the rechristened "Union" ticket.

The Radicals expected Johnson to uphold their views on Reconstruction, and on assuming the presidency he spoke of trying Confederate leaders and breaking up planters' estates. Unlike most Republicans, however, Johnson strongly supported states' rights, and his political shortcomings sparked conflicts almost immediately. Scarred by his humble origins, he became tactless and inflexible when challenged or criticized, alienating even those who sought to work with him.

Johnson moved to return the southern states to the Union quickly. He prescribed a loyalty oath that most white southerners would have to take to regain their civil and political rights and to have their property, except for slaves, restored. High Confederate officials and those with property worth over $20,000 had to apply for individual pardons. Once a state drafted a new constitution and elected state officers and members of Congress, Johnson promised to revoke martial law and recognize the new state government. Suffrage was limited to white citizens who had taken the loyalty oath. This plan was similar to Lincoln's, though more lenient. Only informally did Johnson stipulate that the southern states were to renounce their ordinances of secession, repudiate the Confederate debt, and ratify the proposed Thirteenth Amendment abolishing slavery.

The Failure of Johnson's Program ››

The southern delegates who met to construct new governments were in no mood to follow Johnson's recommendations. Several states merely repealed instead of repudiating their ordinances of secession, rejected the Thirteenth Amendment, or refused to repudiate the Confederate debt.

Nor did the new governments allow African Americans any political rights or provide in any effective way for black education. In addition, each state passed a series of laws, often modeled on its old slave code, that applied only to African Americans. These "**black codes**" did give African Americans some rights that had not been granted to slaves. They legalized marriages from slavery and allowed black southerners to hold and sell property and to sue and be sued in state courts. Yet their primary intent was to keep African Americans as propertyless agricultural laborers with inferior legal rights. The new freedpeople could not serve on juries, testify against whites, or work as they pleased. Mississippi prohibited them from buying or renting farmland, and most states ominously provided that black people who were vagrants could be arrested and hired out to landowners. Many northerners were incensed by the restrictive black codes, which violated their conception of freedom.

black codes laws passed by southern states in 1865 and 1866, modeled on the slave codes in effect before the Civil War. The codes did grant African Americans some rights not enjoyed by slaves, but their primary purpose was to keep African Americans as propertyless agricultural laborers.

Southern voters under Johnson's plan also defiantly elected prominent Confederate military and political leaders to office. At this point, Johnson could have called for new elections or admitted that a different program of Reconstruction was needed. Instead he caved in. For all his harsh rhetoric, he shrank from the prospect of social upheaval, and as the lines of ex-Confederates waiting to see him lengthened, he began issuing special pardons almost as fast as they could be printed. Publicly Johnson put on a bold face, announcing that Reconstruction had been successfully completed. But many members of Congress were deeply alarmed, and the stage was set for a serious confrontation.

Johnson's Break with Congress >>

The new Congress was by no means of one mind. A small number of Democrats and a few conservative Republicans backed the president's program of immediate and unconditional restoration. At the other end of the spectrum, a larger group of Radical Republicans, led by Thaddeus Stevens, Charles Sumner, Benjamin Wade, and others, was bent on remaking southern society in the image of the North. Reconstruction must "revolutionize Southern institutions, habits, and manners," insisted Representative Stevens, ". . . or all our blood and treasure have been spent in vain."

As a minority, the Radicals needed the aid of the moderate Republicans, the largest bloc in Congress. Led by William Pitt Fessenden and Lyman Trumbull, the moderates had no desire to foster social revolution or promote racial equality in the South. But they wanted to keep Confederate leaders from reassuming power, and they were convinced that the former slaves needed federal protection. Otherwise, Trumbull declared, the freedpeople would "be tyrannized over, abused, and virtually reenslaved."

The central issue dividing Johnson and the Radicals was the place of African Americans in American society. Johnson accused his opponents of seeking "to Africanize the southern half of our country," while the Radicals championed civil and political rights for African Americans. The only way to maintain loyal governments and develop a Republican party in the South, Radicals argued, was to give black men the ballot. Moderates agreed that the new southern governments were too harsh toward African Americans, but they feared that too great an emphasis on black civil rights would alienate northern voters.

In December 1865, when southern representatives to Congress appeared in Washington, a majority in Congress voted to exclude them. Congress also appointed a joint committee, chaired by Senator Fessenden, to look into Reconstruction.

The growing split with the president became clearer when Congress passed a bill extending the life of the Freedmen's Bureau. Created in March 1865, the bureau provided emergency food, clothing, and medical care to war refugees (including white southerners) and took charge of settling freedpeople on abandoned lands. The new bill gave the bureau the added responsibilities of supervising special courts to resolve disputes involving freedpeople and establishing schools for black southerners. Although this bill passed with virtually unanimous Republican support, Johnson vetoed it.

Johnson also vetoed a civil rights bill designed to overturn the more flagrant provisions of the black codes. The law made African Americans citizens of the United States and granted them the right to own property, make contracts, and have access to courts as parties and witnesses. For most Republicans Johnson's action was the last straw, and in April 1866 Congress overrode his veto. Congress then approved a slightly revised Freedmen's Bureau bill in July and promptly overrode the president's veto. Johnson's refusal to compromise drove the moderates into the arms of the Radicals.

BACKSTORY
Manning the Barricades

When President Johnson defied the Tenure of Office Act by firing Secretary of War Edwin Stanton, Stanton barricaded himself in his office and refused to turn over the key. He remained there for several weeks, meals being brought to him. Worries ran so high that the president might use force to expel him that two members of Congress organized a company of 100 guards to deter any attack.

The Fourteenth Amendment

>> To prevent unrepentant Confederates from taking over the reconstructed state governments and denying African Americans basic freedoms, the Joint Committee on Reconstruction proposed an amendment to the Constitution, which passed both houses of Congress with the necessary two-thirds vote in June 1866.

The amendment guaranteed repayment of the national war debt and prohibited repayment of the Confederate debt. To counteract the president's wholesale pardons, it disqualified prominent Confederates from holding office. Because moderates balked at giving the vote to African Americans, the amendment merely gave Congress the right to reduce the representation of any state that did not have impartial male suffrage. The practical effect of this provision, which Radicals labeled a "swindle," was to allow northern states to retain white suffrage, since unlike southern states they had few African Americans in their populations and thus would not be penalized.

The amendment's most important provision, Section 1, defined an American citizen as anyone born in the United States or naturalized, thereby automatically making African Americans citizens. Section 1 also prohibited states from abridging "the privileges or immunities" of citizens, depriving "any person of life, liberty, or property, without due process of law," or denying "any person . . . equal protection of the laws." The framers of the amendment probably intended to prohibit laws that applied to one race only, such as the black codes, or that made certain acts felonies when committed by black but not white people, or that decreed different penalties for the same crime when committed by white and black lawbreakers. The framers probably did not intend to prevent segregation (the legal separation of the races) in schools and public places.

Johnson denounced the amendment and urged southern states not to ratify it. Ironically, of the seceded states only the president's own state ratified the amendment, and Congress readmitted Tennessee with no further restrictions. The telegram sent to Congress by a longtime foe of Johnson officially announcing Tennessee's approval ended: "Give my respects to the dead dog in the White House."

The Election of 1866

>> When Congress blocked his policies, Johnson undertook a speaking tour of the East and Midwest in the fall of 1866 to drum up popular support. But the president found it difficult to convince northern audiences that white southerners were fully repentant. Only months earlier white mobs in Memphis and New Orleans had attacked black residents and killed nearly 100 in two major race riots. "The negroes now know, to their sorrow, that it is best not to arouse the fury of the white man," boasted one Memphis newspaper. When the president encountered hostile audiences during his northern campaign, he made matters only worse by trading insults and proclaiming that the Radicals were traitors.

bloody shirt political campaign tactic of "waving the bloody shirt," used by Republicans against Democrats; it invoked the deaths and casualties from the Civil War as a reason to vote for Republicans as the party of the Union, rather than the Democrats, who had often opposed the war.

Not to be outdone, the Radicals vilified Johnson as a traitor aiming to turn the country over to former rebels. Resorting to the tactic of "waving the **bloody shirt**," they appealed to voters by reviving bitter memories of the war. In a classic example of such rhetoric, Governor Oliver Morton of Indiana proclaimed that "every bounty jumper, every deserter, every sneak who ran away from the draft" was a Democrat; every "New York rioter in 1863 who burned up little children in colored asylums called himself a Democrat. In short, the Democratic party may be described as a common sewer."

Voters soundly repudiated Johnson, as the Republicans won more than a two-thirds majority in both houses of Congress. The Radicals had reached the height of their power, propelled by genuine alarm among northerners that Johnson's policies would lose the fruits of the Union's victory. Johnson was a president virtually without a party.

Did the South or the North win the Civil War?

> Resorting to the **tactic** of "waving the **bloody shirt**," [Radicals] **appealed** to voters by reviving **bitter memories** of the war.

CONGRESSIONAL RECONSTRUCTION

With a clear mandate in hand, congressional Republicans passed their own program of Reconstruction, beginning with the first Reconstruction Act in March 1867. Like all later pieces of Reconstruction legislation, it was repassed over Johnson's veto.

Placing the 10 unreconstructed states under military commanders, the act provided that in enrolling voters, officials were to include black adult males but not former Confederates, who were barred from holding office under the Fourteenth Amendment. Delegates to the state conventions were to frame constitutions that provided for black suffrage and disqualified prominent ex-Confederates from office. The first state legislatures to meet under the new constitution were required to ratify the Fourteenth Amendment. Once these steps were completed and Congress approved the new state constitution, a state could send representatives to Congress.

White southerners found these requirements so obnoxious that officials took no steps to register voters. Congress then enacted a second Reconstruction Act, also in March, ordering the local military commanders to put the machinery of Reconstruction into motion. Johnson's efforts to limit the power of military commanders produced a third act, passed in July, that upheld their superiority in all matters.

« This politician is literally "waving the bloody shirt"—using the bitter memories of the Civil War to rouse voters to side with Republicans.

When the first election was held in Alabama to ratify the new state constitution, whites boycotted it in sufficient numbers to prevent a majority of voters from participating. Undaunted, Congress passed the fourth Reconstruction Act (March 1868), which required ratification of the constitution by only a majority of those voting rather than those who were registered.

By June 1868 Congress had readmitted the representatives of seven states. Texas, Virginia, and Mississippi did not complete the process until 1869. Georgia finally followed in 1870.

Post-Emancipation Societies in the Americas

>> With the exception of Haiti's revolution (1791–1804), the United States was the only society in the Americas in which the destruction of slavery was accomplished by violence. But the United States, uniquely among these societies, enfranchised former slaves almost immediately after the emancipation. Thus in the United States former masters and slaves battled for control of the state in ways that did not occur in other post-emancipation societies. In most of the Caribbean, property requirements for voting left the planters in political control. Jamaica, for example, with a population of 500,000 in the 1860s, had only 3,000 voters.

Moreover, in reaction to political efforts to mobilize disfranchised black peasants, Jamaican planters dissolved the assembly and reverted to being a Crown colony governed from London. Of the sugar islands, all but Barbados adopted the same policy, thereby blocking the potential for any future black peasant democracy. Nor did any of these societies have the counterparts of

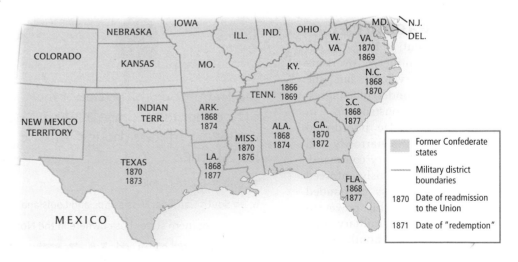

THE SOUTHERN STATES DURING RECONSTRUCTION

The Grant Administration

>> In 1868 Grant was elected president—and Republicans were shocked. Their candidate, a great war hero, had won by a margin of only 300,000 votes. Furthermore, with an estimated 450,000 black Republican votes cast in the South, a majority of whites had voted Democratic. The election helped convince Republican leaders that an amendment securing black suffrage throughout the nation was necessary.

In February 1869 Congress sent the Fifteenth Amendment to the states for ratification. It forbade any state to deny the right to vote on grounds of race, color, or previous condition of servitude. It did not forbid literacy and property requirements, as some Radicals wanted, because the moderates feared that only a conservative version of the amendment could be ratified. As a result, loopholes remained that even-

disfranchisement denial of a citizen's right to vote. } tually allowed southern states to **disfranchise** African Ameri-

cans. Furthermore, advocates of women's suffrage such as Lucy Stone and Susan B. Anthony were bitterly disappointed when Congress refused to prohibit voting discrimination on the basis of sex as well as race. The amendment was ratified in March 1870.

As a general, Ulysses S. Grant's quiet manner and well known resolution served him well. As president, he proved much less certain of his goals, and therefore less effective at corralling politicians than at maneuvering troops.

A series of scandals wracked his administration, so much so that "Grantism" soon became a code word in American politics for corruption, cronyism, and venality. Although Grant did not profit personally, he remained loyal to his friends and displayed little zeal to root out wrongdoing. Nor was Congress immune from the lowered tone of public life. In such a climate ruthless state machines, led by men who favored the status quo, came to dominate the party.

As corruption in both the North and the South worsened, reformers became more interested in cleaning up government than in protecting black rights. Congress in 1872 passed an amnesty act, allowing many more ex-Confederates to serve in southern governments. That same year liberal Republicans broke with the Republican party and nominated for president Horace Greeley, the editor of the New York *Tribune*. A one-time Radical, Greeley had become disillusioned with Reconstruction and urged a restoration of home rule in the South as well as adoption of civil service reform. Democrats decided to back the Liberal Republican ticket. The Republicans renominated Grant, who, despite the defection of a number of prominent Radicals, won an easy victory.

>> Grant swings from a trapeze while supporting a number of associates accused of corruption. Among those holding on are Secretary of the Navy George M. Robeson (*top center*), who was accused of accepting bribes for awarding Navy contracts; Secretary of War William W. Belknap (*top right*), who was forced to resign for selling Indian post traderships; and the president's private secretary, Orville Babcock (*bottom right*), who was implicated in the Whiskey Ring scandal. Although not personally involved in the scandals during his administration, Grant was reluctant to dismiss from office supporters accused of wrongdoing.

Growing Northern Disillusionment >>

During Grant's second term, Congress passed the Civil Rights Act of 1875, the last major piece of Reconstruction legislation. This law prohibited racial discrimination in public accommodations, transportation, places of amusement, and juries. At the same time, Congress rejected a ban on segregation in public schools, which was almost universally practiced in the North as well as the South. The federal government made little attempt to enforce the law, however, and in 1883 the Supreme Court struck down its provisions, except the one relating to juries.

Despite passage of the Civil Rights Act, many northerners were growing disillusioned with Reconstruction. They were repelled by the corruption of the southern governments, they were tired of the violence and disorder that accompanied elections in the South, and they had little faith in black Americans. William Dodge, a wealthy New York capitalist and an influential Republican, wrote in 1875 that the South could never develop its resources "till confidence in her state governments can be restored, and this will never be done by federal bayonets." It had been a mistake, he went on, to make black southerners feel "that the United States government was their special friend, rather than those . . . among whom they must live and for whom they must work. We have tried this long enough," he concluded. "Now let the South alone."

As the agony of the war became more distant, the Panic of 1873, which precipitated a severe four-year depression, diverted public attention to economic issues. Battered by the panic and the corruption issue, the Republicans lost a shocking 77 seats in Congress in the 1874 elections, and along with them control of the House of Representatives for the first time since 1861.

"The truth is our people are tired out with the worn out cry of 'Southern outrages'!!" one Republican concluded. "Hard times and heavy taxes make them wish the 'ever lasting nigger' were in hell or Africa." More and more, Republicans spoke about cutting loose the unpopular southern governments.

The Triumph of White Supremacy >>

Meanwhile, southern Democrats set out to overthrow the remaining Radical governments. Already white Republicans in the South felt heavy pressure to desert their party. To poor

>> "Brute Might Makes Right. Shoot Suffrage to Death," reads the sign above the figure. By the time this cartoon appeared in 1879, terror tactics had "redeemed" the South for white Democrats.

AFTER THE FACT
Minstrels, Carnivals, and Ghosts

The costumes of Ku Klux Klan night riders—pointed hoods and white sheets—have become a staple of history books. In fact, not all the KKK wore costumes, and those who did sported a variety of outfits. But why use such outlandish, often elaborate disguises? To hide the identity of members, according to some accounts, or to terrorize freedpeople into thinking they were being menaced by Confederate ghosts. But clearly African Americans knew these were living, mortal enemies. Though simpler masks would have hidden identities, the guns that they brandished were far more frightening than any "ghostly" robes.

One historian has suggested that the KKK performances took their cues from traditions already a part of American popular culture: the costumes of Mardi Gras and similar carnivals, as well as the humorous sketches of minstrel shows. In behaving like minstrel performers or carnival revelers, KKK members may have had other audiences in mind. Northerners who read accounts of their doings could be lulled into thinking that the repressive night rides were just humorous pranks, not a threat to Radical rule. For southern Democrats, KKK rituals provided a way to reassert a sense of white supremacy. Klansmen might have been defeated in war, but their theatrical night rides helped overturn the social order of Reconstruction, just as carousers at carnivals disrupted the night. The ritual garb provided more innocent cover for a campaign of intimidation that often turned deadly.

Mississippi Redeemers

"Seeing that nothing but intimidation would enable them [the Democrats] to carry the election they resorted to it in every possible way . . . At Sulphur Springs they came very near precipitating a bloody riot by beating colored men over the heads with pistols. . . . In Aberdeen . . . the colored men who had gathered . . . to vote were told if they did not leave town within five minutes that the last man would be shot dead in his tracks, and that not a man could vote that day unless he voted the Democratic ticket."

white southerners who lacked social standing, the Democratic appeal to racial solidarity offered special comfort. The large landowners and other wealthy groups that led southern Democrats objected less to black southerners voting, since they were confident that if outside influences were removed, they could control the black vote.

Democrats also resorted to economic pressure to undermine Republican power. In heavily black counties, newspapers published the names of black residents who cast Republican ballots and urged planters to discharge

them. But terror and violence provided the most effective means to overthrow the radical regimes. A number of paramilitary organizations broke up Republican meetings, terrorized white and black Republicans, assassinated Republican leaders, and prevented black citizens from voting. The most notorious of these organizations was the Ku Klux Klan, along with similar groups functioned as an unofficial arm of the Democratic party.

What became known as the Mississippi Plan was inaugurated in 1875, when Democrats decided to use as much violence as necessary to carry the state election. Local papers trumpeted, "Carry the election peaceably if we can, forcibly if we must." Recognizing that northern public opinion had grown sick of repeated federal intervention in southern elections, the Grant administration rejected the request of Republican governor Adelbert Ames for troops to stop the violence. Bolstered by terrorism, the Democrats swept the election in Mississippi. Violence and intimidation prevented as many as 60,000 black and white Republicans from voting, converting the normal Republican majority into a Democratic majority of 30,000. Mississippi had been "redeemed."

The Disputed Election of 1876 >>

The 1876 presidential election was crucial to the final overthrow of Reconstruction. The Republicans nominated Ohio governor Rutherford B. Hayes to oppose Samuel Tilden of New York. Once again, violence prevented an estimated quarter of a million Republican votes from being cast in the South. Tilden had a clear majority of 250,000 in the popular vote, but the outcome in the Electoral College was in doubt because both parties claimed South Carolina, Florida, and Louisiana, the only reconstructed states still in Republican hands.

To arbitrate the disputed returns, Congress established a 15-member electoral commission. By a straight party vote of 8 to 7, the commission awarded the disputed electoral votes—and the presidency—to Hayes.

When angry Democrats threatened a filibuster to prevent the electoral votes from being counted, key Republicans met with southern Democrats and reached an informal understanding, later known as the Compromise of 1877. Hayes's supporters agreed to withdraw federal troops from the South and not oppose the new Democratic state governments. For their part, southern Democrats dropped their opposition to Hayes's election and pledged to respect African Americans' rights.

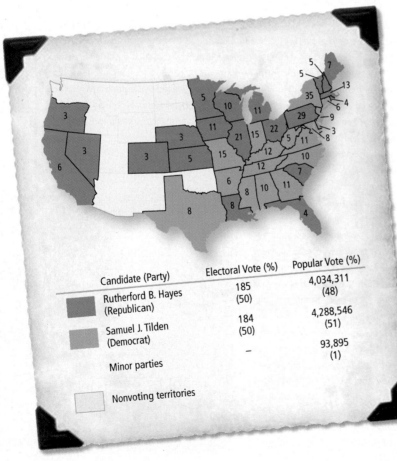

Candidate (Party)	Electoral Vote (%)	Popular Vote (%)
Rutherford B. Hayes (Republican)	185 (50)	4,034,311 (48)
Samuel J. Tilden (Democrat)	184 (50)	4,288,546 (51)
Minor parties	–	93,895 (1)
Nonvoting territories		

ELECTION OF 1876

Without federal support, the last Republican southern governments collapsed, and Democrats took control of the remaining states of the Confederacy. By 1877, the entire South was in the hands of the **Redeemers**, as they called themselves. Reconstruction and Republican rule had come to an end.

{ **Redeemers** southerners who came to power in southern state governments from 1875 to 1877, claiming to have "redeemed" the South from Reconstruction. The Redeemers looked to undo many of the changes wrought by the Civil War.

Racism and the Failure of Reconstruction »

Reconstruction failed for a multitude of reasons. The reforming impulse behind the Republican party of the 1850s had been battered and worn down by the war. The new materialism of industrial America inspired a jaded cynicism in many Americans. In the South, African American voters and leaders inevitably lacked a certain amount of education and experience; elsewhere, Republicans were divided over policies and options.

Yet beyond these obstacles, the sad fact remains that the ideals of Reconstruction were most clearly defeated by a deep-seated racism that permeated American life. Racism stimulated white southern resistance, undercut northern support for black rights, and eventually made northerners willing to write off Reconstruction, and with it the welfare of African Americans. Although Congress could pass a constitutional amendment abolishing slavery, it could not overturn at a stroke the social habits of two centuries.

With the overthrow of Reconstruction, the white South had won back some of the power it had lost in 1865—but not all. In the longer term, the political equations of power had been changed. Even under redeemer governments, African Americans did not return to the social position they had occupied before the war. They were no longer slaves, and black southerners who walked dusty roads in search of family members, sent their children to school, or worshiped in their own black churches knew what a momentous change this was. Even under the exploitative sharecropping system, black income rose significantly in freedom. Then, too, the guarantees of "equal protection" and "due process of law" had been written into the Constitution and would be available for later generations to use in championing once again the Radicals' goal of racial equality.

> Even under **redeemer governments**, African Americans did **not** return to the **social position** they had **occupied before** the war.

But this was a struggle left to future reformers. For the time being, the clear trend was away from change or hope—especially for former slaves like Benjamin Montgomery and his sons, the owners of the old Davis plantations in Mississippi. In the 1870s bad crops, lower cotton prices, and falling land values undermined the Montgomerys' financial position, and in 1875 Jefferson Davis sued to have the sale of Brierfield invalidated. Following the overthrow of Mississippi's Radical government, a white conservative majority of the court awarded Brierfield to Davis in 1878. The Montgomerys lost Hurricane as well.

The waning days of Reconstruction were times filled with such ironies: of governments "redeemed" by violence, of Fourteenth Amendment rights being used by conservative courts to protect not black people but giant corporations, of reformers taking up other causes. Increasingly, the industrial North focused on an economic task: integrating both the South and the West into the Union. In the case of both regions, northern factories sought to use southern and western raw materials to produce goods and to find national markets for those products. Indeed, during the coming decades European nations also scrambled to acquire natural resources and markets. In the onrushing age of imperialism, Western nations would seek to dominate newly acquired colonies in Africa and Asia, with the same disregard for their "subject peoples" that was seen with African Americans, Latinos, and Indians in the United States.

Disowned by its northern supporters and unmourned by public opinion, Reconstruction was over.

CHAPTER SUMMARY

Presidents Abraham Lincoln and Andrew Johnson and the Republican-dominated Congress each developed a program of Reconstruction to quickly restore the Confederate states to the Union.

▌ Lincoln's 10 percent plan required that 10 percent of qualified voters from 1860 swear an oath of loyalty to begin organizing a state government.
▌ Following Lincoln's assassination, Andrew Johnson changed Lincoln's terms and lessened Reconstruction's requirements.

- The more radical Congress repudiated Johnson's state governments and eventually enacted its own program of Reconstruction, which included the principle of black suffrage.
  - Congress passed the Fourteenth and Fifteen Amendments and also extended the life of the Freedmen's Bureau, a unique experiment in social welfare.
  - Congress rejected land reform, however, which would have provided the freedpeople with a greater economic stake.
  - The effort to remove Johnson from office through impeachment failed.
- The Radical governments in the South, led by black and white southerners and transplanted northerners, compiled a mixed record on matters such as racial equality, education, economic issues, and corruption.
- Reconstruction was a time of both joy and frustration for former slaves.
  - Former slaves took steps to reunite their families and establish black-controlled churches.

- They evidenced a widespread desire for land and education.
- Black resistance to the old system of labor led to the adoption of sharecropping.
- The Freedmen's Bureau fostered these new working arrangements and also the beginnings of black education in the South.
- Northern public opinion became disillusioned with Reconstruction during the presidency of Ulysses S. Grant.
- Southern whites used violence, economic coercion, and racism to overthrow the Republican state governments.
- In 1877 Republican leaders agreed to end Reconstruction in exchange for Rutherford B. Hayes's election as president.
- Racism played a key role in the eventual failure of Reconstruction.

Significant Events

Louisiana, Arkansas, and Tennessee establish governments under Lincoln's Reconstruction plan

Freedmen's Bureau established; Johnson becomes president; presidential Reconstruction completed; Thirteenth Amendment ratified

Constitutional conventions in the South; Blacks vote in southern elections

1864   **1865–1866**   **1865**   **1866**   **1867–1868**

Black codes enacted

Civil rights bill passed over Johnson's veto; Memphis and New Orleans riots; Ku Klux Klan organized

Additional Reading

Historians' views of Reconstruction have dramatically changed over the past half century. Modern studies offer a more sympathetic assessment of Reconstruction and the experience of African Americans. Indicative of this trend is Eric Foner, *Reconstruction* (1988), and his briefer treatment (with photographic essays by Joshua Brown) *Forever Free: the Story of Emancipation and Reconstruction* (2005). Michael Les Benedict treats the clash between Andrew Johnson and Congress in *The Impeachment and Trial of Andrew Johnson* (1973). Political affairs in the South during Reconstruction are examined in Dan T. Carter, *When the War Was Over* (1985), and Thomas Holt, *Black over White* (1977), an imaginative study of black political leadership in South Carolina. Hans Trefousse, *Thaddeus Stevens: Nineteenth-Century Egalitarian* (1997), provides a sympathetic reassessment of the influential Radical Republican.

Leon Litwack, *Been in the Storm So Long* (1979), sensitively analyzes the transition of enslaved African Americans to freedom. Heather Andrea Williams, *Self-Taught: African American Education in Slavery and Freedom* (2005), illustrates the black drive for literacy and education. James L. Roark, *Masters without Slaves* (1977), discusses former slaveholders' adjustment to the end of slavery. The dialectic of black-white relations is charted from the antebellum years through Reconstruction and beyond in Steven Hahn, *A Nation under Our Feet: Black Political Struggles in the Rural South from Slavery to the Great Migration* (2003). Two excellent studies of changing labor relations in southern agriculture are Julie Saville, *The Work of Reconstruction* (1995), and John C. Rodrigue, *Reconstruction in the Cane Fields* (2001). For contrasting views of the Freedman's Bureau see George R. Bentley, *A History of the Freedman's Bureau* (1955)—favorable—and Donald Nieman, *To Set the Law in Motion* (1979)—more critical. William Gillette, *Retreat from Reconstruction, 1869–1879* (1980), focuses on national politics and the end of Reconstruction, while Michael Perman, *The Road to Redemption* (1984), looks at developments in the South.

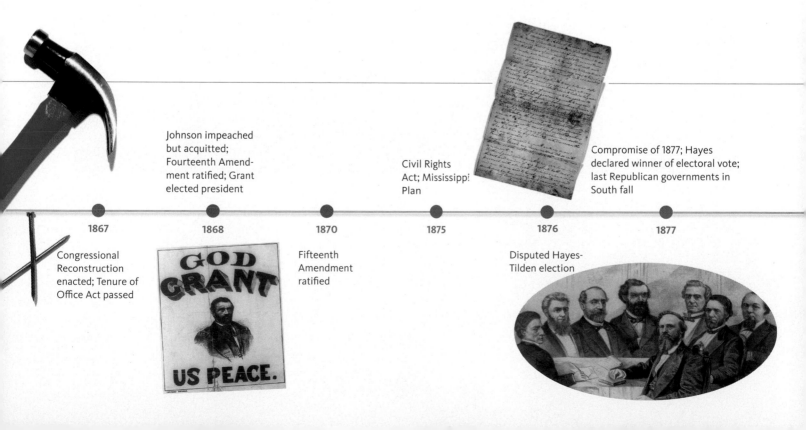

Johnson impeached but acquitted; Fourteenth Amendment ratified; Grant elected president

Civil Rights Act; Mississippi Plan

Compromise of 1877; Hayes declared winner of electoral vote; last Republican governments in South fall

1867 **1868** **1870** **1875** **1876** **1877**

Congressional Reconstruction enacted; Tenure of Office Act passed

GOD GRANT US PEACE.

Fifteenth Amendment ratified

Disputed Hayes-Tilden election

Appendix

- **The Declaration of Independence**

- **The Constitution of the United States of America**

The Declaration of Independence

IN CONGRESS, JULY 4, 1776

The Unanimous Declaration of the Thirteen United States of America

When, in the course of human events, it becomes necessary for one people to dissolve the political bands which have connected them with another, and to assume, among the powers of the earth, the separate and equal station to which the laws of nature and of nature's God entitle them, a decent respect to the opinions of mankind requires that they should declare the causes which impel them to the separation.

We hold these truths to be self-evident, that all men are created equal; that they are endowed by their Creator with certain unalienable rights; that among these, are life, liberty, and the pursuit of happiness. That, to secure these rights, governments are instituted among men, deriving their just powers from the consent of the governed; that, whenever any form of government becomes destructive of these ends, it is the right of the people to alter or to abolish it, and to institute a new government, laying its foundation on such principles, and organizing its powers in such form, as to them shall seem most likely to effect their safety and happiness. Prudence, indeed, will dictate that governments long established, should not be changed for light and transient causes; and, accordingly, all experience hath shown, that mankind are more disposed to suffer, while evils are sufferable, than to right themselves by abolishing the forms to which they are accustomed. But, when a long train of abuses and usurpations, pursuing invariably the same object, evinces a design to reduce them under absolute despotism, it is their right, it is their duty, to throw off such government and to provide new guards for their future security. Such has been the patient sufferance of these colonies, and such is now the necessity which constrains them to alter their former systems of government. The history of the present King of Great Britain is a history of repeated injuries and usurpations, all having, in direct object, the establishment of an absolute tyranny over these States. To prove this, let facts be submitted to a candid world:

He has refused his assent to laws the most wholesome and necessary for the public good.

He has forbidden his governors to pass laws of immediate and pressing importance, unless suspended in their operation till his assent should be obtained; and, when so suspended, he has utterly neglected to attend to them.

He has refused to pass other laws for the accommodation of large districts of people, unless those people would relinquish the right of representation in the legislature; a right inestimable to them, and formidable to tyrants only.

He has called together legislative bodies at places unusual, uncomfortable, and distant from the depository of their public records, for the sole purpose of fatiguing them into compliance with his measures.

He has dissolved representative houses repeatedly for opposing, with manly firmness, his invasions on the rights of the people.

He has refused, for a long time after such dissolutions, to cause others to be elected; whereby the legislative powers, incapable of annihilation, have returned to the people at large for their exercise; the state remaining, in the meantime, exposed to all the danger of invasion from without, and convulsions within.

He has endeavored to prevent the population of these States; for that purpose, obstructing the laws for naturalization of foreigners, refusing to pass others to encourage their migration hither, and raising the conditions of new appropriations of lands.

He had obstructed the administration of justice, by refusing his assent to laws for establishing judiciary powers. He has made judges dependent on his will alone, for the tenure of their offices, and the amount and payment of their salaries.

He has erected a multitude of new offices, and sent hither swarms of officers to harass our people, and eat out their substance.

He has kept among us, in time of peace, standing armies, without the consent of our legislatures.

He has affected to render the military independent of, and superior to, the civil power.

He has combined, with others, to subject us to a jurisdiction foreign to our Constitution, and unacknowledged by our laws; giving his assent to their acts of pretended legislation:

For quartering large bodies of armed troops among us:

For protecting them by a mock trial, from punishment,

for any murders which they should commit on the inhabitants of these States:

For cutting off our trade with all parts of the world:

For imposing taxes on us without our consent:

For depriving us, in many cases, of the benefit of trial by jury:

For transporting us beyond seas to be tried for pretended offences:

For abolishing the free system of English laws in a neighboring province, establishing therein an arbitrary government, and enlarging its boundaries, so as to render it at once an example and fit instrument for introducing the same absolute rule into these colonies:

For taking away our charters, abolishing our most valuable laws, and altering, fundamentally, the powers of our governments:

For suspending our own legislatures, and declaring themselves invested with power to legislate for us in all cases whatsoever.

He has abdicated government here, by declaring us out of his protection, and waging war against us.

He has plundered our seas, ravaged our coasts, burnt our towns, and destroyed the lives of our people.

He is, at this time, transporting large armies of foreign mercenaries to complete the works of death, desolation, and tyranny, already begun, with circumstances of cruelty and perfidy scarcely paralleled in the most barbarous ages, and totally unworthy the head of a civilized nation.

He has constrained our fellow citizens, taken captive on the high seas, to bear arms against their country, to become the executioners of their friends, and brethren, or to fall themselves by their hands.

He has excited domestic insurrections amongst us, and has endeavored to bring on the inhabitants of our frontiers, the merciless Indian savages, whose known rule of warfare is an undistinguished destruction of all ages, sexes, and conditions.

In every stage of these oppressions, we have petitioned for redress, in the most humble terms; our repeated petitions have been answered only by repeated injury. A prince, whose character is thus marked by every act which may define a tyrant, is unfit to be the ruler of a free people.

Nor have we been wanting in attention to our British brethren. We have warned them, from time to time, of attempts made by their legislature to extend an unwarrantable jurisdiction over us. We have reminded them of the circumstances of our emigration and settlement here. We have appealed to their native justice and magnanimity, and we have conjured them, by the ties of our common kindred, to disavow these usurpations, which would inevitably interrupt our connections and correspondence. They, too, have been deaf to the voice of justice and consanguinity. We must, therefore, acquiesce in the necessity which denounces our separation, and hold them as we hold the rest of mankind, enemies in war, in peace, friends.

We, therefore, the representatives of the United States of America, in general Congress assembled, appealing to the Supreme Judge of the world for the rectitude of our intentions, do, in the name, and by the authority of the good people of these colonies, solemnly publish and declare, that these united colonies are, and of right ought to be, free and independent states: that they are absolved from all allegiance to the British Crown, and that all political connection between them and the state of Great Britain is, and ought to be, totally dissolved; and that, as free and independent states, they have full power to levy war, conclude peace, contract alliances, establish commerce, and to do all other acts and things which independent states may of right do. And, for the support of this declaration, with a firm reliance on the protection of Divine Providence, we mutually pledge to each other our lives, our fortunes, and our sacred honor.

The foregoing Declaration was, by order of Congress, engrossed, and signed by the following members:

JOHN HANCOCK

New Hampshire	Massachusetts Bay	Rhode Island	Connecticut
New York	New Jersey	Pennsylvania	John Morton
Delaware	Maryland	Virginia	Benjamin Harrison
North Carolina	South Carolina	Georgia	Roger Sherman
Josiah Bartlett	Samuel Adams	Stephen Hopkins	George Clymer
William Floyd	Richard Stockton	Robert Morris	Thomas Nelson, Jr.
Caesar Rodney	Samuel Chase	George Wythe	Samuel Huntington
William Hooper	Edward Rutledge	Button Gwinnett	James Smith
William Whipple	John Adams	William Ellery	Francis Lightfoot Lee
Philip Livingston	John Witherspoon	Benjamin Rush	William Williams
George Read	William Paca	Richard Henry Lee	George Taylor
Joseph Hewes	Thomas Heyward, Jr.	Lyman Hall	Carter Braxton
Matthew Thornton	Robert Treat Paine	Benjamin Franklin	Oliver Wolcott
Francis Lewis	Francis Hopkinson	Thomas Jefferson	James Wilson
Thomas M'Kean	Thomas Stone	George Walton	George Ross
John Penn	Thomas Lynch, Jr.		
Lewis Morris	Elbridge Gerry		
	John Hart		
	Charles Carroll,		
	of Carrollton		
	Arthur Middleton		
	Abraham Clark		

Resolved, That copies of the Declaration be sent to the several assemblies, conventions, and committees, or counsils of safety, and to the several commanding officers of the continental troops; that it be proclaimed in each of the United States, at the head of the army.

The Constitution of the United States of America[1]

We the People of the United States, in Order to form a more perfect Union, establish Justice, insure domestic Tranquility, provide for the common defence, promote the general Welfare, and secure the Blessings of Liberty to ourselves and our Posterity, do ordain and establish this CONSTITUTION for the United States of America.

ARTICLE I

SECTION 1. All legislative Powers herein granted shall be vested in a Congress of the United States, which shall consist of a Senate and House of Representatives.

SECTION 2. The House of Representatives shall be composed of Members chosen every second Year by the People of the several States, and the Electors in each State shall have the Qualifications requisite for Electors of the most numerous Branch of the State Legislature. No Person shall be a Representative who shall not have attained to the Age of twenty-five Years, and been seven Years a Citizen of the United States, and who shall not, when elected, be an Inhabitant of that State in which he shall be chosen.

[Representatives and direct Taxes[2] shall be apportioned among the several States which may be included within this Union, according to their respective Numbers, which shall be determined by adding to the whole Number of free Persons, including those bound to Service for a Term of Years, and excluding Indians not taxed, three fifths of all other Persons.][3] The actual Enumeration shall be made within three Years after the first Meeting of the Congress of the United States, and within every subsequent Term of ten Years, in such Manner as they shall by Law direct. The Number of Representatives shall not exceed one for every thirty Thousand, but each State shall have at Least one Representative; and until such enumeration shall be made, the State of New Hampshire shall be entitled to chuse three, Massachusetts eight, Rhode- Island and Providence Plantations one, Connecticut five, New York six, New Jersey four, Pennsylvania eight, Delaware one, Maryland six, Virginia ten, North Carolina five, South Carolina five, and Georgia three. When vacancies happen in the Representation from any State, the Executive Authority thereof shall issue Writs of Election to fill such Vacancies. The House of Representatives shall chuse their Speaker and other Officers; and shall have the sole Power of Impeachment.

SECTION 3. The Senate of the United States shall be composed of two Senators from each State, chosen by the Legislature thereof, for six Years; and each Senator shall have one Vote.

Immediately after they shall be assembled in Consequence of the first Election, they shall be divided as equally as may be into three Classes. The Seats of the Senators of the first Class shall be vacated at the Expiration of the second Year, of the second Class at the Expiration of the fourth Year, and of the third Class at the Expiration of the sixth Year, so that one-third may be chosen every second Year; and if Vacancies happen by Resignation, or otherwise, during the Recess of the Legislature of any State, the Executive thereof may make temporary Appointments until the next Meeting of the Legislature, which shall then fill such Vacancies. No Person shall be a Senator who shall not have attained to the Age of thirty Years, and been nine Years a Citizen of the United States, and who shall not, when elected, be an Inhabitant of that State for which he shall be chosen.

The Vice President of the United States shall be President of the Senate, but shall have no vote, unless they be equally divided.

The Senate shall chuse their other Officers, and also a President pro tempore, in the absence of the Vice President, or when he shall exercise the Office of President of the United States.

The Senate shall have the sole Power to try all Impeachments. When sitting for that purpose they shall be on Oath or Affirmation. When the President of the United States is tried, the Chief Justice shall preside: And no person shall be convicted without the Concurrence of two thirds of the Members present.

Judgment in Cases of Impeachment shall not extend further than to removal from Office, and disqualification to hold and enjoy any Office of honor, Trust, or Profit under the United States: but the Party convicted shall nevertheless be liable and subject to Indictment, Trial, Judgment, and Punishment, according to Law.

---

1 This version follows the original Constitution in capitalization and spelling. It is adapted from the text published by the United States Department of the Interior, Office of Education.

2 Altered by the Sixteenth Amendment.

3 Negated by the Fourteenth Amendment.

SECTION 4. The Times, Places and Manner of holding Elections for Senators and Representatives, shall be prescribed in each State by the Legislature thereof; but the Congress may at any time by Law make or alter such Regulations, except as to the Places of Chusing Senators. The Congress shall assemble at least once in every Year, and such Meeting shall be on the first Monday in December, unless they shall by Law appoint a different Day.

SECTION 5. Each House shall be the Judge of the Elections, Returns and Qualifications of its own Members, and a Majority of each shall constitute a Quorum to do Business; but a smaller number may adjourn from day to day, and may be authorized to compel the Attendance of absent Members, in such Manner, and under such Penalties, as each House may provide.

Each House may determine the Rules of its Proceedings, punish its Members for disorderly Behaviour, and, with the Concurrence of two thirds, expel a Member. Each House shall keep a Journal of its Proceedings, and from time to time publish the same, excepting such Parts as may in their Judgment require Secrecy; and the Yeas and Nays of the Members of either House on any question shall, at the Desire of one fifth of those Present, be entered on the Journal.

Neither House, during the Session of Congress, shall, without the Consent of the other, adjourn for more than three days, nor to any other Place than that in which the two Houses shall be sitting.

SECTION 6. The Senators and Representatives shall receive a Compensation for their Services, to be ascertained by Law, and paid out of the Treasury of the United States. They shall in all Cases, except Treason, Felony, and Breach of the Peace, be privileged from Arrest during their Attendance at the Session of their respective Houses, and in going to and returning from the same; and for any Speech or Debate in either House, they shall not be questioned in any other Place.

No Senator or Representative shall, during the Time for which he was elected, be appointed to any civil Office under the Authority of the United States, which shall have been created, or the Emoluments whereof shall have been increased, during such time; and no Person holding any Office under the United States shall be a Member of either House during his continuance in Office.

SECTION 7. All Bills for raising Revenue shall originate in the House of Representatives; but the Senate may propose or concur with Amendments as on other bills. Every Bill which shall have passed the House of Representatives and the Senate, shall, before it become a Law, be presented to the President of the United States; If he approve he shall sign it, but if not he shall return it, with his Objections, to that House in which it shall have originated, who shall enter the Objections at large on their Journal,

and proceed to reconsider it. If after such Reconsideration two thirds of that House shall agree to pass the bill, it shall be sent, together with the objections, to the other House, by which it shall likewise be reconsidered, and if approved by two thirds of that House, it shall become a Law. But in all such Cases the Votes of both Houses shall be determined by Yeas and Nays, and the Names of the Persons voting for and against the Bill shall be entered on the Journal of each House respectively. If any Bill shall not be returned by the President within ten Days (Sundays excepted) after it shall have been presented to him, the Same shall be a Law, in like Manner as if he had signed it, unless the Congress by their Adjournment prevent its Return, in which Case it shall not be a Law. Every Order, Resolution, or Vote to which the Concurrence of the Senate and House of Representatives may be necessary (except on a question of Adjournment) shall be presented to the President of the United States; and before the Same shall take Effect, shall be approved by him, or being disapproved by him, shall be repassed by two thirds of the Senate and House of Representatives, according to the Rules and Limitations prescribed in the Case of a Bill.

SECTION 8. The Congress shall have Power To lay and collect Taxes, Duties, Imposts and Excises, to pay the Debts and provide for the common Defence and general Welfare of the United States; but all Duties, Imposts and Excises shall be uniform throughout the United States;

To borrow money on the credit of the United States;

To regulate Commerce with foreign Nations, and among the several States, and with the Indian Tribes;

To establish an uniform rule of Naturalization, and uniform Laws on the subject of Bankruptcies throughout the United States; To coin Money, regulate the Value thereof, and of foreign Coin, and fix the Standard of Weights and Measures;

To provide for the Punishment of counterfeiting the Securities and current Coin of the United States;

To establish Post Offices and post Roads; To promote the Progress of Science and useful Arts, by securing for limited Times to Authors and Inventors the exclusive Right to their respective Writings and Discoveries;

To constitute Tribunals inferior to the Supreme Court;

To define and punish Piracies and Felonies committed on the high Seas, and Offenses against the Law of Nations;

To declare War, grant Letters of Marque and Reprisal, and make Rules concerning Captures on Land and Water;

To raise and support Armies, but no Appropriation of Money to that Use shall be for a longer Term than two Years;

To provide and maintain a Navy;

To make Rules for the Government and Regulation of the land and naval forces;

To provide for calling forth the Militia to execute the Laws of the Union, suppress Insurrections and repel Invasions;

To provide for organizing, arming, and disciplining the Militia, and for government such Part of them as may be employed in the Service of the United States, reserving to the States respectively, the Appointment of the Officers, and the Authority of training the Militia according to the discipline prescribed by Congress;

To exercise exclusive Legislation in all Cases whatsoever, over such District (not exceeding ten Miles square) as may, by Cession of particular States, and the acceptance of Congress, become the Seat of the Government of the United States, and to exercise like Authority over all Places purchased by the Consent of the Legislature of the State in which the Same shall be, for the Erection of Forts, Magazines, Arsenals, Dock-yards, and other needful Buildings;—And

To make all Laws which shall be necessary and proper for carrying into Execution the foregoing Powers, and all other Powers vested by this Constitution in the Government of the United States, or in any Department or Officer thereof.

SECTION 9. The Migration or Importation of such Persons as any of the States now existing shall think proper to admit, shall not be prohibited by the Congress prior to the Year one thousand eight hundred and eight, but a tax or duty may be imposed on such Importation, not exceeding ten dollars for each Person.

The privilege of the Writ of Habeas Corpus shall not be suspended, unless when in Cases of Rebellion or Invasion the public Safety may require it.

No bill of Attainder or ex post facto Law shall be passed.

No capitation, or other direct, Tax shall be laid unless in Proportion to the Census or Enumeration herein before directed to be taken.

No Tax or Duty shall be laid on Articles exported from any State.

No Preference shall be given by any Regulation of Commerce or Revenue to the Ports of one State over those of another: nor shall Vessels bound to, or from, one State, be obliged to enter, clear, or pay Duties in another.

No Money shall be drawn from the Treasury, but in Consequence of Appropriations made by Law; and a regular Statement and Account of the Receipts and Expenditures of all public Money shall be published from time to time.

No Title of Nobility shall be granted by the United States: And no Person holding any Office of Profit or Trust under them, shall, without the Consent of the Congress, accept of any present, Emolument, Office, or Title, of any kind whatever, from any King, Prince, or foreign State.

SECTION 10. No State shall enter into any Treaty, Alliance, or Confederation; grant Letters of Marque and Reprisal; coin Money; emit Bills of Credit; make any Thing but gold and silver Coin a Tender in Payment of Debts; pass any Bill of Attainder, ex post facto Law, or Law impairing the Obligation of Contracts, or grant any Title of Nobility.

No State shall, without the Consent of the Congress, lay any Imposts or Duties on Imports or Exports, except what may be absolutely necessary for executing its inspection Laws; and the net Produce of all Duties and Imposts, laid by any State on Imports or Exports, shall be for the use of the Treasury of the United States; and all such Laws shall be subject to the Revision and Control of the Congress.

No state shall, without the Consent of Congress, lay any duty of Tonnage, keep Troops, or Ships of War in time of Peace, enter into any Agreement or Compact with another State, or with a foreign Power, or engage in War, unless actually invaded, or in such imminent Danger as will not admit of delay.

ARTICLE II

SECTION 1. The executive Power shall be vested in a President of the United States of America. He shall hold his Office during the Term of four years, and, together with the Vice President, chosen for the same Term, be elected, as follows:

Each State shall appoint, in such Manner as the Legislature thereof may direct, a Number of Electors, equal to the whole Number of Senators and Representatives to which the State may be entitled in the Congress: but no Senator or Representative, or Person holding an Office of Trust or Profit under the United States, shall be appointed an Elector.

[The Electors shall meet in their respective States, and vote by Ballot for two persons, of whom one at least shall not be an Inhabitant of the same State with themselves. And they shall make a List of all the Persons voted for, and of the Number of Votes for each; which List they shall sign and certify, and transmit sealed to the Seat of the Government of the United States, directed to the President of the Senate. The President of the Senate shall, in the Presence of the Senate and House of Representatives, open all the Certificates, and the Votes shall then be counted. The Person having the greatest Number of Votes shall be the President, if such Number be a Majority of the whole Number of Electors appointed; and if there be more than one who have such Majority, and have an equal Number of Votes, then the House of Representatives shall immediately chuse by Ballot one of them for President; and if no Person have a Majority, then from the five highest on the List the said House shall in like Manner chuse the President. But in chusing the President, the Votes shall be taken by States, the Representation from each State having one Vote; a quorum for this Purpose shall consist of a Member or Members from two-thirds of the States, and a Majority of all the States shall be necessary to a Choice. In every

Case, after the Choice of the President, the Person having the greatest Number of Votes of the Electors shall be the Vice President. But if there should remain two or more who have equal votes, the Senate shall chuse from them by Ballot the Vice President.]⁴

The Congress may determine the Time of chusing the Electors, and the Day on which they shall give their Votes; which Day shall be the same throughout the United States.

No person except a natural-born Citizen, or a Citizen of the United States, at the time of the Adoption of this Constitution, shall be eligible to the Office of President; neither shall any Person be eligible to that Office who shall not have attained to the Age of thirty-five years, and been fourteen Years a Resident within the United States.

In Case of the Removal of the President from Office, or of his Death, Resignation, or Inability to discharge the Powers and Duties of the said Office, the same shall devolve on the Vice President, and the Congress may by Law provide for the Case of Removal, Death, Resignation, or Inability, both of the President and Vice President, declaring what Officer shall then act as President, and such Officer shall act accordingly, until the disability be removed, or a President shall be elected.

The President shall, at stated Times, receive for his Services a Compensation, which shall neither be increased nor diminished during the Period for which he shall have been elected, and he shall not receive within that Period any other Emolument from the United States, or any of them.

Before he enter on the execution of his Office, he shall take the following Oath or Affirmation:—"I do solemnly swear (or affirm) that I will faithfully execute the Office of President of the United States, and will, to the best of my Ability, preserve, protect, and defend the Constitution of the United States."

SECTION 2. The President shall be Commander in Chief of the Army and Navy of the United States, and of the Militia of the several States, when called into the actual Service of the United States; he may require the Opinion, in writing, of the principal Officer in each of the executive Departments, upon any subject relating to the Duties of their respective Offices, and he shall have Power to Grant Reprieves and Pardons for Offenses against the United States, except in Cases of Impeachment.

He shall have Power, by and with the Advice and Consent of the Senate, to make Treaties, provided two-thirds of the Senators present concur; and he shall nominate, and by and with the Advice and Consent of the Senate, shall appoint Ambassadors, other public Ministers and Consuls, Judges of the supreme Court, and all other Officers of the United States, whose Appointments are not herein otherwise provided for, and which shall be established by Law: but the Congress may by Law vest the Appoint-

ment of such inferior Officers, as they think proper, in the President alone, in the Courts of Law, or in the Heads of Departments.

The President shall have Power to fill up all Vacancies that may happen during the Recess of the Senate, by granting Commissions which shall expire at the End of their next Session.

SECTION 3. He shall from time to time give to the Congress Information of the State of the Union, and recommend to their Consideration such Measures as he shall judge necessary and expedient; he may, on extraordinary occasions, convene both Houses, or either of them, and in Case of Disagreement between them, with respect to the Time of Adjournment, he may adjourn them to such Time as he shall think proper; he shall receive Ambassadors and other public Ministers; he shall take care that the Laws be faithfully executed, and shall Commission all the Officers of the United States.

SECTION 4. The President, Vice President and all civil Officers of the United States, shall be removed from Office on Impeachment for, and Conviction of, Treason, Bribery, or other high Crimes and Misdemeanors.

ARTICLE III

SECTION 1. The judicial Power of the United States, shall be vested in one supreme Court, and in such inferior Courts as the Congress may from time to time ordain and establish. The Judges, both of the supreme and inferior Courts, shall hold their Offices during good Behaviour, and shall, at stated Times, receive for their Services, a Compensation, which shall not be diminished during their Continuance in Office.

SECTION 2. The judicial Power shall extend to all Cases, in Law and Equity, arising under this Constitution, the Laws of the United States, and Treaties made, or which shall be made, under their Authority;—to all Cases affecting ambassadors, other public ministers and consuls;—to all cases of admiralty and maritime Jurisdiction;— to Controversies to which the United States shall be a Party;—to Controversies between two or more States;—between a State and Citizens of another State;⁵ —between Citizens of different States—between Citizens of the same State claiming Lands under Grants of different States, and between a State, or the Citizens thereof, and foreign States, Citizens, or Subjects. In all Cases affecting Ambassadors, other public Ministers and Consuls, and those in which a State shall be Party, the supreme Court shall have original Jurisdiction. In all the other Cases before mentioned, the

---

4 Revised by the Twelfth Amendment.

5 Qualified by the Eleventh Amendment.

supreme Court shall have appellate Jurisdiction, both as to Law and Fact, with such Exceptions, and under such Regulations as the Congress shall make.

The trial of all Crimes, except in Cases of Impeachment, shall be by Jury; and such Trial shall be held in the State where the said Crimes shall have been committed; but when not committed within any State, the Trial shall be at such Place or Places as the Congress may by Law have directed.

SECTION 3. Treason against the United States, shall consist only in levying War against them, or in adhering to their Enemies, giving them Aid and Comfort. No Person shall be convicted of Treason unless on the Testimony of two Witnesses to the same overt Act, or on Confession in open Court.

The Congress shall have power to declare the Punishment of Treason, but no Attainder of Treason shall work Corruption of Blood, or Forfeiture except during the Life of the Person attainted.

ARTICLE IV

SECTION 1. Full Faith and Credit shall be given in each State to the public Acts, Records, and judicial Proceedings of every other State. And the Congress may by general Laws prescribe the Manner in which such Acts, Records and Proceedings shall be proved, and the Effect thereof.

SECTION 2. The Citizens of each State shall be entitled to all Privileges and Immunities of Citizens in the several States.

A Person charged in any State with Treason, Felony, or other Crime, who shall flee from Justice, and be found in another State, shall on demand of the executive Authority of the State from which he fled, be delivered up, to be removed to the State having Jurisdiction of the crime. No Person held to Service or Labour in one State, under the Laws thereof, escaping into another, shall, in Consequence of any Law or Regulation therein, be discharged from such Service or Labour, but shall be delivered up on Claim of the Party to whom such Service or Labour may be due.

SECTION 3. New States may be admitted by the Congress into this Union; but no new State shall be formed or erected within the Jurisdiction of any other State; nor any State be formed by the Junction of two or more States, or parts of States, without the Consent of the Legislatures of the States concerned as well as of the Congress. The Congress shall have Power to dispose of and make all needful Rules and Regulations respecting the Territory or other Property belonging to the United States; and nothing in this Constitution shall be so construed as to Prejudice any Claims of the United States, or of any particular State.

SECTION 4. The United States shall guarantee to every State in this Union a Republican Form of Government, and shall protect each of them against Invasion; and on Application of the Legislature, or of the Executive (when the Legislature cannot be convened) against domestic Violence.

ARTICLE V

The Congress, whenever two-thirds of both Houses shall deem it necessary, shall propose Amendments to this Constitution, or, on the Application of the Legislatures of two-thirds of the several States, shall call a Convention for proposing Amendments, which, in either Case, shall be valid to all Intents and Purposes, as part of this Constitution, when ratified by the Legislatures of three-fourths of the several States, or by Conventions in three-fourths thereof, as the one or the other Mode of Ratification may be proposed by the Congress; Provided that no Amendment which may be made prior to the Year One thousand eight hundred and eight shall in any Manner affect the first and fourth Clauses in the Ninth Section of the first Article; and that no State, without its Consent, shall be deprived of its equal Suffrage in the Senate.

ARTICLE VI

All Debts contracted and Engagements entered into, before the Adoption of this Constitution, shall be as valid against the United States under this Constitution, as under the Confederation.

This Constitution, and the Laws of the United States which shall be made in Pursuance thereof; and all Treaties made, or which shall be made, under the Authority of the United States, shall be the supreme Law of the Land; and the Judges in every State shall be bound thereby, any Thing in the Constitution or Laws of any State to the Contrary notwithstanding.

The Senators and Representatives before mentioned, and the Members of the several State Legislatures, and all executive and judicial Officers, both of the United States and of the several States, shall be bound by Oath or Affirmation to support this Constitution; but no religious Tests shall ever be required as a qualification to any Office or public Trust under the United States.

ARTICLE VII

The Ratification of the Conventions of nine States shall be sufficient for the Establishment of this Constitution between the States so ratifying the same.

Done in Convention by the Unanimous Consent of the States present the Seventeenth Day of September in the Year of our Lord one thousand seven hundred and Eighty seven, and of the Independence of the United States of America the Twelfth. In Witness whereof We have hereunto subscribed our Names.[6]

GEORGE WASHINGTON
PRESIDENT AND DEPUTY FROM VIRGINIA

New Hampshire	Massachusetts	Connecticut	Georgia
New Jersey	**Pennsylvania**	George Clymer	James Wilson
Delaware	**Maryland**	Pierce Butler	James Madison, Jr.
North Carolina	**South Carolina**	William Samuel Johnson	William Few
John Langdon	Nathaniel Gorham	Thomas FitzSimons	
William Livingston	Benjamin Franklin		**New York**
George Read	James McHenry	**Virginia**	Gouverneur Morris
William Blount	John Rutledge	Roger Sherman	Abraham Baldwin
Nicholas Gilman	Rufus King	Jared Ingersoll	Alexander Hamilton
David Brearley	Thomas Mifflin	John Blair	
Gunning Bedford, Jr.	Daniel of St. Thomas Jenifer		
Richard Dobbs Spaight	Charles Cotesworth Pinckney		
William Paterson	Robert Morris		
John Dickinson	Daniel Carroll		
Hugh Williamson	Charles Pinckney		
Jonathan Dayton			
Richard Bassett			
Jacob Broom			

Articles in Addition to, and Amendment of, the Constitution of the United States of America, Proposed by Congress, and Ratified by the Legislatures of the Several States, Pursuant to the Fifth Article of the Original Constitution[7]

[AMENDMENT I]

Congress shall make no law respecting an establishment of religion, or prohibiting the free exercise thereof; or abridging the freedom of speech, or of the press; or the right of the people peaceably to assemble, and to petition the Government for a redress of grievances.

[AMENDMENT II]

A well regulated Militia, being necessary to the security of a free State, the right of the people to keep and bear Arms shall not be infringed.

[AMENDMENT III]

No Soldier shall, in time of peace, be quartered in any house, without the consent of the Owner, nor in time of war, but in a manner to be prescribed by law.

6 These are the full names of the signers, which in some cases are not the signatures on the document.

7 This heading appears only in the joint resolution submitting the first ten amendments, known as the Bill of Rights.

[AMENDMENT IV]

The right of the people to be secure in their persons, houses, papers, and effects, against unreasonable searches and seizures, shall not be violated, and no Warrants shall issue, but upon probable cause, supported by Oath or affirmation, and particularly describing the place to be searched, and the persons or things to be seized.

[AMENDMENT V]

No person shall be held to answer for a capital or otherwise infamous crime, unless on a presentment or indictment of a Grand Jury, except in cases arising in the land or naval forces, or in the Militia, when in actual service in time of War or public danger; nor shall any person be subject for the same offence to be twice put in jeopardy of life or limb; nor shall be compelled in any criminal case to be a witness against himself, nor be deprived of life, liberty, or property, without due process of law; nor shall private property be taken for public use, without just compensation.

[AMENDMENT VI]

In all criminal prosecutions, the accused shall enjoy the right to a speedy and public trial, by an impartial jury of the State and district wherein the crime shall have been committed, which district shall have been previously ascertained by law, and to be informed of the nature and cause of the accusation; to be confronted with the witnesses against him; to have compulsory process for obtaining witnesses in his favour, and to have the Assistance of Counsel for his defence.

[AMENDMENT VII]

In suits at common law, where the value in controversy shall exceed twenty dollars, the right of trial by jury shall be preserved, and no fact tried by a jury, shall be otherwise reexamined in any Court of the United States, than according to the rules of the common law.

[AMENDMENT VIII]

Excessive bail shall not be required, nor excessive fines imposed, nor cruel and unusual punishments inflicted.

[AMENDMENT IX]

The enumeration of the Constitution, of certain rights, shall not be construed to deny or disparage others retained by the people.

[AMENDMENT X]

The powers not delegated to the United States by the Constitution, nor prohibited by it to the States, are reserved to the States respectively, or to the people. [Amendments I-X, in force 1791.]

[AMENDMENT XI][8]

The Judicial power of the United States shall not be construed to extend to any suit in law or equity, commenced or prosecuted against one of the United States by Citizens of another State, or by Citizens or Subjects of any Foreign State.

[AMENDMENT XII][9]

The Electors shall meet in their respective States and vote by ballot for President and Vice-President, one of whom, at least, shall not be an inhabitant of the same State with themselves; they shall name in their ballots the person voted for as President, and in distinct ballots the person voted for as Vice-President, and they shall make distinct lists of all persons voted for as President, and of all persons voted for as Vice-President, and of the number of votes for each, which lists they shall sign and certify, and transmit sealed to the seat of the government of the United States, directed to the President of the Senate;—The President of the Senate shall, in the presence of the Senate and House of Representatives, open all the certificates and the votes shall then be counted;—The person having the greatest number of votes for President, shall be the President, if such number be a majority of the whole number of Electors appointed; and if no person have such majority, then from the persons having the highest numbers not exceeding three on the list of those voted for as President, the House of Representatives shall choose immediately, by ballot, the President. But in choosing the President, the votes shall be taken by states, the representation from each state having one vote; a quorum for this purpose shall

8 Adopted in 1798.
9 Adopted in 1804.

consist of a member or members from two-thirds of the states, and a majority of all the states shall be necessary to a choice. And if the House of Representatives shall not choose a President whenever the right of choice shall devolve upon them, before the fourth day of March next following, then the Vice-President shall act as President, as in the case of the death or other constitutional disability of the President.—The person having the greatest number of votes as Vice-President, shall be the Vice-President, if such number be a majority of the whole number of Electors appointed, and if no person have a majority, then from the two highest numbers on the list, the Senate shall choose the Vice-President; a quorum for the purpose shall consist of two-thirds of the whole number of Senators, and a majority of the whole number shall be necessary to a choice. But no person constitutionally ineligible to the office of President shall be eligible to that of Vice-President of the United States.

[AMENDMENT XIII][10]

SECTION 1. Neither slavery nor involuntary servitude, except as a punishment for crime whereof the party shall have been duly convicted, shall exist within the United States, or any place subject to their jurisdiction.

SECTION 2. Congress shall have power to enforce this article by appropriate legislation.

[AMENDMENT XIV][11]

SECTION 1. All persons born or naturalized in the United States, and subject to the jurisdiction thereof, are citizens of the United States and of the State wherein they reside. No State shall abridge the privileges or immunities of citizens of the United States; nor shall any State deprive any person of life, liberty, or property, without due process of law; nor deny to any person within its jurisdiction the equal protection of the laws.

SECTION 2. Representatives shall be apportioned among the several States according to their respective numbers, counting the whole number of persons in each State, excluding Indians not taxed. But when the right to vote at any election for the choice of electors for President and Vice-President of the United States, Representatives in Congress, the Executive and Judicial officers of a State, or the members of the Legislature thereof, is denied to any of the male inhabitants of such State, being twentyone years of age, and citizens of the United States, or in any way abridged, except for participation in rebellion, or other crime, the basis of representation therein shall be reduced in the proportion which the number of such male citizens shall bear to the whole number of male citizens twenty-one years of age in such State.

SECTION 3. No person shall be a Senator or Representative in Congress, or elector of President and Vice- President, or hold any office, civil or military, under the United States, or under any State, who, having previously taken an oath, as a member of Congress, or as an officer of the United States, or as a member of any State legislature, or as an executive or judicial officer of any State, to support the Constitution of the United States, shall have engaged in insurrection or rebellion against the same, or given aid or comfort to the enemies thereof. But Congress may by a vote of two-thirds of each House, remove such disability.

SECTION 4. The validity of the public debt of the United States, authorized by law, including debts incurred for payment of pensions and bounties for services in suppressing insurrection or rebellion, shall not be questioned. But neither the United States nor any State shall assume or pay any debts or obligation incurred in aid of insurrection or rebellion against the United States, or any claim for the loss or emancipation of any slave; but all such debts, obligations, and claims shall be held illegal and void.

SECTION 5. The Congress shall have the power to enforce, by appropriate legislation, the provisions of this article.

[AMENDMENT XV][12]

SECTION 1. The right of citizens of the United States to vote shall not be denied or abridged by the United States or by any State on account of race, color, or previous condition of servitude—

SECTION 2. The Congress shall have power to enforce this article by appropriate legislation.

[AMENDMENT XVI][13]

The Congress shall have power to lay and collect taxes on incomes, from whatever source derived, without apportionment among the several States, and without regard to any census or enumeration.

10 Adopted in 1865.
11 Adopted in 1868.

12 Adopted in 1870.
13 Adopted in 1913.

[AMENDMENT XVII][14]

The Senate of the United States shall be composed of two Senators from each State, elected by the people thereof, for six years; and each Senator shall have one vote. The electors in each State shall have the qualifications requisite for electors of the most numerous branch of the State legislatures.

When vacancies happen in the representation of any State in the Senate, the executive authority of such State shall issue writs of election to fill such vacancies: Provided, That the legislature of any State may empower the executive thereof to make temporary appointments until the people fill the vacancies by election as the legislature may direct. This amendment shall not be so construed as to affect the election or term of any Senator chosen before it becomes valid as part of the Constitution.

[AMENDMENT XVIII][15]

SECTION 1. After one year from the ratification of this article the manufacture, sale, or transportation of intoxicating liquors within, the importation thereof into, or the exportation thereof from the United States and all territory subject to the jurisdiction thereof for beverage purposes is hereby prohibited.

SECTION 2. The Congress and the several States shall have concurrent power to enforce this article by appropriate legislation.

SECTION 3. This article shall be inoperative unless it shall have been ratified as an amendment to the Constitution by the legislatures of the several States, as provided in the Constitution, within seven years from the date of the submission hereof to the States by the Congress.

[AMENDMENT XIX][16]

The right of citizens of the United States to vote shall not be denied or abridged by the United States or by any State on account of sex.

Congress shall have power to enforce this article by appropriate legislation.

14 Adopted in 1913.

15 Adopted in 1918.

16 Adopted in 1920.

[AMENDMENT XX][17]

SECTION 1. The terms of the President and Vice-President shall end at noon on the 20th day of January, and the terms of Senators and Representatives at noon on the 3d day of January, of the years in which such terms would have ended if this article had not been ratified; and the terms of their successors shall then begin.

SECTION 2. The Congress shall assemble at least once in every year, and such meeting shall begin at noon on the 3d day of January, unless they shall by law appoint a different day.

SECTION 3. If, at the time fixed for the beginning of the term of the President, the President elect shall have died, the Vice-President elect shall become President. If a President shall not have been chosen before the time fixed for the beginning of his term or if the President elect shall have failed to qualify, then the Vice-President elect shall act as President until a President shall have qualified; and the Congress may by law provide for the case wherein neither a President elect nor a Vice-President elect shall have qualified, declaring who shall then act as President, or the manner in which one who is to act shall be selected, and such person shall act accordingly until a President or Vice-President shall have qualified.

SECTION 4. The Congress may by law provide for the case of the death of any of the persons from whom the House of Representatives may choose a President whenever the right of choice shall have devolved upon them, and for the case of the death of any of the persons from whom the Senate may choose a Vice-President whenever the right of choice shall have devolved upon them.

SECTION 5. Sections 1 and 2 shall take effect on the 15th day of October following the ratification of this article.

SECTION 6. This article shall be inoperative unless it shall have been ratified as an amendment to the Constitution by the legislatures of three-fourths of the several States within seven years from the date of its submission.

17 Adopted in 1933.

[AMENDMENT XXI]¹⁸

SECTION 1. The eighteenth article of amendment to the Constitution of the United States is hereby repealed.

SECTION 2. The transportation or importation into any State, Territory, or possession of the United States for delivery or use therein of intoxicating liquors, in violation of the laws thereof, is hereby prohibited.

SECTION 3. This article shall be inoperative unless it shall have been ratified as an amendment to the Constitution by conventions in the several States, as provided in the Constitution, within seven years from the date of the submission hereof to the States by the Congress.

[AMENDMENT XXII]¹⁹

No person shall be elected to the office of the President more than twice, and no person who has held the office of President, or acted as President, for more than two years of a term to which some other person was elected President shall be elected to the office of the President more than once.

But this Article shall not apply to any person holding the office of President when this Article was proposed by the Congress, and shall not prevent any person who may be holding the office of President, or acting as President, during the term within which this Article becomes operative from holding the office of President or acting as President during the remainder of such term.

This article shall be inoperative unless it shall have been ratified as an amendment to the Constitution by the legislatures of three-fourths of the several states within seven years from the date of its submission to the states by the Congress.

[AMENDMENT XXIII]²⁰

SECTION 1. The District constituting the seat of Government of the United States shall appoint in such manner as the Congress may direct:

A number of electors of President and Vice-President equal to the whole number of Senators and Representatives in Congress to which the District would be entitled if it were a State, but in no event more than the least populous State; they shall be in addition to those appointed by the States, but they shall be considered, for the purpose of the election of President and Vice-President, to be electors appointed by a State; and they shall meet in the District and perform such duties as provided by the twelfth article of amendment.

SECTION 2. The Congress shall have power to enforce this article by appropriate legislation.

[AMENDMENT XXIV]²¹

SECTION 1. The right of citizens of the United States to vote in any primary or other election for President or Vice-President, for electors for President or Vice-President, or for Senator or Representative in Congress, shall not be denied or abridged by the United States or any state by reason of failure to pay any poll tax or other tax.

SECTION 2. The Congress shall have the power to enforce this article by appropriate legislation.

[AMENDMENT XXV]²²

SECTION 1. In case of the removal of the President from office or of his death or resignation, the Vice-President shall become President.

SECTION 2. Whenever there is a vacancy in the office of the Vice President, the President shall nominate a Vice President who shall take office upon confirmation by a majority vote of both Houses of Congress.

SECTION 3. Whenever the President transmits to the President Pro Tempore of the Senate and the Speaker of the House of Representatives his written declaration that he is unable to discharge the powers and duties of his office, and until he transmits to them a written declaration to the contrary, such powers and duties shall be discharged by the Vice-President as Acting President.

SECTION 4. Whenever the Vice-President and a majority of either the principal officers of the executive departments or of such other body as Congress may by law provide, transmit to the President Pro Tempore of the Senate and the Speaker of the House of Representatives their written declaration that the President is unable to discharge the powers and duties of his office, the Vice President shall immediately assume the powers and du-

18 Adopted in 1933.

19 Adopted in 1951.

20 Adopted in 1961.

21 Adopted in 1964.

22 Adopted in 1967.

ties of the office as Acting President.

Thereafter, when the President transmits to the President Pro Tempore of the Senate and the Speaker of the House of Representatives his written declaration that no inability exists, he shall resume the powers and duties of his office unless the Vice President and a majority of either the principal officers of the executive departments or of such other body as Congress may by law provide, transmit within four days to the President Pro Tempore of the Senate and the Speaker of the House of Representatives their written declaration that the President is unable to discharge the powers and duties of his office. Thereupon Congress shall decide the issue, assembling within forty-eight hours for that purpose if not in session. If the Congress, within twenty-one days after receipt of the latter written declaration, or, if Congress is not in session, within twenty-one days after Congress is required to assemble, determines by two-thirds vote of both Houses that the President is unable to discharge the powers and duties of his office, the Vice President shall continue to discharge the same as Acting President; otherwise, the President shall resume the powers and duties of his office.

[AMENDMENT XXVI] [23]

SECTION 1. The right of citizens of the United States, who are eighteen years of age or older, to vote shall not be denied or abridged by the United States or by any State on account of age.

SECTION 1. The Congress shall have power to enforce this article by appropriate legislation.

[AMENDMENT XXVII] [24]

No law, varying the compensation for the services of the Senators and Representatives, shall take effect, until an election of Representatives shall have intervened.

23 Adopted in 1971.
24 Adopted in 1992.

Credits

to; **146 T:** "Black Methodists Holding a Meeting," by Pavel Petrovich Svinin, 1811-1813. Watercolor on paper, 6-9/16 x 9-15/16". Provenance: R.T.H. Halsy, New York. The Metropolitan Museum of Art, Rogers Fund, 1942 (42.95.19). Photo © 1985 The Metropolitan Museum of Art, New York; **146 B:** Derek Dammann/iStockphoto; **147:** Christine Balderas; **148:** Photodisc/PunchStock; **150:** Library of Congress; **152:** Private Collection, Peter Newark American Pictures/The Bridgeman Art Library; **156-157 (left to right):** (top) Library of Congress; (bottom) National Archives and Records Administration (Public); Getty Images; Library of Congress [LC-DIG-ppmsca-17522]; C Squared Studios/Getty Images; Library of Congress [LC-USZC4-6423]; Courtesy of the Library of Congress; Photodisc; **158-159:** Collection of New-York Historical Society/The Bridgeman Art Library; **160:** The Granger Collection, New York; **163:** Eyewire (Photodisc)/PunchStock; **164:** Private Collection; **165:** DaddyBit/iStockphoto; **166:** "Alexander Hamilton", c. 1972, by John Trumbull. Oil on canvas, 30 1/4 x 24 1/8 in. Gift of Avalon Foundation, © 2000 Board of Trustees, National Gallery of Art, Washington, DC; **167:** Réunion des Musées Nationaux / Art Resource, NY; **171:** "The Procession of Victuallers," 1821, by Joseph Yeager. Philadelphia Museum of Art, (1961-7-17); **175:** The Granger Collection, New York; **179:** The British Library; **181:** CMCD/Getty Images; **182:** Library of Congress [LC-DIG-ppmsca-10755]; **184-185 (left to right):** Pixtal/Age Fotostock; The McGraw-Hill Companies Inc./Ken Cavanagh Photographer; Library of Congress [LC-USZ62-13002]; National Archives and Records Administration (Public); Library of Congress [LC-USZ62-20214]; Library of Congress [LC-USZ62-10609]; Library of Congress [LC-USZC4-3616]; Library of Congress [LC-USZC4-3675]; Library of Congress; **186-187:** "Lockport on the Erie Canal," 1832 by Mary Keys. Watercolor on paper. 15-1/4 x 20-1/4 in. Museum Purchase. 55.45. Munson-Williams-Proctor Arts Institute/Art Resource, NY; **188:** Library of Congress; **190:** SuperStock; **192:** Eric Isselée/iStockphoto; **194 T:** Johann Helgason/IStockphoto; **194 B:** Missouri Historical Society (Neg # CT SS831); **195:** Library of Congress; **196:** American Textile History Museum, Lowell MA; **198:** "Pawtucket Falls, Rhode Island" by Jacques Gerard Milbert, 1828-29. Lithograph on India paper. The New York Public Library/Art Resource, NY; **200:** "Calculating," 1844, by Thomas Hicks, American (1823-1890). Oil on canvas, 13 5/8 x 17 in. Gift of Maxim Karolik for the M. and M. Karolik Collection of American Paintings, 1815-1865, 62.273. © 2007 Museum of Fine Arts, Boston. All Rights Reserved.; **201:** Library of Congress [LC-USZ62-89594]; **202-203 (left to right):** Library of Congress [LC-USZC4-12270]; Library of Congress; Library of Congress; Stockbyte/PunchStock; Comstock Images/Alamy; Library of Congress; Library of Congress; CMCD/Getty Images; **204-205:** "The Verdict of the People" by George Caleb Bingham, 1854-55. Saint Louis Art Museum, Gift of Bank of America; **206:** Tennessee State Museum Collection. Photography by June Dorman; **207:** "The Butcher," by Nicolino Calyo, c. 1840-44. Museum of the City of New York, Gift of Mrs. Francis Garvan in memory of Francis Garvan; **330:** The Granger Collection; **210:** "Andrew Jackson," 1835 by Asher B. Durand. The New-York Historical Society, 1858.11; **211:** Brandon Laufenberg/iStockphoto; **212:** Library of Congress [LC-USZC4-6466]; **215:** Courtesy of the J. Paul Getty Museum, Los Angeles, 84.XT.441.3; **217:** Library of Congress; **218:** Museum of the City of New York, The J. Clarence Davies Collection; **222-223 (left to right):** Library of Congress; Library of Congress [LC-USZC2-2753]; Library of Congress; Image Source/Alamy; Library of Congress; Brand X Pictures/PunchStock; Library of Congress [LC-USZC2-3178]; **224-225:** Library of Congress; **226:** Harriet Beecher Stowe Center, Hartford, CT; **227:** Rubberball/Punchstock; **228 T:** Library of Congress; **228 B:** Allen Memorial Art Museum, Gift of Lewis Tappan. Oberlin College; **229:** Royalty-Free/Corbis; **230 T:** Stock Montage, Inc.; **231:** Design Pics/PunchStock; **232:** Concord Free Public Library; **233:** © Lowell Georgia/Corbis; **235 M:** Photofest; **235 B:** Library of Congress; **236:** Library of Congress [LC-USZC4-1298]; **237:** Madison County Historical Society, Oneida, NY; **238:** Rhoda Jenkins/ Coline Jenkins-Sahlin; **240-241 (left to right):** Library of Congress; Library of Congress; Library of Congress; Ingram Publishing/ Fotosearch; C Squared Studios/Getty Images; Library of Congress [LC-USZ62-9797]; Library of Congress; Stockbyte/ PictureQuest; **242-243:** National Archives of Canada, Documentary Art and Photography Division; **244:** The Historic

New Orleans Collection, accession no. 1960.46; **246:** Museum of the City of New York, Harry T. Peters Collection; **251:** The Historic New Orleans Collection, accession no. 1975.93.5; **252:** Basil Hall, Etching 25, "Forty etchings from sketches made with the camera lucida in North America, in 1827 and 1828". Edinburg, London. William L. Clements Library, University of Michigan; **253:** National Archives and Records Administration; **254:** Middle Passage Museum's Collection; **255:** Schomburg Center for Research in Black Culture, New York Public Library, Art Resource, NY; **256-257:** "Lynchburg, Negro Dance," from Sketchbook of Landscapes in the State of Virginia by Lewis Miller, Virginia, ca. 1853, accession 1978.301.1, 17B. Abby Aldrich Rockefeller Folk Art Museum, Williamsburg, VA; **258:** National Museum of American History, Smithsonian Institution; **260-261 (left to right):** Brand X Pictures/PunchStock; Library of Congress [LC-USZC4-2521]; Library of Congress [LC-DIG-cwpbh-02605]; The Palma Collection/Getty Images; Ingram Publishing/Alamy; Ingram Publishing/ Fotosearch; Ingram Publishing/Alamy; Royalty-Free/Corbis; **262-263:** New York Public Library/Art Resource, NY; **264:** National Anthropological Archives, Smithsonian Institution; **266:** Library of Congress; **267 T:** "Market Scene in Mexico, in San Felipe, Coahuila" by Theodore Gentilz. Courtesy Witte Museum; **267 B:** TexPhoto/iStockphoto; **268:** "Sunday at San Miguel, Santa Fe, New Mexico," 1882, by Rudolf Cronau. Courtesy of the Museum of the American West, Autry National Center, 93.99.2; **273:** Government Printing Office, 1898; **274:** Library of Congress [LC-USZ62-1272]; **276 & 277 B:** Library of Congress; **277 T:** "The 'Heathen Chinee' with Pick and Rocker", from Mining Scenes in California Series, ca. 1868. Photograph by Edweard J. Muybrige. Courtesy California Historical Society, San Francisco, FN-138990; **278 T:** Courtesy of The Bancroft Library, University of California, Berkeley; **278 B:** PhotoLink/Getty Images; **281:** Library of Congress; **284-285 (left to right):** Digital Archive Japan/Alamy; Stockbyte/Getty Images; Library of Congress; Library of Congress; Image Club; Library of Congress; Photodisc/Getty Images; Library of Congress [LC-USZC2-3199]; **286-287:** Kansas State Historical Society, FK2.83*15; **289:** Culver Pictures; **294 R:** Juthathip Tybon/iStockphoto; **294 L:** Brasil2/iStockphoto; **296:** Dan Brandenburg/iStockphoto; **297:** Print Collection, Miriam and Ira D. Wallach Division of Arts, Prints and Photographs. New York Public Library, Astor, Lenox and Tilden Foundations; **299 T:** Private Collection, Peter Newark American Pictures/The Bridgeman Art Library; **299 B:** Carlos Rex Arbogast/ AP Images; **300 L-R:** Library of Congress; **301:** Royalty-Free/Corbis; **302:** Library of Congress, Prints & Photographs Division [LC-USZC2-331]; **305:** The New-York Historical Society, PR-022-3-45-13; **306-307 (left to right):** Library of Congress [LC-USZ62-27710]; Siede Preis/Getty Images; Arthur S. Aubry/Getty Images; Library of Congress; Library of Congress; Stockbyte; **308-309:** MPI/Getty Images; **310:** Library of Congress; **311 T:** Library of Congress [LC-DIG-ppmsca-09854]; **311 B:** Library of Congress [LC-USZ62-120480]; **313:** Royalty-Free/Corbis; **318:** Corbis; **319:** The Museum of the Confederacy, Richmond, Virginia; **321:** Department of the Army, U.S. Army Military History Institute Carlisle Barracks, PA; **322:** Library of Congress; **323:** Royalty-Free/Corbis; **324:** Royalty-Free/Corbis; **325:** "Reveille on a Winter Morning" by Henry Bacon. West Point Museum Collections, United States Military Academy; **328:** © 1996 Virginia Historical Society; **329 TL:** Library of Congress; **329 TR:** Valentine Richmond History Center; **329 B:** H P Moore/Getty Images; **330:** Royalty-Free/Corbis; **332-333 (left to right):** Royalty-Free/Corbis; Library of Congress; C Squared Studios/Getty Images; Library of Congress [LC-USZC4-2815]; Royalty-Free/Corbis; Brand X Pictures/PunchStock; Image Club; **334-335:** Library of Congress; **336:** "A Visit from the Old Mistress," by Winslow Homer, 1876. Oil on canvas, 18x24 1/8". National Museum of American Art, Smithsonian Institution, Washington, DC, USA. Gift of William T. Evans. Art Resource, NY; **337:** Harper's Weekly; **338:** Royalty-Free/Corbis; **341:** Puck, 1890; **345:** © Corbis; **347:** Library of Congress; **348:** The Granger Collection, New York; **349 T:** Library of Congress; **349 B:** The New York Public Library/Art Resource, NY.; **350** Alex Stout/iStockphoto; **352-353 (left to right):** Library of Congress LC-DIG-ppmsca-17562]; Library of Congress [LC-B8184-10690]; Comstock/PunchStock; Brian Hagiwara/Brand X Pictures/Getty Images; Library of Congress; Burke/Triolo/Brand X Pictures/Jupiterimages; Library of Congress; **354:** Masterfile Royalty-Free.

Index

A

Abenakis, 64, 72, 73
abolitionism
　beginnings of, 235–237
　opponents and divisions with, 237–238
　party system and, 239–240
　perfection and, 235–238
　schism of 1840, 238
　spread of, 237
　women's rights movement, 238
Acoma pueblo, 41, 42, 43
Actes and Monuments, 67
actual representation, 110
Adams, Charles Francis Jr., 325
Adams, John, 123, 152, 179
　election of 1800, 170
　Marshall, John, judicial review and, 170
　naval war with France and, 168–169
　Republic and presidency of, 168–170
　suppression at home, 169
Adams, John Quincy (son), 183, 189, 207, 208, 210
Adams, Samuel, 111, 113, 152
Adena cultures, 7m
Africa
　Chesapeake society, Atlantic slave trade and,
　　49, 50, 51, 52
　Eurasia and Potuguese wave with, 22–23
　fifteenth century Eurasia and, 21–24
　ivory masks, 23
African Americans. *See also* slaves
　American Revolution and, 133–134
　celebrations, 171–172
　Civil War and, 318
　community, 213–214
　free, 212–213, 215, 257–258
　minstrelsy and, 214, 349
　populations, 161
　racism and, 53, 214, 351
　revivalism and rise of churches, 229
African Methodist Episcopal (AME) Church, 229
age expectancy, 68
agriculture
　Ancient Mexico and, 5–6
　gifts, 9–10
　market revolution and economy with, 191–192
　Southwest and, 6
alcohol, 160, 234, 239
Alcott, Bronson, 231
Algonquins, 14, 15, 62, 63, 64, 72
Alien Acts, 169
allegiance, patterns of, 125
Allen, Ethan, 86
Amazon rainforest, 10
America, 178, 275
　additional reading, 203
　boom to bust with one-day clock and, 187–188
　chapter summary, 202
　development of Lowell Mills in, 197
　distribution of populations in North, 90
　England's entry in, 32–36
　enlightenment in, 91–94
　Great Awakening (aftermath) in, 93–94
　Great Awakening (first) in, 93
　inequality in England and, 94–95
　market revolution in, 189–193

　opening of, 186–203
　politics in England and, 95–96
　prosperity and anxiety in, 201–202
　Republic and turning inward of, 182–184
　restless temper and, 192–193
　rise of factories in, 193–198
　significant events, 202–203
　social structures of market society in, 199–201
　Spain in North and South, 24–29
　Spanish, 28
　transportation network of market economy
　　(1840), 191
　travel times (1800–1830), 190
　Union and sectional changes in, 290–295
America before the European Invasions (Kehoe), 17
American Anti-Slavery Society, 237
American society
　growth of railroad economy, 290–291
　immigration, 293–294
　railroads and prairie environment, 291
　railroads and urban environment, 291
　rising industrialization, 291, 293
　Southern complaints in, 294–295
American Temperance Society, 234
the American Revolution
　additional reading, 137
　African Americans in, 133–134
　American people and, 120–137
　British empire's last days in America and,
　　115–116
　chapter summary, 136
　decision for independence and, 122–124
　fighting begins and, 116–117
　fighting in North, 124–126, 127, 128
　first Continental Congress and, 114–115
　as global war, 128–129
　independence and toward, 114–118
　market, 189–193
　new men and women of, 148–149
　Paine's common sense and, 109, 117–118
　patterns of allegiance, 125
　people and, 120–137
　significant events, 136–137
　smallpox pandemic (1775–1782), 130
　struggle in South, 131–132, 133, 134
　surrender at Yorktown, 134–136
　turning point in, 128–131
　worlds turned upside down, 134–136
Ames, Adelbert, 350
amnesty, 337
Anasazis, 6, 7m, 10, 14
Ancient Mexico
　agriculture in, 5–6
　Anasazis in, 6, 7m, 10, 14
　Aztecs in, 5, 6, 11, 16, 26, 27
　collapse of, 14
　cultures, 5–6
　Mayans in, 6, 7m, 11, 14, 16
　Mesoamerica and, 5–6, 9, 11, 16
　Olmecs in, 5–6, 7m, 11, 14, 16
　Pueblo Bonito, 6
　Toltecs in, 11
Ancient Peoples of the Southwest (Plog), 17
Anderson, Mary, 344
Anderson, Robert, 303, 304
animals, 12–13

Anthony, Susan B., 238, 348
anxiety, 201–202
Apaches, 43
Appalachia, independence and frontier in, 107
Appeal to the Colored Citizens of the World
　(Walker, David), 213, 237
L'Archevêque, Jean, 80, 81–83
Arctic cultures, 9
aristocracy, 150–151
Arkansas, 65
Arnold, Benedict, 128, 134
Arrellano, Estevan, 42
assimilate, 294
Astor, John Jacob, 199
asylum movement, 235
Atchison, David Rice, 297
Atlas of the North American Indian (Waldman), 17
Austin, Moses, 267
Austin, Stephen (son), 267
autonomy, 97
Awful Disclosures of Maria Monk, 296
Aztecs, 5, 6, 11, 16, 26, 27

B

Babcock, Orville, 348
backcountry, settlement of, 84–85
Bacon, Nathaniel, 48–49
Bacon's Rebellion, 48–49
balanced constitution, 95
balances. *See* checks and balances
the Bank War
　bank destroyed, 217–218
　bare-knuckled boxers and, 217–218
　Jackson's impact on presidency and, 218
　national bank and panic of 1819, 216–217
Baptists, 176, 178
Barbary states, 178, 179
barter economy, 163
Bastille prison, 166
Battle of Antietam, 310
Battle of Bull Run, 309–310, 316
Battle of Fallen Timbers, 174
Battle of Horseshoe Bend, 181
Battle of New Orleans, 182
Battle of Seven Days, 316
Battle of Shiloh, 315
Battle of Tippecanoe, 178
Beauregard, Pierre (general), 309
Beaver Wars, 63–64
Beecher, Catharine (daughter), 230, 234
Beecher, Lyman (reverend), 225, 226, 227, 228,
　230, 235, 238
the Beecher family, 225, 226, 227
Belknap, William W., 348
benign neglect, 97
the Bering Strait, 4, 5, 7m, 16
Berkeley, William, 48, 54, 73
Biddle, Nicholas, 216, 217, 218
Birney, James G., 236, 239, 272
black codes, 338, 339
blacks, 342–343. *See also* African Americans;
　slavery; slaves
　Civil War soldiers, 318–319
　experiencing freedom, 344–345
　families, 345

free, 133, 212–213, 257–258
  new working conditions for, 346
  planters and new way of life for, 346–347
  reconstruction and aspirations of, 344–347
  schoolhouse and church, 345–346
the Black Death, 21–22, 67
Bleecker, Ann Eliza, 131
bloody shirt, 340
Blue Jacket, 173
Bodmer, Karl, 11
Boleyn, Anne, 32
Bonaparte, Napoleon, 175, 181, 184
bonds, 321
boom bust cycles, 201
Booth, John Wilkes, 331, 337
border states, 312–313
Boston massacre, imperial crisis and, 112–113
Boston Tea Party, 113
boundaries, 86, *183*
Braddock, Edward (major general), 103
Bradford, Dorothy, 66
Bradford, William, 66, 72
Bridger, Jim, 199
*A Briefe and True Reporte of the New Found Land
  of Virginia* (Hariot), 34
British invasion, 181–182
British navy, 181
Brooke, John, 92
Brooks, Preston S., 297
Brown, John, 288, 301
Brown,,Owen, 288
Brown, Salmon, 288
Brown, William Wells, 237
Brownson, Orestes, 231
bubonic plague. *See* the Black Death
Buchanan, James, 298, 299
Burgoyne, John, 128
Burr, Aaron, 170

C

Cabeza de Vaca, Alvar Núñez, 29
Cabot, John. *See* Cabota, Giovanni
Cabota, Giovanni, 20
caciques (Taino chiefs), 15
Caddos, 82
Cahokia, 8, 10
Calculating, 200
Caldwell, Charles, 347
Calhoun, John C., 189, 207, 208, 215, 259, 281, *281,*
  331
Calvert family, 47, 48–49
Calvin, John, *31,* 32, 36, 65, 70
camp life, 324
campaigns, 282
Campbell, John, 103
cannibalism, 29
Canyon de Chelly, 7
the Caribbean
  Carolinas, Florida, and southeastern slave
    wars, 54, 56
  colonization and Carolinas to, 53–54, *55,*
    56–58
  and founding of Carolinas, 54
  paradise lost, 53–54
  Spanish beachhead in, 24–26
Carleton, Guy (sir), 126, 128
the Carolinas
  Caribbean and founding of, 54
  colonization and Caribbean to, 53–54, *55,*
    56–58
  Florida, and southeastern slave wars, Carib-

bean and, 54, 56
  search for order in, 56–57
carpetbaggers, 343
Carteret, George, 74
Cartier, Jacques, 62
caste system, 253
Catherine of Aragon (queen), 32
Catholics, 66, 296
Cavelier, René Robert, 65, 82
Cayugas, 63
cede, 174
celibate, 43
census, 161
Chaco Canyon, *6, 7m,* 10
Champlain, Samuel de, 62, 63
Charles I (king), 48, 54, 58, 67
Charles II (king), 48, 54, 73
Charleston, 131, *338*
charter, 33
checks and balances, 154
Cherokee Phoenix, 211
Cherokees, 14, 181, 211–212
Chesapeake society, *47*
  Africa, Atlantic slave trade and, 49, 50, 51, 52
  Bacon's rebellion, 48–49
  changes in English policy in, 48
  colonization and changing, 52–53
  Coode's rebellion, 48–49
  in crisis, 48–52
  English and, 44–48
  Maryland's founding and renewal of Indian
    Wars, 47–48
  reform, tobacco boom and, 46
  from servitude to slavery in, 49
  Virginia Company and, 45
  war with Confederacy and, 46–47
Chestnut, Mary, 328
Chevalier, Michael, 193
Chickasaws, 14, 56, 65, 181
children, slaves, 255
China, 21, 279–280
Chippewas, 178
Choctaws, 14, 56, 181
churches, 229, 345–346
Ciboneys, 15
Cincinnati Commercial, 298
civil liberties, 322–323
Civil Rights Act of 1875, 349
the Civil War
  additional reading, 333
  African Americans', 318
  in balance, 328
  Battle of Bull Run and, 309–310, 316
  black soldiers in, 318–319
  blockade and isolate, 313–314
  border states, 312–313
  camp life, 324
  changing face of battle, 324
  chapter summary, 332
  civil liberties and dissent during, 322–323
  confederate financing and government in, 320
  Confederate home front and, 319–320
  demands of total, 311–313
  discipline in, 323–324
  eastern stalemate and, 315–317
  emancipation and, 317–319
  emancipation proclamation and, 317–318
  government finances and economy in, 321
  Grant and, 314–315
  hardening attitudes, 324–325
  hardship and suffering during, 320
  Lincoln's general in, 326–328

logic of events and, 317
  new economy and, 319
  new opportunities for Southern women
    during, 319
  opening moves, 313–317
  political leadership and, 312
  Republic and, 308–333
  rich man's war, 321
  significant events, *332–333*
  soldiers joining, 323–325
  twilight of confederacy in, 329–331
  Union home front and, 321–323
  Union's triumph, 325–328
  women and workforce in, 321–322
Clark, George Rogers, 130, 175
Clark, William, 175
Clay, Henry, 180, 183, 189, 208, 217, 219, 271, 282
Clinton, Henry (sir), 129
Clinton, Hillary, 299
clocks, 187–188
Coe, Michael D., 17
Coercive Acts, 113–114
Colleton, John (sir), 54
Colombo, Cristoforo. *See* Columbus, Christopher
colonies, 41–44, 73–76, *84*
colonization
  additional reading, 79
  adjustment to empire and, 76–78
  African Transatlantic slave trade and, 50–51
  bears on floating islands and, 61–62
  from Caribbean to Carolinas and, 53–54, 55,
    56–58
  changing Chesapeake society and, 52–53
  chapter summary, 59, 78
  Chesapeake and, *47*
  Chesapeake, English society and, 44–48
  Chesapeake society in crisis and, 48–52
  early New England, 69
  founding of New England and, 65–68
  mid-Atlantic colonies and, 73–76
  Mississippi's lure and, 64–65
  New Netherlands, Iroquois and Beaver Wars,
    63–64
  North America and France's, 62–65
  North: conflict and, 60–79
  royal authority in America in 1700, 76–78
  significant events, 58–59, 78–79
  South: conflict and, 38–59
  Spain in Americas and, 24–27, *28,* 29
  Spanish missions in North America and, 44
  stability and order in early New England,
    68–73
  strangers and, 39–40
  Sudbury, Massachusetts, and, *70*
  suggested reading, 59
Columbian exchange, 26–27
Columbus, Christopher, 3, 5, 14, 21, 24
commercial economies, women in semisubsistence and, 162–163
committees of correspondence, 113
Common Sense (Paine), 117, 123
communications, 190–191
the Compromise of 1850, 282, *283*
comptoir (storehouse for dead animal skins), 63
the Confederacy
  Chesapeake society and war with, 46–47
  Constitution to, 151–155
  home front of, 319–320
  Miami and, 173–174
  resources of Union and, *311*
Confiscation Act of 1862, 342

conflicts
  frontier and social, 85–86
  New England communities in, 70–71
  North: colonization and, 60–79
  seaports and social, 89
  South: colonization and, 38–59
Congregationalists, 65
congressional reconstruction
  impeachment and, 342
  land issues and, 342
  post-emancipation societies in Americas and, 341–342
conquistadores, 20
conscription, 320
the Constitution
  additional reading, 158
  chapter summary, 156
  commerce and, 163
  Confederacy and, 151–155
  from confederation to, 151–155
  crisis and, 138–157
  deadlock broken and, 153
  framing federal, 152
  Jay-Gardoqui Treaty and, 151
  ordinance of 1785, *145*
  ratification of, 153–154, *155*
  Republican experiments and, 140–142
  Republican society, 148–151
  Shay's Rebellion and, 151–152
  significant events, *156–157*
  state constitutions and, 140–141
  temptations of peace with, 142–147
  Virginia and New Jersey plans and, 152–153
  Western land claims (1782-1802), *143*
Continental Army, 123
Continental Congress
  first, and revolution, 114–115
  independence and second, 123
contraband, 317
Coode, John, 48–49
Coode's Rebellion, 48–49
Cooper, Anthony Ashley (sir), 54
Copperheads, 322, 323
Cornwallis, Charles (general), 142, *150*
"Cornwallis Turned Nurse, and His Mistress a Soldier," *150*
corporation, 192
Cortés, Hernán, 20, 26, *27*, 29, 30, 35, 41
Corwin, Thomas, 274
cotton
  Deep/Upper South and, 245–247
  distribution of slavery and, 247
  kingdom's social structure, 245–248
  market revolution and trade in, 189
  other crops in South and, *246*
  Rural South and, 247
  slavery as labor system for, 247–248
  South and social structure of, 245–248
  South, other crops and, *246*
Cotton, John, 71
counter-reformation, 63
couriers de bois (runners in the woods), 63
Crawford, William H., 207
Creeks, 14, 56
crisis
  Chesapeake society in, 48–52
  Constitution and, 138–157
  democracy and nullification, 215–216
  enduring cultures and, 14–15
  imperial, 104–111
  North America on eve of contact and, 15–16
  North America's, 14–16

nullification, 215–216
slavery and escape from, 281–284
transformation and, 14–16
Union and worsening, 298–301
Crittenden, John, 303
Crockett, Davy, 269
Cromwell, Oliver, 48
cultures
  Ancient Mexico, 5–6
  decline and life expectancy of, 14–16
  democracy and new political, 207–219
  Eastern Woodlands, 6–7, 7–8
  ecosystems and, 5
  enduring, 14–15
  Great Basin, 8, 15
  Great Plains, 8, 15, 263–265
  Mandan, *11*, 175
  Mayan, 6, *7m*, 11, 14, 16
  nomads in, 4
  North American, 4–9
  Pacific Northwest, 8–9
  pressure on Indian lands and, 175–176
  Republic and political, 171–172
  South and slave, 255–258
  Southwest, 6–7
  Subarctic and Arctic, 9
Curry, John Steuart, *286–287*

D

daguerreotypes, 215
Dartmouth College v. Woodward, 192
Daughters of Liberty, 112
Davis Bend, 335–336
Davis, Henry Winter, 337
Davis, Jefferson, 312, 320, 328, 336
Davis, Joseph (brother), 336
Dawes, William, 116
de Bry, Theodore, 9, 23
de Soto, Hernán, 29
death rates, 46
Decatur, Stephen (captain), 178
Declaration of Independence, 123, *124*
Declaration of the Rights of Man, 221
the Deep South, 245–247. *See also* the South
Delany, Martin, 237
Delawares, 64
democracy
  accommodate or resist, 211
  additional reading, 223
  bank war and, 216–218
  chapter summary, 222
  equality and opportunity with, 207
  free blacks in North and, 212–213
  Indian removal and, 213
  Jacksonian party system and, 220–221
  Jackson's rise to power and, 210–211
  new political culture of, 207–219
  nullification crisis and, 215–216
  race and, 211–214
  racism and, 214
  rise of, 204–223
  significant events, *222–223*
  spread of white manhood suffrage and, *214*
  Trail of Tears and, 211–212
  Van Buren and depression and, 219–220
Democratic Review, 220, 266
The Democratization of American Christianity (Hatch), 227
demographics, 20
depreciated, 217
depression, 219–220

Diamond, Jared, 17
Dias, Bartolomeu, 24
Dickens, Charles, 193, 239
Dickinson, John, 111, 112, 152
A Discourse Concerning Westerne Planting (Hakluyt), 33
disenfranchisement, 348
dissent, 322–323
distilled spirits, annual consumption, per capita, of, *234*. *See also* alcohol
Dix, Dorothea, 235
Dodge, William, 349
domesticity, 229–230
Donaldson, Israel, 288
Doolittle, Amos, 116
Douglas, Stephen A., 282, 288, 295, *299–300*, 299–301, 302
Douglass, Esther, 345
Douglass, Frederick, *237*, 257
Doyle, James, 288
Doyle, Mahala (wife), 288
Drake, Francis (sir), 35
Dred Scott decision, 298–299
Drinker, Elizabeth, 149
Dunmore (lord), 123, 134
Dutch West India Company, 63

E

earthen mounds, *2–3*, 4, 8
East India Company, 113
Eastern Woodlands, 7–8, 8, 14
economic specialization, 199
ecosystems, 5
Edge of Empire (Jasanoff), 104
educational reform, 234
Edward, Jonathan, 93
Edward VI (king), 32
egalitarian, 14
1850s
  caning of Sumner, 297–298
  collapse of second American party system in, 295–296
  election of 1856, 298
  know-nothings in, 296–297
  political realignment of, 295–298
  republicans and bleeding Kansas, 297
elect, 31
election
  1796, 157–158
  1800, *169*, 170
  1824, 208
  1828, 210
  1856, 298
  1866, 340
  1876, 350–351
  sectional, 301–302
Eliot, John, 72, 73
Elizabeth I (queen), 32, 33, 35
Ellis, Powhatan, 206
Ellsworth, Oliver, 152
emancipation
  proclamation, 317–319
  Republic's, 317–319
embargo, 179
Embargo Act, 181
Emerson, Ralph Waldo, 231, 232
empresarios, 267
England. *See also* New England
  ambitions of Gilbert, Raleigh, and Wingina, 33–35
  Anglo-American worlds of North America and, 94–97

charter, 33
Chesapeake society and, 44–48
economic and social development, 94–95
entry into America, 32–36
imperial system before 1760, 96–97
independence and joys of being from, 101–102
inequality in America and, 94–95
politics in America and, 95–96
Reformation in, 32
enlightenment, 91–94
equality, democracy with opportunity and, 207
Eries, 64
Eskimos. *See* Inuits
Esteban, 29
Eurasia
Africa and Portuguese wave in, 22–23
early modern goth and, 22
Europe's place in world, 21–22
fifteenth century Africa and, 21–24
sugar, origins of Atlantic slave trade and, 23–24
Europe
explorations of fifteenth/sixteenth century, *34*
independence and claims to North America by, *105*
place in world, 21–22
principal routes of exploration in, *25*
religious reform divides, 30–32
evangelical, 227
Ex parte Milligan, 322
excise tax, 160
expansion
anti-war and Western, 274
Indians and Western, 271, 273–274
Overland Trail and Western, 270–271
rise of slavery and Western, 262–285
slavery and political origins of, 271–276
slavery, horse and gun frontiers and Sioux nation, *265*
wars and provoking Western, 272–273
Western, 270–276
explorations, *25, 34*

F

factories
industrial work and, 197
labor movement and, 197–198
Lowell mills, environment and, 196
Patch, workers' art and, 198
rise of, 193–198
technological advances and, 194–195
textile, 195–196
Fagan, Brian M., 17
farming, 10, 276–278. *See also* agriculture; landscapers
Farragut, David G. (admiral), 312, 328
Faust, Drew, 317
federalism, 153
Federalists, ideologies of Republicans and, 168
The Federalist Papers (Madison), 154
Ferdinand (king), 22, 24
Fertile Crescent, 11
Fessenden, William Pitt, 339
Fillmore, Millard, 283
Finney, Charles Grandison, 227–228, 233, 235, 238
fishing nets, far horizons of old/new worlds and, 19–20
Fletcher v. Peck, 192
Florida, 31–32, 43, *43,* 54, 56
Florida Indians Planting Maize, 111
Fort Hamilton, 4
Fort Washington, 4
Forten, James, 171–172

1491: New Revelations of the Americas before Columbus (Mann, Charles), 15, 17
fourteenth amendment, 340
Fox, 178, 212
Foxe, John, *67*
France, 166
Adams, John, and naval war with, 168–169
colonization by North America and, 62–65
origins of new, 62–63
Francis I (king), 22
Franciscan monks, 43, 44
Franklin, Benjamin, *85,* 92, 93, 95, 97, 123, *124, 129,* 153, 184
free
African Americans, 212–213, 215, 257–258
black Southerners and slaves, 212, 213, 257–258
slaves, 133, 212–213, 215, 257–258
soil party, 282
freedmen/freedpeople, 318
Freehling, William W., 304
Frémont, John C., 298
French Revolution, political parties, Americans and, 166
Fuller, Margaret, 231
Fulton, Robert, 190

G

Gage, Thomas (general), 115, 116, 121–122
Galloway, Joseph, 124
da Gama, Vasco, 24
Gardoqui, Don Diego de, 151
Garrison, William Lloyd, 235, 236, 237, 238, 239, 259
Gast, John, 266
Gates, Horatio (general), 128, 132
George II (king), 57
George III (king), 101, 110, 111, 117, 123, *141*
Georgia, 250
founding of, 57–58
post war, 343
Worcester v., 212
Germain, George (lord), 123, 126
Gerry, Elbridge, 152
Gibbons v. Ogden, 192
Gilbert, Humphrey, 20, 32–33, 35
Glorious Revolution, 76–77
God. *See also* religions
Beecher family, perfection and kingdom of, *225, 226,* 227
difference between man and, 167
questioning existence of, 70
gold rush, 278–279
goodwives, 71
goth, early modern, 22
government
confederate financing and, 320
economy and financing, 321
Hamilton's financial program for, 164, *165,* 166
reconstruction reforms under new state, 344
Republic and new, 164–166
Washington, George, organizes, 164
graduated income tax, 320
Grant, Ulysses S., 314–315, 328, *329,* 348
Great Basin, cultures, 8, 15
Great Plains, 8, 15, 263–265
Great Temple of the Sun, 6
the Great Awakening
aftermath, 93–94
enlightenment and, 91–94
first, 93
second, 176–177

Greeley, Horace, 317, 348
Green, Duff, 259
Greene, Nathanael, 132–133
Grenville, Richard (sir), 34, 106, 108, 110
Grimké, Angelina, 236, 238
Grimké, Sarah, 236, 238
Guns, Germs, and Steel: The Fates of Human Societies (Diamond), 17

H

habeas corpus, 312
Haitian Revolution, 184
Hakluyt, Richard, 33, 34
Hall, Basil, 252
Hamilton, Alexander, 152, 160, 161, *164, 165, 166,* 170, 171, 192
Hammond, James Henry, 245, 249, 253
Hancock, John, *124*
Handbook of North American Indians (Sturtevant), 17
Handsome Lake, 177
Hariot, Thomas, 34
Harmar, Josiah (general), 173
Harper, William, 216
Harpers Ferry, 301
Harris, Emily Lyles, 319
Harrison, William Henry (general), 178, 181, 220, 269, 271
Hartford Convention, 182
Hatch, Nathan, 227
Hawthorne, Nathaniel, 192, 232
Hayne, Robert, 239
Henry, Patrick, 109, 139, 155, 259
Henry the Navigator (prince), 22
Henry VII (king), 20, 22
Henry VIII (king), 32
Herald of Freedom, 288
Hicks, Thomas, 200
Hidden Cities: The Discovery and Loss of Ancient North American Civilization, 17
Hinds, Josiah, 252
Hobbes, Thomas, 21
Hoe, Robert, 191
Hogarth, William, 106
Hohokams, 6, 10, 14
Homer, Winslow, 336
Hooker, Isabella Beecher, 238
Hooker, Thomas, 70
Hopewell cultures, *7m*
Houdon, Jean Antoine, 167
Houston, Sam, 269
Howe, Daniel Walker, 190
Howe, William (major general), 122, 126, 129
Hudson, Henry, 63
Huguenots, 31–32, 36, 65
Hume, David, 154
Hurons, 14, 62, 63, 64
Hutchinson, Anne, 71

I

Ice Age, 4, 5
ideologies, Federalist and Republican, 168
Illinois, 3, 65
illnesses
animals and, 12–13
the Black Death, 21–22, 67
malaria, 52
scurvy, 66
smallpox, 26, 27, 43, 64, 72, *130,* 175
syphilis, 27
virgin soil epidemic, 26

immigration, 84, 293–294

immune systems, 12. *See also* illnesses

impeachment, 342

imperial crisis

    beginning of colonial resistance and, 108–109

    Boston massacre and, 112–113

    empire strikes back and, 113–114

    Grenville's new measure and, 106, 108

    independence and, 104–114

    international sons of liberty and, 112

    new troubles on frontier and, 104, 106

    resistance organized and, 111–112

    resistance revived and, 113

    riots and resolves with, 109–110

    spirits of independence and, 111

    Stamp Act mob and, 109

    Stamp Act repeal and, 100, 110–111

    Townshend Acts and, 111

imperial system, 96–97

indentures, 46

independence

    additional reading, 119

    American Revolution and decision for, 122–124

    Appalachian frontier (1750-1755), *107*

    chapter summary, 118

    declaration of, 123

    embargo and, 179

    European claims in North America (1750 and 1763), *105*

    imperial crisis and, 104–114

    joys of being English and, 101–102

    loyalists and, 123–124

    Republic and second war for American, 179–182

    toward revolution and, 114–118

    second Continental Congress, 123

    Seven Years' War and, 102, *103, 104*

    significant events, *118–119*

    toward war for American, 100–119

Indian Elder or Chief, 33

Indian Wars, 46, 47–48

Indians. *See also* cultures; specific tribes

    baptized, 43

    Blue Jacket and Little Turtle, 173

    democracy and removal of, *213*

    driven west of Mississippi, 4

    Jefferson and land for, 175–176

    lands, cultures and pressure on, 175–176

    landscapers, 10–11

    North America's, *13m*

    Opechancanough, 47–48

    removal, 213

    Republic, white encroachment and response from, *177*

    Republic, whites in West and, 173–179

    search for North America's empires with, 29–30

    sentiments against, 16

    slavery and, 43

    Squanto, 71

    successful uprising of, 43–44

    taking land from, 70–71

    Tecumseh, 177–178

    uprisings, 56

    Western expansion and, 271, 273–274

industrial work, 197

inflation, 219

innovations and limitations

    agricultural gifts, 9–10

    animals and illness, 12–13

    landscapers, 10–11

North American, 6–13

    shape of problems with, 11–12

The Institutes of the Christian Religion (Calvin), 31

institutions, of the South, 252–255

international sons of liberty, 112

Inuits, 9, 15

Iroquois, 14, 15, 63–64, 97, 98, 177

Iroquois League, 63

Isabella (queen), 22, 24

itinerants, 93

ivory masks, *23*

J

Jackson, Andrew (general), 15–16, 181, 182, 208, *212*, 216, 259, 269, 303, 325

    democracy and party system of, 220–221

    democracy and rise to power, 210–211

    democrats, Whigs, and market, 220–221

    impact on presidency and Bank War, 218

    people's president, 210–211

    political agenda in market economy, 211

    rise to power, 210–211

    social bases of two parties and, 221

James (duke of York), 73

James I (king), 35, 40, 46, 58, 65, 66

James II (king), 76

Jamestown, 3, *45*

Jasanoff, Maya, 104

Jay, John, 151

Jay-Gardoqui Treaty, 151

Jefferson, Thomas, 4, 123, 144, 152, 164, 167, 168, 170, 180, 208, 221, 259

    economic policies, 173

    Indian lands and, 175–176

    new capital city and, 172–173

    philosophy, 173

    in power during Republic, 172–173

Jemmy, 91

Jeremiah, Thomas, 133

Jerome, Chauncey, 187–*188*, 195, 200, 201

Jesuits, 43, 63, *80*

Johnson, Andrew, 336, 337–339, 347

Johnson, Octave, 244

Johnston, Albert (general), 315

Johnston, Joseph, 316

joint stock company, 45

Jones, Betty, 344

Jones, John, 319

Jones, Samuel, 288

Jordan, Daniel (colonel), 242, 249

Joseph, Louis (general), 103

journeymen, 194, 195

judicial review, 170

Judiciary Act of 1801, 170

K

Kansas Free State, 288

Kansas, Union and sacked town in, 287–288

Kansas-Nebraska Act, *296*

Kearny, Stephen W., 42

Kehoe, Alice Beck, 17

Kelly, Abby, 238

Kemble, Fanny, 257

Kennedy, Roger G., 17

Keys, Mary, 186

King Philip's War. *See* Metacom's war

King, Rufus, 152

King William's War, 83

Kingdoms of Gold, Kingdoms of Jade: The Americas before Columbus (Fagan), 17

"kivas," 6

Koontz, Rex, 17

Ku Klux Klan, 349, 350

Kwakiutls, 9

L

La Salle, Sieur de, 65, 82

labor movement, 197–198

landed states, 143

landless states, 143

lands. *See also* the Bering Strait

    bridge, 5

    claims: Constitution and Western, *143*

    issues, 342

    Jefferson and Indian, 175–176

    taking, 70–71

landscapers, 10–11

Lane, Ralph, 34, 35

de Las Casas, Bartolomé, 24

Le Moyne, Jacques, 43

Leaves of Grass (Whitman), 232

Lecompton constitution, 299

Lee, Ann, 232–233

Lee, Richard Henry, 123

Lee, Robert E. (general), 316, 317, 326, *329*

L'Enfant, Pierre Charles, 172

Lenni Lenapes, 75

Leonard, Daniel, 124

Letters on the Condition of Women and the Equality of the Sexes (Grimké, S.), 238

Lewis, Cass, 282

Lewis, Meriwether, 175

The Liberator, 236, 259

limitations. *See* innovations and limitations

Lincoln, Abraham, 302, 328, 330, 337

    10 percent plan and, 337

    Civil War general and, 326–328

    Douglas's debate with, 299–300, 301

    Union and president, *296*

Lincoln-Douglas debates, 299–301

Little Turtle, 173

Livingston, Margaret, 148

Livingston, Robert, 175

Locke, John, 54, 108, 259

Long, Jacob, 160

Louis XIV (king), 77

Louisiana, slavery and colonial society in French, 91

Louis-Philippe (king), 207

the Louisiana Purchase, *174, 183*

Lovejoy, Elijah, 237

Lowell Mills, 194, 196, *197*

the Lowell Offering, 195

loyalists, 123–124

loyalty oath, 337

Luther, Martin, 30–31, 32, 36

M

Madison, Dolly, 182

Madison, James, *152*, 154, 155, 164, 167, 170, 180–181, 182, 189, 259

Madoc (king), 4

Maine law, 239

Makahs, 9

malaria, 52

mammals, large. *See* megafauna

Mandans, *11,* 175

Manifest Destiny

    doctrine's roots, 266

    Mexican borderlands and, 266–267

    slavery, Manifest Destiny and (not so), 266–269

Texas republic and, 268–269
Texas revolution and, 267–268
Manifest Destiny, 266
Mann, Charles C., 14, 15, 17
Mann, Horace, 234
Marbury v. Madison, 170
Marbury, William, 170
market economy, *191, 192,* 211, 228–229
market revolution
    agriculture in market economy and, 191–192
    communications and, 190–191
    cotton trade and, 189
    Marshall, promotion of enterprise and, 192
    new nationalism and, 189
    postal system and, 191
    transportation and, 189–190
market society
    economic specialization and, 199
    materialism in, 199
    social mobility, 200
    social structures and, 199–201
    time and, 200–201
    wealth and emerging middle class in, 199–200
"maroon" communities, 91
Marshall, James, 278
Marshall, John, 170, 192
Mary I (queen), 32, 67
Mary II (queen), 76
Maryland, founding of, 47–48
Masasoits, 72, 73
Massachusetts, 67–68, 70, 72
materialism, 199
Mayans, 6, 7*m*, 11, 14, 16
McClellan, George, 312, 316, 328
McCullough v. Maryland, 192
McDowell, Irvin (general), 309
McGuire, Judith, 320
McKim, Randolph, 310
Meade, George Gordon, 325
megafauna, 4, 5, 10, 11, 12
Mehmed II (sultan), 21
Melville, Herman, 232
Menéndez de Avilés, Pedro, 32, 43
mercantilism, 44
Mesa Verde, 7
Mesoamerica, 5–6, 9, 11, 16
Metacom's war, 72–73
Methodists, 176, 178
Mexico. *See also* Ancient Mexico
    borderlands and slavery, *269*
    borderlands, Manifest Destiny and, 266–267
    Mexicans, 273–274
    Spain's founding of "New," 41–42
    war between U.S. and, 275
Mexico: From the Olmecs to the Aztecs (Coe and
    Koontz), 17
Miami Confederacy, 173–174
Micmacs, 62
mid-Atlantic colonies
    English rule in New York, 73
    founding of New Jersey, 73–74
    patterns of growth in, 74–76
    Quaker odysseys and, 74
    Quakers and politics in, 75–76
middle class, 199–200, 230–231
militias, 127
millennialism, 226
Miller, Lewis, 256
Miller, William, 160
Milner, George R., 17
Ming dynasty, 21
minstrelsy, 214, 349

Mississippi
    colonization and lure of, 64–65
    cultures, 7*m*
    driving Indians west of, 4
    Indians east of, 7–8
    site, 7*m*
Missouri Compromise, 183, 295
Moby-Dick (Melville), 232
Moctezuma, 26, *27,* 41
Moctezuma, Isabel de Tolosa Cortés, 41
Mogollons, 6, 14
Mohawks, 63
Mohegans, 72
Molasses Act of 1733, 106
monocultures, 41
Monroe, James, 175, 182, 183–184, 207
Montagnais, 62, 63
Montcalm (marquis), 103, 104
Montgomery, Benjamin, 336, 351
Moore, James, 56
Mormons, 233, 280
Morris, Gouverneur, 163
Morris, Robert, 152
Morse, Samuel F. B., 190
motherhood, women's education and Republican,
    149–150
Mott, Lucretia, 238
mounds, *2–3,* 4, 8
*The Moundbuilders: Ancient Peoples of Eastern
    North America* (Milner), 17
Mulberry plantation, *57*
Mundus Novus (New World), *24*
Murray, Judith Sargent, 149
Muskogeans, 14
mutiny, 130

N

Narragansetts, 72
Narváez, Pánfilo de, 29
Nast, Thomas, 337
Natchez, 15, 65
nationalism, market revolution and new, 189
Native Americans, 10, 12. *See also* Indians
nativism, 294
naturalization, 169
Navajos, 43
Navigation Acts, 48
Nebraska. *See* Kansas-Nebraska Act
Neutrals, 64
Neville, John (general), 160–161
New Amsterdam, *60–61,* 62
New England
    Anglo-American worlds and, 94–97
    colonization and early, *69*
    communities in conflict, 70–71
    early, *69*
    founding, 65–68
    goodwives and witches in, 71
    Metacom's war and, 72–73
    pilgrim settlement at Plymouth Colony, 66–67
    Puritan movement in, 65–66
    Puritan settlement at Massachusetts Bay,
        67–68
    removal of indigenous people in, 70–71
    stability and order in early, 68–73
New Jersey, 73–74, 126–127, 152–153
New Netherlands, colonization, Iroquois and
    Beaver Wars, 63–64
New York, 73, 126–127
Newfoundland, 20, 24
nomads, 4

Nootkans, 9
North America. *See also* America
    additional reading, 17, 99
    Anglo-American worlds of England and,
        94–97
    boundary disputes and tenant wars in, 86
    chapter summary, 16–17, 99
    colonization by France and, 62–65
    continent of cultures in, 4–9
    crisis and transformation in, 14–16
    distribution of American population in, *90*
    early peoples of, 4–5, 7*m*
    eighteenth century seaports in, 86–89
    enlightenment and awakening in, 91–94
    estimated population by region (1720–1760),
        87
    estimated population of colonial cities,
        (1720–1770), *87*
    on eve of contact, 15–16
    first civilizations of, 2–17
    forces of division in, 83–89
    immigration and natural increase in eigh-
        teenth century, 84
    Indians of, 13*m*
    innovations and limitations in, 6–13
    mosaic of, 80–99
    non-English settlements in British, 84
    overseas trade networks, *96*
    power of hidden past in, 3–4
    search for Indian empires in, 29–30
    settlement of backcountry, 84–85
    settlement patterns, *83*
    Seven Years' War and, 97–98
    significant events, *98–99*
    significant events in, *16–17*
    slave families and communities, 90–91
    slave resistance in eighteenth century
        British, 91
    slavery and colonial society in French
        Louisiana, 91
    social conflict on frontier, 85–86
    Southern slave societies in, 89–91
    Spain's colonization in, 41–44
    Spanish missions in, *44*
    tattooed traveller's tale of, 81–83
the North
    American Revolution and fighting in, 124–126,
        127, 128
    campaigns in New York and New Jersey, 126
    capturing Philadelphia and, 127–128
    conflict and colonization in, 60–79
    disaster for British at Saratoga and, 128
    free blacks in, 212–213
    growing disillusionment in, 349
    laying strategies, 126
    turning point and home front in, 131
    two armies at bay and, 124–126
    winding down war in, 129–130
the Northwest Territory, 144–145
Notes on the State of Virginia (Jefferson), 173
Noyes, John Humphrey, 233
nullification crisis, 215–216

O

Obama, Barack, 299
Oglethorpe, James, 57
Ohio, southern, 2
Olmecs, 5–6, 7*m*, 11, 14, 16
Olmstead, Frederick Law, 252
Oñate, Juan de, 41, 42, 45
Oneidas, 63, 233

Onondagas, 63
Opechancanough, 47–48
opportunity, 207
opposition, 108
Ordinance of 1785, *145*
Osages, 65
O'Sullivan, John L., 266
Ottos, 65
L'Ouverture, Toussaint, 254
Overland Trail, 270–271
Owen, Robert, 233, 239
owners, slave, 249

P

Pacific Northwest, cultures, 8–9
Paine, Thomas, 221
   revolution and common sense of, 109, 117–118
Pamunkeys, 39, 40
panics
   of 1819, 193, 201–202, 216–217
   of 1837, 196
   of 1873, 349
Paquime, 14
Parke Custin, George Washington, 128
parties. *See* political parties
partisan warfare, 132
party system
   abolitionism and, 239–240
   collapse of second American, 295–296
   Maine law and, 239
   reform shaken by, 239–240
past, power of hidden, 3–4
Patch, Sam, 198
paternalism, 195
Paterson, William, 152
patterns, North America's settlement, *83*
Paul, Mary, 194, 196
Pawnees, 65, *80*, 82
Pawtuckets, 72
Paxton Boys, *85*
pays d'en haut (upper country), 64
peace
   Constitution and temptations with, 142–147
   disputes among states and, 143–144
   foreign intrigues and, 142–143
   more democratic West and, 144
   Northwest Territory and, 144–145
   slavery, sectionalism and, 145–147
   temptations of West, 142
   wartime economic disruption, 147
peculiar institution, 147
Penn, William, 74–76
peoples. *See also* African Americans; blacks;
   Indians; whites
   American revolution and, 120–137
   North America's early, 4–5, *7m*
   religion and elect, 31
Pequots, 72
perfection
   abolitionism and, 235–238
   additional reading, 241
   American romanticism and, 231–232
   annual consumption of distilled spirits, per
      capita, *234*
   Beechers, kingdom of God and, 225, *226*, 227
   chapter summary, 240–241
   fires of, 224–241
   party system shaken by reform and, 239–240
   reform age and, 232–235
   revivalism, social order and, 227–229
   significant events, 240–241

women's sphere and, 229–*231*
Perry, Oliver Hazard (commander), 181
Petuns, 64
Philadelphia, capturing, 127–128
Philosopher's Camp, 232
Pickett, George (general), 326
Pierce, Franklin, 295
pilgrims, Separatists, 66, 67
Pinckney, Charles Cotesworth, 179, 180
Pinckney, Thomas, 151, 152, 168, 174
Pinckney's Treaty, 174
Pitt, William, 103, 104, *106*, 111
Pizarro, Francisco, 20, 26, 27, 29
plague. *See* the Black Death
plantations
   Hopeton, Georgia, layout of, *250*
   Mulberry, 57
   post war Georgia, 343
   Southern mistress on, 251
Plog, Stephen, 17
Plummer, Franklin E., 206, 217
Plymouth Colony, 66–67
Plymouths, 3
Pocahontas, 40, *41*
political culture, 207
political festivals, 171
political parties
   Americans, French Revolution and, 166
   democracy and Jackson's system with, 210–211
   perfection and reform of, 239–240
   Republic and emergence of, 166–168
   Washington, George's, neutral course and, 167
political realignment of 1850, 295–298
Polk, James K., 272, 273, 276
Ponce de Léon, Juan, 29
Popé, 42, 43–44, 82
popular sovereignty, 281
populations
   census, 161
   distribution of American, *90*
   free blacks, *212*
   growth, 193, 293
   immigrant growth, 293
   North America and colonial cities', *87*
   North America and estimated regional, *87*
   South and 1860, *249*
Portugal, Eurasia and Africa wave with, 22–23
postal system, 191
Potawatomis, 178
Poverty Point, 8, *16*
Powhatan, 39, 40, 46, 49, 53, 58
predestination, 65
Presbyterians, 65
Prescott, William, 122
present, *4n*
presidential reconstruction
   election of 1866, 340
   fourteenth amendment, 340
   Johnson, A., and, 337–339
   Lincoln's 10 percent plan and, 337
presidios, 267
prison reform, *235*
problems, shape of, 11–12
proslavery arguments, 259
prosperity, 201–202
Prosser, Gabriel, 254
Protestants, 228–229, 231
Pueblo Bonito, *6*
Pueblo Revolt, 43–44
Pueblos, 82
Puritans, 65–68, 70

Q

Quakers, 73, 74, 75–76, *85*
Quapaws, 65

R

race, 211–214
racism, 53, 214, 351
The Radicalism of the American Revolution
   (Wood), 148
railroads, 290–291, *292*, 293
Raleigh, Walter, 20, 32–34, 35
rancheros, 267
ratification, Constitution and, 153–154, *155*
rebellions
   Bacon's, 48–49
   Coode's, 48–49
   Shays's, 151–152
   slaves, 215, 254–256
   Stono, 91
reconquista, 24
Reconstruction
   abandonment of, 347–351
   additional reading, 353
   black and white republicans, 342–344
   black aspirations and, 344–347
   chapter summary, 351–352
   congressional, 341–342
   disputed election of 1876, 350–351
   economic issues, corruption and, 344
   Georgia plantation after war, *343*
   Grant administration and, 348
   growing disillusionment in North with, 349
   minstrels, carnivals, ghosts and, 349
   presidential, 337–340
   racism and failure of, 351
   reforms under new state government and, 344
   secret sale at Davis Bend and, 335–336
   significant events and, *352–353*
   South and, 342–344
   Southern states during, *341*
   Union and, 334–353
   white supremacy and, 349–350
redeemers, 351
The Refiner's Fire (Brooke), 92
reform
   age of, 232–235
   asylum movement and, 235
   educational, 234
   Mormon experience and, 233
   perfection and party system shaken by, 239–240
   socialist communities and, 233–234
   temperance movement and, 234
   utopian communities and, 232–233
Reform Bill of 1832, 209, 260
the Reformation, 32
religions
   Calvin's contributions to, 31, 32, 36, 65, 70
   elect peoples and, 31
   English Reformation, 32
   Europe divided by reforms in, 30–32
   Franciscan monks and, 43, 44
   French Huguenots, birth of Spanish Florida
      and, 31–32
   Jesuits and, 43
   Luther's teaching on, 30–31
   market economy and, 228–229
   Mormons, 233, 280
   Puritans, 65–66, 67–68, 70
   Quakers, 74, 75–76
   slavery and, 256–257

republican motherhood, 149
Republican society
    attack on aristocracy and, 150–151
    motherhood and education for women in, 149–150
    new men of Revolution, 148
    new women of Revolution, 148–149
    seduction literature, women's virtues and, 149
    Wollstonecraft's vindication and, 149
Republicans
    and bleeding Kansas, 297
    Constitution and experiments of, 140–142
    Constitution and society of, 148–151
    ideologies of Federalists and, 168
    Madison and young, 180–181
    society, 148, 149–150, 151
the Republic
    additional reading, 185, 333
    America turns inward, 182–184
    Bull Run and, 309–310
    changing magnitude of battle and, *314*
    chapter summary, 184–185, 332
    Civil War and, 308–333
    Confederate home front and, 319–320
    early (1789–1824), 158–185
    emancipation of, 317–319
    emergence of political parties, 166–168
    gone to be soldiers, 323–325
    Great Awakening (second), 176–177
    Hamilton's financial system, *165*
    Indian response to white encroachment, 177
    Indians and whites in West, 173–179
    Jefferson in power, 172–173
    Louisiana Purchase, *174*
    Missouri Compromise and Union's boundaries in 1820, *183*
    new government in, 164–166
    opening moves and, 313–317
    political culture of, 171–172
    presidency of Adams, John, and, 168–170
    second war for American independence and, 179–182
    semisubsistance in, *162*, 163
    1789: social portrait, 161–163
    significant events, *184–185*, *332–333*
    total war (1861-1865) and, 308–333
    total war demands and, 311–313
    Union and Confederacy resources (1861), *311*
    Union home front and, 321–323
    Union's triumph and, 325–331
    United States and Barbary states (1801–1815), *178*
    war in East (1861–1862), *316*
    war in East (1863–1865), *326*
    war in West (1861–1862), *315*
    war in West (1863–1865), *327*
    War of 1812, 180
resistance
    British North America and slave, 91
    democracy and accommodation or, 211
    imperial crisis and colonial, 108–109
    Miami confederacy and, 173–174
    organized, 111–112
    revived, 113
    slavery and, 254–255
Revenue Act, 106
revivalism
    Finney's new measures and theology, 227–228
    religion and market economy, 228–229
    rise of African American churches, 229
    social order, perfection and, 227–229
revolts, 43–44, 46. *See also* rebellions

revolution. *See* the American Revolution; French Revolution; Glorious Revolution; Haitian Revolution; market revolution
Ribault, Jean, 32
Rice, Sally, 196
Ripley, George, 231, 232
Robeson, George M., *348*
Rolfe, John, 40, 41
romanticism, Transcendentalists and, 231–232
Ross, John, 211
routes, European exploration and principal, *25*
the Rural South, 247
Rush, Benjamin, 149
Russell, William, 310
Rutledge, John, 152

S

"sachem" (Ieader), 72
"sagamore" (Ieader), 72
San Francisco, *278, 279*
San Miguel mission, *268*
Santa Anna, Antonio López, 268, 269
Saratoga, disaster for British at, 128
Sauks, 178, 212
scalawags, 343
schoolhouses, 345–346
Scott, Winfield, 274, 284
Scott, Winfield (general), 312
scurvy, 66
seaports, *21*, 86–89
secession, 302–303, *304*
sectionalism, 145–147
Sedition Acts, 169
seduction literature, 149
self-reliance, 232
semisubsistence economies, 162–163
Semple, Nannie McKenzie, *319*
Seneca Falls convention, 238
Senecas, 63
separation
    of church and state, 70, 71
    of powers, 153
Separatists, 66, 67
serpentine mound, 2
serpents. *See* snakes
settlements, North America's patterns with, *83*
Seven Days' battles. *See* Battle of Seven Days
Seven Years' War, 97–98
    independence and, 102, *103*, 104
    postwar expectations, 104
    years of defeat and, 102–103
    years of victory and, 103–104
1789
    Constitution and commerce in, 163
    Republic and social portrait of, 161–163
    semisubsistence and commercial economies, 162–163
the Shakers, 232
Shawnees, 58, 64, 65, 176
Shays, Daniel (captain), 151–152
Shays's Rebellion, 151–152
Sherman, Roger, 123, 152
Sherman, William Tecumseh (general), 315, 328
Sioux nation, *265*
slave trade, 49, *50, 51,* 52
slavery
    additional reading, 285
    arguments in support of, 259
    chapter summary, 284–285
    Chesapeake society: from servitude to, 49
    colonial society in French Louisiana and, 91

    Compromise of 1850, territorial growth and, *283*
    cotton and distribution of, 247
    defense of, 259–260
    escape from crisis and, 281–284
    indentured, 46
    as labor system for cotton, 247–248
    maintenance of slaves and, 253–254
    Manifest (and not so Manifest) Destiny and, 266–269
    Mexican borderlands and, *269*
    new societies in West and, 276–281
    Overland Trail and, *270*
    peculiar institution of, 252–255
    political origins of expansion and, 271–276
    religion and, 256–257
    resistance to, 254–255
    sectionalism, peace and, 145–147
    significant events, *284–285*
    Sioux expansion, horse and gun frontiers and, *265*
    South and culture of, 255–258
    South and defense of, 259–260
    South and spread of, *248*
    strangers on Great Plains and, 263–265
    trek West and, *270–271*
    U.S.-Mexican War and, 275
    Western expansion and rise of, 262–285
    women and children in, 255
    work, discipline and, 253
slaves, 10. *See also* slavery
    Aztec's, 6, 26
    colonization and African Transatlantic trade in, *50–51*
    community, 257
    culture, 255–258
    Estaben, 29
    Eurasia, sugar and origins of Atlantic trade in, 23–24
    families and communities, 90–91, 255–256
    first narrative written by, 172
    free, 133, 212–213, 215, 257–258
    free black Southerners and former, 257–258
    importing of, 28
    Indian, 43
    Jemmy, 91
    Lord calling and, 256–257
    owners, 249
    rebellions, 215, 254–256
    resistance in eighteenth century British North America, 91
    runaway, 244
    songs/stories of protest and celebration, 256
    Southern societies and, 89–91
    wars, 54, 56
Slidell, John, 273
smallpox, 26, 27, 43, *64,* 72, *130,* 175
Smith, James (reverend), 4
Smith, Jedediah, 199
Smith, John, 66
Smith, Joseph, 233, 280
Smith, Venture, 172
snakes, 2
social mobility, 200
social order, revivalism, perfection and, 227–229
social settings, 245
social sources, 208–210
social structures, market society and, 199–201
socialist communities, 233–234
soldiers
    black Civil War, 318–319
    joining Civil War, 232–325
    Republic's, 323–325

solstices, summer and winter, 2, 3
Sons of Liberty, 111, 112
South Carolina, 215–216, *338*
South Carolina Exposition and Protest, 215
the South
    additional reading, 261
    African Americans in age of revolution in,
      133–134
    American Revolution and struggle in, 131–132,
      133, 134
    American society and complaints from,
      294–295
    beleaguered, 301
    chapter summary, 260–261
    Civil War and women in, 319
    class structure of whites in, 249–252
    conflict and colonization in, 38–59
    cotton and other crops of, *246*
    cotton kingdom's social structure of, 245–248
    Deep and Upper, 245–247
    defense of slavery in, 259–260
    diverse social settings in, *245*
    Greene takes command in, 132–133
    master at home in, 250–251
    old, 242–261
    partisan struggle in, 131–132
    peculiar institution of, 252–255
    plantation layout in Hopeton, Georgia, *250*
    plantation mistresses in, 251
    poor whites in, 252
    population (1860), *249*
    real, 242, 244–245
    reconstruction and, 342–344
    siege of Charleston, 131
    significant events, *260–261*
    slave culture in, 255–258
    slave societies in, 89–91
    slaveowners in, 249
    spread of slavery (1820–1860), *248*
    tidewater and frontier in, 249–250
    yeoman farmers in, 251–252
the Southwest, 6–7, *7m*
Spain
    in Americas, 24–29
    Aztec depiction of, 27
    Aztecs conquered by, 26
    beachhead in Caribbean, 24–26
    colonies in America, *28*
    and colonization in North America, 41–44
    Columbian exchange and, 26–27
    conquistadores, 20
    crown steps in, 27–29
    founding of "New" Mexico by, 41–42
    growth of Florida by, 43
    and missions in North America, *44*
    Popé, Pueblo Revolt and, 43–44
    reconquista, 24
specie, 216
Spicer, Laura, 345
Spiegel, Marcus, 323
spoils system, 210
Squanto, 67, 72
St. Clair, Arthur (general), 174
St. Francis of Assisi, 43
Stafford, Joseph, 92
Stamp Act, 100, 109, 110–111
Stanton, Elizabeth Cady, 238, *238*
Steel, Eliza (mother), 244
Steel, Ferdinand, 244, 251
Stevens, Thaddeus, 339
Stiles, Ezra, 144
Still, William, 237

Stone, Lucy, 238, 348
Stono Rebellion, 91
Stowe, Harriet Beecher, 238, 284, 298
stratified society, 207
Stuart, John, *95*
Sturtevant, William C., 17
Subarctic, cultures, 9
Sudbury, Massachusetts, colonization of, *70*
suffrage, 166, 214
sugar, 41
    act, 107, 108
    Eurasia, Atlantic slave trade origins and, 23–24
    production, *23,* 53–54
Sugar Act, 107, 108
Sumner, Charles, *297–298,* 339
Swain, William, 278
syphilis, 27

T

Tainos, 15
Tallmadge, James, 183
Tammany Society, 159
Taney, Roger, 218, 298
Tappan, Lewis, 237, 238
tariffs, 106
Tarleton, Banastre (colonel), 133
task systems, 89
taxes. *See also* tariffs
    alcohol, 160
    excise, 160
    graduated income, 320
    whiskey, 160
Taylor, Zachary (general), 273, 282
technological advances, 194–195
Tecumseh, 177–178, *179,* 181
Tejanos, 268
temperance movement, 234
tenant wars, 86
Tenochtitlán, 6
Tenskwatawa, 178
Tenure of Office Act, 342
teosinte, 9
Teotihuacán, 5–6
territorial growth, Compromise of 1850, slavery
    and, *283*
Tewas, 44
Texas
    republic, 267–269
    revolution, 267–268
textile factories, 195–196
theocracy, 233
This Republic of Suffering (Faust), 317
Thomas, Sally, 258
Thoreau, Henry David, 232
Ticknor, George, 331
time, 200–201
Timucua Indians, 32
Tinkham, Jim, 309, 310
Tlingits, 9
tobacco, 40, 41, 46
Tocqueville, Alexis de, 191
Toltecs, 11
Townshend Acts, 111
Townshend, Charles, 111
trade
    colonization and African Transatlantic slave,
      49, 50, 51, 52
    cotton, 189
    overseas networks for North America's, *96*
    sugar, Eurasia and origins of Atlantic slave,
      23–24

Tragic Prelude, 286–287
Trail of Tears, 211–212
Transcendentalists, 231–232
Transcontinental Treaty, 183
transformation, crisis and, 14–16
transportation, 189–190, *191*
treasure fleets, 21
treaties
    Ghent, 182
    Guadalupe Hidalgo, 274, 280
    Jay-Gardoqui, 151
    Paris, 104
    Pinckney's, 174
    Transcontinental, 183
Treaty of Ghent, 182
Treaty of Guadalupe Hidalgo, 274, 280
Treaty of Paris, 104
Truth, Sojourner, 237
Tshimshians, 9
Tubman, Harriet, 237
Turner, Nat, 254, 258
turning point
    American Revolution as global war and,
      128–129
    home front in North and, 131
    war in West and, 130–131
    winding down war in North and, 129–130
Tuscaroras, 14, 63
Tyler, John, 271–272

U

Uncle Tom's Cabin (Stowe), *236,* 238, 284, 298
Underground Railroad, 237
the Union
    additional reading, 307
    broken, 286–307
    chapter summary, 306
    divided nation's roots and, 304–305
    growth of railroad network (1850-1860), 292
    home front, 321–323
    Kansas town sacked, 287–288
    Kansas-Nebraska Act, *296*
    Lincoln for president of, *289*
    outbreak of war, 303–304
    political realignment of 1850 and, 295–298
    reconstructing, 334–353
    reconstruction and, 334–353
    Republic and home front of, 321–323
    resources of Confederacy and, *311*
    road to war, 301–305
    secession from, 302–303
    secession patterns, *304*
    sectional changes in American society and,
      290–295
    sectional election and, 301–302
    significant events, *306–307*
    triumph of, 325–331
    worsening crisis, 298–301
United States. *See* America
the Upper South, 245–247
uprisings, Indian, 43–44, 56
urbanization, 193–194
Utes, 43
utopian communities, 232–233

V

Van Buren, Martin, 218, 219–220, 259, 269, 272,
    282
variola major, 131
Vázquez de Coronado, Francisco, 29–30, 38, 41
verbal violence, 171

Vergennes, Charles Gravier de, 128–129
Vesey, Denver, 215
Vespucci, Florentine Amerigo, 24
Vick, Sarah Pierce, *251*
Victorianism, 230
victuallers, *171*
Villasur, Don Pedro de, *80, 82*
A Vindication of the Rights of Women (Wollstone-craft), 149
virgin soil epidemic, 26
Virginia, 45, 46, 152–153
Virginia debate of 1832, 259
virtual representation, 110
A Visit from the Old Mistress, 336
von Steuben (baron), 129, 135

W

Wade, Benjamin, 337, 339
Walden (Thoreau), 232
Walden Pond, 232
Waldman, Carl, 17
Waldo, Daniel, 270, 271
Walker, David, 213, 237
Walker, James, 199
Wampanoags, 67, 72
War of 1812, 183, 188, 189
wars. *See also* the North; the South
    of 1812, *180*
    Adams, John, France and naval, 168–169
    America's independence and, 100–119
    backcountry and partisan, 132
    Bank, 216–218
    Beaver, 63–64
    border states and, 312–313
    Caribbean, Carolinas, Florida, and southeast-ern slave, 54, 56
    civil, 308–333
    Civil War as rich man's, 321
    decision for, 181
    democracy and bank, 216–218
    in East (1861-1862), *316*
    in East (1863-1865), *326*
    expectations post, 104
    Indian, 46
    King Philip's, 72–73
    King William's, 83
    Metacom's, 72–73
    North and winding down, 129–130
    political leadership and, 312
    reconstruction and Georgia plantation after, *343*
    Republic, America's independence and sec-ond, 179–182
    Republic and changing magnitude of, 314
    Republic and demands of total, 311–313
    Republic and total, 308–333
    tenant, 86
    Union and outbreak of, 303–304
    Union and road to, 301–305
    U.S.-Mexican, *275*
    in West (1861-1862), *315*
    in West (1863-1865), *327*
    Western expansion and opposition to, 274
    Western expansion and provoking, 272–273
    Yamasee, 56, 57
Washington, George, 4, 98, 102, 124, 125, 126, 129, 130, 132, 152, 154, 160, 161, 172, 180, 259
    government and neutral course set by, 167
    government organized by, 164
    surrender, 103
    verbal violence against, 171

Washington, Henry, 136
Wayne, "Mad Anthony," 174
The Way of Good and Evil, 228
wealth, 199–200
Webster, David, 216
Weld, Theodore Dwight, 235, 237, 238
Welsh hypothesis, 4
Western expansion
    Indians and, 271, 273–274
    Mexicans and, 273–274
    opposition to war and, 274
    Overland Trail and, 270–271
    to Pacific, 272
    political origins of, 271–276
    price of victory and, 274–275
    provoking war and, 272–273
    rise of slavery and, 262–285
Westos, 58
the West
    farming in, 276–278
    gold rush in, 278–279
    migration from China to, 279–280
    moving frontier and showdown in, 280–281
    restless movement, 193
    rise of slavery and expansion into, 262–285
    San Francisco: instant city, 279
    slavery and new societies in, 276–281
    trek into, 270–271
    turning point and war in, 130–131
    whites, Indians and, 173–177
What Hath God Wrought (Howe, D. W.), 190
the Whigs, 220–221, 259, 269
Whiskey Rebellion, 160
whiskey tax, 160
White, John, 33, 34, 35
Whitefield, George, 93, 94, 227
Whitefield Revival, 93
whites, 342–344
    democracy and spread of manhood suffrage with, *214*
    frontier society and, 176
    Indians in West and, 173–177
    poor Southern, 252
    Republic and West with Indians and, 173–179
    republic, West and, 173–179
    republicans, reconstruction, blacks and, 342–344
    South and class structure of, 249–252
    supremacy, 349–350
Whitman, Walt, 232
Whitney, Eli, 189, 195, 260
Why the Civil War Came, 304
Wilkinson, Eliza, 148
Willard, Abijah, 122
Willard, Emma Hunt, 234
William of Orange (king), 76
Williams, Nancy (wife), 244
Williams, Roger, 70, 71, 72
Williams, Sam, 244
Wilmot, David, 275
Wilson, James, 152
Wingina, 33–35, 40
Winnebagos, 178
Winthrop, John, 68
witches, 71
Wolfe, James (general), 104
Wollstonecraft, Mary, 149
women
    Civil War and Southern, 319
    Civil War and workforce of, 321–322
    ideal of domesticity, 229–230
    middle-class family in transition and, 230–231

Overland Trail and, 271
perfection and sphere of, 229–231
plantation mistresses, 251
Republican motherhood and education for, 149–150
seduction literature and virtues of, 149
semisubsistence and commercial economies and, 162–163
Shaker, 233
slaves, 255
social standing of, 71
women's rights movement and, 238
Wood, Gordon, 148
Woodmason, Charles, 86
Worcester v. Georgia, 212
worlds
    additional reading, 37
    American Revolution and upside down, 134–136
    chapter summary, 36
    England's entry into America, 32–36
    Eurasia and Africa in fifteenth century, 21–24
    European exploration: fifteenth/sixteenth centuries, *34*
    Europe's place in, 21–22
    fishing nets and far horizons in, 19–20
    1400-1600, old and new, 18–37
    North America, England and Anglo-American, 94–97
    principal routes of European exploration, 25
    religious reform divides Europe, 30–32
    search for North America's Indian empires, 29–30
    significant events, *36–37*
    Spain in Americas, 24–29
    Spanish America, ca. 1600, *28*
Wyandots, 178

X

XYZ Affair, 168

Y

Yamasee War, 56, 57
Yamasees, 56
Yorktown, 134–136

Z

Zaldívar, Juan de, 42
Zaldívar, Vincente de, 42
Zheng He, 21